1975

W9-BCE-436

3 0301 00009517 0

book may be kept

FOURTEEN DAYS

HISTORY OF
EUROPEAN MORALS

HISTORY OF
EUROPEAN MORALS

from Augustus to Charlemagne

By William Edward Hartpole Lecky

INTRODUCTION BY C. WRIGHT MILLS

New York
GEORGE BRAZILLER
1955

LIBRARY
College of St. Francis
JOLIET, ILL.

©Copyright 1955 by George Braziller, Inc.

55-37387

Manufactured in The United States of America

170.9
L 461
Rev.

INTRODUCTION
By C. Wright Mills

THOSE who would think about the nature of society and
history in our time have been living off the big men of the
nineteenth century. There has not yet appeared any twen-
tieth-century political theorist, sociologist, historian or
economist whose work is truly up to their level. William
Edward Hartpole Lecky—one of whose books you now hold
in your hand—is among the big nineteenth-century men off
whose work we have been living. The trouble is that many
of us do not know it. It is quite possible to earn a PH.D. in
any American social science today without ever having
opened a book by Lecky. And that is indeed a great pity.

For Lecky is not only an historian; like every great historian, he is as well a philosopher of history. As a philosopher of history, he stresses the role of ideas and of standards; as an historian, he does not merely compile his original findings; he fuses them into a poetic form. As James J.
Auchmuty has recently noted, Lecky would have agreed
fully with G. M. Trevelyan's statement: "Truth is the criterion of historical study; but its impelling motive is poetic.
Its poetry consists in its being true. There we find the syn-
thesis of the scientific and literary views of history."*

The social conditions of Lecky's work were far removed
from those of the historian today: a man of property by
birth, he used his private means for the pursuit of scholar-
ship. He was one of the last of the great line of historians
who were not professors, and which includes Gibbon and
Macauley, Acton and Froude. Lecky traveled widely and

---

*James Johnston Auchmuty, *Lecky: A Biographical and Critical Essay*
(Dublin, Ireland: Hodges, Figgis & Co., 1945), p. 5.

71243

read widely when young; rather than work up routine lectures for undergraduates, he absorbed at his leisure the intellectual climate of his time. He was one of those unspecialized men whose breadth of view and imaginative touch enables them to realize something of the unity of the human mind. That is why — even when we reject Lecky's moral view as somewhat Victorian, his estimate of economic matters as fatuous, his political outlook as querulous and summary — we nevertheless know that here is a man who is full of human sanity and whose general historical outlook is still quite exciting.

W. E. H. Lecky was born near Dublin in 1838. His family, Scotch in origin, had been Irish landlords for 150 years. When William was only a year or so old, his mother died; and, when he was fourteen, his father. Reared by his stepmother, who had remarried, his childhood was rather upset, his education intermittent. He was an unhappy schoolboy at the Royal School at Armagh, where he was sent when thirteen, and later at Chelterham, an English public school he attended. He was independent and solitary to the point of idiosyncrasy, and he remained so throughout his life.

In the eighteen-fifties, Lecky was at Trinity College, Dublin, among a distinguished group of students under the instruction of a first-rate faculty. His private reading while still at the university led him to produce and publish a small book, *The Religious Tendencies of the Age*. After his college career, he toured the principal European cities for four years; and wherever he went, he studied and he wrote. He had decided that he wanted to become an author and a member of parliament as well.

In 1861, he published *Leaders of Public Opinion in Ireland*, which sold 34 copies; but four years later his *History of the Rise and Influence of Rationalism in Europe* ap-

peared. With this book, which was published when he was
only 27 years old, he became a figure in the world of literature; in its first 50 years, it was reprinted over twenty
times.

He moved to London, was elected to the Athenaeum Club,
became a close friend of Carlyle, and devoted virtually his
complete attention to writing. He frequented the British
Museum, the Vatican Library in Rome, the Bibliothèque
Nationale in Paris — and the gallery of the House of Com-
mons. He trained himself to read easily in Greek and Latin,
German and Italian, Spanish and French. In 1869, he published the *History of European Morals*, which like the *Rationalism* was an immediate literary success, and the book
of which Lecky was most proud.

By the age of 30, with these two books to his name, Lecky
was a literary man of London and a man with a European
reputation. These two books are "closely connected," as
Lecky knew. "They are an attempt," he wrote at the time,
"to examine the merits of certain theological opinions according to the historical method — that is, by examining the
causes that produced and favored them and the degrees
and ways in which they benefited or injured mankind. The
Morals is a history of the imposition of those opinions upon
the world and attempts to show how far their success may
be accounted for by natural causes, how far they were connected with pre-existing opinions and in what respects they
were an improvement on pre-existing beliefs. The *Rationalism* is a history of the decay of these opinions, an examination of the causes of that decay and of the manner in which
it has affected the happiness of man. Both books belong to a
very small school of historical writings which began in the
seventeenth century with Vico, was continued by Condorcet,
Herder, Hegel and Comte, and which found its last great

viii

representative in Mr. Buckle ... What characterizes these
writers is that they try to look at history, not as a series of
biographies or accidents or pictures, but as a great organic
whole; that they consider the social and intellectual condition of the world at any given period a problem to be explained, the net result of innumerable influences which it is
the business of the historian to trace; and that they especially believe that intellectual belief has not been due to
arguments or other intellectual causes, but has been very
profoundly modified in many curious ways by social, political and industrial influences."*

1869 was a watershed year in Lecky's work: after the
publication of the *Morals* he wrote modern political history.
His great classic, issued in eight huge volumes as the *History of England in the 18th Century* between 1878 and 1890,
absorbed his energies for some twenty years. In 1871 he had
married a Dutch lady, who was lady-in-waiting to Queen
Sophia of the Netherlands. He lived quietly with her, mainly
in London, working at his books. Two years after the last
volume of his *History* appeared, he was offered, and declined, a chair at Oxford. He did, however, stand for Parliament, and became, for some ten years, the Liberal-
Unionist MP for his old university. It was, he said, "a terrible interruption to literature." But he did manage, in
1896, to produce two indifferent volumes on *Democracy and
Liberty*, as well as a charming little book of moral guidance,
The Map of Life (1899). He died suddenly in 1903 of heart
failure, in the library of his London house.

The best "way into" the works of Lecky is simply to begin
reading any of his major works, which really do not need

*Quoted by H. Montgomery Hyde in his introduction to *A Victorian His-
torian: Private Letters of W. E. H. Lecky, 1859-1878* (London: Home &
Van Thal, 1947), pp. 9-10.

any introduction. For what he is all about is clear: he is all about the nature of man in the course of Western history. The best criticism that can be made of any writer can truly be made of Lecky: if you read one of his major works, you will read the others.

PREFACE

THE questions with which an historian of Morals is chiefly
concerned are the changes that have taken place in the
moral standard and in the moral type. By the first, I
understand the degrees in which, in different ages, recog-
nized virtues have been enjoined and practised. By the
second, I understand the relative importance that in different ages has been attached to different virtues. Thus, for
example, a Roman of the age of Pliny, an Englishman of
the age of Henry VIII., and an Englishman of our own day,
would all agree in regarding humanity as a virtue, and its
opposite as a vice; but their judgments of the acts which
are compatible with a humane disposition would be widely
different. A humane man of the first period might derive a
keen enjoyment from those gladiatorial games, which an
Englishman, even in the days of the Tudors, would regard
as atrociously barbarous; and this last would, in his turn,
acquiesce in many sports which would now be emphatically
condemned. And, in addition to this change of standard,
there is a continual change in the order of precedence which
is given to virtues. Patriotism, chastity, charity, and humility are examples of virtues, each of which has in some ages
been brought forward as of the most supreme and transcendent importance, and the very basis of a virtuous character, and in other ages been thrown into the background,
and reckoned among the minor graces of a noble life. The
heroic virtues, the amiable virtues, and what are called
more especially the religious virtues, form distinct groups,
to which, in different periods, different degrees of prominence have been assigned; and the nature, causes, and

consequences of these changes in the moral type are among the most important branches of history.

In estimating, however, the moral condition of an age, it is not sufficient to examine the ideal of moralists. It is necessary also to enquire how far that ideal has been realised among the people. The corruption of a nation is often reflected in the indulgent and selfish ethics of its teachers; but it sometimes produces a reaction, and impels the moralist to an asceticism which is the extreme opposite of the prevailing spirit of society. The means which moral teachers possess of acting upon their fellows, vary greatly in their nature and efficacy, and the age of the highest moral teaching is often not that of the highest general level of practice. Sometimes we find a kind of aristocracy of virtue, exhibiting the most refined excellence in their teaching and in their actions, but exercising scarcely any appreciable influence upon the mass of the community. Sometimes we find moralists of a much less heroic order, whose influence has permeated every section of society. In addition, therefore, to the type and standard of morals inculcated by the teachers, an historian must investigate the realised morals of the people.

The three questions I have now briefly indicated are those which I have especially regarded in examining the moral history of Europe between Augustus and Charlemagne. As a preliminary to this inquiry, I have discussed at some length the rival theories concerning the nature and obligations of morals, and have also endeavoured to show what virtues are especially appropriate to each successive stage of civilisation, in order that we may afterwards ascertain to what extent the natural evolution has been affected by special agencies. I have then followed the moral history of the Pagan Empire, reviewing the Stoical, the

Eclectic, and the Egyptian philosophies, that in turn flourished, showing in what respects they were the products or expressions of the general condition of society, tracing their influence in many departments of legislation and literature, and investigating the causes of the deep-seated corruption which baffled all the efforts of emperors and philosophers. The triumph of the Christian religion in Europe next demands our attention. In treating this subject, I have endeavoured, for the most part, to exclude all considerations of a purely theological or controversial character, all discussions concerning the origin of the faith in Palestine, and concerning the first type of its doctrine, and to regard the Church simply as a moral agent, exercising its influence in Europe. Confining myself within these limits, I have examined the manner in which the circumstances of the Pagan Empire impeded or assisted its growth, the nature of the opposition it had to encounter, the transformations it underwent under the influence of prosperity, of the ascetic enthusiasm, and of the barbarian invasions, and the many ways in which it determined the moral condition of society. The growing sense of the sanctity of human life, the history of charity, the formation of the legends of the hagiology, the effects of asceticism upon civic and domestic virtues, the moral influence of monasteries, the ethics of the intellect, the virtues and vices of the decaying Christian Empire and of the barbarian kingdoms that replaced it, the gradual apotheosis of secular rank, and the first stages of that military Christianity which attained its climax at the Crusades, have been all discussed with more or less detail; and I have concluded my work by reviewing the changes that have taken place in the position of women, and in the moral questions connected with the relations of the sexes.

In investigating these numerous subjects, it has occasionally, though rarely, happened that my path has intersected that which I had pursued in a former work, and in two or three instances I have not hesitated to repeat facts to which I had there briefly referred. I have thought that such a course was preferable to presenting the subject shorn of some material incident, or to falling into what has always the appearance of an unpleasing egotism, by appealing unnecessarily to my own writings. Although the history of the period I have traced has never, so far as I am aware, been written from exactly the point of view which I have adopted, I have, of course, been for the most part moving over familiar ground, which has been often and ably investigated; and any originality that may be found in this work must lie, not so much in the facts which have been exhumed, as in the manner in which they have been grouped, and in the significance that has been ascribed to them. I have endeavoured to acknowledge the more important works from which I have derived assistance; and if I have not always done so, I trust the reader will ascribe it to the great multitude of the special histories relating to the subjects I have treated, to my unwillingness to overload my pages with too numerous references, and perhaps, in some cases, to the difficulty that all who have been much occupied with a single department of history must sometimes have, in distinguishing the ideas which have sprung from their own reflections, from those which have been derived from books.

There is one writer, however, whom I must especially mention, for his name occurs continually in the following pages, and his memory has been more frequently, and in these latter months more sadly, present to my mind than any other. Brilliant and numerous as are the works of the late Dean Milman, it was those only who had the great privilege of his friendship, who could fully realise the amazing extent and variety of his knowledge; the calm, luminous, and delicate judgment which he carried into so many spheres; the inimitable grace and tact of his conversation, coruscating with the happiest anecdotes, and the brightest and yet the gentlest humour; and, what was perhaps more remarkable than any single faculty, the admirable harmony and symmetry of his mind and character, so free from all the disproportion, and eccentricity, and exaggeration that sometimes make even genius assume the form of a splendid disease. They can never forget those yet higher attributes, which rendered him so unspeakably reverend to all who knew him well — his fervent love of truth, his wide tolerance, his large, generous, and masculine judgments of men and things; his almost instinctive perception of the good that is latent in each opposing party, his disdain for the noisy triumphs and the fleeting popularity of mere sectarian strife, the fond and touching affection with which he dwelt upon the images of the past, combining, even in extreme old age, with the keenest and most hopeful insight into the progressive movements of his time, and with a rare power of winning the confidence and reading the thoughts of the youngest about him. That such a writer should have devoted himself to the department of history, which more than any other has been distorted by ignorance, puerility, and dishonesty, I conceive to be one of the happiest facts in English literature, and (though sometimes diverging from his views) in many parts of the following work I have largely availed myself of his researches.

I cannot conceal from myself that this book is likely to encounter much, and probably angry, contradiction from different quarters and on different grounds. It is strongly opposed to a school of moral philosophy which is at present extremely influential in England; and, in addition to the many faults that may be found in its execution, its very plan must make it displeasing to many. Its subject necessarily includes questions on which it is exceedingly difficult for an English writer to touch, and the portion of history with which it is concerned has been obscured by no common measure of misrepresentation and passion. I have endeavoured to carry into it a judicial impartiality, and I trust that the attempt, however imperfect, may not be wholly useless to my readers.

London: March, 1869

TABLE OF CONTENTS

HISTORY OF
EUROPEAN MORALS

VOLUME I

HISTORY OF
EUROPEAN MORALS.

CHAPTER I.

THE NATURAL HISTORY OF MORALS.

A BRIEF ENQUIRY into the nature and foundations of morals appears an obvious, and, indeed, almost an indispensable preliminary, to any examination of the moral progress of Europe. Unfortunately, however, such an enquiry is beset with serious difficulties, arising in part from the extreme multiplicity of detail which systems of moral philosophy present, and in part from a fundamental antagonism of principles, dividing them into two opposing groups. The great controversy, springing from the rival claims of intuition and utility to be regarded as the supreme regulator of moral distinctions, may be dimly traced in the division between Plato and Aristotle; it appeared more clearly in the division between the Stoics and the Epicureans; but it has only acquired its full distinctness of definition, and the importance of the questions depending on it has only been fully appreciated, in modern times, under the influence of such writers as Cudworth, Clarke, and Butler upon the one side, and Hobbes, Helvétius, and Bentham on the other

Independently of the broad intellectual difficulties which must be encountered in treating this question, there is a difficulty of a personal kind, which it may be advisable at once to meet. There is a disposition in some moralists to resent, as an imputation against their own characters, any charge of immoral consequences that may be brought against the principles they advocate. Now it is a peculiarity of this controversy that every moralist is compelled, by the very nature of the case, to bring such charges against the opinions of his opponents. The business of a moral philosophy is to account for and to justify our moral sentiments, or in other words, to show how we come to have our notions of duty, and to supply us with a reason for acting upon them. If it does this adequately, it is impregnable, and therefore a moralist who repudiates one system is called upon to show that, according to its principles, the notion of duty, or the motives for performing it, could never have been generated. The Utilitarian accuses his opponent of basing the entire system of morals on a faculty that has no existence, of adopting a principle that would make moral duty vary with the latitude and the epoch, of resolving all ethics into an idle sentiment. The intuitive moralist, for reasons I shall hereafter explain, believes that the Utilitarian theory is profoundly immoral. But to suppose that either of these charges extends to the character of the moralist is altogether to misconceive the position which moral theories actually hold in life. Our moral sentiments do not flow from, but long precede our ethical systems; and it is usually only after our characters have been fully formed that we begin to reason about them. It is both possible and very common for the reasoning to be very defective, without any corresponding imperfection in the disposition of the man.

The two rival theories of morals are known by many names, and are subdivided into many groups. One of them is generally described as the stoical, the intuitive, the independent or the sentimental; the other as the epicurean, the inductive, the utilitarian, or the selfish. The moralists of the former school, to state their opinions in the broadest form, believe that we have a natural power of perceiving that some qualities, such as benevolence, chastity, or veracity, are better than others, and that we ought to cultivate them, and to repress their opposites. In other words, they contend, that by the constitution of our nature, the notion of right carries with it a feeling of obligation; that to say a course of conduct is our duty, is in itself, and apart from all consequences, an intelligible and sufficient reason for practising it; and that we derive the first principles of our duties from intuition. The moralist of the opposite school denies that we have any such natural perception. He maintains that we have by nature absolutely no knowledge of merit and demerit, of the comparative excellence of our feelings and actions, and that we derive these notions solely from an observation of the course of life which is conducive to human happiness. That which makes actions good is, that they increase the happiness or diminish the pains of mankind. That which constitutes their demerit is their opposite tendency. To procure 'the greatest happiness for the greatest number,' is therefore the highest aim of the moralist, the supreme type and expression of virtue.

It is manifest, however, that this last school, if it proceeded no further than I have stated, would have failed to accomplish the task which every moralist must undertake. It is easy to understand that experience may show that certain actions are conducive to the happiness of mankind, and that these actions may in consequence be regarded as supremely excellent. The question still remains, why we are bound to perform them. If men, who believe that virtuous actions are those which experience shows to be useful to society, believe also that they are under a natural obligation to seek the happiness of others, rather than their

own, when the two interests conflict, they have certainly no
claim to the title of inductive moralists. They recognise a
móral faculty, or natural sense of moral obligation or duty
as truly as Butler or as Cudworth. And, indeed, a position
very similar to this has been adopted by several intuitive
moralists. Thus Hutchcson, who is the very founder in
modern times of the doctrine of ' a moral sense,' and who
has defended the disinterested character of virtue more
powerfully than perhaps any other moralist, resolved all
virtue into benevolence, or the pursuit of the happiness of
others; but he maintained that the excellence and obligation of benevolence are revealed to us by a 'moral sense.'
Hume, in like manner, pronounced utility to be the criterion
and essential element of all virtue, and is so far undoubtedly
a Utilitaiian; but he asserted also that our pursuit of virtue
is unselfish, and that it springs from a natural feeling of
approbation or d:sapprobation distinct from reason, and produced by a peculiar sense, or taste, which rises up within us
at the contemplation of virtue or of vice.[1] A similar
doctrine has more recently been advocated by Mackintosh.

---

[1] The opinions of Hume on
moral questions are grossly misrepresented by many writers, who
persist in describing them as substantially identical with those of
Bentham. How far Hume was
from denying the existence of a
moral sense, the following passages
will show:—' The final sentence, it
is probable, which pronounces
characters and actions amiable or
odious, praiseworthy or blame-
able . . . depends on some internal
sense or feeling which nature has
made universal in the whole
species.' — *Enquiry   Concerning
Morals,* § 1. 'The hypothesis we
embrace . . . defines virtue to be
whatever mental action or quality
gives to the spectator the pleasing
sentiment of approbation.'—Ibid.
Append. I. 'The crime or immorality is no particular fact or relation which can be the object of the
understanding, but arises entirely
from the sentiment of disapprobation, which, by the structure of
human nature, we unavoidably feel
on the apprehension of barbarity or
treachery.' — Ibid.   'Reason in-
structs us in the several tendencies
of actions, and humanity makes a
distinction in favour of those which
are useful and beneficial.'—Ibid.
'As virtue is an end, and is desirable on its own account without
fee or reward, merely for the immediate satisfaction it conveys, it
is requisite that there should be
some sentiment which it touches,

It is supposed by many that it is a complete description of the Utilitarian system of morals, that it judges all actions and dispositions by their consequences, pronouncing them moral in proportion to their tendency to promote, immoral in proportion to their tendency to diminish, the happiness of man But such a summary is clearly inadequate, for it deals only with one of the two questions which every moralist must answer. A theory of morals must explain not only what constitutes a duty, but also how we obtain the notion of there being such a thing as duty. It must tell us not merely what is the course of conduct we *ought* to pursue, but also what is the meaning of this word ' ought,' and from what source we derive the idea it expresses.

Those who have undertaken to prove that all our morality is a product of experience, have not shrunk from this task, and have boldly entered upon the one path that was open to them. The notion of there being any such feeling as an original sense of obligation distinct from the anticipation of pleasure or pain, they treat as a mere illusion of the imagination. All that is meant by saying we ought to do an action is, that if we do not do it, we shall suffer. A desire to obtain happiness and to avoid pain is the only possible motive to action. The reason, and the only reason, why we should perform virtuous actions, or in other words, seek the good of others, is that on the whole such a course will bring us the greatest amount of happiness.

We have here then a general statement of the doctrine which bases morals upon experience. If we ask what constitutes virtuous, and what vicious actions, we are told that the first are those which increase the happiness or diminish the

---

some internal taste or feeling, or whatever you please to call it, which distinguishes moral good and evil, and which embraces the one and rejects the other.'—Ibid. The two writers to whom Hume was most indebted were Hutcheson and Butler. In some interesting letters to the former (Burton's *Life of Hume*, vol. i.), he discusses the points on which he differed from them.

pains of mankind; and the second are those which have the opposite effect. If we ask what is the motive to virtue, we are told that it is an enlightened self-interest. The words happiness, utility, and interest include, however, many different kinds of enjoyment, and have given rise to many different modifications of the theory.

Perhaps the lowest and most repulsive form of this theory is that which was propounded by Mandeville, in his 'Enquiry into the Origin of Moral Virtue.'[1] According to this writer, virtue sprang in the first instance from the cunning of rulers. These, in order to govern men, found it necessary to persuade them that it was a noble thing to restrain, instead of indulging their passions, and to devote themselves entirely to the good of the community. The manner in which they attained this end was by acting upon the feeling of vanity. They persuaded men that human nature was something nobler than the nature of animals, and that devotion to the community rendered a man pre-eminently great. By statues, and titles, and honours; by continually extolling such men as Regulus or Decius; by representing those who were addicted to useless enjoyments as a low and despicable class, they at last so inflamed the vanity of men as to kindle an intense emulation, and inspire

---

[1] 'The chief thing therefore which lawgivers and other wise men that have laboured for the establishment of society have endeavoured, has been to make the people they were to govern believe that it was more beneficial for everybody to conquer than to indulge his appetites, and much better to mind the public than what seemed his private interest . . . observing that none were either so savage as not to be charmed with praise, or so despicable as patiently to bear contempt, they justly concluded that flattery must be the most powerful argument that could be used to human creatures. Making use of this bewitching engine, they extolled the excellency of our nature above other animals . . . by the help of which we were capable of performing the most noble achievements. Having, by this artful flattery, insinuated themselves into the hearts of men, they began to instruct them in the notions of honour and shame, &c.' —*Enquiry into the Origin of Moral Virtue.*

the most heroic actions. And soon new influences came into play. Men who began by restraining their passions, in order to acquire the pleasure of the esteem of others, found that this restraint saved them from many painful consequences that would have naturally ensued from over-indulgence, and this discovery became a new motive to virtue. Each member of the community moreover found that he himself derived benefit from the self-sacrifice of others, and also that when he was seeking his own interest, without regard to others, no persons stood so much in his way as those who were similarly employed, and he had thus a double reason for diffusing abroad the notion of the excellence of self-sacrifice. The result of all this was that men agreed to stigmatise under the term 'vice' whatever was injurious, and to eulogise as 'virtue.' whatever was beneficial to society.

The opinions of Mandeville attracted, when they were published, an attention greatly beyond their intrinsic merit, but they are now sinking rapidly into deserved oblivion. The author, in a poem called the 'Fable of the Bees,' and in comments attached to it, himself advocated a thesis altogether inconsistent with that I have described, maintaining that 'private vices were public benefits,' and endeavouring, in a long series of very feeble and sometimes very grotesque arguments, to prove that vice was in the highest degree beneficial to mankind. A far greater writer had however already framed a scheme of morals which, if somewhat less repulsive, was in no degree less selfish than that of Mandeville; and the opinions of Hobbes concerning the essence and origin of virtue, have, with no very great variations, been adopted by what may be termed the narrower school of Utilitarians.

According to these writers we are governed exclusively by our own interest.[1] Pleasure, they assure us, is the only

---

[1] 'I conceive that when a man deliberates whether he shall do a thing or not do it, he does nothing else but consider whether it be better for himself to do it or not to do it.'—Hobbes *On Liberty and*

good,[1] and moral good and moral evil mean nothing more
than our voluntary conformity to a law that will bring it to
us.[2] To love good simply as good, is impossible.[3] When we
speak of the goodness of God, we mean only His goodness to

Necessity. 'Good and evil are
names that signify our appetites
and aversions.' — Ibid. *Leviathan,*
part i. ch. xvi. 'Obligation is the
necessity of doing or omitting any
action in order to be happy.'—Gay's
dissertation prefixed to King's *Origin of Evil,* p. 36. 'The only reason
or motive by which individuals can
possibly be induced to the practice
of virtue, must be the feeling immediate or the prospect of future
private happiness.'—Brown *On the
Characteristics,* p. 159. 'En tout
temps, en tout lieu, tant en matière
de morale qu'en matière d'esprit,
c'est l'intérêt personnel qui dicte le
jugement des particuliers, et l'intérêt général qui dicte celui des
nations. . . . Tout homme ne prend
dans ses jugements conseil que de
son intérêt.'—Helvétius *De l'Esprit,*
discours ii. 'Nature has placed
mankind under the governance of
two sovereign masters, pain and
pleasure. It is for them alone to
point out what we ought to do, as
well as to determine what we shall
do. . . . The principle of utility
recognises this subjection, and assumes it for the foundation of that
system, the object of which is to
rear the fabric of felicity by the
hands of reason and of law Systems
which attempt to question it, deal
in sounds instead of sense, in caprice
instead of reason, in darkness instead of light.'—Bentham's *Principles of Morals and Legislation,* ch. i.
'By the principle of utility is meant
that principle which approves or
disapproves of every action whatsoever, according to the tendency

which it appears to have to augment
or diminish the happiness of the
party whose interest is in question.
—Ibid. 'Je regarde l'amour éclairé
de nous-mêmes comme le principe
de tout sacrifice moral.'—D'Alem-
bert quoted by D. Stewart, *Active
and Moral Powers,* vol. i. p. 220.

[1] 'Pleasure is in itself a good;
nay, even setting aside immunity
from pain, the only good; pain is
in itself an evil, and, indeed, without exception, the only evil, or else
the words good and evil have no
meaning.'— Bentham's *Principles
of Morals and Legislation,* ch. x.

[2] 'Good and evil are nothing
but pleasure and pain, or that which
occasions or procures pleasure or
pain to us. Moral good and evil
then is only the conformity or dis-
agreement of our voluntary actions
to some law whereby good or evil
is drawn on us by the will and
power of the law maker, which
good and evil, pleasure or pain, attending our observance or breach
of the law by the decree of the law
maker, is that we call reward or punishment.'—Locke's *Essay,* book ii.
ch. xxviii. 'Take away pleasures
and pains, not only happiness, but
justice, and duty, and obligation,
and virtue, all of which have been
so elaborately held up to view as
independent of them, are so many
empty sounds.'—Bentham's *Springs
of Action,* ch. i. § 15.

[3] 'Il lui est aussi impossible
d'aimer le bien pour le bien, que
d'aimer le mal pour le mal.' —
Helvétius *De l'Esprit,* disc. ii.
ch. v.

us.[1] Reverence is nothing more than our conviction, that one who has power to do us both good and harm, will only do us good.[2] The pleasures of piety arise from the belief that we are about to receive pleasure, and the pains of piety from the belief that we are about to suffer pain from the Deity.[3] Our very affections, according to some of these writers, are all forms of self-love. Thus charity springs partly from our desire to obtain the esteem of others, partly from the expectation that the favours we have bestowed will be reciprocated, and partly, too, from the gratification of the sense of power, by the proof that we can satisfy not only our own desires but also the desires of others.[4] Pity is an emotion arising from a vivid realisation of sorrow that may befall ourselves, suggested by the sight of the sorrows of others. We pity especially those who have not

---

[1] 'Even the goodness which we apprehend in God Almighty, is his goodness to us.'—Hobbes *On Human Nature*, ch. vii. § 3. So Waterland, 'To love God is in effect the same thing as to love happiness, eternal happiness; and the love of happiness is still the love of ourselves.'—*Third Sermon on Self-love*.

[2] 'Reverence is the conception we have concerning another, that he hath the power to do unto us both good and hurt, but not the will to do us hurt.'—Hobbes *On Human Nature*, ch. viii. § 7.

[3] 'The pleasures of piety are the pleasures that accompany the belief of a man's being in the acquisition, or in possession of the good-will or favour of the Supreme Being; and as a fruit of it, of his being in the way of enjoying pleasures to be received by God's special appointment either in this life or in a life to come.'—Bentham's *Principles of Morals and Legislation*, ch. v. 'The pains of piety are the pains that accompany the belief of a man's

being obnoxious to the displeasure of the Supreme Being, and in consequence to certain pains to be inflicted by His especial appointment, either in this life or in a life to come. These may be also called the pains of religion.'—Ibid.

[4] 'There can be no greater argument to a man of his own power, than to find himself able not only to accomplish his own desires, but also to assist other men in theirs; and this is that conception wherein consisteth charity.'—Hobbes *On Hum. Nat.* ch. ix. § 17. 'No man giveth but with intention of good to himself, because gift is voluntary; and of all voluntary acts, the object to every man is his own good.'—Hobbes' *Leviathan*, part i. ch. xv. 'Dream not that men will move their little finger to serve you, unless their advantage in so doing be obvious to them. Men never did so, and never will while human nature is made of its present materials.'—Bentham's *Deontology*, vol. ii. p. 133

deserved calamity, because we consider ourselves to belong to that category ; and the spectacle of suffering against which no forethought could provide, reminds us most forcibly of what may happen to ourselves.[1] Friendship is the sense of the need of the person befriended.[2]

From such a conception of human nature it is easy to divine what system of morals must flow. No character, feeling, or action is naturally better than others, and as long as men are in a savage condition, morality has no existence. Fortunately, however, we are all dependent for many of our pleasures upon others. Co-operation and organisation are essential to our happiness, and these are impossible without

[1] ' Pity is imagination or fiction of future calamity to ourselves, proceeding from the sense of another man's calamity. But when it lighteth on such as we think have not deserved the same, the compassion is greater, because there then appeareth more probability that the same may happen to us ; for the evil that happeneth to an innocent man may happen to every man.'— Hobbes *On Hum. Nat.* ch. ix. § 10. ' La pitié est souvent un sentiment de nos propres maux dans les maux d'autrui. C'est une habile prévoyance des malheurs où nous pouvons tomber. Nous donnons des secours aux autres pour les engager à nous en donner en de semblables occasions, et ces services que nous leur rendons sont, à proprement parler, des biens que nous nous faisons à nous-mêmes par avance.'— La Rochefoucauld, *Maximes*, 264. Butler has remarked that if Hobbes' account were true, the most fearful would be the most compassionate nature ; but this is perhaps not quite just, for Hobbes' notion of pity implies the union of two not absolutely identical, though nearly allied, influences, timidity and ima-

gination. The theory of Adam Smith, though closely connected with, differs totally in consequences from that of Hobbes on this point. He says, ' When I condole with you for the loss of your son, in order to enter into your grief, I do not consider what I, a person of such a character and profession, should suffer if I had a son, and if that son should die — I consider what I should suffer if I was really you. I not only change circumstances with you, but I change persons and characters. My grief, therefore, is entirely upon your account. . . . A man may sympathise with a woman in child-bed, though it is impossible he should conceive himself suffering her pains in his own proper person and character.'— *Moral Sentiments*, part vii. ch. i. § 3.

[2] ' Ce que les hommes ont nommé amitié n'est qu'une société, qu'un ménagement réciproque d'intérêts et qu'un échange de bons offices. Ce n'est enfin qu'un commerce où l'amour-propre se propose toujours quelque chose à gagner.'— La Rochefoucauld, *Max.* 83. See this idea developed at large in Helvétius.

some restraint being placed upon our appetites. Laws are enacted to secure this restraint, and being sustained by rewards and punishments, they make it the interest of the individual to regard that of the community. According to Hobbes, the disposition of man is so anarchical, and the importance of restraining it so transcendent, that absolute government alone is good; the commands of the sovereign are supreme, and must therefore constitute the law of morals. The other moralists of the school, though repudiating this notion, have given a very great and distinguished place to legislation in their schemes of ethics; for all our conduct being determined by our interests, virtue being simply the conformity of our own interests with those of the community, and a judicious legislation being the chief way of securing this conformity, the functions of the moralist and of the legislator are almost identical.[1] But in addition to the rewards and punishments of the penal code, those arising from public opinion—fame or infamy, the friendship or hostility of those about us—are enlisted on the side of virtue. The educating influence of laws, and the growing perception of the identity of interests of the different members of the community, create a public opinion favourable to all the qualities which are 'the means of peaceable, sociable, and comfortable living.'[2] Such are justice, gratitude, modesty,

---

[1] 'La science de la morale n'est autre chose que la science même de la législation.'—Helvétius *De l'Esprit*, ii. 17.

[2] This doctrine is expounded at length in all the moral works of Hobbes and his school. The following passage is a fair specimen of their meaning:—'Moral philosophy is nothing else but the science of what is good and evil in the conversation and society of mankind. Good and evil are names that signify our appetites and aversions, which in different tempers, customs, and doctrines of men are different . . . from whence arise disputes, controversies, and at last war. And therefore, so long as man is in this condition of mere nature (which is a condition of war), his private appetite is the measure of good and evil. And consequently all men agree in this, that peace is good, and therefore also that the ways or means of peace, (which, as I have showed before) are justice, gratitude, modesty.

equity, and mercy; and such, too, are purity and chastity, which, considered in themselves alone, are in no degree more excellent than the coarsest and most indiscriminate lust, but which can be shown to be conducive to the happiness of society, and become in consequence virtues.[1] This education of public opinion grows continually stronger with civilisation, and gradually moulds the characters of men, making them more and more disinterested, heroic, and unselfish. A disinterested, unselfish, and heroic man, it is explained, is one who is strictly engrossed in the pursuit of his own pleasure, but who pursues it in such a manner as to include in its gratification the happiness of others.[2]

It is a very old assertion, that a man who prudently sought his own interest would live a life of perfect virtue. This opinion is adopted by most of those Utilitarians who are least inclined to lay great stress upon religious motives; and as they maintain that every man necessarily pursues exclusively his own happiness, we return by another path to the old Platonic doctrine, that all vice is ignorance. Virtue is a judicious, and vice an injudicious, pursuit of pleasure. Virtue is a branch of prudence, vice is nothing more than

---

equity, mercy, and the rest of the laws of nature are good . . . and their contrary vices evil.'—Hobbes' *Leviathan*, part i. ch. xvi. See, too, a striking passage in Bentham's *Deontology*, vol. ii. p. 132.

[1] As an ingenious writer in the *Saturday Review* (Aug. 10, 1867) expresses it: 'Chastity is merely a social law created to encourage the alliances that most promote the permanent welfare of the race, and to maintain woman in a social position which it is thought advisable she should hold.' See, too, on this view, Hume's *Inquiry concerning Morals*, § 4, and also *note* x.: 'To what other purpose do all

the ideas of chastity and modesty serve? Nisi utile est quod facimus, frustra est gloria.'

[2] 'All pleasure is necessarily self-regarding, for it is impossible to have any feelings out of our own mind. But there are modes of delight that bring also satisfaction to others, from the round that they take in their course. Such are the pleasures of benevolence. Others imply no participation by any second party, as, for example, eating, drinking, bodily warmth, property, and power; while a third class are fed by the pains and privations of fellow-beings, as the delights of sport and tyranny. The

imprudence or miscalculation.[1] He who seeks to improve
the moral condition of mankind has two, and only two,
ways of accomplishing his end.   The first is, to make it
more and more the interest of each to conform to that of
the others ; the second is, to dispel the ignorance which
prevents men from seeing their true interest.[2] If chastity
or truth, or any other of what we regard as virtues, could be
shown to produce on the whole more pain than they destroy,
or to deprive men of more pleasure than they afford, they
would not be virtues, but vices.[3] If it could be shown that

condemnatory phrase, selfishness, applies with especial emphasis to the last-mentioned class, and, in a qualified degree, to the second group; while such terms as unselfishness, disinterestedness, self-devotion, are applied to the vicarious position wherein we seek our own satisfaction in that of others.' —Bain ,On the Emotions and Will, p. 113.

[1] 'Vice may be defined to be a miscalculation of chances, a mistake in estimating the value of pleasures and pains. It is false moral arithmetic.' — Bentham's Deontology, vol. i. p. 131.

[2] 'La récompense, la punition, la gloire et l'infamie soumises à ses volontés sont quatre espèces de divinités avec lesquelles le législateur peut toujours opérer le bien public et créer des hommes illustres en tous les genres. Toute l'étude des moralistes consiste à déterminer l'usage qu'on doit faire de ces récompenses et de ces punitions et les secours qu'on peut tirer pour lier l'intérêt personnel à l'intérêt général '—Helvétius De l'Esprit, i. 22. 'La justice de nos jugements et de nos actions n'est jamais que la rencontre heureuse de notre intérêt avec l'intérêt pub-

lic.'—Ibid. ii. 7. 'To prove that the immoral action is a miscalculation of self-interest, to show how erroneous an estimate the vicious man makes of pains and pleasures, is the purpose of the intelligent moralist. Unless he can do this he does nothing; for, as has been stated above, for a man not to pursue what he deems likely to produce to him the greatest sum of enjoyment, is, in the very nature of things, impossible.'—Bentham's Deontology.

[3] 'If the effect of virtue were to prevent or destroy more pleasure than it produced, or to produce more pain than it prevented, its more appropriate name would be wickedness and folly ; wickedness as it affected others, folly as respected him who practised it.'—Bentham's Deontology, vol. i. p. 142. 'Weigh pains, weigh pleasures, and as the balance stands will stand the question of right and wrong.' — Ibid. vol. i. p. 127. 'Moralis philosophiæ caput est, Faustine fili, ut scias quibus ad beatam vitam perveniri rationibus possit.'—Apuleius, Ad Doct. Platonis, ii. 'Atque ipsa utilitas, justi prope mater et æqui.' - Horace Sat. I. iii. 98.

it is not for our own interest to practise any of what are admitted to be virtues, all obligation to practise them would immediately cease.[1] The whole scheme of ethics may be evolved from the four canons of Epicurus. The pleasure which produces no pain is to be embraced. The pain which produces no pleasure is to be avoided. The pleasure is to be avoided which prevents a greater pleasure, or produces a greater pain. The pain is to be endured which averts a greater pain, or secures a greater pleasure.[2]

So far I have barely alluded to any but terrestrial motives. These, in the opinion of many of the most illustrious of the school, are sufficient, but others—as we shall see, I think, with great reason—are of a different opinion. Their obvious resource is in the rewards and punishments of another world, and these they accordingly present as the motive to virtue. Of all the modifications of the selfish theory, this alone can be said to furnish interested motives for virtue which are invariably and incontestably adequate. If men introduce the notion of infinite punishments and infinite rewards distributed by an omniscient Judge, they can undoubtedly supply stronger reasons for practising virtue than can ever be found for practising vice. While admitting therefore in emphatic terms, that any sacrifice of our pleasure, without the prospect of an equivalent reward, is a simple act of madness, and unworthy of a rational being,[3] these

---

[1] 'We can be obliged to nothing but what we ourselves are to gain or lose something by; for nothing else can be "violent motive" to us. As we should not be obliged to obey the laws or the magistrate unless rewards or punishments, pleasure or pain, somehow or other, depended upon our obedience; so neither should we, without the same reason, be obliged to do what is right, to practise virtue, or to obey the commands of God.'—

Paley's *Moral Philosophy*, book ii. ch. ii.

[2] See Gassendi *Philosophiæ Epicuri Syntagma.* These four canons are a skilful condensation of the argument of Torquatus in Cicero, *De Fin.* i. 2. See, too, a very striking letter by Epicurus himself, given in his life by Diogenes Laërtius.

[3] 'Sanus igitur non est, qui nulla spe majore proposita, iis bonis quibus cæteri utuntur in vita, la-

writers maintain that we may reasonably sacrifice the enjoyments of this life, because we shall be rewarded by far greater enjoyment in the next. To gain heaven and avoid hell should be the spring of all our actions,[1] and virtue is simply prudence extending its calculations beyond the grave.[2]

---

bores et cruciatus et miserias anteponat. . . . . Non aliter his bonis præsentibus abstinendum est quam si sint aliqua majora, propter quæ tanti sit et voluptates omittere et mala omnia sustinere.'—Lactantius, *Div. Inst.* vi. 9. Macaulay, in some youthful essays against the Utilitarian theory (which he characteristically described as 'Not much more laughable than phrenology, and immeasurably more humane than cock-fighting'), maintains the theological form of selfishness in very strong terms. 'What proposition is there respecting human nature which is absolutely and universally true? We know of only one, and that is not only true but identical, that men always act from self-interest.' — Review of Mill's *Essay on Government.* 'Of this we may be sure, that the words "greatest happiness" will never in any man's mouth mean more than the greatest happiness of others, which is consistent with what he thinks his own. . . . This direction (Do as you would be done by) would be utterly unmeaning, as it actually is in Mr. Bentham's philosophy, unless it were accompanied by a sanction. In the Christian scheme accordingly it is accompanied by a sanction of immense force. To a man whose greatest happiness in this world is inconsistent with the greatest happiness of the greatest number, is held out the prospect of an infinite happiness hereafter, from

which he excludes himself by wronging his fellow-creatures here.'— *Answer to the Westminster Review's Defence of Mill.*

[1] 'All virtue and piety are thus resolvable into a principle of self-love. It is what Scripture itself resolves them into by founding them upon faith in God's promises, and hope in things unseen. In this way it may be rightly said that there is no such thing as disinterested virtue. It is with reference to ourselves and for our own sakes that we love even God Himself.'—Waterland, *Third Sermon on Self-love.* 'To risk the happiness of the whole duration of our being in any case whatever, were it possible, would be foolish.'— Robert Hall's *Sermon on Modern Infidelity.* 'In the moral system the means are virtuous practice; the end, happiness.'—Warburton's *Divine Legation,* book ii. Appendix.

[2] 'There is always understood to be a difference between an act of prudence and an act of duty. Thus, if I distrusted a man who owed me a sum of money, I should reckon it an act of prudence to get another person bound with him; but I should hardly call it an act of duty. . . . Now in what, you will ask, does the difference consist, inasmuch as, according to our account of the matter, both, in the one case and the other, in acts of duty as well as acts of prudence, we consider solely what we our-

This calculation is what we mean by the 'religious motive.' [1]
The belief that the nobility and excellence of virtue could
incite us, was a mere delusion of the Pagans.[2]

Considered simply in the light of a prudential scheme,
there are only two possible objections that could be brought
against this theory. It might be said that the amount of
virtue required for entering heaven was not defined, and
that therefore it would be possible to enjoy some vices on
earth with impunity. To this, however, it is answered that
the very indefiniteness of the requirement renders zealous
piety a matter of prudence, and also that there is probably a
graduated scale of rewards and punishments adapted to every
variety of merit and demerit.[3] It might be said too that
present pleasures are at least certain, and that those of
another world are not equally so. It is answered that the
rewards and punishments offered in another world are so
transcendently great, that according to the rules of ordinary

---

selves shall gain or lose by the
act? The difference, and the only
difference, is this: that in the one
case we consider what we shall
gain or lose in the present world;
in the other case, we consider also
what we shall gain or lose in the
world to come.'—Paley's *Moral
Philosophy*, ii. 3.

[1] 'Hence we may see the weakness and mistake of those falsely
religious . . . who are scandalised
at our being determined to the pursuit of virtue through any degree
of regard to its happy consequences
in this life. . . . For it is evident
that the religious motive is precisely of the same kind, only
stronger, as the happiness expected
is greater and more lasting.'—
Brown's *Essays on the Characteristics*, p. 220.

[2] 'If a Christian, who has the
view of happiness and misery in

another life, be asked why a man
must keep his word, he will give
this as a reason, because God, who
has the power of eternal life and
death, requires it of us. But if an
Hobbist be asked why, he will
answer, because the public requires
it, and the Leviathan will punish
you if you do not. And if one of
the old heathen philosophers had
been asked, he would have an
swered, because it was dishonest,
below the dignity of man, and opposite to virtue, the highest perfection
of human nature, to do otherwise.'
—Locke's *Essay*, i. 3.

[3] Thus Paley remarks that—
'The Christian religion hath not
ascertained the precise quantity of
virtue necessary to salvation,' and
he then proceeds to urge the probability of graduated scales of rewards and punishments. (*Moral
Philosophy*, book i. ch. vii.)

prudence, if there were only a probability, or even a bare possibility, of their being real, a wise man should regulate his course with a view to them.[1]

Among these writers, however, some have diverged to a certain degree from the broad stream of utilitarianism, declaring that the foundation of the moral law is not utility, but the will or arbitrary decree of God. This opinion, which was propounded by the schoolman Ockham, and by several other writers of his age,[2] has in modern times found many adherents,[3] and been defended through a variety of motives. Some have upheld it on the philosophical ground that a law can be nothing but the sentence of a lawgiver; others from a desire to place morals in permanent subordination to theology; others in order to answer objections to Christianity derived from apparently immoral acts said to have been sanctioned by the Divinity; and others because having adopted strong Calvinistic sentiments, they were at once profoundly opposed to utilitarian morals, and at the

---

[1] This view was developed by Locke (*Essay on the Human Understanding*, book ii. ch. xxi.) Pascal, in a well-known passage, applied the same argument to Christianity, urging that the rewards and punishments it promises are so great, that it is the part of a wise man to embrace the creed, even though he believes it improbable, if there be but a possibility in its favour.

[2] Cudworth, in his *Immutable Morals*, has collected the names of a number of the schoolmen who held this view. See, too, an interesting note in Miss Cobbe's very learned *Essay on Intuitive Morals*, pp. 18, 19.

[3] E. g. Soame Jenyns, Dr. Johnson, Crusius, Pascal, Paley, and Austin. Warburton is generally quoted in the list, but not I think quite fairly. See his theory, which is rather complicated (*Divine Legation*, i. 4). Waterland appears to have held this view, and also Condillac. See a very remarkable chapter on morals, in his *Traité des Animaux*, part ii. ch. vii. Closely connected with this doctrine is the notion that the morality of God is generically different from the morality of men, which having been held with more or less distinctness by many theologians (Archbishop King being perhaps the most prominent), has found in our own day an able defender in Dr. Mansel. Much information on the history of this doctrine will be found in Dr. Mansel's *Second Letter* to Professor Goldwin Smith (Oxford, 1862).

same time too firmly convinced of the total depravity of human nature to admit the existence of any trustworthy moral sense.[1]

In the majority of cases, however, these writers have proved substantially utilitarians. When asked how we can know the will of God, they answer that in as far as it is not included in express revelation, it must be discovered by the rule of utility; for nature proves that the Deity is supremely benevolent, and desires the welfare of men, and therefore any conduct that leads to that end is in conformity with His will.[2] To the question why the Divine will should be obeyed, there are but two answers. The first, which is that of the intuitive moralist, is that we are under a natural obligation of gratitude to our Creator. The second, which is that of the selfish moralist, is that the Creator has infinite rewards and punishments at His disposal. The latter answer appears usually to have been adopted, and the most eminent member has summed up with great succinctness the opinion of his school. 'The good of mankind,' he says, 'is the subject, the will of God the rule, and everlasting happiness the motive and end of all virtue.'[3]

---

[1] Leibnitz noticed the frequency with which Supralapsarian Calvinists adopt this doctrine. (*Théodicée*, part ii § 176.) Archbishop Whately, who from his connection with the Irish Clergy had admirable opportunities of studying the tendencies of Calvinism, makes a similar remark as the result of his own experience. (*Whately's Life*, vol. ii. p. 339.)

[2] 'God designs the happiness of all His sentient creatures. . . . Knowing the tendencies of our actions, and knowing His benevolent purpose, we know His tacit commands.'—Austin's *Lectures on Jurisprudence*, vol. i. p. 31.   'The

commands which He has revealed we must gather from the terms wherein they are promulgated. The commands which He has not revealed we must construe by the principle of utility.'—Ibid. p. 96. So Paley's *Moral Philosophy*, book ii. ch. iv. v.

[3] Paley's *Moral Philosophy*, book 1. ch. vii. The question of the disinterestedness of the love we should bear to God was agitated in the Catholic Church, Bossuet taking the selfish, and Fénelon the unselfish side. The opinions of Fénelon and Molinos on the subject were authoritatively condemned. In England, the less dogmatic cha

We have seen that the distinctive characteristic of the inductive school of moralists is an absolute denial of the existence of any natural or innate moral sense or faculty enabling us to distinguish between the higher and lower parts of our nature, revealing to us either the existence of a law of duty or the conduct that it prescribes. We have seen that the only postulate of these writers is that happiness being universally desired is a desirable thing, that the only merit they recognise in actions or feelings is their tendency to promote human happiness, and that the only motive to a virtuous act they conceive possible is the real or supposed happiness of the agent. The sanctions of morality thus constitute its obligation, and apart from them the word 'ought' is absolutely unmeaning. Those sanctions, as we have considered them, are of different kinds and degrees of magnitude. Paley, though elsewhere acknowledging the others, regarded the religious one as so immeasurably the first, that he represented it as the one motive of virtue.[1] Locke divided them into Divine rewards and punishments, legal penalties and social penalties;[2] Bentham into physical, political, moral or popular, and religious—the first being the bodily evils that result from vice, the second the enactments of legislators, the third the pleasures and pains arising from social intercourse, the fourth the rewards and punishments of another world.[3]

---

racter of the national faith, and also the fact that the great anti-Christian writer, Hobbes, was the advocate of extreme selfishness in morals, had, I think, a favourable influence upon the ethics of the church. Hobbes gave the first great impulse to moral philosophy in England, and his opponents were naturally impelled to an unselfish theory. Bishop Cumberland led the way, resolving virtue (like Hutcheson) into benevolence.

The majority of divines, however, till the present century, have, I think, been on the selfish side.

[1] *Moral Philosophy*, ii. 3.

[2] *Essay on the Human Understanding*, ii. 28.

[3] *Principles of Morals and Legislation*, ch. iii. Mr. Mill observes that, 'Bentham's idea of the world is that of a collection of persons pursuing each his separate interest or pleasure, and the prevention of whom from jostling one

During the greater part of the sixteenth and seventeenth centuries the controversy in England between those who derived the moral code from experience, and those who derived it from intuitions of the reason, or from a special faculty, or from a moral sense, or from the power of sympathy, turned mainly upon the existence of an unselfish element in our nature. The reality of this existence having been maintained by Shaftesbury, was established with an unprecedented, and I believe an irresistible force, by Hutcheson, and the same question occupies a considerable place in the writings of Butler, Hume, and Adam Smith. The selfishness of the school of Hobbes, though in some degree mitigated, may be traced in every page of the writings of Bentham; but some of his disciples have in this respect deviated very widely from their master, and in their hands the whole tone and complexion of utilitarianism have been changed.[1] The two means by which this transformation

---

another more than is unavoidable, may be attempted by hopes and fears derived from three sources— the law, religion, and public opinion. To these three powers, considered as binding human conduct, he gave the name of sanctions; the political sanction operating by the rewards and penalties of the law; the religious sanction by those expected from the ruler of the universe; and the popular, which he characteristically calls also the moral sanction, operating through the pains and pleasures arising from the favour or disfavour of our fellow-creatures.'—*Dissertations*, vol. i. pp. 362–363.

[1] Hume on this, as on most other points, was emphatically opposed to the school of Hobbes, and even declared that no one could honestly and in good faith deny the reality of an unselfish element

in man. Following in the steps of Butler, he explained it in the following passage:—'Hunger and thirst have eating and drinking for their end, and from the gratification of these primary appetites arises a pleasure which may become the object of another species of desire or inclination that is secondary and interested. In the same manner there are mental passions by which we are impelled immediately to seek particular objects, such as fame or power or vengeance, without any regard to interest, and when these objects are attained a pleasing enjoyment ensues. . . . Now where is the difficulty of conceiving that this may likewise be the case with benevolence and friendship, and that from the original frame of our temper we may feel a desire of another's happiness or good, which by means of has been effected are the recognition of our unselfish or sympathetic feelings, and the doctrine of the association of ideas.

That human nature is so constituted that we naturally take a pleasure in the sight of the joy of others is one of those facts which to an ordinary observer might well appear among the most patent that can be conceived. We have seen, however, that it was emphatically denied by Hobbes, and during the greater part of the last century it was fashionable among writers of the school of Helvétius to endeavour to prove that all domestic or social affections were dictated simply by a need of the person who was beloved. The reality of the pleasures and pains of sympathy was admitted by Bentham;[1] but in accordance with the whole spirit of his philosophy, he threw them as much as possible into the background, and, as I have already noticed, gave them no place in his summary of the sanctions of virtue. The tendency, however, of the later members of the school has been to recognise them fully,[2] though they

---

that affection becomes our own good, and is afterwards pursued, from the combined motives of benevolence and self-enjoyment?'—Hume's *Enquiry concerning Morals*, Appendix II. Compare Butler, 'If there be any appetite or any inward principle besides self-love, why may there not be an affection towards the good of our fellow-creatures, and delight from that affection's being gratified and uneasiness from things going contrary to it?'—*Sermon on Compassion*.

[1] 'By sympathetic sensibility is to be understood the propensity that a man has to derive pleasure from the happiness, and pain from the unhappiness, of other sensitive beings.'—Bentham's *Principles of Morals and Legislation*, ch. vi.

'The sense of sympathy is universal. Perhaps there never existed a human being who had reached full age without the experience of pleasure at another's pleasure, of uneasiness at another's pain. . . . Community of interests, similarity of opinion, are sources from whence it springs.'—*Deontology*, vol. i. pp. 169–170.

[2] 'The idea of the pain of another is naturally painful. The idea of the pleasure of another is naturally pleasurable. . . . In this, the unselfish part of our nature, lies a foundation, even independently of inculcation from without, for the generation of moral feelings'—Mill's *Dissertations*, vol. i. p. 137. See, too, Bain's *Emotions and the Will*, pp. 289, 313; and es

differ as to the source from which they spring. According to one section our benevolent affections are derived from our selfish feelings by an association of ideas in a manner which I shall presently describe. According to the other they are an original part of the constitution of our nature. However they be generated, their existence is admitted, their cultivation is a main object of morals, and the pleasure derived from their exercise a leading motive to virtue. The differences between the intuitive moralists and their rivals on this point are of two kinds. Both acknowledge the existence in human nature of both benevolent and malevolent feelings, and that we have a natural power of distinguishing one from the other; but the first maintain and the second deny that we have a natural power of perceiving that one is better than the other. Both admit that we enjoy a pleasure in acts of benevolence to others, but most writers of the first school maintain that that pleasure follows unsought for, while writers of the other school contend that the desire of obtaining it is the motive of the action.

But by far the most ingenious and at the same time most influential system of utilitarian morals is that which owes its distinctive feature to the doctrine of association of Hartley. This doctrine, which among the modern achievements of ethics occupies on the utilitarian side a position corresponding in importance to the doctrine of innate moral faculties as distinguished from innate moral ideas on the intuitive side, was not absolutely unknown to the ancients, though they never perceived either the extent to which it may be carried or the important consequences that might be deduced from it. Some traces of it may be found in Aris-

---

pecially Austin's *Lectures on Jurisprudence.* The first volume of this brilliant work contains, I think without exception, the best modern statement of the utilitarian theory in its most plausible form—a statement equally remarkable for its ability, its candour, and its uniform courtesy to opponents.

totle,[1] and some of the Epicureans applied it to friendship, maintaining that, although we first of all love our friend on account of the pleasure he can give us, we come soon to love him for his own sake, and apart from all considerations of utility.[2] Among moderns Locke has the merit of having devised the phrase, 'association of ideas;'[3] but he applied it only to some cases of apparently eccentric sympathies or antipathies. Hutcheson, however, closely anticipated both the doctrine of Hartley and the favourite illustration of the school; observing that we desire some things as themselves pleasurable and others only as means to obtain pleasurable things, and that these latter, which he terms ' secondary desires,' may become as powerful as the former. ' Thus, as soon as we come to apprehend the use of wealth or power to gratify any of our original desires we must also desire them. Hence arises the universality of these desires of wealth and power, since they are the means of gratifying all our desires.'[4] The same principles were carried much farther by a clergyman named Gay in a short dissertation which is now almost forgotten, but to which Hartley ascribed the first suggestion of his theory,[5] and in which indeed the most valuable part of it is clearly laid down. Differing altogether from Hutcheson as to the existence of any innate moral sense or principle

---

[1] See a collection of passages from Aristotle, bearing on the subject, in Mackintosh's *Dissertation*.

[2] Cic. *De Finibus*, i. 5. This view is adopted in Tucker's *Light of Nature* (ed. 1842), vol. i. p. 167. See, too, Mill's *Analysis of the Human Mind*, vol. ii. p. 174.

[3] *Essay*, book ii. ch. xxxiii.

[4] Hutcheson *On the Passions*, § 1. The 'secondary desires' of Hutcheson are closely related to the 'reflex affections' of Shaftesbury. ' Not only the outward beings which offer themselves to the sense are the objects of the affection; but the very actions themselves, and the affections of pity, kindness, gratitude, and their contraries, being brought into the mind by reflection become objects. So that by means of this reflected sense, there arises another kind of affection towards those very affections themselves.'— Shaftesbury's *Enquiry concerning Virtue*, book i. part ii. § 3.

[5] See the preface to Hartley *On Man*. Gay's essay is prefixed to Law's translation of Archbishop King *On the Origin of Evil*.

of benevolence in man, Gay admitted that the arguments of
Hutcheson to prove that the adult man possesses a moral
sense were irresistible, and he attempted to reconcile this fact
with the teaching of Locke by the doctrine of 'secondary
desires.' He remarks that in our reasonings we do not always fall back upon first principles or axioms, but sometimes
start from propositions which though not self-evident we
know to be capable of proof. In the same way in justifying
our actions we do not always appeal to the tendency to
produce happiness which is their one ultimate justification,
but content ourselves by showing that they produce some of
the known 'means to happiness.' These 'means to happiness' being continually appealed to as justifying motives
come insensibly to be regarded as ends, possessing an intrinsic
value irrespective of their tendency ; and in this manner it is
that we love and admire virtue even when unconnected with
our interests.[1]

The great work of Hartley expanding and elaborating
these views was published in 1747. It was encumbered by
much physiological speculation into which it is needless for
us now to enter, about the manner in which emotions act
upon the nerves, and although accepted enthusiastically by
Priestley and Belsham, and in some degree by Tucker, I do not
think that its purely ethical speculations had much influence
until they were adopted by some leading utilitarians in the

---

[1] 'The case is this. We first
perceive or imagine some real good ;
i.e. fitness to promote our happiness
in those things which we love or approve of. . . . . Hence those things
and pleasures are so tied together
and associated in our minds, that
one cannot present itself, but the
other will also occur. And the association remains even after that
which at first gave them the connection is quite forgotten, or perhaps
does not exist, but the contrary.'—
Gay's *Essay*, p. lii. 'All affections
whatsoever are finally resolvable
into reason, pointing out private
happiness, and are conversant only
about things apprehended to be
means tending to this end; and
whenever this end is not perceived,
they are to be accounted for from
the association of ideas, and may
properly enough be called habits
—Ibid. p. xxxi.

present century.[1] Whatever may be thought of the truth, it
is impossible to withhold some admiration from the intellectual grandeur of a system which starting from a conception
of human nature as low and as base as that of Mandeville or
Hobbes professes without the introduction of a single new or
nobler element, by a strange process of philosophic alchemy,
to evolve out of this original selfishness the most heroic and
most sensitive virtue. The manner in which this achieve-
ment is effected is commonly illustrated by the passion of
avarice. Money in itself possesses absolutely nothing that is
admirable or pleasurable, but being the means of procuring
us many of the objects of our desire, it becomes associated in
our minds with the idea of pleasure; it is therefore itself
loved; and it is possible for the love of money so completely
to eclipse or supersede the love of all those things which
money procures, that the miser will forego them all, rather
than part with a fraction of his gold.[2]

---

[1] Principally by Mr. James Mill,
whose chapter on association, in his
Analysis of the Human Mind, may
probably rank with Paley's beautiful chapter on happiness, at the
head of all modern writings on the
utilitarian side,—either of them, I
think, being far more valuable than
anything Bentham ever wrote on
morals. This last writer—whose
contempt for his predecessors was
only equalled by his ignorance of
their works, and who has added
surprisingly little to moral science
(considering the reputation he attained), except a barbarous nomen-
clature and an interminable series
of classifications evincing no real
subtlety of thought—makes, as far
as I am aware, no use of the doctrine of association. Paley states
it with his usual admirable clearness. 'Having experienced in some
instances a particular conduct to be

beneficial to ourselves, or observed
that it would be so, a sentiment of
approbation rises up in our minds,
which sentiment afterwards accompanies the idea or mention of the
same conduct, although the private
advantage which first existed no
longer exist.'—Paley, *Moral Philos.*
i. 5. Paley, however, made less
use of this doctrine than might have
been expected from so enthusiastic
an admirer of Tucker. In our own
day it has been much used by Mr.
J. S. Mill.

[2] This illustration, which was
first employed by Hutcheson, is
very happily developed by Gay (p.
lii.). It was then used by Hartley,
and finally Tucker reproduced the
whole theory with the usual illustration without any acknowledg-
ment of the works of his predecessors, employing however, the term
'translation' instead of ' associa-

71243

LIBRARY
College of St. Francis
JOLIET, ILL.

The same phenomenon may be traced, it is said, in a multitude of other forms.[1] Thus we seek power, because it gives us the means of gratifying many desires. It becomes associated with those desires, and is, at last, itself passionately loved. Praise indicates the affection of the eulogist, and marks us out for the affection of others. Valued at first as a means, it is soon desired as an end, and to such a pitch can our enthusiasm rise, that we may sacrifice all earthly things for posthumous praise which can never reach our ear. And the force of association may extend even farther. We love praise, because it procures us certain advantages. We then love it more than these advantages. We proceed by the same process to transfer our affections to those things which naturally or generally procure praise. We at last love what is praiseworthy more than praise, and will endure perpetual obloquy rather than abandon it.[2] To this process, it is said, all our moral sentiments must be ascribed. Man has no natural benevolent feelings. He is at first governed solely by his interest, but the infant learns to associate its pleasures with the idea of its mother, the boy with the idea of his family, the man with those of his class, his church, his country, and at last of all mankind, and in each case an independent affection is at length formed.[3] The sight of suffering in others awakens in the child a painful recollection of his own sufferings, which parents, by appealing to the infant imagination, still further strengthen, and besides, ' when several children are educated together, the pains, the

---

tion' of ideas. See his curious chapter on the subject, *Light of Nature*, book i. ch. xviii.

[1] ' It is the nature of translation to throw desire from the end upon the means, which thenceforward become an end capable of exciting an appetite without prospect of the consequences whereto they dead. Our habits and most of the

desires that occupy human life are of this translated kind.'—Tucker's *Light of Nature*, vol. ii. (ed. 1842), p. 281.

[2] Mill's *Analysis of the Human Mind*. The desire for posthumous fame is usually cited by intuitive moralists as a proof of a naturally disinterested element in man.

[3] Mill's *Analysis*.

Jenials of pleasure, and the sorrows which affect one gradu
ally extend in some degree to all;' and thus the suffering of
others becomes associated with the idea of our own, and the
feeling of compassion is engendered.[1] Benevolence and justice are associated in our minds with the esteem of our fellow-
men, with reciprocity of favours, and with the hope of future
reward. They are loved at first for these, and finally for
themselves, while opposite trains of association produce opposite feelings towards malevolence and injustice.[2] And thus
virtue, considered as a whole, becomes the supreme object of
our affections.   Of all our pleasures, more are derived from
those acts which are called virtuous, than from any other
source. The virtuous acts of others procure us countless
advantages. Our own virtue obtains for us the esteem of
men and return of favours. All the epithets of praise are
appropriated to virtue, and all the epithets of blame to vice.
Religion teaches us to connect hopes of infinite joy with the
one, and fears of infinite suffering with the other. Virtue
becomes therefore peculiarly associated with the idea of
pleasurable things. It is soon loved, independently of and

---

[1] Hartley *On Man*, vol. i. pp.
474-475.

[2] 'Benevolence . . . has also a
high degree of honour and esteem
annexed to it, procures us many
advantages and returns of kindness,
both from the person obliged and
others, and is most closely connected with the hopes of reward in
a future state, and of self-approbation or the moral sense; and the
same things hold with respect to
generosity in a much higher degree.
It is easy therefore to see how such
associations may be formed as to
engage us to forego great pleasure,
or endure great pain for the sake
of others, how these associations
may be attended with so great a
degree of pleasure as to overrule
the positive pain endured or the
negative one from the foregoing of
a pleasure, and yet how there may
be no direct explicit expectation of
reward either from God or man, by
natural consequence or express appointment, not even of the conco-
mitant pleasure that engages the
agent to undertake the benevolent
and generous action; and this I
take to be a proof from the doctrine of association that there is
and must be such a thing as pure
disinterested benevolence; also a
just account of the origin and
nature of it.'—Hartley *On Man*,
vol. i. pp. 473-474. See too Mill's
Analysis, vol. ii. p. 252.

more than these; we feel a glow of pleasure in practising it, and an intense pain in violating it. Conscience, which is thus generated, becomes the ruling principle of our lives,[1] and having learnt to sacrifice all earthly things rather than disobey it, we rise, by an association of ideas, into the loftiest region of heroism.[2]

The influence of this ingenious, though I think in some respect fanciful, theory depends less upon the number than upon the ability of its adherents. Though little known, I believe, beyond England, it has in England exercised a great fascination over exceedingly dissimilar minds,[3] and it does undoubtedly evade some of the objections to the other forms of the inductive theory. Thus, when intuitive moralists contend that our moral judgments, being instantaneous and effected under the manifest impulse of an emotion of sympathy or repulsion, are as far as possible removed from that cold calculation of interests to which the utilitarian reduces them, it is answered, that the association of ideas is

---

[1] Mill's *Analysis*, vol. ii. pp. 244–247.

[2] 'With self-interest,' said Hartley, 'man must begin; he may end in self-annihilation;' or as Coleridge happily puts it, 'Legality precedes morality in every individual, even as the Jewish dispensation preceded the Christian in the world at large.'—*Notes Theological and Political*, p. 340. It might be retorted with much truth, that we begin by practising morality as a duty—we end by practising it as a pleasure, without any reference to duty. Coleridge, who expressed for the Benthamite theories a very cordial detestation, sometimes glided into them himself. 'The happiness of man,' he says, 'is the end of virtue, and truth is the knowledge of the means.' (*The Friend*,

ed. 1850, vol. ii. p. 192) 'What can be the object of human virtue but the happiness of sentient, still more of moral beings?' (*Notes Theol. and Polit.* p. 351.) Leibnitz says, 'Quand on aura appris à faire des actions louables par ambition, on les fera après par inclination.' (*Sur l'Art de connaître les Hommes.*)

[3] E.g. Mackintosh and James Mill. Coleridge in his younger days was an enthusiastic admirer of Hartley; but chiefly, I believe, on account of his theory of vibrations. He named his son after him, and described him in one of his poems as :—

'He of mortal kind
Wisest, the first who marked the ideal tribes
Up the fine fibres through the sentient brain.' *Religious Musings*

sufficient to engender a feeling which is the proximate cause
of our decision.[1] Alone, of all the moralists of this school,
the disciple of Hartley recognises conscience as a real and
important element of our nature,[2] and maintains that it is
possible to love virtue for itself as a form of happiness
without any thought of ulterior consequences.[3] The immense
value this theory ascribes to education, gives it an unusual
practical importance. When we are balancing between a
crime and a virtue, our wills, it is said, are necessarily
determined by the greater pleasure. If we find more pleasure
in the vice than in the virtue, we inevitably gravitate to evil.
If we find more pleasure in the virtue than in the vice, we
are as irresistibly attracted towards good. But the strength
of such motives may be immeasurably enhanced by an early
association of ideas. If we have been accustomed from
childhood to associate our ideas of praise and pleasure with

---

[1] This position is elaborated in
a passage too long for quotation by
Mr. Austin. (*Lectures on Jurisprudence*, vol. i. p. 44.)

[2] Hobbes defines conscience as
'the opinion of evidence' (*On Human Nature*, ch. vi. § 8). Locke as
'our own opinion or judgment of
the moral rectitude or pravity of
our own actions' (*Essay*, book i.
ch. iii. § 8). In Bentham there is
very little on the subject; but in
one place he informs us that 'conscience is a thing of fictitious existence, supposed to occupy a seat
in the mind' (*Deontology*, vol. i. p.
137); and in another he ranks 'love
of duty' (which he describes as an
'impossible motive, in so far as
duty is synonymous to obligation')
as a variety of the 'love of power'
(*Springs of Action*, ii.) Mr. Bain
says, 'conscience is an imitation
within ourselves of the government
without us.' (*Emotions and Will*,
p 313.)

[3] 'However much they [utili-
tarians] may believe (as they do)
that actions and dispositions are
only virtuous because they promote
another end than virtue, yet this
being granted . . . they not only
place virtue at the very head of the
things which are good as means to
the ultimate end, but they also recognise as a psychological fact the
possibility of its being to the individual a good in itself. . . . Virtue,
according to the utilitarian doctrine, is not naturally and originally part of the end, but it is capable of becoming so. . . . What was
once desired as an instrument for
the attainment of happiness has
come to be desired . . . as part of
happiness. . . . Human nature is
so constituted as to desire nothing
which is not either a part of happiness or a means of happiness.'—J.
S. Mill's *Utilitarianism*, pp. 54, 55.
56, 58.

virtue, we shall readily yield to virtuous motives; if with vice, to vicious ones.   This readiness to yield to one or other set of motives, constitutes disposition, which is thus, according to these moralists, altogether an artificial thing the product of education, and effected by association of ideas.[1]

It will be observed, however, that this theory, refined and imposing as it may appear, is still essentially a selfish one.   Even when sacrificing all earthly objects through love of virtue, the good man is simply seeking his greatest enjoyment, indulging a kind of mental luxury which gives him more pleasure than what he foregoes, just as the miser finds more pleasure in accumulation than in any form of expenditure.[2]   There has been, indeed, one attempt to emancipate the

---

[1] 'A man is tempted to commit adultery with the wife of his friend. The composition of the motive is obvious.   He does not obey the motive.   Why?   He obeys other motives which are stronger. Though pleasures are associated with the immoral act, pains are associated with it also—the pains of the injured husband, the pains of the wife, the moral indignation of mankind, the future reproaches of his own mind.   Some men obey the first rather than the second motive.   The reason is obvious. In these the association of the act with the pleasure is from habit unduly strong, the association of the act with pains is from want of habit unduly weak. This is the case of a bad education. . . . Among the different classes of motives, there are men who are more easily and strongly operated on by some, others by others.   We have also seen that this is entirely owing to habits of association. This facility of being acted upon by motives of a particular description, is that

which we call disposition.'—Mill's *Analysis*, vol. ii. pp. 212, 213, &c. Adam Smith says, I think with much wisdom, that 'the great secret of education is to direct vanity to proper objects.'—*Moral Sentiments*, part vi. § 3.

[2] 'Goodness in ourselves is the prospect of satisfaction annexed to the welfare of others, so that we please them for the pleasure we receive ourselves in so doing, or to avoid the uneasiness we should feel in omitting it.   But God is completely happy in Himself, nor can His happiness receive increase or diminution from anything befalling His creatures; wherefore His goodness is pure, disinterested bounty, without any return of joy or satisfaction to Himself.   Therefore it is no wonder we have imperfect notions of a quality whereof we have no experience in our own nature.'—Tucker's *Light of Nature*, vol. i. p. 355.   ' It is the privilege of God alone to act upon pure, disinterested bounty, without the least addition thereby to His own enjy y·

theory from this condition, but it appears to me altogether futile. It has been said that men in the first instance indulge in baneful excesses, on account of the pleasure they afford, but the habit being contracted, continue to practise them after they have ceased to afford pleasure, and that a similar law may operate in the case of the habit of virtue.[1] But the reason why men who have contracted a habit continue to practise it after it has ceased to give them positive enjoyment, is because to desist, creates a restlessness and uneasiness which amounts to acute mental pain. To avoid that pain is the motive of the action.

The reader who has perused the passages I have accumulated in the notes, will be able to judge with what degree of justice utilitarian writers denounce with indignation the imputation of selfishness, as a calumny against their system. It is not, I think, a strained or unnatural use of language to describe as selfish or interested, all actions which a man performs, in order himself to avoid suffering or acquire the

---

ment.'—Ibid. vol. ii. p. 279. On the other hand, Hutcheson asks, 'If there be such disposition in the Deity, where is the impossibility of some small degree of this public love in His creatures, and why must they be supposed incapable of acting but from self-love?'—*Enquiry concerning Moral Good*, § 2.

[1] 'We gradually, through the influence of association, come to desire the means without thinking of the end; the action itself becomes an object of desire, and is performed without reference to any motive beyond itself. Thus far, it may still be objected that the action having, through association, become pleasurable, we are as much as before moved to act by the anticipation of pleasure, namely, the

pleasure of the action itself. But granting this, the matter does not end here. As we proceed in the formation of habits, and become accustomed to will a particular act . . . because it is pleasurable, we at last continue to will it without any reference to its being pleasurable. . . . In this manner it is that habits of hurtful excess continue to be practised, although they have ceased to be pleasurable, and in this manner also it is that the habit of willing to persevere in the course which he has chosen, does not desert the moral hero, even when the reward . . . is anything but an equivalent for the suffering he undergoes, or the wishes he may have to renounce.'—Mill's *Logic* (4th edition), vol. ii. pp. **416, 417.**

greatest possible enjoyment. If this be so, the term selfish is strictly applicable to all the branches of this system.[1] At the same time it must be acknowledged, that there is a broad difference between the refined hedonism of the utilitarians we have last noticed, and the writings of Hobbes, of Mandeville, or of Paley. It must be acknowledged, also, that not a few intuitive or stoical moralists have spoken of the pleasure to be derived from virtue in language little if at all different from these writers.[2] The main object of the earlier members of the inductive school, was to depress human nature to their standard, by resolving all the noblest actions into coarse and selfish elements. The main object of some of the more influential of the later members of this school,

---

[1] 'In regard to interest in the most extended, which is the original and only strictly proper sense of the word disinterested, no human act has ever been or ever can be disinterested. . . . In the only sense in which disinterestedness can with truth be predicated of human actions, it is employed . . . to denote, not the absence of all interest . . . but only the absence of all interest of the self-regarding class. Not but that it is very frequently predicated of human action in cases in which divers interests, to no one of which the appellation of self-regarding can with propriety be denied, have been exercising their influence, and in particular fear of God, or hope from God, and fear of ill-repute, or hope of good repute. If what is above be correct, the most disinterested of men is not less under the dominion of interest than the most interested. The only cause of his being styled disinterested, is its not having been observed that the sort of motive (suppose it sympathy for an indi-

vidual or class) has as truly a corresponding interest belonging to it as any other species of motive has. Of this contradiction between the truth of the case and the language employed in speaking of it, the cause is that in the one case men have not been in the habit of making—as in point of consistency they ought to have made—of the word interest that use which in the other case they have been in the habit of making of it.'—Bentham's *Springs of Action*, ii. § 2.

[2] Among others Bishop Butler, who draws some very subtle distinctions on the subject in his first sermon 'on the love of our neighbour.' Dugald Stewart remarks that 'although we apply the epithet selfish to avarice and to low and private sensuality, we never apply it to the desire of knowledge or to the pursuits of virtue, which are certainly sources of more exquisite pleasure than riches or sensuality can bestow.'—*Active and Moral Powers*, vol. i. p. 19.

has been to sublimate their conceptions of happiness and interest in such a manner, as to include the highest displays of heroism. As we have seen, they fully admit that conscience is a real thing, and should be the supreme guide of our lives, though they contend that it springs originally from selfishness, transformed under the influence of the association of ideas. They acknowledge the reality of the sympathetic feelings, though they usually trace them to the same source. They cannot, it is true, consistently with their principles, recognise the possibility of conduct which is in the strictest sense of the word unselfish, but they contend that it is quite possible for a man to find his highest pleasure in sacrificing himself for the good of others, that the association of virtue and pleasure is only perfect when it leads habitually to spontaneous and uncalculating action, and that no man is in a healthy moral condition who does not find more pain in committing a crime than he could derive pleasure from any of its consequences. The theory in its principle remains unchanged, but in the hands of some of these writers the spirit has wholly altered.

Having thus given a brief, but, I trust, clear and faithful account of the different modifications of the inductive theory, I shall proceed to state some of the principal objections that have been and may be brought against it. I shall then endeavour to define and defend the opinions of those who believe that our moral feelings are an essential part of our constitution, developed by, but not derived from education, and I shall conclude this chapter by an enquiry into the order of their evolution: so that having obtained some notion of the natural history of morals, we may be able, in the ensuing chapters, to judge how far their normal progress has been accelerated or retarded by religious or political agencies.

'Psychology,' it has been truly said, 'is but developed

consciousness.'[1] When moralists assert, that what we call
virtue derives its reputation solely from its utility, and that
the interest or pleasure of the agent is the one motive to
practise it, our first question is naturally how far this theory
agrees with the feelings and with the language of mankind.
But if tested by this criterion, there never was a doctrine
more emphatically condemned than utilitarianism. In all
its stages, and in all its assertions, it is in direct opposition
to common language and to common sentiments. In all
nations and in all ages, the ideas of interest and utility on
the one hand and of virtue on the other, have been regarded
by the multitude as perfectly distinct, and all languages recognise the distinction. The terms honour, justice, rectitude
or virtue, and their equivalents in every language, present to
the mind ideas essentially and broadly differing from the
terms prudence, sagacity, or interest. The two lines of conduct may coincide, but they are never confused, and we have
not the slightest difficulty in imagining them antagonistic.
When we say a man is governed by a high sense of honour,
or by strong moral feeling, we do not mean that he is prudently pursuing either his own interests or the interests of
society. The universal sentiment of mankind represents
self-sacrifice as an essential element of a meritorious act, and
means by self-sacrifice the deliberate adoption of the least
pleasurable course without the prospect of any pleasure in
return. A selfish act may be innocent, but cannot be virtuous, and to ascribe all good deeds to selfish motives, is not
the distortion but the negation of virtue. No Epicurean
could avow before a popular audience that the one end of his
life was the pursuit of his own happiness without an outburst
of indignation and contempt.[2] No man could consciously
make this—which according to the selfish theory is the only
rational and indeed possible motive of action—the deliberate

---

[1] Sir W. Hamilton.   [2] Cic. *De Fin.* lib. ii.

object of all his undertakings, without his character becoming despicable and degraded.   Whether we look within ourselves or examine the conduct either of our enemies or of our friends, or adjudicate upon the characters in history or in fiction, our feelings on these matters are the same.   In exact proportion as we believe a desire for personal enjoyment to be the motive of a good act is the merit of the agent diminished.   If we believe the motive to be wholly selfish the merit is altogether destroyed.   If we believe it to be wholly disinterested the merit is altogether unalloyed.   Hence, the admiration bestowed upon Prometheus, or suffering virtue constant beneath the blows of Almighty malice, or on the atheist who with no prospect of future reward suffered a fearful death, rather than abjure an opinion which could be of no benefit to society, because he believed it to be the truth. Selfish moralists deny the possibility of that which all ages, all nations, all popular judgments pronounce to have been the characteristic of every noble act that has ever been performed.   Now, when a philosophy which seeks by the light of consciousness to decipher the laws of our moral being proves so diametrically opposed to the conclusions arrived at by the great mass of mankind, who merely follow their consciousness without endeavouring to frame systems of philosophy, that it makes most of the distinctions of common ethical language absolutely unmeaning, this is, to say the least, a strong presumption against its truth.   If Molière's hero had been speaking prose all his life without knowing it, this was simply because he did not understand what prose was.   In the present case we are asked to believe that men have been under a total delusion about the leading principles of their lives which they had distinguished by a whole vocabulary of terms.

It is said that the case becomes different when the pleasure sought is not a gross or material enjoyment, but the satisfaction of performed virtue.   I suspect that if men could persuade themselves that the one motive of a virtuous man was the certainty that the act he accomplished would be followed by a glow of satisfaction so intense as more than to compensate for any sacrifice he might have made, the difference would not be as great as is supposed. In fact, however—and the consciousness of this lies, I conceive, at the root of the opinions of men upon the subject—the pleasure of virtue is one which can only be obtained on the express condition of its not being the object sought. Phenomena of this kind are familiar to us all. Thus, for example, it has often been observed that prayer, by a law of our nature and apart from all supernatural intervention, exercises a reflex influence of a very beneficial character upon the minds of the worshippers. The man who offers up his petitions with passionate earnestness, with unfaltering faith, and with a vivid realisation of the presence of an Unseen Being has risen to a condition of mind which is itself eminently favourable both to his own happiness and to the expansion of his moral qualities. But he who expects nothing more will never attain this. To him who neither believes nor hopes that his petitions will receive a response such a mental state is impossible. No Protestant before an image of the Virgin, no Christian before a pagan idol, could possibly attain it. If prayers were offered up solely with a view to this benefit, they would be absolutely sterile and would speedily cease. Thus again, certain political economists have contended that to give money in charity is worse than useless, that it is positively noxious to society, but they have added that the gratification of our benevolent affections is pleasing to ourselves, and that the pleasure we derive from this source may be so much greater than the evil resulting from our gift, that we may justly, according to the 'greatest happiness principle,' purchase this large amount of gratification to ourselves by a slight injury to our neighbours. The political economy involved in this very characteristic specimen of utilitarian ethics I shall hereafter examine. At present it is sufficient to observe that no one who consciously practised benevolence solely from this motive could obtain the pleasure in question. We receive enjoyment from the thought that we have done good. We never could receive that enjoyment if we believed and realised that we were doing harm. The same thing is pre-eminently true of the satisfaction of conscience. A feeling of satisfaction follows the accomplishment of duty for itself, but if the duty be performed solely through the expectation of a mental pleasure conscience refuses to ratify the bargain.

There is no fact more conspicuous in human nature than the broad distinction, both in kind and degree, drawn between the moral and the other parts of our nature. But this on utilitarian principles is altogether unaccountable. If the excellence of virtue consists solely in its utility or tendency to promote the happiness of men, we should be compelled to canonise a crowd of acts which are utterly remote from all our ordinary notions of morality. The whole tendency of political economy and philosophical history which reveal the physiology of societies, is to show that the happiness and welfare of mankind are evolved much more from our selfish than from what are termed our virtuous acts. The prosperity of nations and the progress of civilisation are mainly due to the exertions of men who while pursuing strictly their own interests, were unconsciously promoting the interests of the community. The selfish instinct that leads men to accumulate, confers ultimately more advantage upon the world than the generous instinct that leads men to give. A great historian has contended with some force that intellectual development is more important to societies than moral development. Yet who ever seriously questioned the reality of the distinction that separates these things? The reader will probably exclaim that the key to that distinction is to be found in the motive; but it is one of the paradoxes of the

utilitarian school that the motive of the agent has absolutely
no influence on the morality of the act.   According to Bentham, there is but one motive possible, the pursuit of our own
enjoyment.   The most virtuous, the most vicious, and the
most indifferent of actions, if measured by this test, would
be exactly the same, and an investigation of motives should
therefore be altogether excluded from our moral judgments.[1]
Whatever test we adopt, the difficulty of accounting for the
unique and pre-eminent position mankind have assigned to
virtue will remain.   If we judge by tendencies, a crowd of
objects and of acts to which no mortal ever dreamed of ascribing virtue, contribute largely to the happiness of man.
If we judge by motives, the moralists we are reviewing have
denied all generic difference between prudential and virtuous

---

[1] 'As there is not any sort of
pleasure that is not itself a good,
nor any sort of pain the exemption
from which is not a good, and as
nothing but the expectation of the
eventual enjoyment of pleasure in
some shape, or of exemption from
pain in some shape, can operate in
the character of a motive, a necessary consequence is that if by motive be meant *sort* of motive, there
is not any such thing as a bad
motive.'— Bentham's *Springs of
Action,* ii. § 4.   The first clauses
of the following passage I have already quoted : ' Pleasure is itself a
good, nay, setting aside immunity
from pain, the only good.   Pain is
in itself an evil, and indeed, without exception, the only evil, or else
the words good and evil have no
meaning.   And this is alike true of
every sort of pain, and of every sort
of pleasure.   It follows therefore
immediately and incontestably that
there is no such thing as any sort
of motive that is in itself a bad
one.'— *Principles of Morals and*

Legislation, ch. ix.   'The search
after motive is one of the prominent
causes of men's bewilderment in
the investigation of questions of
morals. . . . But this is a pursuit
in which every moment employed
is a moment wasted.   All motives
are abstractedly good.   No man
has ever had, can, or could have a
motive different from the pursuit of
pleasure or of shunning pain.'—
Deontology, vol. i. p. 126.   Mr.
Mill's doctrine appears somewhat
different from this, but the difference is I think only apparent.   He
says : ' The motive has nothing to
do with the morality of the action,
though much with the worth of the
agent,' and he afterwards explains
this last statement by saying that
the ' motive makes a great difference in our moral estimation of the
agent, especially if it indicates a
good or a bad habitual disposition,
a bent of character from which useful or from which hurtful actions
are likely to arise.'— *Utilitarianism,* 2nd ed. pp. 26-27.

motives. If we judge by intentions, it is certain that however much truth or chastity may contribute to the happiness
of mankind, it is not with philanthropic intentions that those
virtues are cultivated.

It is often said that intuitive moralists in their reasonings
are guilty of continually abandoning their principles by themselves appealing to the tendency of certain acts to promote
human happiness as a justification, and the charge is usually
accompanied by a challenge to show any confessed virtue that
has not that tendency. To the first objection it may be
shortly answered that no intuitive moralist ever dreamed of
doubting that benevolence or charity, or in other words, the
promotion of the happiness of man, is a duty. He maintains
that it not only is so, but that we arrive at this fact by direct
intuition, and not by the discovery that such a course is
conducive to our own interest. But while he cordially
recognises this branch of virtue, and while he has therefore a
perfect right to allege the beneficial effects of a virtue in its
defence, he refuses to admit that all virtue can be reduced to
this single principle. With the general sentiment of mankind
he regards charity as a good thing only because it is of use
to the world. With the same general sentiment of mankind
he believes that chastity and truth have an independent value,
distinct from their influence upon happiness. To the question
whether every confessed virtue is conducive to human happiness, it is less easy to reply, for it is usually extremely difficult to calculate the remote tendencies of acts, and in cases
where, in the common apprehension of mankind, the morality
is very clear, the consequences are often very obscure. Notwithstanding the claim of great precision which utilitarian
writers so boastfully make, the standard by which they profess to measure morals is itself absolutely incapable of defini
tion or accurate explanation. Happiness is one of the most
indeterminate and undefinable words in the language, and
what are the conditions of ' the greatest possible happiness '

no one can precisely say. No two nations, perhaps no two individuals, would find them the same.[1] And even if every virtuous act were incontestably useful, it by no means follows that its virtue is derived from its utility.

It may be readily granted, that as a general rule those acts which we call virtuous, are unquestionably productive of happiness, if not to the agent, at least to mankind in general, but we have already seen that they have by no means that monopoly or pre-eminence of utility which on utilitarian principles, the unique position assigned to them would appear to imply. It may be added, that if we were to proceed in detail to estimate acts by their consequences, we should soon be led to very startling conclusions. In the first place, it is obvious that if virtues are only good because they promote, and vices only evil because they impair the happiness of mankind, the degrees of excellence or criminality must be strictly proportioned to the degrees of utility or the reverse.[2] Every action, every disposition, every class, every condition of society must take its place on the moral scale precisely in accordance with the degree in which it promotes or diminishes human happiness. Now it is extremely questionable, whether some of the most monstrous forms of sensuality which it is scarcely possible to name, cause as much unhappiness as some infirmities of temper, or procrastination or hastiness of judgment. It is scarcely doubtful that a modest, diffident, and retiring nature, distrustful of its own abilities, and shrinking with humility from conflict, produces on the whole less benefit to the world than the self-assertion of an audacious and arrogant nature, which is impelled to every struggle, and de-

---

[1] This truth has been admirably illustrated by Mr. Herbert Spencer (*Social Statics*, pp. 1–8).

[2] 'On évalue la grandeur de la vertu en comparant les biens obtenus aux maux au prix desquels on les achète : l'excédant en bien mesure la valeur de la vertu, comme l'excédant en mal mesure le degré de haine que doit inspirer le vice.' —Ch. Comte, *Traité de Legislation* liv. ii. ch. xii.

velopes every capacity   Gratitude has no doubt done much
to soften and sweeten the intercourse of life, but the corresponding feeling of revenge was for centuries the one bulwark
against social anarchy, and is even now one of the chief
restraints to crime.[1]   On the great theatre of public life,
especially in periods of great convulsions when passions are
fiercely roused, it is neither the man of delicate scrupulosity
and sincere impartiality, nor yet the single-minded religious
enthusiast, incapable of dissimulation or procrastination, who
confers most benefit upon the world.   It is much rather the
astute statesman earnest about his ends but unscrupulous
about his means, equally free from the trammels of conscience
and from the blindness of zeal, who governs because he partly
yields to the passions and the prejudices of his time.   But
however much some modern writers may idolize the heroes
of success, however much they may despise and ridicule those
far nobler men, whose wide tolerance and scrupulous honour

---

[1] M. Dumont, the translator of
Bentham, has elaborated in a rather
famous passage the utilitarian notions about vengeance.   'Toute
espèce de satisfaction entraînant
une peine pour le délinquant produit
naturellement un plaisir de vengeance pour la partie lésee. Ce
plaisir est un gain. Il rappelle la
parabole de Samson. C'est le doux
qui sort du terrible. C'est le miel
recueilli dans la gueule du lion.
Produit sans frais, résultat net
d'une opération nécessaire à d'autres
titres, c'est une jouissance à cultiver
comme toute autre; car le plaisir
de la vengeance considérée ab-
straitement n'est comme tout autre
plaisir qu'un bien en lui-même.'—
Principes du Code pénal, 2me partie,
ch. xvi. According to a very acute
living writer of this school, 'The
criminal law stands to the passion
of revenge in much the same relation as marriage to the sexual appetite' (J. F. Stephen On the Criminal
Law of England, p. 99).   Mr Mill
observes that, 'In the golden rule
of Jesus of Nazareth, we read the
complete spirit of the ethics of utility' (Utilitarianism, p. 24). It is
but fair to give a specimen of the
opposite order of extravagance.
'So well convinced was Father
Claver of the eternal happiness of
almost all whom he assisted,' says
this saintly missionary's biographer, 'that speaking once of some
persons who had delivered a criminal into the hands of justice, he
said, God forgive them; but they
have secured the salvation of this
man at the probable risk of their
own.'—Newman's Anglican Difficulties, p. 205.

rendered them unfit leaders in the fray, it has scarcely yet been contended that the delicate conscientiousness which in these cases impairs utility constitutes vice. If utility is the sole measure of virtue, it is difficult to understand how we could look with moral disapprobation' on any class who prevent greater evils than they cause. But with such a principle we might find strange priestesses at the utilitarian shrine. 'Aufer meretrices de rebus humanis,' said St. Augustine, 'turbaveris omnia libidinibus.'[1]

Let us suppose an enquirer who intended to regulate his life consistently by the utilitarian principle; let us suppose him to have overcome the first great difficulty of his school, arising from the apparent divergence of his own interests from his duty, to have convinced himself that that divergence does not exist, and to have accordingly made the pursuit of duty his single object, it remains to consider what kind of course he would pursue. He is informed that it is a pure illusion to suppose that human actions have any other end or rule than happiness, that nothing is intrinsically good or intrinsically bad apart from its consequences, that no act which is useful can possibly be vicious, and that the utility of an act constitutes and measures its value. One of his first observations will be that in very many special cases acts such as murder, theft, or falsehood, which the world calls criminal, and which in the majority of instances would undoubtedly be hurtful, appear eminently productive of good. Why then, he may ask, should they not in these cases be performed? The answer he receives is that they would not really be useful, because we must consider the remote as well as the immediate consequences of actions, and although in particular instances a falsehood or even a murder might appear beneficial, it is one of the most important interests of mankind

---

[1] *De Ordine*, ii. 4. The experiment has more than once been tried at Venice, Pisa, &c., and always with the results St. Augustine predicted.

that the sanctity of life and property should be preserved, and that a high standard of veracity should be maintained. But this answer is obviously insufficient. It is necessary to show that the extent to which a single act of what the world calls crime would weaken these great bulwarks of society is such as to counterbalance the immediate good which it produces. If it does not, the balance will be on the side of happiness, the murder or theft or falsehood will be useful, and therefore, on utilitarian principles, will be virtuous. Now even in the case of public acts, the effect of the example of an obscure individual is usually small, but if the act be accomplished in perfect secrecy, the evil effects resulting from the example will be entirely absent. It has been said that it would be dangerous to give men permission to perpetrate what men call crimes in secret. This may be a very good reason why the utilitarian should not proclaim such a principle, but it is no reason why he should not act upon it. If a man be convinced that no act which is useful can possibly be criminal, if it be in his power by perpetrating what is called a crime to obtain an end of great immediate utility, and if he is able to secure such absolute secrecy as to render it perfectly certain that his act cannot become an example, and cannot in consequence exercise any influence on the general standard of morals, it appears demonstrably certain that on utilitarian principles he would be justified in performing it. If what we call virtue be only virtuous *because* it is useful, it can only be virtuous *when* it is useful. The question of the morality of a large number of acts must therefore depend upon the probability of their detection,[1]

---

[1] The reader will here observe the very transparent sophistry of an assertion which is repeated ad nauseam by utilitarians. They tell us that a regard to the remote consequences of our actions would lead us to the conclusion that we should never perform an act which would not be conducive to human happiness if it were universally performed, or, as Mr. Austin expresses it, that 'the question is if acts of this class were generally done or generally forborne or omit-

and a little adroit hypocrisy must often, not merely in appearance but in reality, convert a vice into a virtue. The only way by which it has been attempted with any plausibility to evade this conclusion has been by asserting that the act would impair the disposition of the agent, or in other words predispose him on other occasions to perform acts which are generally hurtful to society. But in the first place a single act has no such effect upon disposition as to counteract a great immediate good, especially when, as we have supposed, that act is not a revolt against what is believed to be right, but is performed under the full belief that it is in accordance with the one rational rule of morals, and in the next place, as far as the act would form a habit it would appear to be the habit of in all cases regulating actions by a precise and minute calculation of their utility, which is the very ideal of utilitarian virtue.

If our enquirer happens to be a man of strong imagination and of solitary habits, it is very probable that he will be accustomed to live much in a world of imagination, a world peopled with beings that are to him as real as those of

---

ted, what would be the probable effect on the general happiness or good?' (*Lectures on Jurisprudence*, vol. i. p. 32.) The question is nothing of the kind. If I am convinced that utility alone constitutes virtue, and if I am meditating any particular act, the sole question of morality must be whether that act is on the whole useful, produces a net result of happiness. To determine this question I must consider both the immediate and the remote consequences of the act; but the latter are not ascertained by asking what would be the result if every one did as I do, but by asking how far, as a matter of fact, my act is likely to produce imi-

tators, or affect the conduct and future acts of others. It may no doubt be convenient and useful to form classifications based on the general tendency of different courses to promote or diminish happiness, but such classification cannot alter the morality of particular acts. It is quite clear that no act which produces on the whole more pleasure than pain can on utilitarian principles be vicious. It is, I think, equally clear that no one could act consistently on such a principle without being led to consequences which in the common judgment of mankind are grossly and scandalously immoral.

flesh, with its joys and sorrows, its temptations and its sins. In obedience to the common feelings of our nature he may have struggled long and painfully against sins of the imagination, which he was never seriously tempted to convert into sins of action. But his new philosophy will be admirably fitted to console his mind. If remorse be absent the indulgence of the most vicious imagination is a pleasure, and if this indulgence does not lead to action it is a clear gain, and therefore to be applauded. That a course may be continually pursued in imagination without leading to corresponding actions he will speedily discover, and indeed it has always been one of the chief objections brought against fiction that the constant exercise of the sympathies in favour of imaginary beings is found positively to indispose men to practical benevolence.[1]

Proceeding farther in his course, our moralist will soon find reason to qualify the doctrine of remote consequences, which plays so large a part in the calculations of utilitarianism. It is said that it is criminal to destroy human beings, even when the crime would appear productive of great utility, for every instance of murder weakens the sanctity of life. But experience shows that it is possible for men to be perfectly indifferent to one particular section of human life, without this indifference extending to others. Thus among the ancient Greeks, the murder or exposition of the children of poor parents was continually practised with the most absolute callousness, without exercising any appreciable influence upon the respect for adult life. In the same manner what may be termed religious unveracity, or the habit of propagating what are deemed useful superstitions, with the consciousness of their being false, or at least suppressing or misrepresenting the facts that might invalidate

---

[1] There are some very good remarks on the possibility of living a life of imagination wholly distinct from the life of action in Mr Bain's *Emotions and Will*, p. 246.

them, does not in any degree imply industrial unveracity
Nothing is more common than to find extreme dishonesty in
speculation coexisting with scrupulous veracity in business.
If any vice might be expected to conform strictly to the
utilitarian theory, it would be cruelty; but cruelty to
animals may exist without leading to cruelty to men, and
even where spectacles in which animal suffering forms a
leading element exercise an injurious influence on character,
it is more than doubtful whether the measure of human unhappiness they may ultimately produce is at all equivalent
to the passionate enjoyment they immediately afford.

This last consideration, however, makes it necessary to
notice a new, and as it appears to me, almost grotesque
development of the utilitarian theory. The duty of humanity
to animals, though for a long period too much neglected,
may, on the principles of the intuitive moralist, be easily
explained and justified. Our circumstances and characters
produce in us many and various affections towards all with
whom we come in contact, and our consciences pronounce
these affections to be good or bad. We feel that humanity
or benevolence is a good affection, and also that it is due in
different degrees to different classes. Thus it is not only
natural but right that a man should care for his own family
more than for the world at large, and this obligation
applies not only to parents who are responsible for having
brought their children into existence, and to children who
owe a debt of gratitude to their parents, but also to brothers
who have no such special tie. So too we feel it to be both
unnatural and wrong to feel no stronger interest in our fellow-
countrymen than in other men. In the same way we feel
that there is a wide interval between the humanity it is
both natural and right to exhibit towards animals, and that
which is due to our own species. Strong philanthropy could
hardly coexist with cannibalism, and a man who had no hesitation in destroying human life for the sake of obtaining the skins

of the victims, or of freeing himself from some trifling inconvenience, would scarcely be eulogised for his benevolence. Yet a man may be regarded as very humane to animals who has no scruple in sacrificing their lives for his food, his pleasures, or his convenience.

Towards the close of the last century an energetic agitation in favour of humanity to animals arose in England, and the utilitarian moralists, who were then rising into influence, caught the spirit of their time and made very creditable efforts to extend it.[1] It is manifest, however, that a theory which recognised no other end in virtue than the promotion of human happiness, could supply no adequate basis for the movement. Some of the recent members of the school have accordingly enlarged their theory, maintaining that acts are virtuous when they produce a net result of happiness, and vicious when they produce a net result of suffering, altogether irrespective of the question whether this enjoyment or suffering is of men or animals. In other words, they place the duty of man to animals on exactly the same basis as the duty of man to his fellow-men, maintaining that no suffering can be rightly inflicted on brutes, which does not produce a larger amount of happiness to man.[2]

The first reflection suggested by this theory is, that it

Bentham especially recurs to this subject frequently. See Sir J. Bowring's edition of his works (Edinburgh, 1843), vol. i. pp. 142, 143, 562; vol. x. pp. 549–550.

[2] 'Granted that any practice causes more pain to animals than it gives pleasure to man; is that practice moral or immoral? And if exactly in proportion as human beings raise their heads out of the slough of selfishness they do not with one voice answer "immoral," let the morality of the principle of utility be for ever condemned.'— Mill's *Dissert.* vol. ii. p. 485. 'We

deprive them [animals] of life, and this is justifiable—their pains do not equal our enjoyments. There is a balance of good.'—Bentham's *Deontology*, vol. i. p. 14. Mr. Mill accordingly defines the principle of utility, without any special reference to man. 'The creed which accepts as the foundation of morals, utility or the great happiness principle, holds that actions are right in proportion as they tend to promote happiness, wrong as they tend to produce the reverse of happiness.'—*Utilitarianism*, pp. 9–10.

appears difficult to understand how, on the principles of the inductive school, it could be arrived at. Benevolence, as we have seen, according to these writers begins in interest. We first of all do good to men, because it is for our advantage, though the force of the habit may at last act irrespective of interest. But in the case of animals which cannot resent barbarity, this foundation of self-interest does not for the most part[1] exist. Probably, however, an association of ideas might help to solve the difficulty, and the habit of benevolence generated originally from the social relations of men might at last be extended to the animal world; but that it should be so to the extent of placing the duty to animals on the same basis as the duty to men, I do not anticipate, or (at the risk of being accused of great inhumanity), I must add, desire. I cannot look forward to a time when no one will wear any article of dress formed out of the skin of an animal, or feed upon animal flesh, till he has ascertained that the pleasure he derives from doing so, exceeds the pain inflicted upon the animal, as well as the pleasure of which by abridging its life he has deprived it.[2] And supposing that

---

[1] The exception of course being domestic animals, which may be injured by ill treatment, but even this exception is a very partial one. No selfish reason could prevent any amount of cruelty to animals that were about to be killed, and even in the case of previous ill-usage the calculations of selfishness will depend greatly upon the price of the animal. I have been told that on some parts of the continent diligence horses are systematically under-fed, and worked to a speedy death, their cheapness rendering such a course the most economical.

[2] Bentham, as we have seen, is of opinion that the gastronomic pleasure would produce the requisite excess of enjoyment. Hartley, who has some amiable and beautiful remarks on the duty of kindness to animals, without absolutely condemning, speaks with much aversion of the custom of eating 'our brothers and sisters,' the animals. (*On Man*, vol. ii. pp. 222–223.) Paley, observing that it is quite possible for men to live without flesh-diet, concludes that the only sufficient justification for eating meat is an express divine revelation in the Book of Genesis. (*Moral Philos*. book ii. ch. 11.) Some reasoners evade the main issue by contending that they kill animals because they would otherwise overrun the earth; but this, as Windham said, 'is an indifferent reason for killing fish.'

with such a calculation before him, the utilitarian should continue to feed on the flesh of animals, his principle might carry him to further conclusions, from which I confess I should recoil. If, when Swift was writing his famous essay in favour of employing for food the redundant babies of a half-starving population, he had been informed that, according to the more advanced moralists, to eat a child, and to eat a sheep, rest upon exactly the same ground ; that in the one case as in the other, the single question for the moralist is, whether the repast on the whole produces more pleasure than pain, it must be owned that the di covery would have greatly facilitated his task.

The considerations I have adduced will, I think, be sufficient to show that the utilitarian principle if pushed to its full logical consequences would be by no means as accordant with ordinary moral notions as is sometimes alleged ; that it would, on the contrary, lead to conclusions utterly and outrageously repugnant to the moral feelings it is intended to explain. I will conclude this part of my argument by very briefly adverting to two great fields in which, as I believe, it would prove especially revolutionary.

The first of these is the field of chastity. It will be necessary for me in the course of the present work to dwell at greater length than I should desire upon questions connected with this virtue. At present, I will merely ask the reader to conceive a mind from which all notion of the intrinsic excellence or nobility of purity was banished, and to suppose such a mind comparing, by a utilitarian standard, a period in which sensuality was almost unbridled, such as the age of Athenian glory or the English restoration, with a period of austere virtue. The question which of these societies was morally the best would thus resolve itself solely into the question in which there was produced the greatest amount of enjoyment and the smallest amount of suffering. The pleasures of domestic life, the pleasures resulting from a

freer social intercourse,[1] the different degrees of suffering inflicted on those who violated the law of chastity, the ulterior consequences of each mode of life upon well-being and upon population, would be the chief elements of the comparison. Can any one believe that the balance of enjoyment would be so unquestionably and so largely on the side of the more austere society as to justify the degree of superiority which is assigned to it ?[2]

The second sphere is that of speculative truth. No class of men have more highly valued an unflinching hostility to superstition than utilitarians. Yet it is more than doubtful whether upon their principles it can be justified. Many superstitions do undoubtedly answer to the Greek conception

---

[1] In commenting upon the French licentiousness of the eighteenth century, Hume says, in a passage which has excited a great deal of animadversion :—' Our neighbours, it seems, have resolved to sacrifice some of the domestic to the social pleasures ; and to prefer ease, freedom, and an open commerce, to strict fidelity and constancy. These ends are both good, and are somewhat difficult to reconcile ; nor must we be surprised if the customs of nations incline too much sometimes to the one side, and sometimes to the other.'— *Dialogue.*

[2] There are few things more pitiable than the blunders into which writers have fallen when trying to base the plain virtue of chastity on utilitarian calculations. Thus since the writings of Malthus it has been generally recognised that one of the very first conditions of all material prosperity is to check early marriages, to restrain the tendency of population to multiply more rapidly than the means

of subsistence. Knowing this, what can be more deplorable than to find moralists making such arguments as these the very foundation of morals?—' The first and great mischief, and by consequence the guilt, of promiscuous concubinage consists in its tendency to diminish marriages.' (Paley's *Moral Philosophy,* book iii. part iii. ch. ii.) 'That is always the most happy condition of a nation, and that nation is most accurately obeying the laws of our constitution, in which the number of the human race is most rapidly increasing. Now it is certain that under the law of chastity, that is, when individuals are exclusively united to each other, the increase of population will be more rapid than under any other circumstances.' (Wayland's *Elements of Moral Science,* p. 298, 11th ed., Boston, 1839.) I am sorry to bring such subjects before the reader, but it is impossible to write a history of morals without doing so.

of slavish 'fear of the gods, and have been productive of
unspeakable misery to mankind, but there are very many
others of a different tendency.   Superstitions appeal to our
hopes as well as to our fears.   They often meet and gratify
the inmost longings of the heart.   They offer certainties
when reason can only afford possibilities or probabilities.
They supply conceptions on which the imagination loves
to dwell.   They sometimes even impart a new sanction
to moral truths.   Creating wants which they alone can
satisfy, and fears which they alone can quell, they often
become essential elements of happiness, and their consoling
efficacy is most felt in the languid or troubled hours when
it is most needed.   We owe more to our illusions than to
our knowledge.   The imagination, which is altogether con-
structive, probably contributes more to our happiness than
the reason, which in the sphere of speculation is mainly
critical and destructive.   The rude charm which in the hour
of danger or distress the savage clasps so confidently to his
breast, the sacred picture which is believed to shed a hallowing and protecting influence over the poor man's cottage,
can bestow a more real consolation in the darkest hour of
human suffering than can be afforded by the grandest theories
of philosophy.   The first desire of the heart is to find something on which to lean.   Happiness is a condition of feeling,
not a condition of circumstances, and to common minds one
of its first essentials is the exclusion of painful and harassing
doubt. A system of belief may be false, superstitious, and
reactionary, and may yet be conducive to human happiness if
it furnishes great multitudes of men with what they believe
to be a key to the universe, if it consoles them in those
seasons of agonizing bereavement when the consolations of enlightened reason are but empty words, if it supports their feeble
and tottering minds in the gloomy hours of sickness and of
approaching death.   A credulous and superstitious nature
may be degraded, but in the many cases where superstition

does not assume a persecuting or appalling form it is not
unhappy, and degradation, apart from unhappiness, can have
no place in utilitarian ethics.   No error can be more grave
than to imagine that when a critical spirit is abroad the
pleasant beliefs will all remain, and the painful ones alone
will perish.   To introduce into the mind the consciousness
of ignorance and the pangs of doubt is to inflict or endure
much suffering, which may even survive the period of transition.   'Why is it,' said Luther's wife, looking sadly back
upon the sensuous creed which she had left, 'that in our old
faith we prayed so often and so warmly, and that our
prayers are now so few and so cold?'[1]   It is related of an
old monk named Serapion, who had embraced the heresy of
the anthropomorphites, that he was convinced by a brother
monk of the folly of attributing to the Almighty a human
form.   He bowed his reason humbly to the Catholic creed;
but when he knelt down to pray, the image which his imagination had conceived, and on which for so many years his
affections had been concentrated, had disappeared, and the
old man burst into tears, exclaiming, 'You have deprived me
of my God.'[2]

These are indeed facts which must be deeply painful to
all who are concerned with the history of opinion.   The
possibility of often adding to the happiness of men by diffusing abroad, or at least sustaining pleasing falsehoods, and
the suffering that must commonly result from their dissolution, can hardly reasonably be denied.   There is one, and
but one, adequate reason that can always justify men in
critically reviewing what they have been taught.   It is, the
conviction that opinions should not be regarded as mere
mental luxuries, that truth should be deemed an end distinct
from and superior to utility, and that it is a moral duty to

---

[1] See Luther's *Table Talk*.   *à l'Hist. ecclésiastique*, tome x. p. 57
[2] Tillemont, *Mém. pour servir*

pursue it, whether it leads to pleasure or whether it leads to pain. Among the many wise sayings which antiquity ascribed to Pythagoras, few are more remarkable than his division of virtue into two distinct branches—to be truthful and to do good.[1]

Of the sanctions which, according to the utilitarians, con stitute the sole motives to virtue, there is one, as I have said, unexceptionably adequate. Those who adopt the religious sanction, can always appeal to a balance of interest in favour of virtue; but as the great majority of modern utilitarians confidently sever their theory from all theological considerations, I will dismiss this sanction with two or three remarks.

In the first place, it is obvious that those who regard the arbitrary will of the Deity as the sole rule of morals, render it perfectly idle to represent the Divine attributes as deserving of our admiration. To speak of the goodness of God, either implies that there is such a quality as goodness, to which the Divine acts conform, or it is an unmeaning tautology. Why should we extol, or how can we admire, the perfect goodness of a Being whose will and acts constitute the sole standard or definition of perfection?[2] The theory which teaches that the arbitrary will of the Deity is the one rule of morals, and the anticipation of future rewards and punishments the one reason for conforming to it, consists of two parts. The first annihilates the goodness of God; the second, the virtue of man.

---

[1] Τό τε ἀληθεύειν καὶ τὸ εὐεργετεῖν. (Ælian, *Var. Hist.* xii. 59.) Longinus in like manner divides virtue into εὐεργεσία καὶ ἀλήθεια. (*De Sublim.* § 1.) The opposite view in England is continually expressed in the saying, 'You should never pull down an opinion until you have something to put in its place,' which can only mean, if you are convinced that some religious or other hypothesis is false, you are morally bound to repress or conceal your conviction until you have discovered positive affirmations or explanations as unqualified and consolatory as those you have destroyed.

[2] See this powerfully stated by Shaftesbury. (*Inquiry concerning Virtue*, book i. part iii.) The same objection applies to Dr. Mansel's modification of the theological doctrine—viz. that the origin of morals is not the will but the nature of God.

Another and equally obvious remark is, that while these theologians represent the hope of future rewards, and the fear of future punishments. as the only reason for doing right, one of our strongest reasons for believing in the existence of these rewards and punishments, is our deep-seated feeling of merit and demerit.   That the present disposition of affairs is in many respects unjust, that suffering often attends a course which deserves reward, and happiness a course which deserves punishment, leads men to infer a future state of retribution. Take away the consciousness of desert, and the inference would no longer be made.

A third remark, which I believe to be equally true, but which may not be acquiesced in with equal readiness, is that without the concurrence of a moral faculty, it is wholly impossible to prove from nature that supreme goodness of the Creator, which utilitarian theologians assume.   We speak of the benevolence shown in the joy of the insect glittering in the sunbeam, in the protecting instincts so liberally bestowed among the animal world, in the kindness of the parent to its young, in the happiness of little children, in the beauty and the bounty of nature, but is there not another side to the picture ?   The hideous disease, the countless forms of rapine and of suffering, the entozoa that live within the bodies, and feed upon the anguish of sentient beings, the ferocious instinct of the cat, that prolongs with delight the agonies of its victim, all the multitudinous forms of misery that are manifested among the innocent portion of creation, are not these also the works of nature?   We speak of the Divine veracity. What is the whole history of the intellectual progress of the world but one long struggle of the intellect of man to emancipate itself from the deceptions of nature ?   Every object that meets the eye of the savage awakens his curiosity only to lure him into some deadly error.   The sun that seems a diminutive light revolving around his world ; the moon and the stars that appear formed only to light his path ; the strange fantastic diseases that suggest irresistibly the notion of present dæmons; the terrific phenomena of nature which appear the results, not of blind forces, but of isolated spiritual agencies—all these things fatally, inevitably, invincibly impel him into superstition.   Through long centuries the superstitions thus generated have deluged the world with blood.   Millions of prayers have been vainly breathed to what we now know were inexorable laws of nature.   Only after ages of toil did the mind of man emancipate itself from those deadly errors to which by the deceptive appearances of nature the long infancy of humanity is universally doomed.

And in the laws of wealth how different are the appearances from the realities of things!   Who can estimate the wars that have been kindled, the bitterness and the wretchedness that have been caused, by errors relating to the apparent antagonism of the interests of nations which were so natural that for centuries they entangled the very strongest intellects, and it was scarcely till our own day that a tardy science came to dispel them?

What shall we say to these things?   If induction alone were our guide, if we possessed absolutely no knowledge of some things being in their own nature good, and others in their own nature evil, how could we rise from this spectacle of nature to the conception of an all-perfect Author?   Even if we could discover a predominance of benevolence in the creation, we should still regard the mingled attributes of nature as a reflex of the mingled attributes of its Contriver. Our knowledge of the Supreme Excellence, our best evidence even of the existence of the Creator, is derived not from the material universe but from our own moral nature.[1]   It is

---

[1] 'The one great and binding ground of the belief of God and a hereafter is the law of conscience.' —Coleridge, *Notes Theological and Political*, p. 367.   That our moral faculty is our one reason for maintaining the supreme benevolence of the Deity was a favourite position of Kant.

not of reason but of faith. In other words it springs from that instinctive or moral nature which is as truly a part of our being as is our reason, which teaches us what reason could never teach, the supreme and transcendent excellence of moral good, which rising dissatisfied above this world of sense, proves itself by the very intensity of its aspiration to be adapted for another sphere, and which constitutes at once the evidence of a Divine element within us, and the augury of the future that is before us.[1]

These things belong rather to the sphere of feeling than of reasoning. Those who are most deeply persuaded of their truth, will probably feel that they are unable by argument to express adequately the intensity of their conviction, but they may point to the recorded experience of the best and greatest men in all ages, to the incapacity of terrestrial things to satisfy our nature, to the manifest tendency, both in individuals and nations, of a pure and heroic life to kindle, and of a selfish and corrupt life to cloud, these aspirations, to the historical fact that no philosophy and no scepticism have been able permanently to repress them. The lines of our moral nature tend upwards. In it we have the common root of religion and of ethics, for the same consciousness that tells us that, even when it is in fact the weakest element of our constitution, it is by right supreme, commanding and authoritative, teaches us also that it is Divine. All the nobler religions that have governed mankind, have done so by virtue of the affinity of their teaching with this nature, by speaking, as common religious language correctly describes it, 'to the heart,' by appealing not to self-interest, but to that Divine element of self-sacrifice which is latent in every soul.[2] The reality of this moral nature is the one great

---

[1] 'Nescio quomodo inhæret in mentibus quasi sæculorum quoddam augurium futurorum; idque in maximis ingeniis altissimisque ani-mis et exsistit maxime et apparet facillime.'—Cic. *Tusc. Disp* i. 14.

[2] 'It is a calumny to say that men are roused to heroic actions

question of natural theology, for it involves that connection between our own and a higher nature, without which the existence of a First Cause were a mere question of archæology, and religion but an exercise of the imagination.

I return gladly to the secular sanctions of utilitarianism. The majority of its disciples assure us that these are sufficient to establish their theory, or in other words, that our duty coincides so strictly with our interest when rightly understood, that a perfectly prudent would necessarily become a perfectly virtuous man.[1] Bodily vice they tell us ultimately brings bodily weakness and suffering. Extravagance is followed by ruin; unbridled passions by the loss of domestic peace; disregard for the interests of others by social or legal penalties; while on the other hand, the most moral is also the most tranquil disposition; benevolence is one of the truest of our pleasures, and virtue may become by habit, an essential of enjoyment. As the shopkeeper who has made his fortune, still sometimes continues at the counter, because the daily routine has become necessary to his happiness, so the 'moral hero' may continue to practise that virtue which was at first the mere instrument of his pleasures, as being in itself more precious than all besides.[2]

---

by ease, hope of pleasure, recompense—sugar-plums of any kind in this world or the next. In the meanest mortal there lies something nobler. The poor swearing soldier hired to be shot has his "honour of a soldier," different from drill, regulations, and the shilling a day. It is not to taste sweet things, but to do noble and true things, and vindicate himself under God's heaven as a God-made man, that the poorest son of Adam dimly longs. Show him the way of doing that, the dullest day-drudge kindles into a hero. They wrong man greatly who say he is to be seduced by ease. Difficulty, abnegation, martyrdom, death, are the allurements that act on the heart of man. Kindle the inner genial life of him, you have a flame that burns up all lower considerations.'—Carlyle's *Hero-worship*, p. 237 (ed. 1858).

[1] 'Clamat Epicurus, is quem vos nimis voluptatibus esse deditum dicitis, non posse jucunde vivi nisi sapienter, honeste, justeque vivatur, nec sapienter, honeste, juste nisi jucunde.'—Cicero, *De Fin.* i. 18.

[2] 'The virtues to be complete must have fixed their residence in the heart and become appetites

This theory of the perfect coincidence of virtue and interest rightly understood, which has always been a commonplace of moralists, and has been advocated by many who were far from wishing to resolve virtue into prudence, contains no doubt a certain amount of truth, but only of the most general kind. It does not apply to nations as wholes, for although luxurious and effeminate vices do undoubtedly corrode and enervate national character, the histories of ancient Rome and of not a few modern monarchies abundantly prove that a career of consistent rapacity, ambition, selfishness, and fraud may be eminently conducive to national prosperity.[1] It does not apply to imperfectly organised societies, where the restraints of public opinion are unfelt and where force is the one measure of right. It does not apply except in a very partial degree even to the most civilised of mankind. It is, indeed, easy to show that in a polished community a certain low standard of virtue is essential to prosperity, to paint the evils of unrestrained passions, and to prove that it is better to obey than to violate the laws of society. But if turning from the criminal or the drunkard we were to compare the man who simply falls in with or slightly surpasses the average morals of those about

---

impelling to actions without further thought than the gratification of them; so that after their expedience ceases they still continue to operate by the desire they raise. ... . I knew a mercer who having gotten a competency of fortune, thought to retire and enjoy himself in quiet; but finding he could not be easy without business was forced to return to the shop and assist his former partners gratis, in the nature of a journeyman. Why then should it be thought strange that a man long inured to the practice of moral duties should persevere in them out of liking,

when they can yield him no further advantage?'—Tucker's *Light of Nature*, vol. i. p. 269. Mr. J. S. Mill in his *Utilitarianism* dwells much on the heroism which he thinks this view of morals may produce.

[1] See Lactantius, *Inst. Div.* vi. 9. Montesquieu, in his *Décadence de l'Empire romain*, has shown in detail the manner in which the crimes of Roman politicians contributed to the greatness of their nation. Modern history furnishes only too many illustrations of the same truth.

him, and indulges in a little vice which is neither injurious
to his own health nor to his reputation, with the man who
earnestly and painfully adopts a much higher standard than
that of his time or of his class, we should be driven to another
conclusion.   Honesty it is said is the best policy—a fact,
however, which depends very much upon the condition of
the police force—but heroic virtue must rest upon a different
basis. If happiness in any of its forms be the supreme object
of life, moderation is the most emphatic counsel of our being,
but moderation is as opposed to heroism as to vice.   There
is no form of intellectual or moral excellence which has not
a general tendency to produce happiness if cultivated in
moderation.   There are very few which if cultivated to great
perfection have not a tendency directly the reverse.   Thus a
mind that is sufficiently enlarged to range abroad amid the
pleasures of intellect has no doubt secured a fund of inex-
haustible enjoyment; but he who inferred from this that the
highest intellectual eminence was the condition most favourable to happiness would be lamentably deceived.   The diseased nervous sensibility that accompanies intense mental
exertion, the weary, wasting sense of ignorance and vanity,
the disenchantment and disintegration that commonly follow
a profound research, have filled literature with mournful
echoes of the words of the royal sage, ' In much wisdom is
much grief, and he that increaseth knowledge increaseth
sorrow.'   The lives of men of genius have been for the
most part a conscious and deliberate realisation of the
ancient myth—the tree of knowledge and the tree of life
stood side by side, and they chose the tree of knowledge
rather than the tree of life.

Nor is it otherwise in the realm of morals.[1]   The virtue
which is most conducive to happiness is plainly that which

---

[1] 'That quick sensibility which
is the groundwork of all advances
towards perfection increases the
pungency of pains and vexations.'—
Tucker's *Light of Nature*, ii. 16
§ 4.

can be realised without much suffering, and sustained without much effort. Legal and physical penalties apply only to the grosser and more extreme forms of vice. Social penalties may strike the very highest forms of virtue.[1] That very sentiment of unity with mankind which utilitarians assure us is one day to become so strong as to overpower all unsocial feelings, would make it more and more impossible for men consistently with their happiness to adopt any course, whether very virtuous or very vicious, that would place them out of harmony with the general sentiment of society. It may be said that the tranquillity of a perfectly virtuous mind is the highest form of happiness, and may be reasonably preferred not only to material advantages, but also to the approbation of society; but no man can fully attain, and few can even approximate, to such a condition. When vicious passions and impulses are very strong, it is idle to tell the sufferer that he would be more happy if his nature were radically different from what it is. If happiness be his object, he must regulate his course with a view to the actual condition of his being, and there can be little doubt that his peace would be most promoted by a compromise with vice. The selfish theory of morals applies only to the virtues of temperament, and not to that much higher form of virtue which is sustained in defiance of temperament.[2] We have no doubt a certain pleasure in cultivating our good tendencies, but we have by no means the same pleasure in repressing our bad ones. There are men whose whole lives are spent in willing one thing, and desiring the opposite. In such cases as these

---

[1] This position is forcibly illustrated by Mr. Maurice in his fourth lecture *On Conscience* (1868). It is manifest that a tradesman resisting a dishonest or illegal trade custom, an Irish peasant in a disturbed district revolting against the agrarian conspiracy of his class, or a soldier in many countries conscientiously refusing in obedience to the law to fight a duel, would incur the full force of social penalties, because he failed to do that which was illegal or criminal.

[2] See Brown *On the Characteristics*, pp. 206–209.

virtue clearly involves a sacrifice of happiness; for the suffering caused by resisting natural tendencies is much greater
than would ensue from their moderate gratification.

The plain truth is that no proposition can be more palpably and egregiously false than the assertion that as far as
this world is concerned, it is invariably conducive to the
happiness of a man to pursue the most virtuous career.   Circumstances and disposition will make one man find his
highest happiness in the happiness, and another man in the
misery, of his kind; and if the second man acts according to
his interest, the utilitarian, however much he may deplore
the result, has no right to blame or condemn the agent.   For
that agent is following his greatest happiness, and this, in the
eyes of utilitarians, in one form or another, is the highest, or
to speak more accurately, the only motive by which human
nature can be actuated.

We may remark too that the disturbance or pain which
does undoubtedly usually accompany what is evil, bears no
kind of proportion to the enormity of the guilt.   An irrita-
bility of temper, which is chiefly due to a derangement of the
nervous system, or a habit of procrastination or indecision,
will often cause more suffering than some of the worst vices
that can corrupt the heart.[1]

But it may be said this calculation of pains and pleasures
is defective through the omission of one element.   Although
a man who had a very strong natural impulse towards some
vice would appear more likely to promote the tranquillity of
his nature by a moderate and circumspect gratification of that

---

[1] 'A toothache produces more
violent convulsions of pain than a
phthisis or a dropsy. A gloomy
disposition . . . may be found in
very worthy characters, though it
is sufficient alone to embitter life.
. . . A selfish villain may possess
a spring and alacrity of temper,
which is indeed a good quality, but
which is rewarded much beyond its
merit, and when attended with good
fortune will compensate for the
uneasiness and remorse arising
from all the other vices.'—Hume's
Essays: The Sceptic.

vice, than by endeavouring painfully to repress his natural
tendencies, yet he possesses a conscience which adjudicates
upon his conduct, and its sting or its approval constitutes a
pain or pleasure so intense, as more than to redress the
balance. Now of course, no intuitive moralist will deny,
what for a long time his school may be almost said to have
been alone in asserting, the reality of conscience, or the
pleasures and pains it may afford. He simply denies, and he
appeals to consciousness in attestation of his position, that
those pains and pleasures are so powerful or so proportioned
to our acts as to become an adequate basis for virtue. Conscience, whether we regard it as an original faculty, or as a
product of the association of ideas, exercises two distinct
functions. It points out a difference between right and
wrong, and when its commands are violated, it inflicts a certain measure of suffering and disturbance. The first function
it exercises persistently through life. The second it only
exercises under certain special circumstances. It is scarcely
conceivable that a man in the possession of his faculties should
pass a life of gross depravity and crime without being conscious that he was doing wrong ; but it is extremely possible
for him to do so without this consciousness having any appreciable influence upon his tranquillity. The condition of
their consciences, as Mr. Carlyle observes, has less influence
on the happiness of men than the condition of their livers.
Considered as a source of pain, conscience bears a striking
resemblance to the feeling of disgust. Notwithstanding the
assertion of Dr. Johnson, I venture to maintain that there
are multitudes to whom the necessity of discharging the
duties of a butcher would be so inexpressibly painful and revolting, that if they could obtain flesh diet on no other condition, they would relinquish it for ever. But to those who
are inured to the trade, this repugnance has simply ceased.
It has no place in their emotions or calculations. Nor can
it be reasonably questioned that most men by an assiduous

attendance at the slaughter-house could acquire a similar indifference. In like manner, the reproaches of conscience are doubtless a very real and important form of suffering to a sensitive, scrupulous, and virtuous girl who has committed some trivial act of levity or disobedience; but to an old and hardened criminal they are a matter of the most absolute indifference.

Now it is undoubtedly conceivable, that by an association of ideas men might acquire a feeling that would cause that which would naturally be painful to them to be pleasurable, and that which would naturally be pleasurable to be painful.[1] But the question will immediately arise, why should they respect this feeling? We have seen that, according to the inductive theory, there is no such thing as natural duty. Men enter into life solely desirous of seeking their own happiness. The whole edifice of virtue arises from the observed fact, that owing to the constitution of our nature, and the intimacy of our social relations, it is necessary for our happiness to abstain from some courses that would be immediately pleasurable and to pursue others that are immediately the reverse. Self-interest is the one ultimate reason for virtue, however much

---

[1] At the same time, the following passage contains, I think, a great deal of wisdom and of a kind peculiarly needed in England at the present day :— The nature of the subject furnishes the strongest presumption that no better system will ever, for the future, be invented, in order to account for the origin of the benevolent from the selfish affections, and reduce all the various emotions of the human mind to a perfect simplicity. The case is not the same in this species of philosophy as in physics. Many an hypothesis in nature, contrary to first appearances, has been found, on more accurate scrutiny, solid and satisfactory. . . . But the presumption always lies on the other side in all enquiries concerning the origin of our passions, and of the internal operations of the human mind. The simplest and most obvious cause which can there be assigned for any phenomenon, is probably the true one. . . . The affections are not susceptible of any impression from the refinements of reason or imagination; and it is always found that a vigorous exertion of the latter faculties, necessarily, from the narrow capacity of the human mind, destroys all activity in the former.'—Hume's *Enquiry Concerning Morals*, Append. II.

the moral chemistry of Hartley may disguise and transform
it. Ought or ought not, means nothing more than the prospect of acquiring or of losing pleasure. The fact that one
line of conduct promotes, and another impairs the happiness of
others is, according to these moralists, in the last analysis, no
reason whatever for pursuing the former or avoiding the
latter, unless such a course is that which brings us the
greatest happiness. The happiness may arise from the action
of society upon ourselves, or from our own naturally benevolent disposition, or, again, from an association of ideas, which
means the force of a habit we have formed, but in any case
our own happiness is the one possible or conceivable motive
of action. If this be a true picture of human nature, the
reasonable course for every man is to modify his disposition
in such a manner that he may attain the greatest possible
amount of enjoyment. If he has formed an association of
ideas, or contracted a habit which inflicts more pain than it
prevents, or prevents more pleasure than it affords, his reasonable course is to dissolve that association, to destroy that
habit. This is what he 'ought' to do according to the only
meaning that word can possess in the utilitarian vocabulary.
If he does not, he will justly incur the charge of imprudence,
which is the only charge utilitarianism can consistently bring
against vice.

That it would be for the happiness as it would certainly be
in the power of a man of a temperament such as I have lately
described, to quench that conscientious feeling, which by its
painful reproaches prevents him from pursuing the course
that would be most conducive to his tranquillity, I conceive
to be self-evident. And, indeed, on the whole, it is more
than doubtful whether conscience, considered apart from the
course of action it prescribes, is not the cause of more pain
than pleasure. Its reproaches are more felt than its approval. The self-complacency of a virtuous man reflecting
with delight upon his own exceeding merit, is frequently

spoken of in the writings of moral philosophers,[1] but is
rarely found in actual life where the most tranquil is seldom
the most perfect nature, where the sensitiveness of conscience
increases at least in proportion to moral growth, and where
in the best men a feeling of modesty and humility is always
present to check the exuberance of self-gratulation.

In every sound system of morals and religion the motives
of virtue become more powerful the more the mind is concentrated upon them. It is when they are lost sight of, when
they are obscured by passion, unrealised or forgotten, that

---

[1] 'The pleasing consciousness
and self-approbation that rise up
in the mind of a virtuous man, exclusively of any direct, explicit,
consideration of advantage likely
to accrue to himself from his pos
session of those good qualities'
(Hartley *On Man*, vol. i. p. 493),
form a theme upon which moralists
of both schools are fond of dilating,
in a strain that reminds one irresistibly of the self-complacency of
a famous nursery hero, while reflecting upon his own merits over a
Christmas-pie. Thus Adam Smith
says, 'The man who, not from
frivolous fancy, but from proper
motives, has performed a generous
action, when he looks forward to
those whom he has served, feels
himself to be the natural object of
their love and gratitude, and by
sympathy with them, of the esteem
and approbation of all mankind.
And when he looks backward to
the motive from which he acted,
and surveys it in the light in which
the indifferent spectator will survey it, he still continues to enter
into it, and applauds himself by
sympathy with the approbation of
this supposed impartial judge. In
both these points of view his con-

duct appears to him every way
agreeable. . . . Misery and wretchedness can never enter the breast
in which dwells complete self-sa-
tisfaction.'—*Theory of Moral Sentiments*, part ii. ch. ii. § 2; part iii.
ch. iii. I suspect that many moralists confuse the self-gratulation
which they suppose a virtuous man
to feel, with the delight a religious
man experiences from the sense of
the protection and favour of the
Deity. But these two feelings are
clearly distinct, and it will, I
believe, be found that the latter
is most strongly experienced by the
very men who most sincerely dis-
claim all sense of merit. 'Were
the perfect man to exist,' said that
good and great writer, Archer
Butler, 'he himself would be the
last to know it; for the highest
stage of advancement is the lowest
descent in humility.' At all events,
the reader will observe, that on
utilitarian principles nothing could
be more pernicious or criminal
than that modest, humble, and
diffident spirit, which diminishes
the pleasure of self-gratulation,
one of the highest utilitarian motives to virtue.

they cease to operate. But it is a peculiarity of the utilitarian conception of virtue that it is wholly unable to resist the solvent of analysis, and that the more the mind realises its origin and its nature, the more its influence on character must decline. The pleasures of the senses will always defy the force of analysis, for they have a real foundation in our being. They have their basis in the eternal nature, of things. But the pleasure we derive from the practice of virtue rests, according to this school, on a wholly different basis. It is the result of casual and artificial association, of habit, of a confusion by the imagination of means with ends, of a certain dignity with which society invests qualities or actions that are useful to itself. Just in proportion as this is felt, just in proportion as the mind separates the idea of virtue from that of natural excellence and obligation, and realises the purely artificial character of the connection, just in that proportion will the coercive power of the moral motive be destroyed. The utilitarian rule of judging actions and dispositions by their tendency to promote or diminish happiness, or the maxim of Kant that man should always act so that the rule of his conduct might be adopted as a law by all rational beings may be very useful as a guide in life; but in order that they should acquire moral weight, it is necessary to presuppose the sense of moral obligation, the consciousness that duty, when discovered, has a legitimate claim to be the guiding principle of our lives. And it is this element which, in the eye of reason, the mere artificial association of ideas can never furnish.

If the patience of the reader has enabled him to accompany me through this long train of tedious arguments, he will, I think, have concluded that the utilitarian theory, though undoubtedly held by many men of the purest, and by some men of almost heroic virtue, would if carried to its logical conclusions prove subversive of morality, and especially, and in the very highest degree, unfavourable to self-denial and to heroism. Even if it explains these, it fails to justify them, and conscience being traced to a mere con fusion of the means of happiness with its end, would be wholly unable to resist the solvent of criticism. That this theory of conscience gives a true or adequate description of the phenomenon it seeks to explain, no intuitive moralist will admit. It is a complete though common mistake to suppose that the business of the moralist is merely to explain the genesis of certain feelings we possess. At the root of all morals lies an intellectual judgment which is clearly distinct from liking or disliking, from pleasure or from pain. A man who has injured his position by some foolish but perfectly innocent act, or who has inadvertently violated some social rule, may experience an emotion of self-reproach or of shame quite as acute as if he had committed a crime. But he is at the same time clearly conscious that his conduct is not a fit subject for moral reprobation, that the grounds on which it may be condemned are of a different and of a lower kind. The sense of obligation and of legitimate supremacy, which is the essential and characteristic feature of .conscience, and which distinguishes it from all the other parts of our nature, is wholly unaccounted for by the association of ideas. To say that a certain course of conduct is pleasing, and that a certain amount of pain results from the weakening of feelings that impel men towards it, is plainly different from what men mean when they say we ought to pursue it. The virtue of Hartley is, in its last analysis, but a disease of the imagination. It may be more advantageous to society than avarice; but it is formed in the same manner, and has exactly the same degree of binding force.[1]

---

[1] Hartley has tried in one place to evade this conclusion by an appeal to the doctrine of final causes. He says that the fact that conscience is not an original prin ciple of our nature, but is formed mechanically in the manner I have described, does not invalidate the fact that it is intended for our guide, 'for all the things which have evident final causes, are plain ly brought about by mechanical

These considerations will help to supply an answer to
the common utilitarian objection that to speak of duty as
distinct from self-interest is unmeaning, because it is absurd
to say that we are under an obligation to do any thing when
no evil consequences would result to us from not doing it.
Rewards and punishments it may be answered are undoubtedly necessary to enforce, but they are not necessary to
constitute, duty. This distinction, whether it be real or
not, has at all events the advantage of appearing self-evident
to all who are not philosophers. Thus when a party of
colonists occupy a new territory they divide the unoccupied
land among themselves, and they murder, or employ for the
gratification of their lusts, the savage inhabitants. Both
acts are done with perfect impunity, but one is felt to be
innocent and the other wrong. A lawful government appro-
priates the land and protects the aboriginals, supporting its
enactments by penalties. In the one case the law both
creates and enforces a duty, in the other it only enforces it.
The intuitive moralist simply asserts that we have the power
of perceiving that certain courses of action are higher, nobler.

means;' and he appeals to the milk
in the breast, which is intended for
the sustenance of the young, but
which is nevertheless mechanically
produced. (*On Man*, vol. ii. pp.
338–339.) But it is plain that
this mode of reasoning would justify us in attributing an authoritative character to any habit—e.g.
to that of avarice—which these
writers assure us is in the manner
of its formation an exact parallel to
conscience. The later followers of
Hartley certainly cannot be accused
of any excessive predilection for
the doctrine of final causes, yet we
sometimes find them asking what
great difference it can make whether (when conscience is admitted
by both parties to be real) it is

regarded as an original principle of
our nature, or as a product of
association? Simply this. If by
the constitution of our nature we
are subject to a law of duty which
is different from and higher than
our interest, a man who violates
this law through interested motives, is deserving of reprobation.
If on the other hand there is no
natural law of duty, and if the
pursuit of our interest is the one
original principle of our being, no
one can be censured who pursues
it, and the first criterion of a wise
man will be his determination to
eradicate every habit (conscientious or otherwise) which impedes
him in doing so.

and better than others, and that by the constitution of our
being, this fact, which is generically distinct from the prospect
of pleasure or the reverse, may and ought to be and continually is a motive of action.   It is no doubt possible for a
man to prefer the lower course, and in this case we say he
is deserving of punishment, and if he remains unpunished
we say that it is unjust.   But if there were no power to
reward or punish him, his acts would not be indifferent.
They would still be intelligibly described as essentially base
or noble, shameful though there were none to censure, admirable though there were none to admire.

That men have the power of preferring other objects
than happiness is a proposition which must ultimately be
left to the attestation of consciousness.   That the pursuit of
virtue, however much happiness may eventually follow in
its train, is in the first instance an example of this preference,
must be established by that common voice of mankind which
has invariably regarded a virtuous motive as generically
different from an interested one.   And indeed even when
the conflict between strong passions and a strong sense of
duty does not exist it is impossible to measure the degrees
of virtue by the scale of enjoyment.   The highest nature is
rarely the happiest.   Petronius Arbiter was, very probably,
a happier man than Marcus Aurelius.   For eighteen centuries
the religious instinct of Christendom has recognised its ideal
in the form of a ' Man of Sorrows.'

Considerations such as I have now urged lead the intuitive moralists to reject the principles of the utilitarian.
They acknowledge indeed that the effect of actions upon the
happiness of mankind forms a most important element in
determining their moral quality, but they maintain that
without natural moral perceptions we never should have
known that it was our duty to seek the happiness of mankind when it diverged from our own, and they deny that
virtue was either originally evolved from or is necessarily

proportioned to utility. They acknowledge that in the existing condition of society there is at least a general coincidence between the paths of virtue and of prosperity, but they contend that the obligation of virtue is of such a nature that no conceivable convulsion of affairs could destroy it, and that it would continue even if the government of the world belonged to supreme malice instead of supreme benevolence. Virtue, they believe, is something more than a calculation or a habit. It is impossible to conceive its fundamental principles reversed. Notwithstanding the strong tendency to confuse cognate feelings, the sense of duty and the sense of utility remain perfectly distinct in the apprehension of mankind, and we are quite capable of recognising each separate ingredient in the same act. Our respect for a gallant but dangerous enemy, our contempt for a useful traitor, our care in the last moments of life for the interests of those who survive us, our clear distinction between intentional and unintentional injuries, and between the consciousness of imprudence and the consciousness of guilt, our conviction that the pursuit of interest should always be checked by a sense of duty, and that selfish and moral motives are so essentially opposed, that the presence of the former necessarily weakens the latter, our indignation at those who when honour or gratitude call them to sacrifice their interests pause to calculate remote consequences, the feeling of remorse which differs from every other emotion of our nature—in a word, the universal, unstudied sentiments of mankind all concur in leading us to separate widely our virtuous affections from our selfish ones. Just as pleasure and pain are ultimate grounds of action, and no reason can be given why we should seek the former and avoid the latter, except that it is the constitution of our nature that we should do so, so we are conscious that the words right and wrong express ultimate intelligible motives, that these motives are generically different from the others, that they are of a higher order, and that they carry with them a sense of obligation. Any scheme of morals that omits these facts fails to give an accurate and adequate description of the states of feeling which consciousness reveals. The consciences of men in every age would have echoed the assertion of Cicero that to sacrifice pleasure with a view of obtaining any form or modification of pleasure in return, no more answers to our idea of virtue, than to lend money at interest to our idea of charity. The conception of pure disinterestedness is presupposed in our estimates of virtue. It is the root of all the emotions with which we contemplate acts of heroism. We feel that man is capable of pursuing what he believes to be right although pain and disaster and mental suffering and an early death be the consequence, and although no prospect of future reward lighten upon his tomb. This is the highest prerogative of our being, the point of contact between the human nature and the divine.

In addition to the direct arguments in its support, the utilitarian school owes much of its influence to some very powerful moral and intellectual predispositions in its favour—the first, which we shall hereafter examine, consisting of the tendency manifested in certain conditions of society towards the qualities it is most calculated to produce, and the second of the almost irresistible attraction which unity and precision exercise on many minds. It was this desire to simplify human nature, by reducing its various faculties and complex operations to a single principle or process, that gave its great popularity to the sensational school of the last century. It led most metaphysicians of that school to deny the duality of human nature. It led Bonnet and Condillac to propose an animated statue, endowed with the five senses as channels of ideas, and with faculties exclusively employed in transforming the products of sensation, as a perfect representative of humanity. It led Helvétius to assert that the original faculties of all men were precisely the same, all the difference between what we call genius and what we call stupidity arising from differences of circumstances, and all the difference between men and animals arising mainly from the structure of the human hand. In morals, theories of unification are peculiarly plausible, and I think peculiarly dangerous, because, owing to the interaction of our moral sentiments, and the many transformations that each can undergo, there are few affections that might not under some conceivable circumstances become the parents of every other. When Hobbes, in the name of the philosophy of self-interest, contended that ' Pity is but the imagination of future calamity to ourselves, produced by the sense of another man's calamity ;'[1] when Hutcheson, in the name of the philosophy of benevolence, argued that the vice of intemperance is that it impels us to violence towards others, and weakens our capacity for doing them good ;[2] when other moralists defending the excellence of our nature maintained that compassion is so emphatically the highest of our pleasures that a desire of gratifying it is the cause of our acts of barbarity ;[3] each of these theories,

---

[1] *On Human Nature,* chap. ix. § 10.

[2] *Enquiry concerning Good and Evil.*

[3] This theory is noticed by Hutcheson, and a writer in the *Spectator* (No. 436) suggests that it may explain the attraction of prize-fights. The case of the pleasure derived from fictitious sorrow is a distinct question, and has been admirably treated in Lord Kames' *Essays on Morality.* Bishop Butler n tices (*Second Sermon on Compassion*), that it is possible for the very intensity of a feeling of compassion to divert men from charity by making them ' industriously turn away from the miserable ;' and it is well known that Goethe, on account of this very susceptibility, made it one of the rules of his life to avoid everything that could suggest painful ideas. Hobbes makes the following very characteristic comments on some famous lines of Lucretius : ' From what passion proceedeth it that men take pleasure to behold from the shore the danger of those that are at sea in a tempest or in fight, or from a safe castle to behold two armies charge one another in the field? It is certainly in the whole sum joy, else men would never flock to such a spectacle. Nevertheless, there is both joy and grief, for as there is novelty and remembrance of our own security present, which is delight, so there is also pity, which is grief. But the delight is so far predominant that men usually are

extravagant as it is, contains a germ of undoubted psychological truth.   It is true that a mind intensely apprehensive
of future calamities would on that account receive a shock at
the sight of the calamities of others.   It is true that a very
keen and absorbing sentiment of benevolence would be in
itself sufficient to divert men from any habit that impaired
their power of gratifying it.   It is true that compassion involves a certain amount of pleasure, and conceivable that
this pleasure might be so intensified that we might seek it
by a crime.   The error in these theories is not that they
exaggerate the possible efficacy of the motives, but that
they exaggerate their actual intensity in human nature and
describe falsely the process by which the results they seek to
explain have been arrived at.   The function of observation
in moral philosophy is not simply to attest the moral sentiments we possess, leaving it to the reason to determine
deductively how they may have been formed ; it is rather to
follow them through all the stages of their formation.

And here I may observe that the term inductive, like
most others that are employed in moral philosophy, may give

---

content in such a case to be spectators of the misery of their
friends.' (*On Human Nature*, ch. ix.
§ 19.) Good Christians, according
to some theologians, are expected
to enjoy this pleasure in great
perfection in heaven. 'We may
believe in the next world also the
goodness as well as the happiness
of the blest will be confirmed and
advanced by reflections naturally
arising from the view of the misery
which some shall undergo, which
seems to be a good reason for the
creation of those beings who shall
be finally miserable, and for the
continuation of them in their miserable existence . . . . though in
one respect the view of the misery

which the damned undergo might
seem to detract from the happiness
of the blessed through pity and
commiseration, yet under another,
a nearer and much more affecting
consideration, viz. that all this is
the misery they themselves were
often exposed to and in danger of
incurring, why may not the sense
of their own escape so far overcome
the sense of another's ruin as quite
to extinguish the pain that usually
attends the idea of it, and even
render it productive of some real
happiness?   To this purpose, Lucretius' *Suave mari*,' etc.   (*Law's
notes to his Translation of King's
Origin of Evil*, pp. 477, 479.)

rise to serious misconception. It is properly applied to those
moralists who, disbelieving the existence of any moral sense
or faculty revealing to us what is right and wrong, maintain
that the origin of those ideas is simply our experience of the
tendency of different lines of conduct to promote or impair
true happiness. It appears, however, to be sometimes imagined that inductive moralists alone think that it is by induction or experience that we ought to ascertain what is the
origin of our moral ideas. But this I conceive to be a complete mistake. The basis of morals is a distinct question from
the basis of theories of morals. Those who maintain the
existence of a moral faculty do not, as is sometimes said,
assume this proposition as a first principle of their arguments,
but they arrive at it by a process of induction quite as severe
as any that can be employed by their opponents.[1] They examine, analyse, and classify their existing moral feelings,
ascertain in what respects those feelings agree with or differ
from others, trace them through their various phases, and
only assign them to a special faculty when they think they
have shown them to be incapable of resolution, and generically different from all others.[2]

---

[1] See e.g. Reid's Essays on the
Active Powers, essay iii. ch. v.

[2] The error I have traced in
this paragraph will be found running through a great part of what
Mr. Buckle has written upon
morals—I think the weakest portion of his great work. See, for
example, an elaborate confusion on
the subject, History of Civilisation,
vol. ii. p. 429. Mr. Buckle maintains that all the philosophers of
what is commonly called 'the
Scotch school' (a school founded by
the Irishman Hutcheson, and to
which Hume does not belong),
were incapable of inductive reasoning, because they maintained
the existence of a moral sense or
faculty, or of first principles, incapable of resolution ; and he enters
into a learned enquiry into the
causes which made it impossible
for Scotch writers to pursue or
appreciate the inductive method.
It is curious to contrast this view
with the language of one, who,
whatever may be the value of his
original speculations, is, I conceive,
among the very ablest philosophical
critics of the present century.
'Les philosophes éccssais adop-
tèrent les procédés que Bacon avait
recommandé d'appliquer à l'étude
du monde physique, et les trans-
portèrent dans l'étude du monde

This separation is all that is meant by a moral faculty. We are apt to regard the term as implying a distinct and well defined organ, bearing to the mind the same kind of relation as a limb to the body. But of the existence of such organs, and of the propriety of such material imagery, we know nothing. Perceiving in ourselves a will, and a crowd of intellectual and emotional phenomena that seem wholly different from the properties of matter, we infer the existence of an immaterial substance which wills, thinks, and feels, and can classify its own operations with considerable precision. The term faculty is simply an expression of classification. If we say that the moral faculty differs from the æsthetic faculty, we can only mean that the mind forms certain judgments of moral excellence, and also certain judgments of beauty, and that these two mental processes are clearly distinct. To ask to what part of our nature moral perceptions should be attributed, is only to ask to what train of mental phenomena they bear the closest resemblance.

If this simple, but often neglected, consideration be borne

moral. Ils firent voir que l'induction baconienne, c'est-à-dire, l'induction précédée d'une observation scrupuleuse des phénomènes, est en philosophie comme en physique la seule méthode légitime. C'est un de leurs titres les plus honorables d'avoir insisté sur cette démonstration, et d'avoir en même temps joint l'exemple au précepte. . . . Il est vrai que le zèle des philosophes écossais en faveur de la méthode d'observation leur a presque fait dépasser le but. Ils ont incliné à renfermer la psychologie dans la description minutieuse et continuelle de phénomènes de l'âme sans réfléchir assez que cette description doit faire place à l'induction et au raisonnement déductif, et qu'une philosophie qui se borne- rait à l'observation serait aussi stérile que celle qui s'amuserait à construire des hypothèses sans avoir préalablement observé.'— Cousin, Hist. de la Philos. Morale au xviiime Siècle, Tome 4, p. 14–16. Dugald Stewart had said much the same thing, but he was a Scotchman, and therefore, according to Mr. Buckle (*Hist. of Civ.* ii. pp. 485–86), incapable of understanding what induction was. I may add that one of the principal objec tions M. Cousin makes against Locke is, that he investigated the origin of our ideas before analysing minutely their nature, and the pro priety of this method is one of the points on which Mr. Mill (*Examination of Sir W. Hamilton*) is at issue with M. Cousin.

in mind, the apparent discordance of intuitive moralists will appear less profound than might at first sight be supposed, for each section merely elucidates some one characteristic of moral judgments. Thus Butler insists upon the sense of obligation that is involved in them, contends that this separates them from all other sentiments, and assigns them in consequence to a special faculty of supreme authority called conscience. Adam Smith and many other writers were especially struck by their sympathetic character. We are naturally attracted by humanity, and repelled by cruelty, and this instinctive, unreasoning sentiment constitutes, according to these moralists, the difference between right and wrong. Cudworth, however, the English precursor of Kant, had already anticipated, and later metaphysicians have more fully exhibited, the inadequacy of such an analysis. Justice, humanity, veracity, and kindred virtues not merely have the power of attracting us, we have also an intellectual perception that they are essentially and immutably good, that their nature does not depend upon, and is not relative to, our constitutions; that it is impossible and inconceivable they should ever be vices, and their opposites, virtues. They are, therefore, it is said, intuitions of the reason. Clarke, developing the same rational school, and following in the steps of those moralists who regard our nature as a hierarchy of powers or faculties, with different degrees of dignity, and an appropriate order of supremacy and subordination, maintained that virtue consisted in harmony with the nature of things. Wollaston endeavoured to reduce it to truth, and Hutcheson to benevolence, which he maintained is recognised and approved by what his respect for the philosophy of Locke induced him to call 'a moral sense,' but what Shaftesbury had regarded as a moral ' taste.' The pleasure attending the gratification of this taste, according to Shaftesbury and Henry More, is the motive to virtue. The doctrine of a moral sense or faculty was the basis of the ethics of Reid. Hume maintained that the peculiar quality of virtue is its utility, but that our affections are purely disinterested, and that we arrive at our knowledge of what is virtuous by a moral sense implanted in our nature, which leads us instinctively to approve of all acts that are beneficial to others. Expanding a pregnant hint which had been thrown out by Butler, he laid the foun dation for a union of the schools of Clarke and Shaftesbury, by urging that our moral decisions are not simple, but com- plex, containing both a judgment of the reason, and an emo- tion of the heart. This fact has been elucidated still further by later writers, who have observed that these two elements apply in varying degrees to different kinds of virtue. Accord- ing to Lord Kames, our intellectual perception of right and wrong applies most strictly to virtues like justice or veracity, which are of what is called 'perfect obligation,' or, in other words, are of such a nature, that their violation is a distinct crime, while the emotion of attraction or affection is shown most strongly towards virtues of imperfect obligation, like benevolence or charity. Like Hutcheson and Shaftesbury, Lord Kames notices the analogies between our moral and æsthetical judgments.

These last analogies open out a region of thought widely different from that we have been traversing. The close connection between the good and the beautiful has been always felt, so much so, that both were in Greek expressed by the same word, and in the philosophy of Plato, moral beauty was regarded as the archetype of which all visible beauty is only the shadow or the image. We all feel that there is a strict propriety in the term moral beauty. We feel that there are different forms of beauty which have a natural correspondence to different moral qualities, and much of the charm of poetry and eloquence rests upon this harmony. We feel that we have a direct, immediate, intuitive percep- tion that some objects, such as the sky above us, are beauti- ful, that this perception of beauty is totally different, and

could not possibly be derived, from a perception of their
utility, and that it bears a very striking resemblance to
the instantaneous and unreasoning admiration elicited by a
generous or heroic action. We perceive too, if we examine
with care the operations of our own mind, that an æsthetical
judgment includes an intuition or intellectual perception,
and an emotion of attraction or admiration, very similar to
those which compose a moral judgment. The very idea of
beauty again implies that it should be admired, as the idea
of happiness implies that it should be desired, and the idea of
duty that it should be performed. There is also a striking
correspondence between the degree and kind of uniformity
we can in each case discover. That there is a difference
between right and wrong, and between beauty and ugliness,
are both propositions which are universally felt. That right
is better than wrong, and beauty than ugliness, are equally
unquestioned. When we go further, and attempt to define
the nature of these qualities, we are met indeed by great
diversities of detail, but by a far larger amount of substantial
unity. Poems like the Iliad or the Psalms, springing in the
most dissimilar quarters, have commanded the admiration of
men, through all the changes of some 3,000 years. The charm
of music, the harmony of the female countenance, the majesty
of the starry sky, of the ocean or of the mountain, the gentler
beauties of the murmuring stream or of the twilight shades,
were felt, as they are felt now, when the imagination of the
infant world first embodied itself in written words.   And
in the same way types of heroism, and of virtue, descending
from the remotest ages, command the admiration of mankind. We can sympathise with the emotions of praise or
blame revealed in the earliest historians, and the most ancient
moralists strike a responsive chord in every heart.   The
broad lines remain unchanged. No one ever contended that
justice was a vice or injustice a virtue; or that a summer
sunset was a repulsive object, or that the sores upon a human

body were beautiful. Always, too, the objects of æsthetical admiration were divided into two great classes, the sublime and the beautiful, which in ethics have their manifest counterparts in the heroic and the amiable.

If, again, we examine the undoubted diversities that exist in judgments of virtue and of beauty, we soon discover that in each case a large proportion of them are to be ascribed to the different degrees of civilisation. The moral standard changes within certain limits, and according to a regular process with the evolutions of society. There are virtues very highly estimated in a rude civilisation which sink into comparative insignificance in an organised society, while conversely, virtues that were deemed secondary in the first become primary in the other. There are even virtues that it is impossible for any but highly cultivated minds to recognise. Questions of virtue and vice, such as the difference between humanity and barbarity, or between temperance and intemperance, are sometimes merely questions of degree, and the standard at one stage of civilisation may be much higher than at another. Just in the same way a steady modification of tastes, while a recognition of the broad features of beauty remains unchanged, accompanies advancing civilisation. The preference of gaudy to subdued tints, of colour to form, of a florid to a chaste style, of convulsive attitudes, gigantic figures, and strong emotions, may be looked for with considerable confidence in an uninstructed people. The refining influence of cultivation is in no sphere more remarkable than in the canons of taste it produces, and there are few better measures of the civilisation of a people than the conceptions of beauty it forms, the type or ideal it endeavours to realise.

Many diversities, however, both of moral and æsthetical judgments, may be traced to accidental causes. Some one who is greatly admired, or who possesses great influence, is distinguished by some peculiarity of appearance, or introduces some peculiarity of dress. He will soon find countless

imitators. Gradually the natural sense of beauty will be
come vitiated; the eye and the taste will adjust themselves
to a false and artificial standard, and men will at last judge
according to it with the most absolute spontaneity. In the
same way, if any accidental circumstance has elevated an
indifferent action to peculiar honour, if a religious system
enforces it as a virtue or brands it as a vice, the consciences
of men will after a time accommodate themselves to the sentence, and an appeal to a wider than a local tribunal is
necessary to correct the error. Every nation, again, from its
peculiar circumstances and position, tends to some particular
type, both of beauty and of virtue, and it naturally extols
its national type beyond all others. The virtues of a small
poor nation, living among barren mountains, surrounded by
powerful enemies, and maintaining its independence only by
the most inflexible discipline, watchfulness, and courage, will
be in some degree different from those of a rich people removed from all fear of invasion and placed in the centre of
commerce. The former will look with a very lenient eye on
acts of barbarity or treachery, which to the latter would
appear unspeakably horrible, and will value very highly
certain virtues of discipline which the other will comparatively neglect. So, too, the conceptions of beauty formed by
a nation of negroes will be different from those formed by a
nation of whites; [1] the splendour of a tropical sky or the
savage grandeur of a northern ocean, the aspect of great
mountains or of wide plains, will not only supply nations with
present images of sublimity or beauty, but will also contribute to form their standard and affect their judgments.
Local customs or observances become so interwoven with
our earliest recollections, that we at last regard them as es-

---

[1] M. Ch. Comte, in his very
learned *Traité de Législation*, liv.
iii. ch. iv., has made an extremely
curious collection of instances in
which different nations have made
their own distinctive peculiarities
of colour and form the ideal of
beauty.

sentially venerable, and even in the most trivial matters it requires a certain effort to dissolve the association. There was much wisdom as well as much wit in the picture of the novelist who described the English footman's contempt for the uniforms of the French, 'blue being altogether ridiculous for regimentals, except in the blue guards and artillery;' and I suppose there are few Englishmen into whose first confused impression of France there does not enter a half-instinctive feeling of repugnance caused by the ferocious appearance of a peasantry who are all dressed like butchers.[1]

It has been said[2] that 'the feelings of beauty, grandeur, and whatever else is comprehended under the name of taste, do not lead to action, but terminate in delightful contemplation, which constitutes the essential distinction between them and the moral sentiments to which in some points of view they may doubtless be likened.' This position I conceive to be altogether untenable. Our æsthetical judgment is of the nature of a preference. It leads us to prefer one class of objects to another, and whenever other things are equal, becomes a ground for action. In choosing the persons with whom we live, the neighbourhood we inhabit, the objects that surround us, we prefer that which is beautiful to that which is the reverse, and in every case in which a choice between beauty and deformity is in question, and no counteracting motive intervenes, we choose the former, and avoid the latter. There are no doubt innumerable events in life in which this question does not arise, but there are also very many in which we are not called upon to make a moral judgment. We say a man is actuated by strong moral principle who chooses according to its dictates in every case involving a moral judgment that comes naturally before him,

---

[1] 'How particularly fine the hard theta is in our English terminations, as in that grand word death, for which the Germans gutturise a sound that *puts you in mind of nothing but a loathsome toad.'*— Coleridge's *Table Talk,* p. 181.
[2] Mackintosh, *Dissert.* p. 238.

and who in obedience to its impulse pursues special courses
of action. Corresponding propositions may be maintained
with perfect truth concerning our sense of beauty. In proportion to its strength does it guide our course in ordinary
life, and determine our peculiar pursuits. We may indeed
sacrifice our sense of material beauty to considerations of
utility with much more alacrity than our sense of moral
beauty; we may consent to build a shapeless house sooner
than to commit a dishonourable action, but we cannot voluntarily choose that which is simply deformed, rather than that
which is beautiful, without a certain feeling of pain, and a
pain of this kind, according to the school of Hartley, is the
precise definition of conscience. Nor is it at all difficult to
conceive men with a sense of beauty so strong that they
would die rather than outrage it.

Considering all these things, it is not surprising that many
moralists should have regarded moral excellence as simply
the highest form of beauty, and moral cultivation as the
supreme refinement of taste. But although this manner of
regarding it is, as I think, far more plausible than the theory
which resolves virtue into utility, although the Greek moralists and the school of Shaftesbury have abundantly proved
that there is an extremely close connection between these
orders of ideas, there are two considerations which appear to
show the inadequacy of this theory. We are clearly conscious
of the propriety of applying the epithet 'beautiful' to virtues
such as charity, reverence, or devotion, but we cannot apply
it with the same propriety to duties of perfect obligation,
such as veracity or integrity. The sense of beauty and the
affection that follows it attach themselves rather to modes of
enthusiasm and feeling than to the course of simple duty
which constitutes a merely truthful and upright man.[1] Besides this, as the Stoics and Butler have shown, the position

---

[1] Lord Kames' *Essays on Morality* (1st edition), pp. 55-56.

of conscience in our nature is wholly unique, and clearly separates morals from a study of the beautiful. While each of our senses or appetites has a restricted sphere of operation, it is the function of conscience to survey the whole constitution of our being, and assign limits to the gratification of all our various passions and desires. Differing not in degree, but in kind from the other principles of our nature, we feel that a course of conduct which is opposed to it may be intelligibly described as unnatural, even when in accordance with our most natural appetites, for to conscience is assigned the prerogative of both judging and restraining them all. Its power may be insignificant, but its title is undisputed, and 'if it had might as it has right, it would govern the world.'[1] It is this faculty, distinct from, and superior to, all appetites, passions, and tastes, that makes virtue the supreme law of life, and adds an imperative character to the feeling of attraction it inspires. It is this which was described by Cicero as the God ruling within us; by the Stoics as the sovereignty of reason; by St. Paul as the law of nature; by Butler as the supremacy of conscience.

The distinction of different parts of our nature, as higher or lower, which appears in the foregoing reasoning, and which occupies so important a place in the intuitive system of morals, is one that can only be defended by the way of illustrations. A writer can only select cases in which such distinctions seem most apparent, and leave them to the feelings of his reader. A few examples will, I hope, be sufficient to show that even in our pleasures, we are not simply determined by the amount of enjoyment, but that there is a difference of kind, which may be reasonably described by the epithets, higher or lower.

If we suppose a being from another sphere, who derived his conceptions from a purely rational process, without the

---

[1] See Butler's *Three Sermons on Human Nature*, and the preface

interventior. of the senses, to descend to our world, and to enquire into the principles of human nature, I imagine there are few points that would strike him as more anomalous, or which he would be more absolutely unable to realise, than the different estimates in which men hold the pleasures derived from the two senses of tasting and hearing. Under the first is comprised the enjoyment resulting from the action of certain kinds of food upon the palate. Under the second the charm of music. Each of these forms of pleasure is natural, each can be greatly heightened by cultivation, in each case the pleasure may be vivid, but is very transient, and in neither case do evil consequences necessarily ensue. Yet with so many undoubted points of resemblance, when we turn to the actual world, we find the difference between these two orders of pleasure of such a nature, that a comparison seems absolutely ludicrous. In what then does this difference consist? Not, surely, in the greater intensity of the enjoyment derived from music, for in many cases this superiority does not exist.[1] We are all conscious that in our comparison of these pleasures, there is an element distinct from any consideration of their intensity, duration, or consequences. We naturally attach a faint notion of shame to the one, while we as naturally glory in the other. A very keen sense of the pleasures of the palate is looked upon as in a certain degree discreditable. A man will hardly boast that he is very fond of eating, but he has no hesitation in acknowledging that he is very fond of music. The first

---

[1] Speaking of the animated statue which he regarded as a representative of man, Condillac says, 'Le goût peut ordinairement contribuer plus que l'odorat à son bonheur et à son malheur. . . .. Il y contribue même encore plus que les sons harmonieux, parce que le besoin de nourriture lui rend les saveurs plus nécessaires, et par conséquent les lui fait goûter avec plus de vivacité. La faim pourra la rendre malheureuse, mais dès qu'elle aura remarqué les sensations propres à l'apaiser, elle y déterminera davantage son attention, les désirera avec plus de violence et en jouira avec plus de délire.'—Traité des Sensations, 1re partie, ch. x.

taste lowers, and the second elevates him in his own eyes, and in those of his neighbours.

Again, let a man of cheerful disposition, and of a cultivated but not very fastidious taste, observe his own emotions and the countenances of those around him during the representation of a clever tragedy and of a clever farce, and it is probable that he will come to the conclusion that his enjoyment in the latter case has been both more unmingled and more intense than in the former. He has felt no lassitude, he has not endured the amount of pain that necessarily accompanies the pleasure of pathos, he has experienced a vivid, absorbing pleasure, and he has traced similar emotions in the violent demonstrations of his neighbours. Yet he will readily admit that the pleasure derived from the tragedy is of a higher order than that derived from the farce. Sometimes he will find himself hesitating which of the two he will choose. The love of mere enjoyment leads him to the one. A sense of its *nobler* character inclines him to the other.

A similar distinction may be observed in other departments. Except in the relation of the sexes, it is probable that a more intense pleasure is usually obtained from the grotesque and the eccentric, than from the perfections of beauty. The pleasure derived from beauty is not violent in its nature, and it is in most cases peculiarly mixed with melancholy. The feelings of a man who is deeply moved by a lovely landscape are rarely those of extreme elation. A shade of melancholy steals over his mind. His eyes fill with tears. A vague and unsatisfied longing fills his soul. Yet, troubled and broken as is this form of enjoyment, few persons would hesitate to pronounce it of a higher kind than any that can be derived from the exhibitions of oddity.

If pleasures were the sole objects of our pursuit, and if their excellence were measured only by the quantity of enjoyment they afford, nothing could appear more obvious than that the man would be esteemed most wise who attained his object at least cost. Yet the whole course of civilisation is in a precisely opposite direction. A child derives the keenest and most exquisite enjoyment from the simplest objects. A flower, a doll, a rude game, the least artistic tale, is sufficient to enchant it. An uneducated peasant is enraptured with the wildest story and the coarsest wit. Increased cultivation almost always produces a fastidiousness which renders necessary the increased elaboration of our pleasures. We attach a certain discredit to a man who has retained those of childhood. The very fact of our deriving pleasure from certain amusements creates a kind of humiliation, for we feel that they are not in harmony with the nobility of our nature.[1]

Our judgments of societies resemble in this respect our judgments of individuals. Few persons, I think, who have compared the modes of popular life in stagnant and undeveloped countries like Spain with those in the great centres of industrial civilisation, will venture to pronounce with any confidence that the quantum or average of actual realised enjoyment is greater in the civilised than in the semi-civilised society. An undeveloped nature is by no means necessarily an unhappy nature, and although we possess no accurate gauge of happiness, we may, at least, be certain that its degrees do not coincide with the degrees of prosperity. The tastes and habits of men in a backward society accommodate themselves to the narrow circle of a few pleasures, and pro-

---

[1] This is one of the favourite thoughts of Pascal, who, however, in his usual fashion dwells upon it in a somewhat morbid and exaggerated strain. ' C'est une bien grande misère que de pouvoir prendre plaisir à des choses si basses et si méprisables . . . l'homme est encore plus à plaindre de ce qu'il peut se divertir à ces choses si frivoles et si basses, que de ce qu'il s'afflige de ses misères effectives. . . . D'où vient que cet homme, qui a perdu depuis peu son fils unique, et qui, accablé de procès et de querelles, était ce matin si troublé, n'y pense plus maintenant? Ne vous en étonnez pas; il est tout occupé à voir par où passera un cerf que ses chiens poursuivent. . . . C'est une joie de malade et de frénétique.'— *Pensées* (Misère de l'homme).

bably find in these as complete satisfaction as more civilised men in a wider range; and if there is in the first condition somewhat more of the weariness of monotony, there is in the second much more of the anxiety of discontent. The supe-riority of a highly civilised man lies chiefly in the fact that he belongs to a higher order of being, for he has approached more nearly to the end of his existence, and has called into action a larger number of his capacities. And this is in itself an end. Even if, as is not improbable, the lower animals are happier than man,[1] and semi-barbarians than civilised men, still it is better to be a man than a brute, better to be born amid the fierce struggles of civilisation than in some stranded nation apart from all the flow of enterprise and knowledge. Even in that material civilisation which utili-tarianism delights to glorify, there is an element which the philosophy of mere enjoyment cannot explain.

Again, if we ask the reason of the vast and indisputable superiority which the general voice of mankind gives to mental pleasures, considered as pleasures, over physical ones, we shall find, I think, no adequate or satisfactory answer on the supposition that pleasures owe all their value to the quantity of enjoyment they afford. The former, it is truly said, are more varied and more prolonged than the latter but on the other hand, they are attained with more effort, and they are diffused over a far narrower circle. No one who compares the class of men who derive their pleasure chiefly from field sports or other forms of physical enjoyment with those who derive their pleasure from the highest in tellectual sources; no one who compares the period of boyhood when enjoyments are chiefly animal with early

---

[1] 'Quæ singula improvidam mortalitatem involvunt, solum ut ista certum sit, nihil esse certi, nec miserius quidquam ho-mine, aut superbius.   Cæteris quippe animantium sola victus cura est, in quo sponte naturæ benigni tas sufficit : uno quidem vel præ ferenda cunctis bonis, quod de gloria, de pecunia, ambitione, su perque de morte, non cogitant.'— Plin. *Hist. Nat.* ii. 5.

manhood when they are chiefly intellectual, will be able to discover in the different levels of happiness any justification of the great interval the world places between these pleasures. No painter or novelist, who wished to depict an ideal of perfect happiness, would seek it in a profound student. Without entering into any doubtful questions concerning the relations of the body to all mental states, it may be maintained that bodily conditions have in general more influence upon our enjoyment than mental ones. The happiness of the great majority of men is far more affected by health and by temperament,[1] resulting from physical conditions, which again physical enjoyments are often calculated to produce, than by any mental or moral causes, and acute physical sufferings paralyse all the energies of our nature to a greater extent than any mental distress. It is probable that the American inventor of the first anæsthetic has done more for the real happiness of mankind than all the moral philosophers from Socrates to Mill. Moral causes may teach men patience, and the endurance of felt suffering, or may even alleviate its pangs, but there are temperaments due to phy-

---

[1] Paley, in his very ingenious, and in some respects admirable, chapter on happiness tries to prove the inferiority of animal pleasures, by showing the short time their enjoyment actually lasts, the extent to which they are dulled by repetition, and the cases in which they incapacitate men for other pleasures. But this calculation omits the influence of some animal enjoyments upon health and temperament. The fact, however, that health, which is a condition of body, is the chief source of happiness, Paley fully admits. 'Health,' he says, 'is the one thing needful . . . . when we are in perfect health and spirits, we feel in ourselves a happiness independent of any particular outward gratification. . . . This is an enjoyment which the Deity has annexed to life, and probably constitutes in a great measure the happiness of infants and brutes . . . of oysters, periwinkles, and the like; for which I have sometimes been at a loss to find out amusement.' On the test of happiness he very fairly says, 'All that can be said is that there remains a presumption in favour of those conditions of life in which men generally appear most cheerful and contented; for though the apparent happiness of mankind be not always a true measure of their real happiness, it is the best measure we have.'—*Moral Philosophy*, i. 6.

sical causes from which most sufferings glance almost unfelt.
It is said that when an ancient was asked 'what use is
philosophy?' he answered, 'it teaches men how to die,' and he
verified his words by a noble death; but it has been proved
on a thousand battle-fields, it has been proved on a thousand
scaffolds, it is proved through all the wide regions of China
and India, that the dull and animal nature which feels little
and realises faintly, can meet death with a calm that philosophy can barely rival.[1] The truth is, that the mental
part of our nature is not regarded as superior to the physical
part, because it contributes most to our happiness. The
superiority is of a different kind, and may be intelligibly
expressed by the epithets higher and lower.

And, once more, there is a class of pleasures resulting
from the gratification of our moral feelings which we naturally place in the foremost rank. To the great majority
of mankind it will probably appear, in spite of the doctrine
of Paley, that no multiple of the pleasure of eating pastry
can be an equivalent to the pleasure derived from a generous
action. It is not that the latter is so inconceivably intense.
It is that it is of a higher order.

This distinction of kind has been neglected or denied by
most utilitarian writers;[2] and although an attempt has re-

---

[1] A writer who devoted a great part of his life to studying the deaths of men in different countries, classes, and churches, and to collecting from other physicians information on the subject, says: 'A mesure qu'on s'éloigne des grands foyers de civilisation, qu'on se rapproche des plaines et des montagnes, le caractère de la mort prend de plus en plus l'aspect calme du ciel par un beau crépuscule du soir. . . . En général la mort s'accomplit d'une manière d'autant plus simple et naturelle qu'on est plus libre des innombrables liens de la civilisation.' Lauvergne, De l'agonie de la Mort, tome i. pp. 131-132.

[2] 'I will omit much usual declamation upon the dignity and capacity of our nature, the superiority of the soul to the body, of the rational to the animal part of our constitution, upon the worthiness, refinement, and delicacy of some satisfactions, or the meanness, grossness, and sensuality of others; because I hold that pleasures differ in nothing but in continuance and

cently been made to introduce it into the system, it appears
manifestly incompatible with its principle. If the reality of
the distinction be admitted, it shows that our wills are so far
from tending necessarily to that which produces most enjoy
ment that we have the power even in our pleasures of recognising a higher and a wholly different quality, and of making
that quality rather than enjoyment the object of our choice.
If it be possible for a man in choosing between two pleasures
deliberately to se'ect as preferable, apart from all consideration
of consequences, that which he is conscious gives least enjoy-

intensity.'—Paley's *Moral Philosophy*, book i. ch. vi. Bentham in
like manner said, 'Quantity of
pleasure being equal, pushpin is as
good as poetry,' and he maintained
that the value of a pleasure depends on—its (1) intensity, (2)
duration, (3) certainty, (4) propin-
quity, (5) purity, (6) fecundity, (7)
extent (*Springs of Action*). The
recognition of the 'purity' of a
pleasure might seem to imply the
distinction for which I have contended in the text, but this is not
so. The purity of a pleasure or
pain, according to Bentham, is 'the
chance it has of not being followed
by sensations of the opposite kind :
that is pain if it be a pleasure,
pleasure if it be a pain.'—*Morals
and Legislation,* i. § 8. Mr. Buckle
(*Hist. of Civilisation*, vol. ii. pp. 399
–400) writes in a somewhat similar
strain, but less unequivocally, for
he admits that mental pleasures
are 'more ennobling' than physical
ones. The older utilitarians, as far
as I have observed, did not even
advert to the question. This being
the case, it must have been a matter of surprise as well as of gratification to most intuitive moralists
to find Mr. Mill fully recognising
the existence of different kinds of
pleasure, and admitting that the
superiority of the higher kinds
does not spring from their being
greater in amount.—*Utilitarianism*, pp. 11–12. If it be meant by
this that we have the power of
recognising some pleasures as
superior to others in kind, irrespective of all consideration of
their intensity, their cost, and
their consequences, I submit that
the admission is completely incompatible with the utilitarian theory,
and that Mr. Mill has only succeeded in introducing Stoical elements into his system by loosening
its very foundation. The impossibility of establishing an aristocracy
of enjoyments in which, apart from
all considerations of consequences,
some which give less pleasure and
are less widely diffused are regarded as intrinsically superior to
others which give more pleasure
and are more general, without
admitting into our estimate a moral
element, which on utilitarian principles is wholly illegitimate, has
been powerfully shown since the
first edition of this book by Professor Grote, in his *Examination
of the Utilitarian Philosophy,* chap.
iii.

ment because he recognises in it a greater worthiness, or elevation, it is certain that his conduct is either wholly irrational, or that he is acting on a principle of judgment for which 'the greatest happiness' philosophy is unable to account. Consistently with that philosophy, the terms higher and lower as applied to different parts of our nature, to different regions of thought or feeling, can have no other meaning than that of productive of more or less enjoyment. But if once we admit a distinction of quality as well as a distinction of quantity in our estimate of pleasure, all is changed. It then appears evident that the different parts of our nature to which these pleasures refer, bear to each other a relation of another kind, which may be clearly and justly described by the terms higher and lower; and the assertion that our reason reveals to us intuitively and directly this hierarchy of our being, is a fundamental position of the greatest schools of intuitive moralists. According to these writers, when we say that our moral and intellectual is superior to our animal nature, that the benevolent affections are superior to the selfish ones, that conscience has a legitimate supremacy over the other parts of our being; this language is not arbitrary, or fantastic, or capricious, because it is intelligible. When such a subordination is announced, it corresponds with feelings we all possess, falls in with the natural course of our judgments, with our habitual and unstudied language.

The arguments that have been directed against the theory of natural moral perceptions are of two kinds, the first, which I have already noticed, being designed to show that all our moral judgments may be resolved into considerations of utility; the second resting upon the diversity of these judgments in different nations and stages of civilisation, which, it is said, is altogether inexplicable upon the supposition of a moral faculty. As these variations form the great stumbling-block in the way of the doctrine I am maintaining, and as they constitute a very important part of the history of morals, I shall make no apology for noticing them in some detail.

In the first place, there are many cases in which diversities of moral judgment arise from causes that are not moral, but purely intellectual. Thus, for example, when theologians pronounced loans at interest contrary to the law of nature and plainly extortionate, this error obviously arose from a false notion of the uses of money. They believed that it was a sterile thing, and that he who has restored what he borrowed, has cancelled all the benefit he received from the transaction. At the time when the first Christian moralists treated the subject, special circumstances had rendered the rate of interest extremely high, and consequently extremely oppressive to the poor, and this fact, no doubt, strengthened the prejudice; but the root of the condemnation of usury was simply an error in political economy. When men came to understand that money is a productive thing, and that the sum lent enables the borrower to create sources of wealth that will continue when the loan has been returned, they perceived that there was no natural injustice in exacting payment for this advantage, and usury either ceased to be assailed, or was assailed only upon the ground of positive commands.

Thus again the question of the criminality of abortion has been considerably affected by physiological speculations as to the time when the fœtus in the womb acquires the nature, and therefore the rights, of a separate being. The general opinion among the ancients seems to have been that it was but a part of the mother, and that she had the same right to destroy it as to cauterise a tumour upon her body. Plato and Aristotle both admitted the practice. The Roman law contained no enactment against voluntary abortion till the time of Ulpian. The Stoics thought that the infant received its soul when respiration began. The Justinian code fixed its animation at forty days after conception. In modern legislations it is treated as a distinct being from the moment of conception.[1] It is obvious that the solution of such questions, though affecting our moral judgments, must be sought entirely outside the range of moral feelings.

In the next place, there is a broad distinction to be drawn between duties which rest immediately on the dictates of conscience, and those which are based upon positive commands. The iniquity of theft, murder, falsehood, or adultery rests upon grounds generically distinct from those on which men pronounce it to be sinful to eat meat on Friday, or to work on Sunday, or to abstain from religious assemblies. The reproaches conscience directs against those who are guilty of these last acts are purely hypothetical, conscience enjoining obedience to the Divine commands, but leaving it to reason to determine what those commands may be. The distinction between these two classes of duties becomes apparent on the slightest reflection, and the variations in their relative prominence form one of the most important branches of religious history.

Closely connected with the preceding are the diversities which result from an ancient custom becoming at last, through its very antiquity, or through the confusion of means with ends, an object of religious reverence. Among the many safeguards of female purity in the Roman republic was an enactment forbidding women even to taste wine, and this very intelligible law being enforced with the earliest education, became at last, by habit and traditionary reverence, so incorporated with the moral feelings of the people, that its violation was spoken of as a monstrous crime. Aulus Gellius has preserved a passage in which Cato observes, 'that the husband has an absolute authority over his wife; it is for him to condemn and punish her, if she has been

---

[1] Büchner, *Force et Matière*, pp. 163-164. There is a very curious collection of the speculations of the ancient philosophers on this subject in Plutarch's treatise, *De Placitis Philos.*

guilty of any shameful act, such as drinking wine or committing adultery.'[1] As soon as the reverence for tradition was diminished, and men ventured to judge old customs upon their own merits, they were able, by steadily reflecting upon this belief, to reduce it to its primitive elements, to separate the act from the ideas with which it had been associated, and thus to perceive that it was not necessarily opposed to any of those great moral laws or feelings which their consciences revealed, and which were the basis of all their reasonings on morals.

A confused association of ideas, which is easily exposed by a patient analysis, lies at the root of more serious anomalies. Thus to those who reflect deeply upon moral history, few things, I suppose, are more humiliating than to contrast the admiration and profoundly reverential attachment excited by a conqueror, who through the promptings of simple vanity, through love of fame, or through greed of territory, has wantonly caused the deaths, the sufferings, or the be-

---

[1] Aulus Gellius, *Noctes*, x. 23. The law is given by Dion. Halicarn. Valerius Maximus says, ' Vini usus olim Romanis feminis ignotus fuit, ne scilicet in aliquod dedecus prolaberentur : quia proximus a Libero patre intemperantiæ gradus ad inconcessam Venerem esse consuevit' (Val. Max. ii. 1, § 5). This is also noticed by Pliny (*Hist. Nat.* xiv. 14), who ascribes the law to Romulus, and who mentions two cases in which women were said to have been put to death for this offence, and a third in which the offender was deprived of her dowry. Cato said that the ancient Romans were accustomed to kiss their wives for the purpose of discovering whether they had been drinking wine. The Bona Dea, it is said, was originally a woman named Fatua, who was famous for her modesty and fidelity to her husband, but who, unfortunately, having once found a cask of wine in the house, got drunk, and was in consequence scourged to death by her husband. He afterwards repented of his act, and paid divine honours to her memory, and as a memorial of her death, a cask of wine was always placed upon the altar during the rites. (Lactantius, *Div. Inst.* i. 22.) The Milesians, also, and the inhabitants of Marseilles are said to have had laws forbidding women to drink wine (Ælian, *Hist. Var.* ii. 38). Tertullian describes the prohibition of wine among the Roman women as in his time obsolete, and a taste for it was one of the great trials of St. Monica (*Aug. Conf.* x. 8).

reavements of thousands, with the abhorrence produced by a single act of murder or robbery committed by a poor and ignorant man, perhaps under the pressure of extreme want or intolerable wrong. The attraction of genius and power, which the vulgar usually measure by their material fruits, the advantages acquired by the nation to which he belongs, the belief that battles are decided by providential interference, and that military success is therefore a proof of Divine favour, and the sanctity ascribed to the regal office, have all no doubt conspired to veil the atrocity of the conqueror's career; but there is probably another and a deeper influence behind. That which invests war, in spite of all the evils that attend it, with a certain moral grandeur, is the heroic self-sacrifice it elicits. With perhaps the single exception of the Church, it is the sphere in which mercenary motives have least sway, in which performance is least weighed and measured by strict obligation, in which a disinterested enthusiasm has most scope. A battle-field is the scene of deeds of self-sacrifice so transcendent, and at the same time so dramatic, that in spite of all its horrors and crimes, it awakens the most passionate moral enthusiasm. But this feeling produced by the thought of so many who have sacrificed their life-blood for their flag or for their chief, needs some definite object on which to rest. The multitude of nameless combatants do not strike the imagination. They do not stand out, and are not realised, as distinct and living figures conspicuous to the view. Hence it is that the chief, as the most prominent, becomes the representative warrior; the martyr's aureole descends upon his brow, and thus by a confusion that seems the very irony of fate, the enthusiasm evoked by the self-sacrifice of thousands sheds a sacred glow around the very man whose prodigious egotism had rendered that sacrifice necessary.

Another form of moral paradox is derived from the fact that positive religions may override our moral perceptions in such a manner, that we may consciously admit a moral con tradiction. In this respect there is a strict parallelism between our intellectual and our moral faculties. It is at present the professed belief of at least three-fourths of the Christian Church, and was for some centuries the firm belief of the entire Church, that on a certain night the Founder of the Christian faith, being seated at a supper table, held His own body in His own hand, broke that body, distributed it to His disciples, who proceeded to eat it, the same body remaining at the same moment seated intact at the table, and soon afterwards proceeding to the garden of Gethsemane. The fact of such a doctrine being believed, does not imply that the faculties of those who hold it are of such a nature that they perceive no contradiction or natural absurdity in these statements. The well-known argument derived from the obscurity of the metaphysical notion of substance is intended only in some slight degree to soften the difficulty. The contradiction is clearly perceived, but it is accepted by faith as part of the teaching of the Church.

What transubstantiation is in the order of reason the Augustinian doctrine of the damnation of unbaptised infants, and the Calvinistic doctrine of reprobation, are in the order of morals. Of these doctrines it is not too much to say, that in the form in which they have often been stated, they surpass in atrocity any tenets that have ever been admitted into any pagan creed, and would, if they formed an essential part of Christianity, amply justify the term 'pernicious superstition,' which Tacitus applied to the faith. That a little child who lives but a few moments after birth and dies before it has been sprinkled with the sacred water is in such a sense responsible for its ancestors having 6,000 years before eaten some forbidden fruit that it may with perfect justice be resuscitated and cast into an abyss of eternal fire in expiation of this ancestral crime, that an all-righteous and all-merciful Creator in the full exercise of those attributes deliberately calls into existence sentient beings whom He has from eternity irrevocably destined to endless, unspeakable, unmitigated torture, are propositions which are at once so extravagantly absurd and so ineffably atrocious that their adoption might well lead men to doubt the universality of moral perceptions. Such teaching is in fact simply dæmonism, and dæmonism in its most extreme form. It attributes to the Creator acts of injustice and of barbarity, which it would be absolutely impossible for the imagination to surpass, acts before which the most monstrous excesses of human cruelty dwindle into insignificance, acts which are in fact considerably worse than any that theologians have attributed to the devil. If there were men who while vividly realising the nature of these acts naturally turned to them as the exhibitions of perfect goodness, all systems of ethics founded upon innate moral perceptions would be false. But happily this is not so. Those who embrace these doctrines do so only because they believe that some inspired Church or writer has taught them, and because they are still in that stage in which men consider it more irreligious to question the infallibility of an apostle than to disfigure by any conceivable imputation the character of the Deity. They accordingly esteem it a matter of duty, and a commendable exercise of humility, to stifle the moral feelings of their nature, and they at last succeed in persuading themselves that their Divinity would be extremely offended if they hesitated to ascribe to him the attributes of a fiend. But their moral feelings, though not unimpaired by such conceptions, are not on ordinary subjects generically different from those of their neighbours. With an amiable inconsistency they can even find something to revolt them in the lives of a Caligula or a Nero. Their theological estimate of justice and mercy is isolated. Their doctrine is accepted as a kind of moral miracle, and as is customary with a certain school of theologians, when they

enunciate a proposition which is palpably self-contradictory
they call it a mystery and an occasion for faith.

In this instance a distinct moral contradiction is con·
sciously admitted. In the case of persecution, a strictly
moral and logical inference is drawn from a very immoral
proposition which is accepted as part of a system of dogmatic
theology. The two elements that should be considered in
punishing a criminal are the heinousness of his guilt and the
injury he inflicts. When the greatest guilt and the greatest
injury are combined, the greatest punishment naturally follows. No one would argue against the existence of a moral
faculty, on the ground that men put murderers to death.
When therefore theologians believed that a man was intensely
guilty who held certain opinions, and that he was causing
the damnation of his fellows if he propagated them, there
was no moral difficulty in concluding that the heretic should
be put to death. Selfish considerations may have directed
persecution against heresy rather than against vice, but the
Catholic doctrines of the guilt of error, and of the infallibility
of the Church, were amply sufficient to justify it.

It appears then that a dogmatic system which is accepted
on rational or other grounds, and supported by prospects of
rewards and punishments, may teach a code of ethics differing from that of conscience; and that in this case the voice
of conscience may be either disregarded or stifled. It is
however also true, that it may be perverted. When, for example, theologians during a long period have inculcated
habits of credulity, rather than habits of enquiry; when they
have persuaded men that it is better to cherish prejudice
than to analyse it; better to stifle every doubt of what they
have been taught than honestly to investigate its value, they
will at last succeed in forming habits of mind that will instinctively and habitually recoil from all impartiality and
intellectual honesty. If men continually violate a duty they
may at last cease to feel its obligation. But this, though it

forms a great difficulty in ethical enquiries, is no argument against the reality of moral perceptions, for it is simply a law to which all our powers are subject. A bad intellectual education will produce not only erroneous or imperfect information but also a false ply or habit of judgment. A bad æsthetical education will produce false canons of taste. Systematic abuse will pervert and vitiate even some of our physical perceptions. In each case the experience of many minds under many conditions must be appealed to, to determine the standard of right and wrong, and long and difficult discipline is required to restore the diseased organ to sanity. We may decide particular moral questions by reasoning, but our reasoning is an appeal to certain moral principles which are revealed to us by intuition.

The principal difficulty I imagine which most men have in admitting that we possess certain natural moral perceptions arises from the supposition that it implies the existence of some mysterious agent like the dæmon of Socrates, which gives us specific and infallible information in particular cases. But this I conceive to be a complete mistake. All that is necessarily meant by the adherents of this school is comprised in two propositions. The first is that our will is not governed exclusively by the law of pleasure and pain, but also by the law of duty, which we feel to be distinct from the former, and to carry with it the sense of obligation. The second is that the basis of our conception of duty is an intuitive perception that among the various feelings, tendencies, and impulses that constitute our emotional being, there are some which are essentially good, and ought to be encouraged, and some which are essentially bad, and ought to be repressed. They contend that it is a psychological fact that we are intuitively conscious that our benevolent affections are superior to our malevolent ones, truth to falsehood, justice to injustice, gratitude to ingratitude, chastity to sensuality, and that in all ages and countries the path of virtue has been towards the higher and not towards the lower feelings. It may be that the sense of duty is so weak as to be scarcely perceptible, and then the lower part of our nature will be supreme. It may happen that certain conditions of society lead men to direct their anxiety for moral improvement altogether in one or two channels, as was the case in ancient Greece, where civic and intellectual virtues were very highly cultivated, and the virtue of chastity was almost neglected. It may happen that different parts of our higher nature in a measure conflict, as when a very strong sense of justice checks our benevolent feelings. Dogmatic systems may enjoin men to propitiate certain unseen beings by acts which are not in accordance with the moral law. Special circumstances may influence, and the intermingling of many different motives may obscure and complicate, the moral evolution; but above all these one great truth appears. No one who desires to become holier and better imagines that he does so by becoming more malevolent, or more untruthful, or more unchaste. Every one who desires to attain perfection in these departments of feeling is impelled towards benevolence, towards veracity, towards chastity.[1]

Now it is manifest that according to this theory the moral unity to be expected in different ages is not a unity of standard, or of acts, but a unity of tendency. Men come into the world with their benevolent affections very inferior in power to their selfish ones, and the function of morals is to invert this order. The extinction of all selfish feeling is impossible for an individual, and if it were general, it would result in the dissolution of society. The question of morals must always be a question of proportion or of degree. At

---

[1] 'La loi fondamentale de la morale agit sur toutes les nations bien connues. Il y a mille différences dans les interprétations de cette loi en mille circonstances; mais le fond subsiste toujours le même, et ce fond est l'idée du juste et de l'injuste.'—Voltaire, *Le Philosophe ignorant.*

one time the benevolent affections embrace merely the family, soon the circle expanding includes first a class, then a nation, then a coalition of nations, then all humanity, and finally, its influence is felt in the dealings of man with the animal world. In each of these stages a standard is formed, different from that of the preceding stage, but in each case the same tendency is recognised as virtue.

We have in this fact a simple, and as it appears to me a conclusive, answer to the overwhelming majority of the objections that are continually and confidently urged against the intuitive school. That some savages kill their old parents, that infanticide has been practised without compunction by even civilised nations, that the best Romans saw nothing wrong in the gladiatorial shows, that political or revengeful assassinations have been for centuries admitted, that slavery has been sometimes honoured and sometimes condemned, are unquestionable proofs that the same act may be regarded in one age as innocent, and in another as criminal. Now it is undoubtedly true that in many cases an historical examination will reveal special circumstances, explaining or palliating the apparent anomaly. It has been often shown that the gladiatorial shows were originally a form of human sacrifice adopted through religious motives; that the rude nomadic life of savages rendering impossible the preservation of aged and helpless members of the tribe, the murder of parents was regarded as an act of mercy both by the murderer and the victim; that before an effective administration of justice was organised, private vengeance was the sole preservative against crime,[1] and political assassination against usurpation; that the insensibility of some savages to the criminality of theft arises from the fact that they were accustomed to

---

[1] The feeling in its favour being often intensified by filial affection. 'What is the most beautiful thing on the earth?' said Osiris to Horus. 'To avenge a parent's wrongs,' was the reply.— Plutarch *De Iside et Osiride.*

have all things in common; that the Spartan law, legalising theft, arose partly from a desire to foster military dexterity among the people, but chiefly from a desire to discourage wealth; that slavery was introduced through motives of mercy, to prevent conquerors from killing their prisoners.[1] All this is true, but there is another and a more general answer. It is not to be expected, and it is not maintained, that men in all ages should have agreed about the application of their moral principles. All that is contended for is that these principles are themselves the same. Some of what appear to us monstrous acts of cruelty, were dictated by that very feeling of humanity, the universal perception of the merit of which they are cited to disprove,[2] and even when this is not the case, all that can be inferred is, that the standard of humanity was very low. But still humanity was recognised as a virtue, and cruelty as a vice.

At this point, I may observe how completely fallacious is the assertion that a progressive morality is impossible upon the supposition of an original moral faculty.[3] To such

---

[1] Hence the Justinian code and also St. Augustine (*De Civ. Dei,* xix. 15) derived servus from 'servare,' to preserve, because the victor preserved his prisoners alive.

[2] 'Les habitants du Congo tuent les malades qu'ils imaginent ne pouvoir en revenir; *c'est, disent-ils, pour leur épargner les douleurs de l'agonie.* Dans l'île Formose, lorsqu'un homme est dangereusement malade, on lui passe un nœud coulant au col et on l'étrangle, *pour l'arracher à la douleur.'—* Helvétius, *De l'Esprit,* ii. 13. A similar explanation may be often found for customs which are quoted to prove that the nations where they existed had no sense of chastity. 'C'est pareillement sous la sauvegarde des lois que les

Siamoises, la gorge et les cuisses à moitié découvertes, portées dans les rues sur les palanquins, s'y présentent dans des attitudes très-lascives. Cette loi fut établie par une de leurs reines nommée Tirada, qui, *pour dégoûter les hommes d'un amour plus déshonnête,* crut devoir employer toute la puissance de la beauté.'—*De l'Esprit,* ii. 14.

[3] 'The contest between the morality which appeals to an external standard, and that which grounds itself on internal conviction, is the contest of progressive morality against stationary, of reason and argument against the deification of mere opinion and habit.' (Mill's *Dissertations,* vol. ii. p. 472); a passage with a true Bentham ring. See, too, vol. i.

statements there are two very simple answers. In the first place, although the intuitive moralist asserts that certain qualities are necessarily virtuous, he fully admits that the degree in which they are acted upon, or in other words, the standard of duty, may become progressively higher. In the next place, although he refuses to resolve all virtue into utility, he admits as fully as his opponents, that benevolence, or the promotion of the happiness of man, is a virtue, and that therefore discoveries which exhibit more clearly the true interests of our kind, may throw new light upon the nature of our duty.

The considerations I have urged with reference to humanity, apply with equal force to the various relations of the sexes. When the passions of men are altogether unrestrained, community of wives and all eccentric forms of sensuality will be admitted. When men seek to improve their nature in this respect, their object will be to abridge and confine the empire of sensuality. But to this process of improvement there are obvious limits. In the first place the continuance of the species is only possible by a sensual act. In the next place the strength of this passion and the weakness of humanity are so great, that the moralist must take into account the fact that in all societies, and especially in those in which free scope had long been given to the passions, a large amount of indulgence will arise which is not due to a simple desire of propagating the species. If then incest is prohibited, and community of wives replaced by ordinary polygamy, a moral improvement will have been effected, and a standard of virtue formed. But this standard soon becomes the starting-point of new progress. If we examine the Jewish law, we find the legislator prohibiting adultery, regulating the degrees

158. There is, however, a schism on this point in the utilitarian camp. The views which Mr. Buckle has expressed in his most eloquent chapter on the comparative influence of intellectual and moral agencies in civilisation diverge widely from those of Mr. Mill.

of marriage, but at the same time authorising polygamy, though with a caution against the excessive multiplication of wives.   In Greece monogamy, though not without exceptions, had been enforced, but a concurrence of unfavourable influences prevented any high standard being attained among the men, and in their case almost every form of indulgence beyond the limits of marriage was permitted.   In Rome the standard was far higher.   Monogamy was firmly established. The ideal of female morality was placed as high as among Christian nations.   Among men, however, while unnatural love and adultery were regarded as wrong, simple unchastity before marriage was scarcely considered a fault.   In Catholicism marriage is regarded in a twofold light, as a means for the propagation of the species, and as a concession to the weakness of humanity, and all other sensual enjoyment is stringently prohibited.

In these cases there is a great difference between the degrees of earnestness with which men exert themselves in the repression of their passions, and in the amount of indulgence which is conceded to their lower nature ; [1] but there is no difference in the direction of the virtuous impulse.   While, too, in the case of adultery, and in the production of children, questions of interest and utility do undoubtedly intervene, we are conscious that the general progress turns upon a totally different order of ideas.   The feeling of all men and the language of all nations, the sentiment which though often weakened is never wholly effaced, that this appetite, even in its most legitimate gratification, is a thing to be veiled and withdrawn from sight, all that is known under the names of decency and indecency, concur in proving that we have an innate, intuitive, instinctive perception that there is something degrading in the sensual part of our nature, something

---

[1] ' Est enim sensualitas quædam   vis animæ est superior.' — Peter vis animæ inferior. . . . Ratio vero   Lombard, Sent. ii. 24.

to which a feeling of shame is naturally attached, something that jars with our conception of perfect purity, something we could not with any propriety ascribe to an all-holy being. It may be questioned whether anyone was ever altogether destitute of this perception, and nothing but the most inveterate passion for system could induce men to resolve it into a mere calculation of interests. It is this feeling or instinct which lies at the root of the whole movement I have described, and it is this too that produced that sense of the sanctity of perfect continence which the Catholic church has so warmly encouraged, but which may be traced through the most distant ages, and the most various creeds. We find it among the Nazarenes and Essenes of Judæa, among the priests of Egypt and India, in the monasteries of Tartary, in the histories of miraculous virgins that are so numerous in the mythologies of Asia. Such, for example, was the Chinese legend that tells how when there was but one man with one woman upon earth, the woman refused to sacrifice her virginity even in order to people the globe, and the gods honouring her purity granted that she should conceive beneath the gaze of her lover's eyes, and a virgin-mother became the parent of humanity.[1] In the midst of the sensuality of ancient Greece, chastity was the pre-eminent attribute of sanctity ascribed to Athene and Artemis. 'Chaste daughter of Zeus,' prayed the suppliants in Æschylus, ' thou whose calm eye is never troubled, look down upon us! Virgin, defend the virgins.' The Parthenon, or virgin's temple, was the noblest religious edifice of Athens. Celibacy was an essential condition in a few of the orders of priests, and in several orders of priestesses. Plato based his moral system upon the distinction between the bodily or sensual, and the spiritual or rational part of our nature, the first being the sign of our degradation, and the second of our dignity. The

[1] Helvétius, *De l'Esprit*, discours iv. See too, Dr. Draper's extremely remarkable *History of* *Intellectual Development in Europe* (New York, 1864), pp. 48, 53.

whole school of Pythagoras made chastity one of its leading
virtues, and even laboured for the creation of a monastic
system.   The conception of the celestial Aphrodite, the uniter
of souls, unsullied by the taint of matter, lingered side by
side with that of the earthly Aphrodite or patroness of lust,
and if there was a time when the sculptors sought to pander
to the excesses of passion there was another in which all their
art was displayed in refining and idealising it.   Strabo mentions the existence in Thrace of societies of men aspiring to
perfection by celibacy and austere lives.   Plutarch applauds
certain philosophers who vowed to abstain for a year from
wine and women in order 'to honour God by their continence.'[1]   In Rome the religious reverence was concentrated
more especially upon married life.   The great prominence accorded to the Penates was the religious sanction of domesticity.
So too, at first, was the worship so popular among the Roman
women of the Bona Dea—the ideal wife who according to the
legend had, when on earth, never looked in the face or known
the name of any man but her husband.[2]   'For altar and
hearth' was the rallying cry of the Roman soldier.   But
above all this we find the traces of a higher ideal.   We find
it in the intense sanctity attributed to the vestal virgins
whose continence was guarded by such fearful penalties, and
supposed to be so closely linked with the prosperity of the
state, whose prayer was believed to possess a miraculous
power, and who were permitted to drive through the streets
of Rome at a time when that privilege was refused even to
the Empress.[3]   We find it in the legend of Claudia, who,

---

[1] Plutarch, *De Cohibenda Ira*.

[2] Lactantius, *Div. Inst*. i. 22.
The mysteries of the Bona Dea
became, however, after a time, the
occasion of great disorders.   See
Juvenal, *Sat*. vi.   M. Magnin has
examined the nature of these rites
(*Origines du Théâtre*, pp. 257–259).

[3] The history of the vestals,
which forms one of the most curious
pages in the moral history of Rome,
has been fully treated by the Abbé
Nadal, in an extremely interesting
and well-written memoir, read before the Académie des Belles-
lettres, and republished in **1725**

when the ship bearing the image of the mother of the gods had been stranded in the Tiber, attached her girdle to its prow, and vindicated her challenged chastity by drawing with her virgin hand, the ponderous mass which strong men had sought in vain to move. We find it in the prophetic gift so often attributed to virgins,[1] in the law which sheltered them from the degradation of an execution,[2] in the language of Statius, who described marriage itself as a fault.[3] In Christianity óne great source of the attraction of the faith has been the ascription of virginity to its female ideal. The Catholic monastic system has been so constructed as to draw many thousands from the sphere of active duty; its irrevocable vows have doubtless led to much suffering and not a little crime; its opposition to the normal development of our mingled nature has often resulted in grave aberrations of the imagination, and it has placed its ban upon domestic affections and sympathies which have a very high moral value; but in its central conception that the purely animal side

---

It was believed that the prayer of a vestal could arrest a fugitive slave in his flight, provided he had not got past the city walls. Pliny mentions this belief as general in his time. The records of the order contained many miracles wrought at different times to save the vestals or to vindicate their questioned purity, and also one miracle which is very remarkable as furnishing a precise parallel to that of the Jew who was struck dead for touching the ark to prevent its falling.

[1] As for example the Sibyls and Cassandra. The same prophetic power was attributed in India to virgins.—Clem. Alexandrin. *Strom.* iii. 7.

[2] This custom continued to the worst period of the empire, though it was shamefully and characteris-

tically evaded. After the fall of Sejanus the senate had no compunction in putting his innocent daughter to death, but their religious feelings were shocked at the idea of a virgin falling beneath the axe. So by way of improving matters 'filia constuprata est prius a carnifice, quasi impium esset virginem in carcere perire.'—Dion Cassius, lviii. 11. See too, Tacitus, *Annal.* v. 9. If a vestal met a prisoner going to execution the prisoner was spared, provided the vestal declared that the encounter was accidental. On the reverence the ancients paid to virgins, see Justus Lipsius, *De Vesta et Vestalibus.*

[3] See his picture of the first night of marriage :—

of our being is a low and a degraded side, it reflects, 1 believe, with perfect fidelity the feelings of our nature.[1]

To these considerations some others of a different nature may be added. It is not true that some ancient nations regarded polygamy as good in the same sense as others regarded chastity. There is a great difference between deeming a state permissible and proposing it as a condition of sanctity. If Mohammedans people paradise with images of sensuality, it is not because these form their ideal of holiness. It is because they regard earth as the sphere of virtue, heaven as that of simple enjoyment. If some pagan nations deified sensuality, this was simply because the deification of the forces of nature, of which the prolific energy is one of the most conspicuous, is among the earliest forms of religion, and long precedes the identification of the Deity with a moral ideal.[2]   If there have

---

'Tacitè subit ille supremus Virginitatis amor, primæque modestia culpæ
Confundit   vultus.   Tunc   ora rigantur honestis
Imbribus.'
    Thebaidos, lib. ii. 232-34.

[1] Bees (which Virgil said had in them something of the divine nature) were supposed by the ancients to be the special emblems or models of chastity. It was a common belief that the bee mother begot her young without losing her virginity. Thus in a fragment ascribed to Petronius we read,

Sic sine concubitu textis apis excita ceris
Fervet, et audaci milite castra replet.'
    Petron. *De Varia Animalium Generatione.*
So too Virgil:—
'Quod neque concubitu indulgent nec corpora segnes

In Venerem solvunt aut fœtus nixibus edunt.'—*Georg.* iv. 198-99.

Plutarch says that an unchaste person cannot approach bees, for they immediately attack him and cover him with stings. Fire was also regarded as a type of virginity. Thus Ovid, speaking of the vestals, says :—

'Nataque de flamma corpora nulla vides :
Jure igitur virgo est, quæ semina nulla remittit
    Nec capit, et comites virginitatis amat.'

' The Egyptians believed that there are no males among vultures, and they accordingly made that bird an emblem of nature.' — Ammianus Marcellinus, xvii. 4.

[2] 'La divinité étant considérée comme renfermant en elle toutes les qualités, toutes les forces intellectuelles et morales de l'homme, chacune de ces forces ou de ces

been nations who attached a certain stigma to virginity, this has not been because they esteemed sensuality intrinsically holier than chastity ; but because a scanty, warlike people whose position in the world depends chiefly on the number of its warriors, will naturally make it its main object to encourage population. This was especially the case with the ancient Jews, who always regarded extreme populousness as indissolubly connected with national prosperity, whose religion was essentially patriotic, and among whom the possibility of becoming an ancestor of the Messiah had imparted a peculiar dignity to childbirth. Yet even among the Jews the Essenes regarded virginity as the ideal of sanctity.

The reader will now be in a position to perceive the utter futility of the objections which from the time of Locke have been continually brought against the theory of natural moral perceptions, upon the ground that some actions which were admitted as lawful in one age, have been regarded as immoral in another. All these become absolutely worthless when it is perceived that in every age virtue has consisted in the cultivation of the same feelings, though the standards of excellence attained have been different. The terms higher and lower, nobler or less noble, purer or less pure, represent moral facts with much greater fidelity than the terms right or wrong, or virtue or vice. There is a certain sense in which moral distinctions are absolute and immutable. There is another sense in which they are altogether relative and transient. There are some acts which are so manifestly and grossly opposed to our moral feelings, that they are regarded as wrong in the very earliest stages of the cultivation of these feelings. There are distinctions, such as that between truth and falsehood, which from their nature assume at once a sharpness of definition that separates them from mere

qualités, conçue séparément, s'offrait comme un Être divin. . . . De-là aussi les contradictions les plus choquantes dans les notions que les anciens avaient des attributs divins.'—Maury, *Hist. des Religions de la Grèce antique,* tome i. pp. 578–579.

virtues of degree, though even in these cases there are wide
variations in the amount of scrupulosity that is in different
periods required.   But apart from positive commands, the
sole external rule enabling men to designate acts, not simply
as better or worse, but as positively right or wrong, is, I
conceive, the standard of society ; not an arbitrary standard
like that which Mandeville imagined, but the level which
society has attained in the cultivation of what our moral
faculty tells us is the higher or virtuous part of our nature.
He who falls below this is obstructing the tendency which is
the essence of virtue.   He who merely attains this, may not
be justified in his own conscience, or in other words, by the
standard of his own moral development, but as far as any
external rule is concerned, he has done his duty.   He who
rises above this has entered into the region of things which
it is virtuous to do, but not vicious to neglect—a region
known among Catholic theologians by the name of ' counsels
of perfection.'   No discussions, I conceive, can be more idle
than whether slavery, or the slaughter of prisoners in war,
or gladiatorial shows, or polygamy, are essentially wrong.
They may be wrong now— they were not so once—and when
an ancient countenanced by his example one or other of these,
he was not committing a crime.   The unchangeable proposition for which we contend is this—that benevolence is always
a virtuous disposition—that the sensual part of our nature is
always the lower part.

At this point, however, a very difficult problem naturally
arises.   Admitting that our moral nature is superior to
our intellectual or physical nature, admitting, too, that by
the constitution of our being we perceive ourselves to be
under an obligation to develope our nature to its perfection,
establishing the supreme ascendency of moral motives, the
question still remains whether the disparity between the
different parts of our being is such that no material or intellectual advantage, however great, may be rightly purchased

by any sacrifice of our moral nature, however small. This is the great question of casuistry, the question which divines express by asking whether the end ever justifies the means; and on this subject there exists among theologians a doctrine which is absolutely unrealised, which no one ever dreams of applying to actual life, but of which it may be truly said that though propounded with the best intentions, it would, if acted upon, be utterly incompatible with the very rudiments of civilisation. It is said that an undoubted sin, even the most trivial, is a thing in its essence and in its consequences so unspeakably dreadful, that no conceivable material or intellectual advantage can counterbalance it; that rather than it should be committed, it would be better that any amount of calamity which did not bring with it sin should be endured, even that the whole human race should perish in agonies.[1] If this be the case, it is manifest that the supreme object of humanity should be sinlessness, and it is equally manifest that the means to this end is the absolute suppression of the desires. To expand the circle of wants is necessarily to multiply temptations, and therefore to increase the number of sins. It may indeed elevate the moral standard, for a torpid sinlessness is not a high moral condition; but if every sin be what these theologians assert, if it be a thing deserving eternal agony, and so inconceivably frightful that the ruin of a world is a less evil than its commission, even moral advantages are utterly incommensurate with it. No heightening of the moral tone, no depth or ecstasy of devotion, can for a moment be placed in the balance. The consequences of this doctrine, if applied to actual life, would be

---

[1] 'The Church holds that it were better for sun and moon to drop from heaven, for the earth to fail, and for all the many millions who are upon it to die of starvation in extremest agony, so far as temporal affliction goes, than that one soul, I will not say should be lost, but should commit one single venial sin, should tell one wilful untruth, though it harmed no one, or steal one poor farthing without excuse.'—Newman's *Anglican Difficulties*, p. 190.

so extravagant, that their simple statement is a refutation
A sovereign, when calculating the consequences of a war,
should reflect that a single sin occasioned by that war, a
single blasphemy of a wounded soldier, the robbery of a
single hencoop, the violation of the purity of a single woman,
is a greater calamity than the ruin of the entire commerce of
his nation, the loss of her most precious provinces, the destruction of all her power. He must believe that the evil of
the increase of unchastity, which invariably results from the
formation of an army, is an immeasurably greater calamity
than any material or political disasters that army can possibly
avert. He must believe that the most fearful plague or
famine that desolates his land should be regarded as a
matter of rejoicing, if it has but the feeblest and most transient influence in repressing vice. He must believe that if
the agglomeration of his people in great cities adds but one
to the number of their sins, no possible intellectual or
material advantages can prevent the construction of cities
being a fearful calamity. According to this principle, every
elaboration of life, every amusement that brings multitudes
together, almost every art, every accession of wealth that
awakens or stimulates desires, is an evil, for all these become
the sources of some sins, and their advantages are for the
most part purely terrestrial. The entire structure of civilisation is founded upon the belief that it is a good thing to
cultivate intellectual and material capacities, even at the
cost of certain moral evils which we are often able accurately
to foresee.[1] The time may come when the man who lays the
foundation-stone of a manufacture will be able to predict
with assurance in what proportion the drunkenness and the
unchastity of his city will be increased by his enterprise.

[1] There is a remarkable dissertation on this subject, called 'The
Limitations of Morality,' in a very
ingenious and suggestive little
work of the Benthamite school,
called *Essays by a Barrister* (reprinted from the *Saturday Review*).

Yet he will still pursue that enterprise, and mankind will pronounce it to be good.

The theological doctrine on the subject, considered in its full stringency, though professed by many, is, as I have said, realised and consistently acted on by no one; but the practical judgments of mankind concerning the extent of the superiority of moral over all other interests vary greatly, and this variation supplies one of the most serious objections to intuitive moralists. The nearest practical approach to the theological estimate of a sin may be found in the ranks of the ascetics. Their whole system rests upon the belief that it is a thing so transcendently dreadful as to bear no proportion or appreciable relation to any earthly interests. Starting from this belief, the ascetic makes it the exclusive object of his life to avoid sinning. He accordingly abstains from all the active business of society, relinquishes all worldly aims and ambitions, dulls by continued discipline his natural desires, and endeavours to pass a life of complete absorption in religious exercises. And in all this his conduct is reasonable and consistent. The natural course of every man who adopts this estimate of the enormity of sin is at every cost to avoid all external influences that can prove temptations, and to attenuate as far as possible his own appetites and emotions. It is in this respect that the exaggerations of theologians paralyse our moral being. For the diminution of sins, however important, is but one part of moral progress. Whenever it is forced into a disproportionate prominence, we find tame, languid, and mutilated natures, destitute of all fire and energy, and this tendency has been still further aggravated by the extreme prominence usually given to the virtue of gentleness, which may indeed be attained by men of strong natures and vehement emotions, but is evidently more congenial to a somewhat feeble and passionless character.

Ascetic practices are manifestly and rapidly disappearing, and their decline is a striking proof of the evanescence of the moral notions of which they were the expression, but in many existing questions relating to the same matter, we find perplexing diversity of judgment. We find it in the contrast between the system of education usually adopted by the Catholic priesthood, which has for its pre-eminent object to prevent sins, and for its means a constant and minute supervision, and the English system of public schools, which is certainly not the most fitted to guard against the possibility of sin, or to foster any very delicate scrupulosity of feeling; but is intended, and popularly supposed, to secure the healthy expansion of every variety of capacity.   We find it in the widely different attitudes which good men in different periods have adopted towards religious opinions they believe to be false; some, like the reformers, refusing to participate in any superstitious service, or to withhold on any occasion, or at any cost, their protest against what they regarded as a lie; others, like most ancient, and some modern philosophers and politicians, combining the most absolute personal incredulity with an assiduous observance of superstitious rites, and strongly censuring those who disturbed delusions which are useful or consolatory to the people; while a third class silently, but without protest, withdraw themselves from the observances, and desire that their opinions should have a free expression in literature, but at the same time discourage all proselytising efforts to force them rudely on unprepared minds.   We find it in the frequent conflicts between the political economist and the Catholic priest on the subject of early marriages, the former opposing them on the ground that it is an essential condition of material well-being that the standard of comfort should not be depressed, the latter advocating them on the ground that the postponement of marriages, through prudential motives, by any large body of men, is the fertile mother of sin. We find it most conspicuously in the marked diversities of tolerance manifested in different communities towards amusements which may in themselves be perfectly innocent, but which prove the sources or the occasions of vice. The Scotch Puritans probably represent one extreme, the Parisian society of the empire the other, while the position of average Englishmen is perhaps equidistant between them. Yet this difference, great as it is, is a difference not of principle, but of degree. No Puritan seriously desires to suppress every clan-gathering, every highland game which may have occasioned an isolated fit of drunkenness, though he may be unable to show that it has prevented any sin that would otherwise have been committed. No Frenchman will question that there is a certain amount of demoralisation which should not be tolerated, however great the enjoyment that accompanies it. Yet the one dwells almost exclusively upon the moral, the other upon the attractive, nature of a spectacle. Between these there are numerous gradations, which are shown in frequent disputes about the merits and demerits of the racecourse, the ball, the theatre, and the concert. Where then, it may be asked, is the line to be drawn? By what rule can the point be determined at which an amusement becomes vitiated by the evil of its consequences?

To these questions the intuitive moralist is obliged to answer, that such a line cannot be drawn, that such a rule does not exist. The colours of our moral nature are rarely separated by the sharp lines of our vocabulary. They fade and blend into one another so imperceptibly, that it is impossible to mark a precise point of transition. The end of man is the full development of his being in that symmetry and proportion which nature has assigned it, and such a development implies that the supreme, the predominant motive of his life, should be moral. If in any society or individual this ascendency does not exist, that society or that individual is in a diseased and abnormal condition. But the superiority of the moral part of our nature, though unquestionable, is indefinite not infinite, and the prevailing standard is not at all times the same. The moralist can only lay down general

principles.   Individual feeling or the general sentiment of
society must draw the application.

The vagueness that on such questions confessedly hangs
over the intuitive theory, has always been insisted upon by
members of the opposite school, who 'in the greatest happiness principle' claim to possess a definite formulary, enabling
them to draw boldly the frontier line between the lawful and
the illicit, and to remove moral disputes from the domain of
feeling to that of demonstration.   But this claim, which forms
the great attraction of the utilitarian school, is, if I mistake
not, one of the grossest of impostures.   We compare with
accuracy and confidence the value of the most various
material commodities, for we mean by this term, exchange-
able value, and we have a common measure of exchange.
But we seek in vain for such a measure enabling us to compare different kinds of utility or happiness.   Thus, to take a
very familiar example, the question may be proposed, whether
excursion trains from a country district to a seaport town
produce more good than evil, whether a man governed by
moral principles should encourage or oppose them.   They
give innocent and healthy enjoyment to many thousands,
they enlarge in some degree the range of their ideas, they can
hardly be said to prevent any sin that would otherwise have
been committed, they give rise to many cases of drunkenness,
each of which, according to the theological doctrine we have
reviewed, should be deemed a more dreadful calamity than
the earthquake of Lisbon, or a visitation of the cholera, but
which have not usually any lasting terrestrial effects; they
also often produce a measure, and sometimes no small measure,
of more serious vice, and it is probable that hundreds of
women may trace their first fall to the excursion train.   We
have here a number of advantages and disadvantages, the
first being intellectual and physical, and the second moral.
Nearly all moralists would acknowledge that a few instances
of immorality would not prevent the excursion train being,
on the whole, a good thing.   All would acknowledge that

very numerous instances would more than counterbalance its advantages. The intuitive moralist confesses that he is unable to draw a precise line, showing where the moral evils outweigh the physical benefits. In what possible respect the introduction of Benthamite formularies improves the matter, I am unable to understand. No utilitarian would reduce the question to one of simple majority, or would have the cynicism to balance the ruin of one woman by the day's enjoyment of another. The impossibility of drawing, in such cases, a distinct line of division, is no argument against the intuitive moralist, for that impossibility is shared to the full extent by his rival.

There are, as we have seen, two kinds of interest with which utilitarian moralists are concerned—the private interest which they believe to be the ultimate motive, and the public interest which they believe to be the end, of all virtue. With reference to the first, the intuitive moralist denies that a selfish act can be a virtuous or meritorious one. If a man when about to commit a theft, became suddenly conscious of the presence of a policeman, and through fear of arrest and punishment were to abstain from the act he would otherwise have committed, this abstinence would not appear in the eyes of mankind to possess any moral value ; and if he were determined partly by conscientious motives, and partly by fear, the presence of the latter element would, in proportion to its strength, detract from his merit. But although selfish considerations are distinctly opposed to virtuous ones, it would be a mistake to imagine they can never ultimately have a purely moral influence. In the first place, a well-ordered system of threats and punishments marks out the path of virtue with a distinctness of definition it could scarcely have otherwise attained. In the next place, it often happens that when the mind is swayed by a conflict of motives, the expectation of reward or punishment will so reinforce or support the virtuous motives, as to secure their victory ; and, as every triumph of these motives increases their strength and weakens the opposing principles, a step will thus have been made towards moral perfection, which will render more probable the future triumph of unassisted virtue.

With reference to the interests of society, there are two distinct assertions to be made. The first is, that although the pursuit of the welfare of others is undoubtedly one form of virtue, it does not include all virtue, or, in other words, that there are forms of virtue which, even if beneficial to mankind, do not become virtuous on that account, but have an intrinsic excellence which is not proportioned to or dependent on their utility. The second is, that there may occasionally arise considerations of extreme and overwhelming utility that may justify a sacrifice of these virtues. This sacrifice may be made in various ways—as, when a man undertakes an enterprise which is in itself perfectly innocent, but which in addition to its great material advantages will, as he well knows, produce a certain measure of crime ; or when, abstaining from a protest, he tacitly countenances beliefs which he considers untrue, because he regards them as transcendently useful ; or again, when, for the benefit of others, and under circumstances of great urgency, he utters a direct falsehood, as, for example, when by such means alone he can save the life of an innocent man.[1] But the fact, that in these cases considerations of extreme utility are suffered to over-

---

[1] The following passage, though rather vague and rhetorical, is not unimpressive: 'Oui, dit Jacobi, je mentirais comme Desdemona mourante, je tromperais comme Oreste quand il veut mourir à la place de Pylade, j'assassinerais comme Timoléon, je serais parjure comme Épaminondas et Jean de Witt, je me déterminerais au suicide comme Caton, je serais sacri- lége comme David ; car j'ai la certitude en moi-même qu'en pardonnant à ces fautes suivant la lettre l'homme exerce le droit souverain que la majesté de son être lui confère ; il appose le sceau de sa divine nature sur la grâce qu'il accorde.' — Barchou de Penhoen, *Hist. de la Philos. allemande,* tome i. p. 295.

ride considerations of morality, is in no degree inconsistent with the facts, that the latter differ in kind from the former, that they are of a higher nature, and that they may supply adequate and legitimate motives of action not only distinct from, but even in opposition to utility. Gold and silver are different metals. Gold is more valuable than silver; yet a very small quantity of gold may be advantageously exchanged for a very large quantity of silver.

The last class of objections to the theory of natural moral perceptions which it is necessary for me to notice, arises from a very mischievous equivocation in the word natural.[1] The term natural man is sometimes regarded as synonymous with man in his primitive or barbarous condition, and sometimes as expressing all in a civilised man that is due to nature as distinguished from artificial habits or acquirements. This equivocation is especially dangerous, because it implies one of the most extravagant excesses to which the sensational philosophy could be pushed—the notion that the difference between a savage and a civilised man is simply a difference of acquisition, and not at all a difference of development. In accordance with this notion, those who deny original moral distinctions have ransacked the accounts of travellers for examples of savages who appeared destitute of moral sentiments, and have adduced them as conclusive evidence of their position. Now it is, I think, abundantly evident that these narratives are usually exceedingly untrustworthy.[2] They

---

[1] This equivocation seems to me to lie at the root of the famous dispute whether man is by nature a social being, or whether, as Hobbes averred, the state of nature is a state of war. Few persons who have observed the recent light thrown on the subject will question that the primitive condition of man was that of savage life, and fewer still will question that savage life is a state of war. On the other hand, it is, I think, equally certain that man necessarily becomes a social being in exact proportion to the development of the capacities of his nature.

[2] One of the best living authorities on this question writes: 'The asserted existence of savages so low as to have no moral standard is too groundless to be discussed. Every human tribe has its general views as to what conduct is right and what

have been in most cases collected by uncritical and unphilo
sophical travellers, who knew little of the language and still
less of the inner life of the people they described, whose means
of information were acquired in simply traversing the country,
who were more struck by moral paradox, than by unostentatious virtue, who were proverbially addicted to embellishing
and exaggerating the singularities they witnessed, and who
very rarely investigated their origin.   It should not be forgotten that the French moralists of the last century, who insisted most strongly on this species of evidence, were also the
dupes of one of the most curious delusions in the whole compass of literary history.   Those unflinching sceptics who
claimed to be the true disciples of the apostle who believed
nothing that he had not touched, and whose relentless criticism played with withering effect on all the holiest feelings
of our nature, and on all the tenets of traditional creeds, had
discovered one happy land where the ideal had ceased to be a
dream.   They could point to one people whose pure and
rational morality, purged from all the clouds of bigotry and
enthusiasm, shone with an almost dazzling splendour above the
ignorance and superstition of Europe.   Voltaire forgot to gibe,
and Helvétius kindled into enthusiasm, when China and the
Chinese rose before their minds, and to this semi-barbarous
nation they habitually attributed maxims of conduct that
neither Roman nor Christian virtue had ever realised.

But putting aside these considerations, and assuming the
fidelity of the pictures of savage life upon which these
writers rely, they fail to prove the point for which they are
adduced.   The moralists I am defending, assert that we
possess a natural power of distinguishing between the higher
and lower parts of our nature.   But the eye of the mind, like

---

wrong, and each generation hands
the standard on to the next.   Even
in the details of their moral standards, wide as their differences are,
there is yet wider agreement
throughout the human race.'—
Tylor on Primitive Society, *Contemporary Review*, April 1873, **p. 702.**

the eye of the body, may be closed. Moral and rational faculties may be alike dormant, and they will certainly be so if men are wholly immersed in the gratification of their senses. Man is like a plant, which requires a favourable soil for the full expansion of its natural or innate powers.¹ Yet those powers both rational and moral are there, and when quickened into action, each will discharge its appointed functions. If it could be proved that there are savages who are absolutely destitute of the progressive energy which distinguishes reason from instinct and of the moral aspiration which constitutes virtue, this would not prove that rational or moral faculties form no part of their nature. If it could be shown that there is a stage of barbarism in which man knows, feels and does nothing that might not be known, felt and done by an ape, this would not be sufficient to reduce him to the level of the brute. There would still be this broad distinction between them—the one possesses a capacity for development which the other does not possess. Under favourable circumstances the savage will become a reasoning,

---

¹ The distinction between innate faculties evolved by experience and innate ideas independent of experience, and the analogy between the expansion of the former and that of the bud into the flower has been very happily treated by Reid. (*On the Active Powers*, essay iii. chap. viii. p. 4.) Professor Sedgwick, criticising Locke's notion of the soul being originally like a sheet of white paper, beautifully says: 'Naked man comes from his mother's womb, endowed with limbs and senses indeed well fitted to the material world, yet powerless from want of use; and as for knowledge, his soul is one unvaried blank; yet has this blank been already touched by a celestial hand, and when plunged in the colours which sur-

round it, it takes not its tinge from accident but design, and comes forth covered with a glorious pattern.' (*On the Studies of the University*, p. 54.) Leibnitz says: 'L'esprit n'est point une table rase. Il est tout plein de caractères que la sensation ne peut que découvrir et mettre en lumière au lieu de les y imprimer. Je me suis servi de la comparaison d'une pierre de marbre qui a des veines plutôt que d'une pierre de marbre tout unie. . . . S'il y avait dans la pierre des veines qui marquassent la figure d'Hercule préférablement à d'autres figures, ... Hercule y serait comme inné en quelque façon, quoiqu'il fallût du travail pour découvrir ces veines.' —*Critique de l'Essai sur l'Entendement.*

progressive, and moral man : under no circumstances can a similar transformation be effected in the ape. It may be as difficult to detect the oakleaf in the acorn as in the stone ; yet the acorn may be converted into an oak : the stone will always continue to be a stone.[1]

The foregoing pages will, I trust, have exhibited with sufficient clearness the nature of the two great divisions of moral philosophy—the school which proceeds from the primitive truth that all men desire happiness, and endeavours out of this fact to evolve all ethical doctrines, and the school which traces our moral systems to an intuitive perception that certain parts of our nature are higher or better than others.   It is obvious that this difference concerning the origin of our moral conceptions forms part of the very much wider metaphysical question, whether our ideas are derived exclusively from sensation or whether they spring in part from the mind itself. The latter theory in antiquity was chiefly represented by the Platonic doctrine of pre-existence, which rested on the conviction that the mind has the power of drawing from its own depths certain conceptions or ideas which cannot be explained by any post-natal experience, and must therefore, it was said, have been acquired in a previous

---

[1] The argument against the intuitive moralists derived from savage life was employed at some length by Locke. Paley then adopted it, taking a history of base ingratitude related by Valerius Maximus, and asking whether a savage would view it with disapprobation. (*Moral Phil.* book i. ch. 5.)   Dugald Stewart (*Active and Moral Powers*, vol. i. pp. 230–231) and other writers have very fully answered this but the same objection has been revived in another form by Mr. Austin, who supposes (*Lectures on Jurisprudence*, vol. i. pp. 82–83) a savage who first meets a hunter carrying a dead deer, kills the hunter and steals the deer, and is afterwards himself assailed by another hunter whom he kills. Mr. Austin asks whether the savage would perceive a moral difference between these two acts of homicide? Certainly not. In this early stage of development, the savage recognises a duty of justice and humanity to the members of his tribe, but to no one beyond this circle. He is in a 'state of war' with the foreign hunter. He has a right to kill the hunter and the hunter an equal right to kill him.

existence. In the seventeenth century it took the orm of a doctrine of innate ideas. But though this theory in the form in which it was professed by Lord Herbert of Cherbury and assailed by Locke has almost disappeared, the doctrine that we possess certain faculties which by their own expansion, and not by the reception of notions from without, are not only capable of, but must necessarily attain, certain ideas, as the bud must necessarily expand into its own specific flower, still occupies a distinguished place in the world of speculation, and its probability has been greatly strengthened by recent observations of the range and potency of instinct in animals. From some passages in his Essay, it appears that Locke himself had a confused perception of this distinction,[1] which was by no means unknown to previous writers; and after the publication of the philosophy of Locke it was clearly exhibited by Shaftesbury and Leibnitz, and incidentally noticed by Berkeley long before Kant established his distinction between the form and the matter of our knowledge, between ideas which are received *a priori* and ideas which are received *a posteriori*. The existence or non-existence of this source of ideas forms the basis of the opposition between the inductive philosophy of England and the French philosophy of the eighteenth century on the one hand, and the German and

---

[1] Everyone who is acquainted with metaphysics knows that there has been an almost endless controversy about Locke's meaning on this point. The fact seems to be that Locke, like most great originators of thought, and indeed more than most, often failed to perceive the ultimate consequences of his principles, and partly through some confusion of thought, and partly through unhappiness of expression, has left passages involving the conclusions of both schools. As a matter of history the sensual school of Condillac grew professedly out of his philosophy. In defence of the legitimacy of the process by which these writers evolved their conclusions from the premisses of Locke, the reader may consult the very able lectures of M. Cousin on Locke. The other side has been treated, among others, by Dugald Stewart in his *Dissertation*, by Professor Webb in his *Intellectualism of Locke*, and by Mr. Rogers in an essay reprinted from the *Edinburgh Review*.

Scotch philosophies, as well as the French eclecticism of the nineteenth century upon the other. The tendency of the first school is to restrict as far as possible the active powers of the human mind, and to aggrandise as far as possible the empire of external circumstances. The other school dwells especially on the instinctive side of our nature, and maintains the existence of certain intuitions of the reason, certain categories or original conceptions, which are presupposed in all our reasonings and cannot be resolved into sensations. The boast of the first school is that its searching analysis leaves no mental phenomenon unresolved, and its attraction is the extreme simplicity it can attain. The second school multiplies faculties or original principles, concentrates its attention mainly upon the nature of our understanding, and asserts very strongly the initiative force both of our will and of our intellect.

We find this connection between a philosophy based upon the senses, and a morality founded upon utility from the earliest times. Aristotle was distinguished among the ancients for the emphasis with which he dwelt upon the utility of virtue, and it was from the writings of Aristotle that the schoolmen derived the famous formulary which has become the motto of the school of Locke. Locke himself devoted especial research to the refutation of the doctrine of a natural moral sense, which he endeavoured to overthrow by a catalogue of immoral practices that exist among savages, and the hesitation he occasionally exhibited in his moral doctrine corresponds not unfaithfully to the obscurity thrown over his metaphysics by the admission of reflection as a source of ideas. If his opponent Leibnitz made pleasure the object of moral action, it was only that refined pleasure which is produced by the contemplation of the happiness of others. When, however, Condillac and his followers, removing reflection from the position Locke had assigned it, reduced the philosophy of sensation to its simplest expression, and when the Scotch and German writers elaborated the principles of the opposite school, the moral tendencies of both were indisputably manifested. Everywhere the philosophy of sensation was accompanied by the morals of interest, and the ideal philosophy, by an assertion of the existence of a moral faculty, and every influence that has affected the prevailing theory concerning the origin of our ideas, has exercised a corresponding influence upon the theories of ethics.

The great movement of modern thought, of which Bacon was at once the highest representative and one of the chief agents, has been truly said to exhibit a striking resemblance, and at the same time a striking contrast, to the movement of ancient thought, which was effected chiefly by the genius of Socrates. In the name of utility, Socrates diverted the intellect of antiquity from the fantastic cosmogonies with which it had long been occupied, to the study of the moral nature of man. In the name of the same utility Bacon laboured to divert the modern intellect from the idle metaphysical speculations of the schoolmen to natural science, to which newly discovered instruments of research, his own sounder method, and a cluster of splendid intellects, soon gave an unprecedented impulse. To the indirect influence of this movement, perhaps, even more than to the direct teaching of Gassendi and Locke, may be ascribed the great ascendency of sensational philosophy among modern nations, and it is also connected with some of the most important differences between ancient and modern history. Among the ancients the human mind was chiefly directed to philosophical speculations, in which the law seems to be perpetual oscillation, while among the moderns it has rather tended towards physical science, and towards inventions, in which the law is perpetual progress. National power, and in most cases even national independence, implied among the ancients the constant energy of high intellectual or moral qualities. When the heroism or the genius of the people had relaxed, when an enervating philosophy or the lassitude that often accompanies civilisation arrived, the whole edifice speedily tottered, the sceptre was transferred to another state, and the same history was elsewhere reproduced. A great nation bequeathed indeed to its successors works of transcendent beauty in art and literature, philosophies that could avail only when the mind had risen to their level, examples that might stimulate the heroism of an aspiring people, warnings that might sometimes arrest it on the path to ruin. But all these acted only through the mind. In modern times, on the other hand, if we put aside religious influences, the principal causes of the superiority of civilised men are to be found in inventions which when once discovered can never pass away, and the effects of which are in consequence in a great measure removed from the fluctuations of moral life. The causes which most disturbed or accelerated the normal progress of society in antiquity were the appearance of great men, in modern times they have been the appearance of great inventions. Printing has secured the intellectual achievements of the past, and furnished a sure guarantee of future progress. Gunpowder and military machinery have rendered the triumph of barbarians impossible. Steam has united nations in the closest bonds. Innumerable mechanical contrivances have given a decisive preponderance to that industrial element which has coloured all the developments of our civilisation. The leading characteristics of modern societies are in consequence marked out much more by the triumphs of inventive skill than by the sustained energy of moral causes.

Now it will appear evident, I think, to those who reflect carefully upon their own minds, and upon the course of history, that these three things, the study of physical science, inventive skill, and industrial enterprise, are connected in such a manner, that when in any nation there is a long-sustained tendency towards one, the others will naturally follow. This connection is partly that of cause and effect, for success in either of these branches facilitates success in the others, a knowledge of natural laws being the basis of many of the most important inventions, and being itself acquired by the aid of instruments of research, while industry is manifestly indebted to both. But besides this connection, there is a connection of congruity. The same cast or habit of thought developes itself in these three forms. They all represent the natural tendencies of what is commonly called the practical as opposed to the theoretical mind, of the inductive or experimental as opposed to the deductive or ideal, of the cautious and the plodding as opposed to the imaginative and the ambitious, of the mind that tends naturally to matter as opposed to that which dwells naturally on ideas. Among the ancients, the distaste for physical science, which the belief in the capricious divine government of all natural phenomena, and the distaste for industrial enterprise which slavery produced, conspired to favour the philosophical tendency, while among the moderns physical science and the habits of industrial life continually react upon one another.

There can be no question that the intellectual tendencies of modern times are far superior to those of antiquity, both in respect to the material prosperity they effect, and to the uninterrupted progress they secure. Upon the other hand, it is, I think, equally unquestionable that this superiority is purchased by the sacrifice of something of dignity and elevation of character. It is when the cultivation of mental and moral qua ities is deemed the primary object, when the mind and its interests are most removed from the things of sense, that great characters are most frequent, and the standard of heroism is most high. In this, as in other cases, the law of congruity is supreme. The mind that is concentrated most on the properties of matter, is predisposed to derive all ideas from the senses, while that which dwells naturally upon its own operations inclines to an ideal philosophy, and the prevailing system of morals depends largely upon the distinction.

In the next place, we may observe that the practical

consequences, so far as ethics are concerned,[1] of the opposition between the two great schools of morals, are less than might be inferred from the intellectual chasm that separates them. Moralists grow up in the atmosphere of society, and experience all the common feelings of other men. Whatever theory of the genesis of morals they may form, they commonly recognise as right the broad moral principles of the world, and they endeavour—though I have attempted to show not always successfully—to prove that these principles may be accounted for and justified by their system. The great practical difference between the schools lies, not in the difference of the virtues they inculcate, but in the different degrees of prominence they assign to each, in the different casts of mind they represent and promote. As Adam Smith observed, a system like that of the Stoics, which makes self-control the ideal of excellence, is especially favourable to the heroic qualities, a system like that of Hutcheson, which resolves virtue into benevolence, to the amiable qualities, and utilitarian systems to the industrial virtues. A society in which any one of these three forms of moral excellence is especially prominent, has a natural tendency towards the corresponding theory of ethics; but, on the other hand, this theory, when formed, reacts upon and strengthens the moral tendency that elicited it. The Epicureans and the Stoics can each claim a great historical fact in their favour. When every other Greek school modified or abandoned the teaching of its founder, the disciples of Epicurus at Athens preserved their hereditary faith unsullied and unchanged.[2] On the other hand, in the

---

[1] I make this qualification, because I believe that the denial of a moral nature in man capable of perceiving the distinction between duty and interest and the rightful supremacy of the former, is both philosophically and actually subversive of natural theology.

[2] See the forcible passage in the life of Epicurus by Diogenes Laërtius. So Mackintosh: 'It is remarkable that, while, of the three professors who sat in the Porch from Zeno to Posidonius, every one either softened or exaggerated the doctrines of his predecessor, and

Roman empire, almost every great character, almost every effort in the cause of liberty, emanated from the ranks of Stoicism, while Epicureanism was continually identified with corruption and with tyranny. The intuitive school, not having a clear and simple external standard, has often proved somewhat liable to assimilate with superstition and mysticism, to become fantastic, unreasoning, and unpractical, while the prominence accorded to interest, and the constant intervention of calculation in utilitarian systems, have a tendency to depress the ideal, and give a sordid and unheroic ply to the character. The first, dwelling on the moral initiative, elevates the tone and standard of life. The second, revealing the influence of surrounding circumstances upon character, leads to the most important practical reforms.[1] Each school has thus proved in some sense at once the corrective and the complement of the other. Each when pushed to its extreme results, produces evils which lead to the reappearance of its rival.

Having now considered at some length the nature and

---

while the beautiful and reverend philosophy of Plato had in his own Academy degenerated into a scepticism which did not spare morality itself, the system of Epicurus remained without change; his disciples continued for ages to show personal honour to his memory in a manner which may seem unaccountable among those who were taught to measure propriety by a calculation of palpable and outward usefulness.'—*Dissertation on Ethical Philosophy*, p. 85, ed. 1836. See, too, Tennemann (*Manuel de la Philosophie*, ed. Cousin, tome i. p. 211).

[1] Thus e.g. the magnificent chapters of Helvétius on the moral effects of despotism, form one of the best modern contributions to political ethics. We have a curious illustration of the emphasis with which this school dwells on the moral importance of institutions in a memoir of M. De Tracy, *On the best Plan of National Education*, which appeared first towards the close of the French Revolution, and was reprinted during the Restoration. The author, who was one of the most distinguished of the disciples of Condillac, argued that the most efficient of all ways of educating a people is, the establishment of a good system of police, for the constant association of the ideas of crime and punishment in the minds of the masses is the one effectual method of creating moral habits, which will continue to act when the fear of punishment is removed.

tendencies of the theories according to which men test and classify their moral feelings, we may pass to an examination of the process according to which these feelings are developed, or, in other words, of the causes that lead societies to elevate their moral standard and determine their preference of some particular kinds of virtue. The observations I have to offer on this subject will be of a somewhat miscellaneous character, but they will all, I trust, tend to show the nature of the changes that constitute moral history, and to furnish us with some general principles which may be applied in detail in the succeeding chapters.

It is sufficiently evident, that, in proportion to the high organisation of society, the amiable and the social virtues will be cultivated at the expense of the heroic and the ascetic. A courageous endurance of suffering is probably the first form of human virtue, the one conspicuous instance in savage life of a course of conduct opposed to natural impulses, and pursued through a belief that it is higher or nobler than the opposite. In a disturbed, disorganised, and warlike society, acts of great courage and great endurance are very frequent, and determine to a very large extent the course of events; but in proportion to the organisation of communities the occasions for their display, and their influence when displayed, are alike restricted. Besides this the tastes and habits of civilisation, the innumerable inventions designed to promote comfort and diminish pain, set the current of society in a direction altogether different from heroism, and somewhat emasculate, though they refine and soften, the character. Asceticism again—including under this term, not merely the monastic system, but also all efforts to withdraw from the world in order to cultivate a high degree of sanctity—belongs naturally to a society which is somewhat rude, and in which isolation is frequent and easy. When men become united in very close bonds of co-operation, when industrial enterprise becomes very ardent, and the prevailing impulse is strongly towards material wealth and luxurious enjoyments, virtue is regarded chiefly or solely in the light of the interests of society, and this tendency is still further strengthened by the educational influence of legislation, which imprints moral distinctions very deeply on the mind, but at the same time accustoms men to measure them solely by an external and utilitarian standard.[1] The first table of the law gives way to the second. Good is not loved for itself, but as the means to an end. All that virtue which is required to form upright and benevolent men is in the highest degree useful to society, but the qualities which constitute a saintly or spiritual character as distinguished from one that is simply moral and amiable, have not the same direct, uniform and manifest tendency to the promotion of happiness, and they are accordingly little valued.[2] In savage life the animal

---

[1] An important intellectual revolution is at present taking place in England. The ascendency in literary and philosophical questions which belonged to the writers of books is manifestly passing in a very great degree to weekly and even daily papers, which have long been supreme in politics, and have begun within the last ten years systematically to treat ethical and philosophical questions. From their immense circulation, their incontestable ability and the power they possess of continually reiterating their distinctive doctrines, from the impatience, too, of long and elaborate writings, which newspapers generate in the public, it has come to pass that these periodicals exercise probably a greater influence than any other productions of the day, in forming the ways of thinking of ordinary educated Englishmen. The many consequences, good and evil, of this change it will be the duty of future literary historians to trace, but there is one which is, I think, much felt in the sphere of ethics. An important effect of these journals has been to evoke a large amount of literary talent in the lawyer class. Men whose professional duties would render it impossible for them to write long books, are quite capable of treating philosophical subjects in the form of short essays, and have in fact become conspicuous in these periodicals. There has seldom, I think, before, been a time when lawyers occupied such an important literary position as at present, or when legal ways of thinking had so great an influence over English philosophy; and this fact has been eminently favourable to the progress of utilitarianism.

[2] There are some good remarks on this point in the very striking chapter on the present condition of Christianity in Wilberforce's *Practical View.*

nature being supreme, these higher qualities are unknown
In a very elaborate material civilisation the prevailing atmosphere is not favourable either to their production or their
appreciation.   Their place has usually been in an intermediate stage.

On the other hand, there are certain virtues that are the
natural product of a cultivated society.   Independently of
all local and special circumstances, the transition of men
from a barbarous or semi-civilised to a highly organised state
necessarily brings with it the destruction or abridgment of
the legitimate sphere of revenge, by transferring the office of
punishment from the wronged person to a passionless tribunal
appointed by society ; [1] a growing substitution of pacific for
warlike occupations, the introduction of refined and intellectual tastes which gradually displace amusements that
derive their zest from their barbarity, the rapid multiplication of ties of connection between all classes and nations,
and also the strengthening of the imagination by intellectual
culture.   This last faculty, considered as the power of realisation, forms the chief tie between our moral and intellectual
natures.   In order to pity suffering we must realise it, and
the intensity of our compassion is usually proportioned to
the vividness of our realisation.[2]   The most frightful catastrophe in South America, an earthquake, a shipwreck, or a
battle, will elicit less compassion than the death of a single
individual who has been brought prominently before our eyes.
To this cause must be chiefly ascribed the extraordinary
measure of compassion usually bestowed upon a conspicuous

---

[1] See Reid's *Essays on the Active Powers*, iii. 4.

[2] I say usually proportioned, because it is, I believe, possible for men to realise intensely suffer-ing. and to derive pleasure from that very fact. This is especially the case with vindictive cruelty, but it is not, I think, altogether confined to that sphere. This ques-tion we shall have occasion to examine when discussing the gla-diatorial shows. Most cruelty, however, springs from callousness, which is simply dulness of imag-ination.

condemned criminal, the affection and enthusiasm that centre upon sovereigns, and many of the glaring inconsistencies of our historical judgments. The recollection of some isolated act of magnanimity displayed by Alexander or Cæsar moves us more than the thought of the 30,000 Thebans whom the Macedonian sold as slaves, of the 2,000 prisoners he crucified at Tyre, of the 1,100,000 men on whose corpses the Roman rose to fame. Wrapt in the pale winding-sheet of general terms the greatest tragedies of history evoke no vivid images in our minds, and it is only by a great effort of genius that an historian can galvanise them into life. The irritation displayed by the captive of St. Helena in his bickerings with his gaoler affects most men more than the thought of the nameless thousands whom his insatiable egotism had hurried to the grave. Such is the frailty of our nature that we are more moved by the tears of some captive princess, by some trifling biographical incident that has floated down the stream of history, than by the sorrows of all the countless multitudes who perished beneath the sword of a Tamerlane, a Bajazet, or a Zenghis Khan.

If our benevolent feelings are thus the slaves of our imaginations, if an act of realisation is a necessary antecedent and condition of compassion, it is obvious that any influence that augments the range and power of this realising faculty is favourable to the amiable virtues, and it is equally evident that education has in the highest degree this effect. To an uneducated man all classes, nations, modes of thought and existence foreign to his own are unrealised, while every increase of knowledge brings with it an increase of insight, and therefore of sympathy. But the addition to his knowledge is the smallest part of this change. The realising faculty is itself intensified. Every book he reads, every intellectual exercise in which he engages, accustoms him to rise above the objects immediately present to his senses, to extend his realisations into new spheres, and reproduce in his imagination

the thoughts, feelings, and characters of others, with a vividness inconceivable to the savage.   Hence, in a great degree,
the tact with which a refined mind learns to discriminate
and adapt itself to the most delicate shades of feeling, and
hence too the sensitive humanity with which, in proportion
to their civilisation, men realise and recoil from cruelty.

We have here, however, an important distinction to
draw.   Under the name of cruelty are comprised two kinds
of vice, altogether different in their causes and in most of
their consequences.   There is the cruelty which springs from
callousness and brutality, and there is the cruelty of vindictiveness.   The first belongs chiefly to hard, dull, and somewhat lethargic characters, it appears most frequently in
strong and conquering nations and in temperate climates,
and it is due in a very great degree to defective realisation.
The second is rather a feminine attribute, it is usually displayed in oppressed and suffering communities, in passionate
natures, and in hot climates.   Great vindictiveness is often
united with great tenderness, and great callousness with
great magnanimity, but a vindictive nature is rarely magnanimous, and a brutal nature is still more rarely tender.   The
ancient Romans exhibited a remarkable combination of great
callousness and great magnanimity, while by a curious
contrast the modern Italian character verges manifestly
towards the opposite combination.   Both forms of cruelty
are, if I mistake not, diminished with advancing civilisation,
but by different causes and in different degrees.   Callous
cruelty disappears before the sensitiveness of a cultivated
imagination.   Vindictive cruelty is diminished by the substitution of a penal system for private revenge.

The same intellectual culture that facilitates the realisation of suffering, and therefore produces compassion, facilitates also the realisation of character and opinions, and
therefore produces charity.   The great majority of uncharit-
able judgments in the world may be traced to a deficiency of

imagination. The chief cause of sectarian animosity, is the incapacity of most men to conceive hostile systems in the light in which they appear to their adherents, and to enter into the enthusiasm they inspire. The acquisition of this power of intellectual sympathy is a common accompaniment of a large and cultivated mind, and wherever it exists, it assuages the rancour of controversy. The severity of our judgment of criminals is also often excessive, because the imagination finds it more easy to realise an action than a state of mind. Any one can conceive a fit of drunkenness or a deed of violence, but few persons who are by nature very sober or very calm can conceive the natural disposition that predisposes to it. A good man brought up among all the associations of virtue reads of some horrible crime. his imagination exhausts itself in depicting its circumstances, and he then estimates the guilt of the criminal, by asking himself, 'How guilty should *I* be, were I to perpetrate such an act?' To realise with any adequacy the force of a passion we have never experienced, to conceive a type of character radically different from our own, above all, to form any just appreciation of the lawlessness and obtuseness of moral temperament, inevitably generated by a vicious education, requires a power of imagination which is among the rarest of human endowments. Even in judging our own conduct, this feebleness of imagination is sometimes shown, and an old man recalling the foolish actions, but having lost the power of realising the feelings, of his youth, may be very unjust to his own past. That which makes it so difficult for a man of strong vicious passions to unbosom himself to a naturally virtuous man, is not so much the virtue as the ignorance of the latter. It is the conviction that he cannot possibly understand the force of a passion he has never felt. That which alone renders tolerable to the mind the thought of judgment by an all-pure Being, is the union of the attribute of omniscience with that of purity, for perfect knowledge implies a perfect power of realisation. The further our analysis extends, and the more our realising faculties are cultivated, the more sensible we become of the influence of circumstances both upon character and upon opinions, and of the exaggerations of our first estimates of moral inequalities. Strong antipathies are thus gradually softened down. Men gain much in charity, but they lose something in zeal.

We may push, I think, this vein of thought one step farther. Our imagination, which governs our affections, has in its earlier and feebler stages little power of grasping ideas, except in a personified and concrete form, and the power of rising to abstractions is one of the best measures of intellectual progress. The beginning of writing is the hieroglyphic or symbolical picture; the beginning of worship is fetishism or idolatry; the beginning of eloquence is pictorial, sensuous, and metaphorical; the beginning of philosophy is the myth. The imagination in its first stages concentrates itself on individuals; gradually by an effort of abstraction it rises to an institution or well-defined organisation; it is only at a very advanced stage that it can grasp a moral and intellectual principle. Loyalty, patriotism, and attachment to a cosmopolitan cause are therefore three forms of moral enthusiasm respectively appropriate to three successive stages of mental progress, and they have, I think, a certain analogy to idolatrous worship, church feeling, and moral culture, which are the central ideas of three stages of religious history.

The reader will readily understand that generalisations of this kind can pretend to nothing more than an approximate truth. Our knowledge of the laws of moral progress is like that of the laws of climate. We lay down general rules about the temperature to be expected as we approach or recede from the equator, and experience shows that they are substantially correct; but yet an elevated plain, or a chain of mountains, or the neighbourhood of the sea, will often in some degree derange our calculations. So, too, in the history of moral changes, innumerable special agencies, such as religious or political institutions, geographical conditions, traditions, antipathies, and affinities, exercise a certain retarding, accelerating, or deflecting influence, and somewhat modify the normal progress. The proposition for which I am contending is simply that there is such a thing as a natural history of morals, a defined and regular order, in which our moral feelings are unfolded ; or, in other words, that there are certain groups of virtues which spring spontaneously out of the circumstances and mental conditions of an uncivilised people, and that there are others which are the normal and appropriate products of civilisation. The virtues of uncivilised men are recognised as virtues by civilised men, but they are neither exhibited in the same perfection, nor given the same position in the scale of duties. Of these moral changes none are more obvious than the gradual decadence of heroism both active and passive, the increase of compassion and of charity, and the transition from the enthusiasm of loyalty to those of patriotism and liberty.

Another form of virtue which usually increases with civilisation is veracity, a term which must be regarded as including something more than the simple avoidance of direct falsehood. In the ordinary intercourse of life it is readily understood that a man is offending against truth, not only when he utters a deliberate falsehood, but also when in his statement of a case he suppresses or endeavours to conceal essential facts, or makes positive assertions without having conscientiously verified their grounds. The earliest form in which the duty of veracity is enforced is probably the observance of vows, which occupy a position of much prominence in youthful religions. With the subsequent progress of civilisation, we find the successive inculcation of three forms of veracity, which may be termed respectively industrial, political, and philosophical. By the first I understand that accuracy of statement or fidelity to engagements which is commonly meant when we speak of a truthful man. Though in some cases sustained by the strong sense of honour which accompanies a military spirit, this form of veracity is usually the special virtue of an industrial nation, for although industrial enterprise affords great temptations to deception, mutual confidence, and therefore strict truthfulness, are in these occupations so transcendently important that they acquire in the minds of men a value they had never before possessed. Veracity becomes the first virtue in the moral type, and no character is regarded with any kind of approbation in which it is wanting. It is made more than any other the test distinguishing a good from a bad man. We accordingly find that even where the impositions of trade are very numerous, the supreme excellence of veracity is cordially admitted in theory, and it is one of the first virtues that every man aspiring to moral excellence endeavours to cultivate. This constitutes probably the chief moral superiority of nations pervaded by a strong industrial spirit over nations like the Italians, the Spaniards, or the Irish, among whom that spirit is wanting. The usual characteristic of the latter nations is a certain laxity or instability of character, a proneness to exaggeration, a want of truthfulness in little things, an infidelity to engagements from which an Englishman, educated in the habits of industrial life, readily infers a complete absence of moral principle. But a larger philosophy and a deeper experience dispel his error. He finds that where the industrial spirit has not penetrated, truthfulness rarely occupies in the popular mind the same prominent position in the catalogue of virtues. It is not reckoned among the fundamentals of morality, and it is possible and even common to find in these nations—what would be scarcely possible in an industrial society—men who are habitually dishonest and untruthful in small things, and whose lives are nevertheless influenced by a deep religious feeling, and adorned by the consistent practice of some of the most difficult and most painful virtues. Trust in Providence, content and resignation in extreme poverty and suffering, the most genuine amiability and the most sincere readiness to assist their brethren, an adherence to their religious opinions which no persecutions and no bribes can shake, a capacity for heroic, transcendent, and prolonged self-sacrifice, may be found in some nations in men who are habitual liars and habitual cheats.

The promotion of industrial veracity is probably the single form in which the growth of manufactures exercises a favourable influence upon morals. It is possible, however, for this virtue to exist in great perfection without any corresponding growth of political veracity, or in other words, of that spirit of impartiality which in matters of controversy desires that all opinions, arguments, and facts should be fully and fairly stated. This habit of what is commonly termed 'fair play' is especially the characteristic of free communities, and it is pre-eminently fostered by political life. The practice of debate creates a sense of the injustice of suppressing one side of a case, which gradually extends through all forms of intellectual life, and becomes an essential element in the national character. But beyond all this there is a still higher form of intellectual virtue. By enlarged intellectual culture, especially by philosophic studies, men come at last to pursue truth for its own sake, to esteem it a duty to emancipate themselves from party spirit, prejudices, and passion, and through love of truth to cultivate a judicial spirit in controversy. They aspire to the intellect not of a sectarian but of a philosopher, to the intellect not of a partisan but of a statesman.

Of these three forms of a truthful spirit the two last may be said to belong exclusively to a highly civilised society. The last especially can hardly be attained by any but a cultivated mind, and is one of the latest flowers of virtue that bloom in the human heart. The growth, however, both of

political and philosophical veracity has been unnaturally retarded by the opposition of theologians, who made it during
many centuries a main object of their policy to suppress all
writings that were opposed to their views, and who, when
this power had escaped their grasp, proceeded to discourage
in every way impartiality of mind and judgment, and to
associate it with the notion of sin.

To the observations I have already made concerning the
moral effects of industrial life, I shall at present add but
two. The first is that an industrial spirit creates two wholly
different types of character—a thrifty character and a speculating character. Both types grow out of a strong sense of
the value and a strong desire for the attainment of material
comforts, but they are profoundly different both in their
virtues and their vices. The chief characteristic of the one
type is caution, that of the other enterprise. Thriftiness is
one of the best regulators of life. It produces order, sobriety,
moderation, self-restraint, patient industry, and all that cast
of virtues which is designated by the term respectability;
but it has also a tendency to form contracted and ungenerous
natures, incapable of enthusiasm or lively sympathy. The
speculating character, on the other hand, is restless, fiery, and
uncertain, very liable to fall into great and conspicuous vices,
impatient of routine, but by no means unfavourable to strong
feelings, to great generosity or resolution. Which of these
two forms the industrial spirit assumes depends upon local
circumstances. Thriftiness flourishes chiefly among men
placed outside the great stream of commerce, and in positions
where wealth is only to be acquired by slow and steady industry, while the speculating character is most common in
the great centres of enterprise and of wealth.

In the next place, it may be remarked that industrial
habits bring forethought into a new position in the moral
type. In early stages of theological belief, men regarding

every incident that happens to them as the result of a special divine decree, sometimes esteem it a test of faith and a form of duty to take no precautions for the future, but to leave questions of food and clothing to Providential interposition. On the other hand, in an industrial civilisation, prudent forethought is regarded not simply as lawful, but as a duty, and a duty of the very highest order. A good man of the industrial type deems it a duty not to marry till he has ensured the maintenance of a possible family; if he possesses children, he regulates his expenses not simply by the relation of his income to his immediate wants, but with a constant view to the education of his sons, to the portioning of his daughters, to the future necessities and careers of each member of his family. Constant forethought is the guiding principle of his whole life. No single circumstance is regarded as a better test of the civilisation of a people than the extent to which it is diffused among them. The old doctrine virtually disappears, and is interpreted to mean nothing more than that we should accept with resignation what no efforts and no forethought could avert.

This change is but one of several influences which, as civilisation advances, diminish the spirit of reverence among mankind. Reverence is one of those feelings which, in utilitarian systems, would occupy at best a very ambiguous position; for it is extremely questionable whether the great evils that have grown out of it in the form of religious superstition and political servitude have not made it a source of more unhappiness than happiness. Yet, however doubtful may be its position if estimated by its bearing on happiness and on progress, there are few persons who are not conscious that no character can attain a supreme degree of excellence in which a reverential spirit is wanting. Of all the forms of moral goodness it is that to which the epithet beautiful may be most emphatically applied. Yet the habits of advancing civilisation are, if I mistake not, on the whole inimical to its growth. For reverence grows out of a sense of constant dependence. It is fostered by that condition of religious thought in which men believe that each incident that befalls them is directly and specially ordained, and when every event is therefore fraught with a moral import. It is fostered by that condition of scientific knowledge in which every portentous natural phenomenon is supposed to be the result of a direct divine interposition, and awakens in consequence emotions of humility and awe. It is fostered in that stage of political life when loyalty or reverence for the sovereign is the dominating passion, when an aristocracy, branching forth from the throne, spreads habits of deference and subordination through every village, when a revolutionary, a democratic, and a sceptical spirit are alike unknown. Every great change, either of belief or of circumstances, brings with it a change of emotions. The self-assertion of liberty, the levelling of democracy, the dissecting-knife of criticism, the economical revolutions that reduce the relations of classes to simple contracts, the agglomeration of population, and the facilities of locomotion that sever so many ancient ties, are all incompatible with the type of virtue which existed before the power of tradition was broken, and when the chastity of faith was yet unstained. Benevolence, uprightness, enterprise, intellectual honesty, a love of freedom, and a hatred of superstition are growing around us, but we look in vain for that most beautiful character of the past, so distrustful of self, and so trustful of others, so simple, so modest, and so devout, which even when, Ixion-like, it bestowed its affections upon a cloud, made its very illusions the source of some of the purest virtues of our nature. In a few minds, the contemplation of the sublime order of nature produces a reverential feeling, but to the great majority of mankind it is an incontestable though mournful fact, that the discovery of controlling and unchanging law deprives phenomena of their moral signifi-

:ance, and nearly all the social and political spheres in which reverence was fostered have passed away. Its most beautiful displays are not in nations like the Americans or the modern French, who have thrown themselves most fully into the tendencies of the age, but rather in secluded regions like Styria or the Tyrol. Its artistic expression is found in no work of modern genius, but in the mediæval cathedral, which, mellowed but not impaired by time, still gazes on us in its deathless beauty through the centuries of the past. A superstitious age, like every other phase of human history, has its distinctive virtaes, which must necessarily decline before a new stage of progress can be attained.

The virtues and vices growing out of the relation between the sexes are difficult to treat in general terms, both on account of the obvious delicacy of the subject, and also because their natural history is extremely obscured by special causes. In the moral evolutions we have as yet examined, the normal influences are most powerful, and the importance of deranging and modifying circumstances is altogether subsidiary. The expansion of the amiable virtues, the decline of heroism and loyalty, and the growth of industrial habits spring out of changes which necessarily take place under almost all forms of civilisation,[1] and the broad features of the movement are therefore in almost all nations substantially the same. But in the history of sensuality, special causes, such as slavery, religious doctrines, or laws affecting marriage, have been the most powerful agents. The immense changes effected in this field by the Christian religion I shall hereafter examine. In the present chapter I shall content myself with two or three very general remarks relating to the nature of the vice, and to the effect of different stages of civilisation upon its progress.

---

[1] The principal exception being where slavery, coexisting with advanced civilisation, retards or prevents the growth of industrial habits.

There are, I conceive, few greater fallacies than are involved in the method so popular among modern writers of judging the immorality of a nation by its statistics of illegitimate births.   Independently of the obvious defect of this method in excluding simple prostitution from our comparison, it altogether neglects the fact that a large number of illegitimate births arise from causes totally different from the great violence of the passions.   Such, for example, is the notion prevailing in many country districts of England, that the marriage ceremony has a retrospective virtue, cancelling previous immorality; and such too is the custom so general among some classes on the Continent of forming permanent connections without the sanction either of a legal or a religious ceremony.   However deeply such facts may be reprehended and deplored, it would be obviously absurd to infer from them that the nations in which they are most prominent are most conspicuous for the uncontrolled violence of their sensual passions.   In Sweden, which long ranked among the lowest in the moral scale, if measured by the number of illegitimate births, the chief cause appears to have been the difficulties with which legislators surrounded marriage.[1]   Even in displays of actual and violent passion, there are distinctions to be drawn which statistics are wholly unable to reach.   The coarse, cynical, and ostentatious sensuality which forms the most repulsive feature of the French character, the dreamy, languid, and æsthetical sensuality of the Spaniard or the Italian, the furtive and retiring sensuality of some northern nations, though all forms of the same vice, are widely different feelings, and exercise widely different effects upon the prevailing disposition.

In addition to the very important influence upon public morals which climate, I think, undoubtedly exercises in

---

[1] See Mr. Laing's *Travels in Sweden*. A similar cause is said to have had a similar effect in Bavaria.

stimulating or allaying the passions, it has a powerful indirect action upon the position, character, and tastes of women, by determining the prevalence of indoor or out-of-door life, and also the classes among whom the gift of beauty is diffused. In northern countries the prevailing cast of beauty depends rather on colour than on form. It consists chiefly of a freshness and delicacy of complexion which severe labour and constant exposure necessarily destroy, and which is therefore rarely found in the highest perfection among the very poor. But the southern type is essentially democratic. The fierce rays of the sun only mellow and mature its charms. Its most perfect examples may be found in the hovel as in the palace, and the effects of this diffusion of beauty may be traced both in the manners and the morals of the people.

It is probable that the observance of this form of virtue is naturally most strict in a rude and semi-civilised but not barbarous people, and that a very refined civilisation is not often favourable to its growth. Sensuality is the vice of young men and of old nations. A languid epicureanism is the normal condition of nations which have attained a high intellectual or social civilisation, but which, through political causes, have no adequate sphere for the exertion of their energies. The temptation arising from the great wealth of some, and from the feverish longing for luxury and exciting pleasures in others, which exists in all large towns, has been peculiarly fatal to female virtue, and the whole tendency of the public amusements of civilisation is in the same direction. The rude combats which form the chief enjoyments of barbarians produce cruelty. The dramatic and artistic tastes and the social habits of refined men produce sensuality. Education raises many poor women to a stage of refinement that makes them suitable companions for men of a higher rank, and not suitable for those of their own. Industrial pursuits have, indeed, a favourable influence in promoting habits of self-restraint, and especially in checking the licence of military life; but on the other hand, they greatly increase temptation by encouraging postponement of marriage, and in communities, even more than in individuals, moral inequalities are much more due to differences of temptation than to differences of self-restraint. In large bodies of men a considerable increase of temptation always brings with it an increase, though not necessarily a proportionate increase, of vice. Among the checks on excessive multiplication, the historical influence of voluntary continence has been, it must be feared, very small. Physical and moral evils have alone been decisive, and as these form the two opposite weights, we unhappily very frequently find that the diminution of the one has been followed by the increase of the other. The nearly universal custom of early marriages among the Irish peasantry has alone rendered possible that high standard of female chastity that intense and jealous sensitiveness respecting female honour, for which, among many failings and some vices, the Irish poor have long been pre-eminent in Europe; but these very marriages are the most conspicuous proofs of the national improvidence, and one of the most fatal obstacles to industrial prosperity. Had the Irish peasants been less chaste, they would have been more prosperous. Had that fearful famine, which in the present century desolated the land, fallen upon a people who thought more of accumulating subsistence than of avoiding sin, multitudes might now be living who perished by literal starvation on the dreary hills of Limerick or Skibbereen.

The example of Ireland furnishes us, however, with a remarkable instance of the manner in which the influence of a moral feeling may act beyond the circumstances that gave it birth. There is no fact in Irish history more singular than the complete, and, I believe, unparalleled absence among the Irish priesthood of those moral scandals which in every continental country occasionally prove the danger of vows of celibacy. The unsuspected purity of the Irish priests in this respect is the more remarkable, because, the government of the country being Protestant, there is no special inquisitorial legislation to ensure it, because of the almost unbounded influence of the clergy over their parishioners, and also because if any just cause of suspicion existed, in the fierce sectarianism of Irish public opinion, it would assuredly be magnified. Considerations of climate are quite inadequate to explain this fact; but the chief cause is, I think, sufficiently obvious. The habit of marrying at the first development of the passions has produced among the Irish peasantry, from whom the priests for the most part spring, an extremely strong feeling of the iniquity of irregular sexual indulgence, which retains its power even over those who are bound to perpetual celibacy.

It will appear evident from the foregoing considerations that, while the essential nature of virtue and vice is unaltered, there is a perpetual, and in some branches an orderly and necessary change, as society advances, both in the proportionate value attached to different virtues in theory, and in the perfection in which they are realised in practice. It will appear too that, while there may be in societies such a thing as moral improvement, there is rarely or never, on a large scale, such a thing as unmixed improvement. We may gain more than we lose, but we always lose something. There are virtues which are continually dying away with advancing civilisation, and even the lowest stage possesses its distinctive excellence. There is no spectacle more piteous or more horrible to a good man than that of an oppressed nationality writhing in anguish beneath a tyrant's yoke; but there is no condition in which passionate, unquestioning self-sacrifice and heroic courage, and the true sentiment of fraternity are more grandly elicited, and it is probable that the triumph of liberty will in these forms not only lessen the moral performances, but even weaken the moral capacities of mankind. War is, no doubt, a fearful evil, but it is the seed-plot of magnanimous virtues, which in a pacific age must wither and decay.   Even the gambling-table fosters among its more skilful votaries a kind of moral nerve, a capacity for bearing losses with calmness, and controlling the force of the desires, which is scarcely exhibited in equal perfection in any other sphere.

There is still so great a diversity of civilisation in existing nations that traversing tracts of space is almost like traversing tracts of time, for it brings us in contact with living representatives of nearly every phase of past civilisation.   But these differences are rapidly disappearing before the unparalleled diffusion and simplification of knowledge, the still more amazing progress in means of locomotion, and the political and military causes that are manifestly converting Europe into a federation of vast centralised and democratic States.   Even to those who believe that the leading changes are on the whole beneficial, there is much that is melancholy in this revolution.   Those small States which will soon have disappeared from the map of Europe, besides their vast superiority to most great empires in financial prosperity, in the material well-being of the inhabitants, and in many cases in political liberty, pacific tastes, and intellectual progress, form one of the chief refuges of that spirit of content, repose, and retrospective reverence which is pre-eminently wanting in modern civilisation, and their security is in every age one of the least equivocal measures of international morality.   The monastic system, however pernicious when enlarged to excess, has undoubtedly contributed to the happiness of the world, by supplying an asylum especially suited to a certain type of character ; and that vindictive and short-sighted revolution which is extirpating it from Europe is destroying one of the best correctives of the excessive industrialism of our age.   It is for the advantage of a nation that it should attain the most advanced existing type of progress, but it is extremely questionable whether it is for the advantage of the community at large that all nations should attain the same type, even when it is the most advanced. The influence of very various circumstances is absolutely necessary to perfect moral development. Hence, one of the great political advantages of class representation, which brings within the range of politics a far greater variety both of capacities and moral qualities than can be exhibited when one class has an exclusive or overwhelmingly preponderating influence, and also of heterogeneous empires, in which different degrees of civilisation produce different kinds of excellence which react upon and complete one another. In the rude work of India and Australia a type of character is formed which England could ill afford to lose.

The remarks I have now made will be sufficient, I hope, to throw some light upon those great questions concerning the relations of intellectual and moral progress which have of late years attracted so large an amount of attention. It has been contended that the historian of human progress should concentrate his attention exclusively on the intellectual elements; for there is no such thing as moral history, morals being essentially stationary, and the rudest barbarians being in this respect as far advanced as ourselves. In opposition to this view, I have maintained that while what may be termed the primal elements of morals are unaltered, there is a perpetual change in the standard which is exacted, and also in the relative value attached to particular virtues, and that these changes constitute one of the most important branches of general history. It has been contended by other writers that, although such changes do take place, and although they play an extremely great part in the world, they must be looked upon as the result of intellectual causes, changes in knowledge producing changes in morals. In this view, as we have seen, there is some truth, but it can only, I think, be accepted with great qualification. It is one of the plainest of facts that neither the individuals nor the ages most distinguished for intellectual achievements have been most distinguished for moral excellence, and that a high intellectual and material civilisation has often coexisted with much depravity. In some respects the conditions of intellectual growth are not favourable to moral growth. The agglomeration of men in great cities—which are always the centres of progress and enlightenment—is one of the most important causes of material and intellectual advance : but great towns are the peculiar seed-plots of vice, and it is extremely questionable whether they produce any special and equivalent efflorescence of virtue, for even the social virtues are probably more cultivated in small populations, where men live in more intimate relations. Many of the most splendid outbursts of moral enthusiasm may be traced to an overwhelming force of conviction rarely found in very culti-vated minds, which are keenly sensible to possibilities of error, conflicting arguments, and qualifying circumstances. Civilisation has on the whole been more successful in repress-ing crime than in repressing vice. It is very favourable to the gentler, charitable, and social virtues, and, where slavery does not exist, to the industrial virtues, and it is the especial nurse of the intellectual virtues ; but it is in general not equally favourable to the production of self-sacrifice, enthu-siasm, reverence, or chastity.

The moral changes, however, which are effected by civili-sation may ultimately be ascribed chiefly to intellectual causes, for these lie at the root of the whole structure of civilised life. Sometimes, as we have seen, intellectual causes act directly, but more frequently they have only an indirect in-fluence, producing habits of life which in their turn produce new conceptions of duty. The morals of men are more go-verned by their pursuits than by their opinions. A type of virtue is first formed by circumstances, and men afterwards make it the model upon which their theories are framed. Thus geographical or other circumstances, that make one nation military and another industrial, will produce in each a realised type of excellence, and corresponding conceptions about the relative importance of different virtues widely different from those which are produced in the other, and this may be the case although the amount of knowledge in the two communities is substantially equal.

Having discussed these questions as fully as the nature of my subject requires, I will conclude this chapter by noticing a few very prevalent errors in the moral judgments of history, and will also endeavour to elucidate some important consequences that may be deduced from the nature of moral types.

It is probable that the moral standard of most men is much lower in political judgments than in private matters in which their own interests are concerned. There is nothing more common than for men who in private life are models of the most scrupulous integrity to justify or excuse the most flagrant acts of political dishonesty and violence; and we should be altogether mistaken if we argued rigidly from such approvals to the general moral sentiments of those who utter them. Not unfrequently too, by a curious moral paradox, political crimes are closely connected with national virtues. A people who are submissive, gentle, and loyal, fall by reason of these very qualities under a despotic government; but this uncontrolled power has never failed to exercise a most pernicious influence on rulers, and their numerous acts of rapacity and aggression being attributed in history to the nation they represent, the national character is wholly misinterpreted.[1] There are also particular kinds both of virtue and of vice which appear prominently before the world, while others of at least equal influence almost escape the notice of history. Thus, for example, the sectarian animosities, the horrible persecutions, the blind hatred of progress, the ungenerous support of every galling disqualification and restraint, the intense class selfishness, the obstinately protracted defence of intellec-

---

[1] This has been, I think, especially the case with the Austrians.

tual and political superstition, the childish but whimsically ferocious quarrels about minute dogmatic distinctions, or dresses,
or candlesticks, which constitute together the main features of
ecclesiastical history, might naturally, though very unjustly,
lead men to place the ecclesiastical type in almost the lowest
rank, both intellectually and morally. These are, in fact, the
displays of ecclesiastical influence which stand in bold relief
in the pages of history. The civilising and moralising influence of the clergyman in his parish, the simple, unostentatious, unselfish zeal with which he educates the ignorant,
guides the erring, comforts the sorrowing, braves the horrors
of pestilence, and sheds a hallowing influence over the dying
hour, the countless ways in which, in his little sphere, he
allays evil passions, and softens manners, and elevates and
purifies those around him—all these things, though very evident to the detailed observer, do not stand out in the same
vivid prominence in historical records, and are continually
forgotten by historians. It is always hazardous to argue
from the character of a corporation to the character of the
members who compose it, but in no other case is this method
of judgment so fallacious as in the history of ecclesiastics, for
there is no other class whose distinctive excellences are less
apparent, and whose mental and moral defects are more
glaringly conspicuous in corporate action. In different nations,
again, the motives of virtue are widely different, and serious
misconceptions arise from the application to one nation of the
measure of another. Thus the chief national virtues of the
French people result from an intense power of sympathy,
which is also the foundation of some of their most beautiful
intellectual qualities, of their social habits, and of their unrivalled influence in Europe. No other nation has so habitual and vivid a sympathy with great struggles for freedom
beyond its border. No other literature exhibits so expansive
and œcumenical a genius, or expounds so skilfully, or appre-
ciates so generously, foreign ideas. In hardly any other land

would a disinterested war for the support of a suffering nationality find so large an amount of support. The national crimes of France are many and grievous, but much will be forgiven her because she loved much. The Anglo-Saxon nations, on the other hand, though sometimes roused to strong but transient enthusiasm, are habitually singularly narrow, unappreciative, and unsympathetic. The great source of their national virtue is the sense of duty, the power of pursuing a course which they believe to be right, independently of all considerations of sympathy or favour, of enthusiasm or success. Other nations have far surpassed them in many qualities that are beautiful, and in some qualities that are great. It is the merit of the Anglo-Saxon race that beyond all others it has produced men of the stamp of a Washington or a Hampden ; men careless, indeed, for glory, but very careful of honour; who made the supreme majesty of moral rectitude the guiding principle of their lives, who proved in the most trying circumstances that no allurements of ambition, and no storms of passion, could cause them to deviate one hair's breadth from the course they believed to be their duty. This was also a Roman characteristic—especially that of Marcus Aurelius. The unweary, unostentatious, and inglorious crusade of England against slavery may probably be regarded as among the three or four perfectly virtuous pages comprised in the history of nations.

Although it cannot be said that any virtue is the negation of another, it is undoubtedly true that virtues are naturally grouped according to principles of affinity or congruity, which are essential to the unity of the type. The heroical, the amiable, the industrial, the intellectual virtues form in this manner distinct groups ; and in some cases the development of one group is incompatible, not indeed with the existence, but with the prominence of others. Content cannot be the leading virtue in a society animated by an intense industrial spirit, nor submission nor tolerance of injuries in a society

formed upon a military type, nor intellectual virtues in a
society where a believing spirit is made the essential of goodness, yet each of these conditions is the special sphere of some
particular class of virtues.   The distinctive beauty of a moral
type depends not so much on the elements of which it is composed, as on the proportions in which those elements are
combined.   The characters of Socrates, of Cato, of Bayard,
of Fénelon, and of St. Francis are all beautiful, but they
differ generically, and not simply in degrees of excellence.
To endeavour to impart to Cato the distinctive charm of St.
Francis, or to St. Francis that of Cato, would be as absurd
as to endeavour to unite in a single statue the beauties of the
Apollo and the Laocoon, or in a single landscape the beauties
of the twilight and of the meridian sun.   Take away pride
from the ancient Stoic or the modern Englishman, and you
would have destroyed the basis of many of his noblest virtues, but humility was the very principle and root of the
moral qualities of the monk.   There is no quality virtuous
in a woman that is not also virtuous in a man, yet that
disposition or hierarchy of virtues which constitutes a perfect
woman would be wholly unsuited for a perfect man.   The
moral is in this respect like the physical type.   The beauty
of man is not the beauty of woman, nor the beauty of the
child as the beauty of the adult, nor the beauty of an Italian
as the beauty of an Englishwoman.   All types of character
are not good, as all types of countenance are not beautiful ;
but there are many distinct casts of goodness, as there are
many distinct casts of beauty.

This most important truth may be stated in a somewhat
different form.   Whenever a man is eminently deficient in
any virtue, it, of course, follows that his character is imperfect,
but it does not necessarily follow that he is not in other respects moral and virtuous.   There is, however, usually some
one virtue, which I may term rudimentary, which is brought
forward so prominently before the world, as the first condi-

tion of moral excellence, that it may be safely inferred that a
man who has absolutely neglected it is entirely indifferent to
moral culture.   Rudimentary virtues vary in different ages,
nations, and classes.   Thus, in the great republics of anti
quity patriotism was rudimentary, for it was so assiduously
cultivated, that it appeared at once the most obvious and the
most essential of duties.   Among ourselves much private
virtue may co-exist with complete indifference to national
interests.   In the monastic period, and in a somewhat different form in the age of chivalry, a spirit of reverential obedience was rudimentary, and the basis of all moral progress ;
but we may now frequently find a good man without it, his
moral energies having been cultivated in other directions.
Common truthfulness and honesty, as I have already said,
are rudimentary virtues in industrial societies, but not in
others.   Chastity, in England at least, is a rudimentary
female virtue, but scarcely a rudimentary virtue among men,
and it has not been in all ages, and is not now in all countries, rudimentary among women.   There is no more important task devolving upon a moral historian, than to discover
in each period the rudimentary virtue, for it regulates in a
great degree the position assigned to all others.

From the considerations I have urged, it will appear that
there is considerable danger in proposing too absolutely a
single character, however admirable, as the model to which
all men must necessarily conform.   A character may be
perfect in its own kind, but no character can possibly embrace all types of perfection ; for, as we have seen, the perfection of a type depends not only upon the virtues that
constitute it, but also upon the order and prominence assigned
to them.   All that can be expected in an ideal is, that it
should be perfect of its own kind, and should exhibit the
type most needed in its age, and most widely useful to mankind.   The Christian type is the glorification of the amiable,
as the Stoic type was that of the heroic qualities, and this is

one of the reasons why Christianity is so much more fitted than Stoicism to preside over civilisation, for the more society is organised and civilised, the greater is the scope for the amiable, and the less for the heroic qualities.

The history of that moral intolerance which endeavours to reduce all characters to a single type has never, I think, been examined as it deserves, and I shall frequently have occasion to advert to it in the following pages.   No one can have failed to observe how common it is for men to make their own tastes or excellences the measure of all goodness, pronouncing all that is broadly different from them to be imperfect or low, or of a secondary value.   And this, which is usually attributed to vanity, is probably in most cases much more due to feebleness of imagination, to the difficulty most men have in conceiving in their minds an order of character fundamentally different from their own.   A good man can usually sympathise much more with a very imperfect character of his own type than with a far more perfect one of a different type.   To this cause, quite as much as to historical causes or occasional divergences of interest, may be traced the extreme difficulty of effecting cordial international friendships, especially in those cases when a difference of race coincides with the difference of nationality.   Each nation has a distinct type of excellence, each esteems the virtues in which it excels, and in which its neighbours are often most deficient, incomparably the greatest.   Each regards with especial antipathy the vices from which it is most free, and to which its neighbours may be most addicted.   Hence arises a mingled feeling of contempt and dislike, from which the more enlightened minds are, indeed, soon emancipated, but which constitutes the popular sentiment.

The type of character of every individual depends partly upon innate temperament and partly upon external circumstances.   A warlike, a refined, an industrial society each evokes and requires its specific qualities, and produces its appropriate type. If a man of a different type arise—if, for example, a man formed by nature to exhibit to the highest perfection the virtues of gentleness or meekness, be born in the midst of a fierce military society—he will find no suitable scope for action, he will jar with his age, and his type will be regarded with disfavour. And the effect of this opposition is not simply that he will not be appreciated as he deserves, he will also never succeed in developing his own distinctive virtues as they would have been developed under other circumstances. Everything will be against him – the force of education, the habits of society, the opinions of mankind, even his own sense of duty. All the highest models of excellence about him being formed on a different type, his very efforts to improve his being will dull the qualities in which nature intended him to excel. If, on the other hand, a man with naturally heroic qualities be born in a society which pre-eminently values heroism, he will not only be more appreciated, he will also, under the concurrence of favourable circumstances, carry his heroism to a far higher point than would otherwise have been possible. Hence changing circumstances produce changing types, and hence, too, the possibility of moral history and the necessity of uniting it with general history. Religions, considered as moral teachers, are realised and effective only when their moral teaching is in conformity with the tendency of their age. If any part of it is not so, that part will be either openly abandoned, or refined away, or tacitly neglected. Among the ancients, the co-existence of the Epicurean and Stoical schools, which offered to the world two entirely different archetypes of virtue, secured in a very remarkable manner the recognition of different kinds of excellence ; for although each of these schools often attained a pre-eminence, neither ever succeeded in wholly destroying or discrediting the other.

Of the two elements that compose the moral condition of mankind, our generalised knowledge is almost restricted to

one. We know much of the ways in which political, social, or intellectual causes act upon character, but scarcely anything of the laws that govern innate disposition, of the reasons and extent of the natural moral diversities of individuals or races. I think, however, that most persons who reflect upon the subject will conclude that the progress of medicine, revealing the physical causes of different moral predispositions, is likely to place a very large measure of knowledge on this point within our reach. Of all the great branches of human knowledge, medicine is that in which the accomplished results are most obviously imperfect and provisional, in which the field of unrealised possibilities is most extensive, and from which, if the human mind were directed to it, as it has been during the past century to locomotive and other industrial inventions, the most splendid results might be expected. Our almost absolute ignorance of the causes of some of the most fatal diseases, and the empirical nature of nearly all our best medical treatment, have been often recognised. The medicine of inhalation is still in its infancy, and yet it is by inhalation that Nature produces most of her diseases, and effects most of her cures. The medical power of electricity, which of all known agencies bears most resemblance to life, is almost unexplored. The discovery of anæsthetics has in our own day opened out a field of inestimable importance, and the proved possibility, under certain physical conditions, of governing by external suggestions the whole current of the feelings and emotions, may possibly contribute yet further to the alleviation of suffering, and perhaps to that euthanasia which Bacon proposed to physicians as an end of their art. But in the eyes both of the philanthropist and of the philosopher, the greatest of all results to be expected in this, or perhaps any other field, are, I conceive, to be looked for in the study of the relations between our physical and our moral natures. He who raises moral pathology to a science, expanding, systema-

tising, and applying many fragmentary observations that
have been already made, will probably take a place among
the master intellects of mankind.   The fastings and bleed-
ings of the mediæval monk, the medicines for allaying or
stimulating the sensual passions, the treatment of nervous
diseases, the moral influences of insanity and of castration, the
researches of phrenology, the moral changes that accompany
the successive stages of physical developments, the instances
of diseases which have altered, sometimes permanently, the
whole complexion of the character, and have acted through
the character upon all the intellectual judgments,[1] are
examples of the kind of facts with which such a science
would deal.   Mind and body are so closely connected that
even those who most earnestly protest against materialism
readily admit that each acts continually upon the other.
The sudden emotion that quickens the pulse, and blanches or
flushes the cheek, and the effect of fear in predisposing to an
epidemic, are familiar instances of the action of the mind
upon the body, and the more powerful and permanent influence of the body upon the disposition is attested by countless observations.   It is probable that this action extends to
all parts of our moral constitution, that every passion or
characteristic tendency has a physical predisposing cause, and
that if we were acquainted with these, we might treat by
medicine the many varieties of moral disease as systematically
as we now treat physical disease.   In addition to its incalculable
practical importance, such knowledge would have a great
philosophical value, throwing a new light upon the filiation
of our moral qualities, enabling us to treat exhaustively the
moral influence of climate, and withdrawing the great question of the influence of race from the impressions of isolated
observers to place it on the firm basis of experiment.   It

---

[1] See some remarkable in-
stances of this in Cabanis, *Rap-*   *ports du Physique et du Moral de*
l'Homme.

would thus form the complement to the labours of the historian.

Such discoveries are, however, perhaps far from attainment, and their discussion does not fall within the compass of this work. My present object is simply to trace the action of external circumstances upon morals, to examine what have been the moral types proposed as ideal in different ages, in what degree they have been realised in practice, and by what causes they have been modified, impaired, or destroyed.

CHAPTER II.

THE PAGAN EMPIRE.

ONE of the first facts that must strike a student who examines the ethical teaching of the ancient civilisations is how imperfectly that teaching was represented, and how feebly it was influenced by the popular creed. The moral ideals had at no time been sought in the actions of the gods, and long before the triumph of Christianity, polytheism had ceased to have any great influence upon the more cultivated intellects of mankind.

In Greece we may trace from the earliest time the footsteps of a religion of nature, wholly different from the legends of the mythology. The language in which the first Greek dramatists asserted the supreme authority and universal providence of Zeus was so emphatic, that the Christian Fathers commonly attributed it either to direct inspiration or to a knowledge of the Jewish writings, while later theologians of the school of Cudworth have argued from it in favour of the original monotheism of our race. The philosophers were always either contemptuous or hostile to the prevailing legends. Pythagoras is said to have declared that he had seer. Hesiod tied to a brazen pillar in hell, and Homer hung upon a tree surrounded by serpents, on account of the fables they had invented about the gods.[1] Plato, for the same reason, banished the poets from his republic. Stilpo turned to

---

[1] Diog. Laërt. *Pythag.*

ridicule the whole system of sacrifices,[1] and was exiled from Athens for denying that the Athene of Phidias was a goddess.[2] Xenophanes remarked that each nation attributed to the gods its distinctive national type, the gods of the Æthiopians being black, the gods of the Thracians fair and blue-eyed.[3] Diagoras and Theodorus are said to have denied, and Protagoras to have questioned the existence of the gods,[4] while the Epicureans deemed them wholly indifferent to human affairs, and the Pyrrhonists pronounced our faculties absolutely incapable of attaining any sure knowledge, either human or divine. The Cynic Antisthenes said that there were many popular gods, but there was only one god of nature.[5] The Stoics, reproducing an opinion which was supported by Aristotle and attributed to Pythagoras,[6] believed in an all-pervading soul of nature, but unlike some modern schools which have adopted this view, they asserted in emphatic language the doctrine of Providence, and the self-consciousness of the Deity.

In the Roman republic and empire, a general scepticism had likewise arisen among the philosophers as the first fruit of intellectual development, and the educated classes were speedily divided between avowed or virtual atheists, like the Epicureans,[7] and pure theists, like the Stoics and the Platonists. The first, represented by such writers as Lucretius and Petronius, regarded the gods simply as the creations of fear, denied every form of Providence, attributed the world

---

[1] Plutarch, *De Profectibus in Virt.*

[2] Diog. Laërt. *Stilpo.*

[3] Clem. Alexand. *Strom.* vii.

[4] Cicero, *De Nat. Deorum,* i. 1.

[5] Lactant. *Inst. Div* i. 5.

[6] 'Pythagoras ita definivit quid esset Deus: Animus qui per universas mundi partes, omnemque naturam commeans atque diffusus, ex quo omnia quae nascuntur animalia vitam capiunt.' — Ibid.

Lactantius in this chapter has collected several other philosophic definitions of the Divinity. See too Plutarch, *De Placit. Philos.* Tertullian explains the stoical theory by an ingenious illustration: 'Stoici enim volunt Deum sic per materiem decucurrisse quomodo mel per favos.'—Tert. *De Anima.*

[7] As Cicero says: 'Epicurus re tollit, oratione relinquit, deos.'— *De Nat. Deor.* i. 44.

to a concurrence of atoms, and life to spontaneous generation, and regarded it as the chief end of philosophy to banish as illusions of the imagination every form of religious belief. The others formed a more or less pantheistic conception of the Deity, asserted the existence of a Providence,[1] but treated with great contempt the prevailing legends which they endeavoured in various ways to explain. The first systematic theory of explanation appears to have been that of the Sicilian Euhemerus, whose work was translated by Ennius. He pretended that the gods were originally kings, whose history and genealogies he professed to trace, and who after death had been deified by mankind.[2] Another attempt, which in the first period of Roman scepticism was more generally popular, was that of some of the Stoics, who regarded the gods as personifications of the different attributes of the Deity, or of different forces of nature. Thus Neptune was the sea, Pluto was fire, Hercules represented the strength of God, Minerva His wisdom, Ceres His fertilising energy.[3] More than a hundred years before the Empire, Varro had declared that 'the soul of the world is God, and that its parts are true divinities.'[4] Virgil and Manilius described, in lines of singular beauty, that universal spirit, the principle of all life, the efficient cause of all motion, which

---

[1] Sometimes, however, they restricted its operation to the great events of life. As an interlocutor in Cicero says : 'Magna dii curant, parva neg igunt.'—Cic. De Natur. Deor. ii. 66. Justin Martyr notices (Trypho, i.) that some philosophers maintained that God cared for the universal or species, but not for the individual. Seneca maintains that the Divinity has determined all things by an inexorable law of destiny, which He has decreed, but which He Himself obeys. (De Provident. v.)

[2] See on this theory Cicero. De Natur. Deor. i. 42 ; Lactantius, Inst. Div. i. 11.

[3] Diog. Laërt. Vit. Zeno. St. Aug. De Civ. Dei, iv. 11. Maximus of Tyre, Dissert. x. (in some editions xxix.) § 8. Seneca, De Beneficiis, iv. 7–8. Cic. De Natur. Deor. i. 15. Cicero has devoted the first two books of this work to the stoical theology. A full review of the allegorical and mythical interpretations of paganism is given by Eusebius, Evang. Præpar. lib. iii.

[4] St. Aug. De Civ. vii. 5.

permeates and animates the globe. Pliny said that 'the world and sky, in whose embrace all things are enclosed, must be deemed a god, eternal, immense, never begotten, and never to perish. To seek things beyond this is of no profit to man, and they transcend the limits of his faculties.'[1] Cicero had adopted the higher Platonic conception of the Deity as mind freed from all taint of matter,[2] while Seneca celebrated in magnificent language ' Jupiter the guardian and ruler of the universe, the soul and spirit, the lord and master of this mundane sphere, . . . the cause of causes; upon whom all things hang. . . . Whose wisdom oversees the world that it may move uncontrolled in its course, . . . from whom all things proceed, by whose spirit we live, . . . who comprises all we see.'[3]   Lucan, the great poet of stoicism, rose to a still higher strain, and to one which still more accurately expressed the sentiments of his school, when he described Jupiter as that majestic, all-pervasive spirit, whose throne is virtue and the universe.[4]   Quintilian defended the subjugation of the world beneath the sceptre of a single man, on the ground that it was an image of the government of God.   Other philosophers contented themselves with asserting the supreme authority of Jupiter Maximus, and reducing the other divinities to mere administrative and angelic functions, or, as the Platonists expressed it, to the position of dæmons.   According to some of the Stoics, a final catastrophe would consume the universe, the resuscitated spirits of men and all these minor gods, and the whole creation being absorbed into the great parent spirit, God

---

Plin. *Hist. Nat.* ii. 1.

'Nec vero Deus ipse qui intelligitur a nobis, alio modo intelligi potest nisi mens soluta quædam et libera, segregata ab omni concretione mortali, omnia sentiens et movens, ipsæque prædita motu sempiterno.'—*Tusc. Quæst.* i. 27.

[3] Senec. *Quæst. Nat.* ii. 45.

[4] ' Estne Dei sedes, nisi terra et pontus et aër,

Et cœlum et virtus? Superos quil quærimus ultra?

Jupiter est quodcumque vides, quodcumque moveris.'

Pharsal. ix. 578-80.

would be all in all. The very children and old women ridiculed Cerberus and the Furies[1] or treated them as mere
metaphors of conscience.[2] In the deism of Cicero the popular divinities were discarded, the oracles refuted and ridiculed,
the whole system of divination pronounced a political imposture, and the genesis of the miraculous traced to the exuberance of the imagination, and to certain diseases of the judgment.[3] Before the time of Constantine, numerous books
had been written against the oracles.[4] The greater number
of these had actually ceased, and the ablest writers justly
saw in this cessation an evidence of the declining credulity
of the people, and a proof that the oracles had been a fruit
of that credulity.[5] The Stoics, holding, as was their custom,
aloof from direct religious discussion, dissuaded their disciples from consulting them, on the ground that the gifts of
fortune were of no account, and that a good man should be
content with his conscience, making duty and not success the
object of his life.[6] Cato wondered that two augurs could

---

[1] 'Quæve anus tam excors in-
veniri potest, quæ illa, quæ quondam credebantur apud inferos por-
tenta, extimescat?'—Cic. De Nat.
Deor. ii. 2.
'Esse aliqu s Manes et subterranea
regna . . .
Nec pueri credunt nisi qui nondum
ære lavantur.'
    Juv. Sat. ii. 149, 152.
See on this subject a good review
by the Abbé Freppel, Les Pères Apo-
stoliques, leçon viii.

[2] Cicero, De Leg. i. 14; Macrobius, In. Som. Scip. i. 10.

[3] See his works De Divinatione
and De Nat. Deorum, which form
a curious contrast to the religious
conservatism of the De Legibus,
which was written chi fly from a
political point of view.

[4] Eusebius, Præp. Evang. lib. iv.

[5] The oracles first gave their
answers in verse, but their bad
poetry was ridiculed, and they
gradually sank to prose, and at
last ceased. Plutarch defended the
inspiration of the bad poetry on the
ground that the inspiring spirit
availed itself of the natural faculties
of the pries ess for the expression
of its infallible t uths—a theory
which is still much in vogue among
Biblic l critics, and is, I believe,
called dynamical inspiration. See
Fontenelle, Hist. des Oracles (1st
ed.), pp. 292–293.

[6] See the f mous description of
Cato refusing to consult the oracle
of Jupiter Ammon in Lucan, Phars.
ix.; and a so Arrian, ii. 7. Seneca
beautifully says, 'Vis deos pro
pitiare? bonus esto. Satis illos
coluit quisquis imitatus est.'—Ep.
xcv.

meet with gravity.[1] The Roman general Sertorius made the forgery of auspicious omens a continual resource in warfare.[2] The Roman wits made divination the favourite subject of their ridicule.[3] The denunciation which the early Greek moralists launched against the popular ascription of immoral deeds to the gods was echoed by a long series of later philosophers,[4] while Ovid made these fables the theme of his mocking *Metamorphoses*, and in his most immoral poem proposed Jupiter as a model of vice. With an irony not unlike that of Isaiah, Horace described the carpenter deliberating whether he should convert a shapeless log into a bench or into a god.[5] Cicero, Plutarch, Maximus of Tyre, and Dion Chrysostom either denounced idolatry or defended the use of images simply on the ground that they were signs and symbols of the Deity,[6] well suited to aid the devotions

---

[1] Cicero, *De Divin*. ii. 24.

[2] Aulus Gellius, *Noct. Att.* xv. 22.

[3] See a long string of witticisms collected by Legendre, *Traité de l'Opinion, ou Mémoires pour servir a l'Histoire de l'Esprit humain* (Venise, 1735), tome i. pp. 386–387.

[4] See Cicero, *De Natura Deorum*; Seneca, *De Brev. Vit.* c. xvi. ; Plin. *Hist. Nat.* ii. 5 ; Plutarch, *De Superstitione*.

[5] ' Olim truncus eram ficulnus, inutile lignum,
Cum faber, incertus scamnum faceretne Priapum,
Maluit esse Deum.'
Sat. I. viii. 1–3.

[6] There is a very curious discussion on this subject, reported to have taken place between Apollonius of Tyana and an Egyptian priest. The former defended the Greek fashion of worshipping the Divinity under the form of the human image, sculptured by Phidias and Praxiteles, this being the noblest form we can conceive, and therefore the least inadequate to the Divine perfections. The latter defended the Egyptian custom of worshipping animals, because, as he said, it is blasphemous to attempt to conceive an image of the Deity, and the Egyptians therefore concentrate the imagination of the worshipper on objects that are plainly merely allegorical or symbolical, and do not pretend to offer any such image (*Philos. Apoll. of Tyana*, vi. 19). Pliny shortly says, ' Effigiem Dei formamque quærere imbecillitatis humanæ reor' (*Hist. Nat.* ii. 5). See too Max. Tyrius. Diss. xxxviii. There was a legend that Numa forbade all idols, and that for 200 years they were unknown in Rome (Plutarch, *Life of Numa*). Dion Chrysostom said that the Gods need no statues or sacrifices, but that by these means we attest our devotion to them (*Orat.* xxxi.) On the vanity of rich idols see Plutarch, *De Superstitione*; Seneca, *Ep.* xxxi.

of the ignorant. Seneca[1] and the whole school of Pythagoras objected to the sacrifices.

These examples will be sufficient to show how widely the
philosophic classes in Rome were removed from the professed
religion of the State, and how necessary it is to seek elsewhere the sources of their moral life. But the opinions of
learned men never reflect faithfully those of the vulgar,
and the chasm between the two classes was even wider than
at present before the dawn of Christianity and the invention
of printing. The atheistic enthusiasm of Lucretius and the
sceptical enthusiasm of some of the disciples of Carneades
were isolated phenomena, and the great majority of the
ancient philosophers, while speculating with the utmost
freedom in private, or in writings that were read by the few,
countenanced, practised, and even defended the religious
rites that they despised. It was believed that many different
paths adapted to different nations and grades of knowledge
converge to the same Divinity, and that the most erroneous
religion is good if it forms good dispositions and inspires
virtuous actions. The oracle of Delphi had said that the
best religion is that of a man's own city. Polybius and
Dionysius of Halicarnassus, who regarded all religions
simply as political agencies, dilated in rapturous terms upon
the devotion of the Romans and the comparative purity of
their creed.[2] Varro openly professed the belief that there
are religious truths which it is expedient that the people
should not know, and falsehoods which they should believe to
be true.[3] The Academic Cicero and the Epicurean Cæsar were
both high officers of religion. The Stoics taught that
every man should duly perform the religious ceremonies of
his country.[4]

But the Roman religion, even in its best days, though an

---

[1] Lact. *Inst. Div.* vi. 25.

[2] Dion. Halic. ii.; Polyb. vi. 56.

[3] St. Aug. *De Civ. Dei*, iv. 31.

[4] Epictetus, *Enchir.* xxxix.

admirable system of moral discipline, was never an independent source of moral enthusiasm. It was the creature of
the State, and derived its inspiration from political feeling.
The Roman gods were not, like those of the Greeks, the
creations of an unbridled and irreverent fancy, nor, like
those of the Egyptians, representations of the forces of nature ;
they were for the most part simple allegories, frigid personifications of different virtues, or presiding spirits imagined
for the protection of different departments of industry.   The
religion established the sanctity of an oath, it gave a kind of
official consecration to certain virtues, and commemorated
special instances in which they had been displayed ; its local
character strengthened patriotic feeling, its worship of the
dead fostered a vague belief in the immortality of the soul,[1]
it sustained the supremacy of the father in the family, surrounded marriage with many imposing solemnities, and
created simple and reverent characters profoundly submissive
to an over-ruling Providence and scrupulously observant of
sacred rites.   But with all this it was purely selfish. It was
simply a method of obtaining prosperity, averting calamity,
and reading the future. Ancient Rome produced many
heroes, but no saint. Its self-sacrifice was patriotic, not religious. Its religion was neither an independent teacher nor
a source of inspiration, although its rites mingled with and
strengthened some of the best habits of the people.

But these habits, and the religious reverence with which
they were connected, soon disappeared amid the immorality
and decomposition that marked the closing years of the Republic and the dawn of the Empire. The stern simplicity of life,
which the censors had so zealously and often so tyrannically

---

[1] Cicero, speaking of the worship
of deified men, says, 'indicat omnium quidem animos immortales
esse, sed fortium bonorumque
divinos.' — De Leg. ii. 11.   The
Roman worship of the dead, which
was the centre of the domestic
religion, has been recently investigated with much ability by M.
Coulanges (La Cité antique)

enforced,[1] was exchanged for a luxury which first appeared after the return of the army of Manlius from Asia,[2] increased to immense proportions after the almost simultaneous conquests of Carthage, Corinth, and Macedonia,[3] received an additional stimulus from the example of Antony,[4] and at last, under the Empire, rose to excesses which the wildest Oriental orgies have never surpassed.[5] The complete subversion of the social and political system of the Republic, the anarchy of civil war, the ever-increasing concourse of strangers, bringing with them new philosophies, customs, and gods, had dissolved or effaced all the old bonds of virtue. The simple juxtaposition of many forms of worship effected what could not have been effected by the most sceptical literature or the most audacious philosophy. The moral influence of religion was almost annihilated. The feeling of reverence was almost extinct. Augustus solemnly degraded the statue of Neptune because his fleet had been wrecked.[6] When Germanicus died, the populace stoned or overthrew the altars of the gods.[7] The idea of sanctity was so far removed from the popular divinities that it became a continual complaint that prayers were offered which the most depraved would blush to pronounce aloud.[8] Amid the corruption of the Empire, we meet with many noble efforts of reform made by philosophers or by emperors, but we find

[1] On the minute supervision exercised by the censors on all the details of domestic life, see Aul. Gell. Noct. ii. 24 ; iv. 12, 20.

[2] Livy, xxxix. 6.

[3] Vell. Paterculus, i. 11–13 ; Eutropius, iv 6. Sallust ascribed the decadence of Rome to the destruction of its rival, Carthage.

[4] Plutarch, De Adulatore et Amico.

[5] There is much curious information about the growth of Roman luxury in Pliny (Hist. Nat. lib.

xxxiv.). The movement of decomposition has been lately fully traced by Mommsen (Hist. of Rome); Döllinger (Jew and Gentile); Denis (Hist. des Idées morales dans l'Antiquité) ; Pressensé (Hist. des trois premiers Siècles); in the histories of Champagny, and in the beautiful closing chapters of the Apôtres of Renan.

[6] Sueton. Aug. xvi.

[7] Ibid. Calig. v.

[8] Persius, Sat. ii.; Horace, Ep. i. 16, vv. 57–60.

scarcely a trace of the moral influence of the old religion. The
apotheosis of the emperors consummated its degradation. The
foreign gods were identified with those of Rome, and all
their immoral legends associated with the national creed.[1]
The theatre greatly extended the area of scepticism. Cicero
mentions the assenting plaudits with which the people heard
the lines of Ennius, declaring that the gods, though real
beings, take no care for the things of man.[2] Plutarch tells
of a spectator at a theatre rising up with indignation after a
recital of the crimes of Diana, and exclaiming to the actor.
'May you have a daughter like her whom you have described!'[3] St. Augustine and other of the Fathers long after
ridiculed the pagans who satirised in the theatres the very
gods they worshipped in the temples.[4]   Men were still
profoundly superstitious, but they resorted to each new religion as to a charm or talisman of especial power, or a system of magic revealing the future.   There existed, too, to a
very large extent, a kind of superstitious scepticism which
occupies a very prominent place in religious history.   There
were multitudes who, declaring that there were no gods, or
that the gods never interfered with human affairs, professed
with the same breath an absolute faith in all portents,
auguries, dreams, and miracles. Innumerable natural objects,
such as comets, meteors, earthquakes, or monstrous births,
were supposed to possess a kind of occult or magical virtue,
by which they foreshadowed, and in some cases influenced,

[1] See, on the identification of
the Greek and Egyptian myths,
Plutarch's De Iside et Osiride. The
Greek and Roman gods were habi-
tually regarded as identical, and
Cæsar and Tacitus, in like manner,
identified the deities of Gaul and
Germany with those of their own
country. See Döllinger, Jew and
Gentile, vol ii. pp. 160-165.

[2] 'Ego deûm genus esse semper
dixi et dicam cœlitum;
Sed eos non curare opinor quid agat
hominum genus.'
Cicero adds: 'magno plausu lo-
quitur assentiente populo.' — De
Divin. ii. 50.
[3] Plutarch, De Superstitione.
[4] St. Aug. De Civ. Dei, vi. 6;
Tertul. Apol. 15; Arnobius, Adv.
Gentes, iv.

the destinies of men. Astrology, which is the special representative of this mode of thought, rose to great prominence.
The elder Pliny notices that in his time a belief was rapidly
gaining ground, both among the learned and among the vulgar, that the whole destiny of man is determined by the star that
presides over his nativity; that God, having ordained this,
never interferes with human affairs, and that the reality
of the portents is due to this pre-ordainment.[1] One of the
later historians of the Empire remarks that numbers who
denied the existence of any divinity believed nevertheless
that they could not safely appear in public, or eat or bathe,
unless they had first carefully consulted the almanac to
ascertain the position of the planet Mercury, or how far the
moon was from the Crab.[2] Except, perhaps, among the peasants in the country districts, the Roman religion, in the
last years of the Republic, and in the first century of the
Empire, scarcely existed, except in the state of a superstition,
and he who would examine the true moral influence of the
time must turn to the great schools of philosophy which had
been imported from Greece.

The vast place which the rival systems of Zeno and Epicurus occupy in the moral history of mankind, and especially in the closing years of the empire of paganism, may

---

[1] 'Pars alia et hanc pellit, as-
troque suo eventus assignat,
nascendi legibus; semelque in
omnes futuros unquam Deo decretum; in reliquum vero otium
datum. Sedere cœpit sententia
hæc pariterque et eruditum vulgus
et rude in eam cursu vadit. Ecce
fulgurum monitus, oraculorum
præscita, aruspicum prædicta,
atque etiam parva dictu, in auguriis
sternumenta et offensiones pedum.'
—Hist. Nat. ii. 5. Pliny himself
expresses great doubt about astrology giving many examples of men
with different destinies. who had
been born at the same time, and
therefore under the same stars (vii.
50). Tacitus expresses complete
doubt about the existence of Providence. (Ann. vi. 22.) Tiberius is
said to have been very indifferent
to the gods and to the worship of
the temples, being wholly addicted
to astrology and convinced that all
things were pre-ordained. (Suet.
Tib. lxix.)

[2] Ammianus Marcellinus, xxviii.
4.

easily lead us to exaggerate the creative genius of their founders, who, in fact, did little more than give definitions or intellectual expression to types of excellence that had at all times existed in the world.   There have ever been stern, upright, self-controlled, and courageous men, actuated by a pure sense of duty, capable of high efforts of self-sacrifice, somewhat intolerant of the frailties of others, somewhat hard and unsympathising in the ordinary intercourse of society, but rising to heroic grandeur as the storm lowered upon their path, and more ready to relinquish life than the cause they believed to be true.   There have also always been men of easy tempers and of amiable disposition, gentle, benevolent, and pliant, cordial friends and forgiving enemies, selfish at heart, yet ever ready, when it is possible, to unite their gratifications with those of others, averse to all enthusiasm, mysticism, utopias, and superstition, with little depth of character or capacity for self-sacrifice, but admirably fitted to impart and to receive enjoyment, and to render the course of life easy and harmonious.   The first are by nature Stoics, and the second Epicureans, and if they proceed to reason about the *summum bonum* or the affections, it is more than probable that in each case their characters will determine their theories.   The first will estimate self-control above all other qualities, will disparage the affections, and will endeavour to separate widely the ideas of duty and of interest, while the second will systematically prefer the amiable to the heroic, and the utilitarian to the mystical.

But while it is undoubtedly true that in these matters character usually determines opinion, it is not less true that character is itself in a great measure governed by national circumstances.   The refined, artistic, sensual civilisations of Greece and Asia Minor might easily produce fine examples of the Epicurean type, but Rome was from the earliest times pre-eminently the home of stoicism.   Long before the Romans had begun to reason about philosophy, they had exhibited it in action, and in their speculative days it was to this doctrine that the noblest minds naturally tended. A great nation engaged in perpetual wars in an age when success in warfare depended neither upon wealth nor upon mechanical genius, but upon the constant energy of patriotic enthusiasm, and upon the unflinching maintenance of military discipline, the whole force of the national character tended to the production of a single definite type. In the absolute authority accorded to the father over the children, to the husband over the wife, to the master over the slave, we may trace the same habits of discipline that proved so formidable in the field. Patriotism and military honour were indissolubly connected in the Roman mind. They were the two sources of national enthusiasm, the chief ingredients of the national conception of greatness. They determined irresistibly the moral theory which was to prove supreme.

Now war, which brings with it so many demoralising influences, has, at least, always been the great school of heroism. It teaches men how to die. It familiarises the mind with the idea of noble actions performed under the influence, not of personal interest, but of honour and of enthusiasm. It elicits in the highest degree strength of character, accustoms men to the abnegation needed for simultaneous action, compels them to repress their fears, and establish a firm control over their affections. Patriotism, too, leads them to subordinate their personal wishes to the interests of the society in which they live. It extends the horizon of life, teaching men to dwell among the great men of the past, to derive their moral strength from the study of heroic lives, to look forward continually, through the vistas of a distant future, to the welfare of an organisation which will continue when they have passed away. All these influences were developed in Roman life to a degree which can now never be reproduced. War, for the reasons I have stated, was far more than at present the school of heroic virtues. Patriotism, in the absence of any strong theological passion, had assumed a transcendent power. The citizen, passing continually from political to military life, exhibited to perfection the moral effects of both. The habits of command formed by a long period of almost universal empire, and by the aristocratic organisation of the city, contributed to the elevation, and also to the pride, of the national character.

It will appear, I think, sufficiently evident, from these considerations, that the circumstances of the Roman people tended inevitably to the production of a certain type of character, which, in its essential characteristics, was the type of stoicism. In addition to the predisposition which leads men in their estimate of the comparative excellence of different qualities to select for the highest eulogy those which are most congruous to their own characters, this fact derives a great importance from the large place which the biographical element occupied in ancient ethical teaching. Among Christians the ideals have commonly been either supernatural beings or men who were in constant connection with supernatural beings, and these men have usually been either Jews or saints, whose lives were of such a nature as to isolate them from most human sympathies, and to efface as far as possible the national type. Among the Greeks and Romans the examples of virtue were usually their own fellow-countrymen; men who had lived in the same moral atmosphere, struggled for the same ends, acquired their reputation in the same spheres, exhibited in all their intensity the same national characteristics as their admirers. History had assumed a didactic character it has now almost wholly lost. One of the first tasks of every moralist was to collect traits of character illustrating the precepts he enforced. Valerius Maximus represented faithfully the method of the teachers of antiquity when he wrote his book giving a catalogue of different moral qualities, and illustrating each by a profusion of examples derived from the history of his own or of foreign nations.

'Whenever,' said Plutarch, 'we begin an enterprise, or take possession of a charge, or experience a calamity, we place before our eyes the example of the greatest men of our own or of bygone ages, and we ask ourselves how Plato or Epaminondas, Lycurgus or Agesilaus, would have acted. Looking into these personages as into a faithful mirror, we can remedy our defects in word or deed. . . . Whenever any perplexity arrives, or any passion disturbs the mind, the student of philosophy pictures to himself some of those who have been celebrated for their virtue, and the recollection sustains his tottering steps and prevents his fall.'[1]

Passages of this kind continually occur in the ancient moralists,[2] and they show how naturally the highest type of national excellence determined the prevailing school of moral philosophy, and also how the influence of the heroic period of national history would act upon the best minds in the subsequent and wholly different phases of development. It was therefore not surprising that during the Empire, though the conditions of national life were profoundly altered, Stoicism should still be the philosophical religion, the great source and regulator of moral enthusiasm. Epicureanism had, indeed, spread widely in the Empire,[3] but it proved little more than a principle of disintegration or an apology for vice, or at best the religion of tranquil and indifferent natures animated by no strong moral enthusiasm. It is indeed true that Epicurus had himself been a man of the most blameless character, that his doctrines were at first carefully distinguished from the coarse sensuality of the Cyrenaic school which had preceded them, that they admitted in theory almost every form of virtue, and that the school had produced

---

[1] *De Profectibus in Virt.* It was originally the custom at Roman feasts to sing to a pipe the actions and the virtues of the greatest men. (Cic. *Tusc. Quæst.* iv.)

[2] E.g. Epictetus, *Ench.* lii.

Seneca is full of similar exhortations.

[3] According to Cicero, the first Latin work on philosophy was by the Epicurean Amafanius. (*Tusc. Quæst.* iv.)

many disciples who, if they had not attained the highest
grades of excellence, had at least been men of harmless lives,
intensely devoted to their master, and especially noted for
the warmth and constancy of their friendships.[1] But a
school which placed so high a value on ease and pleasure was
eminently unfit to struggle against the fearful difficulties that
beset the teachers of virtue amid the anarchy of a military
despotism, and the virtues and the vices of the Romans were
alike fatal to its success.   All the great ideals of Roman excellence belonged to a different type.   Such men as a Decius
or a Regulus would have been impossible in an Epicurean
society, for even if their actuating emotion were no nobler than
a desire for posthumous fame, such a desire could never grow
powerful in a moral atmosphere charged with the shrewd,
placid, unsentimental utilitarianism of Epicurus.   On the
other hand, the distinctions the Epicureans had drawn between more or less refined pleasures and their elevated
conceptions of what constitutes the true happiness of men,
were unintelligible to the Romans, who knew how to sacri·

---

[1] See on the great perfection of
the character of Epicurus his life
by Diogenes Laërtius, and on the
purity of the philosophy he taught
and the degree in which it was distorted and misrepresented by his
Roman followers. Seneca *De Vita
Beata*, c. xii. xiii. and *Ep.* xxi.
Gassendi, in a very interesting little
work entitled *Philosophiæ Epicuri
Syntagma*, has abundantly proved
the possibility of uniting Epicurean
principles with a high code of
morals.   But probably the most
beautiful picture of the Epicurean
system is the first book of the *De
Finibus*, in which Cicero endeavours
to paint it as it would have been
painted by its adherents.   When
we remember that the writer of
this book was one of the most
formidable and unflinching opponents of Epicureanism in all the
ancient world, it must be owned
that it would be impossible to find
a grander example of that noble
love of truth, that sublime and
scrupulous justice to opponents,
which was the pre-eminent glory of
ancient philosophers, and which,
after the destruction of philosophy,
was for many centuries almost unknown in the world.   It is impossible to doubt that Epicureanism
was logically compatible with a very
high degree of virtue.   It is, I
think, equally impossible to doubt
that its practical tendency was towards vice.

fice enjoyment, but who, when pursuing it, gravitated
naturally to the coarsest forms. The mission of Epicureanism was therefore chiefly negative. The anti-patriotic tendency
of its teaching contributed to that destruction of national
feeling which was necessary to the rise of cosmopolitanism,
while its strong opposition to theological beliefs, supported by
the genius and enthusiasm of Lucretius, told powerfully upon
the decaying faith.

Such being the functions of Epicureanism, the construc-
tive or positive side of ethical teaching devolved almost
exclusively upon Stoicism; for although there were a few
philosophers who expressed themselves in strong opposition to
some portions of the Stoical system, their efforts usually
tended to no more than a modification of its extreme and
harshest features. The Stoics asserted two cardinal principles
—that virtue was the sole legitimate object to be aspired to,
and that it involved so complete an ascendancy of the reason
as altogether to extinguish the affections. The Peripatetics
and many other philosophers, who derived their opinions
chiefly from Plato, endeavoured to soften down the exaggeration of these principles. They admitted that virtue was
an object wholly distinct from interest, and that it should be
the leading motive of life; but they maintained that happiness was also a good, and a certain regard for it legitimate.
They admitted that virtue consisted in the supremacy of the
reason over the affections, but they allowed the exercise of
the latter within restricted limits. The main distinguishing
features, however, of Stoicism, the unselfish ideal and the
controlling reason, were acquiesced in, and each represents
an important side of the ancient conception of excellence
which we must now proceed to examine.

In the first we may easily trace the intellectual expression
of the high spirit of self-sacrifice which the patriotic enthusiasm had elicited. The spirit of patriotism has this peculiar characteristic, that, while it has evoked acts of heroism

which are both very numerous and very sublime, it has done
so without presenting any prospect of personal immortality
as a reward. Of all the forms of human heroism, it is probably the most unselfish. The Spartan and the Roman died
for his country because he loved it. The martyr's ecstasy of
hope had no place in his dying hour. He gave up all he
had, he closed his eyes, as he believed, for ever, and he asked
for no reward in this world or in the next. Even the hope
of posthumous fame—the most refined and supersensual of
all that can be called reward—could exist only for the most
conspicuous leaders. It was examples of this nature that
formed the culminations or ideals of ancient systems of
virtue, and they naturally led men to draw a very clear and
deep distinction between the notions of interest and of duty.
It may, indeed, be truly said, that while the conception of
what constituted duty was often very imperfect in antiquity,
the conviction that duty, as distinguished from every modification of selfishness, should be the supreme motive of life
was more clearly enforced among the Stoics than in any later
society.

The reader will probably have gathered from the last
chapter that there are four distinct motives which moral
teachers may propose for the purpose of leading men to
virtue. They may argue that the disposition of events is
such that prosperity will attend a virtuous life, and adversity a vicious one—a proposition they may prove by pointing
to the normal course of affairs, and by asserting the existence
of a special Providence in behalf of the good in the present
world, and of rewards and punishments in the future. As
far as these latter arguments are concerned, the efficacy of
such teaching rests upon the firmness with which certain
theological tenets are held, while the force of the first considerations will depend upon the degree and manner in
which society is organised, for there are undoubtedly some
conditions of society in which a perfectly upright life has

not even a general tendency to prosperity. The peculiar circumstances and dispositions of individuals will also influence largely the way in which they receive such teaching, and, as Cicero observed, 'what one utility has created, another will often destroy.'

They may argue, again, that vice is to the mind what disease is to the body, and that a state of virtue is in consequence a state of health. Just as bodily health is desired for its own sake, as being the absence of a painful, or at least displeasing state, so a well-ordered and virtuous mind may be valued for its own sake, and independently of all the external good to which it may lead, as being a condition of happiness; and a mind distracted by passion and vice may be avoided, not so much because it is an obstacle in the pursuit of prosperity, as because it is in itself essentially painful and disturbing. This conception of virtue and vice as states of health or sickness, the one being in itself a good and the other in itself an evil, was a fundamental proposition in the ethics of Plato.[1] It was admitted, but only to a subsidiary place, by the Stoics,[2] and has passed more or less

---

[1] Mr. Grote gives the following very clear summary of Plato's ethical theory, which he believes to be original:—'Justice is in the mind a condition analogous to good health and strength in the body. Injustice is a condition analogous to sickness, corruption, impotence in the body. . . . To possess a healthy body is desirable for its consequences as a means towards other constituents of happiness, but it is still more desirable in itself as an essential element of happiness *per se*, i.e., the negation of sickness, which would of itself make us miserable. . . . In like manner, the just mind blesses the possessor twice: first and chiefly by bringing to him happiness in itself; next, also, as it leads to ulterior happy results. The unjust mind is a curse to its possessor in itself and apart from results, though it also leads to ulterior results which render it still more a curse to him.'—Grote's *Plato*, vol. iii p. 131. According to Plutarch, Aristo of Chio defined virtue as 'the health of the soul.' (*De Virtute Morali.*)

[2] 'Beata est ergo vita conveniens naturæ suæ; quæ non aliter contingere potest quam si primum sana mens est et in perpetuâ possessione sanitatis suæ.'—Seneca, *De Vita Beata*, c. iii.

into all the succeeding systems. It is especially favourable to large and elevating conceptions of self-culture, for it leads men to dwell much less upon isolated acts of virtue or vice than upon the habitual condition of mind from which they spring.

It is possible, in the third place, to argue in favour of virtue by offering as a motive that sense of pleasure which follows the deliberate performance of a virtuous act. This emotion is a distinct and isolated gratification following a distinct action, and may therefore be easily separated from that habitual placidity of temper which results from the extinction of vicious and perturbing impulses. It is this theory which is implied in the common exhortations to enjoy 'the luxury of doing good,' and though especially strong in acts of benevolence, in which case sympathy with the happiness created intensifies the feeling, this pleasure attends every kind of virtue.

These three motives of action have all this common characteristic, that they point as their ultimate end to the happiness of the agent. The first seeks that happiness in external circumstances; the second and third in psychological conditions. There is, however, a fourth kind of motive which may be urged, and which is the peculiar characteristic of the intuitive school of moralists and the stumbling-block of its opponents. It is asserted that we are so constituted that the notion of duty furnishes in itself a natural motive of action of the highest order, wholly distinct from all the refinements and modifications of self-interest. The coactive force of this motive is altogether independent of surrounding circumstances, and of all forms of belief. It is equally true for the man who believes and for the man who rejects the Christian faith, for the believer in a future world and for the believer in the mortality of the soul. It is not a question of happiness or unhappiness, of reward or punishment, but of a generically different nature. Men feel that a certain course of life is the natural end of their being, and they feel bound, even at the expense of happiness, to pursue it. They feel that certain acts are essentially good and noble, and others essentially base and vile, and this perception leads them to pursue the one and to avoid the other, irrespective of all considerations of enjoyment.

I have recurred to these distinctions, which were more fully discussed in the last chapter, because the school of philosophy we are reviewing furnishes the most perfect of all historical examples of the power which the higher of these motives can exercise over the mind. The coarser forms of self-interest were in stoicism absolutely condemned. It was one of the first principles of these philosophers that all things that are not in our power should be esteemed indifferent; that the object of all mental discipline should be to withdraw the mind from all the gifts of fortune, and that prudence must in consequence be altogether excluded from the motives of virtue. To enforce these principles they continually dilated upon the vanity of human things, and upon the majesty of the independent mind, and they indulged, though scarcely more than other sects, in many exaggerations about the impassive tranquillity of the sage.[1] In the Roman empire stoicism flourished at a period which, beyond almost any other, seemed unfavourable to such teaching. There were reigns when, in the emphatic words of Tacitus, 'virtue was a sentence of death.' In no period had brute force more completely triumphed, in none was the thirst for material advantages more intense, in very few was vice more ostentatiously glorified. Yet in the midst of all these circumstances the Stoics taught a philosophy which was not a compromise, or an attempt to moderate the popular excesses, but which

---

[1] The famous paradox that 'the sage could be happy even in the bull of Phalaris,' comes from the writings not of Zeno but of Epicurus —though the Stoics adopted and greatly admired it. (Cic. *Tusc.* ii. See Gassendi, *Philos. Epicuri Syntagma*, pars iii. c. 1.)

was rather in its austere sanctity the extreme antithesis of all that the prevailing examples and their own interests could dictate. And these men were no impassioned fanatics, fired with the prospect of coming glory. They were men from whose motives of action the belief in the immortality of the soul was resolutely excluded. In the scepticism that accompanied the first introduction of philosophy into Rome, in the dissolution of the old fables about Tartarus and the Styx, and the dissemination of Epicureanism among the people, this doctrine had sunk very low, notwithstanding the beautiful reasonings of Cicero and the religious faith of a few who clung like Plutarch to the mysteries in which it was perpetuated. An interlocutor in Cicero expressed what was probably a common feeling when he acknowledged that, with the writings of Plato before him, he could believe and realise it; but when he closed the book, the reasonings seemed to lose their power, and the world of spirits grew pale and unreal.[1] If Ennius could elicit the plaudits of a theatre when he proclaimed that the gods took no part in human affairs, Cæsar could assert in the senate, without scandal and almost without dissent, that death was the end of all things.[2] Pliny, perhaps the greatest of Roman scholars, adopting the sentiment of all the school of Epicurus, describes the belief in a future life as a form of madness, a puerile and a pernicious illusion.[3] The opinions of the Stoics were wavering and uncertain. Their first doctrine was that the soul of man has a future and independent, b it not

---

[1] 'Sed nescio quomodo dum lego assentior; cum posui librum et mecum ipse de immortalitate animorum cœpi cogitare, assensio omnis illa elabitur.'—Cic. *Tusc.* i.

[2] Sallust, *Catilina*, cap. li.

[3] See that most impressive passage (*Hist. Nat.* vii. 56). That the sleep of annihilation is the happiest end of man is a favourite thought of Lucretius. Thus:

' Nil igitur mors est, ad nos neque pertinet hilum,
Quandoquidem natura animi mortalis habetur.'—iii. 842.

This mode of thought has been recently expressed in Mr. Swinburne's very beautiful poem on *The Garden of Proserpine.*

an eternal existence, that it survives until the last conflagration which was to destroy the world, and absorb all finite
things into the all-pervading soul of nature. Chrysippus,
however, restricted to the best and noblest souls this future
existence, which Cleanthes had awarded to all,[1] and among the
Roman Stoics even this was greatly doubted. The belief
that the human soul is a detached fragment of the Deity
naturally led to the belief that after death it would be
reabsorbed into the parent Spirit. The doctrine that there is
no real good but virtue deprived the Stoics of the argument
for a future world derived from unrequited merit and unpunished crime, and the earnestness with which they contended
that a good man should act irrespectively of reward inclined
them, as it is said to have inclined some Jewish thinkers,[2] to
the denial of the existence of the reward.[3] Panætius, the
founder of Roman stoicism, maintained that the soul perished
with the body,[4] and his opinion was followed by Epictetus,[5]
and Cornutus.[6] Seneca contradicted himself on the subject.[7]

---

[1] Diog. Laërtius. The opinion
of Chrysippus seems to have prevailed, and Plutarch (*De Placit.
Philos.*) speaks of it as that of the
school. Cicero sarcastically says,
'Stoici autem usuram nobis lar-
giuntur, tanquam cornicibus: diu
mansuros aiunt animos; semper,
negant.'—*Tusc. Disp.* i. 31.

[2] It has been very frequently asserted that Antigonus of Socho
having taught that virtue should
be practised for its own sake, his
disciple, Zadok, the founder of the
Sadducees, inferred the non-existence of a future world; but the
evidence for this whole story is
exceedingly unsatisfactory. The
reader may find its history in a
very remarkable article by Mr.
Twisleton on *Sadducees*, in Smith's
Biblical Dictionary.

[3] On the Stoical opinions about
a future life see Martin, *La Vie
future* (Paris, 1858); Courdaveaux
*De l'immortalité de l'âme dans le
Stoïcisme* (Paris, 1857); and Alger's
*Critical Hist. of the Doctrine of a
Future Life* (New York, 1866).

[4] His arguments are met by
Cicero in the *Tusculans*.

[5] See a collection of passages
from his discourses collected by M.
Courdaveaux, in the introduction to
his French translation of that book.

[6] Stobæus, *Eclog. Physic.* lib. i.
cap. 52.

[7] In his consolations to Marcia,
he seems to incline to a belief in
the immortality, or at least the
future existence, of the soul. In
many other passages, however, he
speaks of it as annihilated at
death.

Marcus Aurelius never rose beyond a vague and mournful aspiration. Those who believed in a future world believed in it faintly and uncertainly, and even when they accepted it as a fact, they shrank from proposing it as a motive. The whole system of Stoical ethics, which carried self-sacrifice to a point that has scarcely been equalled, and exercised an influence which has rarely been surpassed, was evolved without any assistance from the doctrine of a future life.[1] Pagan antiquity has bequeathed us few nobler treatises of morals than the 'De Officiis' of Cicero, which was avowedly an expansion of a work of Panætius.[2] It has left us no grander example than that of Epictetus, the sickly, deformed slave of a master who was notorious for his barbarity, enfranchised late in life, but soon driven into exile by Domitian; who, while sounding the very abyss of human misery, and looking forward to death as to simple decomposition, was yet so filled with the sense of the Divine presence that his life was one continued hymn to Providence, and his writings and his example, which appeared to his contemporaries almost the ideal of human goodness, have not lost their consoling power through all the ages and the vicissitudes they have survived.[3]

---

[1] 'Les Stoïciens ne faisaient aucunement dépendre la morale de la perspective des peines ou de la rémunération dans une vie future. . . . La croyance à l'immortalité de l'âme n'appartenait donc, selon leur manière de voir, qu'à la physique, c'est-à-dire à la psychologie.' —Degerando. *Hist. de la Philos.* tome iii. p. 56.

[2] 'Panætius igitur, qui sine controversia de officiis accuratissime disputavit, quemque nos, correctione quadam adhibita, potissimum secuti sumus.'—*De Offic.* iii. 2.

[3] Marcus Aurelius thanks Providence, as for one of the great blessings of his life, that he had been made acquainted with the writings of Epictetus. The story is well known how the old philosopher warned his master, who was beating him, that he would soon break his leg, and when the leg was broken, calmly remarked, 'I told you you would do so.' Celsus quoted this in opposition to the Christians, asking, 'Did your leader under suffering ever say anything so noble?' Origen finely replied, 'He did what was still nobler—He kept silence.' A Christian anchorite (some say St. Nilus, who lived in the beginning of the fifth century)

There was, however, another form of immortality which exercised a much greater influence among the Roman moralists. The desire for reputation, and especially for posthumous reputation—that 'last infirmity of noble minds'[1]—assumed an extraordinary prominence among the springs of Roman heroism, and was also the origin of that theatrical and overstrained phraseology which the greatest of ancient moralists rarely escaped.[2] But we should be altogether in error if we inferred, as some have done, that paganism never rose to the conception of virtue concealing itself from the world, and consenting voluntarily to degradation. No characters were more highly appreciated in antiquity than those of men who, through a sense of duty, opposed the strong current of popular favour; of men like Fabius, who consented for the sake of their country to incur the reputation that is most fatal to a soldier;[3] of men like Cato, who remained unmoved among the scoffs, the insults, and the ridicule of an angry crowd.[4] Cicero, expounding the principles of Stoicism, declared that no one has attained to true philosophy who has not learnt that all vice should be avoided, 'though it were concealed from the eyes of gods and men,'[5] and that no deeds are more laudable than those which are done without ostentation, and far from the sight of men.[6]

---

was so struck with the *Enchiridion* of Epictetus, that he adapted it to Christian use. The conversations of Epictetus, as reported by Arrian, are said to have been the favourite reading of Toussaint l'Ouverture.

[1] Tacitus had used this expression before Milton: 'Quando etiam sapientibus cupido gloriæ novissima exuitur.'—*Hist.* iv. 6.

[2] Two remarkable instances have come down to us of eminent writers begging historians to adorn and even exaggerate their acts. See the very curious letters of Cicero to the historian Lucceius (*Ep. ad Divers.* v. 12); and of the younger Pliny to Tacitus (*Ep.* vii. 33). Cicero has himself confessed that he was too fond of glory.

[3] 'Unus homo nobis cunctando restituit rem;
Non ponebat enim rumores ante salutem.'—Ennius.

[4] See the beautiful description of Cato's tranquillity under insults. Seneca, *De Ira*, ii. 33; *De Const. Sap.* 1, 2.

[5] *De Officiis*, iii. 9.

[6] *Tusc.* ii. 26.

The writings of the Stoics are crowded with sentences to the same effect. 'Nothing for opinion, all for conscience.'[1] 'He who wishes his virtue to be blazed abroad is not labouring for virtue but for fame.'[2] 'No one is more virtuous than the man who sacrifices the reputation of a good man rather than sacrifice his conscience.'[3] 'I do not shrink from praise, but I refuse to make it the end and term of right.'[4] 'If you do anything to please men, you have fallen from your estate.'[5] 'Even a bad reputation nobly earned is pleasing.'[6] 'A great man is not the less great when he lies vanquished and prostrate in the dust.'[7] 'Never forget that it is possible to be at once a divine man, yet a man unknown to all the world.'[8] 'That which is beautiful is beautiful in itself; the praise of man adds nothing to its quality.'[9] Marcus Aurelius, following an example that is ascribed to Pythagoras, made it a special object of mental discipline, by continually meditating on death, and evoking, by an effort of the imagination, whole societies that had passed away, to acquire a realised sense of the vanity of posthumous fame. The younger Pliny painted faithfully the ideal of Stoicism when he described one of his friends as a man 'who did nothing for ostentation, but all for conscience; who sought the reward of virtue in itself, and not in the praise of man.'[10] Nor were the Stoics less emphatic in distinguishing the obligation from the attraction of virtue. It was on this point that they separated from the more refined Epicureans, who were often willing to sublimate to the highest degree the kind of pleasure they proposed as an object, provided only it were admitted that pleasure is necessarily the ultimate end of our actions. But this the Stoics firmly denied. 'Pleasure,' they

---

[1] Seneca, *De Vit. Beat.* c. xx.
[2] Seneca, *Ep.* cxiii.
[3] Seneca, *Ep.* lxxxi.
[4] Persius, *Sat.* i. 45-47.
[5] Epictetus, *Ench.* xxiii.

[6] Seneca, *De Ira*, iii. 41.
[7] Seneca, *Cons. ad Helv.* xiii.
[8] Marc. Aur. vii. 67
[9] Marc. Aur. iv. 20.
[10] Pliny, *Ep.* i. 22.

argued, 'is the companion, not the guide, of our course.'[1]
'We do not love virtue because it gives us pleasure, but it
gives us pleasure because we love it.'[2] 'The wise man will
not sin, though both gods and men should overlook the deed,
for it is not through the fear of punishment or of shame
that he abstains from sin. It is from the desire and obligation of what is just and good.'[3] 'To ask to be paid for
virtue is as if the eye demanded a recompense for seeing, or
the feet for walking.'[4] In doing good, man 'should be like
the vine which has produced grapes, and asks for nothing
more after it has produced its proper fruit.'[5] His end,
according to these teachers, is not to find peace either in life
or in death. It is to do his duty, and to tell the truth.

The second distinguishing feature of Stoicism I have
noticed was the complete suppression of the affections to
make way for the absolute ascendancy of reason. There are
two great divisions of character corresponding very nearly to
the Stoical and Epicurean temperaments I have described—
that in which the will predominates, and that in which the
desires are supreme. A good man of the first class is one
whose will, directed by a sense of duty, pursues the course he
believes to be right, in spite of strong temptations to pursue
an opposite course, arising either from his own passions and
tendencies, or from the circumstances that surround him. A
good man of the second class is one who is so happily constituted that his sympathies and desires instinctively tend to
virtuous ends. The first character is the only one to which
we can, strictly speaking, attach the idea of merit, and it is
also the only one which is capable of rising to high efforts of

---

[1] 'Non dux, sed comes voluptas.'
—De Vit. Beat. c. viii.

[2] 'Voluptas non est merces nec
causa virtutis sed accessio; nec quia
delectat placet sed quia placet delectat.'—Ibid., c. ix.

[3] Peregrinus apud Aul. Gellius,
xii. 11. Peregrinus was a Cynic,
but his doctrine on this point was
identical with that of the Stoics.

[4] Marc. Aurel. ix. 42.

[5] Marc. Aurel. v. 6.

continuous and heroic self-sacrifice; but on the other hand there is a charm in the spontaneous action of the unforced desires which disciplined virtue can perhaps never attain. The man who is consistently generous through a sense of duty, when his natural temperament impels him to avarice, and when every exercise of benevolence causes him a pang, deserves in the very highest degree our admiration; but he whose generosity costs him no effort, but is the natural gratification of his affections, attracts a far larger measure of our love. Corresponding to these two casts of character, we find two distinct theories of education, the aim of the one being chiefly to strengthen the will, and that of the other to guide the desires. The principal examples of the first are the Spartan and Stoical systems of antiquity, and, with some modifications, the asceticism of the Middle Ages. The object of these systems was to enable men to endure pain, to repress manifest and acknowledged desires, to relinquish enjoyments, to establish an absolute empire over their emotions. On the other hand, there is a method of education which was never more prevalent than in the present day, which exhausts its efforts in making virtue attractive, in associating it with all the charms of imagination and of prosperity, and in thus insensibly drawing the desires in the wished-for direction. As the first system is especially suited to a disturbed and military society, which requires and elicits strong efforts of the will, and is therefore the special sphere of heroic virtues, so the latter belongs naturally to a tranquil and highly orga-nised civilisation, which is therefore very favourable to the amiable qualities, and it is probable that as civilisation advances, the heroic type will, in consequence, become more and more rare, and a kind of self-indulgent goodness more common. The circumstances of the ancient societies led them to the former type, of which the Stoics furnished the extreme expression in their doctrine that the affections are of the nature of a disease[1]—a doctrine which they justified by the same kind of arguments as those which are now often employed by metaphysicians to prove that love, anger, and the like can only be ascribed by a figure of speech to the Deity. Perturbation, they contended, is necessarily imperfection, and none of its forms can in consequence be ascribed to a perfect being. We have a clear intuitive perception that reason is the highest, and should be the directing, power of an intelligent being; but every act which is performed at the instigation of the emotions is withdrawn from the empire of reason. Hence it was inferred that while the will should be educated to act habitually in the direction of virtue, even the emotions that seem most fitted to second it should be absolutely proscribed. Thus Seneca has elaborated at length the distinction between clemency and pity, the first being one of the highest virtues, and the latter a positive vice. Clemency, he says, is an habitual disposition to gentleness in the application of punishments. It is that moderation which remits something of an incurred penalty, it is the opposite of cruelty, which is an habitual disposition to rigour. Pity, on the other hand, bears to clemency the same kind of relation as superstition to religion. It is the weakness of a feeble mind that flinches at the sight of suffering. Clemency is an act of judgment, but pity disturbs the judgment. Clemency adjudicates upon the proportion between suffering and guilt. Pity contemplates only suffering, and gives no

---

[1] Seneca, however, in one of his letters (*Ep.* lxxv.), subtilises a good deal on this point. He draws a distinction between affections and maladies. The first, he says, are irrational, and therefore reprehensible movements of the soul, which, if repeated and unrepressed, tend to form an irrational and evil habit, and to the last he in this letter restricts the term disease. He illustrates this distinction by observing that colds and any other slight ailments, if unchecked and neglected, may produce an organic disease. The wise man, he says, is wholly free from moral disease, but no man can completely emancipate himself from affections, though he should make this his constant object.

thought to its cause. Clemency, in the midst of its noblest efforts, is perfectly passionless; pity is unreasoning emotion. Clemency is an essential characteristic of the sage; pity is only suited for weak women and for diseased minds. 'The sage will console those who weep, but without weeping with them; he will succour the shipwrecked, give hospitality to the proscribed, and alms to the poor, . . . restore the son to the mother's tears, save the captive from the arena, and even bury the criminal; but in all this his mind and his counten ance will be alike untroubled. He will feel no pity. He will succour, he will do good, for he is born to assist his fellows, to labour for the welfare of mankind, and to offer to each one his part. . . . His countenance and his soul will betray no emotion as he looks upon the withered legs, the tattered rags, the bent and emaciated frame of the beggar. But he will help those who are worthy, and, like the gods, his leaning will be towards the wretched. . . . It is only diseased eyes that grow moist in beholding tears in other eyes, as it is no true sympathy, but only weakness of nerves, that leads some to laugh always when others laugh, or to yawn when others yawn.' [1]

Cicero, in a sentence which might be adopted as the motto of Stoicism, said that Homer 'attributed human qualities to the gods; it would have been better to have imparted divine qualities to men.' The remarkable passage I have just cited serves to show the extremes to which the Stoics pushed this imitation. And indeed, if we compare the different virtues that have flourished among Pagans and Christians, we invariably find that the prevailing type of excellence among the former is that in which the will and judgment, and among the latter that in which the emotions, are most prominent. Friendship rather than love, hospitality rather than charity, magnanimity rather than tenderness,

---

[1] *De Clem.* ii. 6, 7.

clemency rather than sympathy, are the characteristics of ancient goodness. The Stoics, who carried the suppression of the emotions farther than any other school, laboured with great zeal to compensate the injury thus done to the benevolent side of our nature, by greatly enlarging the sphere of reasoned and passionless philanthropy. They taught, in the most emphatic language, the fraternity of all men, and the consequent duty of each man consecrating his life to the welfare of others. They developed this general doctrine in a series of detailed precepts, which, for the range, depth, and beauty of their charity, have never been surpassed. They even extended their compassion to crime, and adopting the paradox of Plato, that all guilt is ignorance,[1] treated it as an involuntary disease, and declared that the only legitimate ground of punishment is prevention.[2] But, however fully they might reconcile in theory their principles with the widest and most active benevolence, they could not wholly counteract the practical evil of a system which declared war against the whole emotional side of our being, and reduced human virtue to a kind of majestic egotism; proposing as examples Anaxagoras, who, when told that his son had died, simply observed, 'I never supposed that I had begotten an immortal;' or Stilpo, who, when his country had been ruined, his native city captured, and his daughters carried away as slaves or as concubines, boasted that he had lost nothing, for the sage is independent of circumstances.[3] The framework or theory of

[1] 'Peccantes vero quid habet cur oderit, cum error illos in hujusmodi delicta compellat?'—Sen. De Ira, i. 14. This is a favourite thought of Marcus Aurelius, to which he reverts again and again. See, too, Arrian, i. 18.

[2] 'Ergo ne homini quidem nocebimus quia peccavit sed ne peccet, nec unquam ad præteritum sed ad futurum pœna referetur.'—Ibid. ii. 31. In the philosophy of Plato, on the other hand, punishment was chiefly expiatory and purificatory. (Lerminier Introd. à l'Histoire du Droit, p. 123.)

[3] Seneca, De Constant. Sap. v. Compare and contrast this famous sentence of Anaxagoras with that of one of the early Christian hermits. Someone told the hermit that his father was dead. 'Cease your blasphemy,' he answered, 'my father is immortal.' — Socrates, Eccl. Hist. iv. 23.

benevolence might be there, but the animating spirit was
absent.   Men who taught that the husband or the father
should look with perfect indifference on the death of his wife
or his child, and that the philosopher, though he may shed
tears of pretended sympathy in order to console his suffering
friend, must suffer no real emotion to penetrate his breast,[1]
could never found a true or lasting religion of benevolence.
Men who refused to recognise pain and sickness as evils were
scarcely likely to be very eager to relieve them in others.

In truth, the Stoics, who taught that all virtue was conformity to nature, were, in this respect, eminently false to
their own principle.   Human nature, as revealed to us by
reason, is a composite thing, a constitution of many parts
differing in kind and dignity, a hierarchy in which many
powers are intended to co-exist, but in different positions of
ascendancy or subordination.   To make the higher part of
our nature our whole nature, is not to restore but to mutilate humanity, and this mutilation has never been attempted
without producing grave evils.   As philanthropists, the
Stoics, through their passion for unity, were led to the extirpation of those emotions which nature intended as the chief
springs of benevolence.   As speculative philosophers, they
were entangled by the same desire in a long train of pitiable
paradoxes.   Their famous doctrines that all virtues are equal,
or, more correctly, are the same, that all vices are equal, that
nothing is an evil which does not affect our will, and that
pain and bereavement are, in consequence, no ills,[2] though

---

[1] Epictetus, *Ench.* 16, 18.

[2] The dispute about whether
anything but virtue is a good, was,
in reality, a somewhat childish
quarrel about words; for the Stoics,
who indignantly denounced the
Peripatetics for maintaining the
affirmative, admitted that health,
friends, &c., should be sought not
as 'goods' but as 'preferables.'

See a long discussion on this matter
in Cicero (*De Finib.* lib. iii. iv.).
The Stoical doctrine of the equality
of all vices was formally repudiated
by Marcus Aurelius, who maintained (ii. 10), with Theophrastus,
that faults of desire were worse
than faults of anger.   The other
Stoics, while dogmatically asserting
the equality of all virtues as well

partially explained away and frequently disregarded by the
Roman Stoics, were yet sufficiently prominent to give their
teaching something of an unnatural and affected appearance.
Prizing only a single object, and developing only a single side
of their nature, their minds became narrow and their views
contracted. Thus, while the Epicureans, urging men to
study nature in order to banish superstition, endeavoured to
correct that ignorance of physical science which was one of
the chief impediments to the progress of the ancient mind,
the Stoics for the most part disdained a study which was
other than the pursuit of virtue.[1] While the Epicurean poet
painted in magnificent language the perpetual progress of
mankind, the Stoic was essentially retrospective, and exhausted his strength in vain efforts to restore the simplicity
of a by-gone age. While, too, the school of Zeno produced
many of the best and greatest men who have ever lived, it
must be acknowledged that its records exhibit a rather unusual number of examples of high professions falsified in
action, and of men who, displaying in some forms the most
undoubted and transcendent virtue, fell in others far below
the average of mankind. The elder Cato, who, though not
a philosopher, was a model of philosophers, was conspicuous
for his inhumanity to his slaves.[2] Brutus was one of the
most extortionate usurers of his time, and several citizens

---

as the equality of all vices in their
particular judgments graduated
their praise or blame much in the
same way as the rest of the world.

[1] See Seneca (*Ep.* lxxxix.). Seneca himself, however, has devoted
a work to natural history, but the
general tendency of the school was
certainly to concentrate all attention upon morals, and all, or nearly
all the great naturalists were Epicureans. Cicero puts into the
mouth of the Epicurean the sentence, 'Omnium autem rerum natura cognita levamur superstitione,
liberamur mortis metu, non con-
turbamur ignoratione rerum' (*De
Fin.* i.); and Virgil expressed an
eminently Epicurean sentiment in
his famous lines :—
'Felix, qui potuit rerum cognoscere
    causas,
Quique metus omnes et inexorabile
    fatum
Subjecit pedibus, strepitumque
    Acherontis avari.'
                    Georg. 490–492.
[2] Plutarch, *Cato Major.*

of Salamis died of starvation, imprisoned because they could not pay the sum he demanded.[1]   No one eulogised more eloquently the austere simplicity of life which Stoicism advocated than Sallust, who in a corrupt age was notorious for his rapacity.   Seneca himself was constitutionally a nervous and timid man, endeavouring, not always with success, to support himself by a sublime philosophy.   He guided, under circumstances of extreme difficulty, the cause of virtue, and his death is one of the noblest antiquity records; but his life was deeply marked by the taint of flattery, and not free from the taint of avarice, and it is unhappily certain that he lent his pen to conceal or varnish one of the worst crimes of Nero.   The courage of Lucan failed signally under torture, and the flattery which he bestowed upon Nero, in his 'Pharsalia,' ranks with the Epigrams of Martial as probably the extreme limit of sycophancy to which Roman literature descended.

While, too, the main object of the Stoics was to popularise philosophy, the high standard of self-control they exacted rendered their system exceedingly unfit for the great majority of mankind, and for the ordinary condition of affairs.   Life is history, not poetry.   It consists mainly of little things, rarely illumined ·by flashes of great heroism, rarely broken by great dangers, or demanding great exertions. A moral system, to govern society, must accommodate itself to common characters and mingled motives.   It must be capable of influencing natures that can never rise to an heroic level.   It must tincture, modify, and mitigate where it cannot eradicate or transform.   In Christianity there are always a few persons seeking by continual and painful efforts to reverse or extinguish the ordinary feelings of humanity, but in the great majority of cases the influence of the religious principle upon the mind, though very real, is not of a nature

---

[1] Cicero, *Ad Attic.* vi. 2.

to cause any serious strain or struggle. It is displayed in a certain acquired spontaneity of impulse. It softens the character, purifies and directs the imagination, blends insensibly with the habitual modes of thought, and, without revolutionising, gives a tone and bias to all the forms of action. But Stoicism was simply a school of heroes. It recognised no gradations of virtue or vice. It condemned all emotions, all spontaneity, all mingled motives, all the principles, feelings, and impulses upon which the virtue of common men mainly depends. It was capable of acting only on moral natures that were strung to the highest tension, and it was therefore naturally rejected by the multitude.

The central conception of this philosophy of self-control was the dignity of man. Pride, which looks within, making man seek his own approbation, as distinguished from vanity, which looks without, and shapes its conduct according to the opinions of others, was not only permitted in Stoicism, it was even its leading moral agent. The sense of virtue, as I have elsewhere observed, occupies in this system much the same place as the sense of sin in Christianity. Sin, in the conception of the ancients, was simply disease, and they deemed it the part of a wise man to correct it, but not to dwell upon its circumstances. In the many disquisitions which Epictetus and others have left us concerning the proper frame of mind in which man should approach death, repentance for past sin has absolutely no place, nor do the ancients appear to have ever realised the purifying and spiritualising influence it exercises upon character. And while the reality of moral disease was fully recognised, while a lofty and indeed unattainable ideal was continually proposed, no one doubted the essential excellence of human nature, and very few doubted the possibility of man acquiring by his own will a high degree of virtue. In this last respect there was a wide difference between the teaching of the Roman moralists and of the Greek poets.[1] Homer continually represents courage, anger, and the like, as the direct inspiration of Heaven. Æschylus, the great poet of fatalism, regards every human passion as but a single link in the great chain of causes forged by the inexorable will of Zeus.   There are, indeed, few grander things in poetry than his picture of the many and various motives that urged Clytemnestra to the slaughter of Agamemnon—revenge for her murdered daughter, love for Ægisthus, resentment at past breaches of conjugal duty, jealousy of Cassandra, all blending in that fierce hatred that nerved her arm against her husband's life ; while above all this tumult of passion the solemn song of Cassandra proclaimed that the deed was but the decree of Heaven, the harvest of blood springing from the seed of crime, the accomplishment of the ancient curse that was destined to cling for ever to the hapless race of Atreus.   Before the body of the murdered king, and in presence of the wildest paroxysms of human passion, the bystanders bowed their heads, exclaiming, ' Zeus has willed it—Zeus the supreme Ruler, the God who does all; for what can happen in the world without the will of Zeus ?'

But conceptions of this kind had little or no place in the philosophy of Rome.   The issue of human enterprises and the disposition of the gifts of fortune were recognised as under the control of Providence ; but man was master of his own feelings, and was capable of attaining such excellence that he might even challenge comparison with the gods.   Audacious as such sentiments may now appear, they were common to most schools of Roman moralists.   ' We boast justly of our own virtue,' said the eclectic Cicero, ' which we could not do if we derived it from the Deity and not from ourselves.'

This contrast is noticed and largely illustrated by M. Montée n his interesting little work Le Stoïcisme à Rome, and also by Legendre in his Traité de l'Opinion, ou Mémoires pour servir à l'histoire de l'esprit humain (Venise, 1735).

'All morta's judge that fortune is to be received from the gods
and wisdom from ourselves.'[1]   The Epicurean Horace, in his
noblest ode, described the just man, confident in his virtue,
undaunted amid the crash of worlds, and he tells us to pray
only for those things which Jupiter gives and takes away.
'He gives life, he gives wealth; an untroubled mind I secure
for myself.'[2]   'The calm of a mind blest in the consciousness
of its virtue,' was the expression of supreme felicity the
Epicureans had derived from their master.[3]   Lucretius, in a
magnificent passage, designates Epicurus as a god, and boasts
that the popular divinities dwindle into insignificance before
him.   Ceres, he says, gave men corn, and Bacchus wine, but
Epicurus the principles of virtue.   Hercules conquered monsters, Epicurus conquered vice.[4]   'Pray,' said Juvenal, 'for a
healthy mind in a healthy body.   Ask for a brave soul
unscared by death. . . .   But there are things you can give
yourself.'[5]   'Misfortune, and losses, and calumny,' said Seneca,
'disappear before virtue as the taper before the sun.'[6]   'In one
point the sage is superior to God.   God owes it to His nature
not to fear, but the sage owes it to himself.   Sublime
condition! he joins the frailty of a man to the security of a
god.'[7]   'Except for immortality,' he elsewhere writes, 'the
sage is like to God.'[8]   'It is the characteristic of a wise man,'

---

[1] 'Atque hoc quidem omnes mor-
tales sic habent . . . commodita-
tem prosperitatemque vitæ a diis
se habere, virtutem autem nemo
unquam acceptam deo retulit. Ni-
mirum recte. Propter virtutem
enim jure laudamur et in virtute
recte gloriamur. Quod non con-
tingeret si id donum a deo, non a
nobis haberemus.'—Cicero, De Nat.
Deor. iii. 36.

[2] Ep. i. 18.

[3] Seneca Ep. lxvi.

[4] Lucretius, v. It was a Greek
proverb, that Apollo begat Æsculapius to heal the body, and Plato
to heal the soul. (Legendre, Traité
de l'Opinion, tome i. p. 197.)

[5] 'Orandum est ut sit mens sana
in corpore sano:

Fortem posce animum, mortis ter-
rore carentem. . . .

Monstro, quod ipse tibi possis dare.'
          Juvenal, Sat. x. 356.
Marcus   Aurelius   recommends
prayer, but only that we may be
freed from evil desires.   (ix. 11.)

[6] Seneca. Ep. lxvi.

[7] Ibid. Ep. liii.

[8] De Const. Sap. viii.

added Epictetus, 'that he looks for all his good and evil from himself.'· 'As far as his rational nature is concerned, he is in no degree inferior to the gods.'[2]

There were, however, other veins of thought exhibited in stoicism which greatly modified and sometimes positively contradicted this view of the relations of man to the Deity. The theology of the Stoics was an ill-defined, uncertain, and somewhat inconsistent Pantheism; the Divinity was especially worshipped under the two aspects of Providence and moral goodness, and the soul of man was regarded as 'a detached fragment of the Deity,'[3] or as at least pervaded and accompanied by a divine energy. 'There never,' said Cicero, 'was a great man, without an inspiration from on high.'[4] 'Nothing,' said Seneca, 'is closed to God. He is present in our conscience. He intervenes in our thoughts.'[5] 'I tell thee, Lucilius,' he elsewhere writes, 'a sacred spirit dwells within us, the observer and the guardian of our good and evil deeds. . . . No man is good without God. Who, save by His assistance, can rise above fortune? He gives noble and lofty counsels. A God (what God I know not) dwells in every good man.'[6] 'Offer to the God that is in thee,' said Marcus Aurelius, 'a manly being, a citizen, a soldier at his post ready to depart from life as soon as the trumpet sounds.'[7] 'It is sufficient to believe in the Genius who is within us, and to honour him by a pure worship.'[8]

Passages of this kind are not unfrequent in Stoical writings. More commonly, however, virtue is represented as a human act imitating God. This was the meaning of

---

[1] *Ench.* xlviii.

[2] Arrian, i. 12.

[3] Arrian, ii. 8. The same doctrine is strongly stated in Seneca, *Ep.* xcii.

[4] Cicero, *De Nat. Deor.* ii. 66.

[5] *Ep.* lxxxiii. Somewhat similar sentiments are attributed to Thales and Bion (Diog. Laërt.).

[6] *Ep.* xli. There are some beautiful sentiments of this kind in Plutarch's treatise, *De Sera Numinis Vindicta.* It was a saying of Pythagoras, that 'we become better as we approach the gods.'

[7] Marc. Aur. iii. 5.

[8] Marcus Aurelius.

the Platonic maxim, 'follow God,' which the Stoics continually
repeated, which they developed in many passages of the most
touching and beautiful piety, and to which they added the duty
of the most absolute and unquestioning submission to the
decrees of Providence.   Their doctrine on this latter point
harmonised well with their antipathy to the emotional side
of our being. 'To weep, to complain, to groan, is to rebel ;'[1]
'to fear, to grieve, to be angry, is to be a deserter.'[2] 'Re
member that you are but an actor, acting whatever part the
Master has ordained. It may be short, or it may be long.
If He wishes you to represent a poor man, do so heartily ; if
a cripple, or a magistrate, or a private man, in each case
act your part with honour.'[3] 'Never say of anything that
you have lost it, but that you have restored it ; your wife and
child die—you have restored them ; your farm is taken from
you—that also is restored.   It is seized by an impious man.
What is it to you by whose instrumentality He who gave it
reclaims it?'[4] 'God does not keep a good man in prosperity ;
He tries, He strengthens him, He prepares him for Himself.'[5]
'Those whom God approves, whom He loves, He hardens,
He proves, He exercises ; but those whom He seems to
indulge and spare, He preserves for future ills.'[6]   With a
beautiful outburst of submissive gratitude, Marcus Aurelius
exclaims, 'Some have said, Oh, dear city of Cecrops !—but
thou, canst thou say, Oh, dear city of Jupiter ? . . . All that
is suitable to thee, oh world, is suitable to me.'[7]

These passages, which might be indefinitely multiplied,
serve to show how successfully the Stoics laboured, by dilating
upon the conception of Providence, to mitigate the arrogance
which one aspect of their teaching unquestionably displayed.
But in this very attempt another danger was incurred, upon

---

[1] Seneca, *Præf. Nat. Quæst.* iii.
[2] Marc. Aur. x. 25.
[3] Epict. *Ench.* xvii.
[4] Epict. *Ench.* xi.
[5] Seneca, *De Prov.* i.
[6] Ibid. iv.
[7] Marc. Aurel. ii. 2, 3.

which a very large proportion of the moral systems of all ages
have been wrecked. A doctrine which thus enjoins absolute
submission to the decrees of Providence,[1] which proscribes
the affections, and which represents its disciples as altogether
independent of surrounding circumstances, would in most
conditions of society have led necessarily to quietism, and
proved absolutely incompatible with active virtue. Fortunately, however, in the ancient civilisations the idea of virtue
had from the earliest times been so indissolubly connected
with that of political activity that the danger was for a long
period altogether avoided. The State occupied in antiquity
a prominence in the thoughts of men which it never has
attained in modern times. The influence of patriotism
thrilled through every fibre of moral and intellectual life.
The most profound philosophers, the purest moralists, the
most sublime poets, had been soldiers or statesmen. Hence
arose the excessive predominance occasionally accorded to
civic virtues in ancient systems of ethics, and also not a few
of their most revolting paradoxes. Plato advocated community of wives mainly on the ground that the children
produced would be attached more exclusively to their country.[2]
Aristotle may be almost said to have made the difference
between Greek and barbarian the basis of his moral code.

---

[1] The language in which the
Stoics sometimes spoke of the
inexorable determination of all
things by Providence would appear
logically inconsistent with free will.
In fact, however, the Stoics asserted the latter doctrine in unequivocal language, and in their
practical ethics even exaggerated
its power. Aulus Gellius (*Noct.
Att.* vi. 2) has preserved a passage
in which Chrysippus exerted his
subtlety in reconciling the two
things. See, too, Arrian, i. 17.

[2] We have an extremely curious
illustration of this mode of thought
in a speech of Archytas of Taren-
tum on the evils of sensuality,
which Cicero has preserved. He
considers the greatest of these evils
to be that the vice predisposes men
to unpatriotic acts. 'Nullam capi-
taliorem pestem quam corporis
voluptatem, hominibus a natura
datam. . . . . Hinc patriæ prodi-
tiones, hinc rerumpublicarum ever-
siones, hinc cum hostibus clandes-
tina colloquia nasci,' etc.—Cicero,
De Senect. xii.

The Spartan legislation was continually extolled as an ideal, as the Venetian constitution by the writers of the seventeenth century. On the other hand, the contact of the spheres of speculation and of political activity exercised in one respect a very beneficial influence upon ancient philosophies. Patriotism almost always occupied a prominence in the scale of duties, which forms a striking contrast to the neglect or discredit into which it has fallen among modern teachers. We do, indeed, read of an Anaxagoras pointing to heaven as to his true country, and pronouncing exile to be no evil, as the descent to the infernal regions is the same from every land ;[1] but such sentiments, though not unknown among the Epicureans and the Cynics, were diametrically opposed to the prevailing tone. Patriotism was represented as a moral duty, and a duty of the highest order. Cicero only echoed the common opinion of antiquity in that noble passage, in which he asserts that the love we owe our country is even holier and more profound than that we owe our nearest kinsman, and that he can have no claim to the title of a good man who even hesitates to die in its behalf.[2]

A necessary consequence of this prominence of patriotism was the practical character of most ancient ethics. We find, indeed, moralists often exhorting men to moderate their ambition, consoling them under political adversity, and urging that there are some circumstances under which an upright man should for a time withdraw from public affairs ;[3] but the general duty of taking part in political life was emphatically asserted, and the vanity of the quietist theory of life not only maintained, but even somewhat exaggerated. Thus

---

Diog. Laërt. *Anax.*

[2] 'Cari sunt parentes, cari liberi, propinqui, familiares ; sed omnes omnium caritates patria una complexa est ; pro qua quis bonus dubitet mortem oppetere si ei sit profuturus ? '--*De Offic.* i. 17.

[3] See Seneca, *Consol. ad Helviam* and *De Otio Sapien.* ; and Plutarch, *De Exilio.* The first of these works is the basis of one of the most beautiful compositions in the English language, Bolingbroke's *Reflections on Exile.*

Cicero declared that ' all virtue is in action.'[1] The younger Pliny mentions that he once lamented to the Stoic Euphrates the small place which his official duties left for philosophical pursuits; but Euphrates answered that the discharge of public affairs and the administration of justice formed a part, and the most important part, of philosophy, for he who is so engaged is but practising the precepts of the schools.[2] It was a fundamental maxim of the Stoics that humanity is a body in which each limb should act solely and continually with a view to the interests of the whole. Marcus Aurelius, the purest mind of the sect, was for nineteen years the active ruler of the civilised globe. Thrasea, Helvidius, Cornutus, and a crowd of others who had adopted Stoicism as a religion, lived, and in many cases died, in obedience to its precepts, struggling for the liberties of their country in the darkest hours of tyranny.

Men who had formed such high conceptions of duty, who had bridled so completely the tumult of passion, and whose lives were spent in a calm sense of virtue and of dignity, were little likely to be assailed by the superstitious fears that are the nightmare of weaker men. The preparation for death was deemed one of the chief ends of philosophy.[3] The thought of a coming change assisted the mind in detaching itself from the gifts of fortune, and the extinction of all superstitious terrors completed the type of self-reliant majesty which Stoicism had chosen for its ideal. But while it is certain that no philosophers expatiated upon death with a grander eloquence, or met it with a more placid courage, it can hardly be denied that their constant disquisitions forced it into an unhealthy prominence, and somewhat discoloured their whole view of life. ' The Stoics,' as Bacon has said, ' bestowed too much cost on death, and by their preparations

---

[1] De Officiis.
[2] Epist. i. 10.
[3] ' Tota enim philosophorum

vita, ut ait idem, commentatio mortis est.'—Cicero, Tusc. i. 30, ad fin.

made it more fearful.'[1]   There is a profound wisdom in the
maxims of Spinoza, that ' the proper study of a wise man is
not how to die, but how to live,' and that 'there is no subject
on which the sage will think less than death.'[2]   A life of
active duty is the best preparation for the end, and so large
a part of the evil of death lies in its anticipation, that an
attempt to deprive it of its terrors by constant meditation
almost necessarily defeats its object, while at the same time
it forms an unnaturally tense, feverish, and tragical character,
annihilates the ambition and enthusiasm that are essential to
human progress, and not unfrequently casts a chill and a
deadness over the affections.

Among the many half-pagan legends that were connected
with Ireland during the middle ages, one of the most beautiful
is that of the islands of life and of death.   In a certain lake
in Munster it is said there were two islands; into the first
death could never enter, but age and sickness, and the weariness of life, and the paroxysms of fearful suffering were all
known there, and they did their work till the inhabitants,
tired of their immortality, learned to look upon the opposite
island as upon a haven of repose: they launched their barks
upon the gloomy waters; they touched its shore and they
were at rest.[3]

This legend, which is far more akin to the spirit of
paganism than to that of Christianity, and is in fact only
another form of the myth of Tithonus, represents with great
fidelity the aspect in which death was regarded by the exponents of Stoicism.   There was much difference of opinion
and of certitude in the judgments of the ancient philosophers

---

[1] *Essay on Death.*
[2] Spinoza, *Ethics*, iv. 67.
[3] Camden.   Montalembert notices a similar legend as existing
in Brittany (*Les Moines d'Occident*,
tome ii. p. 287).   Procopius (*De*
Bello Goth. iv. 20) says that it is
impossible for men to live in the
west of Britain, and that the district is believed to be inhabited by
the souls of the dead.

concerning the future destinies of the soul, but they were
unanimous in regarding death simply as a natural rest, and
in attributing the terrors that were connected with it to a
diseased imagination.   Death, they said, is the only evil that
does not afflict us when present.   While we are, death is not,
when death has come we are not.   It is a false belief that it
only follows, it also precedes, life.   It is to be as we were
before we were born.   The candle which has been extinguished is in the same condition as before it was lit, and the
dead man as the man unborn.   Death is the end of all sorrow.
It either secures happiness or ends suffering.   It frees the
slave from his cruel master, opens the prison door, calms the
qualms of pain, closes the struggles of poverty.   It is the last
and best boon of nature, for it frees man from all his cares.
It is at worst but the close of a banquet we have enjoyed.
Whether it be desired or whether it be shunned, it is no
curse and no evil, but simply the resolution of our being into
its primitive elements, the law of our nature to which it is
our duty cheerfully to conform.

Such were the leading topics that were employed in that
beautiful literature of 'Consolations,' which the academic
Crantor is said to have originated, and which occupies so
large a place in the writings of Cicero, Plutarch, and the
Stoics.   Cicero, like all the school of Plato, added to these
motives a very firm and constant reference to the immortality
of the soul.   Plutarch held the same doctrine with equal assurance, but he gave it a much less conspicuous position in
his 'Consolations,' and he based it not upon philosophical
grounds, but upon the testimonies of the oracles, and upon
the mysteries of Bacchus.[1]   Among the Stoics the doctrine
shone with a faint and uncertain light, and was seldom or
never adopted as a motive.   But that which is most impressive to a student who turns from the religious literature of

---

[1] In his *De Sera Numinis Vindicta* and his *Consolatio ad Uxorem.*

Christianity to the pagan philosophies, is the complete
absence in the latter of all notion concerning the penal character of death. Death, according to Socrates,[1] either
extinguishes life or emancipates it from the thraldom of the
body. Even in the first case it is a blessing, in the last it is
the greatest of boons. 'Accustom yourself,' said Epicurus,
'to the thought that death is indifferent; for all good and all
evil consist in feeling, and what is death but the privation of
feeling?'[2] 'Souls either remain after death,' said Cicero, 'or
they perish in death. If they remain they are happy; if they
perish they are not wretched.'[3] Seneca, consoling Polybius
concerning the death of his brother, exhorts his friend to
think, 'if the dead have any sensations, then my brother, let
loose as it were from a lifelong prison, and at last enjoying
his liberty, looks down from a loftier height on the wonders
of nature and on all the deeds of men, and sees more clearly
those divine things which he had so long sought in vain to
understand. But why should I be afflicted for one who is
either happy or is nothing? To lament the fate of one who
is happy is envy; to lament the fate of a nonentity is
madness.'[4]

But while the Greek and Roman philosophers were on
this point unanimous, there was a strong opposing current in
the popular mind. The Greek word for superstition signifies
literally, fear of gods or dæmons, and the philosophers
sometimes represent the vulgar as shuddering at the thought
of death, through dread of certain endless sufferings to which
it would lead them. The Greek mythology contains many
fables on the subject. The early Greek vases occasionally

[1] In the *Phædo, passim.* See,
too, Marc. Aurelius, ii. 12.
[2] See a very striking letter of
Epicurus quoted by Diogenes Laërt.
in his life of that philosopher.
Except a few sentences, quoted by
other writers, these letters were all
that remained of the works of
Epicurus, till the recent discovery
of one of his treatises at Hercula-
neum.
[3] *Tusc. Quæst.* i.
[4] *Consol. ad Polyb.* xxvii.

represent scenes of infernal torments, not unlike those of the mediæval frescoes.[1] The rapture with which Epicureanism was received, as liberating the human mind from the thraldom of superstitious terrors, shows how galling must have been the yoke. In the poem of Lucretius, in occasional passages of Cicero and other Latin moralists, above all, in the treatise of Plutarch 'On Superstition,' we may trace the deep impression these terrors had made upon the populace, even during the later period of the Republic, and during the Empire. To destroy them was represented as the highest function of philosophy. Plutarch denounced them as the worst calumny against the Deity, as more pernicious than atheism, as the evil consequences of immoral fables, and he gladly turned to other legends which taught a different lesson. Thus it was related that when, during a certain festival at Argos, the horses that were to draw the statue of Juno to the temple were detained, the sons of the priestess yoked themselves to the car, and their mother, admiring their piety, prayed the goddess to reward them with whatever boon was the best for man. Her prayer was answered —they sank asleep and died.[2] In like manner the architects of the great temple of Apollo at Delphi, prayed the god to select that reward which was best. The oracle told them in reply to spend seven days in rejoicing, and on the following night their reward would come. They too died in sleep.[3] The swan was consecrated to Apollo because its dying song was believed to spring from a prophetic impulse.[4] The Spanish Celts raised temples, and sang hymns of praise to death.[5] No

---

[1] Maury, *Hist. des Religions de la Grèce antique*, tom. i. pp. 582–588. M. Ravaisson, in his Memoir on Stoicism (*Acad. des Inscriptions et Belles-lettres*, tom. xxi.) has enlarged on the terrorism of paganism, but has, I think, exaggerated it. Religious which selected games as the natural form of devotion can never have had any very alarming character.

[2] Plutarch, *Ad Apollonium.*

[3] Ibid.

[4] Cic. *Tusc. Quæst.* i.

[5] Philost. Apoll. of Tyan. v. 4. Hence their passion for suicide.

philosopher of antiquity ever questioned that a good man, reviewing his life, might look upon it without shame and even
with positive complacency, or that the reverence with which
men regard heroic deaths is a foretaste of the sentence of the
Creator.   To this confidence may be traced the tranquil
courage, the complete absence of all remorse, so conspicuous
in the closing hours of Socrates, and of many other of the
sages of antiquity.   There is no fact in religious history
more startling than the radical change that has in this
respect passed over the character of devotion.   It is said of
Chilon, one of the seven sages of Greece, that at the close of
his career he gathered his disciples around him, and con-
gratulated himself that in a long life he could recall but a
single act that saddened his dying hour.   It was that, in a
perplexing dilemma, he had allowed his love of a friend in
some slight degree to obscure his sense of justice.[1]   The
writings of Cicero in his old age are full of passionate aspirations to a future world, unclouded by one regret or by one
fear.   Seneca died tranquilly, bequeathing to his friends 'the
most precious of his possessions, the image of his life.'[2]   Titus
on his deathbed declared that he could remember only a single act with which to reproach himself.[3]   On the last night
in which Antoninus Pius lived, the tribune came to ask for
the pass-word of the night.   The dying emperor gave him
' æquanimitas.'[4]   Julian, the last great representative of his
expiring creed, caught up the same majestic strain.   Amid

---

which Silius Italicus commemo-
rates in lines which I think very
beautiful:—

' Prodiga gens animæ et properare
     facillima mortem ;
Namque ubi transcendit florentes
     viribus annos
Impatiens ævi, spernit novisse
     senectam
Et fati modus in dextra est.'—i.
225-228.

Valerius Maximus (ii. vi. § 12)
speaks of Celts who celebrated the
birth of men with lamentation, and
their deaths with joy.
  [1] Aulus Gellius, *Noctes*, i. 3.
  [2] Tacitus, *Annales*, xv. 62.
  [3] Sueton. *Titus*, 10.
  [4] Capitolinus, *Antoninus*.

the curses of angry priests, and the impending ruin of the
cause he loved, he calmly died in the consciousness of his
virtue; and his death, which is among the most fearless
that antiquity records, was the last protest of philosophic
paganism against the new doctrine that had arisen.[1]

It is customary with some writers, when exhibiting the
many points in which the ancient philosophers anticipated
Christian ethics, to represent Christianity as if it were merely
a development or authoritative confirmation of the highest
teaching of paganism, or as if the additions were at least of
such a nature that there is but little doubt that the best and
purest spirits of the pagan world, had they known them,
would have gladly welcomed them. But this conception,
which contains a large amount of truth if applied to the
teaching of many Protestants, is either grossly exaggerated or
absolutely false if applied to that of the patristic period or of
mediæval Catholicism. On the very subject which the philosophers deemed the most important their unanimous
conclusion was the extreme antithesis of the teaching of
Catholicism. The philosophers taught that death is 'a law
and not a punishment;'[2] the fathers taught that it is a penal
infliction introduced into the world on account of the sin of
Adam, which was also the cause of the appearance of all
noxious plants, of all convulsions in the material globe, and,
as was sometimes asserted, even of a diminution of the light of
the sun. The first taught that death was the end of suffering;
they ridiculed as the extreme of folly the notion that

---

[1] See the beautiful account of
his last hours given by Ammianus
Marcellinus and reproduced by
Gibbon. There are some remarks
well worth reading about the death
of Julian, and the state of thought
that rendered such a death possible,
in Dr. Newman's *Discourses on
University Education*, lect. ix.

[2] 'Lex non pœna mors' was a
favourite saying among the ancients. On the other hand, Tertullian very distinctly enunciated
the patristic view, 'Qui autem
primordia hominis novimus, auden-
ter determinamus mortem non ex
natura secutam hominem sed ex
culpa.'—*De Anima*, 52.

physical evils could await those whose bodies had been reduced to ashes, and they dwelt with emphatic eloquence upon the approaching, and, as they believed, final extinction of superstitious terrors. The second taught that death to the vast majority of the human race is but the beginning of end-less and excruciating tortures—tortures before which the most ghastly of terrestrial sufferings dwindle into insig-nificance—tortures which no courage could defy—which none but an immortal being could endure. The first represented man as pure and innocent until his will had sinned; the second represented him as under a sentence of condemnation at the very moment of his birth. 'No funeral sacrifices,' said a great writer of the first school, 'are offered for children who die at an early age, and none of the ceremonies practised at the funerals of adults are performed at their tombs, for it is believed that infants have no hold upon earth or upon terres-trial affections. . . . The law forbids us to honour them because it is irreligious to lament for those pure souls who have passed into a better life and a happier dwelling-place.'[1] 'Whosoever shall tell us,' said a distinguished exponent of the patristic theology, 'that infants shall be quickened in Christ who die without partaking in His Sacrament, does both contradict the Apostle's teaching and condemn the whole Church. . . . And he that is not quickened in Christ must remain in that condemnation of which the Apostle speaks, "by one man's offence condemnation came upon all men to condemnation." To which condemnation infants are born liable as all the Church believes.'[2] The one school endeavoured to plant its foundations in the moral nature of mankind, by proclaiming that man can become acceptable to the Deity by his own virtue, and by this alone, that all sacri-fices, rites, and forms are indifferent, and that the true worship of God is the recognition and imitation of His

---

[1] Plutarch, *Ad Uxorem.*   [2] St. Augustine, *Epist.* 166

goodness. According to the other school, the most heroic efforts of human virtue are insufficient to avert a sentence of eternal condemnation, unless united with an implicit belief in the teachings of the Church, and a due observance of the rites it enjoins. By the philosophers the ascription of anger and vengeance to the Deity, and the apprehension of future torture at His hands, were unanimously repudiated;[1] by the priests the opposite opinion was deemed equally censurable.[2]

These are fundamental points of difference, for they relate to the fundamental principles of the ancient philosophy. The main object of the pagan philosophers was to dispel the terrors the imagination had cast around death, and by destroying this last cause of fear to secure the liberty of man. The main object of the Catholic priests has been to make death in itself as revolting and appalling as possible, and by representing escape from its terrors as hopeless, except by complete subjection to their rule, to convert it into an instrument of government. By multiplying the dancing or warning skeletons, and other sepulchral images representing the loathsomeness of death without its repose; by substituting inhumation for incremation, and concentrating the imagination on the ghastliness of decay; above all, by peopling the unseen world with demon phantoms and with excruciating tortures, the Catholic Church succeeded in making death in itself unspeakably terrible, and in thus preparing men for the consolations it could offer. Its legends, its ceremonies, its art,[3] its dog-

---

[1] 'At hoc quidem commune est omnium philosophorum, non eorum modo qui deum nihil habere ipsum negotii dicunt, et nihil exhibere alteri; sed eorum etiam, qui deum semper agere aliquid et moliri volunt, numquam nec irasci deum nec nocere.'—Cic. De Offic. iii. 28.

[2] See the refutation of the philosophic notion in Lactantius, De Ira Dei.

[3] 'Revelation,' as Lessing observes in his essay on this subject, 'has made Death the "king of terrors," the awful offspring of sin and the dread way to its punishment; though to the imagination of the ancient heathen world,

matic teaching, all conspired to this end, and the history of its miracles is a striking evidence of its success. The great majority of superstitions have ever clustered around two centres—the fear of death and the belief that every phenomenon of life is the result of a special spiritual interposition. Among the ancients they were usually of the latter kind. Auguries, prophecies, interventions in war, prodigies avenging the neglect of some rite or marking some epoch in the fortunes of a nation or of a ruler, are the forms they usually assumed. In the middle ages, although these were very common, the most conspicuous superstitions took the form of visions of purgatory or hell, conflicts with visible demons, or Satanic miracles. Like those mothers who govern their children by persuading them that the dark is crowded with spectres that will seize the disobedient, and who often succeed in creating an association of ideas which the adult man is unable altogether to dissolve, the Catholic priests resolved to base their power upon the nerves ; and as they long exercised an absolute control over education, literature, and art, they succeeded in completely reversing the teaching of ancient philosophy, and in making the terrors of death for centuries the nightmare of the imagination.

There is, indeed, another side to the picture. The vague uncertainty with which the best pagans regarded death passed away before the teaching of the Church, and it was often replaced by a rapture of hope, which, however, the doctrine of purgatory contributed at a later period largely to quell. But, whatever may be thought of the justice of the Catholic conception of death or of its influence upon human happiness, it is plain that it is radically different from that of the pagan philosophers. That man is not only an imperfect but a fallen being, and that death is the penal consequence of his sin,

---

Greek or Etrurian, he was a youthful genius—the twin brother of Sleep, or a lusty boy with a torch held downwards.'—Coleridge's *Biographia Litteraria*, cap. xxii., note by Sara Coleridge.

was a doctrine profoundly new · to mankind, and it has
exercised an influence of the most serious character upon the
moral history of the world.

The wide divergence of the classical from the Catholic
conception of death appears very plainly in the attitude which
each system adopted towards suicide.   This is, perhaps, the
most striking of all the points of contrast between the teaching of antiquity, and especially of the Roman Stoics, on the one
hand, and that of almost all modern moralists on the other.
It is indeed true that the ancients were by no means unanimous in their approval of the act.   Pythagoras, to whom so
many of the wisest sayings of antiquity are ascribed, is said
to have forbidden men ' to depart from their guard or station
in life without the order of their commander, that is, of God.'[1]
Plato adopted similar language, though he permitted suicide
when the law required it, and also when men had been struck
down by intolerable calamity, or had sunk to the lowest
depths of poverty.[2]   Aristotle condemned it on civic grounds,
as being an injury to the State.[3]   The roll of Greek suicides
is not long, though it contains some illustrious names, among
others those of Zeno and Cleanthes.[4]   In Rome, too, where
suicide acquired a greater prominence, its lawfulness was by
no means accepted as an axiom, and the story of Regulus,

---

[1] 'Vetat Pythagoras injussu
imperatoris, id est Dei, de præsidio
et statione vitæ decedere.'—Cic. De
Senec. xx. If we believe the very
untrustworthy evidence of Diog.
Laërtius (Pythagoras) the philosopher himself committed suicide by
starvation.

[2] See his Laws, lib. ix. In his
Phædon, however, Plato went further, and condemned all suicide.
Libanius says (De Vita Sua) that
the arguments of the Phædon prevented him from committing suicide
after the death of Julian. On the
other hand, Cicero mentions a certain Cleombrotus, who was so
fascinated by the proof of the
immortality of the soul in the
Phædon that he forthwith cast
himself into the sea. Cato, as
is well known, chose this work
to study, the night he committed
suicide.

[3] Arist. Ethic. v.

[4] See a list of these in Lactantius' Inst. Div. iii. 18. Many of
these instances rest on very doubtful evidence.

whether it be a history or a legend, shows that the patient endurance of suffering was once the supreme ideal.[1] Virgil painted in gloomy colours the condition of suicides in the future world.[2] Cicero strongly asserted the doctrine of Pythagoras, though he praised the suicide of Cato.[3] Apuleius, expounding the philosophy of Plato, taught that 'the wise man never throws off his body except by the will of God.'[4] Cæsar, Ovid, and others urged that in extreme distress it is easy to despise life, and that true courage is shown in enduring it.[5] Among the Stoics themselves, the belief that no man may shrink from a duty co-existed with the belief that every man has a right to dispose of his own life. Seneca, who emphatically advocated suicide, admits that there were some who deemed it wrong, and he himself attempted to moderate what he termed 'the passion for suicide', that had arisen among his disciples.[6] Marcus Aurelius wavers a little on the subject, sometimes asserting the right of every man to leave life when

---

[1] Adam Smith's *Moral Sentiments*, part vii. § 2.

[2] 'Proxima deinde tenent mœsti loca qui sibi lethum
Insontes peperere manu, lucemque perosi
Projecere animas. Quam vellent æthere in alto
Nunc et pauperiem et duros perferre labores.'—*Æneid*, vi. 434-437.

[3] Cicero has censured suicide in his *De Senectute*, in the *Somn. Scipionis*, and in the *Tusculans*. Concerning the death of Cato, he says, that the occasion was such as to constitute a divine call to leave life.—*Tusc.* i.

[4] Apuleius, *De Philos Plat.* lib. i.

[5] Thus Ovid :—

'Rebus in adversis facile est contemnere vitam,
Fortiter ille facit qui miser esse potest.'

See, too, Martial, xi. 56.

[6] Especially *Ep.* xxiv. Seneca desires that men should not commit suicide with panic or trepidation. He says that those condemned to death should await their execution, for 'it is a folly to die through fear of death ;' and he recommends men to support old age as long as their faculties remain unimpaired. On this last point, however, his language is somewhat contradictory. There is a good review of the opinions of the ancients in general, and of Seneca in particular, on this subject in Justus Lipsius' *Manuductio ad Stoicam Philosophiam*, lib. iii. dissert. 22, 23, from which I have borrowed much.

he pleases, sometimes inclining to the Platonic doctrine that man is a soldier of God, occupying a post which it is criminal to abandon.[1] Plotinus and Porphyry argued strongly against all suicide.[2]

But, notwithstanding these passages, there can be no question that the ancient view of suicide was broadly and strongly opposed to our own. A general approval of it floated down through most of the schools of philosophy, and even to those who condemned it, it never seems to have assumed its present aspect of extreme enormity. This was in the first instance due to the ancient notion of death ; and we have also to remember that when a society once learns to tolerate suicide, the deed, in ceasing to be disgraceful, loses much of its actual criminality, for those who are most firmly convinced that the stigma and suffering it now brings upon the family of the deceased do not constitute its entire guilt, will readily acknowledge that they greatly aggravate it. In the conditions of ancient thought, this aggravation did not exist. Epicurus exhorted men ' to weigh carefully, whether they would prefer death to come to them, or would themselves

---

[1] In his *Meditations*, ix. 3, he speaks of the duty of patiently awaiting death. But in iii. 1, x. 8, 22–32, he clearly recognises the right of suicide in some cases, especially to prevent moral degeneracy. It must be remembered that the *Meditations* of Marcus Aurelius were private notes for his personal guidance, that all the Stoics admitted it to be wrong to commit suicide in cases where the act would be an injury to society, and that this consideration in itself would be sufficient to divert an emperor from the deed. Antoninus, the uncle, predecessor, and model of M. Aurelius, had considered it his duty several times to prevent Hadrian from committing

suicide (Spartianus, *Hadrianus*). According to Capitolinus, Marcus Aurelius in his last illness purposely accelerated his death by abstinence. The duty of not hastily, or through cowardice, abandoning a path of duty, and the right of man to quit life when it appears intolerable, are combined very clearly by Epictetus, *Arrian*, i. 9; and the latter is asserted in the strongest manner, i. 24–25.

[2] Porphyry, *De Abst. Carnis*, ii. 47 ; Plotinus, 1st Enn. ix. Porphyry says (*Life of Plotinus*) that Plotinus dissuaded him from suicide. There is a good epitome of the arguments of this school against suicide in Macrobius, *In Som. Scip.* 1.

go to death; '[1] and among his disciples, Lucretius, the illustrious poet of the sect, died by his own hand,[2] as did also Cassius the tyrannicide, Atticus the friend of Cicero,[3] the voluptuary Petronius,[4] and the philosopher Diodorus.[5] Pliny described the lot of man as in this respect at least superior to that of God, that man has the power of flying to the tomb,[6] and he represented it as one of the greatest proofs of the bounty of Providence, that it has filled the world with herbs, by which the weary may find a rapid and a painless death.[7] One of the most striking figures that a passing notice of Cicero brings before us, is that of Hegesias, who

[1] Quoted by Seneca, *Ep.* xxvi. Cicero states the Epicurean doctrine to be, 'Ut si tolerabiles sint dolores, feramus, sin minus æquo animo e vita, cum ea non placet, tanquam e theatro, exeamus' (*De Finib.* i. 15); and again, 'De Diis immortalibus sine ullo metu vera sentit. Non dubitat, si ita melius sit, de vita migrare.'—Id. i. 19.

[2] This is noticed by St. Jerome.

[3] Corn. Nepos, *Atticus.* He killed himself when an old man, to shorten a hopeless disease.

[4] Petronius, who was called the arbitrator of tastes ('elegantiæ arbiter'), was one of the most famous voluptuaries of the reign of Nero. Unlike most of his contemporaries, however, he was endowed with the most exquisite and refined taste; his graceful manners fascinated all about him, and made him in matters of pleasure the ruler of the Court. Appointed Proconsul of Bithynia, and afterwards Consul, he displayed the energies and the abilities of a statesman. A Court intrigue threw him out of favour; and believing that his death was resolved on, he determined to anticipate it by sui-

cide. Calling his friends about him, he opened his veins, shut them, and opened them again; prolonged his lingering death till he had arranged his affairs; discoursed in his last moments, not about the immortality of the soul or the dogmas of philosophers, but about the gay songs and epigrams of the hour; and partaking of a cheerful banquet, died as recklessly as he had lived. (Tacit. *Annal.* xvi. 18–19.) It has been a matter of much dispute whether or not this Petronius was the author of the *Satyricon*, one of the most licentious and repulsive works in Latin literature.

[5] Seneca, *De Vita Beata*, xix.

[6] 'Imperfectæ vero in homine naturæ præcipua solatia, ne Deum quidem posse omnia; namque nec sibi potest mortem consciscere si velit, quod homini dedit optimum in tantis vitæ pœnis.'—*Hist. Nat* ii. 5.

[7] *Hist. Nat.* ii. 63. We need not be surprised at this writer thus speaking of sudden death, 'Mortes repentinæ (hoc est summa vitæ felicitas),' vii. 54.

was surnamed by the ancients 'the orator of death.' A conspicuous member of that Cyrenaic school which esteemed the
pursuit of pleasure the sole end of a rational being, he taught
that life was so full of cares, and its pleasure so fleeting and so
alloyed, that the happiest lot for man was death; and such
was the power of his eloquence, so intense was the fascination
he cast around the tomb, that his disciples embraced with
rapture the consequence of his doctrine, multitudes freed
themselves by suicide from the troubles of the world, and the
contagion was so great, that Ptolemy, it is said, was compelled
to banish the philosopher from Alexandria.[1]

But it was in the Roman Empire and among the Roman
Stoics that suicide assumed its greatest prominence, and its
philosophy was most fully elaborated. From an early period
self-immolation, like that of Curtius or Decius, had been
esteemed in some circumstances a religious rite, being, as has
been well suggested, probably a lingering remnant of the
custom of human sacrifices,[2] and towards the closing days of
paganism many influences conspired in the same direction.
The example of Cato, who had become the ideal of the
Stoics, and whose dramatic suicide was the favourite subject of their eloquence,[3] the indifference to death produced
by the great multiplication of gladiatorial shows, the many
instances of barbarian captives, who, sooner than slay their
fellow-countrymen, or minister to the pleasures of their conquerors, plunged their lances into their own necks, or found

---

[1] *Tusc. Quæst.* lib. 1. Another
remarkable example of an epidemic
of suicide occurred among the
young girls of Miletus. (*Aul. Gell.*
xv. 10.)

[2] Sir Cornewall Lewis, *On the
Credibility of Early Roman History*,
vol. ii. p. 430. See, too, on this
class of suicides, Cromaziano, *Isto-
rica Critica del Suicidio* (Venezia,
1788), pp. 81–82. The real name
of the author of this book (which
is, I think, the best history of suicide) was Buonafede. He was a
Celestine monk. The book was
first published at Lucca in 1761.
It was translated into French in
1841.

[3] Senec. *De Provid.* ii. ; *Ep*
xxiv.

otner and still more horrible roads to freedom,[1] the custom
of compelling political prisoners to execute their own sentence,
and, more than all, the capricious and atrocious tyranny
of the Cæsars,[2] had raised suicide into an extraordinary
prominence. Few things are more touching than the passionate joy with which, in the reign of Nero, Seneca clung
to it as the one refuge for the oppressed, the last bulwark
of the tottering mind. ' To death alone it is due that life
is not a punishment, that, erect beneath the frowns of
fortune, I can preserve my mind unshaken and master of
itself. I have one to whom I can appeal. I see before me
the crosses of many forms. . . . I see the rack and the scourge,
and the instruments of torture adapted to every limb and to
every nerve; but I also see Death. She stands beyond my
savage enemies, beyond my haughty fellow-countrymen.
Slavery loses its bitterness when by a step I can pass to
liberty. Against all the injuries of life, I have the refuge of
death.'[3] ' Wherever you look, there is the end of evils. You
see that yawning precipice—there you may descend to
liberty. You see that sea, that river, that well—liberty sits
at the bottom. . . . Do you seek the way to freedom ?—you
may find it in every vein of your body.'[4] ' If I can choose
between a death of torture and one that is simple and easy,
why should I not select the latter ? As I choose the ship
in which I will sail, and the house I will inhabit, so I will
choose the death by which I will leave life. . . . In no matter more than in death should we act according to our desire.
Depart from life as your impulse leads you, whether it be by
the sword, or the rope, or the poison creeping through the
veins ; go your way, and break the chains of slavery. Man
should seek the approbation of others in his life ; his death

---

[1] See some examples of this in
Seneca, *Ep.* lxx.
[2] See a long catalogue of suicides arising from this cause, in
Cromaziano, *Ist. del Suicidio*, pp
112- 14.
[3] *Consol. ad Marc.* c. xx.
[4] *De Ira*, iii. 15

concerns himself alcne. That is the best which pleases him
most. . . . The eternal law has decreed nothing better than
this, that life should have but one entrance and many exits.
Why should I endure the agonies of disease, and the cruelties
of human tyranny, when I can emancipate myself from all
my torments, and shake off every bond? For this reason,
but for this alone, life is not an evil—that no one is obliged
to live. The lot of man is happy, because no one continues
wretched but by his fault. If life pleases you, live. If not,
you have a right to return whence you came.'[1]

These passages, which are but a few selected out of very
many, will sufficiently show the passion with which the most
influential teacher of Roman Stoicism advocated suicide. As
a general proposition, the law recognised it as a right, but
two slight restrictions were after a time imposed.[2] It had

---

[1] *Ep.* lxx.

[2] See Donne's *Biathanatos* (London, 1700), pp. 56–57. Gibbon's *Decline and Fall,* ch. xliv. Blackstone, in his chapter on suicide, quotes the sentence of the Roman lawyers on the subject : 'Si quis impatientia doloris aut tædio vitæ aut morbo aut furore aut pudore mori maluit non animadvertatur in eum.' Ulpian expressly asserts that the wills of suicides were recognised by law, and numerous examples of the act, notoriously prepared and publicly and gradually accomplished, prove its legality in Rome. Suetonius, it is true, speaks of Claudius accusing a man for having tried to kill himself (Claud. xvi.), and Xiphilin says (lxix. 8) that Hadrian gave special permission to the philosopher Euphrates to commit suicide, 'on account of old age and disease ;' but in the first case it appears from the context that a reproach and not a legal action was meant, while Euphrates, I suppose, asked permission to show his loyalty to the emperor, and not as a matter of strict necessity. There were, however, some Greek laws condemning suicide, probably on civic grounds. Josephus mentions (*De Bell. Jud.* iii. 8) that in some nations 'the right hand of the suicide was amputated, and that in Judea the suicide was only buried after sunset.' A very strange law, said to have been derived from Greece, is reported to have existed at Marseilles. Poison was kept by the senate of the city, and given to those who could prove that they had sufficient reason to justify their desire for death, and all other suicide was forbidden. The law was intended, it was said, to prevent hasty suicide, and to make deliberate suicide as rapid and painless as possible. (Valer. Maximus, ii. 6, § 7.) In the Reign

become customary with many men who were accused of political offences to commit suicide before trial, in order to prevent the ignominious exposure of their bodies and the confiscation of their goods; but Domitian closed this resource by ordaining that the suicide of an accused person should entail the same consequences as his condemnation. Hadrian afterwards assimilated the suicide of a Roman soldier to desertion.[1] With these exceptions, the liberty appears to have been absolute, and the act was committed under the most various motives. The suicide of Otho, who is said to have killed himself to avoid being a second time a cause of civil war, was extolled as equal in grandeur to that of Cato.[2] In the Dacian war, the enemy, having captured a distinguished Roman general named Longinus, endeavoured to extort terms from Trajan as a condition of his surrender, but Longinus, by taking poison, freed the emperor from his embarrassment.[3] On the death of Otho, some of his soldiers, filled with grief and admiration, killed themselves before his corpse,[4] as did also a freedman of Agrippina, at the funeral of the empress.[5] Before the close of the Republic, an enthusiastic partisan of one of the factions in the chariot races flung himself upon the pile on which the body of a favourite coachman was consumed, and perished in the flames.[6] A Roman, unmenaced in his

---

of Terror in France, a law was made similar to that of Domitian. (Carlyle's *Hist. of the French Revolution*, book v. c. ii.)

[1] Compare with this a curious 'order of the day,' issued by Napoleon in 1802, with the view of checking the prevalence of suicide among his soldiers. (Lisle, *Du Suicide*, pp. 462–463.)

[2] See Suetonius, *Otho*, c. x.–xi., and the very fine description in Tacitus, *Hist.* lib. ii. c. 47–49. Martial compares the death of Otho to that of Cato:

'Sit Cato, dum vivit, sane vel Cæsare major;
Dum moritur, numquid major Othone fuit?'—*Ep.* vi. 32.

[3] Xiphilin, lxviii. 12.
[4] Tacit. *Hist.* ii. 49. Suet. *Otho*, 12. Suetonius says that, in addition to these, many soldiers who were not present killed themselves on hearing the news.
[5] Ibid. *Annal.* xiv. 9.
[6] Plin. *Hist. Nat.* vii. 54. The opposite faction attributed this suicide to the maddening effects of the perfumes burnt on the pile.

fortune, and standing high in the favour of his sovereign, killed himself under Tiberius, because he could not endure to witness the crimes of the empire.[1] Another, being afflicted by an incurable malady, postponed his suicide till the death of Domitian, that at least he might die free, and on the assassination of the tyrant, hastened cheerfully to the tomb.[2] The Cynic Peregrinus announced that, being weary of life, he would on a certain day depart, and, in presence of a large concourse, he mounted the funeral pile.[3] Most frequently, however, death was regarded as 'the last physician of disease,'[4] and suicide as the legitimate relief from intolerable suffering. 'Above all things,' said Epictetus, 'remember that the door is open. Be not more timid than boys at play. As they, when they cease to take pleasure in their games, declare they will no longer play, so do you, when all things begin to pall upon you, retire ; but if you stay, do not complain.'[5] Seneca declared that he who waits the extremity of old age is not ' far removed from a coward,' 'as he is justly regarded as too much addicted to wine who drains the flask to the very dregs.' ' I will not relinquish old age,' he added, ' if it leaves my better part intact. But if it begins to shake my mind, if it destroys its faculties one by one, if it leaves me not life but breath, I will depart from the putrid or tottering edifice. I will not escape by death from disease so long as it may be healed, and leaves my mind unimpaired. I will not raise my hand against myself on account of pain, for so to die is to be conquered. But if I know that I must suffer without hope of relief, I will depart, not through fear of the pain itself, but because it prevents all for which I would live.'[6] 'Just as a landlord,' said Musonius, ' who has not received his rent, pulls

---

[1] Tacit. *Annal.* vi. 26.

[2] Plin. *Ep.* i. 12.

[3] This history is satirically and unfeelingly told by Lucian. See, too, Ammianus Marcellinus, **xxix.** 1.

[4] Sophocles.

[5] Arrian, i. 24.

[6] Seneca, *Ep.* lviii.

down the doors, removes the rafters, and fills up the well, so
l seem to be driven out of this little body, when nature,
which has let it to me, takes away, one by one, eyes and
ears, hands and feet. I will not, therefore, delay longer, but
will cheerfully depart as from a banquet.'[1]

This conception of suicide as an euthanasia, an abridg
ment of the pangs of disease, and a guarantee against the
dotage of age, was not confined to philosophical treatises.
We have considerable evidence of its being frequently put in
practice. Among those who thus abridged their lives was
Silius Italicus, one of the last of the Latin poets.[2] The
younger Pliny describes in terms of the most glowing admiration the conduct of one of his friends, who, struck down by
disease, resolved calmly and deliberately upon the path he
should pursue. He determined, if the disease was only dangerous and long, to yield to the wishes of his friends and
await the struggle; but if the issue was hopeless, to die by
his own hand. Having reasoned on the propriety of this
course with all the tranquil courage of a Roman, he summoned a council of physicians, and, with a mind indifferent
to either fate, he calmly awaited their sentence.[3] The same
writer mentions the case of a man who was afflicted with a
horrible disease, which reduced his body to a mass of sores.
His wife, being convinced that it was incurable, exhorted her
husband to shorten his sufferings; she nerved and encouraged
him to the effort, and she claimed it as her privilege to
accompany him to the grave. Husband and wife, bound

---

[1] Stobæus. One of the most
deliberate suicides recorded was
that of a Greek woman of ninety
years old.—Val. Maxim. ii. 6, § 8.

[2] Plin. *Ep*. iii. 7. He starved
himself to death.

[3] *Ep*. i. 22. Some of Pliny's
expressions are remarkable:—'Id
ego arduum in primis et præcipua
laude dignum puto. Nam impetu

quodam et instinctu procurrere ad
mortem, commune cum multis
deliberare vero et causas ejus ex
pendere, utque suaserit ratio, vitæ
mortisque consilium suscipere vel
ponere, ingentis est animi.' In
this case the doctors pronounced
that recovery was possible, and
the suicide was in consequence
averted.

together, plunged into a lake.[1] Seneca, in one of his letters, has left us a detailed description of the death-bed of one of the Roman suicides. Tullius Marcellinus, a young man of remarkable abilities and very earnest character, who had long ridiculed the teachings of philosophy, but had ended by em-bracing it with all the passion of a convert, being afflicted with a grave and lingering though not incurable disease, resolved at length upon suicide. He gathered his friends around him, and many of them entreated him to continue in life. Among them, however, was one Stoical philosopher, who addressed him in what Seneca terms the very noblest of discourses. He exhorted him not to lay too much stress upon the ques-tion he was deciding, as if existence was a matter of great im-portance. He urged that life is a thing we possess in common with slaves and animals, but that a noble death should in-deed be prized, and he concluded by recommending suicide. Marcellinus gladly embraced the counsel which his own wishes had anticipated. According to the advice of his friend, he distributed gifts among his faithful slaves, consoled them on their approaching bereavement, abstained during three days from all food, and at last, when his strength had been wholly exhausted, passed into a warm bath and calmly died, describing with his last breath the pleasing sensations that accompanied receding life.[2]

The doctrine of suicide was indeed the culminating point of Roman Stoicism. The proud, self-reliant, unbending cha-racter of the philosopher could only be sustained when he felt that he had a sure refuge against the extreme forms of suf-fering or of despair. Although virtue is not a mere creature of interest, no great system has ever yet flourished which did not present an ideal of happiness as well as an ideal of duty. Stoicism taught men to hope little, but to fear nothing.

---

[1] Lib. vi. *Ep.* xxiv.
[2] *Ep.* lxxvii. On the former career of Marcellinus, see *Ep.* xxix.

It did not array death in brilliant colours, as the path to positive felicity, but it endeavoured to divest it, as the end of suffering, of every terror. Life lost much of its bitterness when men had found a refuge from the storms of fate, a speedy deliverance from dotage and pain. Death ceased to be terrible when it was regarded rather as a remedy than as a sentence. Life and death in the Stoical system were attuned to the same key. The deification of human virtue, the total absence of all sense of sin, the proud stubborn will that deemed humiliation the worst of stains, appeared alike in each. The type of its own kind was perfect. All the virtues and all the majesty that accompany human pride, when developed to the highest point, and directed to the noblest ends, were here displayed. All those which accompany humility and self-abasement were absent.

I desire at this stage of our enquiry to pause for a moment, in order to retrace briefly the leading steps of the foregoing argument, and thus to bring into the clearest light the connection which many details and quotations may have occasionally obscured. Such a review will show at a single glance in what respects Stoicism was a result of the pre-existent state of society, and in what respects it was an active agent, how far its influence was preparing the way for Christian ethics, and how far it was opposed to them.

We have seen, then, that among the Romans, as among other people, a very clear and definite type of moral excellence was created before men had formed any clear intellectual notions of the nature and sanctions of virtue. The characters of men are chiefly governed by their occupations, and the republic being organised altogether with a view to military success, it had attained all the virtues and vices of a military society. We have seen, too, that at all times, but most especially under the conditions of ancient warfare, military life is very unfavourable to the amiable, and very favourable to the heroic virtues. The Roman had learnt to value force

very highly. Being continually engaged in inflicting pain,
his natural or instinctive humanity was very low. His moral
feelings were almost bounded by political limits, acting only,
and with different degrees of intensity, towards his class, his
country, and its allies. Indomitable pride was the most
prominent element of his character. A victorious army
which is humble or diffident, or tolerant of insult, or
anxious to take the second place, is, indeed, almost a contradiction of terms. The spirit of patriotism, in its relation to
foreigners, like that of political liberty in its relation to
governors, is a spirit of constant and jealous self-assertion ;
and although both are very consonant with high morality and
great self-devotion, we rarely find that the grace of genuine
humility can flourish in a society that is intensely pervaded
by their influence. The kind of excellence that found most
favour in Roman eyes was simple, forcible, massive, but
coarse-grained. Subtilty of motives, refinements of feelings,
delicacies of susceptibility, were rarely appreciated.

This was the darker side of the picture. On the other
hand, the national character, being formed by a profession in
which mercenary considerations are less powerful, and splendid
examples of self-devotion more frequent, than in any other,
had early risen to a heroic level. Death being continually
confronted, to meet it with courage was the chief test of
virtue. The habits of men were unaffected, frugal, honourable,
and laborious. A stern discipline pervading all ages and
classes of society, the will was trained, to an almost unexampled degree, to repress the passions, to endure suffering
and opposition, to tend steadily and fearlessly towards an unpopular end. A sense of duty was very widely diffused, and
a deep attachment to the interests of the city became the
parent of many virtues.

Such was the type of excellence the Roman people had
attained at a time when its intellectual cultivation produced
philosophical discussions, and when numerous Greek pro-

fessors, attracted partly by political events, and partly by the patronage of Scipio Æmilianus, arrived at Rome, bringing with them the tenets of the great schools of Zeno and Epicurus, and of the many minor sects that clustered around them. Epicureanism being essentially opposed to the pre-existing type of virtue, though it spread greatly, never attained the position of a school of virtue. Stoicism, taught by Panætius of Rhodes, and soon after by the Syrian Posidonius, became the true religion of the educated classes. It furnished the principles of virtue, coloured the noblest literature of the time, and guided all the developments of moral enthusiasm.

The Stoical system of ethics was in the highest sense a system of independent morals. It taught that our reason reveals to us a certain law of nature, and that a desire to conform to this law, irrespectively of all considerations of reward or punishment, of happiness or the reverse, is a possible and a sufficient motive of virtue. It was also in the highest sense a system of discipline. It taught that the will, acting under the complete control of the reason, is the sole principle of virtue, and that all the emotional part of our being is of the nature of a disease. Its whole tendency was therefore to dignify and strengthen the will, and to degrade and suppress the desires. It taught, moreover, that man is capable of attaining an extremely high degree of moral excellence, that he has nothing to fear beyond the present life, that it is essential to the dignity and consistence of his character that he should regard death without dismay, and that he has a right to hasten it if he desires.

It is easy to see that this system of ethics was strictly consonant with the type of character the circumstances of the Roman people had formed. It is also manifest that while the force of circumstances had in the first instance secured its ascendancy, the energy of will which it produced would enable it to offer a powerful resistance to the tendencies of an altered condition of society. This was pre-eminently shown in the history of Roman Stoicism. The austere purity of the writings of Seneca and his school is a fact probably unique in history, when we consider, on the one hand, the intense and undisguised depravity of the Empire, and on the other, the prominent position of most of the leading Stoics in the very centre of the stream. More than once in later periods did great intellectual brilliancy coincide with general depravity, but on none of these occasions was this moral phenomenon reproduced. In the age of Leo X., in the age of the French Regency, or of Lewis XV., we look in vain for high moral teaching in the centre of Italian or of Parisian civilisation. The true teachers of those ages were the reformers, who arose in obscure towns of Germany or Switzerland, or that diseased recluse who, from his solitude near Geneva, fascinated Europe by the gleams of a dazzling and almost peerless eloquence, and by a moral teaching which, though often feverish, paradoxical, and unpractical, abounded in passages of transcendent majesty and of the most entrancing purity and beauty. But even the best moral teachers who rose in the centres of the depraved society felt the contagion of the surrounding vice. Their ideal was depressed, their austerity was relaxed, they appealed to sordid and worldly motives, their judgments of character were wavering and uncertain, their whole teaching was of the nature of a compromise. But in ancient Rome, if the teachers of virtue acted but feebly upon the surrounding corruption, their own tenets were at least unstained. The splendour of the genius of Cæsar never eclipsed the moral grandeur of the vanquished Cato, and amid all the dramatic vicissitudes of civil war and of political convulsion, the supreme authority of moral distinctions was never forgotten. The eloquence of Livy was chiefly employed in painting virtue, the eloquence of Tacitus in branding vice. The Stoics never lowered their standard because of the depravity around them, and if we trace in their teaching any reflection of the prevailing worship of enjoyment, it is only in the passionate intensity with which they dwelt upon the tranquillity of the tomb.

But it is not sufficient for a moral system to form a bulwark against vice, it must also be capable of admitting those extensions and refinements of moral sympathies which advancing civilisation produces, and the inflexibility of its antagonism to evil by no means implies its capacity of enlarging its conceptions of good. During the period which elapsed between the importation of Stoical tenets into Rome and the ascendancy of Christianity, an extremely important transformation of moral ideas had been effected by political changes, and it became a question how far the new elements could coalesce with the Stoical ideal, and how far they tended to replace it by an essentially different type. These changes were twofold, but were very closely connected. They consisted of the increasing prominence of the benevolent or amiable, as distinguished from the heroic qualities, and of the enlargement of moral sympathies, which having at first comprised only a class or a nation, came at last, by the destruction of many artificial barriers, to include all classes and all nations. The causes of these changes—which were the most important antecedents of the triumph of Christianity—are very complicated and numerous, but it will, I think, be possible to give in a few pages a sufficiently clear outline of the movement.

It originated in the Roman Empire at the time when the union of the Greek and Latin civilisations was effected by the conquest of Greece. The general humanity of the Greeks had always been incomparably greater than that of the Romans. The refining influence of their art and literature, their ignorance of gladiatorial games, and their comparative freedom from the spirit of conquest, had separated them widely from their semi-barbarous conquerors, and had given a peculiar softness and tenderness to their ideal

characters. Pericles, who, when the friends who had
gathered round his death-bed, imagining him to be insensible,
were recounting his splendid deeds, told them that they had
forgotten his best title to fame—that 'no Athenian had ever
worn mourning on his account;' Aristides, praying the gods
that those who had banished him might never be compelled
by danger or suffering to recall him; Phocion, when unjustly
condemned, exhorting his son never to avenge his death, all
represent a type of character of a milder kind than that
which Roman influences produced. The plays of Euripides
had been to the ancient world the first great revelation of
the supreme beauty of the gentler virtues. Among the many
forms of worship that flourished at Athens, there was an
altar which stood alone, conspicuous and honoured beyond
all others. The suppliants thronged around it, but no image
of a god, no symbol of dogma was there. It was dedicated
to Pity, and was venerated through all the ancient world as
the first great assertion among mankind of the supreme
sanctity of Mercy.[1]

But while the Greek spirit was from a very early period

---

[1] See the very beautiful lines of
Statius:—

'Urbe fuit media nulli concessa
     potentum
Ara Deum, mitis posuit Clementia
     sedem :
Et miseri fecere sacram, sine sup-
     plice numquam
Illa novo; nulla damnavit vota
     repulsa.
Auditi quicunque rogant, noc-
     tesque diesque
Ire datum, et solis numen placare
     querelis.
Parca superstitio; non thurea
     flamma, nec altus
Accipitur sanguis, lachrymis al-
     taria sudant. . .

Nulla autem effigies, nulli com
     missa metallo
Forma Deæ, mentes habitare et
     pectora gaudet.
Semper habet trepidos, semper
     locus horret egenis
Cœtibus, ignotæ tantum felicibus
     aræ.'—*Thebaid*, xii. 481–496.

This altar was very old, and was
said to have been founded by the
descendants of Hercules. Diodorus
of Sicily, however, makes a Syra-
cusan say that it was brought from
Syracuse (lib. xiii 22). Marcus
Aurelius erected a temple to 'Bene-
ficentia' on the Capitol. (Xiphilin,
lib. lxxi. 34.)

distinguished for its humanity, it was at first as far removed from cosmopolitanism as that of Rome. It is well known that Phrynichus was fined because in his 'Conquest of Miletus' he had represented the triumph of barbarians over Greeks.[1] His successor, Æschylus, deemed it necessary to violate all dramatic probabilities by making the Persian king and courtiers continually speak of themselves as barbarians. Socrates, indeed, had proclaimed himself a citizen of the world,[2] but Aristotle taught that Greeks had no more duties to barbarians than to wild beasts, and another philosopher was believed to have evinced an almost excessive range of sympathy when he declared that his affections extended beyond his own State, and included the whole people of Greece. But the dissolving and disintegrating philosophical discussions that soon followed the death of Socrates, strengthened by political events, tended powerfully to destroy this feeling. The traditions that attached Greek philosophy to Egypt, the subsequent admiration for the schools of India to which Pyrrho and Anaxarchus are said to have resorted,[3] the prevalence of Cynicism and Epicureanism, which agreed in inculcating indifference to political life, the complete decomposition of the popular national religions, and the incompatibility of a narrow local feeling with great knowledge and matured civilisation, were the intellectual causes of the change, and the movement of expansion received a great political stimulus when Alexander eclipsed the glories of Spartan and Athenian history by the vision of universal empire, accorded to the conquered nations the privileges of the conquerors, and

---

[1] Herodotus, vi. 21.

[2] See Arrian's *Epictetus*, i. 9. The very existence of the word φιλανθρωπία shows that the idea was not altogether unknown.

[3] Diog. Laërt. *Pyrrho*. There was a tradition that Pythagoras had himself penetrated to India, and learnt philosophy from the gymnosophists. (Apuleius, *Florid* lib. ii. c. 15.)

create l in Alexandria a great centre both of commercial intercourse and of philosophical eclecticism.[1]

It is evident, therefore, that the prevalence of Greek ideas
in Rome would be in a two-fold way destructive of narrow
national feelings. It was the ascendancy of a people who
were not Romans, and of a people who had already become
in a great degree emancipated from local sentiments. It is
also evident that the Greeks having had for several centuries
a splendid literature, at a time when the Romans had none,
and when the Latin language was still too rude for literary
purposes, the period in which the Romans first emerged from
a purely military condition into an intelligent civilisation
would bring with it an ascendancy of Greek ideas. Fabius
Pictor and Cincius Alimentus, the earliest native Roman historians, both wrote in Greek,[2] and although the poems of
Ennius, and the 'Origines' of Marcus Cato, contributed
largely to improve and fix the Latin language, the precedent
was not at once discontinued.[3]   After the conquest of Greece,
the political ascendancy of the Romans and the intellectual
ascendancy of Greece were alike universal.[4]   The conquered

---

[1] This aspect of the career of
Alexander was noticed in a remarkable passage of a treatise
ascribed to Plutarch (*De Fort.
Alex.*). 'Conceiving he was sent
by God to be an umpire between
all, and to unite all together, he
reduced by arms those whom he
could not conquer by persuasion,
and formed of a hundred diverse
nations one single universal body,
mingling, as it were, in one cup of
friendship the customs, marriages,
and laws of all.   He desired that
all should regard the whole world
as their common country, . . . that
every good man should be esteemed
a Hellene, every evil man a barbarian.'   See on this subject the
third lecture of Mr. Merivale (whose

translation of Plutarch I have borrowed) *On the Conversion of the
Roman Empire.*

[2] They were both born about
B.C. 250.   See Sir C. Lewis, *Credibility of Early Roman History*,
vol. i. p. 82.

[3] Aulus Gellius mentions the
indignation of Marcus Cato against
a consul named Albinus, who had
written in Greek a Roman history,
and prefaced it by an apology for
his faults of style, on the ground
that he was writing in a foreign
language. (*Noct Att.* xi. 8.)

[4] See a vivid picture of the
Greek influence upon Rome, in
Mommsen's *Hist. of Rome* (Eng.
trans.), vol. iii. pp. 423–426.

people, whose patriotic feelings had been greatly enfeebled by
the influences I have noticed, acquiesced readily in their new
condition, and notwithstanding the vehement exertions of the
conservative party, Greek manners, sentiments, and ideas
soon penetrated into all classes, and moulded all the forms of
Roman life.   The elder Cato, as an acute observer has
noticed, desired all Greek philosophers to be expelled from
Rome.   The younger Cato made Greek philosophers his most
intimate friends.[1] Roman virtue found its highest expression
in Stoicism.   Roman vice sheltered itself under the name of
Epicurus.   Diodorus of Sicily and Polybius first sketched in
Greek the outlines of universal history.   Dionysius of Halicarnassus explored Roman antiquities.   Greek artists and
Greek architects thronged the city; but the first, under
Roman influence, abandoned the ideal for the portrait, and
the second degraded the noble Corinthian pillar into the bastard composite.[2] The theatre, which now started into sudden
life, was borrowed altogether from the Greeks.   Ennius and
Pacuvius imitated Euripides; Cæcilius, Plautus, Terence,
and Nævius devoted themselves chiefly to Menander.   Even
the lover in the days of Lucretius painted his lady's charms
in Greek.[3] Immense sums were given for Greek literary
slaves, and the attractions of the capital drew to Rome nearly
all that was brilliant in Athenian society.

While the complete ascendancy of the intellect and
manners of Greece was destroying the simplicity of the old
Roman type, and at the same time enlarging the range of

[1] Plin. *Hist. Nat.* vii. 31.
[2] See Friedlænder, *Mœurs romaines du règne d'Auguste à la fin
des Antonins* (French trans., 1865),
tome i. pp. 6–7.
[3] See the curious catalogue of
Greek love terms in vogue (Lucretius, lib. iv. line 1160, &c.). Juve-

nal, more than a hundred years
later, was extremely angry with
the Roman ladies for making love
in Greek (*Sat.* vi. lines 190–195).
Friedlænder remarks that there is
no special term in Latin for to ask
in marriage (tome i. p. 354).

Roman sympathies, an equally powerful influence was breaking down the aristocratic and class feeling which had so long
raised an insurmountable barrier between the nobles and the
plebeians. Their long contentions had issued in the civil
wars, the dictatorship of Julius Cæsar, and the Empire, and
these changes in a great measure obliterated the old lines of
demarcation. Foreign wars, which develop with great intensity distinctive national types, and divert the public mind
from internal changes, are usually favourable to the conservative spirit; but civil wars are essentially revolutionary, for
they overwhelm all class barriers and throw open the highest
prizes to energy and genius. Two very remarkable and altogether unprecedented illustrations of this truth occurred at
Rome. Ventidius Bassus, by his military skill, and by the
friendship of Julius Cæsar, and afterwards of Antony, rose
from the position of mule-driver to the command of a Roman
army, and at last to the consulate,[1] which was also attained,
about 40 B.C., by the Spaniard Cornelius Balbus.[2] Augustus,
though the most aristocratic of emperors, in order to discourage celibacy, permitted all citizens who were not senators
to intermarry with freedwomen. The empire was in several
distinct ways unfavourable to class distinctions. It was for
the most part essentially democratic, winning its popularity
from the masses of the people, and crushing the senate, which
had been the common centre of aristocracy and of freedom.
A new despotic power, bearing alike on all classes, reduced
them to an equality of servitude. The emperors were themselves in many cases the mere creatures of revolt, and their
policy was governed by their origin. Their jealousy struck

---

[1] Aul. Gell. *Noct.* xv. 4; Vell.
Paterculus, ii. 65. The people were
much scandalised at this elevation,
and made epigrams about it. There
is a curious catalogue of men who
at different times rose in Rome from
low positions to power and dignity.
in Legendre, *Traité de l'Opinion*,
tome ii. pp. 254–255.

[2] Dion Cassius, xlviii. 32. Plin
Hist. Nat. v. 5; vii. 44.

down many of the nobles, while others were ruined by the public games, which it became customary to give, or by the luxury to which, in the absence of political occupations, they were impelled, and the relative importance of all was diminished by the new creations. The ascendancy of wealth began to pass into new quarters. Delators, or political informers, encouraged by the emperors, and enriched by the confiscated properties of those whose condemnation they had procured, rose to great influence. From the time of Caligula, for several reigns, the most influential citizens were freedmen, who occupied the principal offices in the palace, and usually obtained complete ascendancy over the emperors. Through them alone petitions were presented. By their instrumentality the Imperial favours were distributed. They sometimes dethroned the emperors. They retained their power unshaken through a succession of revolutions. In wealth, in power, in the crowd of their courtiers, in the splendour of their palaces in life, and of their tombs in death, they eclipsed all others, and men whom the early Roman patricians would have almost disdained to notice, saw the proudest struggling for their favour.[1]

Together with these influences many others of a kindred nature may be detected. The colonial policy which the Gracchi had advocated was carried out at Narbonne, and during the latter days of Julius Cæsar, to the amazement and scandal of the Romans, Gauls of this province obtained seats in the senate.[2] The immense extent of the empire made it necessary for numerous troops to remain during long periods of time in distant provinces, and the foreign habits that were thus acquired began the destruction of the exclusive feelings of the Roman army, which the subsequent enrolment of

[1] The history of the influence of freedmen is minutely traced by Friedlænder, *Mœurs romaines du règne d'Auguste à la fin des Antonins,* tome i. pp. 58–93. Statius and Martial sang their praises.

[2] See Tacit. *Ann.* vi. 23–26.

barbarians completed. The public games, the immense luxury, the concentration of power, wealth, and genius, made Rome the centre of a vast and ceaseless concourse of strangers, the focus of all the various philosophies and religions of the empire, and its population soon became an amorphous, hetero‧geneous mass, in which all nations, customs, languages, and creeds, all degrees of virtue and vice, of refinement and barbarism, of scepticism and credulity, intermingled and inter‧acted.   Travelling had become more easy and perhaps more frequent than it has been at any other period before the nineteenth century. The subjection of the whole civilised world to a single rule removed the chief obstacles to locomotion. Magnificent roads, which modern nations have rarely rivalled and never surpassed, intersected the entire empire, and relays of post-horses enabled the voyager to proceed with an astonishing rapidity. The sea, which, after the destruction of the fleets of Carthage, had fallen almost completely under the dominion of pirates, had been cleared by Pompey. The European shores of the Mediterranean and the port of Alexandria were thronged with vessels. Romans traversed the whole extent of the empire on political, military, or commercial errands, or in search of health, or knowledge, or pleasure.[1] The entrancing beauties of Como and of Tempe, the luxurious manners of Baiæ and Corinth, the schools, commerce, climate, and temples of Alexandria, the soft winters of Sicily, the artistic wonders and historic recollections of Athens and the Nile, the great colonial interests of Gaul, attracted their thousands, while Roman luxury needed the products of the remotest lands, and the demand for animals for the amphitheatre spread Roman enterprise into the wildest deserts. In the capital, the toleration accorded to different creeds was such that the city soon became a miniature of the

---

[1] On the Roman journeys, see the almost exhaustive dissertation of Friedlænder, tome ii.

world. Almost every variety of charlatanism and of belief displayed itself unchecked, and boasted its train of proselytes. Foreign ideas were in every form in the ascendant. Greece, which had presided over the intellectual development of Rome, acquired a new influence under the favouring policy of Hadrian, and Greek became the language of some of the later as it had been of the earliest writers. Egyptian religions and philosophies excited the wildest enthusiasm. As early as the reign of Augustus there were many thousands of Jewish residents at Rome,[1] and their manners and creed spread widely among the people.[2] The Carthaginian Apuleius,[3] the Gauls Florus and Favorinus, the Spaniards Lucan, Columella, Martial, Seneca, and Quintilian, had all in their different departments a high place in Roman literature or philosophy.

In the slave world a corresponding revolution was taking place. The large proportion of physicians and sculptors who were slaves, the appearance of three or four distinguished authors in the slave class, the numerous literary slaves imported from Greece, and the splendid examples of courage, endurance, and devotion to their masters furnished by slaves during the civil wars, and during some of the worst periods of the Empire, were bridging the chasm between the servile and the free classes, and the same tendency was more powerfully stimulated by the vast numbers and overwhelming influence of the freedmen. The enormous scale and frequent

---

Joseph. (*Antiq.* xvii. 11, § 1) says above 8.000 Jews resident in Rome took part in a petition to Cæsar. If these were all adult males, the total number of Jewish residents must have been extremely large.

[2] See the famous fragment of Seneca cited by St. Augustin (*De Civ. Dei*, vi. 11): 'Usque eo sceleratissimæ gentis consuetudo convaluit, ut per omnes jam terras recepta sit: victi victoribus leges dederunt.' There are numerous scattered allusions to the Jews in Horace, Juvenal, and Martial.

[3] The Carthaginian influence was specially conspicuous in early Christian history. Tertullian and Cyprian (both Africans) are justly regarded as the founders of Latin theology. (See Milman's *Latin Christianity* (ed. 1867), vol. i. pp. 35-36.)

fluctuations of the great Roman establishments, and the innumerable captives reduced to slavery after every war, rendered manumission both frequent and easy, and it was soon regarded as a normal result of faithful service. Many slaves bought their freedom out of the savings which their masters always permitted them to make. Others paid for it by their labour after their emancipation. Some masters emancipated their slaves in order to obtain their part in the distribution of corn, others to prevent the discovery of their own crimes by the torture of their slaves, others through vanity, being desirous of having their funerals attended by a long train of freedmen, very many simply as a reward for long service.[1] The freedman was still under what was termed the patronage of his former master; he was bound to him by what in a later age would have been called a feudal tie, and the political and social importance of a noble depended in a very great degree upon the multitude of his clients. The children of the emancipated slave were in the same relation to the patron, and it was only in the third generation that all disqualifications and restraints were abrogated. In consequence of this system, manumission was often the interest of the master. In the course of his life he enfranchised individual slaves. On his death-bed or by his will he constantly emancipated multitudes. Emancipation by testament acquired such dimensions, that Augustus found it necessary to restrict the power; and he made several limitations, of which the most important was that no one should emancipate by his will more than one hundred of his slaves.[2] It was once proposed that the slaves should be distinguished by a special dress, but the proposition was abandoned because their number was so great that to

---

[1] Milc had emancipated some slaves to prevent them from being tortured as witnesses. (Cic. Pro Milo.) This was made illegal. The other reasons for enfranchise-ment are given by Dion. Halicarn. Antiq. lib. iv.

[2] This subject is fully treated by Wallon, Hist. de l'Esclavage dans l'Antiquité.

reveal to them their strength would be to place the city at their mercy.[1] Even among those who were not slaves, the element that was derived from slavery soon preponderated. The majority of the free population had probably either themselves been slaves, or were descended from slaves, and men with this tainted lineage penetrated to all the offices of the State.[2] 'There was,' as has been well said, 'a circulation of men from all the universe. Rome received them slaves, and sent them back Romans.'[3]

It is manifest how profound a change had taken place since the Republican days, when the highest dignities were long monopolised by a single class, when the censors repressed with a stringent severity every form or exhibition of luxury, when the rhetoricians were banished from the city, lest the faintest tinge of foreign manners should impair the stern simplicity of the people, and when the proposal to transfer the capital to Veii, after a great disaster, was rejected on the ground that it would be impious to worship the Roman deities anywhere but on the Capitol, or for the Flamens and the Vestals to emigrate beyond the walls.[4]

The greater number of these tendencies to universal fusion or equality were blind forces resulting from the stress of circumstances, and not from any human forethought, or were agencies that were put in motion for a different object. It must, however, be acknowledged that a definite theory of policy had a considerable part in accelerating the movement. The policy of the Republic may be broadly described as a policy of conquest, and that of the Empire as a policy of preservation. The Romans having acquired a vast dominion, were met by the great problem which every first-class power is called upon to solve—by what means many communities,

---

[1] Senec. *De Clemen.* i. 24.
See, on the prominence and the insolence of the freedmen, Tacit. *Annal.* iii. 26–27.

[3] Montesquieu, *Décadence des Romains*, ch. xiii.
[4] See the very curious speech attributed to Camillus (Livy, v. 52)

with different languages, customs, characters, and traditions, can be retained peaceably under a single ruler. In modern times, this difficulty has been most successfully met by local legislatures, which, if they supply a 'line of cleavage,' a nucleus around which the spirit of opposition may form, have on the other hand the priceless advantage of giving the annexed people a large measure of self-government, a centre and safety-valve of local public opinion, a sphere for local ambitions, and a hierarchy of institutions adapted to the distinctive national type. Under no other conditions can a complex empire be carried on with so little strain, or effort, or humiliation, or its inevitable final dissolution be effected with so little danger or convulsion. But local legislatures, which are the especial glory of English statesmanship, belong exclusively to modern civilisation. The Roman method of conciliation was, first of all, the most ample toleration of the customs, religion, and municipal freedom of the conquered, and then their gradual admission to the privileges of the conqueror. By confiding to them in a great measure the defence of the empire, by throwing open to them the offices of State, and especially by according to them the right of Roman citizenship, which had been for centuries jealously restricted to the inhabitants of Rome, and was afterwards only conceded to Italy and Cisalpine Gaul, the emperors sought to attach them to their throne. The process was very gradual, but the whole movement of political emancipation attained its completion when the Imperial throne was occupied by the Spaniard Trajan, and by Pertinax, the son of a freedman, and when an edict of Caracalla extended the rights of Roman citizenship to all the provinces of the empire.

It will appear evident, from the foregoing sketch, that the period which elapsed between Panætius and Constantine exhibited an irresistible tendency to cosmopolitanism. The convergence, when we consider the number, force, and harmony of the influences that composed it, is indeed unexampled

in history. The movement extended through all the fields of
religious, philosophical, political, industrial, military, and domestic life. The character of the people was completely transformed, the landmarks of all its institutions were removed,
the whole principle of its organisation was reversed. It would
be impossible to find a more striking example of the manner
in which events govern character, destroying old habits and
associations, and thus altering that national type of excellence
which is, for the most part, the expression or net moral result
of the national institutions and circumstances. The effect of
the movement was, no doubt, in many respects evil, and some
of the best men, such as the elder Cato and Tacitus, opposed
it, as leading to the demoralisation of the empire; but if it
increased vice, it also gave a peculiar character to virtue. It
was impossible that the conception of excellence, formed in a
society where everything conspired to deepen class divisions
and national jealousies and antipathies, should be retained
unaltered in a period of universal intercourse and amalgamation. The moral expression of the first period is obviously
to be found in the narrower military and patriotic virtues;
that of the second period in enlarged philanthropy and
sympathy.

The Stoical philosophy was admirably fitted to preside over
this extension of sympathies. Although it proved itself in
every age the chief school of patriots, it recognised also, from
the very first, and in the most unequivocal manner, the fraternity of mankind. The Stoic taught that virtue alone is a
good, and that all other things are indifferent; and from this
position he inferred that birth, rank, country, or wealth are
the mere accidents of life, and that virtue alone makes one
man superior to another. He taught also that the Deity is
an all-pervading Spirit, animating the universe, and revealed
with especial clearness in the soul of man; and he concluded
that all men are fellow-members of a single body, united by
participation in the same Divine Spirit. These two doctrines

formed part of the very first teaching of the Stoics, but it was
the special glory of the Roman teachers, and an obvious result
of the condition of affairs I have described, to have brought
them into full relief.   One of the most emphatic as well as
one of the earliest extant assertions of the duty of ' charity to
the human race,'[1] occurs in the treatise of Cicero upon duties,
which was avowedly based upon Stoicism.   Writing at a
period when the movement of amalgamation had for a generation been rapidly proceeding,[2] and adopting almost without
restriction the ethics of the Stoics, Cicero maintained the
doctrine of universal brotherhood as distinctly as it was afterwards maintained by the Christian Church.   ' This whole
world,' he tells us, ' is to be regarded as the common city of
gods and men.'[3]   ' Men were born for the sake of men, that
each should assist the others.'[4]   ' Nature ordains that a man
should wish the good of every man, whoever he may be, for
this very reason, that he is a man.'[5]   ' To reduce man to the
duties of his own city and to disengage him from duties to
the members of other cities, is to break the universal society
of the human race.'[6]   ' Nature has inclined us to love men,
and this is the foundation of the law.'[7]   The same principles
were reiterated with increasing emphasis by the later Stoics.
Adopting the well-known line which Terence had translated
from Menander, they maintained that man should deem
nothing human foreign to his interest.   Lucan expatiated
with all the fervour of a Christian poet upon the time when
' the human race will cast aside its weapons, and when all
nations will learn to love.'[8]   ' The whole universe,' said

---

[1] ' Caritas generis humani.'—*De
Finib.*   So, too, he speaks (*De Leg.*
i. 23) of every good man as ' civis
totius mundi.'

[2] He speaks of Rome as ' civitas
ex nationum conventu constituta.'

[3] *De Legib.* i. 7.   [4] *De Offic.*

[5] Ibid. iii. 6.

[6] *De Offic.* iii. 6.

[7] *De Legib.* i. 15.

[8] ' Tunc genus humanum positis
     sibi consulat armis,
   Inque vicem gens omnis amet.'
     — *Pharsalia*, vi.

Seneca, 'which you see around you, comprising all things, both divine and human, is one. We are members of one great body. Nature has made us relatives when it begat us from the same materials and for the same destinies. She planted in us a mutual love, and fitted us for a social life.'[1] 'What is a Roman knight, or freedman, or slave? These are but names springing from ambition or from injury.'[2] 'I know that my country is the world, and my guardians are the gods.'[3] 'You are a citizen,' said Epictetus, 'and a part of the world. . . . The duty of a citizen is in nothing to consider his own interest distinct from that of others, as the hand or foot, if they possessed reason and understood the law of nature, would do and wish nothing that had not some relation to the rest of the body.'[4] 'An Antonine,' said Marcus Aurelius, ' my country is Rome ; as a man, it is the world.'[5]

So far Stoicism appears fully equal to the moral require-ments of the age. It would be impossible to recognise more cordially or to enforce more beautifully that doctrine of universal brotherhood for which the circumstances of the Roman Empire had made men ripe. Plato had said that no one is born for himself alone, but that he owes himself in part to his country, in part to his parents, and in part to his friends. The Roman Stoics, taking a wider survey, declared that man is born not for himself but for the whole world.[6] And their doctrine was perfectly consistent with the original principles of their school.

But while Stoicism was quite capable of representing the widening movement, it was not equally capable of representing the softening movement of civilisation. Its condemnation

---

[1] *Ep.* xcv.
[2] *Ep.* xxxi.
[3] *De Vita Beato* xx.
[4] Arrian, ii. 10.
[5] vi. 44.

[6] ' Hæc duri immota Catonis

Secta fuit, servare modum, finemque tenere,
Naturamque sequi, patriæque impendere vitam,
Nec sibi sed toti genitum se credere mundo.'
Lucan, *Phars.* ii. 380-383.

of the affections, and its stern, tense ideal, admirably fitted
for the struggles of a simple military age, were unsuited for
the mild manners and luxurious tastes of the age of the
Antonines. A class of writers began to arise who, like the
Stoics, believed virtue, rather than enjoyment, to be the
supreme good, and who acknowledged that virtue consisted
solely of the control which the enlightened will exercises
over the desires, but who at the same time gave free scope to
the benevolent affections and a more religious and mystical
tone to the whole scheme of morals. Professing various
speculative doctrines, and calling themselves by many names
—eclectics, peripatetics, or Platonists—they agreed in forming or representing a moral character, less strong, less sublime,
less capable of endurance and heroism, less conspicuous for
energy of will, than that of the Stoics, but far more tender
and attractive. The virtues of force began to recede, and the
gentler virtues to advance, in the moral type. Insensibility
to suffering was no longer professed; indomitable strength
was no longer idolised, and it was felt that weakness and
sorrow have their own appropriate virtues.[1] The works of
these writers are full of delicate touches which nothing but
strong and lively feelings could have suggested. We find this
in the well-known letter of Pliny on the death of his slaves,[2]
in the frequent protests against the ostentation of indifference
with which the Stoics regarded the loss of their friends, in
many instances of simple, artless pathos, which strike the
finest chords of our nature. When Plutarch, after the death
of his daughter, was writing a letter of consolation to his wife,

---

[1] There is a passage on this
subject in one of the letters of
Pliny, which I think extremely remarkable, and to which I can recall
no pagan parallel :—' Nuper me
cujusdam amici languor admonuit,
optimos esse nos dum infirmi sumus.
Quem enim infirmum aut avaritia
aut libido solicitat? Non amoribus
servit, non appetit honores . . .
tunc deos, tunc hominem esse se
meminit.'—Plin. Ep. vii. 26.

[2] Ep. viii. 16. He says : ' Hominis est enim affici dolore, sentire,
resistere tamen, et solatia admittere,
non solatiis non egere.'

we find him turning away from all the commonplaces of the Stoics as the recollection of one simple trait of his little child rushed upon his mind :—'She desired her nurse to press even her dolls to the breast. She was so loving that she wished everything that gave her pleasure to share in the best of what she had.'

Plutarch, whose fame as a biographer has, I think, unduly eclipsed his reputation as a moralist, may be justly regarded as the leader of this movement, and his moral writings may be profitably compared with those of Seneca, the most ample exponent of the sterner school. Seneca is not unfrequently self-conscious, theatrical, and overstrained. His precepts have something of the affected ring of a popular preacher. The imperfect fusion of his short sentences gives his style a disjointed and, so to speak, granulated character, which the Emperor Caligula happily expressed when he compared it to sand without cement; yet he often rises to a majesty of eloquence, a grandeur both of thought and of expression, that few moralists have ever rivalled. Plutarch, though far less sublime, is more sustained, equable, and uniformly pleasing. The Montaigne of antiquity, his genius coruscates playfully and gracefully around his subject; he delights in illustrations which are often singularly vivid and original, but which, by their excessive multiplication, appear sometimes rather the texture than the ornament of his discourse. A gentle, tender spirit, and a judgment equally free from paradox, exaggeration, and excessive subtilty, are the characteristics of all he wrote. Plutarch excels most in collecting motives of consolation; Seneca in forming characters that need no consolation. There is something of the woman in Plutarch; Seneca is all a man. The writings of the first resemble the strains of the flute, to which the ancients attributed the power of calming the passions and charming away the clouds of sorrow, and drawing men by a gentle suasion into the paths of virtue; the writings of the other are like the trumpet-blast, which kindles the soul with an heroic courage. The first is most fitted to console a mother sorrowing over her dead child, the second to nerve a brave man, without flinching and without illusion, to grapple with an inevitable fate.

The elaborate letters which Seneca has left us on distinctive tenets of the Stoical school, such as the equality of vices or the evil of the affections, have now little more than an historic interest; but the general tone of his writings gives them a permanent importance, for they reflect and foster a certain type of excellence which, since the extinction of Stoicism, has had no adequate expression in literature. The prevailing moral tone of Plutarch, on the other hand, being formed mainly on the prominence of the amiable virtues, has been eclipsed or transcended by the Christian writers, but his definite contributions to philosophy and morals are more important than those of Seneca. He has left us one of the best works on superstition, and one of the most ingenious works on Providence, we possess. He was probably the first writer who advocated very strongly humanity to animals on the broad ground of universal benevolence, as distinguished from the Pythagorean doctrine of transmigration, and he was also remarkable, beyond all his contemporaries, for his high sense of female excellence and of the sanctity of female love.

The Romans had at all times cared more for the practical tendency of a system of philosophy than for its logical or speculative consistency. One of the chief attractions of Stoicism, in their eyes, had been that its main object was not to build a system of opinion, but to propose a pattern of life,[1] and Stoicism itself was only adapted to the Roman character after it had been simplified by Panætius.[2] Although the system could never free itself altogether from that hardness which rendered it so unsuited for an advanced civilisation, it

---

[1] This characteristic of Stoicism is well noticed in Grant's *Aristotle*, vol. i. p. 254. The first volume of this work contains an extremely good review of the principles of the Stoics.

[2] Cic. *De Finib.* lib. iv

was profoundly modified by the later Stoics, who rarely scrupled to temper it by the admixture of new doctrines. Seneca himself was by no means an unmixed Stoic. If Epictetus was more nearly so, this was probably because the extreme hardship he underwent made him dwell more than his contemporaries upon the importance of fortitude and endurance. Marcus Aurelius was surrounded by the disciples of the most various schools, and his Stoicism was much tinctured by the milder and more religious spirit of Platonism. The Stoics, like all other men, felt the moral current of the time, though they yielded to it less readily than some others. In Thrasea, who occupied in his age a position analogous to that of Cato in an earlier period, we find little or nothing of the asperity and hardness of his great prototype. In the writings of the later Stoics, if we find the same elements as in those of their predecessors, these elements are at least combined in different proportions.

In the first place, Stoicism became more essentially religious. The Stoical character, like all others of a high order, had always been reverential; but its reverence differed widely from that of Christians. It was concentrated much less upon the Deity than upon virtue, and especially upon virtue as exhibited in great men. When Lucan, extolling his hero, boasted that 'the gods favoured the conquering cause, but Cato the conquered,' or when Seneca described ' the fortune of Sulla ' as ' the crime of the gods,' these sentences, which sound to modern ears grossly blasphemous appear to have excited no murmur. We have already seen the audacious language with which the sage claimed an equality with the Divinity. On the other hand, the reverence for virtue apart from all conditions of success, and especially for men of the stamp of Cato, who through a strong moral conviction struggled bravely, though unsuccessfully, against force, genius, or circumstances, was perhaps more steady and more passionate than in any later age. The duty of absolute

submission to Providence, as I have already shown, was con
tinually inculcated, and the pantheistic notion of all virtue
being a part or emanation of the Deity was often asserted,
but man was still the centre of the Stoic's scheme, the ideal
to which his reverence and devotion aspired.   In later
Stoicism this point of view was gradually changed. Without
any formal abandonment of their pantheistic conceptions, the
language of philosophers recognised with much greater clearness a distinct and personal Divinity.   Every page of Epictetus and Marcus Aurelius is impregnated with the deepest
religious feeling.   'The first thing to learn,' said the former,
'is that there is a God, that His knowledge pervades the
whole universe, and that it extends not only to our acts but
to our thoughts and feelings. . . .   He who seeks to please
the gods must labour as far as lies in him to resemble them.
He must be faithful as God is faithful, free as He is free,
beneficent as He is beneficent, magnanimous as He is magnanimous.'[1]   'To have God for our maker and father and
guardian, should not that emancipate us from all sadness and
from all fear?'[2] 'When you have shut your door and
darkened your room, say not to yourself you are alone. God
is in your room, and your attendant genius likewise. Think
not that they need the light to see what you do.[3] What can
I, an old man and a cripple, do but praise God? If I were
a nightingale, I would discharge the office of a nightingale;
if a swan, that of a swan. But I am a reasonable being;
my mission is to praise God, and I fulfil it; nor shall I ever,
as far as lies in me, shrink from my task, and I exhort you
to join in the same song of praise.'[4]

The same religious character is exhibited, if possible,
in a still greater degree in the 'Meditations of Marcus
Aurelius; but in one respect the ethics of the emperor differ

---

[1] Arrian, *Epict.* ii. 14   [3] Ibid. i. 14.
[2] Ibid. i. 9.   [4] Ibid. i. 16.

widely from those of the slave. In Epictetus we invariably
find the strongest sense of the majesty of man. As the child
of the Deity, as a being capable of attaining the most exalted
virtue, he magnified him to the highest point, and never
more so than in the very passage in which he exhorted his
disciples to beware of haughtiness. The Jupiter Olympus of
Phidias, he reminds them, exhibits no arrogance, but the
unclouded serenity of perfect confidence and strength.[1]
Marcus Aurelius, on the other hand, dwelt rather on the
weakness than on the force of man, and his meditations
breathe a spirit, if not of Christian humility, at least of the
gentlest and most touching modesty. He was not, it is true,
like some later saints, who habitually apply to themselves
language of reprobation which would be exaggerated if applied
to the murderer or the adulterer. He did not shrink from
recognising human virtue as a reality, and thanking Providence for the degree in which he had attained it, but he
continually reviewed with an unsparing severity the weaknesses of his character, he accepted and even solicited reproofs
from every teacher of virtue, he made it his aim, in a position
of supreme power, to check every emotion of arrogance and
pride, and he set before him an ideal of excellence which
awed and subdued his mind.

Another very remarkable feature of later Stoicism was its
increasingly introspective character. In the philosophy of
Cato and Cicero, virtue was displayed almost exclusively in
action. In the later Stoics, self-examination and purity of
thought were continually inculcated. There are some writers who, with an obstinacy which it is more easy to explain
than to excuse, persist, in defiance of the very clearest
evidence to the contrary, in representing these virtues as
exclusively Christian, and in maintaining, without a shadow
of proof, that the place they undeniably occupy in the later

[1] Arrian, ii. 8.

Roman moralists was due to the direct or indirect influence of the new faith. The plain fact is that they were fully known to the Greeks, and both Plato and Zeno even exhorted men to study their dreams, on the ground that these often reveal the latent tendencies of the disposition.[1]   Pythagoras urged his disciples daily to examine themselves when they retired to rest,[2] and this practice soon became a recognised part of the Pythagorean discipline.[3]   It was introduced into Rome with the school before the close of the Republic.   It was known in the time of Cicero[4] and Horace.[5]   Sextius, one of the masters of Seneca, a philosopher of the school of Pythagoras, who flourished chiefly before the Christian era, was accustomed daily to devote a portion of time to self-examination ; and Seneca, who at first inclined much to the tenets of Pythagoras,[6] expressly tells us that it was from Sextius he learnt the practice.[7]   The increasing prominence of the Pythagorean philosophy which accompanied the invasion of Oriental creeds, the natural tendency of the empire, by closing the avenues of political life, to divert the attention from action to emotion, and also the increased latitude allowed to the play of the sympathies or affections by the later Stoics, brought this emotional part of virtue into great prominence.   The letters of Seneca are a kind of moral medicine applied for the most part to the cure of different

---

[1] Plutarch, *De Profect. in Virt.* This precept was enforced by Bishop Sanderson in one of his sermons. (Southey's *Commonplace Book*, vol. i. p. 92.)

[2] Diog. Laërt. *Pythagoras.*

[3] Thus Cicero makes Cato say : ‘ Pythagoreorumque more, exercendæ memoriæ gratia, quid quoque die dixerim, audiverim, egerim, commemoro vesperi.’—*De Senect.* x.

[4] Ibid.

[5] *Sermon,* i. 4.

[6] He even gave up, for a time, eating meat, in obedience to the Pythagorean principles. (*Ep.* cviii.) Seneca had two masters of this school, Sextius and Sotion. He was at this time not more than seventeen years old. (See Aubertin, *Étude critique sur les Ràpports supposés entre Sénèque et St. Paul,* p. 156.)

[7] See his very beautiful description of the self-examination of Sextius and of himself. (*De Ira,* iii. 36.)

infirmities of character. Plutarch, in a beautiful treatise on
'The Signs of Moral Progress,' treated the culture of the
feelings with delicate skill. The duty of serving the Divinity
with a pure mind rather than by formal rites became a
commonplace of literature, and self-examination one of the
most recognised of duties. Epictetus urged men so to purify
their imaginations, that at the sight of a beautiful woman
they should not even mentally exclaim, ' Happy her husband ! ' [1] The meditations of Marcus Aurelius, above all,
are throughout an exercise of self-examination, and the duty
of watching over the thoughts is continually inculcated.

It was a saying of Plutarch that Stoicism, which sometimes exercised a prejudicial and hardening influence upon
characters that were by nature stern and unbending, proved
peculiarly useful as a cordial to those which were naturally
gentle and yielding. Of this truth we can have no better
illustration than is furnished by the life and writings of
Marcus Aurelius, the last and most perfect representative
of Roman Stoicism. A simple, childlike, and eminently
affectionate disposition, with little strength of intellect or
perhaps originally of will, much more inclined to meditation,
speculation, solitude, or friendship, than to active and public
life, with a profound aversion to the pomp of royalty and
with a rather strong natural leaning to pedantry, he had
embraced the fortifying philosophy of Zeno in its best form,
and that philosophy made him perhaps as nearly a perfectly
virtuous man as has ever appeared upon our world. Tried
by the chequered events of a reign of nineteen years, presiding over a society that was profoundly corrupt, and over a
city that was notorious for its license, the perfection of his
character awed even calumny to silence, and the spontaneous
sentiment of his people proclaimed him rather a god than a
man.[2] Very few men have ever lived concerning whose

---

[1] Arrian, ii. 18. Compare the
Manual of Epictetus, xxxiv.

[1] 'Quod de Romulo ægre credi
tum est, omnes pari consensu

inner life we can speak so confidently. His ' Meditations,
which form one of the most impre sive, form also one of the
truest books in the whole range of religious literature.   They
consist of rude fragmentary notes without literary skill or
arrangement, written for the most part in hasty, broken, and
sometimes almost unintelligible sentences amid the turmoil
of a camp,[1] and recording, in accents of the most penetrating
sincerity, the struggles, doubts, and aims of a soul of which,
to employ one of his own images, it may be truly said that it
possessed the purity of a star, which needs no veil to hide its
nakedness.   The undisputed master of the whole civilised
world, he set before him as models such men as Thrasea and
Helvidius, as Cato and Brutus, and he made it his aim to
realise the conception of a free State in which all citizens are
equal, and of a royalty which makes it its first duty to respect
the liberty of the citizens.[2]   His life was passed in unremitting
activity.   For nearly twelve years he was absent with armies
in the distant provinces of the empire ; and although his political capacity has been much and perhaps justly questioned,
it is impossible to deny the unwearied zeal with which he discharged the duties of his great position.   Yet few men have
ever carried farther the virtue of little things, the delicate
moral tact and the minute scruples which, though often
exhibited by women and by secluded religionists, very rarely
survive much contact with active life.   The solicitude with
which he endeavoured to persuade two jealous rhetoricians
to abstain during their debates from retorts that might
destroy their friendship,[3] the careful gratitude with which, in
a camp in Hungary, he recalled every moral obligation he

---

praesumserunt, Marcum cœlo re-
ceptum esse.'—Aur. Vict. *Epit.* xvi.
' Deusque etiam nunc habetur.'—
Capitolinus.
    [1] The first book of his *Medita-
tions* was written on the borders of

the Granua, in Hungary.
    [2] i. 14.
    [3] See his touching letter to
Fronto, who was about to engage
in a debate with Herod Atticus.

could trace, even to the most obscure of his tutors,[1] his
anxiety to avoid all pedantry and mannerism in his conduct,[2]
and to repel every voluptuous imagination from his mind,[3]
his deep sense of the obligation of purity,[4] his laborious
efforts to correct a habit of drowsiness into which he had
fallen, and his self-reproval when he had yielded to it,[5]
become all, I think, inexpressibly touching when we remember that they were exhibited by one who was the
supreme ruler of the civilised globe, and who was continually
engaged in the direction of the most gigantic interests. But
that which is especially remarkable in Marcus Aurelius is
the complete absence of fanaticism in his philanthropy.
Despotic monarchs sincerely anxious to improve mankind are
naturally led to endeavour, by acts of legislation, to force
society into the paths which they believe to be good, and
such men, acting under such motives, have sometimes been
the scourges of mankind. Philip II. and Isabella the
Catholic inflicted more suffering in obedience to their consciences than Nero and Domitian in obedience to their lusts.
But Marcus Aurelius steadily resisted the temptation. 'Never
hope,' he once wrote, 'to realise Plato's Republic. Let it be
sufficient that you have in some slight degree ameliorated
mankind, and do not think that amelioration a matter of
small importance. Who can change the opinions of men?
and without a change of sentiments what can you make but
reluctant slaves and hypocrites?'[6] He promulgated many
laws inspired by a spirit of the purest benevolence. He

---

[1] i 6-15. The eulogy he
passed on his Stoic master Apollonius is worthy of notice. Apollonius furnished him with an
example of the combination of
extreme firmness and gentleness.

[2] E.g. 'Beware of Cæsarising.'
(vi. 30.) 'Be neither a tragedian
nor a courtesan.' (v. 28.) 'Be

just and temperate and a follower
of the gods; but be so with simplicity, for the pride of modesty is
the worst of all.' (xii. 27.)

[3] iii. 4.
[4] i. 17.
[5] v. 1.
[6] ix. 29.

mitigated the gladiatorial shows.   He treated with invariable
deference the senate, which was the last bulwark of political
freedom.   He endowed many chairs of philosophy which
were intended to diffuse knowledge and moral teaching
through the people.   He endeavoured by the example of his
Court to correct the extravagances of luxury that were prevalent, and he exhibited in his own career a perfect model of
an active and conscientious administrator ; but he made no
rash efforts to force the people by stringent laws out of the
natural channel of their lives.   Of the corruption of his subjects he was keenly sensible, and he bore it with a mournful
but gentle patience.   We may trace in this respect the milder
spirit of those Greek teachers who had diverged from Stoicism, but it was especially from the Stoical doctrine that all
vice springs from ignorance that he derived his rule of life,
and this doctrine, to which he repeatedly recurred, imparted
to all his judgments a sad but tender charity.   'Men were
made for men ; correct them, then, or support them.'[1]   'If
they do ill, it is evidently in spite of themselves and through
ignorance.'[2]   'Correct them if you can ; if not, remember
that patience was given you to exercise it in their behalf.'[3]
' It would be shameful for a physician to deem it strange that
a man was suffering from fever.'[4]   'The immortal gods consent for countless ages to endure without anger, and even to
surround with blessings, so many and such wicked men ; but
thou who hast so short a time to live, art thou already weary,
and that when thou art thyself wicked?'[5]   'It is involuntarily that the soul is deprived of justice, and temperance,
and goodness, and all other virtues.   Continually remember
this ; the thought will make you more gentle to all mankind.'[6]
' It is right that man should love those who have offended
him.   He will do so when he remembers that all men are his

---

[1] viii. 59.
[2] xi. 18.
[3] ix. 11.

[4] viii. 15.
[5] vii. 70.
[6] vii. 63.

relations, and that it is through ignorance and involuntarily
that they sin—and then we all die so soon.'[1]

The character of the virtue of Marcus Aurelius, though
exhibiting the softening influence of the Greek spirit which
in his time pervaded the empire, was in its essentials strictly
Roman.[2] Though full of reverential gratitude to Providence,
we do not find in him that intense humility and that deep
and subtle religious feeling which were the principles of
Hebrew virtue, and which have given the Jewish writers so
great an ascendancy over the hearts of men.   Though borne
naturally and instinctively to goodness, his 'Meditations' do
not display the keen æsthetical sense of the beauty of virtue
which was the leading motive of Greek morals, and which the
writing of Plotinus afterwards made very familiar to the
Roman world.   Like most of the best Romans, the principle
of his virtue was the sense of duty, the conviction of the
existence of a law of nature to which it is the aim and purpose of our being to conform.   Of secondary motives he
appears to have been little sensible.   The belief in a superintending Providence was the strongest of his religious
convictions, but even that was occasionally overcast.   On the
subject of a future world his mind floated in a desponding
doubt.   The desire for posthumous fame he deemed it his duty
systematically to mortify.   While most writers of his school
regarded death chiefly as the end of sorrows, and dwelt upon
it in order to dispel its terrors, in Marcus Aurelius it is
chiefly represented as the last great demonstration of the
vanity of earthly things.   Seldom, indeed, has such active
and unrelaxing virtue been united with so little enthusiasm,

---

[1] vii. 22.
[2] Mr. Maurice, in this respect,
compares and contrasts him very
happily with Plutarch.   'Like
Plutarch, the Greek and Roman
characters were in Marcus Aurelius
remarkably blended; but, unlike

Plutarch, the foundation of his
mind was Roman.   He was a
student that he might more effectually carry on the business of an
emperor.'—*Philosophy of the First
Six Centuries*, p. 32.

and been cheered by so little illusion of success. 'There is
but one thing,' he wrote, 'of real value—to cultivate truth
and justice, and to live without anger in the midst of lying
and unjust men.'[1]

The command he had acquired over his feelings was so
great that it was said of him that his countenance was never
known to betray either elation or despondency.[2] We, however,
who have before us the records of his inner life, can have no
difficulty in detecting the deep melancholy that overshadowed
his mind, and his closing years were darkened by many and
various sorrows. His wife, whom he dearly loved and
deeply honoured, and who, if we may believe the Court
scandals that are reported by historians, was not worthy of
his affection,[3] had preceded him to the tomb. His only surviving son had already displayed the vicious tendencies that
afterwards made him one of the worst of rulers. The philosophers, who had instructed him in his youth, and to whom
he had clung with an affectionate friendship, had one by one
disappeared, and no new race had arisen to supply their
place. After a long reign of self-denying virtue, he saw the
decadence of the empire continually more apparent. The
Stoical school was rapidly fading before the passion for
Oriental superstitions. The barbarians, repelled for a time,
were again menacing the frontiers, and it was not difficult to
foresee their future triumph. The mass of the people had

---

[1] vi. 47.

[2] Capitolinus, Aurelius Victor.

[3] M. Suckau, in his admirable
Étude sur Marc-Aurèle, and M.
Renan, in a very acute and learned
*Examen de quelques faits relatifs à
l'impératrice Faustine* (read before
the Institut, August 14, 1867),
have shown the extreme uncertainty of the stories about the
debaucheries of Faustina, which
the biographers of Marcus Aurelius
have collected. It will be observed
that the emperor himself has left
an emphatic testimony to her
virtue, and to the happiness he
derived from her (i. 17); that the
earliest extant biographer of Marcus Aurelius was a generation
later; and that the infamous
character of Commodus naturally
predisposed men to imagine that
he was not the son of so perfect an
emperor.

become too inert and too corrupt for any efforts to regenerate them. A fearful pestilence, followed by many minor calamities, had fallen upon the land and spread misery and panic through many provinces. In the midst of these calamities, the emperor was struck down with a mortal illness, which he bore with the placid courage he had always displayed, exhibiting in almost the last words he uttered his forgetfulness of self and his constant anxiety for the condition of his people.[1] Shortly before his death he dismissed his attendants, and, after one last interview, his son, and he died as he long had lived, alone.[2]

Thus sank to rest in clouds and darkness the purest and gentlest spirit of all the pagan world, the most perfect model of the later Stoics. In him the hardness, asperity, and arrogance of the sect had altogether disappeared, while the affectation its paradoxes tended to produce was greatly mitigated. Without fanaticism, superstition, or illusion, his whole life was regulated by a simple and unwavering sense of duty. The contemplative and emotional virtues which Stoicism had long depressed, had regained their place, but the active virtues had not yet declined. The virtues of the hero were still deeply honoured, but gentleness and tenderness had acquired a new prominence in the ideal type.

But while the force of circumstances was thus developing the ethical conceptions of antiquity in new directions, the mass of the Roman people were plunged in a condition of depravity which no mere ethical teaching could adequately correct. The moral condition of the empire is, indeed, in some respects one of the most appalling pictures on record, and writers have much more frequently undertaken to paint or even to exaggerate its enormity than to investigate the circumstances by which it may be explained. Such circumstances,

---

[1] 'Quid me fletis, et non magis cogitatis?' Capitolinus, *M. Aurelius.*
de pestilentia et communi morte
[2] Ibid.

however, must unquestionably exist. There is no reason to believe that the innate propensities of the people were worse during the Empire than during the best days of the Republic. The depravity of a nation is a phenomenon which, like all others, may be traced to definite causes, and in the instance before us they are not difficult to discover.

I have already said that the virtue of the Romans was a military and patriotic virtue, formed by the national insti tutions, and to which religious teaching was merely accessory. The domestic, military, and censorial discipline, concurring with the general poverty and also with the agricultural pur- suits of the people, had created the simplest and most austere habits, while the institutions of civic liberty provided ample spheres for honourable ambition. The nobles, being the highest body in a free State, and being at the same time con- tinually confronted by a formidable opposition under the guidance of the tribunes, were ardently devoted to public life. The dangerous rivalry of the surrounding Italian States, and afterwards of Carthage, demanded and secured a constant vigilance. Roman education was skilfully designed to elicit heroic patriotism, and the great men of the past became the ideal figures of the imagination. Religion hallowed the local feeling by rites and legends, instituted many useful and domestic habits, taught men the sanctity of oaths, and, by fostering a continual sense of a superintending Providence, gave a depth and solemnity to the whole character.

Such were the chief influences by which the national type of virtue had been formed, but nearly all of these were cor- roded or perverted by advancing civilisation. The domestic and local religion lost its ascendancy amid the increase of scepticism and the invasion of a crowd of foreign superstitions The simplicity of manners, which sumptuary laws and the institution of the censorship had long maintained, was replaced ..y the extravagances of a Babylonian luxury. The aristocratic dignity perished with the privileges on which it reposed. The patriotic energy and enthusiasm died away in a universal empire which embraced all varieties of language, custom, and nationality.

But although the virtues of a poor and struggling community necessarily disappear before increasing luxury, they are in a normal condition of society replaced by virtues of a different stamp. Gentler manners and enlarged benevolence follow in the train of civilisation, greater intellectual activity and more extended industrial enterprise give a new importance to the moral qualities which each of these require, the circle of political interests expands, and if the virtues that spring from privilege diminish, the virtues that spring from equality increase.

In Rome, however, there were three great causes which impeded the normal development—the Imperial system, the institution of slavery, and the gladiatorial shows. Each of these exercised an influence of the widest and most pernicious character on the morals of the people. To trace those influences in all their ramifications would lead me far beyond the limits I have assigned to the present work, but I shall endeavour to give a concise view of their nature and general character.

The theory of the Roman Empire was that of a representative despotism. The various offices of the Republic were not annihilated, but they were gradually concentrated in a single man. The senate was still ostensibly the depository of supreme power, but it was made in fact the mere creature of the Emperor, whose power was virtually uncontrolled. Political spies and private accusers, who in the latter days of the Republic had been encouraged to denounce plots against the State, began under Augustus to denounce plots against the Emperor; and the c'ass being enormously increased under Tiberius, and stimulated by the promise of part of the confiscated property, they menaced every leading politician and even every wealthy man. The nobles were gradually depressed, ruined, or driven by the dangers of public life into orgies of private luxury. The poor were conciliated, not by any increase of liberty or even of permanent prosperity, but by gratuitous distributions of corn and by public games, while, in order to invest themselves with a sacred character, the emperors adopted the religious device of an apotheosis.

This last superstition, of which some traces may still be found in the titles appropriated to royalty, was not wholly a suggestion of politicians. Deified men had long occupied a prominent place in ancient belief, and the founders of cities had been very frequently worshipped by the inhabitants.[1] Although to more educated minds the ascription of divinity to a sovereign was simply an unmeaning flattery, although it in no degree prevented either innumerable plots against his life, or an unsparing criticism of his memory, yet the popular reverence not unfrequently anticipated politicians in representing the emperor as in some special way under the protection of Providence. Around Augustus a whole constellation of miraculous stories soon clustered. An oracle, it was said, had declared his native city destined to produce a ruler of the world. When a child, he had been borne by invisible hands from his cradle, and placed on a lofty tower, where he was found with his face turned to the rising sun. He rebuked the frogs that croaked around his grandfather's home, and they became silent for ever. An eagle snatched a piece of bread from his hand, soared into the air, and then, descending, presented it to him again. Another eagle dropped at his feet a chicken, bearing a laurel-branch in its beak. When his body was burnt, his image was seen rising to heaven above the flames. When another man tried to sleep in the bed in which the Emperor had been born, the profane intruder was

---

[1] Many examples of this are given by Coulanges, *La Cité antique*, pp. 177–178.

dragged forth by an unseen hand. A patrician named Lætorius, having been condemned for adultery, pleaded in mitigation of the sentence that he was the happy possessor of the spot of ground on which Augustus was born.[1] An Asiatic town, named Cyzicus, was deprived of its freedom by Tiberius, chiefly because it had neglected the worship of Augustus.[2] Partly, no doubt, by policy, but partly also by that spontaneous process by which in a superstitious age conspicuous characters so often become the nuclei of legends,[3] each emperor was surrounded by a supernatural aureole. Every usurpation, every break in the ordinary line of succession, was adumbrated by a series of miracles; and signs, both in heaven and earth, were manifested whenever an emperor was about to die.

Of the emperors themselves, a great majority, no doubt, accepted their divine honours as an empty pageant, and more than one exhibited beneath the purple a simplicity of tastes and character which the boasted heroes of the Republic had never surpassed. It is related of Vespasian that, when dying, he jested mournfully on his approaching dignity, observing, as he felt his strength ebbing away, ' I think I am becoming a god.'[4] Alexander Severus and Julian refused to accept the ordinary language of adulation, and of those who did not reject it we know that many looked upon it as a modern sovereign looks upon the phraseology of petitions or the ceremonies of the Court. Even Nero was so far from being intoxicated with his Imperial dignity that he continually sought triumphs as a singer or an actor, and it was his artistic skill, not his divine prerogatives, that excited his vanity.[5] Caligula, however, who appears to have been literally deranged,[6]

---

[1] All this is related by Suetonius, *August.*
[2] Tacit. *Annal.* iv. 36.
[3] See, e.g., the sentiments of the people about Julius Cæsar,
Sueton. *J. C.* lxxxviii.
[4] Sueton. *Vesp.* xxiii.
[5] ' Qualis artifex pereo' were his dying words.
[6] See Sueton. *Calig.* 1.

is said to have accepted his divinity as a serious fact, to have
substituted his own head for that of Jupiter on many of the
statues,[1] and to have once started furiously from his seat
during a thunderstorm that had interrupted a gladiatorial
show, shouting with frantic gestures his imprecations against
Heaven, and declaring that the divided empire was indeed
intolerable, that either Jupiter or himself must speedily suc-
cumb.[2] Heliogabalus, if we may give any credence to his
biographer, confounded all things, human and divine, in
hideous and blasphemous orgies, and designed to unite all
forms of religion in the worship of himself.

A curious consequence of this apotheosis was that the
images of the emperors were invested with a sacred character
like those of the gods. They were the recognised refuge of
the slave or the oppressed,[4] and the smallest disrespect to
them was resented as a heinous crime. Under Tiberius,
slaves and criminals were accustomed to hold in their hands
an image of the emperor, and, being thus protected, to pour
with impunity a torrent of defiant insolence upon their masters
or judges.[5] Under the same emperor, a man having, when
drunk, accidentally touched a nameless domestic utensil with
a ring on which the head of the emperor was carved, he was
immediately denounced by a spy.[6] A man in this reign was
accused of high treason for having sold an image of the emperor with a garden.[7] It was made a capital offence to beat
a slave, or to undress, near a statue of Augustus, or to enter
a brothel with a piece of money on which his head was en-
graved,[8] and at a later period a woman, it is said, was ac-

---

[1] Sueton. *Calig.* xxii. A statue
of Jupiter is said to have burst out
laughing just before the death of
this emperor.

[2] Seneca, *De Ira*, i. 46 ; Sueton.
Calig. xxii.

[3] Lampridius, *Heliogab.*

[4] Senec. *De Clemen.* i. 18.

[5] Tacit. *Annal.* iii. 36

[6] Senec. *De Benefic.* iii. 26.

[7] Tacit. *Annal.* i. 73. Tiberius
refused to allow this case to be proceeded with. See, too, Philost.
Apollonius of Tyana, i. 15.

[8] Suet. *Tiber.* lviii.

tually executed for undressing before the statue of Domitian.[1]

It may easily be conceived that men who had been raised
to this pinnacle of arrogance and power, men who exercised
uncontrolled authority in the midst of a society in a state of
profound corruption, were often guilty of the most atrocious
extravagances. In the first period of the Empire more especially, when traditions were not yet formed, and when experience had not yet shown the dangers of the throne, the brains
of some of its occupants reeled at their elevation, and a kind
of moral insanity ensued. The pages of Suetonius remain as
an eternal witness of the abysses of depravity, the hideous,
intolerable cruelty, the hitherto unimagined extravagances of
nameless lust that were then manifested on the Palatine, and
while they cast a fearful light· upon the moral chaos into
which pagan society had sunk, they furnish ample evidence
of the demoralising influences of the empire. The throne was,
it is true, occupied by some of the best as well as by some of
the worst men who have ever lived; but the evil, though
checked and mitigated, was never abolished. The corruption
of a Court, the formation of a profession of spies, the encouragement given to luxury, the distributions of corn, and the
multiplication of games, were evils which varied greatly in
their degrees of intensity, but the very existence of the empire
prevented the creation of those habits of political life which
formed the moral type of the great republics of antiquity.
Liberty, which is often very unfavourable to theological
systems, is almost always in the end favourable to morals :
for the most effectual method that has been devised for diverting men from vice is to give free scope to a higher ambition.
This scope was absolutely wanting in the Roman Empire,
and the moral condition, in the absence of lasting political
habits, fluctuated greatly with the character of the Emperors.

---

[1] 'Mulier quædam, quod semel   damnata et interfecta est.'—Xiphi-
exuerat ante statuam Domitiani,   lin, lxvii. 12.

The results of the institution of slavery were probably even more serious. In addition to its manifest effect in encouraging a tyrannical and ferocious spirit in the masters, it cast a stigma upon all labour, and at once degraded and impoverished the free poor. In modern societies the formation of an influential and numerous middle class, trained in the sober and regular habits of industrial life, is the chief guarantee of national morality, and where such a class exists, the disorders of the upper ranks, though undoubtedly injurious, are never fatal to society. The influence of great outbursts of fashionable depravity, such as that which followed the Restoration in England, is rarely more than superficial. The aristocracy may revel in every excess of ostentatious vice, but the great mass of the people, at the loom, the counter, or the plough, continue unaffected by their example, and the habits of life into which they are forced by the condition of their trades preserve them from gross depravity. It was the most frightful feature of the corruption of ancient Rome that it extended through every class of the community. In the absence of all but the simplest machinery, manufactures, with the vast industrial life they beget, were unknown. The poor citizen found almost all the spheres in which an honourable livelihood might be obtained wholly or at least in a very great degree preoccupied by slaves, while he had learnt to regard trade with an invincible repugnance. Hence followed the immense increase of corrupt and corrupting professions, as actors, pantomimes, hired gladiators, political spies, ministers to passion, astrologers, religious charlatans, pseudo-philosophers, which gave the free classes a precarious and occasional subsistence, and hence, too, the gigantic dimensions of the system of clientage. Every rich man was surrounded by a train of dependants, who lived in a great measure at his expense, and spent their lives in ministering to his passions and flattering his vanity. And, above all, the public distribution of corn, and occasionally of money, was carried on to such an extent, that, so far as the first necessaries of life were concerned, the whole poor free population of Rome was supported gratuitously by the Government. To effect this distribution promptly and lavishly was the main object of the Imperial policy, and its consequences were worse than could have resulted from the most extravagant poor-laws or the most excessive charity. The mass of the people were supported in absolute idleness by corn, which was given without any reference to desert, and was received, not as a favour, but as a right, while gratuitous public amusements still further diverted them from labour.

Under these influences the population rapidly dwindled away. Productive enterprise was almost extinct in Italy, and an unexampled concurrence of causes made a vicious celibacy the habitual condition. Already in the days of Augustus the evil was apparent, and the dangers which in later reigns drove the patricians still more generally from public life, drove them more and more into every extravagance of sensuality. Greece, since the destruction of her liberty, and also the leading cities of Asia Minor and of Egypt, had become centres of the wildest corruption, and Greek and Oriental captives were innumerable in Rome. Ionian slaves of a surpassing beauty, Alexandrian slaves, famous for their subtle skill in stimulating the jaded senses of the confirmed and sated libertine, became the ornaments of every patrician house, the companions and the instructors of the young. The disinclination to marriage was so general, that men who spent their lives in endeavouring by flatteries to secure the inheritance of wealthy bachelors became a numerous and a notorious class. The slave population was itself a hotbed of vice, and it contaminated all with which it came in contact; while the attractions of the games, and especially of the public baths, which became the habitual resort of the idle, combined with the charms of the Italian climate, and with the miserable domestic architecture that was general, to draw the poor

citizens from indoor life. Idleness, amusements, and a oare
subsistence were alone desired, and the general practice of
abortion among the rich, and of infanticide and exposition in
all classes, still further checked the population.

The destruction of all public spirit in a population so
situated was complete and inevitable. In the days of the
Republic a consul had once advocated the admission of a brave
Italian people to the right of Roman citizenship, on the
ground that 'those who thought only of liberty deserved to
be Romans.'[1] In the Empire all liberty was cheerfully bartered for games and corn, and the worst tyrant could by
these means be secure of popularity. In the Republic, when
Marius threw open the houses of those he had proscribed, to
be plundered, the people, by a noble abstinence, rebuked the
act, for no Roman could be found to avail himself of the
permission.[2] In the Empire, when the armies of Vitellius
and Vespasian were disputing the possession of the city, the
degenerate Romans gathered with delight to the spectacle as
to a gladiatorial show, plundered the deserted houses, encouraged either army by their reckless plaudits, dragged out
the fugitives to be slain, and converted into a festival the
calamity of their country.[3] The degradation of the national
character was permanent. Neither the teaching of the
Stoics, nor the government of the Antonines, nor the triumph
of Christianity could restore it. Indifferent to liberty, the
Roman now, as then, asks only for an idle subsistence and
for public spectacles, and countless monasteries and ecclesiastical pageants occupy in modern Rome the same place as
did the distributions of corn and the games of the amphitheatre in the Rome of the Cæsars.

It must be remembered, too, that while public spirit had

---

[1] 'Eos demum, qui nihil præter-
quam de libertate cogitent, dignos
esse, qui Romani fiant.'— Livy, viii.
21.

[2] Valerius Maximus, iv. 3, § 14.
[3] See the picture of this scene
in Tacitus, Hist. iii. 83.

thus decayed in the capital of the empire, there existed no independent or rival power to reanimate by its example the smouldering flame. The existence in modern Europe of many distinct nations on the same level of civilisation, but with different forms of government and conditions of national life secures the permanence of some measure of patriotism and liberty. If these perish in one nation, they survive in another, and each people affects those about it by its rivalry or example. But an empire which comprised all the civilised globe could know nothing of this political interaction. In religious, social, intellectual, and moral life, foreign ideas were very discernible, but the enslaved provinces could have no influence in rekindling political life in the centre, and those which rivalled Italy in their civilisation, even surpassed it in their corruption and their servility.

In reviewing, however, the conditions upon which the moral state of the empire depended, there are still two very important centres or seed-plots of virtue to which it is necessary to advert. I mean the pursuit of agriculture and the discipline of the army. A very early tradition, which was attributed to Romulus, had declared that warfare and agriculture were the only honourable occupations for a citizen,[1] and it would be difficult to overrate the influence of the last in forming temperate and virtuous habits among the people. It is the subject of the only extant work of the elder Cato. Virgil had adorned it with the lustre of his poetry. A very large part of the Roman religion was intended to symbolise its stages or consecrate its operations. Varro expressed an eminently Roman sentiment in that beautiful sentence which Cowper has introduced into English poetry, 'Divine Providence made the country, but human art the town.'[2] The reforms of Vespasian consisted chiefly

---

[1] Dion. Halicarnass.
[2] 'Divina Natura dedit agros; ars humana ædificavit urbes.'

of the elevation to high positions of the agriculturists of the provinces. Antoninus, who was probably the most perfect of all the Roman emperors, was through his whole reign a zealous farmer.

As far as the distant provinces were concerned, it is pro-bable that the Imperial system was on the whole a good. The scandalous rapacity of the provincial governors, which disgraced the closing years of the Republic, and which is im-mortalised by the indignant eloquence of Cicero, appears to have ceased, or at least greatly diminished, under the super-vision of the emperors. Ample municipal freedom, good roads, and for the most part wise and temperate rulers, secured for the distant sections of the empire a large measure of prosperity. But in Italy itself, agriculture, with the habits of life that attended it, speedily and fatally decayed. The peasant proprietor soon glided hopelessly into debt. The immense advantages which slavery gave the rich gradually threw nearly all the Italian soil into their hands. The peasant who ceased to be proprietor found himself excluded by slave labour from the position of a hired cultivator, while the gratuitous distributions of corn drew him readily to the metropolis. The gigantic scale of these distributions induced the rulers to obtain their corn in the form of a tribute from distant countries, chiefly from Africa and Sicily, and it almost ceased to be cultivated in Italy. The land fell to waste, or was cultivated by slaves or converted into pasture, and over vast tracts the race of free peasants entirely disappeared.

This great revolution, which profoundly affected the moral condition of Italy, had long been impending. The debts of the poor peasants, and the tendency of the patricians to monopolise the conquered territory, had occasioned some of the fiercest contests of the Republic, and in the earliest days of the Empire the blight that seemed to have fallen on the Italian soil was continually and pathetically lamented. Livy, Varro, Columella, and Pliny have noticed it in the

most emphatic terms,[1] and Tacitus observed that as early
as the reign of Claudius, Italy, which had once supplied the
distant provinces with corn, had become dependent for the
very necessaries of life upon the winds and the waves.[2] The
evil was indeed of an almost hopeless kind. Adverse winds,
or any other accidental interruption of the convoys of corn,
occasioned severe distress in the capital; but the prospect of
the calamities that would ensue if any misfortune detached
the great corn-growing countries from the empire, might well
have appalled the politician. Yet the combined influence of
slavery, and of the gratuitous distributions of corn, acting in
the manner I have described, rendered every effort to revive
Italian agriculture abortive, and slavery had taken such deep
root that it would have been impossible to abolish it, while
no emperor dared to encounter the calamities and rebellion
that would follow a suspension or even a restriction of the
distributions.[3] Many serious efforts were made to remedy
the evil.[4] Alexander Severus advanced money to the poor
to buy portions of land, and accepted a gradual payment
without interest from the produce of the soil. Pertinax
settled poor men as proprietors on deserted land, on the sole
condition that they should cultivate it. Marcus Aurelius
began, and Aurelian and Valentinian continued, the system of
settling great numbers of barbarian captives upon the Italian
soil, and compelling them as slaves to till it. The introduction

---

[1] See a collection of passages
from these writers in Wallon, *Hist.
de l'Esclavage*, tome ii. pp. 378–379.
Pliny, in the first century, noticed
(*Hist. Nat.* xviii. 7) that the *lati-
fundia*, or system of large properties, was ruining both Italy and the
provinces, and that six landlords
whom Nero killed were the pos-
sessors of half Roman Africa.

[2] Tacit. *Annal.* xii. 43. The
same complaint had been made still

earlier by Tiberius, in a letter to
the Senate. (*Annal.* iii. 54.)

[3] Augustus, for a time, contemplated abolishing the distributions,
but soon gave up the idea. (Suet.
Aug. xlii.) He noticed that it had
the effect of causing the fields to
be neglected.

[4] M. Wallon has carefully traced
this history. (*Hist. de l'Esclav.*
tome iii. pp. 294–297.)

of this large foreign element into the heart of Italy was eventually one of the causes of the downfall of the empire, and it is also about this time that we first dimly trace the condition of serfdom or servitude to the soil into which slavery afterwards faded, and which was for some centuries the general condition of the European poor. But the economical and moral causes that were destroying agriculture in Italy were too strong to be resisted, and the simple habits of life which agricultural pursuits promote had little or no place in the later empire.

A somewhat less rapid but in the end not less complete decadence had taken place in military life. The Roman army was at first recruited exclusively from the upper classes, and the service, which lasted only during actual warfare, was gratuitous. Before the close of the Republic, however, these conditions had disappeared. Military pay is said to have been instituted at the time of the siege of Veii.[1] Some Spaniards who were enrolled during the rivalry of Rome and Carthage were the first example of the employment of foreign mercenaries by the former.[2] Marius abolished the property qualification of the recruits.[3] In long residences in Spain and in the Asiatic provinces discipline gradually relaxed, and the historian who traced the progress of Oriental luxury in Rome dwelt with a just emphasis upon the ominous fact that it had first been introduced into the city by soldiers.[4] The civil wars contributed to the destruction of the old military traditions, but being conducted by able generals it is probable that they had more effect upon the patriotism than upon the discipline of the army. Augustus reorganised the whole military system, establishing a body of soldiers known as the Prætorian guard, and dignified with some special privileges, permanently in Rome, while the

---

[1] Livy, iv. 59–60. Florus, i. 12.   [3] Sallust, *Bell. Jugurth.* 84-86.
[2] Livy, xxiv. 49.   [4] Livy, xxxix. 6.

other legions were chiefly mustered upon the frontiers
During his long reign, and during that of Tiberius, both
sections were quiescent, but the murder of Caligula by his
soldiers opened a considerable period of insubordination.
Claudius, it was observed, first set the fatal example of purchasing his safety from his soldiers by bribes.[1] The armies
of the provinces soon discovered that it was possible to elect
an emperor outside Rome, and Galba, Otho, Vitellius, and
Vespasian were all the creatures of revolt. The evil was,
however, not yet past recovery. Vespasian and Trajan enforced discipline with great stringency and success. The
emperors began more frequently to visit the camps. The
number of the soldiers was small, and for some time the
turbulence subsided. The history of the worst period of the
Empire, it has been truly observed, is full of instances of brave
soldiers trying, under circumstances of extreme difficulty,
simply to do their duty. But the historian had soon occasion
to notice again the profound influence of the voluptuous
Asiatic cities upon the legions.[2] Removed for many years
from Italy, they lost all national pride, their allegiance was
transferred from the sovereign to the general, and when the
Imperial sceptre fell into the hands of a succession of incom-
petent rulers, they habitually urged their commanders to
revolt, and at last reduced the empire to a condition of military anarchy. A remedy was found for this evil, though
not for the luxurious habits that had been acquired, in the
division of the empire, which placed each army under the
direct supervision of an emperor, and it is probable that at a
later period Christianity diminished the insubordination,
though it may l ave also diminished the military fire, of the
soldiers.[3] But other and still more powerful causes were in

---

[1] 'Primus Cæsarum fidem mi-
litis etiam præmio pigneratus.'—
Suet. *Claud*. x.

[2] Se Tacitus, *Annal*. xiii. 35;
Hist. ii. 69.

[3] M. Sismondi thinks that the
influence of Christianity in subduing the spirit of revolt, if not in
the army, at least in the people
was very great. He says: 'Il est

operation preparing the military downfall of Rome. The habits of inactivity which the Imperial policy had produced, and which, through a desire for popularity, most emperors laboured to encourage, led to a profound disinclination for the hardships of military life. Even the Prætorian guard, which was long exclusively Italian, was selected after Septimus Severus from the legions on the frontiers,[1] while, Italy being relieved from the regular conscription, these were recruited solely in the provinces, and innumerable barbarians were subsidised. The political and military consequences of this change are sufficiently obvious. In an age when, artillery being unknown, the military superiority of civilised nations over barbarians was far less than at present, the Italians had become absolutely unaccustomed to real war, and had acquired habits that were beyond all others incompatible with military discipline, while many of the barbarians who menaced and at last subverted the empire had been actua'ly trained by Roman generals. The moral consequence is equally plain—military discipline, like agricultural labour, ceased to have any part among the moral influences of Italy.

To those who have duly estimated the considerations I have enumerated, the downfall and moral debasement of the empire can cause no surprise, though they may justly wonder that its agony should have been so protracted, that it should have produced a multitude of good and great men, both

---

remarquable qu'en cinq ans, sept prétendans au trône, tous bien supérieurs à Honorius en courage, en talens et en vertus, furent successivement envoyés captifs à Ravenne ou punis de mort, que le peuple applaudit toujours à ces jugemens et ne se sépara point de l'autorité légitime, tant la doctrine du droit divin des rois que les évêques avoient commencé à prêcher sous Théodose avoit fait de progrès,

et tant le monde romain sembloit determiné à périr avec un monarque imbécile plutôt que tenté de se donner un sauveur.'—*Hist. de la Chute de l'Empire romain*, tome i. p. 221.

[1] See Gibbon, ch. v.; Merivale's *Hist. of Rome*, ch. lxvii. It was thought that troops thus selected would be less likely to revolt Constantine abolished the Prætorians.

pagan and Christian, and that these should have exercised
so wide an influence as they unquestionably did. Almost
every institution or pursuit by which virtuous habits would
naturally have been formed had been tainted or destroyed,
while agencies of terrific power were impelling the people to
vice. The rich, excluded from most honourable paths of ambition, and surrounded by countless parasites who inflamed
their every passion, found themselves absolute masters of innumerable slaves who were their willing ministers, and often
their teachers, in vice. The poor, hating industry and destitute of all intellectual resources, lived in habitual idleness,
and looked upon abject servility as the normal road to
fortune. But the picture becomes truly appalling when we
remember that the main amusement of both classes was the
spectacle of bloodshed, of the death, and sometimes of the
torture, of men.

The gladiatorial games form, indeed, the one feature of
Roman society which to a modern mind is almost inconceivable in its atrocity. That not only men, but women, in an
advanced period of civilisation—men and women who not
only professed but very frequently acted upon a high code of
morals—should have made the carnage of men their habitual
amusement, that all this should have continued for centuries,
with scarcely a protest, is one of the most startling facts in
moral history. It is, however, perfectly normal, and in no
degree inconsistent with the doctrine of natural moral perceptions, while it opens out fields of ethical enquiry of a very
deep though painful interest.

These games, which long eclipsed, both in interest and in
influence, every other form of public amusement at Rome,[1]

---

[1] The gladiatorial shows are
treated incidentally by most Roman
historians, but the three works from
which I have derived most assistance in this part of my subject are
the *Saturnalia* of Justus Lipsius,
Magnin, *Origines du Théâtre* (an
extremely learned and interesting
book, which was unhappily never
completed), and Friedlænder's

were originally religious ceremonies celebrated at the tombs of the great, and intended as human sacrifices to appease the Manes of the dead.[1] They were afterwards defended as a means of sustaining the military spirit by the constant spectacle of courageous death,[2] and with this object it was customary to give a gladiatorial show to soldiers before their departure to a war.[3] In addition to these functions they had a considerable political importance, for at a time when all the regular organs of liberty were paralysed or abolished, the ruler was accustomed in the arena to meet tens of thousands of his subjects, who availed themselves of the opportunity to present their petitions, to declare their grievances, and to censure freely the sovereign or his ministers.[4] The games

Roman Manners from Augustus to the Antonines (the second volume of the French translation). M. Wallon has also compressed into a few pages (*Hist. de l'Esclavage,* tome ii. pp. 129–139) much information on the subject.

[1] Hence the old name of *bustuarii* (from *bustum,* a funeral pile) given to gladiators (Nieupoort, *De Ritibus Romanorum,* p. 514). According to Pliny (*Hist. Nat.* xxx. 3), 'regular human sacrifices were only abolished in Rome by a decree of the senate, B.C. 97,' and there are some instances of them at a still later period. Much information about them is collected by Sir C. Lewis, *Credibility of Roman History,* vol. ii. p. 430; Merivale, *Conversion of the Roman Empire,* pp. 230–233; Legendre. *Traité de l'Opinion,* vol. i. pp. 229–231. Porphyry, in his *De Abstinentia Carnis,* devoted considerable research to this matter. Games were habitually celebrated by wealthy private individuals, during the early part of the empire, at the funerals of their relatives, but their mortuary cha-

racter gradually ceased, and after Marcus Aurelius they had become mere public spectacles, and were rarely celebrated at Rome by private men. (See Wallon, *Hist. de l'Esclav.* tome ii. pp. 135–136.) The games had then really passed into their purely secular stage, though they were still nominally dedicated to Mars and Diana, and though an altar of Jupiter Latiaris stood in the centre of the arena. (Nieupoort, p. 365.)

[2] Cicero, *Tusc.* lib. ii.

[3] Capitolinus, *Maximus et Balbinus.* Capitolinus says this is the most probable origin of the custom, though others regarded it as a sacrifice to appease Nemesis by an offering of blood.

[4] Much curious information on this subject may be found in Friedländer, *Mœurs romaines,* liv. vi. ch. i. Very few Roman emperors ventured to disregard or to repress these outcries, and they led to the fall of several of the most powerful ministers of the empire. On the whole these games represent the strangest and most ghastly form

are said to have been of Etruscan origin; they were first
introduced into Rome, B.C. 264, when the two sons of a man
named Brutus compelled three pair of gladiators to fight at
the funeral of their father,[1*] and before the close of the
Republic they were common on great public occasions, and,
what appears even more horrible, at the banquets of the
nobles.[2] The rivalry of Cæsar and Pompey greatly multiplied them, for each sought by this means to ingratiate himself with the people. Pompey introduced a new form of
combat between men and animals.[3] Cæsar abolished the old
custom of restricting the mortuary games to the funerals of
men, and his daughter was the first Roman lady whose tomb
was desecrated by human blood.[4] Besides this innovation,
Cæsar replaced the temporary edifices in which the games
had hitherto been held by a permanent wooden amphitheatre,
shaded the spectators by an awning of precious silk, compelled
the condemned persons on one occasion to fight with silver
lances,[5] and drew so many gladiators into the city that the
Senate was obliged to issue an enactment restricting their
number.[6] In the earliest years of the Empire, Statilius
Taurus erected the first amphitheatre of stone.[7] Augustus

political liberty has ever assumed.
On the other hand, the people
readily bartered all genuine freedom
for abundant games.

[1] Valer. Maximus, ii. 4, § 7.

[2] On the gladiators at banquets,
see J. Lipsius, *Saturnalia*, lib. i., c.
vi., Magnin; *Origines du Théâtre*,
pp. 380–385. This was originally
an Etruscan custom, and it was
also very common at Capua. As
Silius Italicus says:—

'Exhilarare viris convivia cæde
Mos olim, et miscere epulis spec-
tacula dira.'
Verus, the colleague of Marcus
Aurelius, was especially addicted to
this kind of entertainment. (Capi-

tolinus, *Verus*.) See, too, Athenæus,
iv. 40, 41.

[3] Senec. *De Brevit. Vit.* c. xiii.

[4] Sueton. *J. Cæsar*, xxvi. Pliny
(*Ep.* vi. 34) commends a friend for
having given a show in memory of
his departed wife.

[5] Pliny, *Hist. Nat.* xxxiii. 16.

[6] Sueton. *Cæsar*, x.; Dion Cassius, xliii. 24.

[7] Sueton. *Aug.* xxix. The history of the amphitheatres is given
very minutely by Friedlænder, who,
like nearly all other antiquaries,
believes this to have been the first
of stone. Pliny mentions the existence, at an earlier period, of two
connected wooden theatres, which

ordered that not more than 120 men should fight on a single occasion, and that no prætor should give more than two spectacles in a single year,[1] and Tiberius again fixed the maximum of combatants,[2] but notwithstanding these attempts to limit them the games soon acquired the most gigantic proportions. They were celebrated habitually by great men in honour of their dead relatives, by officials on coming into office, by conquerors to secure popularity, and on every occasion of public rejoicing, and by rich tradesmen who were desirous of acquiring a social position.[3] They were also among the attractions of the public baths. Schools of gladiators—often the private property of rich citizens—existed in every leading city of Italy, and, besides slaves and criminals, they were thronged with freemen, who voluntarily hired themselves for a term of years. In the eyes of multitudes, the large sums that were paid to the victor, the patronage of nobles and often of emperors, and still more the delirium of popular enthusiasm that centred upon the successful gladiator, outweighed all the dangers of the profession. A complete recklessness of life was soon engendered both in the spectators and the combatants. The 'lanistæ,' or purveyors of gladiators, became an important profession. Wandering bands of gladiators traversed Italy, hiring themselves for the provincial amphitheatres. The influence of the games gradually pervaded the whole texture of Roman life. They became the common-place of conversation.[4] The children imitated them in their play.[5] The philosophers drew from

swung round on hinges and formed an amphitheatre. (*Hist. Nat.* xxxvi. 21.)

[1] Dion Cassius, liv. 2. It appears, however, from an inscription, that 10,000 gladiators fought in the reign and by the command of Augustus. Wallon, *Hist. de l'Esclavage*, tome, ii. p. 133.

[2] Sueton. *Tiber.* xxxiv. Nero

made another slight restriction (Tacit. *Annal.* xiii. 31), which appears to have been little observed.

[3] Martial notices (*Ep.* iii. 59) and ridicules a spectacle given by a shoemaker at Bologna, and by a fuller at Modena.

[4] Epictetus, *Enchir.* xxxiii. § 2
[5] Arrian, iii. 15.

them their metaphors and illustrations. The artists pourtrayed them in every variety of ornament.[1] The vestal
virgins had a seat of honour in the arena.[2] The Colosseum,
which is said to have been capable of containing more than
80,000 spectators, eclipsed every other monument of Imperial
splendour, and is even now at once the most imposing and
the most characteristic relic of pagan Rome.

In the provinces the same passion was displayed. From
Gaul to Syria, wherever the Roman influence extended, the
spectacles of blood were introduced, and the gigantic remains
of amphitheatres in many lands still attest by their ruined
grandeur the sca'e on which they were pursued. In the
reign of Tiberius, more than 20,000 persons are said to have
perished by the fall of the amphitheatre at the suburban town
of Fidenæ.[3] Under Nero, the Syracusans obtained, as a
special favour, an exemption from the law which limited the
number of gladiators.[4] Of the vast train of prisoners brought
by Titus from Judea, a large proportion were destined by the
conqueror for the provincial games.[5] In Syria, where they
were introduced by Antiochus Epiphanes, they at first produced rather terror than pleasure ; but the effeminate Syrians
soon learned to contemplate them with a passionate enjoyment,[6] and on a single occasion Agrippa caused 1,400 men to
fight in the amphitheatre at Berytus.[7] Greece alone was in

---

[1] See these points minutely
proved in Friedlænder.

[2] Suet. *Aug.* xliv. This was
noticed before by Cicero. The
Christian poet Prudentius dwelt on
this aspect of the games in some
forcible lines :—

Virgo modesta jubet converso
pollice rumpi
Ne lateat pars ulla animæ vitalibus
imis
Altius impresso dum palpitat ense
socutor.'

[3] Sueton. *Tiberius,* xl. Tacitus,
who gives a graphic description of
the disaster (*Annal.* iv. 62–63),
says 50,000 persons were killed or
wounded.

[4] Tacit. *Annal.* xiii. 49.

[5] Joseph. *Bell. Jud.* vi. 9.

[6] See the very curious picture
which Livy has given (xli. 20) of
the growth of the fascination.

[7] Joseph. *Antiq. Jud.* xix. 7

some degree an exception. When an attempt was made to introduce the spectacle into Athens, the cynic philosophei Demonax appealed successfully to the better feelings of the people by exclaiming, 'You must first overthrow the altar of Pity.'[1] The games are said to have afterwards penetrated to Athens, and to have been suppressed by Apollonius of Tyana;[2] but with the exception of Corinth, where a very large foreign population existed, Greece never appears to have shared the general enthusiasm.[3]

One of the first consequences of this taste was to render the people absolutely unfit for those tranquil and refined amusements which usually accompany civilisation. To men who were accustomed to witness the fierce vicissitudes of deadly combat, any spectacle that did not elicit the strongest excitement was insipid. The only amusements that at all rivalled the spectacles of the amphitheatre and the circus were those which appealed strongly to the sensual passions, such as the games of Flora, the postures of the pantomimes, and the ballet.[4] Roman comedy, indeed, flourished for a short period, but only by throwing itself into the same career. The pander and the courtesan are the leading characters of Plautus, and the more modest Terence never attained an equal popularity. The different forms of vice have a continual tendency to act and react upon one another, and the intense craving after excitement which the amphitheatre must necessarily have produced, had probably no

---

[1] Lucian, *Demonax.*

[2] Philost. *Apoll.* iv. 22.

[3] Friedlænder, tome ii. pp. 95–96. There are, however, several extant Greek inscriptions relating to gladiators, and proving the existence of the shows in Greece. Pompeii, which was a Greek colony, had a vast amphitheatre, which we may still admire; and, under Nero, games were prohibited at Pompeii

for ten years, in consequence of a riot that broke out during a gladiatorial show. (Tacit. *Annal.* xiv. 17.) After the defeat of Perseus, Paulus Emilius celebrated a show in Macedonia. (Livy, xli. 20.)

[4] These are fully discussed by Magnin and Friedlænder. There is a very beautiful description of a ballet, representing the 'Judgment of Paris,' in Apuleius, *Metamorph.* x.

sm ll influence in stimulating the orgies of sensuality which Tacitus and Suetonius describe.

But if comedy could to a certain extent flourish with the gladiatorial games, it was not so with tragedy. It is, indeed, true that the tragic actor can exhibit displays of more intense agony and of a grander heroism than were ever witnessed in the arena. His mission is not to paint nature as it exists in the light of day, but nature as it exists in the heart of man. His gestures, his tones, his looks, are such as would never have been exhibited by the person he represents, but they display to the audience the full intensity of the emotions which that person would have felt, but which he would have been unable adequately to reveal. But to those who were habituated to the intense realism of the amphitheatre, the idealised suffering of the stage was unimpressive. All the genius of a Siddons or a Ristori would fail to move an audience who had continually seen living men fall bleeding and mangled at their feet. One of the first functions of the stage is to raise to the highest point the susceptibility to disgust. When Horace said that Medea should not kill her children upon the stage, he enunciated not a mere arbitrary rule, but one which grows necessarily out of the development of the drama. It is an essential characteristic of a refined and cultivated taste to be shocked and offended at the spectacle of bloodshed; and the theatre, which somewhat dangerously dissociates sentiment from action, and causes men to waste their compassion on ideal sufferings, is at least a barrier against the extreme forms of cruelty by developing this susceptibility to the highest degree. The gladiatorial games, on the other hand, destroyed all sense of disgust, and therefore all refinement of taste, and they rendered the permanent triumph of the drama impossible.[1]

---

[1] Pacuvius and Accius were the founders of Roman tragedy. The abridger, Vellerus Paterculus, who is the only Roman historian who pays any attention to literary history, boasts that the latter might

It is abundantly evident, both from history and from present experience, that the instinctive shock, or natural feeling of disgust, caused by the sight of the sufferings of men is not generically different from that which is caused by the sight of the sufferings of animals. The latter, to those who are not accustomed to it, is intensely painful. The former continually becomes by use a matter of absolute indifference. If the repugnance which is felt in the one case appears greater than in the other, it is not on account of any innate sentiment which commands us to reverence our species, but simply because our imagination finds less difficulty in realising human than animal suffering, and also because education has strengthened our feelings in the one case much more than in the other. There is, however, no fact more clearly established than that when men have regarded it as not a crime to kill some class of their fellow-men, they have soon learnt to do so with no more natural compunction or hesitation than they would exhibit in killing a wild animal. This is the normal condition of savage men. Colonists and Red Indians even now often shoot each other with precisely the same indifference as they shoot beasts of prey, and the whole history of warfare—especially when warfare was conducted on more savage principles than at present—is an illustration of the fact. Startling, therefore, as it may now appear, it is in no degree unnatural that Roman spectators should have contemplated with perfect equanimity the slaughter of men. The Spaniard, who is brought in infancy to the bull-ring, soon learns to gaze with indifference or with pleasure upon sights before which the unpractised eye of the stranger quails with horror, and the same process would be equally efficacious had the spectacle been the sufferings of men.

We now look back with indignation upon this indifference;

---

rank honourably with the best Greek tragedians. He adds, 'ut in illis [the Greeks] limæ, in hoc pœne plus videatur fuisse sanguinis.'— *Hist. Rom.* ii. 9.

but yet, although it may be hard to realise, it is probably true that there is scarcely a human being who might not by custom be so indurated as to share it. Had the most bene-volent person lived in a country in which the innocence of these games was deemed axiomatic, had he been taken to them in his very childhood, and accustomed to associate them with his earliest dreams of romance, and had he then been left simply to the play of the emotions, the first paroxysm of horror would have soon subsided, the shrinking repugnance that followed would have grown weaker and weaker, the feeling of interest would have been aroused, and the time would probably come in which it would reign alone. But even this absolute indifference to the sight of human suffering does not represent the full evil resulting from the gladiatorial games. That some men are so constituted as to be capable of taking a real and lively pleasure in the simple contem-plation of suffering as suffering, and without any reference to their own interests, is a proposition which has been strenu-ously denied by those in whose eyes vice is nothing more than a displacement, or exaggeration, of lawful self-regarding feelings, and others, who have admitted the reality of the phenomenon, have treated it as a very rare and exceptional disease.[1] That it is so—at least in its extreme forms—in the present condition of society, may reasonably be hoped, though I imagine that few persons who have watched the habits of boys would question that to take pleasure in giving at least some degree of pain is sufficiently common, and though it is not quite certain that all the sports of adult men would be entered into with exactly the same zest if their victims were not sentient beings. But in every society in which atrocious punishments have been common, this side of human nature

---

[1] Thus, e.g., Hobbes: 'Alienæ calamitatis contemptus nominatur crudelitas, proceditque a propriæ securitatis opinione. Nam ut ali- quis sibi placeat in malis alienis sine alio fine, videtur mihi im-possibile.'—*Leviathan*, pars i. c. vi.

has acquired an undoubted prominence.   It is related of
Claudius that his special delight at the gladiatorial shows
was in watching the countenances of the dying, for he had
learnt to take an artistic pleasure in observing the variations
of their agony.[1]   When the gladiator lay prostrate it was
customary for the spectators to give the sign with their
thumbs, indicating whether they desired him to be spared or
slain, and the giver of the show reaped most popularity
when, in the latter case, he permitted no consideration of
economy to make him hesitate to sanction the popular
award.[2]

Besides this, the mere desire for novelty impelled the
people to every excess or refinement of barbarity.[3]   The
simple combat became at last insipid, and every variety of
atrocity was devised to stimulate the flagging interest.   At
one time a bear and a bull, chained together, rolled in fierce
contest along the sand ; at another, criminals dressed in the
skins of wild beasts were thrown to bulls, which were maddened by red-hot irons, or by darts tipped with burning
pitch.   Four hundred bears were killed on a single day under
Caligula ;   three hundred on another day under Claudius.
Under Nero, four hundred tigers fought with bulls and elephants ; four hundred bears and three hundred lions were
slaughtered by his soldiers.   In a single day, at the dedication
of the Colosseum by Titus, five thousand animals perished.
Under Trajan, the games continued for one hundred and
twenty-three successive days.[4]   Lions, tigers, elephants, rhi-

---

Sueton. *Claudius*, xxxiv.

[2]   ' Et verso pollice vulgi
Quemlibet occidunt populariter.'—
Juvenal, *Sat.* iii. 36–37.

[3]   Besides the many incidental
notices scattered through the Roman historians, and through the
writings of Seneca, Plutarch, Juvenal and Pliny, we have a curious

little book, *De Spectaculis*, by
Martial—a book which is not more
horrible from the atrocities it recounts than from the perfect absence of all feeling of repulsion or
compassion it everywhere displays.
[4]   These are but a few of the many
examples given by Magnin, who
has collected a vast array of authorities on the subject. (*Origines*

noceroses, hippopotami, giraffes, bulls, stags, even crocodiles
and serpents, were employed to give novelty to the spectacle
Nor was any form of human suffering wanting. The first
Gordian, when edile, gave twelve spectacles, in each of which
from one hundred and fifty to five hundred pair of gladiators
appeared.[1] Eight hundred pair fought at the triumph of
Aurelian.[2] Ten thousand men fought during the games of
Trajan.[3] Nero illumined his gardens during the night by
Christians burning in their pitchy shirts.[4] Under Domitian.
an army of feeble dwarfs was compelled to fight,[5] and, more
than once, female gladiators descended to perish in the arena.[6]
A criminal personating a fictitious character was nailed to a
cross, and there torn by a bear.[7] Another, representing
Scævola, was compelled to hold his hand in a real flame.[8] A
third, as Hercules, was burnt alive upon the pile.[9] So intense

---

du Théâtre, pp. 445–453.) M.
Mongez has devoted an interesting
memoir to ' Les animaux promenés
ou tués dans le cirque.' (*Mém. de
l'Acad. des Inscrip. et Belles-lettres*,
tome x.) See, too, Friedlænder. Pliny
rarely gives an account of any wild
animal without accompanying it by
statistics about its appearances in
the arena. The first instance of a
wild beast hunt in the amphitheatre
is said to be that recorded by Livy
(xxxix. 22), which took place about
80 B.C.

[1] Capitolinus, *Gordiani.*
[2] Vopiscus, *Aurelian.*
[3] Xiphilin, lxviii. 15.
[4] Tacit. *Annal.* xv. 44.
[5] Xiphilin, lxvii. 8; Statius,
Sylv. i. 6.
[6] During the Republic, a rich
man ordered in his will that
some women he had purchased for
the purpose should fight in the
funeral games to his memory, but
the people annulled the clause.
(Athenæus, iv. 39.) Under Nero

and Domitian, female gladiators
seem to have been not uncommon.
See Statius, *Sylv.* i. 6; Sueton.
Domitian, iv.; Xiphilin, lxvii. 8.
Juvenal describes the enthusiasm
with which Roman ladies practised
with the gladiatorial weapons (*Sat.*
vi. 248, &c.), and Martial (*De
Spectac.* vi.) mentions the combats
of women with wild beasts. One,
he says, killed a lion. A combat
of female gladiators, under Severus,
created some tumult, and it was
decreed that they should no longer
be permitted. (Xiphilin, lxxv. 16.)
See Magnin, pp. 434–435.

[7] Martial, *De Spectac.* vii.
[8] Ibid. *Ep.* viii. 30.
[9] Tertullian, *Ad Nation.* i. 10.
One of the most ghastly features
of the games was the comic aspect
they sometimes assumed. This was
the case in the combats of dwarfs.
There were also combats by blind-
folded men. Petronius (*Satyricon*,
c. xlv.) has given us a horrible description of the maimed and feeble

was the craving for blood, that a prince was less unpopular if
he neglected the distribution of corn than if he neglected the
games ; and Nero himself, on account of his munificence in
this respect, was probably the sovereign who was most
beloved by the Roman multitude. Heliogabalus and Galerius
are reported, when dining, to have regaled themselves with
the sight of criminals torn by wild beasts. It was said of the
latter that ' he never supped without human blood.' [1]

It is well for us to look steadily on such facts as these.
They display more vividly than any mere philosophical disquisition the abyss of depravity into which it is possible for
human nature to sink.   They furnish us with striking proofs
of the reality of the moral progress we have attained, and
they enable us in some degree to estimate the regenerating
influence that Christianity has exercised in the world.   For
the destruction of the gladiatorial games is all its work.
Philosophers, indeed, might deplore them, gentle natures
might shrink from their contagion, but to the multitude they
possessed a fascination which nothing but the new religion
could overcome.

Nor was this fascination surprising, for no pageant has
ever combined more powerful elements of attraction.   The
magnificent circus, the gorgeous dresses of the assembled
Court, the contagion of a passionate enthusiasm thrilling
almost visibly through the mighty throng, the breathless
silence of expectation, the wild cheers bursting simultaneously
from eighty thousand tongues, and echoing to the farthest
outskirts of the city, the rapid alternations of the fray, the

---

men who were sometimes compelled to fight.   People afflicted
with epilepsy were accustomed to
drink the blood of the wounded
gladiators, which they believed to
be a sovereign remedy.   (Pliny,
Hist. Nat. xxviii. 2 ; Tertul.
Apol. ix.)

[1] 'Nec unquam sine humano
cruore cœnabat.'—Lactan. *De Mort.
Persec.* Much the same thing is
told of the Christian emperor Justinian II., who lived at the end of
the seventh century. (Sismondi,
*Hist. de la Chute de l'Empire
Romain,* tome ii. p. 85.)

deeds of splendid courage that were manifested, were all well fitted to entrance the imagination. The crimes and servitude of the gladiator were for a time forgotten in the blaze of glory that surrounded him. Representing to the highest degree that courage which the Romans deemed the first of virtues, the cynosure of countless eyes, the chief object of conversation in the metropolis of the universe, destined, if victorious, to be immortalised in the mosaic and the sculpture,[1] he not unfrequently rose to heroic grandeur. The gladiator Spartacus for three years defied the bravest armies of Rome. The greatest of Roman generals had chosen gladiators for his body-guard.[2] A band of gladiators, faithful even to death, followed the fortunes of the fallen Antony, when all besides had deserted him.[3] Beautiful eyes, trembling with passion, looked down upon the fight, and the noblest ladies in Rome, even the empress herself, had been known to crave the victor's love.[4] We read of gladiators lamenting that the games occurred so seldom,[5] complaining bitterly if they were not permitted to descend into the arena,[6] scorning to fight except with the most powerful antagonists,[7] laughing aloud as their wounds were dressed,[8] and at last, when prostrate in the dust, calmly turning their throats to the sword of the conqueror.[9] The enthusiasm that gathered round them was so intense that special laws were found necessary, and were sometimes insufficient to prevent patricians from enlisting in their ranks,[10] while the tranquil

---

[1] Winckelmann says the statue called 'The Dying Gladiator' does not represent a gladiator. At a later period, however, statues of gladiators were not uncommon, and Pliny notices (*Hist. Nat.* xxxv. 33) paintings of them. A fine specimen of mosaic portraits of gladiators is now in the Lateran Museum.

[2] Plutarch's *Life of Cæsar.*

[3] Dion Cassius, li. 7.

[4] Faustina, the wife of Marcus Aurelius, was especially accused of this weakness. (Capitolinus, *Marcus Aurelius.*)

[5] Seneca, *De Provident.* iv.

[6] Arrian's *Epictetus*, i. 29.

[7] Seneca, *De Provident.* iii.

[8] Aulus Gellius, xii. 5.

[9] Cicero, *Tusc.* lib. ii.

[10] Some Equites fought under Julius Cæsar, and a senator named

courage with which they never failed to die supplied the philosopher with his most striking examples.[1] The severe continence that was required before the combat, contrasting vividly with the licentiousness of Roman life, had even invested them with something of a moral dignity; and it is a singularly suggestive fact that of all pagan characters the gladiator was selected by the Fathers as the closest approximation to a Christian model.[2] St. Augustine tells us how one of his friends, being drawn to the spectacle, endeavoured by closing his eyes to guard against a fascination he knew to be sinful. A sudden cry caused him to break his resolution, and he never could withdraw his gaze again.[3]

And while the influences of the amphitheatre gained a complete ascendancy over the populace, the Roman was not without excuses that could lull his moral feelings to repose. The games, as I have said, were originally human sacrifices—religious rites sacred to the dead—and it was argued that the death of the gladiator was both more honourable and more

---

Fulvius Setinus wished to fight, but Cæsar prevented him. (Suet. *Cæsar*, xxxix.; Dion Cassius, xliii. 23.) Nero, according to Suetonius, compelled men of the highest rank to fight. Laws prohibiting patricians from fighting were several times made and violated. (Friedlænder, pp. 39–41.) Commodus is said to have been himself passionately fond of fighting as a gladiator. Much, however, of what Lampridius relates on this point is perfectly incredible. On the other hand, the profession of the gladiator was constantly spoken of as infamous; but this oscillation between extreme admiration and contempt will surprise no one who has noticed the tone continually adopted about prize-fighters in England, and about the members of some other professions on the Continent. Juvenal dwells (*Sat.* viii. 197–210) with great indignation on an instance of a patrician fighting,

[1] 'Quis mediocris gladiator ingemuit, quis vultum mutavit unquam?'—Cic. *Tusc. Quæst.* lib. ii.

[2] E.g. Clem. Alex. *Strom.* iii. There is a well-known passage of this kind in Horace, *Ars Poet.* 412–415. The comparison of the good man to an athlete or gladiator, which St. Paul employed, occurs also in Seneca and Epictetus, from which some have inferred that they must have known the writings of the Apostle. M. Denis, however, has shown (*Idées morales dans l'Antiquité*, tome ii. p. 240) that the same comparison had been used, before the rise of Christianity, by Plato, Æschines, and Cicero.

[3] *Confess.* vi. 8.

merciful than that of the passive victim, who, in the Homeric age, was sacrificed at the tomb. The combatants were either professional gladiators, slaves, criminals, or military captives. The lot of the first was voluntary. The second had for a long time been regarded as almost beneath or beyond a freeman's care; but when the enlarging circle of sympathy had made the Romans regard their slaves as 'a kind of second human nature,'[1] they perceived the atrocity of exposing them in the games, and an edict of the emperor forbade it.[2] The third had been condemned to death, and as the victorious gladiator was at least sometimes pardoned,[3] a permission to fight was regarded as an act of mercy. The fate of the fourth could not strike the early Roman with the horror it would now inspire, for the right of the conquerors to massacre their prisoners was almost universally admitted.[4] But, beyond the point of desiring the games to be in some degree restricted, extremely few of the moralists of the Roman Empire ever advanced. That it was a horrible and demoralising thing to make the spectacle of the deaths, even of guilty men, a form of popular amusement, was a position which no Roman school had attained, and which was only reached by a very few individuals. Cicero observes, 'that the gladiatorial spectacles appear to some cruel and inhuman,' and, he adds, 'I know not whether as they are now conducted it is not so, but when guilty men are compelled to fight, no better discipline against suffering and death can be

---

[1] '[Servi] etsi per fortunam in omnia obnoxii, tamen quasi secundum hominum genus sunt.'—Florus, *Hist.* iii. 20.

[2] Macrinus, however, punished fugitive slaves by compelling them to fight as gladiators. (Capitolinus, *Macrinus.*)

[3] Tacit. *Annal.* xii. 56. According to Friedlænder, however, there were two classes of criminals.

One class were condemned only to fight, and pardoned if they conquered; the others were condemned to fight till death, and this was considered an aggravation of capital punishment.

[4] 'Ad conciliandum plebis favorem effusa largitio, quum spectaculis indulget, supplicia quondam hostium artem facit.'—Florus, iii. 12.

presented to the eye. [1] Seneca, it is true, adopts a far nobler
language. He denounced the games with a passionate
eloquence. He refuted indignantly the argument derived
from the guilt of the combatants, and declared that under
every form and modification these amusements were brutalising, savage, and detestable. [2] Plutarch went even farther,
and condemned the combats of wild beasts on the ground
that we should have a bond of sympathy with all sentient
beings, and that the sight of blood and of suffering is necessarily and essentially depraving. [3] To these instances we
may add Petronius, who condemned the shows in his poem
on the civil war; Junius Mauricus, who refused to permit
the inhabitants of Vienne to celebrate them, and replied to
the remonstrances of the emperor, ' Would to Heaven it were
possible to abolish such spectacles, even at Rome !' [4] and,
above all, Marcus Aurelius, who, by compelling the gladiators
to fight with blunted swords, rendered them for a time comparatively harmless. [5] But these, with the Athenian remonstrances I have already noticed, are almost the only instances
now remaining of pagan protests against the most conspicuous
as well as the most atrocious feature of the age. Juvenal,
whose unsparing satire has traversed the whole field of
Roman manners, and who denounces fiercely all cruelty to
slaves, has repeatedly noticed the gladiatorial shows, but on
no single occasion does he intimate that they were inconsistent
with humanity. Of all the great historians who recorded
them, not one seems to have been conscious that he was
recording a barbarity, not one appears to have seen in them

---

[1] *Tusc. Quæst.* ii. 17.
[2] See his magnificent letter on
the subject. (*Ep.* vii.)
[3] In his two treatises *De Esu
Carnium.*
[4] Pliny. *Ep.* iv. 22.
[5] Xiphilin, lxxi. 29. Capitolinus,
M. Aurelius. The emperor also

once carried off the gladiators to a
war with his army, much to the
indignation of the people. (Capit.)
He has himself noticed the extreme
weariness he felt at the public
amusements he was obliged to
attend. (vii. 3.)

any greater evils than an increasing tendency to pleasure and the excessive multiplication of a dangerous class. The Roman sought to make men brave and fearless, rather than gentle and humane, and in his eyes that spectacle was to be applauded which steeled the heart against the fear of death, even at the sacrifice of the affections. Titus and Trajan, in whose reigns, probably, the greatest number of shows were compressed into a short time, were both men of conspicuous clemency, and no Roman seems to have imagined that the fact of 3,000 men having been compelled to fight under the one, and 10,000 under the other, cast the faintest shadow upon their characters. Suetonius mentions, as an instance of the amiability of Titus, that he was accustomed to jest with the people during the combats of the gladiators,[1] and Pliny especially eulogised Trajan because he did not patronise spectacles that enervate the character, but rather those which impel men 'to noble wounds and to the contempt of death.'[2] The same writer, who was himself in many ways conspicuous for his gentleness and charity, having warmly commended a friend for acceding to a petition of the people of Verona, who desired a spectacle, adds this startling sentence : 'After so general a request, to have refused would not have been firmness—it would have been cruelty.'[3] Even in the closing years of the fourth century, the præfect Symmachus, who was regarded as one of the most estimable pagans of his age, collected some Saxon prisoners to fight in honour of his son. They strangled themselves in prison, and Symmachus lamented the misfortune that had befallen him from their 'impious hands,' but endeavoured to calm his feelings by recalling the patience of Socrates and the precepts of philosophy.[4]

---

[1] Sueton. *Titus*, viii.

[2] ' Visum est spectaculum inde non enerve nec fluxum, nec quod animos virorum molliret et frangeret, sed quod ad pulchra vulnera contemptumque mortis accenderet.'

Pliny, *Paneg.* xxxiii.

[3] ' Præterea tanto consensu rogabaris, ut negare non constans sed durum videretur.'—Plin. *Epist.* vi. 34.

[4] **Symmach.** *Epist.* ii. 46.

While, however, I have no desire to disguise or palliate
the extreme atrocity of this aspect of Roman life, there are
certain very natural exaggerations, against which it is necessary for us to guard.   There are in human nature, and more
especially in the exercise of the benevolent affections, inequalities, inconsistencies, and anomalies, of which theorists
do not always take account.   We should be altogether in
error if we supposed that a man who took pleasure in a
gladiatorial combat in ancient Rome was necessarily as inhuman as a modern would be who took pleasure in a similar
spectacle.   A man who falls but a little below the standard
of his own merciful age is often in reality far worse than a
man who had conformed to the standard of a much more
barbarous age, even though the latter will do some things
with perfect equanimity from which the other would recoil
with horror.   We have a much greater power than is sometimes supposed of localising both our benevolent and malevolent feelings.   If a man is very kind, or very harsh to some
particular class, this is usually, and on the whole justly, regarded as an index of his general disposition, but the
inference is not infallible, and it may easily be pushed too
far.   There are some who appear to expend all their kindly
feelings on a single class, and to treat with perfect indifference all outside it.   There are others who regard a certain
class as quite outside the pale of their sympathies, while in
other spheres their affections prove lively and constant.
There are many who would accede without the faintest reluctance to a barbarous custom, but would be quite incapable
of an equally barbarous act which custom had not consecrated.   Our affections are so capricious in their nature that
it is continually necessary to correct by detailed experience
the most plausible deductions.   Thus, for example, it is a
very unquestionable and a very important truth that cruelty
to animals naturally indicates and promotes a habit of mind
which leads to cruelty to men; and that, on the other hand,

an affectionate and merciful disposition to animals commonly
implies a gentle and amiable nature.   But, if we adopted
this principle as an infallible criterion of humanity, we should
soon find ourselves at fault. To the somewhat too hackneyed
anecdote of Domitian gratifying his savage propensities by
killing flies,[1] we might oppose Spinoza, one of the purest,
most gentle, most benevolent of mankind, of whom it is re
lated that almost the only amusement of his life was putting
flies into spiders' webs and watching their struggles and their
deaths.[2]   It has been observed that a very large proportion
of the men who during the French Revolution proved themselves most absolutely indifferent to human suffering were
deeply attached to animals.   Fournier was devoted to a
squirrel, Couthon to a spaniel, Panis to two gold pheasants
Chaumette to an aviary, Marat kept doves.[3] Bacon has
noticed that the Turks, who are a cruel people, are nevertheless conspicuous for their kindness to animals, and he mentions the instance of a Christian boy who was nearly stoned
to death for gagging a long-billed fowl.[4] In Egypt there are
hospitals for superannuated cats, and the most loathsome
insects are regarded with tenderness; but human life is
treated as if it were of no account, and human suffering
scarcely elicits a care.[5] The same contrast appears more or

---

[1] Sueton. *Domitian.* iii. It is
very curious that the same emperor, about the same time (the
beginning of his reign), had such a
horror of bloodshed that he resolved
to prohibit the sacrifice of oxen.
(Suet. *Dom.* ix.)

[2] 'Pendant qu'il restait au logis,
il n'était incommode à personne;
il y passait la meilleure partie de
son temps tranquillement dans sa
chambre. . . . Il se divertissait
aussi quelquefois à fumer une pipe
de tabac; ou bien lorsqu'il voulait
se relâcher l'esprit un peu plus
longtemps, il cherchait des arai-

gnées qu'il faisait battre ensemble,
ou des mouches qu'il jetait dans la
toile d'araignée, et regardait ensuite cette bataille avec tant de
plaisir qu'il éclatait quelquefois de
rire.'—Colerus, *Vie de Spinoza.*

[3] This is noticed by George
Duval in a curious passage of his
Souvenirs de la Terreur, quoted by
Lord Lytton in a note to his *Zanoni.*

[4] *Essay on Goodness.*

[5] This contrast has been noticed
by Archbishop Whately in a lecture
on Egypt. See, too, Legendre,
Traité de l'Opinion, tome ii. p. 371.

less in all Eastern nations. On the other hand, travellers are unanimous in declaring that in Spain an intense passion for the bull-fight is quite compatible with the most active benevolence and the most amiable disposition. Again, to pass to another sphere, it is not uncommon to find conquerors, who will sacrifice with perfect callousness great masses of men to their ambition, but who, in their dealings with isolated individuals, are distinguished by an invariable clemency. Anomalies of this kind continually appear in the Roman population. The very men who looked down with delight when the sand of the arena was reddened with human blood, made the theatre ring with app'ause when Terence, in his famous line, proclaimed the universal brotherhood of man. When the senate, being unable to discover the murderer of a patrician, resolved to put his four hundred slaves to death, the people rose in open rebellion against the sentence.[1] A knight named Erixo, who in the days of Augustus had so scourged his son that he died of the effects, was nearly torn to pieces by the indignant population.[2] The elder Cato deprived a senator of his rank, because he had fixed an execution at such an hour that his mistress could enjoy the spectacle.[3] Even in the amphitheatre there were certain traces of a milder spirit. Drusus, the people complained, took too visible a pleasure at the sight of blood;[4] Caligula was too curious in watching death;[5] Caracalla, when a boy, won enthusiastic p!audits by shedding tears at the execution of criminals.[6] Among the most popular spectacles at Rome was rope-dancing, and then, as now, the cord being stretched at a great height above the ground, the apparent, and indeed

[1] Tacit. Annal. xiv. 45.
[2] Senec. De Clemen. i. 14.
[3] Val. Max. ii. 9. This writer speaks of 'the eyes of a mistress delighting in human blood' with as much horror as if the gladiatorial games were unknown. Livy gives a rather different version of this story.
[4] Tacit. Annal. i. 76.
[5] Sueton. Calig. xi.
[6] Spartian. Caracalla. Tertullian mentions that his nurse was a Christian.

real, danger added an evil zest to the performances. In the reign of Marcus Aurelius an accident had occurred, and the emperor, with his usual sensitive humanity, ordered that no rope-dancer should perform without a net or a mattress being spread out below. It is a singularly curious fact that this precaution, which no Christian nation has adopted, continued in force during more than a century of the worst period of the Roman Empire, when the blood of captives was poured out like water in the Colosseum.[1] The standard of humanity was very low, but the sentiment was still manifest, though its displays were capricious and inconsistent.

The sketch I have now drawn will, I think, be sufficient to display the broad chasm that existed between the Roman moralists and the Roman people. On the one hand we find a system of ethics, of which when we consider the range and beauty of its precepts, the sublimity of the motives to which it appealed, and its perfect freedom from superstitious elements, it is not too much to say that though it may have been equalled, it has never been surpassed. On the other hand, we find a society almost absolutely destitute of moralising institutions, occupations, or beliefs, existing under an economical and political system which inevitably led to general depravity, and passionately addicted to the most brutalising amusements. The moral code, while it expanded in theoretical catholicity, had contracted in practical application. The early Romans had a very narrow and imperfect standard of duty, but their patriotism, their military system, and their enforced simplicity of life had made that standard essentially popular. The later Romans had attained a very high and spiritual conception of duty, but the philosopher

---

[1] Capitolinus, *Marcus Aurelius.* Capitolinus, who wrote under Diocletian, says that in his time the custom of spreading a net under the rope-dancer still continued. I do not know when it ceased at Rome, but St. Chrysostom mentions that in his time it had been abolished in the East. — Jortin's *Remarks on Ecclesiastical History,* ii. 71 (ed. 1846).

with his group of disciples, or the writer with his few readers had scarcely any point of contact with the people. The great practical problem of the ancient philosophers was how they could act upon the masses. Simply to tell men what is virtue, and to extol its beauty, is insufficient. Something more must be done if the characters of nations are to be moulded and inveterate vices eradicated.

This problem the Roman Stoics were incapable of meeting, but they did what lay in their power, and their efforts, though altogether inadequate to the disease, were by no means contemptible. In the first place they raised up many great and good rulers who exerted all the influence of their position in the cause of virtue. In most cases these reforms were abolished on the accession of the first bad emperor, but there were at least some that remained. It has been observed that the luxury of the table, which had acquired the most extravagant proportions during the period that elapsed between the battle of Actium and the reign of Galba, began from this period to decline, and the change is chiefly attributed to Vespasian, who had in a measure reformed the Roman aristocracy by the introduction of many provincials, and who made his court an example of the strictest frugality.[1] The period from the accession of Nerva to the death of Marcus Aurelius, comprising no less than eighty-four years, exhibits a uniformity of good government which no other despotic monarchy has equalled. Each of the five emperors who then reigned deserves to be placed among the best rulers who have ever lived. Trajan and Hadrian, whose personal characters were most defective, were men of great and conspicuous genius. Antoninus and Marcus Aurelius, though less distinguished as politicians, were among the most perfectly virtuous men who have ever sat on a throne. During forty years of this period, perfect, unbroken peace reigned

---

[1] Tacit. *Ann.* iii. 55.

over the entire civilised globe. The barbarian encroachments had not yet begun. The distinct nationalities that
composed the Empire, gratified by perfect municipal and by
perfect intellectual freedom, had lost all care for political
liberty, and little more than three hundred thousand soldiers
guarded a territory which is now protected by much more
than three millions.[1]

In creating this condition of affairs, Stoicism, as the chief
moral agent of the Empire, had a considerable though not a
preponderating influence. In other ways its influence was
more evident and exclusive. It was a fundamental maxim
of the sect, 'that the sage should take part in public life,'[2]
and it was therefore impossible that Stoicism should flourish
without producing a resuscitation of patriotism. The same
moral impulse which transformed the Neoplatonist into a
dreaming mystic and the Catholic into a useless hermit,
impelled the Stoic to the foremost post of danger in the
service of his country. While landmark after landmark of
Roman virtue was submerged, while luxury and scepticism
and foreign habits and foreign creeds were corroding the
whole framework of the national life, amid the last paroxysms of expiring liberty, amid the hideous carnival of
vice that soon followed upon its fall, the Stoic remained unchanged, the representative and the sustainer of the past.
A party which had acquired the noble title of the Party of
Virtue, guided by such men as Cato or Thrasea or Helvidius
or Burrhus, upheld the banner of Roman virtue and Roman
liberty in the darkest hours of despotism and of apostasy
Like all men who carry an intense religious fervour into
politics, they were often narrow-minded and intolerant, blind
to the inevitable changes of society, incapable of compromise,
turbulent and inopportune in their demands,[3] but they more

---

[1] Champagny, *Les Antonins*,
tome ii. pp. 179–200.

[2] πολιτεύεσθαι τον σόφον.—Diog.
Laërt. *Zeno.*

[3] Thus Tigellinus spoke of
'Stoicorum arrogantia sectaque quæ
turbidos et negotiorum appetentes
faciat.'—Tacit. *Ann.* xiv. 57. The

than redeemed their errors by their noble constancy and
courage. The austere purity of their lives, and the heroic
grandeur of their deaths, kept alive the tradition of Roman
liberty even under a Nero or a Domitian. While such men
existed it was felt that all was not lost. There was still a
rallying point of freedom, a seed of virtue that might germi
nate anew, a living protest against the despotism and the
corruption of the Empire.

A third and still more important service which Stoicism
rendered to popular morals was in the formation of Roman
jurisprudence.[1] Of all the many forms of intellectual exertion in which Greece and Rome struggled for the mastery
this is perhaps the only one in which the superiority of the
latter is indisputable. ' To rule the nations' was justly pronounced by the Roman poet the supreme glory of his
countrymen, and their administrative genius is even now unrivalled in history. A deep reverence for law was long one
of their chief moral characteristics, and in order that it
might be inculcated from the earliest years it was a part of
the Roman system of education to oblige the children to

---

accusation does not appear to have
been quite untrue, for Vespasian,
who was a very moderate emperor,
thought it necessary to banish
nearly all the philosophers from
Rome on account of their factious-
ness. Sometimes the Stoics showed
their independence by a rather
gratuitous insolence   Dion Cassius relates that, when Nero was
thinking of writing a poem in 400
books, he asked the advice of the
Stoic Cornutus, who said, that
no one would read so long a work.
' But,' answered Nero, ' your favourite Chrysippus wrote still more
numerous books.' ' True,' rejoined
Cornutus, ' but then they were of
use to humanity.' On the other

hand, Seneca is justly accused of
condescending too much to the
vices of Nero in his efforts to mitigate their effects.
    [1] The influence of Stoicism on
Roman law has been often exa-
mined. See, especially, Degerando,
Hist. de la Philosophie (2nd ed.),
tome iii. pp. 202-204 ; Laferrière,
*De l'Influence du Stoïcisme sur les
Jurisconsultes   romains* ; Denis,
*Théories et Idées morales dans
l'Antiquité,* tome ii. pp. 187-217 ;
Troplong, *Influence du Christianisme
sur le Droit civil des Romains* ;
Merivale, *Conversion of the Roman
Empire,* lec. iv. ; and the great work
of Gravina, *De Ortu et Progressu
Juris civilis.*

repeat by rote the code of the decemvirs.[1] The laws of the
Republic, however, being an expression of the contracted,
local, military, and sacerdotal spirit that dominated among
the people, were necessarily unfit for the political and intellectual expansion of the Empire, and the process of renova-
tion which was begun under Augustus by the Stoic Labeo,[2]
was continued with great zeal under Hadrian and Alexander
Severus, and issued in the famous compilations of Theodosius
and Justinian. In this movement we have to observe two
parts. There were certain general rules of guidance laid
down by the great Roman lawyers which constituted what
may be called the ideal of the jurisconsults—the ends to
which their special enactments tended—the principles of
equity to guide the judge when the law was silent or ambiguous. There were also definite enactments to meet specific
cases. The first part was simply borrowed from the Stoics,
whose doctrines and method thus passed from the narrow
circle of a philosophical academy and became the avowed
moral beacons of the civilised globe. The fundamental difference between Stoicism and early Roman thought was that
the former maintained the existence of a bond of unity
among mankind which transcended or annihilated all class
or national limitations. The essential characteristic of the
Stoical method was the assertion of the existence of a certain
law of nature to which it was the end of philosophy to conform. These tenets were laid down in the most unqualified
language by the Roman lawyers. 'As far as natural law is
concerned,' said Ulpian, 'all men are equal.'[3] 'Nature,'
said Paul, 'has established among us a certain relationship.'[4]
'By natural law,' Ulpian declared, 'all men are born free.'[5]

---

[1] Cic. De Legib. ii. 4, 23.
[2] There were two rival schools,
that of Labeo and that of Capito.
The first was remarkable for its
strict adherence to the letter of
the law—the second for the lati
tude of interpretation it admitted
[3] Dig. lib. i. tit. 17–32.
[4] Ibid. i. tit. 1–3.
[5] Ibid. i. tit. 1–4.

'Slavery was defined by Florentinus as 'a custom of the law of nations, by which one man, contrary to the law of nature, is subjected to the dominion of another.'[1] In accordance with these principles it became a maxim among the Roman lawyers that in every doubtful case where the alternative of slavery or freedom was at issue, the decision of the judge should be towards the latter.[2]

The Roman legislation was in a twofold manner the child of philosophy. It was in the first place itself formed upon the philosophical model, for, instead of being a mere empirical system adjusted to the existing requirements of society, it laid down abstract principles of right to which it endeavoured to conform;[3] and, in the next place, these principles were borrowed directly from Stoicism. The prominence the sect had acquired among Roman moralists, its active intervention in public affairs, and also the precision and brevity of its phraseology, had recommended it to the lawyers,[4] and the

---

[1] *Dig.* lib. i. tit. 4-5.

[2] Laferrière, p. 32.   Wallon, *Hist. de l'Esclavage dans l'Antiquité,* tome iii. pp. 71-80. M. Wallon gives many curious instances of legal decisions on this point.

[3] To prove that this is the correct conception of law was the main object of Cicero's treatise *De Legibus.* Ulpian defined jurisprudence as 'divinarum atque humanarum rerum notitia, justi atque injusti scientia.'—*Dig.* lib. i. tit. 1-10. So Paul 'Id quod semper æquum ac bonum est jus dicitur ut est jus naturale.'—*Dig.* lib. i. tit. 1-11. And Gaius, 'Quod vero naturalis ratio inter omnes homines constituit . . . vocatur jus gentium.'—*Dig.* lib. i. tit. 1-9. The Stoics had defined true wisdom as 'rerum divinarum atque humanarum scientia.'—Cic. *De Offic.* i. 43.

[4] Cicero compares the phraseology of the Stoics with that of the Peripatetics, maintaining that the precision of the former is well adapted to legal discussions, and the redundancy of the latter to oratory. 'Omnes fere Stoici prudentissimi in disserendo sint et id arte faciant, sintque architecti pene verborum; iidem traducti a disputando ad dicendum, inopes reperiantur: unum excipio Catonem. . . . . Peripateticorum institutis commodius fingeretur oratio . . . . nam ut Stoicorum astrictior est oratio, aliquantoque contracti r quam aures populi requirunt: sic illorum liberior et latior quam patitur consuetudo judiciorum et fori.'—*De Claris Oratoribus.* A very judicious historian of philosophy observes: 'En général à Rome le petit nombre d'hommes livrés à la méditation et à l'enthousiasme préférèrent Pythagore et

union then effected between the legal and philosophical spirit is felt to the present day. To the Stoics and the Roman lawyers is mainly due the clear recognition of the existence of a law of nature above and beyond all human enactments which has been the basis of the best moral and of the most influential though most chimerical political speculation of later ages, and the renewed study of Roman law was an important element in the revival that preceded the Reformation.

It is not necessary for my present purpose to follow into very minute detail the application of these principles to practical legislation. It is sufficient to say, that there were few departments into which the catholic and humane principles of Stoicism were not in some degree carried. In the political world, as we have already seen, the right of Roman citizenship, with the protection and the legal privileges attached to it, from being the monopoly of a small class, was gradually but very widely diffused. In the domestic sphere, the power which the old laws had given to the father of the family, though not destroyed, was greatly abridged, and an important innovation, which is well worthy of a brief notice, was thus introduced into the social system of the Empire.

It is probable that in the chronology of morals, domestic virtue takes the precedence of all others; but in its earliest phase it consists of a single article—the duty of absolute submission to the head of the household. It is only at a later period, and when the affections have been in some degree evoked, that the reciprocity of duty is felt, and the whole tendency of civilisation is to diminish the disparity between the different members of the family. The process by which the wife from a simple slave becomes the companion and

---

Platon; les hommes du monde et ceux qui cultivaient les sciences naturelles s'attachèrent à Épicure; les orateurs et les hommes d'État à la nouvelle Académie; les jurisconsultes au Portique.' — Degerando, *Hist. de la Philos.* tome iii. p. 196.

equal of her husband, I shall endeavour to trace in a future chapter. The relations of the father to his children are profoundly modified by the new position the affections assume in education, which in a rude nation rests chiefly upon authority, but in a civilised community upon sympathy. In Rome the absolute authority of the head of the family was the centre and archetype of that whole system of discipline and subordination which it was the object of the legislator to sustain. Filial reverence was enforced as the first of duties. It is the one virtue which Virgil attributed in any remarkable degree to the founder of the race. The marks of external respect paid to old men were scarcely less than in Sparta.[1] It was the boast of the lawyers that in no other nation had the parent so great an authority over his children.[2] The child was indeed the absolute slave of his father, who had a right at any time to take away his life and dispose of his entire property. He could look to no time during the life of his father in which he would be freed from the thraldom. The man of fifty, the consul, the general, or the tribune, was in this respect in the same position as the infant, and might at any moment be deprived of all the earnings of his labour, driven to the most menial employments, or even put to death, by the paternal command.[3]

There can, I think, be little question that this law, at least in the latter period of its existence, defeated its own

[1] See a very remarkable passage in Aulus Gellius, *Noct.* ii. 15.

[2] 'Fere enim nulli alii sunt homines qui talem in filios suos habeant potestatem qualem nos habemus.'—Gaius.

[3] A full statement of these laws is given by Dion. Halicarn. ii. 4. It was provided that if a father sold his son and if the son was afterwards enfranchised by the purchaser, he became again the slave of his father, who might sell him a second, and, if manumission again ensued, a third time. It was only on the third sale that he passed for ever out of the parental control. A more merciful law, attributed to Numa, provided that when the son married (if that marriage was with the consent of the father), the father lost the power of selling him. In no other way, however, was his authority even then abridged.

object. There are few errors of education to which more unhappy homes may be traced than this—that parents have sought tô command the obedience, before they have sought to win the confidence, of their children. This was the path which the Roman legislator indicated to the parent, and its natural consequence was to chill the sympathies and arouse the resentment of the young. Of all the forms of virtue filial affection is perhaps that which appears most rarely in Roman history. In the plays of Plautus it is treated much as conjugal fidelity was treated in England by the playwriters of the Restoration. An historian of the reign of Tiberius has remarked that the civil wars were equally remarkable for the many examples they supplied of the devotion of wives to their husbands, of the devotion of slaves to their masters, and of the treachery or indifference of sons to their fathers.[1]

The reforms that were effected during the pagan empire did not reconstruct the family, but they at least greatly mitigated its despotism. The profound change of feeling that had taken place on the subject is shown by the contrast between the respectful, though somewhat shrinking, acquiescence, with which the ancient Romans regarded parents who had put their children to death,[2] and the indignation excited under Augustus by the act of Erixo. Hadrian, apparently by a stretch of despotic power, banished a man who had assassinated his son.[3] Infanticide was forbidden, though

---

[1] Velleius Paterculus, ii. 67. A great increase of parricide was noticed during the Empire (Senec. *De Clem.* i. 23). At first, it is said, there was no law against parricide, for the crime was believed to be too atrocious to be possible.

[2] Numerous instances of these executions are collected by Livy, Val. Maximus, &c.; their history is fully given by Cornelius van Bynkershoek, 'De Jure occidendi, vendendi, et exponendi liberos apud veteres Romanos,' in his works (Cologne, 1761).

[3] This proceeding of Hadrian, which is related by the lawyer Marcian, is doubly remarkable, because the father had surprised his son in adultery with his stepmother. Now a Roman had originally not only absolute authority over the life of his son, but also the right of killing any one whom he found committing adultery with his wife. Yet Marcian praises the severity

not seriously repressed, but the right of putting to death an adult child had long been obsolete, when Alexander Severus formally withdrew it from the father. The property of children was also in some slight degree protected. A few instances are recorded of wills that were annulled because they had disinherited legitimate sons,[1] and Hadrian, following a policy that had been feebly initiated by his two predecessors, gave the son an absolute possession of whatever he might gain in the military service. Diocletian rendered the sale of children by the fathers, in all cases, illegal.[2]

In the field of slavery the legislative reforms were more important. This institution, indeed, is one that meets us at every turn of the moral history of Rome, and on two separate occasions in the present chapter I have already had occasion to notice it. I have shown that the great prominence of the slave element in Roman life was one of the causes of the enlargement of sympathies that characterises the philosophy of the Empire, and also that slavery was in a very high degree, and in several distinct ways, a cause of the corruption of the free classes. In considering the condition of the slaves themselves, we may distinguish, I think, three periods. In the earlier and simpler days of the Republic, the head of the family was absolute master of his slaves, but circumstances in a great measure mitigated the evil of the despotism. The slaves were very few in number. Each Roman proprietor had commonly one or two who assisted him in cultivating the soil, and superintended his property when he was absent in the army. In the frugal habits of the time, the master was brought into the most intimate connection with his

---

of Hadrian, 'Nam patria potestas in pietate debet, non atrocitate, consistere.'—*Digest.* lib. xlviii. tit. 9, § 5.

[1] Valer. Max. vii. 7.

[2] See, on all this subject, Gibbon, *Decline and Fall*, ch. xliv.; Trop-
long, *Influence du Christianisme sur le Droit*, ch. ix.; Denis, *Hist. des Idées morales*, tome ii. pp. 107–120; Laferrière, *Influence du Stoïcisme sur les Jurisconsultes*, pp. 37–44.

slaves. He shared their labours and their food, and the
control he exercised over them, in most cases probably differed
little from that which he exercised over his sons. Under
such circumstances, great barbarity to slaves, though always
possible, was not likely to be common, and the protection of
religion was added to the force of habit. Hercules, the god
of labour, was the special patron of slaves. There was a
legend that Sparta had once been nearly destroyed by an
earthquake sent by Neptune to avenge the treacherous murder
of some Helots.[1] In Rome, it was said, Jupiter had once in
a dream commissioned a man to express to the senate the
divine anger at the cruel treatment of a slave during the
public games.[2] By the pontifical law, slaves were exempted
from field labours on the religious festivals.[3] The Saturnalia
and Matronalia, which were especially intended for their
benefit, were the most popular holidays in Rome, and on
these occasions the slaves were accustomed to sit at the same
table with their masters.[4]

Even at this time, however, it is probable that great
atrocities were occasionally committed. Everything was
permitted by law, although it is probable that the censor in
cases of extreme abuse might interfere, and the aristocratic
feelings of the early Roman, though corrected in a measure
by the associations of daily labour, sometimes broke out in a
fierce scorn for all classes but his own. The elder Cato, who
may be regarded as a type of the Romans of the earlier
period, speaks of slaves simply as instruments for obtaining
wealth, and he encouraged masters, both by his precept and
his example, to sell them as useless when aged and infirm.[5]

---

[1] Ælian, *Hist. Var.* vi. 7.
[2] Livy, ii. 36; Cicero, *De Divin.* ii. 26.
[3] Cicero, *De Legibus,* ii. 8–12. Cato, however, maintained that slaves might on those days be employed on work which did not require oxen. — Wallon, *Hist. de l'Esclavage,* tome ii. p. 215.
[4] See the *Saturnalia* of Macrobius.
[5] See his *Life* by Plutarch, and his book on agriculture.

In the second period, the condition of slaves had greatly deteriorated. The victories of Rome, especially in the East, had introduced into the city innumerable slaves [1] and the wildest luxury, and the despotism of the master remained unqualified by law, while the habits of life that had originally mitigated it had disappeared. The religious sentiments of the people were at the same time fatally impaired, and many new causes conspired to aggravate the evil. The passion for gladiatorial shows had begun, and it continually produced a savage indifference to the infliction of pain. The servile wars of Sicily, and the still more formidable revolt of Spartacus, had shaken Italy to the centre, and the shock was felt in every household. 'As many enemies as slaves,' had become a Roman proverb. The fierce struggles of barbarian captives were repaid by fearful punishments, and many thousands of revolted slaves perished on the cross. An atrocious law, intended to secure the safety of the citizens, provided that if a master were murdered, all the slaves in his house, who were not in chains or absolutely helpless through illness, should be put to death. [2]

Numerous acts of the most odious barbarity were committed. The well-known anecdotes of Flaminius ordering a slave to be killed to gratify, by the spectacle, the curiosity of

[1] The number of the Roman slaves has been a matter of much controversy. M. Dureau de la Malle (*Econ. politique des Romains*) has restricted it more than any other writer. Gibbon (*Decline and Fall*, chap. ii.) has collected many statistics on the subject, but the fullest examination is in M. Wallon's admirable *Hist. de l'Esclavage*. On the contrast between the character of the slaves of the Republic and those of the Empire, see Tac. *Ann.* xiv. 44.

[2] Tacit. *Annal.* xiii. 32; xiv. 42–45. Wallon, *Hist. de l'Esclav.*

ii. 293. I have already noticed the indignant rising of the people caused by the proposal to execute the 400 slaves of the murdered Pedanius. Their interposition was however (as Tacitus informs us), unavailing, and the slaves, guarded against rescue by a strong band of soldiers, were executed. It was proposed to banish the freedmen who were in the house, but Nero interposed and prevented it. Pliny notices (*Ep.* viii. 14) the banishment of the freedmen of a murdered man.

a guest; of Vedius Pollio feeding his fish on the flesh of slaves; and of Augustus sentencing a slave, who had killed and eaten a favourite quail, to crucifixion, are the extreme examples that are recorded; for we need not regard as an historical fact the famous picture in Juvenal of a Roman lady, in a moment of caprice, ordering her unoffending servant to be crucified. We have, however, many other very horrible glimpses of slave life at the close of the Republic and in the early days of the Empire. The marriage of slaves was entirely unrecognised by law, and in their case the words adultery, incest, or polygamy had no legal meaning. Their testimony was in general only received in the law-courts when they were under torture. When executed for a crime, their deaths were of a most hideous kind. The ergastula, or private prisons, of the masters were frequently their only sleeping-places. Old and infirm slaves were constantly exposed to perish on an island of the Tiber. We read of slaves chained as porters to the doors, and cultivating the fields in chains. Ovid and Juvenal describe the fierce Roman ladies tearing their servants' faces, and thrusting the long pins of their brooches into their flesh. The master, at the close of the Republic, had full power to sell his slave as a gladiator, or as a combatant with wild beasts.[1]

All this is very horrible, but it must not be forgotten that there was another side to the picture. It is the custom of many ecclesiastical writers to paint the pagan society of the Empire as a kind of pandemonium, and with this object they collect the facts I have cited, which are for the most part narrated by Roman satirists or historians, as examples of the most extreme and revolting cruelty; they represent them as fair specimens of the ordinary treatment of the servile class, and they simply exclude from their con-

[1] See all this fully illustrated in Wallon. The plays of Plautus and the Roman writers on agriculture contain numerous allusions to the condition of slaves.

sideration the many qualifying facts that might be alleged
Although the marriage of a slave was not legally recognised,
it was sanctioned by custom, and it does not appear to have
been common to separate his family.[1] Two customs to which
I have already referred distinguish ancient slavery broadly
from that of modern times. The peculium, or private property of slaves, was freely recognised by masters, to whom,
however, after the death of the slave, part or all of it usually
reverted,[2] though some masters permitted their slaves to
dispose of it by will.[3] The enfranchisement of slaves was
also carried on to such an extent as seriously to affect the
population of the city. It appears from a passage in Cicero
that an industrious and well-conducted captive might commonly look forward to his freedom in six years.[4] Isolated
acts of great cruelty undoubtedly occurred; but public
opinion strongly reprehended them, and Seneca assures us
that masters who ill-treated their slaves were pointed at and
insulted in the streets.[5] The slave was not necessarily the
degraded being he has since appeared. The physician who
tended the Roman in his sickness, the tutor to whom he
confided the education of his son, the artists whose works
commanded the admiration of the city, were usually slaves.
Slaves sometimes mixed with their masters in the family, ate
habitually with them at the same table,[6] and were regarded
by them with the warmest affection. Tiro, the slave and
afterwards the freedman of Cicero, compiled his master's
letters, and has preserved some in which Cicero addressed

---

[1] Wallon, tome ii. pp. 209–210,
357. There were no laws till the
time of the Christian emperors
against separating the families of
slaves, but it was a maxim of the
jurisconsults that in forced sales
they should not be separated.
(Wallon, tome iii. pp. 55–56.)
[2] Ibid. tome ii. pp. 211–213.
[3] Plin. Epist. viii. 16. It was

customary to allow the public or
State slaves to dispose of half their
goods by will. (Wallon, tome iii.
p. 59.)
[4] Wallon, tome ii. p. 419. This
appears from an allusion of Cicero,
Philip. viii. 11.
[5] Senec. De Clem. i. 18.
[6] Ibid. Ep. xlvii.

him in terms of the most sincere and delicate friendship. I have already referred to the letter in which the younger Pliny poured out his deep sorrow for the death of some of his slaves, and endeavoured to console himself with the thought that as he had emancipated them before their death, at least they had died free.[1] Epictetus passed at once from slavery to the friendship of an emperor.[2] The great multiplication of slaves, though it removed them from the sympathy of their masters, must at least have in most cases alleviated their burdens. The application of torture to slave witnesses, horrible as it was, was a matter of rare occurrence, and was carefully restricted by law.[3] Much vice was undoubtedly fostered, but yet the annals of the civil wars and of the Empire are crowded with the most splendid instances of the fidelity of slaves. In many cases they refused the boon of liberty and defied the most horrible tortures rather than betray their masters, accompanied them in their flight when all others had abandoned them, displayed undaunted courage and untiring ingenuity in rescuing them from danger, and in some cases saved the lives of their owners by the deliberate sacrifice of their own.[4] This was, indeed, for some time the pre-eminent virtue of Rome, and it proves conclusively that the masters were not so tyrannical, and that the slaves were not so degraded, as is sometimes alleged.

The duty of humanity to slaves had been at all times one

---

[1] Pliny, *Ep.* viii. 16.

[2] Spartianus, *Hadrianus.*

[3] Compare Wallon, tome ii. p. 186; tome iii. pp. 65–66. Slaves were only to be called as witnesses in cases of incest, adultery, murder, and high treason, and where it was impossible to establish the crime without their evidence. Hadrian considered that the reality of the crime must have already acquired a strong probability, and the jurisconsult Paul laid down that at least two free witnesses should be heard before slaves were submitted to torture, and that the offer of an accused person to have his slaves tortured that they might attest his innocence should not be accepted.

[4] Numerous and very noble instances of slave fidelity are given by Seneca, *De Benefic.* iii. 19–27; Val. Max. vi. 8; and in Appian's *History of the Civil Wars.* See, too, Tacit. *Hist.* i. 3.

of those which the philosophers had most ardently inculcated. Plato and Aristotle, Zeno and Epicurus, were, on
this point, substantially agreed.[1] The Roman Stoics gave
the duty a similar prominence in their teaching, and Seneca
especially has filled pages with exhortations to masters to
remember that the accident of position in no degree affects
the real dignity of men, that the slave may be free by virtue
while the master may be a slave by vice, and that it is the
duty of a good man to abstain not only from all cruelty, but
even from all feeling of contempt towards his slaves.[2] But
these exhortations, in which some have imagined that they
have discovered the influence of Christianity, were, in
fact, simply an echo of the teaching of ancient Greece, and
especially of Zeno, the founder of Stoicism, who had laid down,
long before the dawn of Christianity, the broad principles
that ' all men are by nature equal, and that virtue alone establishes a difference between them.'[3] The softening influence
of the peace of the Antonines assisted this movement of
humanity, and the slaves derived a certain incidental benefit
from one of the worst features of the despotism of the
Cæsars. The emperors, who continually apprehended plots
against their lives or power, encouraged numerous spies
around the more important of their subjects, and the facility
with which slaves could discover the proceedings of their
masters inclined the Government in their favour.

Under all these influences many laws were promulgated

---

[1] Aristotle had, it is true, declared slavery to be part of the law
of nature—an opinion which, he
said, was rejected by some of his
contemporaries ; but he advocated
humanity to slaves quite as emphatically as the other philosophers
(*Economics*, i. 5). Epicurus was
conspicuous even among Greek
philosophers for his kindness to
slaves, and he associated some of

his own with his philosophical labours. (Diog. Laërt. *Epicurus*.)
[2] *De Benef*. iii. 18–28; *De Vita
Beata*, xxiv.; *De Clem*. i. 18, and
especially *Ep*. xlvii. Epictetus, as
might be expected from his history,
frequently recurs to the duty. Plutarch writes very beautifully upon
it in his treatise *De Cohibenda Ira*.
[3] Diog. Laërt. *Zeno*.

which profoundly altered the legal position of the slaves, and opened what may be termed the third period of Roman slavery. The Petronian law, which was issued by Augustus, or, more probably, by Nero, forbade the master to condemn his slave to combat with wild beasts without a sentence from a judge.[1] Under Claudius, some citizens exposed their sick slaves on the island of Æsculapius in the Tiber, to avoid the trouble of tending them, and the emperor decreed that if the slave so exposed recovered from his sickness he should become free, and also, that masters who killed their slaves instead of exposing them should be punished as murderers.[2] It is possible that succour was afforded to the abandoned slave in the temple of Æsculapius,[3] and it would appear from these laws that the wanton slaughter of a slave was already illegal. About this time the statue of the emperor had become an asylum for slaves.[4] Under Nero, a judge was appointed to hear their complaints, and was instructed to punish masters who treated them with barbarity, made them the instruments of lust, or withheld from them a sufficient quantity of the necessaries of life.[5] A considerable pause appears to have ensued; but Domitian made a law, which was afterwards reiterated, forbidding the Oriental custom of mutilating slaves for sensual purposes, and the reforms were renewed with great energy in the period of the Antonines. Hadrian and his two successors formally deprived masters of the right of killing their slaves; forbade them to sell slaves to the lanistæ, or speculators in gladiators; destroyed the ergastula, or private prisons; ordered that, when a master was murdered, those slaves only should be

---

Bodin thinks it was promulgated by Nero, and he has been followed by Troplong and Mr. Merivale. Champagny (*Les Antonins*, tome ii. p. 115) thinks that no law after Tiberius was called *lex*.

[2] Sueton. *Claud.* xxv.; Dion Cass. lx. 29.

[3] See Dumas, *Secours publics chez les Anciens* (Paris, 1813), pp 125–130.

[4] Senec. *De Clem.* i. 18.

[5] Senec. *De Benef.* iii. 22.

tortured who were within hearing;[1] appointed officers through
all the provinces to hear the complaints of slaves; enjoined
that no master should treat his slaves with excessive severity;
and commanded that, when such severity was proved, the
master should be compelled to sell the slave he had ill-
treated.[2] When we add to these laws the broad maxims of
equity asserting the essential equality of the human race,
which the jurists had borrowed from the Stoics, and which
supplied the principles to guide the judges in their decisions,
it must be admitted that the slave code of Imperial Rome
compares not unfavourably with those of some Christian
nations.

While a considerable portion of the principles, and even
much of the phraseology, of Stoicism passed into the system
of public law, the Roman philosophers had other more direct
means of acting on the people. On occasions of family
bereavement, when the mind is most susceptible of impressions, they were habitually called in to console the survivors.
Dying men asked their comfort and support in the last hours
of their life. They became the directors of conscience to
numbers who resorted to them for a solution of perplexing
cases of practical morals, or under the influence of despondency or remorse.[3] They had their special exhortations

---

[1] Spartian. *Hadrianus.* Hadrian
exiled a Roman lady for five years
for treating her slaves with atrocious cruelty. (*Digest.* lib. i. tit. 6,
§ 2.)

[2] See these laws fully examined
by Wallon, tome iii. pp. 51–92,
and also Laferrière, *Sur l'Influence
du Stoïcisme sur le Droit.* The
jurisconsults gave a very wide scope
to their definitions of cruelty. A
master who degraded a literary
slave, or a slave musician, to some
coarse manual employment, such
as a porter, was decided to have

ill-treated him. (Wallon, tome iii.
p. 62.)

[3] Thus, e.g., Livia called in the
Stoic Areus to console her after
the death of Drusus (Senec. *Ad
Marc.*). Many of the letters of
Seneca and Plutarch are written
to console the suffering. Cato,
Thrasea, and many others appear
to have fortified their last hours
by conversation with philosophers.
The whole of this aspect of Stoicism
has been admirably treated by M.
Martha (*Les Moralistes de l'Empire
Romain*).

for every vice, and their remedies adapted to every variety of character. Many cases were cited of the conversion of the vicious or the careless, who had been sought out and fasci nated by the philosopher,[1] and who, under his guidance, had passed through a long course of moral discipline, and had at last attained a high degree of virtue. Education fell in a great degree into their hands. Many great families kept a philosopher among them in what in modern language might be termed the capacity of a domestic chaplain,[2] while a system of popular preaching was created and widely diffused.

Of these preachers there were two classes who differed greatly in their characters and their methods. The first, who have been very happily termed the 'monks of Stoicism,'[3] were the Cynics, who appear to have assumed among the later moralists of the Pagan empire a position somewhat resembling that of the mendicant orders in Catholicism. In a singularly curious dissertation of Epictetus,[4] we have a picture of the ideal at which a Cynic should aim, and it is impossible in reading it not to be struck by the resemblance it bears to the missionary friar. The Cynic should be a man devoting his entire life to the instruction of mankind. He must be unmarried, for he must have no family affections to divert or to dilute his energies. He must wear the meanest dress sleep upon the bare ground, feed upon the simplest food, abstain from all earthly pleasures, and yet exhibit to the world the example of uniform cheerfulness and content. No one, under pain of provoking the Divine anger, should embrace such a career, unless he believes himself to be called

---

[1] We have a pleasing picture of the affection philosophers and their disciples sometimes bore to one another in the lines of Persius (*Sat.* v.) to his master Cornutus.

[2] Grant's *Aristotle*, vol. i. pp. 277-278.

[3] Champagny, *Les Antonins*, tome i. p. 405.

[4] Arrian, iii. 22. Julian has also painted the character of the true Cynic, and contrasted it with that of the impostors who assumed the garb. See Neander's *Life of Julian* (London, 1850), p. 94.

and assisted by Jupiter. It is his mission to go among men as the ambassador of God, rebuking, in season and out of season, their frivolity, their cowardice, and their vice. He must stop the rich man in the market-place. He must preach to the populace in the highway. He must know no respect and no fear. He must look upon all men as his sons, and upon all women as his daughters. In the midst of a jeering crowd, he must exhibit such a placid calm that men may imagine him to be of stone. Ill-treatment, and exile, and death must have no terror in his eyes, for the discipline of his life should emancipate him from every earthly tie; and, when he is beaten, 'he should love those who beat him, for he is at once the father and the brother of all men.'

A curious contrast to the Cynic was the philosophic rhetorician, who gathered around his chair all that was most brilliant in Roman or Athenian society. The passion for oratory which the free institutions of Greece had formed, had survived the causes that produced it, and given rise to a very singular but a very influential profession; which, though excluded from the Roman Republic, acquired a great development after the destruction of political liberty. The rhetoricians were a kind of itinerant lecturers, who went about from city to city, delivering harangues that were often received with the keenest interest. For the most part, neither their characters nor their talents appear to have deserved much respect. Numerous anecdotes are recorded of their vanity and rapacity, and their success was a striking proof of the decadence of public taste.[1] They had cultivated the his-

---

[1] Seneca the rhetorician (father of the philosopher) collected many of the sayings of the rhetoricians of his time. At a later period, Philostratus wrote the lives of eminent rhetoricians, Quintilian discussed their rules of oratory, and Aulus Gellius painted the whole society in which they moved. On their injurious influence upon eloquence, see Petronius, *Satyricon*, i. 2. Much curious information about the rhetoricians is collected in Martha, *Moralistes de l'Empire Romain*, and in Nisard, *Etudes sur les Poetes Latins de la Décadence*, art. Juvenal

trionic part of oratory with the most minute attention. The
arrangement of their hair, the folds of their dresses, all their
postures and gestures were studied with artistic care. They
had determined the different kinds of action that are appropriate for each branch of a discourse and for each form of
eloquence. Sometimes they personated characters in Homer
or in ancient Greek history, and delivered speeches which
those characters might have delivered in certain conjunctures
of their lives. Sometimes they awakened the admiration of
their audience by making a fly, a cockroach, dust, smoke, a
mouse, or a parrot the subject of their eloquent eulogy.[1]
Others, again, exercised their ingenuity in defending some
glaring paradox or sophism, or in debating some intricate
case of law or morals, or they delivered literary lectures
remarkable for a minute but captious and fastidious criticism.
Some of the rhetoricians recited only harangues prepared
with the most elaborate care, others were ready debaters, and
they travelled from city to city, challenging opponents to discuss some subtle and usually frivolous question. The poet
Juvenal and the satirist Lucian had both for a time followed
this profession. Many of the most eminent acquired immense
wealth, travelled with a splendid retinue, and excited transports of enthusiasm in the cities they visited. They were often
charged by cities to appear before the emperor to plead for a
remission of taxes, or of the punishment due for some offence.
They became in a great measure the educators of the people
and contributed very largely to form and direct their taste.

---

[1] 'Cependant ces orateurs n'é-
taient jamais plus admirés que
lorsqu'ils avaient le bonheur de
trouver un sujet où la louange fut
un tour de force. . . . Lucien a fait
l'éloge de la mouche; Fronton de
la poussière, de la fumée, de la négli-
gence; Dion Chrysostome de la
chevelure, du perroquet, etc. Au
cinquième siècle, Synésius, qui fut
un grand évêque, fera le panégy
rique de la calvitie, long ouvrage
où toutes les sciences sont mises à
contribution pour apprendre aux
hommes ce qu'il y a non-seulement
de bonheur mais aussi de mérite à
être chauve.'—Martha, *Moralistes
de l'Empire Romain* (ed. 1865), p.
275.

It had been from the first the custom of some philosophers to adopt this profession, and to expound in the form of rhetorical lectures the principles of their school. In the Flavian period and in the age of the Antonines, this alliance of philosophy, and especially of Stoical philosophy, with rhetoric became more marked, and the foundation of liberally endowed chairs of rhetoric and philosophy by Vespasian, Hadrian, and Marcus Aurelius contributed to sustain it. Discourses of the Platonist Maximus of Tyre, and of the Stoic Dion Chrysostom, have come down to us, and they are both of a high order of intrinsic merit. The first turn chiefly on such subjects as the comparative excellence of active and contemplative life, the pure and noble conceptions of the Divine nature which underlie the fables or allegories of Homer, the dæmon of Socrates, the Platonic notions of the Divinity, the duty of prayer, the end of philosophy, and the ethics of love.[1] Dion Chrysostom, in his orations, expounded the noblest and purest theism, examined the place which images should occupy in worship, advocated humanity to slaves, and was, perhaps, the earliest writer in the Roman Empire who denounced hereditary slavery as illegitimate.[2] His life was very eventful and very noble. He had become famous as a sophist and rhetorician, skilled in the laborious frivolities of the profession. Calamity, however, and the writings of Plato induced him to abandon them and devote himself exclusively to the improvement of mankind. Having defended with a generous rashness a man who had been proscribed by the tyranny of Domitian, he was compelled to fly from Rome in the garb of a beggar; and, carrying with him only a work of Plato and a speech of Demosthenes, he travelled to the most distant frontiers of the empire. He gained his livelihood by the work of his

[1] There is a good review of the teaching of Maximus in Champagny, *Les Antonins*, tome ii. pp. 207–215.

[2] *Orat.* xv.; *De Servitute.*

hands, for he refused to receive money for his discourses ; but he taught and captivated the Greek colonists who were scattered among the barbarians, and even the barbarians themselves. Upon the assassination of Domitian, when the legions hesitated to give their allegiance to Nerva, the eloquence of Dion Chrysostom overcame their irresolution. By the same eloquence he more than once appeased seditions in Alexandria and the Greek cities of Asia Minor. He preached before Trajan on the duties of royalty, taking a line of Homer for his text. He electrified the vast and polished audience assembled at Athens for the Olympic games as he had before done the rude barbarians of Scythia. Though his taste was by no means untainted by the frivolities of the rhetorician, he was skilled in all the arts that awaken curiosity and attention, and his eloquence commanded the most various audiences in the most distant lands. His special mission, however, was to popularise Stoicism by diffusing its principles through the masses of mankind.[1]

The names, and in some cases a few fragments, of the writings of many other rhetorical philosophers, such as Herod Atticus, Favorinus, Fronto, Taurus, Fabianus, and Julianus, have come down to us, and each was the centre of a group of passionate admirers, and contributed to form a literary society in the great cities of the empire. We have a vivid picture of this movement in the ' Attic Nights ' of Aulus Gellius—a work which is, I think, one of the most curious and instructive in Latin literature, and which bears to the literary society of the period of the Antonines much the same relation as the writings of Helvétius bear to the Parisian society on the eve of the Revolution. Helvétius, it is said, collected the materials for his great work on ' Mind ' chiefly from the conversation of the drawing-rooms of Paris at a time when that conversation had attained a degree of

---

[1] See the singularly charming essay on Dion Chrysostom, in M. Martha's book.

perfection which even Frenchmen had never before equalled.
He wrote in the age of the 'Encyclopædia,' when the social
and political convulsions of the Revolution were as yet unfelt; when the first dazzling gleams of intellectual freedom
had flashed upon a society long clouded by superstition and
aristocratic pride; when the genius of Voltaire and the peerless
conversational powers of Diderot, irradiating the bold philosophies of Bacon and Locke, had kindled an intellectual
enthusiasm through all the ranks of fashion;[1] and when the
contempt for the wisdom and the methods of the past was
only equalled by the prevailing confidence in the future.
Brilliant, graceful, versatile, and superficial, with easy
eloquence and lax morals, with a profound disbelief in moral
excellence, and an intense appreciation of intellectual beauty,
disdaining all pedantry, superstition, and mystery, and with
an almost fanatical persuasion of the omnipotence of analysis,
he embodied the principles of his contemporaries in a philosophy which represents all virtue and heroism as but disguised self-interest; he illustrated every argument, not by
the pedantic learning of the schools, but by the sparkling
anecdotes and acute literary criticisms of the drawing-room,
and he thus produced a work which, besides its intrinsic
merits, was the most perfect mirror of the society from which
it sprang.[2] Very different, both in form, subject, and
tendency, but no less truly representative, was the work of
Aulus Gellius. It is the journal, or common-place book, or
miscellany of a scholar moving in the centre of the literary
society of both Rome and Athens during the latter period of

---

[1] Mr. Buckle, in his admirable
chapter on the 'Proximate Causes
of the French Revolution' (*Hist. of
Civilisation*, vol. i.), has painted this
fashionable enthusiasm for knowledge with great power, and illustrated it with ample learning.

[2] The saying of Mme. Dudeffand

about Helvétius is well known:
'C'est un homme qui a dit le secret
de tout le monde.' How truly Helvétius represented this fashionable
society appears very plainly from
the vivid portrait of it in the
Nouvelle Héloïse, part ii. letter
xvii., a masterpiece of its kind.

the Antonines, profoundly imbued with its spirit, and devoting his leisure to painting its leading figures, and compiling the substance of their teaching. Few books exhibit a more curious picture of the combination of intense child-like literary and moral enthusiasm with the most hopeless intellectual degeneracy. Each prominent philosopher was surrounded by a train of enthusiastic disciples, who made the lecture-room resound with their applause,[1] and accepted him as their monitor in all the affairs of life. He rebuked publicly every instance of vice or of affectation he had observed in their conduct, received them at his own table, became their friend and confidant in their troubles, and sometimes assisted them by his advice in their professional duties.[2] Taurus, Favorinus, Fronto, and Atticus were the most prominent figures, and each seems to have formed, in the centre of a corrupt society, a little company of young men devoted with the simplest and most ardent earnestness to the cultivation of intellectual and moral excellence. Yet this society was singularly puerile. The age of genius had closed, and the age of pedantry had succeeded it. Minute, curious, and fastidious verbal criticism of the great writers of the past was the chief occupation of the scholar, and the whole tone of his mind had become retrospective and even archaic. Ennius was esteemed a greater poet than Virgil, and Cato a greater prose writer than Cicero. It was the affectation of some to tesselate their conversation with antiquated and obsolete words.[3] The study of etymologies had risen into great favour, and curious questions of grammar and pro-

---

[1] Musonius tried to stop this custom of applauding the lecturer. (Aul. Gell. *Noct.* v. i.) The habits that were formed in the schools of the rhetoricians were sometimes carried into the churches, and we have notices of preachers (especially St. Chrysostom) being vocife- rously applauded.

[2] Thus Gellius himself consulted Favorinus about a perplexing case which he had, in his capacity of magistrate, to determine, and received from his master a long dissertation on the duties of a judge (xiv. 2).

[3] i. 10.

nunciation were ardently debated. Logic, as in most ages of intellectual poverty, was greatly studied and prized. Bold speculations and original thought had almost ceased, but it was the delight of the philosophers to throw the arguments of great writers into the form of syllogisms, and to debate them according to the rules of the schools. The very amusements of the scholars took the form of a whimsical and puerile pedantry. Gellius recalls, with a thrill of emotion, those enchanting evenings when, their more serious studies being terminated, the disciples of Taurus assembled at the table of their master to pass the happy hours in discussing such questions as when a man can be said to die, whether in the last moment of life or in the first moment of death ; or when he can be said to get up, whether when he is still on his bed or when he has just left it.[1] Sometimes they proposed to one another literary questions, as what old writer had employed some common word in a sense that had since become obsolete ; or they discussed such syllogisms as these :—' You have what you have not lost ; you have not lost horns, therefore you have horns.' ' You are not what I am. I am a man ; therefore you are not a man.'[2] As moralists, they exhibited a very genuine love of moral excellence, but the same pedantic and retrospective character. They were continually dilating on the regulations of the censors and the customs of the earliest period of the Republic. They acquired the habit of never enforcing the simplest lesson without illustrating it by a profusion of ancient examples and by detached sentences from some philosopher, which they employed much as texts of Scripture are often employed in the writings of the Puritans.[3] Above all, they

---

[1] *Noct. Att.* vi. 13. They called these questions *symposiacæ*, as being well fitted to stimulate minds already mellowed by wine.

[2] xviii. 2.

[3] We have a curious example of this in a letter of Marcus Aurelius preserved by Gallicanus in his *Life of Avidius Cassius.*

delighted in cases of conscience, which they discussed with the subtilty of the schoolmen.

Lactantius has remarked that the Stoics were especially noted for the popular or democratic character of their teaching.[1] To their success in this respect their alliance with the rhetoricians probably largely contributed; but in other ways it hastened the downfall of the school. The useless speculations, refinements, and paradoxes which the subtle genius of Chrysippus had connected with the simple morals of Stoicism, had been for the most part thrown into the background by the early Roman Stoics; but in the teaching of the rhetoricians they became supreme. The endowments given by the Antonines to philosophers attracted a multitude of impostors, who wore long beards and the dress of the philosopher, but whose lives were notoriously immoral. The Cynics especially, professing to reject the ordinary conventionalities of society, and being under none of that discipline or superintendence which in the worst period has secured at least external morality among the mendicant monks, continually threw off every vestige of virtue and of decency. Instead of moulding great characters and inspiring heroic actions, Stoicism became a school of the idlest casuistry, or the cloak for manifest imposture.[2] The very generation which saw Marcus Aurelius on the throne, saw also the extinction of the influence of his sect.

The internal causes of the decadence of Stoicism, though very powerful, are insufficient to explain this complete

---

[1] 'Senserunt hoc Stoici qui servis et mulieribus philosophandum esse dixerunt.'—Lact. *Nat. Div.* iii. 25. Zeno was often reproached for gathering the poorest and most sordid around him when he lectured. (Diog. Laërt. *Zeno*.)

[2] This decadence was noticed and rebuked by some of the leading philosophers. See the language of Epictetus in Arrian, ii. 19, iv. 8, and of Herod Atticus in Aul. Gell. i. 2, ix. 2. St. Augustine speaks of the Cynics as having in his time sunk into universal contempt. See much evidence on this subject in Friedlænder, *Hist. des Mœurs Romaines*, tome iv. 378–385.

eclipse. The chief cause must be found in the fact that the minds of men had taken a new turn, and their enthusiasm was flowing rapidly in the direction of Oriental religions, and, under the guidance of Plotinus, Porphyry, Iamblichus, and Proclus, of a mythical philosophy which was partly Egyptian and partly Platonic. It remains for me, in concluding this review of the Pagan empire, to indicate and explain this last transformation of Pagan morals.

It was in the first place a very natural reaction against the extreme aridity of the Stoical casuistry, and also against the scepticism which Sextus Empiricus had revived, and in this respect it represents a law of the human mind which has been more than once illustrated in later times. Thus, the captious, unsatisfying, intellectual subtleties of the schoolmen were met by the purely emotional and mystical school of St. Bonaventura, and afterwards of Tauler, and thus the adoration of the human intellect, that was general in the philosophy of the last century, prepared the way for the complete denial of its competency by De Maistre and by Lamennais.

In the next place, mysticism was a normal continuation of the spiritualising movement which had long been advancing. We have already seen that the strong tendency of ethics, from Cato to Marcus Aurelius, was to enlarge the prominence of the emotions in the type of virtue. The formation of a gentle, a spiritual, and, in a word, a religious character had become a prominent part of moral culture, and it was regarded not simply as a means, but as an end. Still, both Marcus Aurelius and Cato were Stoics. They both represented the same general cast or conception of virtue, although in Marcus Aurelius the type had been profoundly modified. But the time was soon to come when the balance between the practical and the emotional parts of virtue, which had been steadily changing, should be decisively turned in favour of the latter, and the type of Stoicism was then necessarily discarded.

A concurrence of political and commercial causes had arisen, very favourable to the propagation of Oriental beliefs. Commerce had produced a constant intercourse between Egypt and Italy. Great numbers of Oriental slaves, passionately devoted to their national religions, existed in Rome; and Alexandria, which combined a great intellectual development with a geographical and commercial position exceedingly favourable to a fusion of many doctrines, soon created a school of thought which acted powerfully upon the world. Four great systems of eclecticism arose; Aristobulus and Philo tinctured Judaism with Greek and Egyptian philosophy. The Gnostics and the Alexandrian fathers united, though in very different proportions, Christian doctrines with the same elements; while Neoplatonism, at least in its later forms, represented a fusion of the Greek and Egyptian mind. A great analogy was discovered between the ideal philosophy of Plato and the mystical philosophy that was indigenous to the East, and the two systems readily blended.[1]

But the most powerful cause of the movement was the intense desire for positive religious belief, which had long been growing in the Empire. The period when Roman incredulity reached its extreme point had been the century that preceded and the half century that followed the birth of Christ. The sudden dissolution of the old habits of the Republic effected through political causes, the first comparison of the multitudinous religions of the Empire and also the writings of Euhemerus had produced an absolute religious disbelief which Epicureanism represented and encouraged. This belief, however, as I have already noticed, co-existed with numerous magical and astrological superstitions, and

---

[1] This movement is well treated by Vacherot, *Hist. de l'École d'Alexandrie.*

the ignorance of physical science was so great, and the conception of general laws so faint, that the materials for a great
revival of superstition still remained. From the middle of
the first century, a more believing and reverent spirit began
to arise. The worship of Isis and Serapis forced its way into
Rome in spite of the opposition of the rulers. Apollonius of
Tyana, at the close of the Flavian period, had endeavoured
to unite moral teaching with religious practices ; the oracles,
which had long ceased, were partially restored under the
Antonines ; the calamities and visible decline of the Empire
withdrew the minds of men from that proud patriotic worship of Roman greatness, which was long a substitute for
religious feeling ; and the frightful pestilence that swept over
the land in the reigns of Marcus Aurelius and his successor
was followed by a blind, feverish, and spasmodic superstition.
Besides this, men have never acquiesced for any considerable
time in a neglect of the great problems of the origin, nature,
and destinies of the soul, or dispensed with some form of religious worship and aspiration. That religious instincts are
as truly a part of our nature as are our appetites and our
nerves, is a fact which all history establishes, and which
forms one of the strongest proofs of the reality of that
unseen world to which the soul of man continually tends.
Early Roman Stoicism, which in this respect somewhat
resembled the modern positive school, diverted for the most
part its votaries from the great problems of religion, and
attempted to evolve its entire system of ethics out of existing
human nature, without appealing to any external supernatural sanction. But the Platonic school, and the Egyptian
school which connected itself with the name of Pythagoras,
were both essentially religious. The first aspired to the
Deity as the source and model of virtue, admitted dæmons
or subordinate spiritual agents acting upon mankind, and explained and purified, in no hostile spirit, the popular religions. The latter made the state of ecstasy or quietism its

ideal condition, and sought to purify the mind by theurgy or special religious rites. Both philosophies conspired to effect a great religious reformation, in which the Greek spirit usually represented the rational, and the Egyptian the mystical, element.

Of the first, Plutarch was the head. He taught the supreme authority of reason. He argued elaborately that superstition is worse than atheism, for it calumniates the character of the Deity, and its evils are not negative, but positive. At the same time, he is far from regarding the Mythology as a tissue of fables. Some things he denies. Others he explains away. Others he frankly accepts. He teaches for the most part a pure monotheism, which he reconciles with the common belief, partly by describing the different divinities as simply popular personifications of Divine attributes, and partly by the usual explanation of dæmons. He discarded most of the fables of the poets, applying to them with fearless severity the tests of human morality, and rejecting indignantly those which attribute to the Deity cruel or immoral actions. He denounces all religious terrorism, and draws a broad line of distinction between both the superstitious and idolatrous conception of the Deity on the one hand, and the philosophical conception on the other. ' The superstitious man believes in the gods, but he has a false idea of their nature. Those good beings whose providence watches over us with so much care, those beings so ready to forget our faults, he represents as ferocious and cruel tyrants, taking pleasure in tormenting us. He believes the founders of brass, the sculptors of stone, the moulders of wax ; he attributes to the gods a human form ; he adorns and worships the image he has made, and he listens not to the philosophers, and men of knowledge who associate the Divine image, not with bodily beauty, but with grandeur and majesty, with gentleness and goodness.'[1] On the other hand,

---

[1] *De Superstitione.*

Plutarch believed that there was undoubtedly a certain super-natural basis in the Pagan creed ; he believed in oracles ; he defended, in a very ingenious essay, hereditary punishment, and the doctrine of a special Providence ; he admitted a future retribution, though he repudiated the notion of physical torment ; and he brought into clear relief the moral teaching conveyed in some of the fables of the poets.

The position which Plutarch occupied under Trajan, Maximus of Tyre occupied in the next generation. Like Plutarch, but with a greater consistency, he maintained a pure monotheistic doctrine, declaring that ' Zeus is that most ancient and guiding mind that begot all things—Athene is prudence—Apollo is the sun.'[1] Like Plutarch, he developed the Platonic doctrine of dæmons as an explanation of much of the mythology, and he applied an allegorical interpretation with great freedom to the fables of Homer, which formed the text-book or the Bible of Paganism. By these means he endeavoured to clarify the popular creed from all elements inconsistent with a pure monotheism, and from all legends of doubtful morality, while he sublimated the popular worship into a harmless symbolism.   ' The gods,' he assures us, ' them-selves need no images,' but the infirmity of human nature re-quires visible signs ' on which to rest.'   ' Those who possess such faculties, that with a steady mind they can rise to heaven, and to God, are in no need of statues.   But such men are very rare.'   He then proceeds to recount the different ways by which men have endeavoured to represent or symbolise the Divine nature, as the statues of Greece, the animals of Egypt, or the sacred flame of Persia.   ' The God,' he continues, ' the Father and the Founder of all that exists, older than the sun, older than the sky, greater than all time, than every age, and than all the works of nature, whom no words can express, whom no eye can see . . . What can we

---

[1] *Dissertations*, x. § 8 (ed. Davis, London, 1740). In some editions this is *Diss.* xxix.

say concerning his images? Only let men understand that there is but one Divine nature; but whether the art of Phidias chiefly preserves his memory among the Greeks, or the worship of animals among the Egyptians, a river among these, or a flame among those, I do not blame the variety of the representations—only let men understand that there is but one; only let them love one, let them preserve one in their memory.'[1]

A third writer who, nearly at the same time as Maximus of Tyre, made some efforts in the same direction, was Apuleius, who, however, both as a moral teacher, and in his freedom from superstition, was far inferior to the preceding. The religion he most admired was the Egyptian; but in his philosophy he was a Platonist, and in that capacity, besides an exposition of the Platonic code of morals, he has left us a singularly clear and striking disquisition on the doctrine of dæmons. 'These dæmons,' he says, 'are the bearers of blessings and prayers between the inhabitants of earth and heaven, carrying prayers from the one and assistance from the other . . . By them also, as Plato maintained in his "Banquet," all revelations, all the various miracles of magicians, all kinds of omens, are ruled. They have their several tasks to perform, their different departments to govern; some directing dreams, others the disposition of the entrails, others the flight of birds . . . The supreme deities do not descend to these things—they leave them to the intermediate divinities.'[2] But these intermediate spirits are not simply the agents of supernatural phenomena—they are also the guardians of our virtue and the recorders of our actions. 'Each man has in life witnesses and guards of his deeds, visible to no one, but always present, witnessing not only every act but every thought. When life has ended and we must return whence we came, the same genius who had

---

[1] *Dissert.* xxxviii.　　　　[2] *De Dæmone Socratis.*

charge over us, takes us away and hurries us in his custody to judgment, and then assists us in pleading our cause. If any thing is falsely asserted he corrects it—if true, he substantiates it, and according to his witness our sentence is determined.'[1]

There are many aspects in which these attempts at re ligious reform are both interesting and important. They are interesting, because the doctrine of dæmons, mingled, it is true, with the theory of Euhemerus about the origin of the deities, was universally accepted by the Fathers as the true explanation of the Pagan theology, because the notion and, after the third century, even the artistic type of the guardian genius reappeared in that of the guardian angel, and because the transition from polytheism to the conception of a single deity acting by the delegation or ministration of an army of subsidiary spirits, was manifestly fitted to prepare the way for the reception of Christianity. They are interesting, too, as showing the anxiety of the human mind to sublimate its religious creed to the level of the moral and intellectual standard it had attained, and to make religious ordinances in some degree the instruments of moral improvement. But they are interesting above all, because the Greek and Egyptian methods of reform represent with typical distinctness the two great tendencies of religious thought in all succeeding periods. The Greek spirit was essentially rationalistic and eclectic; the Egyptian spirit was essentially mystical and devotional. The Greek sat in judgment upon his religion. He modified, curtailed, refined, allegorised, or selected. He treated its inconsistencies or absurdities, or immoralities, with precisely the same freedom of criticism as those he encountered in ordinary life. The Egyptian, on the other hand, bowed low before the Divine presence.

---

[1] *De Dæmone Socratis.* See, on the office of dæmons or genii, Arrian i. 14, and a curious chapter in Ammianus Marcell. xxi. 14. See, too, Plotinus, 3rd *Enn.* lib. iv.

He veiled his eyes, he humbled his reason, he represented the introduction of a new element into the moral life of Europe, the spirit of religious reverence and awe.

'The Egyptian deities,' it was observed by Apuleius, 'were chiefly honoured by lamentations, and the Greek divinities by dances.' [1] The truth of the last part of this very significant remark appears in every page of Greek history. No nation had a richer collection of games and festivals growing out of its religious system; in none did a light, sportive, and often licentious fancy play more fearlessly around the popular creed, in none was religious terrorism more rare. The Divinity was seldom looked upon as holier than man, and a due observance of certain rites and ceremonies was deemed an ample tribute to pay to him. In the Egyptian system the religious ceremonies were veiled in mystery and allegory. Chastity, abstinence from animal food, ablutions, long and mysterious ceremonies of preparation or initiation, were the most prominent features of worship. The deities representing the great forces of nature, and shrouded by mysterious symbols, excited a degree of awe which no other ancient religion approached.

The speculative philosophy, and the conceptions of morals, that accompanied the inroad of Oriental religions, were of a kindred nature. The most prominent characteristic of the first was its tendency to supersede the deductions of the reason by the intuitions of ecstasy. Neoplatonism, and the philosophies that were allied to it, were fundamentally pantheistic,[2] but they differed widely from the pantheism of the Stoics. The Stoics identified man with God, for the purpose of glorifying man—the Neoplatonists for the purpose of aggrandising God. In the conception of the first, man, independent, self controlled, and participating in the highest

---

[1] *De Dæmone Socratis.*

[2] I should except Plotinus, however, who was faithful in this point to Plato, and was in consequence much praised by the Christian Fathers.

nature of the universe, has no superior in creation. According to the latter, man is almost a passive being, swayed and permeated by a divine impulse. Yet he is not altogether divine. The divinity is latent in his soul, but dulled, dimmed, and crushed by the tyranny of the body. ' To bring the God that is in us into conformity with the God that is in the universe,' to elicit the ideas that are graven in the mind, but obscured and hidden by the passions of the flesh—above all, to subdue the body, which is the sole obstacle to our complete fruition of the Deity—was the main object of life. Porphyry described all philosophy as an anticipation of death—not in the Stoical sense of teaching us to look calmly on our end, but because death realises the ideal of philosophy, the complete separation of soul and body. Hence followed an ascetic morality, and a supersensual philosophy. ' The greatest of all evils,' we are told, ' is pleasure; because by it the soul is nailed or riveted to the body, and thinks that true which the body persuades it, and is thus deprived of the sense of divine things.' [1] ' Justice, beauty, and goodness, and all things that are formed by them, no eye has ever seen, no bodily sense can apprehend. Philosophy must be pursued by pure and unmingled reason and with deadened senses; for the body disturbs the mind, so that it cannot follow after wisdom. As long as it is lost and mingled in the clay, we shall never sufficiently possess the truth we desire.' [2]

But the reason which is thus extolled as the revealer of truth must not be confounded with the process of reasoning. It is something quite different from criticism, analysis, comparison, or deduction. It is essentially intuitive, but it only acquires its power of transcendental intuition after a

---

[1] 'Omnium malorum maximum voluptas, qua tanquam clavo et fibula anima corpori nectitur; putatque vera quæ et corpus suadet, et ita spoliatur rerum divinarum aspectu.' — Iamblichus, *De Secta Pythagor.* (Romæ, 1556), p. 38, Plotinus, 1st *Enn.* vi. 6.

[2] *De Sect. Pyth.* pp. 36, 37.

long process ot discipline. When a man passes from the
daylight into a room which is almost dark, he is at first
absolutely unable to see the objects around him ; but gradu
ally his eye grows accustomed to the feeble light, the outline
of the room becomes dimly visible, object after object emerges
into sight, until at last, by intently gazing, he acquires the
power of seeing around him with tolerable distinctness. In
this fact we have a partial image of the Neoplatonic doctrine
of the knowledge of divine things. Our soul is a dark chamber.
darkened by contact with the flesh, but in it there are graven
divine ideas, there exists a living divine element. The eye of
reason, by long and steady introspection, can learn to decipher these characters ; the will, aided by an appointed course
of discipline, can evoke this divine element, and cause it to
blend with the universal spirit from which it sprang. The
powers of mental concentration, and of metaphysical abstraction, are therefore the highest intellectual gifts; and quietism,
or the absorption of our nature in God, is the last stage of virtue.
' The end of man,' said Pythagoras, ' is God.' The mysterious
' One,' the metaphysical abstraction without attributes and
without form which constitutes the First Person of the Alexandrian Trinity, is the acme of human thought, and the condition
of ecstasy is the acme of moral perfection. Plotinus, it was
said, had several times attained it. Porphyry, after years of
discipline, once, and but once.[1] The process of reasoning is
here not only useless, but pernicious. ' An innate knowledge
of the gods is implanted in our minds prior to all reasoning.'[2]
In divine things the task of man is not to create or to
acquire, but to educe. His means of perfection are not
dialectics or research, but long and patient meditation, silence,
abstinence from the distractions and occupations of life, the
subjugation of the flesh, a life of continual discipline, a
constant attendance on those mysterious rites which detach

---

[1] Porphyry, *Life of Plotinus.*   [2] Iamblichus, *De Mysteriis,* 1.

him from material objects, overawe and elevate his mind, and quicken his realisation of the Divine presence.[1]

The system of Neoplatonism represents a mode of thought which in many forms, and under many names, may be traced through the most various ages and creeds. Mysticism, transcendentalism, inspiration, and grace, are all words expressing the deep-seated belief that we possess fountains of knowledge apart from all the acquisitions of the senses; that there are certain states of mind, certain flashes of moral and intellectual illumination, which cannot be accounted for by any play or combination of our ordinary faculties. For the sobriety, the timidity, the fluctuations of the reasoning spirit, Neoplatonism substituted the transports of the imagination; and, though it cultivated the power of abstraction, every other intellectual gift was sacrificed to the discipline of asceticism. It made men credulous, because it suppressed that critical spirit which is the sole barrier to the ever-encroaching imagination; because it represented superstitious rites as especially conducive to that state of ecstasy which was the condition of revelation; because it formed a nervous, diseased, expectant temperament, ever prone to hallucinations, ever agitated by vague and uncertain feelings that were readily attributed to inspiration. As a moral system it carried, indeed, the purification of the feelings and imagination to a higher perfection than any preceding school, but it had the deadly fault of separating sentiment from action. In this respect it was well fitted to be the close, the final suicide, of Roman philosophy. Cicero assigned a place of happiness in the future world to all who faithfully served the State.[2] The Stoics had taught that all virtue was vain that did not issue in action. Even Epictetus, in his portrait of the

---

[1] See, on this doctrine of ecstasy, Vacherot, *Hist. de l'École d'Alexandrie*, tome i. p. 576, &c.

[2] 'Sic habeto, omnibus qui patriam conservaverint, adjuverint, auxerint, certum esse in cœlo ac definitum locum ubi beati ævo sempiterno fruantur.'—Cic. *Somn. Scip.*

ascetic cynic—even Marcus Aurelius, in his minute self-examination—had never forgotten the outer world. The early Platonists, though they dwelt very strongly on mental discipline, were equally practical. Plutarch reminds us that the same word is used for light, and for man,[1] for the duty of man is to be the light of the world; and he shrewdly remarked that Hesiod exhorted the husbandman to pray for the harvest, but to do so with his hand upon the plough. Apuleius, expounding Plato, taught 'that he who is inspired by nature to seek after good must not deem himself born for himself alone, but for all mankind, though with diverse kinds and degrees of obligation, for he is formed first of all for his country, then for his relations, then for those with whom he is joined by occupation or knowledge.' Maximus of Tyre devoted two noble essays to showing the vanity of all virtue which exhausts itself in mental transports without radiating in action among mankind. 'What use,' he asked, 'is there in knowledge unless we do those things for which knowledge is profitable? What use is there in the skill of the physician unless by that skill he heals the sick, or in the art of Phidias unless he chisels the ivory or the gold. . . . Hercules was a wise man, but not for himself, but that by his wisdom he might diffuse benefits over every land and sea. . . Had he preferred to lead a life apart from men, and to follow an idle wisdom, Hercules would indeed have been a Sophist, and no one would call him the son of Zeus. For God himself is never idle; were He to rest, the sky would cease to move, and the earth to produce, and the rivers to flow into the ocean, and the seasons to pursue their appointed course.'[2] But the Neoplatonists, though they sometimes spoke of civic

---

[1] Φῶς, which, according to Plutarch (who here confuses two distinct words), is poetically used for man (*De Latenter Vivendo*). A similar thought occurs in M. Aurelius, who speaks of the good man as light which only ceases to shine when it ceases to be.

[2] *Diss.* xxi. § 6.

virtues, regarded the condition of ecstasy as not only transcending, but including all, and that condition could only be
arrived at by a passive life.   The saying of Anaxagoras, that
his mission was to contemplate the sun, the stars, and the
course of nature, and that this contemplation was wisdom,'
was accepted as an epitome of their philosophy.[1]   A senator
named Rogantianus, who had followed the teaching of
Plotinus, acquired so intense a disgust for the things of life,
that he left all his property, refused to fulfil the duties of a
prætor, abandoned his senatorial functions, and withdrew
himself from every form of business and pleasure.   Plotinus,
instead of reproaching him, overwhelmed him with eulogy,
selected him as his favourite disciple, and continually represented him as the model of a philosopher.[2]

The two characteristics I have noticed—the abandonment of civic duties, and the discouragement of the critical
spirit—had from a very early period been manifest in the
Pythagorean school.[3]   In the blending philosophies of the
third and fourth centuries, they became continually more
apparent.   Plotinus was still an independent philosopher,
inheriting the traditions of Greek thought, though not the
traditions of Greek life, building his system avowedly by a
rational method, and altogether rejecting theurgy or religious
magic.   His disciple, Porphyry, first made Neoplatonism
anti-Christian, and, in his violent antipathy to the new faith,
began to convert it into a religious system.   Iamblichus,
who was himself an Egyptian priest, completed the trans-

---

[1] Iamblichus, *De Sect. Pythagoræ*,
p. 35.

[2] Porphyry, *Life of Plotinus*, cap.
vii.; Plotinus, 1st *Enn.* iv. 7.   See
on this subject Degerando, *Hist.
de la Philos.* iii. p. 383.

[3] Thus it was said of Apollonius
that in his teaching at Ephesus he
did not speak after the manner of
the followers of Socrates, but en-

deavoured to detach his disciples
from all occupation other than philosophy.—*Philostr. Apoll. of Tyana*,
iv. 2.   Cicero notices the aversion
the Pythagoreans of his time displayed to argument: 'Quum ex
iis quæreretur quare ita esset, re-
spondere solitos, Ipse dixit; ipse
autem erat Pythagoras.'—*De Nat
Deor.* i. 5.

formation,[1] resolved all moral discipline into theurgy, and sacrificed all reasoning to faith.[2] Julian attempted to realise the conception of a revived Paganism, blending with and purified by philosophy. In every form the appetite for miracles and for belief was displayed. The theory of dæmons completely superseded the old Stoical naturalism, which regarded the different Pagan divinities as allegories or personifications of the Divine attributes. The Platonic ethics were again, for the most part, in the ascendant, but they were deeply tinctured by a foreign element. Thus, suicide was condemned by the Neoplatonists, not merely on the principle of Plato, that it is an abandonment of the post of duty to which the Deity has called us, but also on the quietist ground, that perturbation is necessarily a pollution of the soul, and that, as mental perturbation accompanies the act, the soul of the suicide departs polluted from the body.[3] The belief in a future world, which was the common glory of the schools of Pythagoras and of Plato, had become universal. As Roman greatness, in which men had long seen the reward of virtue, faded rapidly away, the conception of 'a city of God' began to grow more clearly in the minds of men, and the countless slaves who were among the chief propagators of Oriental faiths, and who had begun to exercise an unprecedented influence in Roman life, turned with a natural and a touching eagerness towards a happier and a freer world.[4] The incredulity of Lucretius, Cæsar, and Pliny had

---

[1] See Vacherot, tome ii. p. 66.

[2] See Degerando, *Hist. de la Philosophie*, tome iii. pp. 400, 401.

[3] Plotinus, 1st *Enn.* ix.

[4] See a strong passage, on the universality of this belief, in Plotinus, 1st *Enn.* i. 12, and Origen, *Cont. Cels.* vii. A very old tradition represented the Egyptians as the first people who held the doctrine of the immortality of the soul.

Cicero (*Tusc. Quæst.*) says that the Syrian Pherecydes, master of Pythagoras, first taught it. Maximus of Tyre attributes its origin to Pythagoras, and his slave Zamolxis was said to have introduced it into Greece. Others say that Thales first taught it. None of these assertions have any real historical value.

disappeared. Above all, a fusion had been effected between moral discipline and religion, and the moralist sought his chief means of purification in the ceremonies of the temple.

I have now completed the long and complicated task to which the present chapter has been devoted. I have endeavoured to exhibit, so far as can be done, by a description of general tendencies, and by a selection of quotations, the spirit of the long series of Pagan moralists who taught at Rome during the period that elapsed between the rise of Roman philosophy and the triumph of Christianity. My object has not been to classify these writers with minute accuracy, according to their speculative tenets, but rather, as I had proposed, to exhibit the origin, the nature, and the fortunes of the general notion or type of virtue which each moralist had regarded as supremely good. History is not a mere succession of events connected only by chronology. It is a chain of causes and effects. There is a great natural difference of degree and direction in both the moral and intellectual capacities of individuals, but it is not probable that the general average of natural morals in great bodies of men materially varies. When we find a society very virtuous or very vicious —when some particular virtue or vice occupies a peculiar prominence, or when important changes pass over the moral conceptions or standard of the people—we have to trace in these things simply the action of the circumstances that were dominant. The history of Roman ethics represents a steady and uniform current, guided by the general conditions of society, and its progress may be marked by the successive ascendancy of the Roman, the Greek, and the Egyptian spirit.

In the age of Cato and Cicero the character of the ideal was wholly Roman, although the philosophical expression of that character was derived from the Greek Stoics. It exhibited all the force, the grandeur, the hardness, the practical tendency which Roman circumstances had early created, combined with that catholicity of spirit which resulted from very recent political and intellectual changes. In the course of time, the Greek element, which represented the gentler and more humane spirit of antiquity, gained an ascendancy. It did so by simple propagandism, aided by the long peace of the Antonines, by the effeminate habits produced by the increasing luxury, by the attractions of the metropolis, which had drawn multitudes of Greeks to Rome, by the patronage of the Emperors, and also by the increasing realisation of the doctrine of universal brotherhood, which Panætius and Cicero had asserted, but of which the full consequences were only perceived by their successors. The change in the type of virtue was shown in the influence of eclectic, and for the most part Platonic, moralists, whose special assaults were directed against the Stoical condemnation of the emotions, and in the gradual softening of the Stoical type. In Seneca the hardness of the sect, though very apparent, is broken by precepts of a real and extensive benevolence, though that benevolence springs rather from a sense of duty than from tenderness of feeling. In Dion Chrysostom the practical benevolence is not less prominent, but there is less both of pride and of callousness. Epictetus embodied the sternest Stoicism in his Manual, but his dissertations exhibit a deep religious feeling and a wide range of sympathies. In Marcus Aurelius the emotional elements had greatly increased, and the amiable qualities began to predominate over the heroic ones. We find at the same time a new stress laid upon purity of thought and imagination, a growing feeling of reverence, and an earnest desire to reform the popular religion.

This second stage exhibits a happy combination of the Roman and Greek spirits. Disinterested, strictly practical, averse to the speculative subtilties of the Greek intellect, Stoicism was still the religion of a people who were the rulers and the organisers of the world, whose enthusiasm was essentially patriotic, and who had learnt to sacrifice everything but pride to the sense of duty. It had, however, become amiable, gentle, and spiritual. It had gained much in beauty, while it had lost something in force. In the world of morals, as in the world of physics, strength is nearly allied to hardness. He who feels keenly is easily moved, and a sensitive sympathy which lies at the root of an amiable character is in consequence a principle of weakness. The race of great Roman Stoics, which had never ceased during the tyranny of Nero or Domitian, began to fail. In the very moment when the ideal of the sect had attained its supreme perfection, a new movement appeared, the philosophy sank into disrepute, and the last act of the drama began.

In this, as in the preceding ones, all was normal and regular. The long continuance of despotic government had gradually destroyed the active public spirit of which Stoicism was the expression. The predominance of the subtile intellect of Greece, and the multiplication of rhetoricians, had converted the philosophy into a school of disputation and of casuistry. The increasing cultivation of the emotions continued, till what may be termed the moral centre was changed, and the development of feeling was deemed more important than the regulation of actions. This cultivation of the emotions predisposed men to religion. A reaction, intensified by many minor causes, set in against the scepticism of the preceding generation, and Alexandria gradually became the moral capital of the empire. The Roman type speedily disappeared. A union was effected between superstitious rites and philosophy, and the worship of Egyptian deities prepared the way for the teaching of the Neoplatonists, who combined the most visionary part of the speculations of Plato with the ancient philosophies of the East. In Plotinus we find most of the first; in Iamblichus most of the second. The minds of men, under their influence, grew introspective, credulous, and superstitious, and found their ideal states in the hallucinations of ecstasy and the calm of an unpractical mysticism.

Such were the influences which acted in turn upon a society which, by despotism, by slavery, and by atrocious amusements, had been debased and corrupted to the very core. Each sect which successively arose contributed something to remedy the evil. Stoicism placed beyond cavil the great distinctions between right and wrong. It inculcated the doctrine of universal brotherhood, it created a noble literature and a noble legislation, and it associated its moral system with the patriotic spirit which was then the animating spirit of Roman life. The early Platonists of the Empire corrected the exaggerations of Stoicism, gave free scope to the amiable qualities, and supplied a theory of right and wrong, suited not merely for heroic characters and for extreme emergencies, but also for the characters and the circumstances of common life. The Pythagorean and Neoplatonic schools revived the feeling of religious reverence, inculcated humility, prayerfulness, and purity of thought, and accustomed men to associate their moral ideals with the Deity, rather than with themselves.

The moral improvement of society was now to pass into other hands. A religion which had long been increasing in obscurity began to emerge into the light. By the beauty of its moral precepts, by the systematic skill with which it governed the imagination and habits of its worshippers, by the strong religious motives to which it could appeal, by its admirable ecclesiastical organisation and, it must be added, by its unsparing use of the arm of power, Christianity soon eclipsed or destroyed all other sects, and became for many centuries the supreme ruler of the moral world. Combining the Stoical doctrine of universal brotherhood, the Greek predilection for the amiable qualities, and the Egyptian spirit of reverence and religious awe, it acquired from the first an intensity and universality of influence which none of the philosophies it had superseded had approached. I have now to examine the moral causes that governed the rise of this religion in Rome, the ideal of virtue it presented, the degree and manner in which it stamped its image upon the character of nations, and the perversions and distortions it underwent.

CHAPTER III.

THE CONVERSION OF ROME.

THERE is no fact in the history of the human mind more remarkable than the complete unconsciousness of the importance and the destinies of Christianity, manifested by the Pagan writers before the accession of Constantine. So large an amount of attention has been bestowed on the ten or twelve allusions to it they furnish, that we are sometimes apt to forget how few and meagre those allusions are, and how utterly impossible it is to construct from them, with any degree of certainty, a history of the early Church. Plutarch and the elder Pliny, who probably surpass all other writers of their time in the range of their illustrations, and Seneca, who was certainly the most illustrious moralist of his age, never even mention it. Epictetus and Marcus Aurelius have each adverted to it with a passing and contemptuous censure. Tacitus describes in detail the persecution by Nero, but treats the suffering religion merely as 'an execrable superstition;' while Suetonius, employing the same expression, reckons the persecution among the acts of the tyrant that were either laudable or indifferent. Our most important document is the famous letter of the younger Pliny. Lucian throws some light both on the extent of Christian charity, and on the aspect in which Christians were regarded by the religious jugglers of their age, and the long series of Pagans who wrote the lives of the Emperors in that most critical period from the accession of Hadrian, almost to the eve of the triumph of the Church, among a crowd of details concerning the dresses, games, vices, and follies of the Court, supply us with six or seven short notices of the religion that was transforming the world.

The general silence of the Pagan writers on this subject did not arise from any restrictions imposed upon them by authority, for in this field the widest latitude was conceded, nor yet from the notions of the dignity of history, or the importance of individual exertions, which have induced some historians to resolve their task into a catalogue of the achievements of kings, statesmen, and generals. The conception of history, as the record and explanation of moral revolutions, though of course not developed to the same prominence as among some modern writers, was by no means unknown in antiquity,[1] and in many branches our knowledge of the social changes of the Roman Empire is extremely copious. The dissolution of old beliefs, the decomposition of the entire social and moral system that had arisen under the Republic, engaged in the very highest degree the attention of the literary classes, and they displayed the most commendable diligence in tracing its stages. It is very curious and instructive to contrast the ample information they have furnished us concerning the growth of Roman luxury, with their almost absolute silence concerning the growth of Christianity. The moral importance of the former movement they clearly recognised, and they have accordingly preserved so full a record of all the changes in dress, banquets, buildings, and spectacles, that it would be possible to write with the most minute detail the whole history of Roman luxury, from the day when a censor deprived an elector of his vote because his garden was negli-

---

[1] We have a remarkable instance of the clearness with which some even of the most insignificant historians recognised the folly of confining history to the biographies of the Emperors, in the opening chapter of Capitolinus, *Life of Macrinus.* Tacitus is full of beautiful episodes, describing the manners and religion of the people.

gently cultivated, to the orgies of Nero or Heliogabalus.
The moral importance of the other movement they altogether
overlooked, and their oversight leaves a chasm in history
which can never be supplied.

That the greatest religious change in the history of man
kind should have taken place under the eyes of a brilliant
galaxy of philosophers and historians, who were profoundly
conscious of the decomposition around them, that all of these
writers should have utterly failed to predict the issue of the
movement they were observing, and that, during the space
of three centuries, they should have treated as simply contemptible an agency which all men must now admit to have
been, for good or for evil, the most powerful moral lever that
has ever been applied to the affairs of man, are facts well
worthy of meditation in every period of religious transition.
The explanation is to be found in that broad separation between the spheres of morals and of positive religion we have
considered in the last chapter. In modern times, men who
were examining the probable moral future of the world, would
naturally, and in the first place, direct their attention to the
relative positions and the probable destinies of religious institutions. In the Stoical period of the Roman Empire,
positive religion had come to be regarded as merely an art
for obtaining preternatural assistance in the affairs of life,
and the moral amelioration of mankind was deemed altogether external to its sphere. Philosophy had become to the
educated most literally a religion. It was the rule of life, the
exposition of the Divine nature, the source of devotional feeling   The numerous Oriental superstitions that had deluged
the city were regarded as peculiarly pernicious and contemptible, and of these none was less likely to attract the favour
of the philosophers than that of the Jews,[1] who were noto-

---

[1] The passages relating to the
Jews in Roman literature are collected in Aubertin's *Rapports sup-*
posés entre Sénèque et St. Paul,
Champagny, *Rome et Judée,* tome i.
pp. 134–137.

rious as the most sordid, the most turbulent,[1] and the most
unsocial[2] of the Oriental colonists. Of the ignorance of their
tenets, displayed even by the most eminent Romans, we have
a striking illustration in the long series of grotesque fables
concerning their belief, probably derived from some satirical
pamphlet, which Tacitus has gravely inserted in his history.[3]
Christianity, in the eyes of the philosopher, was simply a sect
of Judaism.

Although I am anxious in the present work to avoid, as
far as possible, all questions that are purely theological, and
to consider Christianity merely in its aspect as a moral agent,
it will be necessary to bestow a few preliminary pages upon
its triumph in the Roman Empire, in order to ascertain how
far that triumph was due to moral causes, and what were its
relations to the prevailing philosophy. There are some
writers who have been so struck with the conformity between
some of the doctrines of the later Stoics and those of Christianity that they have imagined that Christianity had early
obtained a decisive influence over philosophy, and that the
leading teachers of Rome had been in some measure its
disciples. There are others who reduce the conversion of
the Roman Empire to a mere question of evidences, to the
overwhelming proofs the Christian teachers produced of the
authenticity of the Gospel narratives. There are others,
again, who deem the triumph of Christianity simply miraculous. Everything, they tell us, was against it. The course
of the Church was like that of a ship sailing rapidly and
steadily to the goal, in direct defiance of both wind and tide,
and the conversion of the Empire was as literally supernatural as the raising of the dead, or the sudden quelling of
the storm.

On the first of these theories it will not, I think, be

---

[1] Cicero, *pro Flacco*, 28; Sueton.　　[2] Juvenal, *Sat.* xiv
Claudius, 25.　　[3] *Hist.* v

necessary, after the last chapter, to expatiate at length.   It is admitted that the greatest moralists of the Roman Empire either never mentioned Christianity, or mentioned it with contempt ; that they habitually disregarded the many re- ligions which had arisen among the ignorant ; and that we have no direct evidence of the slightest value of their ever having come in contact with or favoured the Christians. The supposition that they were influenced by Christianity rests mainly upon their enforcement of the Christian duty of self-examination, upon their strong assertion of the universal brotherhood of mankind, and upon the delicate and expansive humanity they at last evinced.   But although on all these points the later Stoics approximated much to Christianity, we have already seen that it is easy to discover in each case the cause of the tendency.   The duty of self-examination was simply a Pythagorean precept, enforced in that school long before the rise of Christianity, introduced into Stoicism when Pythagoreanism became popular in Rome, and confessedly borrowed from this source.   The doctrine of the universal brotherhood of mankind was the manifest expression of those political and social changes which reduced the whole civilised globe to one great empire, threw open to the most distant tribes the right of Roman citizenship, and subverted all those class divisions around which moral theories had been formed.   Cicero asserted it as emphatically as Seneca.   The theory of pantheism, representing the entire creation as one great body, pervaded by one Divine soul, harmonised with it ; and it is a curious fact that the very phraseology concerning the fellow-membership of all things in God, which has been most confidently adduced by some modern writers as proving the connection between Seneca and Christianity, was selected by Lactantius as the clearest illustration of the pantheism of Stoicism.[1]   The humane character of the later Stoical teach-

---

[1] Lact. *Inst. Div.* vii. 3.

ing was obviously due to the infusion of the Greek element
into Roman life, which began before the foundation of the
Empire, and received a new impulse in the reign of Hadrian,
and also to the softening influence of a luxurious civilisation,
and of the long peace of the Antonines.   While far inferior
to the Greeks in practical and realised humanity, the Romans
never surpassed their masters in theoretical humanity except
in one respect.   The humanity of the Greeks, though very
earnest, was confined within a narrow circle.   The social and
political circumstances of the Roman Empire destroyed the
barrier.

The only case in which any plausible arguments have been
urged in favour of the notion that the writings of the Stoics
were influenced by the New Testament is that of Seneca.
This philosopher was regarded by all the mediæval writers
as a Christian, on the ground of a correspondence with St.
Paul, which formed part of a forged account of the martyrdom of St. Peter and St. Paul, attributed to St. Linus.
These letters, which were absolutely unnoticed during the
first three centuries, and are first mentioned by St. Jerome,
are now almost universally abandoned as forgeries;[1] but
many curious coincidences of phraseology have been pointed
out between the writings of Seneca and the epistles of St.
Paul; and the presumption derived from them has been
strengthened by the facts that the brother of Seneca was that
Gallio who refused to hear the disputes between St. Paul and
the Jews, and that Burrhus, who was the friend and colleague of Seneca, was the officer to whose custody St. Paul
had been entrusted at Rome.   Into the minute verbal critic-

---

[1] See their history fully investigated in Aubertin.   Augustine
followed Jerome in mentioning the
letters, but neither of these writers
asserted their genuineness.   Lactantius, nearly at the same time
(*Inst. Div.* vi. 24), distinctly spoke
of Seneca as a Pagan, as Tertullian
(*Apol.* 50) had done before.   The
immense number of forged documents is one of the most disgraceful
features of the Church history of
the first few centuries.

ism to which this question had given rise,[1] it is not necessary for me to enter. It has been shown that much of what was deemed Christian phraseology grew out of the pantheistic notion of one great body including, and one Divine mind animating and guiding, all existing things; and many other of the pretended coincidences are so slight as to be altogether worthless as an argument. Still I think most persons who review what has been written on the subject will conclude that it is probable some fragments at least of Christian language had come to the ears of Seneca. But to suppose that his system of morals is in any degree formed after the model or under the influence of Christianity, is to be blind to the most obvious characteristics of both Christianity and Stoicism; for no other moralist could be so aptly selected as representing their extreme divergence. Reverence and humility, a constant sense of the supreme majesty of God and of the weakness and sinfulness of man, and a perpetual reference to another world, were the essential characteristics of Christianity, the source of all its power, the basis of its distinctive type. Of all these, the teaching of Seneca is the direct antithesis. Careless of the future world, and profoundly convinced of the supreme majesty of man, he laboured to emancipate his disciples 'from every fear of God and man;' and the proud language in which he claimed for the sage an equality with the gods represents, perhaps, the highest point to which philosophic arrogance has been carried. The Jews, with whom the Christians were then universally identified, he emphatically describes as 'an accursed race.'[2] One man, indeed, there was

---

[1] Fleury has written an elaborate work maintaining the connection between the apostle and the philosopher. Troplong (*Influence du Christianisme sur le Droit*) has adopted the same view. Aubertin, in the work I have already cited, has maintained the opposite view (which is that of all or nearly all English critics) with masterly skill and learning. The Abbé Dourif (*Rapports du Stoïcisme et du Christianisme*) has placed side by side the passages from each writer which are most alike.

[2] Quoted by St. Augustine.— *De Civ. Dei*, vi. 11.

among the later Stoics who had almost realised the Christian type, and in whose pure and gentle nature the arrogance of his school can be scarcely traced; but Marcus Aurelius, who of all the Pagan world, if we argued by internal evidence alone, would have been most readily identified with Christianity, was a persecutor of the faith, and he has left on record in his 'Meditations' his contempt for the Christian martyrs. [1]

The relation between the Pagan philosophers and the Christian religion was a subject of much discussion and of profound difference of opinion in the early Church. [2] While the writers of one school apologised for the murder of Socrates, described the martyred Greek as the 'buffoon of Athens,' [3] and attributed his inspiration to diabolical influence; [4] while they designated the writings of the philosophers as 'the schools of heretics,' and collected with a malicious assiduity all the calumnies that had been heaped upon their memory— there were others who made it a leading object to establish a close affinity between Pagan philosophy and the Christian revelation. Imbued in many instances, almost from child-hood, with the noble teaching of Plato, and keenly alive to the analogies between his philosophy and their new faith, these writers found the exhibition of this resemblance at once deeply grateful to themselves and the most successful way of dispelling the prejudices of their Pagan neighbours. The success that had attended the Christian prophecies attributed to the Sibyls and the oracles, the passion for eclecticism, which the social and commercial position of Alexandria had generated, and also the example of the Jew Aristobulus, who had some time before contended that the Jewish

---

[1] xi. 3.

[2] The history of the two schools has been elaborately traced by Ritter, Pressensé, and many other writers. I would especially refer to the fourth volume of De-gerando's most fascinating *His-toire de la Philosophie.*

[3] 'Scurra Atticus,' Min. Felix, *Octav.* This term is said by Cicero to have been given to Socrates by Zeno. (Cic. *De Nat. Deor.* i. 34.)

[4] Tertull. *De Anima,* 39.

writings had been translated into Greek, and had been the
source of much of the Pagan wisdom, encouraged them in
their course.   The most conciliatory, and at the same time
the most philosophical school, was the earliest in the Church.
Justin Martyr—the first of the Fathers whose writings possess any general philosophical interest—cordially recognises
the excellence of many parts of the Pagan philosophy, and
even attributes it to a Divine inspiration, to the action of
the generative or 'seminal Logos,' which from the earliest
times had existed in the world, had inspired teachers like
Socrates and Musonius, who had been persecuted by the
dæmons, and had received in Christianity its final and perfect
manifestation.[1]   The same generous and expansive apprecia
tion may be traced in the writings of several later Fathers,
although the school was speedily disfigured by some grotesque
extravagances.   Clement of Alexandria—a writer of wide
sympathies, considerable originality, very extensive learning,
but of a feeble and fantastic judgment—who immediately
succeeded Justin Martyr, attributed all the wisdom of antiquity to two sources.   The first source was tradition; for
the angels, who had been fascinated by the antediluvian
ladies, had endeavoured to ingratiate themselves with their
fair companions by giving them an abstract of the metaphysical and other learning which was then current in heaven,
and the substance of these conversations, being transmitted
by tradition, supplied the Pagan philosophers with their
leading notions.   The angels did not know everything, and
therefore the Greek philosophy was imperfect; but this event
formed the first great epoch in literary history.   The second
and most important source of Pagan wisdom was the Old
Testament,[2] the influence of which many of the early Christians traced in every department of ancient wisdom.   Plato had

---

[1] See especially his *Apol.* ii. 8,
12, 13. He speaks of the σπερματικὸς
λόγος.

[2] See, on all this, Clem. Alex.
Strom. v., and also i. 22.

borrowed from it all his philosophy, Homer the noblest con
ceptions of his poetry, Demosthenes the finest touches of his
eloquence. Even Miltiades owed his military skill to an
assiduous study of the Pentateuch, and the ambuscade by
which he won the battle of Marathon was imitated from
the strategy of Moses.[1]   Pythagoras, moreover, had been
himself a circumcised Jew.[2]   Plato had been instructed in
Egypt by the prophet Jeremiah.   The god Serapis was no
other than the patriarch Joseph, his Egyptian name being
manifestly derived from his great-grandmother Sarah.[3]

Absurdities of this kind, of which I have given extreme
but by no means the only examples, were usually primarily
intended to repel arguments against Christianity, and they
are illustrations of the tendency which has always existed in
an uncritical age to invent, without a shadow of foundation,
the most elaborate theories of explanation rather than recognise the smallest force in an objection.   Thus, when the
Pagans attempted to reduce Christianity to a normal product
of the human mind, by pointing to the very numerous Pagan
legends which were precisely parallel to the Jewish histories,

---

[1] St. Clement repeats this twice
(*Strom.* i. 24, v. 14). The writings
of this Father are full of curious,
and sometimes ingenious, attempts
to trace different phrases of the
great philosophers, orators, and
poets to Moses. A vast amount of
learning and ingenuity has been
expended in the same cause by
Eusebius. (*Præp. Evan.* xii. xiii.)
The tradition of the derivation of
Pagan philosophy from the Old
Testament found in general little
favour among the Latin writers.
There is some curious information
on this subject in Waterland's
'Charge to the Clergy of Middle-
sex, to prove that the wisdom of
the ancients was borrowed from

revelation; delivered in 1731.' It
is in the 8th volume of Waterland's
works (ed. 1731).
[2] St. Clement (*Strom.* i.) mentions that some think him to have
been Ezekiel, an opinion which St.
Clement himself does not hold.
See, on the patristic notions about
Pythagoras, Legendre, *Traité de
l'Opinion*, tome i. p. 164.
[3] This was the opinion of Julius
Firmicus Maternus, a Latin writer
of the age of Constantine, 'Nam
quia Saræ pronepos fuerat . . .
Serapis dictus est Græco sermone,
hoc est Σαρâs ἄπο.'—Julius Firmicus Maternus, *De Errore Pro-
fanarum Religionum*, cap. xiv.

it was answered that the dæmons were careful students of prophecy, that they foresaw with terror the advent of their Divine Conqueror, and that, in order to prevent men believing in him, they had invented, by anticipation, a series of legends resembling the events which were foretold.[1] More frequently, however, the early Christians retorted the accusations of plagiarism, and by forged writings attributed to Pagan authors, or, by pointing out alleged traces of Jewish influence in genuine Pagan writings, they endeavoured to trace through the past the footsteps of their faith. But this method of assimilation, which culminated in the Gnostics, the Neoplatonists, and especially in Origen, was directed not to the later Stoics of the Empire, but to the great philosophers who had preceded Christianity. It was in the writings of Plato, not in those of Epictetus or Marcus Aurelius, that the Fathers of the first three centuries found the influence of the Jewish Scriptures, and at the time when the passion for discovering these connections was most extravagant, the notion of Seneca and his followers being inspired by the Christians was unknown.

Dismissing then, as altogether groundless, the notion that Christianity had obtained a complete or even a partial influence over the philosophic classes during the period of Stoical ascendancy, we come to the opinion of those who suppose that the Roman Empire was converted by a system of evidences—by the miraculous proofs of the divinity of Christianity, submitted to the adjudication of the people. To estimate this view aright, we have to consider both the capacity of the men of that age for judging miracles, and also—which is a different question—the extent to which such evidence would weigh upon their minds. To treat this subject satis-

---

[1] Justin Martyr, *Apol.* i. 54; Trypho, 69–70. There is a very curious collection of Pagan legends that were parallel to Jewish incidents, in La Mothe le Vayer, let. xciii.

factorily, it may be advisable to enter at some little length into the broad question of the evidence of the miraculous.

With the exception of a small minority of the priests of the Catholic Church, a general incredulity on the subject of miracles now underlies the opinions of almost all educated men. Nearly every one, however cordially he may admit some one particular class of miracles, as a general rule regards the accounts of such events, which are so frequent in all old historians, as false and incredible, even when he fully believes the natural events that are authenticated by the same testimony. The reason of this incredulity is not alto-gether the impossibility or even extreme natural improba-bility of miracles; for, whatever may be the case with some, there is at least one class or conception of them which is perfectly free from logical difficulty. There is no contradic-tion involved in the belief that spiritual beings, of power and wisdom immeasurably transcending our own, exist, or that, existing, they might, by the normal exercise of their powers, perform feats as far surpassing the understanding of the most gifted of mankind, as the electric telegraph and the prediction of an eclipse surpass the faculties of a savage. Nor does the incredulity arise, I think, as is commonly asserted, from the want of that amount and kind of evidence which in other departments is deemed sufficient. Very few of the minor facts of history are authenticated by as much evidence as the Stigmata of St. Francis, or the miracle of the holy thorn, or those which were said to have been wrought at the tomb of the Abbé Paris. We believe, with tolerable assurance, a crowd of historical events on the testi-mony of one or two Roman historians; but when Tacitus and Suetonius describe how Vespasian restored a blind man to sight, and a cripple to strength,[1] their deliberate

---

[1] Suet. *Vesp.* 7; Tacit. *Hist.* iv. 81. There is a slight difference between the two historians about the second miracle. Suetonius

assertions do not even beget in our minds a suspicion that the narrative may possibly be true. We are quite certain that miracles were not ordinary occurrences in classical or mediæval times, but nearly all the contemporary writers from whom we derive our knowledge of those periods were convinced that they were.

If, then, I have correctly interpreted the opinions of ordinary educated people on this subject, it appears that the common attitude towards miracles is not that of doubt, of hesitation, of discontent with the existing evidence, but rather of absolute, derisive, and even unexamining incredulity. Such a fact, when we consider that the antecedent possibility of at least some miracles is usually admitted, and in the face of the vast mass of tradition that may be adduced in their favour, appears at first sight a striking anomaly, and the more so because it can be shown that the belief in miracles had in most cases not been reasoned down, but had simply faded away.

In order to ascertain the process by which this state of mind has been attained, we may take an example in a sphere which is happily removed from controversy. There are very few persons with whom the fictitious character of fairy tales has not ceased to be a question, or who would hesitate to disbelieve or even to ridicule any anecdote of this nature which was told them, without the very smallest examination of its evidence. Yet, if we ask in what respect the existence of fairies is naturally contradictory or absurd, it would be difficult to answer the question. A fairy is simply a being

---

says it was the leg, Tacitus that it was the hand, that was diseased. The god Serapis was said to have revealed to the patients that they would be cured by the emperor. Tacitus says that Vespasian did not believe in his own power; that it was only after much persuasion he was induced to try the experiment; that the blind man was well known in Alexandria, where the event occurred, and that eye-witnesses who had no motive to lie still attested the miracle.

possessing a moderate share of human intelligence, with little or no moral faculty, with a body pellucid, winged, and volatile, like that of an insect, with a passion for dancing, and, perhaps, with an extraordinary knowledge of the properties of different plants. That such beings should exist, or that, existing, they should be able to do many things beyond human power, are propositions which do not present the smallest difficulty. For many centuries their existence was almost universally believed. There is not a country, not a province, scarcely a parish, in which traditions of their appearance were not long preserved. So great a weight of tradition, so many independent trains of evidence attesting statements perfectly free from intrinsic absurdity, or even improbability, might appear sufficient, if not to establish conviction, at least to supply a very strong *primâ facie* case, and ensure a patient and respectful investigation of the subject.

It has not done so, and the reason is sufficiently plain. The question of the credibility of fairy tales has not been resolved by an examination of evidence, but by an observation of the laws of historic development. Wherever we find an ignorant and rustic population, the belief in fairies is found to exist, and circumstantial accounts of their apparitions are circulated. But invariably with increased education this belief passes away. It is not that the fairy tales are refuted or explained away, or even narrowly scrutinised. It is that the fairies cease to appear. From the uniformity of this decline, we infer that fairy tales are the normal product of a certain condition of the imagination; and this position is raised to a moral certainty when we find that the decadence of fairy tales is but one of a long series of similar transformations.

When the savage looks around upon the world and begins to form his theories of existence, he falls at once into three great errors, which become the first principles of his subse-

quent opinions. He believes that this earth is the centre of
the universe, and that all the bodies encircling it are intended
for its use; that the disturbances and dislocations it presents,
and especially the master curse of death, are connected with
some event in his history, and also that the numerous phenomena and natural vicissitudes he sees around him are due
to direct and isolated volitions, either of spirits presiding
over, or of intelligences inherent in, matter. Around these
leading conceptions a crowd of particular legends speedily
cluster. If a stone falls beside him, he naturally infers that
some one has thrown it. If it be an aërolite, it is attributed to some celestial being. Believing that each comet,
tempest, or pestilence results from a direct and isolated act,
he proceeds to make theories regarding the motives that
have induced his spiritual persecutors to assail him, and the
methods by which he may assuage their anger. Finding
numerous distinct trains or series of phenomena, he invents
for each appropriate presiding spirits. Miracles are to him
neither strange events nor violations of natural law, but
simply the unveiling or manifestation of the ordinary government of the world.

With these broad intellectual conceptions several minor
influences concur. A latent fetichism, which is betrayed in
that love of direct personification, or of applying epithets
derived from sentient beings to inanimate nature, which
appears so largely in all poetry and eloquence, and especially
in those of an early period of society, is the root of a great
part of our opinions. If—to employ a very familiar illustration—the most civilised and rational of mankind will
observe his own emotions, when by some accident he has
struck his head violently against a door-post, he will probably
find that his first exclamation was not merely of pain but of
anger, and of anger directed against the wood. In a moment
reason checks the emotion; but if he observes carefully his
own feelings, he may easily convince himself of the uncon

scious fetichism which is latent in his mind, and which, in
the case of a child or a savage, displays itself without
reserve. Man instinctively ascribes volition to whatever
powerfully affects him. The feebleness of his imagination
conspires with other causes to prevent an uncivilised man from
rising above the conception of an anthropomorphic Deity,
and the capricious or isolated acts of such a being form his
exact notion of miracles. The same feebleness of imagination
makes him clothe all intellectual tendencies, all conflicting
emotions, all forces, passions, or fancies, in material forms.
His mind naturally translates the conflict between opposing
feelings into a history of the combat between rival spirits.
A vast accumulation of myths is spontaneously formed—each
legend being merely the material expression of a moral fact.
The simple love of the wonderful, and the complete absence
of all critical spirit, aid the formation.

In this manner we find that in certain stages of society,
and under the action of the influences I have stated, an ac-
cretion of miraculous legends is naturally formed around
prominent personages or institutions. We look for them as
we look for showers in April, or for harvest in autumn. We
can very rarely show with any confidence the precise manner
in which a particular legend is created or the nucleus of
truth it contains, but we can analyse the general causes
that have impelled men towards the miraculous ; we can
show that these causes have never failed to produce the
effect, and we can trace the gradual alteration of mental
conditions invariably accompanying the decline of the belief.
When men are destitute of critical spirit, when the notion of
uniform law is yet unborn, and when their imaginations are
still incapable of rising to abstract ideas, histories of miracles
are always formed and always believed, and they continue to
flourish and to multiply until these conditions have altered.
Miracles cease when men cease to believe and to expect them.
In periods that are equally credulous, they multiply or

diminish in proportion to the intensity with which the imagination is directed to theological topics. A comparison of the
histories of the most different nations shows the mythical
period to have been common to all; and we may trace in
many quarters substantially the same miracles, though varied
by national characteristics, and with a certain local cast and
colouring. As among the Alps the same shower falls as rain
in the sunny valleys, and as snow among the lofty peaks, so
the same intellectual conceptions which in one moral latitude
take the form of nymphs, or fairies, or sportive legends, appear in another as dæmons or appalling apparitions. Sometimes we can discover the precise natural fact which the
superstition had misread. Thus, epilepsy, the phenomenon
of nightmare, and that form of madness which leads men
to imagine themselves transformed into some animal, are,
doubtless, the explanation of many tales of demoniacal possession, of incubi, and of lycanthropy. In other cases we may
detect a single error, such as the notion that the sky is close
to the earth, or that the sun revolves around the globe, which
had suggested the legend. But more frequently we can give
only a general explanation, enabling us to assign these legends
to their place, as the normal expression of a certain stage of
knowledge or intellectual power; and this explanation is
their refutation. We do not say that they are impossible, or
even that they are not authenticated by as much evidence as
many facts we believe. We only say that, in certain conditions of society, illusions of the kind inevitably appear. No
one can prove that there are no such things as ghosts; but if
a man whose brain is reeling with fever declares that he has
seen one, we have no great difficulty in forming an opinion
about his assertion.

The gradual decadence of miraculous narratives which
accompanies advancing civilisation may be chiefly traced to
three causes. The first is that general accuracy of observation
and of statement which all education tends more or less to

produce, which checks the amplifications of the undisciplined
imagination, and is speedily followed by a much stronger
moral feeling on the subject of truth than ever exists in a
r de civilisation. The second is an increased power of abstraction, which is likewise a result of general education, and
which, by correcting the early habit of personifying all phenomena, destroys one of the most prolific sources of legends,
and closes the mythical period of history. The third is the
progress of physical science, which gradually dispels that conception of a universe governed by perpetual and arbitrary
interference, from which, for the most part, these legends
originally sprang. The whole history of physical science is
one continued revelation of the reign of law. The same law
that governs the motions of a grain of dust, or the light of the
glowworm's lamp, is shown to preside over the march of the
most majestic planet or the fire of the most distant sun. Countless phenomena, which were for centuries universally believed
to be the results of spiritual agency, portents of calamity, or
acts of Divine vengeance, have been one by one explained, have
been shown to rise from blind physical causes, to be capable of
prediction, or amenable to human remedies. Forms of
madness which were for ages supposed to result from possession, are treated successfully in our hospitals. The advent of
the comet is predicted. The wire invented by the sceptic
Franklin defends the crosses on our churches from the lightning stroke of heaven. Whether we examine the course of
the planets or the world of the animalculæ; to whatever field
of physical nature our research is turned, the uniform,
invariable result of scientific enquiry is to show that even the
most apparently irregular and surprising phenomena are
governed by natural antecedents, and are parts of one great
connected system. From this vast concurrence of evidence,
from this uniformity of experience in so many spheres, there
arises in the minds of scientific men a conviction, amounting
to absolute moral certainty, that the whole course of physical

nature is governed by law, that the notion of the perpetual interference of the Deity with some particular classes of its phenomena is false and unscientific, and that the theological habit of interpreting the catastrophes of nature as Divine warnings or punishments, or disciplines, is a baseless and a pernicious superstition.

The effects of these discoveries upon miraculous legends are of various kinds. In the first place, a vast number which have clustered around the notion of the irregularity of some phenomenon which is proved to be regular—such as the innumerable accounts collected by the ancients to corroborate their opinion of the portentous nature of comets—are directly overthrown. In the next place, the revelation of the inter-dependence of phenomena greatly increases the improbability of some legends which it does not actually disprove. Thus, when men believed the sun to be simply a lamp revolving around and lighting our world, they had no great difficulty in believing that it was one day literally arrested in its course, to illuminate an army which was engaged in mas-sacring its enemies; but the case became different when it was perceived that the sun was the centre of a vast system of worlds, which a suspension of the earth's motion must have reduced to chaos, without a miracle extending through it all. Thus, again, the old belief that some animals became for the first time carnivorous in consequence of the sin of Adam, ap-peared tolerably simple so long as this revolution was sup-posed to be only a change of habits or of tastes; but it became more difficult of belief when it was shown to involve a change of teeth; and the difficulty was, I suppose, still further aggravated when it was proved that, every animal having digestive organs specially adapted to its food, these also must have been changed.

In the last place, physical science exercises a still wider influence by destroying what I have called the centre ideas out of which countless particular theories were evolved, of

which they were the natural expression, and upon which
their permanence depends. Proving that our world is not
the centre of the universe, but is a simple planet, revolving
with many others around a common sun ; proving that the
disturbances and sufferings of the world do not result from
an event which occurred but 6,000 years ago; that long
before that period the earth was dislocated by the most
fearful convulsions; that countless generations of sentient
animals, and also, as recent discoveries appear conclusively
to show, of men, not only lived but died ; proving, by an
immense accumulation of evidence, that the notion of a
universe governed by isolated acts of special intervention is
untrue—physical science had given new directions to the
currents of the imagination, supplied the judgment with new
measures of probability, and thus affected the whole circle of
our beliefs.

With most men, however, the transition is as yet but
imperfectly accomp'ished, and that part of physical nature
which science has hitherto failed to explain is regarded as a
sphere of special interposition. Thus, multitudes who recognise the fact that the celestial phenomena are subject to
inflexible law, imagine that the dispensation of rain is in
some sense the result of arbitrary interpositions, determined
by the conduct of mankind. Near the equator, it is true, it
is tolerably constant and capable of prediction ; but in proportion as we recede from the equator, the rainfall becomes more
variable, and consequently, in the eyes of some, supernatural, and although no scientific man has the faintest doubt
that it is governed by laws as inflexible as those which determine the motions of the planets, yet because, owing to the great
complexity of the determining causes, we are unable fully to
explain them, it is still customary to speak of 'plagues of
rain and water' sent on account of our sins, and of 'scarcity
and dearth, which we most justly suffer for our iniquity.'
Corresponding language is employed about the forms of

disease and death which science has but imperfectly explained. If men are employed in some profession which
compels them to inhale steel filings or noxious vapours, or if
they live in a pestilential marsh, the diseases that result
from these conditions are not regarded as a judgment or a
discipline, for the natural cause is obvious and decisive. But
if the conditions that produced the disease are very subtle
and very complicated; if physicians are incapable of tracing
with certainty its nature or its effects; if, above all, it
assumes the character of an epidemic, it is continually treated
as a Divine judgment. The presumption against this view
arises not only from the fact that, in exact proportion as
medical science advances, diseases are proved to be the necessary consequence of physical conditions, but also from many
characteristics of unexplained disease which unequivocally
prove it to be natural. Thus, cholera, which is frequently
treated according to the theological method, varies with the
conditions of temperature, is engendered by particular forms
of diet, follows the course of rivers, yields in some measure to
medical treatment, can be aggravated or mitigated by courses
of conduct that have no relation to vice or virtue, takes its
victims indiscriminately from all grades of morals or opinion.
Usually, when definite causes are assigned for a supposed
judgment,• they lead to consequences of the most grotesque
absurdity. Thus, when a deadly and mysterious disease fell
upon the cattle of England, some divines, not content with
treating it as a judgment, proceeded to trace it to certain
popular writings containing what were deemed heterodox
opinions about the Pentateuch, or about the eternity of punishment. It may be true that the disease was imported from
a country where such speculations are unknown; that the
authors objected to had no cattle; that the farmers, who
chiefly suffered by the disease, were for the most part absolutely unconscious of the existence of these books, and if they

knew them would have indignantly repudiated them; that the town populations, who chiefly read them, were only affected indirectly by a rise in the price of food, which falls with perfect impartiality upon the orthodox and upon the heterodox; that particular counties were peculiarly sufferers, without being at all conspicuous for their scepticism; that similar writings appeared in former periods, without cattle being in any respect the worse; and that, at the very period at which the plague was raging, other countries, in which far more audacious speculations were rife, enjoyed an absolute immunity. In the face of all these consequences, the theory has been confidently urged and warmly applauded.

It is not, I think, sufficiently observed how large a proportion of such questions are capable of a strictly inductive method of discussion. If it is said that plagues or pestilences are sent as a punishment of error or of vice, the assertion must be tested by a comprehensive examination of the history of plagues on the one hand, and of periods of great vice and heterodoxy on the other. If it be said that an influence more powerful than any military agency directs the course of battles, the action of this force must be detected as we would detect electricity, or any other force, by experiment. If the attribute of infallibility be ascribed to a particular Church, an inductive reasoner will not be content with enquiring how far an infallible Church would be a desirable thing, or how far certain ancient words may be construed as a prediction of its appearance; he will examine, by a wide and careful survey of ecclesiastical history, whether this Church has actually been immutable and consistent in its teaching, whether it has never been affected by the ignorance or the passion of the age; whether its influence has uniformly been exerted on the side which proved to be true; whether it has never supported by its authority scientific views which were afterwards demonstrated to be false, or countenanced and

consolidated popular errors, or thrown obstacles in the path
of those who were afterwards recognised as the enlighteners
of mankind. If ecclesiastical deliberations are said to be
specially inspired or directed by an illuminating and supernatural power, we should examine whether the councils and
convocations of clergymen exhibit a degree and harmony of
wisdom that cannot reasonably be accounted for by the play
of our unassisted faculties. If institutions are said to owe
their growth to special supernatural agencies, distinct from
the ordinary system of natural laws, we must examine
whether their courses are so striking and so peculiar that
natural laws fail to explain them. Whenever, as in the case
of a battle, very many influences concur to the result, it will
frequently happen that that result will baffle our predictions.
It will also happen that strange coincidences, such as the
frequent recurrence of the same number in a game of chance,
will occur. But there are limits to these variations from
what we regard as probable. If, in throwing the dice, we
uniformly attained the same number, or if in war the army
which was most destitute of all military advantages was uniformly victorious, we should readily infer that some special
cause was operating to produce the result. We must remember, too, that in every great historical crisis the prevalence
of either side will bring with it a long train of consequences,
and that we only see one side of the picture. If Hannibal,
after his victory at Cannæ, had captured and burnt Rome,
the vast series of results that have followed from the ascendancy of the Roman Empire would never have taken place,
but the supremacy of a maritime, commercial, and comparatively pacific power would have produced an entirely different
series, which would have formed the basis and been the
essential condition of all the subsequent progress ; a civilisation, the type and character of which it is now impossible to
conjecture, would have arisen, and its theologians would
probably have regarded the career of Hannibal as one

of the most manifest instances of special interposition on record.

If we would form sound opinions on these matters, we must take a very wide and impartial survey of the phenomena of history. We must examine whether events have tended in a given direction with a uniformity or a persistence that is not naturally explicable. We must examine not only the facts that corroborate our theory, but also those which oppose it.

That such a method is not ordinarily adopted must be manifest to all. As Bacon said, men 'mark the hits, but not the misses;' they collect industriously the examples in which many, and sometimes improbable, circumstances have converged to a result which they consider good, and they simply leave out of their consideration the circumstances that tend in the opposite direction. They expatiate with triumph upon the careers of emperors who have been the unconscious pioneers or agents in some great movement of human progress, but they do not dwell upon those whose genius was expended in a hopeless resistance, or upon those who, like Bajazet or Tamerlane, having inflicted incalculable evils upon mankind, passed away, leaving no enduring fruit behind them. A hundred missionaries start upon an enterprise, the success of which appears exceedingly improbable. Ninety-nine perish and are forgotten. One missionary succeeds, and his success is attributed to supernatural interference, because the probabilities were so greatly against him. It is observed that a long train of political or military events ensured the triumph of Protestantism in certain nations and periods. It is forgotten that another train of events destroyed the same faith in other lands, and paralysed the efforts of its noblest martyrs. We are told of showers of rain that followed public prayer; but we are not told how often prayers for rain proved abortive, or how much longer than usual the dry weather had already continued when they were offered.[1]   As the old philosopher observed, the votive tablets of those who escaped are suspended in the temple, while those who were shipwrecked are forgotten.

Unfortunately, these inconsistencies do not arise simply from intellectual causes. A feeling which was intended to be religious, but which was in truth deeply the reverse, once led men to shrink from examining the causes of some of the more terrible of physical phenomena, because it was thought that these should be deemed special instances of Divine interference, and should, therefore, be regarded as too sacred for investigation.[2] In the world of physical science this mode of thought has almost vanished, but a corresponding sentiment may be often detected in the common judgments of history. Very many well-meaning men—censuring the pursuit of truth in the name of the God of Truth—while they regard it as commendable and religious to collect facts illustrating

---

[1] The following is a good specimen of the language which may still be uttered, apparently without exciting any protest, from the pulpit in one of the great centres of English learning: ' But we have prayed, and not been heard, at least in this present visitation. Have we deserved to be heard ? In former visitations it was observed commonly how the cholera lessened from the day of the public humiliation. When we dreaded famine from long - continued drought, on the morning of our prayers the heaven over our head was of brass; the clear burning sky showed no token of change. Men looked with awe at its unmitigated clearness. In the evening was the cloud like a man's hand ; the relief was come.' (And then the author adds, in a note): ' This describes what I myself saw on the Sunday morning in

Oxford, on returning from the early communion at St. Mary's at eight. There was no visible change till the evening.'—Pusey's *Miracles of Prayer*, preached at Oxford, 1866.

[2] E.g. : 'A master of philosophy, travelling with others on the way, when a fearful thunderstorm arose, checked the fear of his fellows, and discoursed to them of the natural reasons of that uproar in the clouds, and those sudden flashes wherewith they seemed (out of the ignorance of causes) to be too much affrighted : in the midst of his philosophical discourse he was struck dead with the dreadful eruption which he slighted. What could this be but the finger of that God who will have his works rather entertained with wonder and trembling than with curious scanning ? '—Bishop Hall, *The Invisible World*, § vi.

or corroborating the theological theory of life, consider it irreverent and wrong to apply to those facts, and to that theory, the ordinary severity of inductive reasoning.

What I have written is not in any degree inconsistent with the belief that, by the dispensation of Providence, moral causes have a natural and often overwhelming influence upon happiness and upon success, nor yet with the belief that our moral nature enters into a very real, constant, and immediate contact with a higher power. Nor does it at all disprove the possibility of Divine interference with the order even of physical nature. A world governed by special acts of intervention, such as that which mediæval theologians imagined, is perfectly conceivable, though it is probable that most impartial enquirers will convince themselves that this is not the system of the planet we inhabit; and if any instance of such interference be sufficiently attested, it should not be rejected as intrinsically impossible. It is, however, the fundamental error of most writers on miracles, that they confine their attention to two points—the possibility of the fact, and the nature of the evidence. There is a third element, which in these questions is of capital importance : the predisposition of men in certain stages of society towards the miraculous, which is so strong that miraculous stories are then invariably circulated and credited, and which makes an amount of evidence that would be quite sufficient to establish a natural fact, altogether inadequate to establish a supernatural one. The positions for which I have been contending are that a perpetual interference of the Deity with the natural course of events is the earliest and simplest notion of miracles, and that this notion, which is implied in so many systems of belief, arose in part from an ignorance of the laws of nature, and in part also from an incapacity for inductive reasoning, which led men merely to collect facts coinciding with their preconceived opinions, without attending to those that were inconsistent with them. By this method there is no superstition that could not be defended. Volumes have been written giving perfectly authentic histories of wars, famines, and pestilences that followed the appearance of comets. There is not an cmen, not a prognostic, however childish, that has not, in the infinite variety of events, been occasionally veii fied, and to minds that are under the influence of a super stitious imagination these occasional verifications more than outweigh all the instances of error. Simple knowledge is wholly insufficient to correct the disease. No one is so firmly convinced of the reality of lucky and unlucky days, and of supernatural portents, as the sailor, who has spent his life ir watching the deep, and has learnt to read with almost unerring skill the promise of the clouds. No one is more persuaded of the superstitions about fortune than the habitual gambler. Sooner than abandon his theory, there is no extravagance of hypothesis to which the superstitious man will not resort. The ancients were convinced that dreams were usually supernatural. If the dream was verified, this was plainly a prophecy. If the event was the exact opposite of what the dream foreshadowed, the latter was still supernatural, for it was a recognised principle that dreams should sometimes be interpreted by contraries. If the dream bore no relation to subsequent events, unless it were transformed into a fantastic allegory, it was still supernatural, for allegory was one of the most ordinary forms of revelation. If no ingenuity of interpretation could find a prophetic meaning in a dream, its supernatural character was even then not necessarily destroyed; for Homer said there was a special portal through which deceptive visions passed into the mind, and the Fathers declared that it was one of the occupations of the dæmons to perplex and bewilder us with unmeaning dreams.

To estimate aright the force of the predisposition to the miraculous should be one of the first tasks of the enquirer into its reality; and no one, I think, can examine the subject with impartiality without arriving at the conclusion that in many periods of history it has been so strong as to accumulate around pure delusions an amount of evidence far greater than would be sufficient to establish even improbable natural facts. Through the entire duration of Pagan Rome, it was regarded as an unquestionable truth. established by the most ample experience, that prodigies of various kinds announced every memorable event, and that sacrifices had the power of mitigating or arresting calamity. In the Republic, the Senate itself officially verified and explained the prodigies.[1] In the Empire there is not an historian, from Tacitus down to the meanest writer in the Augustan history, who was not convinced that numerous prodigies foreshadowed the accession and death of every sovereign, and every great catastrophe that fell upon the people. Cicero could say with truth that there was not a single nation of antiquity, from the polished Greek to the rudest savage, which did not admit the existence of a real art enabling men to foretell the future, and that the splendid temples of the oracles, which for so many centuries commanded the reverence of mankind, sufficiently attested the intensity of the belief.[2] The reality of the witch miracles was established by a critical tribunal, which, however imperfect, was at least the most searching then existing in the world, by the judicial decisions of the law courts of every European country, supported by the unanimous voice of public opinion, and corroborated by the investigation of some of the ablest men during several centuries. The belief that the king's touch can cure scrofula flourished in the most brilliant periods of English history.[3] It was unshaken by

---

[1] Sir C. Lewis *On the Credibility of Roman Hist.* vol. i. p. 50.

[2] Cic. *De Divin.* lib. i. c. 1.

[3] 'The days on which the miracle [of the king's touch] was to be wrought were fixed at sittings of the Privy Council, and were solemnly notified by the clergy to all the parish churches of the realm. When the appointed time came, several divines in full canonicals stood round the canopy of state. The surgeon of the royal household introduced the sick. A

the most numerous and public experiments.   It was asserted
by the privy council, by the bishops of two religions, by the
general voice of the clergy in the palmiest days of the English Church, by the University of Oxford, and by the enthusiastic assent of the people.   It survived the ages of the
Reformation, of Bacon, of Milton, and of Hobbes.   It was
by no means extinct in the age of Locke, and would probably
have lasted still longer, had not the change of dynasty at the
Revolution assisted the tardy scepticism.[1]   Yet there is now

---

passage of Mark xvi. was read.
When the words "They shall lay
their hands on the sick and they
shall recover,"had been pronounced,
there was a pause and one of the
sick was brought to the king. His
Majesty stroked the ulcers. . . .
Then came the Epistle, &c. The
Service may still be found in the
Prayer Books of the reign of Anne.
Indeed, it was not until some time
after the accession of George I.
that the University of Oxford
ceased to reprint the office of healing, together with the Liturgy.
Theologians of eminent learning,
ability, and virtue gave the sanction of their authority to this
mummery, and, what is stranger
still, medical men of high note
believed, or affected to believe, it.
. . . Charles II., in the course of
his reign, touched near 100,000
persons. . . . In 1682 he performed the rite 8,500 times. In
1684 the throng was such that six
or seven of the sick were trampled
to death. James, in one of his
progresses, touched 800 persons in
the choir of the cathedral of Ches-
ter.'—Macaulay's *History of England*, c. xiv.
[1] One of the surgeons of Charles
II. named John Brown, whose
official duty it was to superintend

the ceremony, and who assures us
that he has witnessed many thousands touched, has written an extremely curious account of it,
called *Charisma Basilicon* (London,
1684).   This miraculous power
existed exclusively in the English
and French royal families, being
derived, in the first, from Edward
the Confessor, in the second, from
St. Lewis.   A surgeon attested
the reality of the disease before
the miracle was performed.   The
king hung a riband with a gold
coin round the neck of the person
touched; but Brown thinks the
gold, though possessing great virtue, was not essential to the cure.
He had known cases where the
cured person had sold, or ceased to
wear, the medal, and his disease
returned.   The gift was unimpaired by the Reformation, and an
obdurate Catholic was converted
on finding that Elizabeth, after
the Pope's excommunication, could
cure his scrofula. Francis I. cured
many persons when prisoner in
Spain. Charles I., when a prisoner,
cured a man by his simple benediction, the Puritans not permitting
him to touch him. His blood had
the same efficacy ; and Charles II.,
when an exile in the Netherlands,
still retained it. There were, how-

scarcely an educated man who will defend these miracles. Considered abstractedly, indeed, it is perfectly conceivable that Providence might have announced coming events by prodigies, or imparted to some one a miraculous power, or permitted evil spirits to exist among mankind and assist them in their enterprises.   The evidence establishing these miracles is cumulative, and it is immeasurably greater than the evidence of many natural facts, such as the earthquakes at Antioch, which no one would dream of questioning. We disbelieve the miracles, because an overwhelming experience proves that in certain intellectual conditions, and under the influence of certain errors which we are enabled to trace, superstitions of this order invariably appear and flourish, and that, when these intellectual conditions have passed, the prodigies as invariably cease, and the whole fabric of superstition melts silently away.

It is extremely difficult for an ordinary man, who is little conversant with the writings of the past, and who unconsciously transfers to other ages the critical spirit of his own, to realise the fact that histories of the most grotesquely extravagant nature could, during the space of many centuries, be continually propounded without either provoking the smallest question or possessing the smallest truth.   We may, however, understand something of this credulity when we remember the diversion of the ancient mind from physical science to speculative

---

ever, some 'Atheists, Sadducees, and ill-conditioned Pharisees' who even then disbelieved it; and Brown gives the letter of one who went, a complete sceptic, to satisfy his friends, and came away cured and converted.   It was popularly, but Brown says erroneously, believed that the touch was peculiarly efficacious on Good Friday.   An official register was kept, for every month in the reign of Charles II., of the persons touched, but two years and a half appear to be wanting. The smallest number touched in one year was 2,983 (in 1669); the total, in the whole reign, 92,107. Brown gives numbers of specific cases with great detail. Shakspeare has noticed the power (*Macbeth*, Act iv. Scene 3). Dr. Johnson, when a boy, was touched by Queen Anne; but at that time few persons, except Jaccbites, believed the miracle.

philosophy; the want of the many checks upon error which printing affords; the complete absence of that habit of cautious, experimental research which Bacon and his contemporaries infused into modern philosophy; and, in Christian times, the theological notion that the spirit of belief is a virtue, and the spirit of scepticism a sin.   We must remember, too, that before men had found the key to the motions of the heavenly bodies—before the false theory of the vortices and the true theory of gravitation—when the multitude of apparently capricious phenomena was very great, the notion that the world was governed by distinct and isolated influences was that which appeared most probable even to the most rational intellect.   In such a condition of knowledge—which was that of the most enlightened days of the Roman Empire— the hypothesis of universal law was justly regarded as a rash and premature generalisation.   Every enquirer was confronted with innumerable phenomena that were deemed plainly miraculous.   When Lucretius sought to banish the supernatural from the universe, he was compelled to employ much ingenuity in endeavouring to explain, by a natural law, why a miraculous fountain near the temple of Jupiter Ammon was hot by night and cold by day, and why the temperature of wells was higher in winter than in summer.[1] Eclipses were supposed by the populace to foreshadow calamity; but the Roman soldiers believed that by beating drums and cymbals they could cause the moon's disc to regain its brightness.[2]   In obedience to dreams, the great Emperor

---

[1] Lucretius, lib. vi.   The poet says there are certain seeds of fire in the earth, around the water, which the sun attracts to itself, but which the cold of the night represses, and forces back upon the water.

The fountain of Jupiter Ammon, and many others that were deemed miraculous, are noticed by Pliny, *Hist. Nat.* ii. 106.

'Fly not yet; the fount that played
In times of old through Ammon's
      shade,
Though icy cold by day it ran,
Yet still, like souls of mirth, began
To burn when night was near.'---
      Moore's *Melodies.*

[2] Tacit. *Annal.* i. 28.   Long afterwards, the people of Turin were accustomed to greet every

Augustus went begging money through the streets of Rome,[1] and the historian who records the act himself wrote to Pliny, entreating the postponement of a trial.[2] The stroke of the lightning was an augury,[3] and its menace was directed especially against the great, who cowered in abject terror during a thunder-storm. Augustus used to guard himself against thunder by wearing the skin of a sea-calf.[4] Tiberius, who professed to be a complete freethinker, had greater faith in laurel leaves.[5] Caligula was accustomed during a thunder-storm to creep beneath his bed.[6] During the games in honour of Julius Cæsar, a comet appearing for seven days in the sky, the people believed it to be the soul of the dead,[7] and a temple was erected in its honour.[8] Sometimes we find this credulity broken by curious inconsistencies of belief, or semi-rationalistic explanations. Livy, who relates with perfect faith innumerable prodigies, has observed, never-

---

eclipse with loud cries, and St. Maximus of Turin energetically combated their superstition. (Ceillier, *Hist. des Auteurs sacrés*, tome xiv. p. 607.)

[1] Suet. *Aug.* xci.

[2] See the answer of the younger Pliny (*Ep.* i. 18), suggesting that dreams should often be interpreted by contraries. A great many instances of dreams that were believed to have been verified are given in Cic. (*De Divinatione*, lib. i.) and Valerius Maximus (lib. i. c. vii.). Marcus Aurelius (Capitolinus) was said to have appeared to many persons after his death in dreams, and predicted the future.

[3] The augurs had noted eleven kinds of lightning with different significations. (Pliny, *Hist. Nat.* ii. 53.) Pliny says all nations agree in clapping their hands when it lightens (xxviii. 5). Cicero very shrewdly remarked that the

Roman considered lightning a good omen when it shone upon his left, while the Greeks and barbarians believed it to be auspicious when it was upon the right. (Cic. *De Divinat.* ii. 39.) When Constantine prohibited all other forms of magic, he especially authorised that which was intended to avert hail and lightning. (*Cod. Theod.* lib. ix. tit. xvi. l. 3.)

[4] Suet. *Aug.* xc.

[5] Ibid. *Tiber.* lxix. The virtue of laurel leaves, and of the skin of a sea-calf, as preservatives against lightning, are noticed by Pliny (*Hist. Nat.* ii. 56), who also says (xv. 40) that the laurel leaf is believed to have a natural antipathy to fire, which it shows by its angry crackling when in contact with that element.

[6] Suet. *Calig.* ii.

[7] Suet. *Jul. Cæs.* lxxxviii.

[8] Plin. *Hist. Nat.* ii. 23.

theless, that the more prodigies are believed, the more they
are announced.[1] Those who admitted most fully the reality
of the oracles occasionally represented them as natural,
contending that a prophetic faculty was innate in all men,
though dormant in most; that it might be quickened into
action by sleep, by a pure and ascetic life, or in the prostra-
tion that precedes death, or in the delirium produced by
certain vapours; and that the gradual enfeebling of the last
was the cause of the cessation of the oracles.[2] Earthquakes

---

[1] 'Prodigia eo anno multa nun-
tiata sunt, quæ quo magis credebant simplices ac religiosi homines
eo plura nuntiabantur' (xxiv. 10).
Compare with this the remark of
Cicero on the oracles: 'Quando
autem illa vis evanuit? An postquam homines minus creduli esse
cœperunt?' (De Div. ii. 57.)

[2] This theory, which is developed at length by the Stoic, in
the first book of the De Divinatione of Cicero, grew out of the
pantheistic notion that the human
soul is a part of the Deity, and
therefore by nature a participator
in the Divine attribute of prescience.
The soul, however, was crushed by
the weight of the body; and there
were two ways of evoking its prescience—the ascetic way, which
attenuates the body, and the magical way, which stimulates the
soul. Apollonius declared that
his power of prophecy was not due
to magic, but solely to his abstinence from animal food. (Philost.
Ap. of Tyana, viii. 5.) Among
those who believed the oracles,
there were two theories. The first
was that they were inspired by
dæmons or spirits of a degree lower
than the gods. The second was,
that they were due to the action
of certain vapours which emanated
from the taverns beneath the

temples, and which, by throwing
the priestess into a state of delirium, evoked her prophetic
powers. The first theory was that
of the Platonists, and it was
adopted by the Christians, who,
however, changed the signification
of the word dæmon. The second
theory, which appears to be due
to Aristotle (Baltus, Réponse à
l'Histoire des Oracles, p. 132), is
noticed by Cic. De Div. i. 19; Plin.
H. N. ii. 95; and others. It is
closely allied to the modern belief
in clairvoyance. Plutarch, in his
treatise on the decline of the oracles,
attributes that decline sometimes to
the death of the dæmons (who were
believed to be mortal), and sometimes to the exhaustion of the
vapours. The oracles themselves,
according to Porphyry (Fontenelle,
Hist. des Oracles, pp. 220–222, first
ed.), attributed it to the second
cause. Iamblichus (De Myst. § iii.
c. xi.) combines both theories, and
both are very clearly stated in the
following curious passage: 'Quam-
quam Platoni credam inter deos
atque homines, natura et loco
medias quasdam divorum potes-
tates intersitas, easque divinai iones
cunctas et magorum miracula
gubernare. Quin et illud mecum
reputo, posse animum humanum,
præsertim, puerilem et simplicem,

were believed to result from supernatural interpositions, and
to call for expiatory sacrifices, but at the same time they
had direct natural antecedents. The Greeks believed that
they were caused by subterranean waters, and they accordingly sacrificed to Poseidon. The Romans were uncertain as
to their physical antecedents, and therefore inscribed no
name on the altar of expiation.[1] Pythagoras is said to have
attributed them to the strugglings of the dead.[2] Pliny,
after a long discussion, decided that they were produced by
air forcing itself through fissures of the earth, but he immediately proceeds to assert that they are invariably the
precursors of calamity.[3] The same writer, having recounted
the triumph of astronomers in predicting and explaining
eclipses, bursts into an eloquent apostrophe to those great
men who had thus reclaimed man from the dominion of
superstition, and in high and enthusiastic terms urges them
to pursue still further their labour in breaking the thraldom
of ignorance.[4] A few chapters later he professes his unhesi-
tating belief in the ominous character of comets.[5] The
notions, too, of magic and astrology, were detached from all
theological belief, and might be found among many who were
absolute atheists.[6]

These few examples will be sufficient to show how fully
the Roman soil was prepared for the reception of miraculous
histories, even after the writings of Cicero and Seneca, in the

seu carminum avocamento, sive
odorum delenimento, soporari, et
ad oblivionem præsentium exter-
nari: et paulisper remota corporis
memoria, redigi ac redire ad naturam suam, quæ est immortalis
scilicet et divina; atque ita veluti
quodam sopore futura rerum præ-
sagire.'—Apuleius, *Apolog.*
[1] Aul. Gell. *Noct.* ii. 28. Florus,
however (*Hist.* i. 19), mentions a
Roman general appeasing the goddess Earth on the occasion of an

earthquake that occurred during a
battle.
[2] Ælian, *Hist. Var.* iv. 17.
[3] *Hist. Nat.* ii. 81–86.
[4] Ibid. ii. 9.
[5] Ibid. ii. 23.
[6] I have referred in the last
chapter to a striking passage of
Am. Marcellinus on this combination. The reader may find some
curious instances of the superstitions of Roman sceptics in Cham
pagry, *Les Antonins*, tome iii. p. 46

brilliant days of Augustus and the Antonines. The feebleness of the uncultivated mind, which cannot rise above
material conceptions, had indeed passed away, the legends of
the popular theology had lost all power over the educated,
but at the same time an absolute ignorance of physical science
and of inductive reasoning remained. The facility of belief
that was manifested by some of the most eminent men,
even on matters that were not deemed supernatural, can only
be realised by those who have an intimate acquaintance with
their works. Thus, to give but a few examples, that great
naturalist whom I have so often cited tells us with the utmost gravity how the fiercest lion trembles at the crowing of
a cock ; [1] how elephants celebrate their religious ceremonies ; [2]
how the stag draws serpents by its breath from their holes,
and then tramples them to death ; [3] how the salamander is
so deadly that the food cooked in water, or the fruit grown
on trees it has touched, are fatal to man ; [4] how, when a ship
is flying before so fierce a tempest that no anchors or chains
can hold it, if only the remora or echinus fastens on its keel,
it is arrested in its course, and remains motionless and rooted
among the waves.[5] On matters that would appear the most
easily verified, he is equally confident. Thus, the human
saliva, he assures us, has many mysterious properties. If a
man, especially when fasting, spits into the throat of a serpent, it is said that the animal speedily dies.[6] It is certain
that to anoint the eyes with spittle is a sovereign remedy
against ophthalmia.[7] If a pugilist, having struck his adversary, spits into his own hand, the pain he caused instantly

---

[1] viii. 19. This is also mentioned by Lucretius.

[2] viii. 1.

[3] viii. 50. This was one of the
reasons why the early Christians
sometimes adopted the stag as a
symbol of Christ.

[4] xxix. 23.

[5] xxxii. 1.

[6] vii. 2.

[7] xxviii. 7. The blind man
restored to sight by Vespasian was
cured by anointing his eyes with
spittle. (Suet. *Vesp.* 7 ; Tacit.
Hist. iv. 81.)

ceases. If he spits into his hand before striking, the blow is the more severe.[1] Aristotle, the greatest naturalist of Greece, had observed that it was a curious fact that on the sea-shore no animal ever dies except during the ebbing of the tide. Several centuries later, Pliny, the greatest naturalist of an empire that was washed by many tidal seas, directed his attention to this statement. He declared that, after careful observations which had been made in Gaul, it had been found to be inaccurate, for what Aristotle stated of all animals was in fact only true of man.[2] It was in 1727 and the two following years, that scientific observations made at Rochefort and at Brest finally dissipated the delusion.[3]

Volumes might be filled with illustrations of how readily, in the most enlightened days of the Roman Empire, strange, and especially miraculous, tales were believed, even under circumstances that would appear to give every facility for the detection of the imposture. In the field of the supernatural, however, it should be remembered that a movement, which I have traced in the last chapter, had produced a very exceptional amount of credulity during the century and a half that preceded the conversion of Constantine. Neither the writings of Cicero and Seneca, nor even those of Pliny and Plutarch, can be regarded as fair samples of the belief of the educated. The Epicurean philosophy which rejected, the Academic philosophy which doubted, and the Stoic philosophy which simplified and sublimated superstition, had alike disappeared. The ' Meditations ' of Marcus Aurelius closed the period of Stoical influence, and the ' Dialogues ' of Lucian were the last solitary protest of expiring scepticism.[4] The aim of the philosophy of Cicero had been to ascertain truth

---

[1] Ibid. The custom of spitting in the hand before striking still exists among pugilists.

[2] ii. 101.

[3] Legendre, *Traité de l' Opinion*, tome ii. p. 17. The superstition is, however, said still to linger in many sea-coast towns.

[4] Lucian is believed to have died about two years before Marcus Aurelius.

by the free exercise of the critical powers. The aim of the
Pythagorean philosophy was to attain the state of ecstasy,
and to purify the mind by religious rites. Every philosopher
soon plunged into magical practices, and was encircled, in the
eyes of his disciples, with a halo of legend. Apollonius of
Tyana, whom the Pagans opposed to Christ, had raised the
dead, healed the sick, cast out devils, freed a young man from
a lamia or vampire with whom he was enamoured, prophesied,
seen in one country events that were occurring in another,
and filled the world with the fame of his miracles and of his
sanctity.[1] A similar power, notwithstanding his own dis-
claimer, was popularly attributed to the Platonist Apuleius.[2]

---

[1] See his very curious Life by
Philostratus. This Life was written at the request of Julia Domna,
the wife of Septimus Severus,
whether or not with the intention
of opposing the Gospel narrative is
a question still fiercely discussed.
Among the most recent Church
historians, Pressensé maintains the
affirmative, and Neander the negative. Apollonius was born at nearly
the same time as Christ, but out-
lived Domitian. The traces of his
influence are widely spread through
the literature of the empire.
Eunapius calls him ''Aπολλώνιος ὁ
ἐκ Τυάνων, οὐκέτι φιλόσοφος ἀλλ'
ἦν τι θεῶν τε καὶ ἀνθρώπου μέσον.'
—Lives of the Sophists. Xiphilin
relates (lxvii. 18) the story, told
also by Philostratus, how Apollonius, being at Ephesus, saw the
assassination of Domitian at Rome.
Alexander Severus placed (Lampridius Severus) the statue of
Apollonius with those of Orpheus,
Abraham, and Christ, for worship
in his oratory. Aurelian was reported to have been diverted from
his intention of destroying Tyana
by the ghost of the philosopher,
who appeared in his tent, rebuked
him, and saved the city (Vopiscus,
Aurelian); and, lastly, the Pagan
philosopher Hierocles wrote a book
opposing Apollonius to Christ,
which was answered by Eusebius.
The Fathers of the fourth century
always spoke of him as a great
magician. Some curious passages
on the subject are collected by M
Chassang, in the introduction to
his French translation of the work
of Philostratus.

[2] See his defence against the
charge of magic. Apuleius, who
was at once a brilliant rhetorician,
the writer of an extremely curious
novel (The Metamorphoses, or
Golden Ass), and of many other
works, and an indefatigable student
of the religious mysteries of his time,
lived through the reigns of Hadrian
and his two successors. After his
death his fame was for about a century apparently eclipsed; and it
has been noticed as very remarkable that Tertullian, who lived a
generation after Apuleius, and who,
like him, was a Carthaginian, has
never even mentioned him. During
the fourth century his reputation re-

Lucian has left us a detailed account of the impostures by which the philosopher Alexander endeavoured to acquire the fame of a miracle-worker.[1]   When a magician plotted against Plotinus, his spells recoiled miraculously against himself; and when an Egyptian priest endeavoured by incantations to evoke the guardian dæmon of the philosopher, instead of a dæmon the temple of Isis was irradiated by the presence of a god.[2] Porphyry was said to have expelled an evil dæmon from a bath.[3]   It was reported among his disciples that when Iamblichus prayed he was raised (like the saints of another creed) ten cubits from the ground, and that his body and his dress assumed a golden hue.[4]   It was well known that he had at Gadara drawn forth from the waters of two fountains their guardian spirits, and exhibited them in bodily form to his disciples.[5]   A woman named Sospitra had been visited by two spirits under the form of aged Chaldeans, and had been endowed with a transcendent beauty and with a superhuman knowledge.   Raised above all human frailties, save only love and death, she was able to see at once the deeds which were done in every land, and the people, dazzled by her beauty and her wisdom, ascribed to her a share of the omnipresence of the Deity.[6]

Christianity floated into the Roman Empire on the wave of credulity that brought with it this long train of Oriental

---

vived, and Lactantius, St. Jerome, and St. Augustine relate that many miracles were attributed to him, and that he was placed by the Pagans on a level with Christ, and regarded by some as even a greater magician.   See the sketch of his life by M. Bétoland prefixed to the Panckoucke edition of his works.

[1] *Life of Alexander*. There is an extremely curious picture of the religious jugglers, who were wandering about the Empire, in the eighth and ninth books of the *Metamorphoses* of Apuleius.   See, too, Juvenal, *Sat.* vi. 510–585.

[2] Porphyry's *Life of Plotinus*.

[3] Eunapius, *Porph.*

[4] Ibid. *Iamb.*   Iamblichus himself only laughed at the report.

[5] Eunapius, *Iamb.*

[6] See her life in Eunapius, *Œdescus.* Ælian and the rhetorician Aristides are also full of the wildest prodigies.   There is an interesting dissertation on this subject in Friedlænder (*Trad. Franc.* tome iv. p. 177–186).

superstitions and legends.   In its moral aspect it was broadly
distinguished from the systems around it, but its miracles
were accepted by both friend and foe as the ordinary accompaniments of religious teaching.   The Jews, in the eyes of
the Pagans, had long been proverbial for their credulity,[1] and
the Christians inherited a double measure of their reputation.
Nor is it possible to deny that in the matter of the miraculous the reputation was deserved.   Among the Pagans the
theory of Euhemerus, who believed the gods to be but deified
men, had been the stronghold of the Sceptics, while the
Platonic notion of dæmons was adopted by the more believing
philosophers.   The Christian teachers combined both theories,
maintaining that deceased kings had originally supplied the
names of the deities, but that malevolent dæmons had taken
their places ; and without a single exception the Fathers
maintained the reality of the Pagan miracles as fully as their
own.[2]   The oracles, as we have seen, had been ridiculed and
rejected by numbers of the philosophers, but the Christians
unanimously admitted their reality.   They appealed to a long
series of oracles as predictions of their faith ; and there is, I
believe, no example of the denial of their supernatural character in the Christian Church till 1696, when a Dutch
Anabaptist minister named Van Dale, in a remarkable book,[3]

---

[1] 'Credat   Judæus   Apella.'—
Hor. Sat. v. 100.

[2] This appears from all the
writings of the Fathers.   There
were, however, two forms of Pagan
miracles about which there was
some hesitation in the early Church
—the beneficent miracle of healing and the miracle of prophecy.
Concerning the first, the common
opinion was that the dæmons only
cured diseases they had themselves
caused, or that, at least, if they ever
(in order to enthral men more effectually) cured purely natural dis

eases, they did it by natural means,
which their superior knowledge
and power placed at their disposal.
Concerning prophecy, it was the
opinion of some of the Fathers that
intuitive prescience was a Divine
prerogative, and that the prescience
of the dæmons was only acquired
by observation.   Their immense
knowledge enabled them to forecast
events to a degree far transcending human faculties, and they employed this power in the oracles.

[3] De Origine ac Progressu Idola
triæ (Amsterdam).

which was abridged and translated by Fontenelle, asserted, in opposition to the unanimous voice of ecclesiastical authority, that they were simple impostures—a theory which is now almost universally accepted. To suppose that men who held these opinions were capable, in the second or third centuries, of ascertaining with any degree of just confidence whether miracles had taken place in Judæa in the first century, is grossly absurd; nor would the conviction of their reality have made any great impression on their minds at a time when miracles were supposed to be so abundantly diffused.

In truth, the question of the reality of the Jewish miracles must be carefully distinguished from that of the conversion of the Roman Empire. With the light that is furnished to us by modern investigations and habits of thought, we weigh the testimony of the Jewish writers; but most of the more judicious of modern apologists, considering the extreme credulity of the Jewish people, decline to make the question simply one of evidence, and occupy themselves chiefly in endeavouring to show that miracles are possible, that those recorded in the Biblical narratives are related in such a manner, and are so interwoven with the texture of a simple and artless narrative, as to carry with them an internal proof of their reality; that they differ in kind from later miracles, and especially that the character and destinies of Christianity are such as to render its miraculous origin antecedently probable. But in the ages when the Roman Empire was chiefly converted, all sound and discriminating historical investigation of the evidence of the early miracles was impossible, nor was any large use made of those miracles as proofs of the religion. The rhetorician Arnobius is probably the only one of the early apologists who gives, among the evidences of the faith, any prominent place to the miracles of Christ.[1] When

---

[1] This characteristic of early Christian apology is forcibly exhibited by Pressensé, *Hist. des trois premiers Siècles*, 2ᵐᵉ série, tome ii.

evidential reasoning was employed, it was usually an appeal
not to miracles, but to prophecy. But here again the opinions
of the patristic age must be pronounced absolutely worthless.
To prove that events had taken place in Judæa, accurately
corresponding with the prophecies, or that the prophecies
were themselves genuine, were both tasks far transcending
the critical powers of the Roman converts. The wild extravagance of fantastic allegory, commonly connected with
Origen, but which appears at a much earlier date in the
writings of Justin Martyr and Irenæus, had thrown the interpretation of prophecy into hopeless confusion, while the
deliberate and apparently perfectly unscrupulous forgery of a
whole literature, destined to further the propagation either
of Christianity as a whole, or of some particular class of
tenets that had arisen within its border,[1] made criticism at
once pre-eminently difficult and necessary. A long series of
oracles were cited, predicting in detail the sufferings of Christ.
The prophecies forged by the Christians, and attributed by
them to the heathen Sibyls, were accepted as genuine by the
entire Church, and were continually appealed to as among
the most powerful evidences of the faith. Justin Martyr
declared that it was by the instigation of dæmons that it had
been made a capital offence to read them.[2] Clement of
Alexandria preserved the tradition that St. Paul had urged
the brethren to study them.[3] Celsus designated the Christians
Sibyllists, on account of the pertinacity with which they insisted upon them.[4] Constantine the Great adduced them in
a solemn speech before the Council of Nice.[5] St. Augustine
notices that the Greek word for a fish, which, containing the
initial letters of the name and titles of Christ, had been

---

[1] The immense number of these
forged writings is noticed by all
candid historians, and there is, I
believe, only one instance of any
attempt being made to prevent
this pious fraud. A priest was degraded for having forged some
voyages of St. Paul and St. Thecla.
(Tert. *De Baptismo*, 17.)
[2] *Apol*. i.   [3] *Strom*. vi. c. 5.
[4] Origen, *Cont. Cels.* v.
[5] *Oratio* (apud Euseb.) xviii.

adopted by the Early Church as its sacred symbol, contains also the initial letters of some prophetic lines ascribed to the Sibyl of Erythra.[1] The Pagans, it is true, accused their opponents of having forged or interpolated these prophecies;[2] but there was not a single Christian writer of the patristic period who disputed their authority, and there were very few even of the most illustrious who did not appeal to them. Unanimously admitted by the Church of the Fathers, they were unanimously admitted during the middle ages, and an allusion to them passed into the most beautiful lyric of the Missal. It was only at the period of the Reformation that the great but unhappy Castellio pointed out many passages in them which could not possibly be genuine. He was followed, in the first years of the seventeenth century, by a Jesuit named Possevin, who observed that the Sibyls were known to have lived at a later period than Moses, and that many passages in the Sibylline books purported to have been written before Moses. Those passages, therefore, he said, were interpolated; and he added, with a characteristic sagacity, that they had doubtless been inserted by Satan, for the purpose of throwing suspicion upon the books.[3] It was in 1649 that a French Protestant minister, named Blondel, ventured for the first time in the Christian Church to denounce these writings as deliberate and clumsy forgeries, and after much angry controversy his sentiment has acquired an almost undisputed ascendancy in criticism.

But although the opinion of the Roman converts was extremely worthless, when dealing with past history or with literary criticism, there was one branch of miracles concerning which their position was somewhat different. Contem-

---

[1] *De Civ. Dei*, xviii. 23.

[2] Constantine, *Oratio* xix. 'His testimoniis quidam revicti solent eo confugere ut aiant non esse illa carmina Sibyllina, sed a nostris conficta atque composita.'—Lactant. *Div. Inst.* iv. 15.

[3] Antonius Possevinus, *Apparatus Sacer* (1606), verb. 'Sibylla.'

porary miracles, often of the most extraordinary cnaracter, but usually of the nature of visions, exorcisms, or healing the sick, were from the time of Justin Martyr uniformly represented by the Fathers as existing among them,[1] and they continue steadily along the path of history, till in the pages of Evagrius and Theodoret, in the Lives of Hilarion and Paul, by St. Jerome, of Antony, by St. Athanasius, and of Gregory Thaumaturgus, by his namesake of Nyssa, and in the Dialogues of St. Gregory the Great, they attain as grotesque an extravagance as the wildest mediæval legends. Few things are more striking than the assertions hazarded on this matter by some of the ablest of the Fathers. Thus, St. Irenæus assures us that all Christians possessed the power of working miracles; that they prophesied, cast out devils, healed the sick, and sometimes even raised the dead; that some who had been thus resuscitated lived for many years among them, and that it would be impossible to reckon the wonderful acts that were daily performed.[2] St. Epiphanius tells us that some rivers and fountains were annually transformed into wine, in attestation of the miracle of Cana; and he adds that he had himself drunk of one of these fountains, and his brethren of another.[3] St. Augustine notices that miracles were less frequent and less widely known than formerly, but that many still occurred, and some of them he had himself witnessed. Whenever a miracle was reported, he ordered that a special examination into its circumstances should be made, and that the depositions of the witnesses should be read publicly to the people. He tells us, besides many other miracles, that Gamaliel in a dream revealed to a priest named Lucianus the place where the bones of St. Stephen were buried; that those bones, being thus discovered, were brought to Hippo, the diocese of which St. Augustine was bishop; that they raised

---

[1] This subject is fully treated by Middleton in his *Free Enquiry*, whom I have closely followed.

[2] Irenæus, *Contr. Hæres.* ii. 32

[3] Epiphan. *Adv. Hæres.* ii. 30.

five dead persons to life ; and that, although only a portion
of the miraculous cures they effected had been registered, the
certificates drawn up in two years in the diocese, and by the
orders of the saint, were nearly seventy. In the adjoining
diocese of Calama they were incomparably more numerous.[1]
In the height of the great conflict between St. Ambrose and
the Arian Empress Justina, the saint declared that it had
been revealed to him by an irresistible presentiment—or, as
St. Augustine, who was present on the occasion, says, in a
dream—that relics were buried in a spot which he indicated.
The earth being removed, a tomb was found filled with blood,
and containing two gigantic skeletons, with their heads
severed from their bodies, which were pronounced to be those
of St. Gervasius and St. Protasius, two martyrs of remarkable physical dimensions, who were said to have suffered about
300 years before. To prove that they were genuine relics, the
bones were brought in contact with a blind man, who was
restored to sight, and with demoniacs, who were cured; the
dæmons, however, in the first place, acknowledging that the
relics were genuine; that St. Ambrose was the deadly enemy
of the powers of hell ; that the Trinitarian doctrine was true ;
and that those who rejected it would infallibly be damned.
The next day St. Ambrose delivered an invective against all
who questioned the miracle. St. Augustine recorded it in
his works, and spread the worship of the saints through
Africa. The transport of enthusiasm with which the miracles
were greeted at Milan enabled St. Ambrose to overcome
every obstacle ; but the Arians treated them with a derisive
incredulity, and declared that the pretended demoniacs had
been bribed by the saint.[2]

Statements of this kind, which are selected from very

St. Aug. *De Civ. Dei*, xxii. 8.
[2] This history is related by St.
Ambrose in a letter to his sister
Marcellina ; by St. Paulinus of
Nola, in his *Life of Ambrose ;* and
by St. Augustine, *De Civ. Dei*, xxii.
8 ; *Confess.* ix. 7.

many tnat are equally positive, though not equally precise.
suggest veins of thought of obvious interest and importance.
We are now, however, only concerned with the fact, that,
with the exception of one or two isolated miracles, such
as the last I have noticed, and of one class of miracles
which I shall proceed to describe, these prodigies, whether
true or false, were wrought for the exclusive edification of
confirmed believers. The exceptional miracles were those of
exorcism, which occupied a very singular position in the early
Church. The belief that certain diseases were inflicted by
Divine agency was familiar to the ancients, but among the
early Greeks the notion of diabolical possession appears to
have been unknown. A dæmon, in the philosophy of Plato,
though inferior to·a deity, was not an evil spirit, and it is extremely doubtful whether the existence of evil dæmons was
known either to the Greeks or Romans till about the time of
the advent of Christ.[1] The belief was introduced with the
Oriental superstitions which then poured into Rome, and it
brought in its train the notions of possession and exorcism.
The Jews, who in their own country appear to have regarded
it as a most ordinary occurrence to meet men walking about
visibly possessed by devils, and who professed to have learnt
from Solomon the means of expelling them, soon became the
principal exorcists, accomplishing their feats partly by adjuration, and partly by means of a certain miraculous root
named Baaras. Josephus assures us that he had himself, in
the reign of Vespasian, seen a Jew named Eleazar drawing
by these means a dæmon through the nostrils of a possessed
person, who fell to the ground on the accomplishment of the
miracle ; while, upon the command of the magician, the

---

[1] Plutarch thought they were
known by Plato, but this opinion
has been much questioned. See a
very learned discussion on the subject in Farmer's *Dissertation on*
Miracles, pp. 129–140; and Fontenelle, *Hist. des Oracles*, pp. 23,
27. Porphyry speaks much of evil
dæmons.

devil, to prove that it had really left his victim, threw down
a cup of water which had been placed at a distance.[1] The
growth of Neoplatonism and kindred philosophies greatly
strengthened the belief, and some of the later philosophers,
as well as many religious charlatans, practised exorcism.
But, of all classes, the Christians became in this respect the
most famous. From the time of Justin Martyr, for about
two centuries, there is, I believe, not a single Christian
writer who does not solemnly and explicitly assert the reality
and frequent employment of this power;[2] and although, after
the Council of Laodicea, the instances became less numerous,
they by no means ceased. The Christians fully recognised
the supernatural power possessed by the Jewish and Gentile
exorcists, but they claimed to be in many respects their
superiors. By the simple sign of the cross, or by repeating
the name of their Master, they professed to be able to cast
out devils which had resisted all the enchantments of Pagan

---

[1] Josephus, *Antiq.* viii. 2, § 5.

[2] This very curious subject is
fully treated by Baltus (*Réponse à
l'Histoire des Oracles*, Strasburg,
1707, published anonymously in
reply to Van Dale and Fontenelle), who believed in the reality
of the Pagan as well as the
patristic miracles; by Bingham
(*Antiquities of the Christian Church*,
vol. i. pp. 316–324), who thinks
the Pagan and Jewish exorcists
were impostors, but not the Christians; and by Middleton (*Free
Enquiry*, pp. 80–93), who disbe-
lieves in all the exorcists after the
apostolic times. It has also been
the subject of a special controversy in England, carried on by
Dodwell, Church, Farmer, and
others. Archdeacon Church says:
'If we cannot vindicate them [the
Fathers of the first three centuries]
on this article, their credit must
be lost for ever; and we must be
obliged to decline all further defence of them. It is impossible
for any words more strongly to ex
press a claim to this miracle than
those used by all the best writers
of the second and third centuries.'
—*Vindication of the Miracles of
the First Three Centuries*, p. 199.
So, also, Baltus: 'De tous les
anciens auteurs ecclésiastiques,
n'y en ayant pas un qui n'ait parlé
de ce pouvoir admirable que les
Chrétiens avoient de chasser les
démons' (p. 296). Gregory of
Tours describes exorcism as sufficiently common in his time, and
mentions having himself seen a
monk named Julian cure by his
words a possessed person. (*Hist.*
iv. 32.)

exorcists, to silence the oracles, tc compel the dæmons to con fess the tiuth of the Christian faith. Sometimes their power extended still further. Dæmons, we are told, were accustomed to enter into animals, and these also were expelled by the Christian adjuration. St. Jerome, in his ' Life of St. Hilarion,' has given us a graphic account of the courage with which that saint confronted, and the success with which he relieved, a possessed camel.[1] In the reign of Julian, the very bones of the martyr Babylas were sufficient to silence the oracle of Daphne ; and when, amid the triumphant chants of the Christians, the relics, by the command of Julian, were removed, the lightning descended from heaven and consumed the temple.[2]   St. Gregory Thaumaturgus having expelled the dæmons from an idol temple, the priest, finding his means of subsistence destroyed, came to the saint, imploring him to permit the oracles to be renewed.   St. Gregory, who was then on his journey, wrote a note containing the words ' Satan, return,' which was immediately obeyed, and the priest, awe-struck by the miracle, was converted to Christianity.[3] Tertullian, writing to the Pagans in a time of persecution, in language of the most deliberate earnestness, challenges his opponents to bring forth any person who is

[1] *Vit. Hilar.* Origen notices that cattle were sometimes possessed by devils. See Middleton's *Free Enquiry*, pp. 88, 89.

[2] The miracle of St. Babylas is the subject of a homily by St. Chrysostom, and is related at length by Theodoret, Sozomen, and Socrates. Libanius mentions that, by command of Julian, the bones of St. Babylas were removed from the temple. The Christians said the temple was destroyed by lightning ; the Pagans declared it was burnt by the Christians, and Julian ordered measures of reprisal to be taken. Amm. Marcellinis, however, mentions a report that the fire was caused accidentally by one of the numerous candles employed in the ceremony.   The people of Antioch defied the emperor by chanting, as they removed the relics, ' Confounded be all they that trust in graven images.'

[3] See the *Life of Gregory Thaumaturgus*, by Gregory of Nyssa.   St. Gregory the Great assures us (*Dial.* iii. 10) that Sabinus, Bishop of Placentia, wrote a letter to the river Po, which had overflowed its banks and flooded some church lands.   When the letter was thrown into the stre im the waters at once subsided.

possessed by a dæmon or any of those virgins or prophets who
are supposed to be inspired by a divinity. He asserts that,
in reply to the interrogation of any Christian, the dæmons
will be compelled to confess their diabolical character; he
invites the Pagans, if it be otherwise, to put the Christian
immediately to death; and he proposes this as at once the
simplest and most decisive demonstration of the faith.[1]
Justin Martyr,[2] Origen,[3] Lactantius,[4] Athanasius,[5] and
Minucius Felix,[6] all in language equally solemn and explicit,
call upon the Pagans to form their opinions from the confessions wrung from their own gods. We hear from them,
that when a Christian began to pray, to make the sign of the
cross, or to utter the name of his Master in the presence of a
possessed or inspired person, the latter, by screams and frightful contortions, exhibited the torture that was inflicted, and
by this torture the evil spirit was compelled to avow its
nature. Several of the Christian writers declare that this
was generally known to the Pagans. In one respect, it was
observed, the miracle of exorcism was especially available for
evidential purposes; for, as dæmons would not expel dæmons,
it was the only miracle which was necessarily divine.

It would be curious to examine the manner in which the
challenge was received by the Pagan writers; but unhappily,
the writings which were directed against the faith having
been destroyed by the Christian emperors, our means of information on this point are very scanty. Some information,

---

[1] 'Edatur hic aliquis sub tri-
bunalibus vestris, quem dæmone agi
constet. Jussus a quolibet Christiano loqui spiritus ille, tam se
dæmonem confitebitur de vero,
quam alibi deum de falso. Æque
producatur aliquis ex iis qui de
deo pati existimantur, qui aris
inhalantes numen de nidore conci-
piunt . . . nisi se dæmones con-
fessi fuerint, Christiano mentiri
non audentes, ibidem illius Chri-
tiani procacissimi sanguinem fun-
dite. Quid isto opere manifestius ?
quid hæc probatione fidelius ?'—
Tert. *Apol.* xxiii.
[2] *Apol.* i.; *Trypho*
[3] *Cont. Cels.* vii.
[4] *Inst. Div.* iv. 27
[5] *Life of Antony.*
[6] *Octavius.*

however, we possess, and it would appear to show that, among the educated classes at least, these phenomena did not extort any great admiration. The eloquent silence about diabolical possession observed by the early philosophers, when discussing such questions as the nature of the soul and of the spiritual world, decisively show that in their time possession had not assumed any great prominence or acquired any general credence. Plutarch, who admitted the reality of evil dæmons, and who was the most strenuous defender of the oracles, treats the whole class of superstitions to which exorcism belongs with much contempt.[1] Marcus Aurelius, in recounting the benefits he had received from different persons with whom he had been connected, acknowledges his debt of gratitude to the philosopher Diognetus for having taught him to give no credence to magicians, jugglers, and expellers of dæmons.[2] Lucian declares that every cunning juggler could make his fortune by going over to the Christians and preying upon their simplicity.[3] Celsus described the Christians as jugglers performing their tricks among the young and the credulous.[4] The most decisive evidence, however, we possess, is a law of Ulpian, directed, it is thought, against the Christians, which condemns those ' who use incantations or imprecations, or (to employ the common word of impostors) exorcisms.'[5] Modern criticism has noted a few facts which may throw some light upon this obscure subject. It has been observed that the

---

[1] De Superstitione.
[2] i. 6.
[3] De Mort. Peregrin.
[4] Origen, Adv. Cels. vi. Compare the curious letter which Vopiscus (Saturninus) attributes to Hadrian, ' Nemo illic [i.e. in Egypt] archisynagogus Judæorum, nemo Samarites, nemo Christianorum presbyter, non mathematicus, non aruspex, non aliptes.'
[5] ' Si incantavit, si imprecatus est, si (ut vulgari verbo impostorum utor) exorcizavit.'—Bingham, Antiquities of the Christian Church (Oxf., 1855), vol. i. p. 318. This law is believed to have been directed specially against the Christians, because these were very prominent as exorcists, and because Lactantius (Inst. Div. v. 11) says that Ulpian had collected the laws against them.

symptoms of possession were for the most part identical with those of lunacy or epilepsy ; that it is quite possible that the excitement of an imposing religious ceremony might produce or suspend the disorder ; that leading questions might in these cases be followed by the desired answers; and that some passages from the Fathers show that the exorcisms were not always successful, or the cures always permanent.   It has been observed, too, that at first the power of exorcism was open to all Christians without restraint; that this licence, in an age when religious jugglers were very common, and in a Church whose members were very credulous, gave great facilities to impostors ; that when the Laodicean Council, in the fourth century, forbade any one to exorcise, except those who were duly authorised by the bishop, these miracles speedily declined ; and that, in the very beginning of the fifth century, a physician named Posidonius denied the existence of possession.[1]

To sum up this whole subject, we may conclude that what is called the evidential system had no prominent place in effecting the conversion of the Roman Empire.   Historical criticisms were far too imperfect to make appeals to the miracles of former days of any value, and the notion of the wide diffusion of miraculous or magical powers, as well as the generally private character of the alleged miracles of the Patristic age, made contemporary wonders very unimpressive. The prophecies attributed to the Sibyls, and the practice of exorcism, had, however, a certain weight; for the first were connected with a religious authority, long and deeply revered at Rome, and the second had been forced by several circumstances into great prominence.   But the effect even of these may be safely regarded as altogether subsidiary, and the main causes of the conversion must be looked for in another and a wider sphere.

---

[1] Philostorgius, *Hist. Eccl.* viii. 10.

These causes were the general tendencies of the age
They are to be found in that vast movement of mingled
scepticism and credulity, in that amalgamation or dissolution
of many creeds, in that profound transformation of habits, of
feelings, and of ideals, which I have attempted to paint in
the last chapter.   Under circumstances more favourable to
religious proselytism than the world had ever before known,
with the path cleared by a long course of destructive cri
ticism, the religions and philosophies of mankind were
struggling for the mastery in that great metropolis where
all were amply represented, and in which alone the destinies
of the world could be decided.   Among the educated a frigid
Stoicism, teaching a majestic but unattainable grandeur, and
scorning the support of the affections, the hope of another
world, and the consolations of worship, had for a time been in
the ascendant, and it only terminated its noble and most
fruitful career when it had become manifestly inadequate
to the religious wants of the age.   Among other classes,
religion after religion ran its conquering course.   The Jews,
although a number of causes had made them the most hated
of all the Roman subjects, and although their religion, from
its intensely national character, seemed peculiarly unsuited
for proselytism, had yet, by the force of their monotheism,
their charity, and their exorcisms, spread the creed of Moses
far and wide.   The Empress Poppæa is said to have been a
proselyte.   The passion of Roman women for Jewish rites
was one of the complaints of Juvenal.   The Sabbath and the
Jewish fasts became familiar facts in all the great cities, and
the antiquity of the Jewish law the subject of eager discussion.   Other Oriental religions were even more successful.
The worship of Mithra, and, above all, of the Egyptian
divinities, attracted their thousands, and during more than
three centuries the Roman writings are crowded with allusions to their progress.   The mysteries of the Bona Dea,[1] the

---

[1] See Juvenal, *Sat.* vi. 314–335.

solemn worship of Isis, the expiatory rites that cleansed the
guilty soul, excited a very delirium of enthusiasm. Juvenal
describes the Roman women, at the dawn of the winter day,
breaking the ice of the Tiber to plunge three times into its
sacred stream, dragging themselves on bleeding knees in
penance around the field of Tarquin, offering to undertake
pilgrimages to Egypt to seek the holy water for the shrine of
Isis, fondly dreaming that they had heard the voice of the
goddess.[1] Apuleius has drawn a graphic picture of the solemn
majesty of her processions, and the spell they cast upon the
most licentious and the most sceptical.[2] Commodus, Caracalla,
and Heliogabalus were passionately devoted to them.[3] The
temples of Isis and Serapis, and the statues of Mithra, are
among the last prominent works of Roman art. In all other
forms the same credulity was manifested. The oracles that
had been silent were heard again; the astrologers swarmed
in every city; the philosophers were surrounded with an
atmosphere of legend; the Pythagorean school had raised
credulity into a system. On all sides, and to a degree unparalleled in history, we find men who were no longer
satisfied with their old local religion, thirsting for belief,
passionately and restlessly seeking for a new faith.

In the midst of this movement, Christianity gained its
ascendancy, and we can be at no loss to discover the cause of
its triumph. No other religion, under such circumstances,
had ever combined so many distinct elements of power and
attraction. Unlike the Jewish religion, it was bound by no
local ties, and was equally adapted for every nation and for
every class. Unlike Stoicism, it appealed in the strongest
manner to the affections, and offered all the charm of a sympathetic worship. Unlike the Egyptian religions, it united
with its distinctive teaching a pure and noble system of

See Juvenal, *Sat.* vi. 520–530. [3] See their *Lives*, by Lampri-
[2] *Metamorphoses*, book x. dius and Spartianus.

ethics, and proved itself capable of realising it in action. It proclaimed, amid a vast movement of social and national amalgamation, the universal brotherhood of mankind. Amid the softening influence of philosophy and civilisation, it taught the supreme sanctity of love. To the slave, who had never before exercised so large an influence over Roman religious life, it was the religion of the suffering and the oppressed. To the philosopher it was at once the echo of the highest ethics of the later Stoics, and the expansion of the best teaching of the school of Plato. To a world thirsting for prodigy, it offered a history replete with wonders more strange that those of Apollonius; while the Jew and the Chaldean could scarcely rival its exorcists, and the legends of continual miracles circulated among its followers. To a world deeply conscious of political dissolution, and prying eagerly and anxiously into the future, it proclaimed with a thrilling power the immediate destruction of the globe—the glory of all its friends, and the damnation of all its foes. To a world that had grown very weary gazing on the cold and passionless grandeur which Cato realised, and which Lucan sung, it presented an ideal of compassion and of love—a Teacher who could weep by the sepulchre of His friend, who was touched with the feeling of our infirmities. To a world, in fine, distracted by hostile creeds and colliding philosophies, it taught its doctrines, not as a human speculation, but as a Divine revelation, authenticated much less by reason than by faith. 'With the heart man believeth unto righteousness;' 'He that doeth the will of my Father will know the doctrine, whether it be of God;' 'Unless you believe you cannot understand;' 'A heart naturally Christian;' 'The heart makes the theologian,' are the phrases which best express the first action of Christianity upon the world. Like all great religions, it was more concerned with modes of feeling than with modes of thought. The chief cause of its success was the congruity of its teaching with the spiritual

nature of mankind. It was because it was true to the moral
sentiments of the age, because it represented faithfully the
supreme type of excellence to which men were then tending,
because it corresponded with their religious wants, aims, and
emotions, because the whole spiritual being could then expand and expatiate under its influence, that it planted its
roots so deeply in the hearts of men.

To all these elements of attraction, others of a different
order must be added. Christianity was not merely a moral
influence, or a system of opinions, or an historical record, or
a collection of wonder-working men; it was also an institution definitely, elaborately, and skilfully organised, possessing a weight and a stability which isolated or undisciplined
teachers could never rival, and evoking, to a degree before
unexampled in the world, an enthusiastic devotion to its
corporate welfare, analogous to that of the patriot to his
country. The many forms of Pagan worship were pliant in
their nature. Each offered certain advantages or spiritual
gratifications; but there was no reason why all should not
exist together, and participation in one by no means implied
disrespect to the others. But Christianity was emphatically
exclusive; its adherent was bound to detest and abjure the
faiths around him as the workmanship of dæmons, and to
consider himself placed in the world to destroy them. Hence
there sprang a stern, aggressive, and at the same time disciplined enthusiasm, wholly unlike any other that had been
witnessed upon earth. The duties of public worship; the
sacraments, which were represented as the oaths of the
Christian warrior; the fasts and penances and commemorative
days, which strengthened the Church feeling; the intervention of religion in the most solemn epochs of life, conspired
to sustain it. Above all, the doctrine of salvation by belief,
which then for the first time flashed upon the world; the
persuasion, realised with all the vividness of novelty, that
Christianity opened out to its votaries eternal happiness,

while all beyond its pale were doomed to an eternity of torture, supplied a motive of action as powerful as it is perhaps possible to conceive. It struck alike the coarsest chords of hope and fear, and the finest chords of compassion and love. The polytheist, admitting that Christianity might possibly be true, was led by a mere calculation of prudence to embrace it, and the fervent Christian would shrink from no suffering to draw those whom he loved within its pale. Nor were other inducements wanting. To the confessor was granted in the Church a great and venerable authority, such as the bishop could scarcely claim.[1] To the martyr, besides the fruition of heaven, belonged the highest glory on earth. By winning that bloodstained crown, the meanest Christian slave might gain a reputation as glorious as that of a Decius or a Regulus. His body was laid to rest with a sumptuous splendour;[2] his relics, embalmed or shrined, were venerated with an almost idolatrous homage. The anniversary of his birth into another life was commemorated in the Church, and before the great assembly of the saints his heroic sufferings were recounted.[3] How, indeed, should he not be envied? He had passed away into eternal bliss. He had left upon earth an abiding name. By the 'baptism of blood' the sins of a life had been in a moment effaced.

Those who are accustomed to recognise heroic enthusiasm as a normal product of certain natural conditions, will have no difficulty in understanding that, under such circumstances

---

[1] The conflict between St. Cyprian and the confessors, concerning the power of remitting penances claimed by the latter, though it ended in the defeat of the confessors, shows clearly the influence they had obtained.

[2] 'Thura plane non emimus; si Arabiæ queruntur scient Sabæi pluris et carioris suas merces Christianis sepeliendis profligari quam diis fumigandis.'—*Apol.* 42. Sometimes the Pagans burnt the bodies of the martyrs, in order to prevent the Christians venerating their relics.

[3] Many interesting particulars about these commemorative festivals are collected in Cave's *Primitive Christianity*, part i. c. vii. The anniversaries were called ' Natalia, or birth-days.

as I have described, a transcendent courage should have been
evoked.   Men seemed indeed to be in love with death.   Believing, with St. Ignatius, that they were 'the wheat of
God,' they panted for the day when they should be 'ground
by the teeth of wild beasts into the pure bread of Christ!
Beneath this one burning enthusiasm all the ties of earthly
love were snapt in twain.   Origen, when a boy, being restrained by force from going forth to deliver himself up to
the persecutors, wrote to his imprisoned father, imploring
him not to let any thought of his family intervene to quench
his resolution or to deter him from sealing his faith with
his blood.   St. Perpetua, an only daughter, a young mother
of twenty-two, had embraced the Christian creed, confessed
it before her judges, and declared herself ready to endure
for it the martyr's death.   Again and again her father came
to her in a paroxysm of agony, entreating her not to deprive
him of the joy and the consolation of his closing years.
He appealed to her by the memory of all the tenderness
he had lavished upon her – by her infant child — by his
own gray hairs, that were soon to be brought down in
sorrow to the grave.   Forgetting in his deep anguish all
the dignity of a parent, he fell upon his knees before his
child, covered her hands with kisses, and, with tears streaming from his eyes, implored her to have mercy upon him.
But she was unshaken though not untouched; she saw her
father, frenzied with grief, dragged from before the tribunal;
she saw him tearing his white beard, and lying prostrate and
broken-hearted on the prison floor; she went forth to die for
a faith she loved more dearly—for a faith that told her that
her father would be lost for ever.[1]   The desire for martyrdom
became at times a form of absolute madness, a kind of epidemic of suicide, and the leading minds of the Church found it
necessary to exert all their authority to prevent their followers

---

[1] See her acts in Ruinart.

from thrusting themselves into the hands of the persecutors.[1] Tertullian mentions how, in a little Asiatic town, the entire population once flocked to the proconsul, declaring themselves to be Christians, and imploring him to execute the decree of the emperor and grant them the privilege of martyrdom. The bewildered functionary asked them whether, if they were so weary of life, there were no precipices or ropes by which they could end their days; and he put to death a small number of the suppliants, and dismissed the others.[2]   Two illustrious Pagan moralists and one profane Pagan satirist have noticed this passion with a most unpleasing scorn. 'There are some,' said Epictetus, 'whom madness, there are others, like the Galilæans, whom custom, makes indifferent to death.'[3] 'What mind,' said Marcus Aurelius, 'is prepared, if need be, to go forth from the body, whether it be to be extinguished, or to be dispersed, or to endure?—prepared by deliberate reflection, and not by pure obstinacy, as is the custom of the Christians.'[4] 'These wretches,' said Lucian, speaking of the Christians, 'persuade themselves that they are going to be altogether immortal, and to live for ever; wherefore they despise death, and many of their own accord give themselves up to be slain.'[5]

'I send against you men who are as greedy of death as you are of pleasures,' were the words which, in after days, the

[1] St. Clem. Alex. *Strom.* iv. 10. There are other passages of the same kind in other Fathers.

[2] *Ad Scapul.*v. Eusebius (*Martyrs of Palestine*, ch. iii.) has given a detailed account of six young men, who in the very height of the Galerian persecution, at a time when the most hideous tortures were applied to the Christians, voluntarily gave themselves up as believers. Sulp. Severus (*Hist.* ii. 32), speaking of the voluntary martyrs under Diocletian, says that Christians

then 'longed for death as they now long for bishoprics.' 'Cogi qui potest, nescit mori,' was the noble maxim of the Christians.

[3] Arrian, iv. 7. It is not certain, however, that this passage alludes to the Christians. The followers of Judas of Galilee were called Galilæans, and they were famous for their indifference to death. See Joseph. *Antiq.* xviii. 1.

[4] xi. 3.

[5] *Peregrinus.*

Mohametan chief addressed to the degenerate Christians of Syria, and which were at once the presage and the explanation of his triumph. Such words might with equal propriety have been employed by the early Christian leaders to their Pagan adversaries. The zeal of the Christians and of the Pagans differed alike in degree and in kind. When Constantine made Christianity the religion of the State, it is probable that its adherents were but a minority in Rome. Even in the days of Theodosius the senate was still wedded to Paganism;[1] yet the measures of Constantine were both natural and necessary. The majority were without inflexible belief, without moral enthusiasm, without definite organisation, without any of those principles that inspire the heroism either of resistance or aggression. The minority formed a serried phalanx, animated by every motive that could purify, discipline, and sustain their zeal. When once the Christians had acquired a considerable position, the question of their destiny was a simple one. They must either be crushed or they must reign. The failure of the persecution of Diocletian conducted them inevitably to the throne.

It may indeed be confidently asserted that the conversion of the Roman Empire is so far from being of the nature of a miracle or suspension of the ordinary principles of human nature, that there is scarcely any other great movement on record in which the causes and effects so manifestly correspond. The apparent anomalies of history are not inconsiderable, but they must be sought for in other quarters. That within the narrow limits and scanty population of the Greek States should have arisen men who, in almost every conceivable form of genius, in philosophy, in epic, dramatic and lyric poetry, in written and spoken eloquence, in statesmanship, in sculpture, in painting, and probably also in music, should have

---

[1] Zosimus.

attained almost or altogether the highest limits of human perfection—that the creed of Mohamet should have preserved its pure monotheism and its freedom from all idolatrous tendencies, when adopted by vast populations in that intellectual condition in which, under all other creeds, a gross and material worship has proved inevitable, both these are facts which we can only very imperfectly explain. Considerations of climate, and still more of political, social, and intellectual customs and institutions, may palliate the first difficulty, and the attitude Mohamet assumed to art may supply us with a partial explanation of the second; but I suppose that, after all has been said, most persons will feel that they are in presence of phenomena very exceptional and astonishing. The first rise of Christianity in Judæa is a subject wholly apart from this book. We are examining only the subsequent movement in the Roman Empire. Of this movement it may be boldly asserted that the assumption of a moral or intellectual miracle is utterly gratuitous. Never before was a religious transformation so manifestly inevitable. No other religion ever combined so many forms of attraction as Christianity, both from its intrinsic excellence, and from its manifest adaptation to the special wants of the time. One great cause of its success was that it produced more heroic actions and formed more upright men than any other creed; but that it should do so was precisely what might have been expected.

To these reasonings, however, those who maintain that the triumph of Christianity in Rome is naturally inexplicable, reply by pointing to the persecutions which Christianity had to encounter. As this subject is one on which many misconceptions exist, and as it is of extreme importance on account of its connection with later persecutions, it will be necessary briefly to discuss it.

It is manifest that the reasons that may induce a ruler to suppress by force some forms of religious worship or opinion,

are very various. He may do so on moral grounds, because
they directly or indirectly produce immorality; or on religious
grounds, because he believes them to be offensive to the
Deity ; or on political grounds, because they are injurious
either to the State or to the Government ; or on corrupt
grounds, because he desires to gratify some vindictive or
avaricious passion. From the simple fact, therefore, of a
religious persecution we cannot at once infer the principles
of the persecutor, but must examine in detail by which of the
above motives, or by what combination of them, he has been
actuated.

Now, the persecution which has taken place at the instigation of the Christian priests differs in some respects broadly
from all others. It has been far more sustained, systematic,
and unflinching. It has been directed not merely against
acts of worship, but also against speculative opinions. It has
been supported not merely as a right, but also as a duty. It
has been advocated in a whole literature of theology, by the
classes that are especially devout, and by the most opposing
sects, and it has invariably declined in conjunction with a
large portion of theological dogmas.

I have elsewhere examined in great detail the history of
persecutions by Christians, and have endeavoured to show
that, while exceptional causes have undoubtedly occasionally
occurred, they were, in the overwhelming majority of cases,
simply the natural, legitimate, and inevitable consequence of
a certain portion of the received theology. That portion is the
doctrine that correct theological opinions are essential to
salvation, and that theological error necessarily involves
guilt. To these two opinions may be distinctly traced
almost all the sufferings that Christian persecutors have
caused, almost all the obstructions they have thrown in the
path of human progress ; and those sufferings have been so
grievous that it may be reasonably questioned whether
superstition has not often proved a greater curse than vice,

and that obstruction was so pertinacious, that the contraction of theological influence has been at once the best measure, and the essential condition of intellectual advance. The notion that he might himself be possibly mistaken in his opinions, which alone could cause a man who was tnoroughly imbued with these principles to shrink from persecuting, was excluded by the theological virtue of faith, which, whatever else it might involve, implied at least an absolute unbroken certainty, and led the devotee to regard all doubt, and therefore all action based upon doubt, as sin.

To this general cause of Christian persecution I have shown that two subsidiary influences may be joined. A large portion of theological ethics was derived from writings in which religious massacres, on the whole the most ruthless and sanguinary upon record, were said to have been directly enjoined by the Deity, in which the duty of suppressing idolatry by force was given a greater prominence than any article of the moral code, and in which the spirit of intolerance has found its most eloquent and most passionate expressions.[1] Besides this, the destiny theologians represented as awaiting the misbeliever was so ghastly and so appalling as to render it almost childish to lay any stress upon the earthly suffering that might be inflicted in the extirpation of error.

That these are the true causes of the great bulk of Christian persecution, I believe to be one of the most certain as well as one of the most important facts in history. For the detailed proof I can only refer to what I have elsewhere written; but I may here notice that that proof combines every conceivable kind of evidence that in such a question can be demanded. It can be shown that these principles would naturally lead men to persecute. It can be shown that from the time of Constantine to the time when the

---

[1] 'Do I not hate them, O Lord, that hate thee ?—yea, I hate them with a perfect hatred.'

rationalistic spirit wrested the bloodstained sword from the priestly hand, persecution was uniformly defended upon them—defended in long, learned, and elaborate treatises, by the best and greatest men the Church had produced, by sects that differed on almost all other points, by multitudes who proved in every conceivable manner the purity of their zeal. It can be shown, too, that toleration began with the distinction between fundamental and non-fundamental doctrines, expanded in exact proportion to the growing latitudinarianism, and triumphed only when indifference to dogma had become a prevailing sentiment among legislators. It was only when the battle had been won—when the anti-dogmatic party, acting in opposition to the Church, had rendered persecution impossible—that the great body of theologians revised their arguments, and discovered that to punish men for their opinions was wholly at variance with their faith. With the merits of this pleasing though somewhat tardy conversion I am not now concerned; but few persons, I think, can follow the history of Christian persecution without a feeling of extreme astonishment that some modern writers, not content with maintaining that the doctrine of exclusive salvation *ought* not to have produced persecution, have ventured, in defiance of the unanimous testimony of the theologians of so many centuries, to dispute the plain historical fact that it *did* produce it. They argue that the Pagans, who did not believe in exclusive salvation, persecuted, and that therefore that doctrine cannot be the cause of persecution. The answer is that no sane man ever maintained that all the persecutions on record were from the same source. We can prove by the clearest evidence that Christian persecutions sprang chiefly from the causes I have alleged. The causes of Pagan persecutions, though different, are equally manifest, and I shall proceed shortly to indicate them.

They were partly political and partly religious. The Governments in most of the ancient States, in the earlier

stages of their existence, undertook the complete education
of the people; professed to control and regulate all the details
of their social life, even to the dresses they wore, or the
dishes that were served upon their tables; and, in a word, to
mould their whole lives and characters into a uniform type.
Hence, all organisations and corporations not connected with
the State, and especially all that emanated from foreign
countries, were looked upon with distrust or antipathy. But
this antipathy was greatly strengthened by a religious consideration. No belief was more deeply rooted in the ancient
mind than that good or bad fortune sprang from the intervention of spiritual beings, and that to neglect the sacred
rites was to bring down calamity upon the city. In the
diminutive Greek States, where the function of the Government was immensely enlarged, a strong intolerance existed,
which extended for some time not merely to practices, but to
writings and discourses. The well-known persecutions of
Anaxagoras, Theodorus, Diagoras, Stilpo, and Socrates; the
laws of Plato, which were as opposed to religious as to domestic
freedom; and the existence in Athens of an inquisitorial
tribunal,[1] sufficiently attested it. But long before the final
ruin of Greece, speculative liberty had been fully attained.
The Epicurean and the Sceptical schools developed unmolested,
and even in the days of Socrates, Aristophanes was able to
ridicule the gods upon the stage.

In the earlier days of Rome religion was looked upon as
a function of the State; its chief object was to make the gods
auspicious to the national policy,[2] and its principal ceremonies
were performed at the direct command of the Senate. The
national theory on religious matters was that the best religion

---

[1] See Renan's *Apôtres*, p. 314.

[2] M. Pressensé very truly says
cf the Romans, 'Leur religion était
essentiellement un art—l'art ·de
découvrir les desseins des dieux et
l'agir sur eux par des rites variés.'

—*Hist. des Trois premiers Siècles*,
tome i. p. 192. Montesquieu has
written an interesting essay on the
political nature of the Roman re
ligion.

is always that of a man's own country. At the same time, the widest tolerance was granted to the religions of conquered nations. The temples of every god were respected by the Roman army. Before besieging a city, the Romans were accustomed to supplicate the presiding deities of that city. With the single exception of the Druids, whose human sacrifices it was thought a matter of humanity to suppress,[1] and whose fierce rebellions it was thought necessary to crush, the teachers of all national religions continued unmolested by the conqueror.

This policy, however, applied specially to religious rites practised in the countries in which they were indigenous. The liberty to be granted to the vast confluence of strangers attracted to Italy during the Empire was another question. In the old Republican days, when the censors regulated with the most despotic authority the minutest affairs of life, and when the national religion was interwoven with every detail of political and even domestic transactions, but little liberty could be expected. When Carneades endeavoured to inculcate his universal scepticism upon the Romans, by arguing alter-nately for and against the same proposition, Cato immediately urged the Senate to expel him from the city, lest the people should be corrupted by his teaching.[2] For a similar reason all rhetoricians had been banished from the Republic.[3] The most remarkable, however, and at the same time the extreme expression of Roman intolerance that has descended to us, is the advice which Mæcenas is represented as having given to Octavius Cæsar, before his accession to the throne. 'Always,' he said, 'and everywhere, worship the gods according to the rites of your country, and compel others to the same worship. Pursue with your hatred and with punish-

---

[1] Sueton. *Claud.* xxv.
[2] Plin. *Hist. Nat.* vii. 31.
[3] Tacit. *De Orat.* xxxv.; Aul. Gell. *Noct.* xv. 11. It would ap-pear, from this last authority, that the rhetoricians were **twice ex-**pelled.

ments those who introduce foreign religions, not only for the
sake of the gods—the despisers of whom can assuredly never
do anything great—but also because they who introduce new
divinities entice many to use foreign laws.   Hence arise conspiracies, societies, and assemblies, things very unsuited to
an homogeneous empire.   Tolerate no despiser of the gods,
and no religious juggler.   Divination is necessary, and therefore let the aruspices and augurs by all means be sustained,
and let those who will, consult them; but the magicians must
be utterly prohibited, who, though they sometimes tell the
truth, more frequently, by false promises, urge men on to
conspiracies.' [1]

This striking passage exhibits very clearly the extent to
which in some minds the intolerant spirit was carried in
antiquity, and also the blending motives that produced it.
We should be, however, widely mistaken if we regarded it as
a picture of the actual religious policy of the Empire.   In
order to realise this, it will be necessary to notice separately
liberty of speculation and liberty of worship.

When Asinius Pollio founded the first public library in
Rome, he placed it in the Temple of Liberty.   The lesson
which was thus taught to the literary classes was never forgotten.   It is probable that in no other period of the history
of the world was speculative freedom so perfect as in the
Roman Empire.   The fearless scrutiny of all notions of
popular belief, displayed in the writings of Cicero, Seneca,
Lucretius, or Lucian, did not excite an effort of repression.
Philosophers were, indeed, persecuted by Domitian and Vespasian for their ardent opposition to the despotism of the
throne,[2] but on their own subjects they were wholly untram-

---

[1] Dion Cassius, lii. 36. Most
historians believe that this speech
represents the opinions, not of the
Augustan age, but of the age of
the writer who relates it.

[2] On the hostility of Vespasian
to philosophers, see Xiphilin, lxvi.
13; on that of Domitian, the Letters of Pliny and the Agricola of
Tacitus.

melled. The Greek writers consoled themselves for the extinction of the independence of their country by the reflection
that in the sphere of intellect the meddling policy of the
Greek States was replaced by an absolute and a majestic
freedom.[1] The fierceness of the opposition of sects faded
beneath its influence. Of all the speculative conflicts of
antiquity, that which most nearly approached the virulence
of later theological controversies was probably that between
the Stoics and the Epicureans; but it is well worthy of notice
that some of the most emphatic testimonies to the moral
goodness of Epicurus have come from the writings of his
opponents.

But the policy of the Roman rulers towards religious
rites was very different from, and would at first sight appear
to be in direct opposition to, their policy towards opinions.
An old law, which Cicero mentions, expressly forbade the
introduction of new religions,[2] and in the Republican days
and the earliest days of the Empire there are many instances
of its being enforced. Thus, in A.U.C. 326, a severe drought
having led men to seek help from new gods, the Senate
charged the ædiles to allow none but Roman deities to be
worshipped.[3] Lutatius, soon after the first Punic war, was
forbidden by the Senate to consult foreign gods, 'because,'
said the historian, 'it was deemed right the Republic should
be administered according to the national auspices, and not
according to those of other lands.'[4] During the second Punic
war, a severe edict of the Senate enjoined the suppression of
certain recent innovations.[5] About A.U.C. 615 the prætor
Hispalus exiled those who had introduced the worship of
the Sabasian Jupiter.[6] The rites of Bacchus, being accompanied by gross and scandalous obscenity, were suppressed,

---

[1] See a remarkable passage in
Dion Chrysostom, *Or.* lxxx. *De
Libertate.*
[2] Cic. *De Legib.* ii. 11; Tertull.
Apol. v.

[3] Livy, iv. 30.
[4] Val. Maximus, i. 3, § 1.
[5] Livy, xxv. 1.
[6] Val. Max. i. 3, § 2.

the consul, in a remarkable speech, calling upon the people to
revive the religious policy of their ancestors.[1] The worship
of Isis and Serapis only gained its footing after a long struggle,
and no small amount of persecution. The gross immorality
it sometimes favoured, its wild and abject superstition, so
thoroughly alien to the whole character of Roman life and
tradition, and also the organisation of its priesthood, rendered
it peculiarly obnoxious to the Government. When the first
edict of suppression was issued, the people hesitated to destroy
a temple which seemed so venerable in their eyes, and the
consul Æmilius Paulus dispelled their fears by seizing an
axe and striking the first blow himself.[2] During the latter
days of the Republic, edicts had commanded the destruction
of the Egyptian temples. Octavius, however, in his younger
days, favoured the new worship, but, soon after, it was again
suppressed.[3] Under Tiberius it had once more crept in; but
the priests of Isis having enabled a patrician named Mundus
to disguise himself as the god Anubis, and win the favours of a
devout worshipper, the temple, by order of the emperor, was
destroyed, the images were thrown into the Tiber, the priests
were crucified, and the seducer was banished.[4] Under the same
emperor four thousand persons were exiled to Sardinia, as
affected with Jewish and Egyptian superstitions. They were
commissioned to repress robbers; but the Roman historian

[1] See the account of these proceedings, and of the very remarkable speech of Postumius, in Livy, xxxix. 8–19. Postumius notices the old prohibition of foreign rites, and thus explains it: — 'Judicabant enim prudentissimi viri omnis divini humanique juris, nihil æque dissolvendæ religionis esse, quam ubi non patrio sed externo ritu sacrificaretur.' The Senate, though suppressing these rites on account of the outrageous immoralities connected with them, decreed, that if any one thought it a matter of religious duty to perform religious ceremonies to Bacchus, he should be allowed to do so on applying for permission to the Senate, provided there were not more than five assistants, no common purse, and no presiding priest.

[2] Val. Max. i. 3.

[3] See Dion Cassius, xl. 47; xlii. 26; xlvii. 15; liv. 6.

[4] Joseph. Antiq. xviii. 3.

observed, with a characteristic scorn, that if they died through the unhealthiness of the climate, it would be but a 'small loss.'[1]

These measures represent together a considerable amount of religious repression, but they were produced exclusively by notions of policy or discipline. They grew out of that intense national spirit which sacrificed every other interest to the State, and resisted every form of innovation, whether secular or religious, that could impair the unity of the national type, and dissolve the discipline which the predominance of the military spirit and the stern government of the Republic had formed. They were also, in some cases, the result of moral scandals. When, however, it became evident that the internal condition of the Republic was unsuited for the Empire, the rulers frankly acquiesced in the change, and from the time of Tiberius, with the single exception of the Christians, perfect liberty of worship seems to have been granted to the professors of all religions in Rome.[2] The old law upon the subject was not revoked, but it was not generally enforced. Sometimes the new creeds were expressly authorised. Sometimes they were tacitly permitted. With a single exception, all the religions of the world raised their heads unmolested in the 'Holy City.'[3]

The liberty, however, of professing and practising a foreign worship did not dispense the Roman from the obligation of performing also the sacrifices or other religious rites of his own land. It was here that whatever religious fanaticism mingled with Pagan persecutions was displayed. Eusebius tells us that religion was divided by the Romans

---

[1] Tacit. *Annal.* ii. 85.

[2] Tacitus relates (*Ann.* xi. 15) that under Claudius a senatus consultus ordered the pontiffs to take care that the old Roman (or, more properly, Etruscan) system of divination was observed, since the influx of foreign superstitions had led to its disuse; but it does not appear that this measure was intended to interfere with any other form of worship.

[3] 'Sacrosanctam istam civitatem accedo.'—Apuleius, *Metam.* lib. x. It is said that there were at one time no less than 420 ædes sacræ in Rome. Nieupoort, *De Ritibus Romanorum* (1716), p. 276

into three parts—the mythology, or legends that had descended from the poets; the interpretations or theories by which the philosophers endeavoured to rationalise, filter, or explain away these legends; and the ritual or official religious observances. In the first two spheres perfect liberty was accorded, but the ritual was placed under the control of the Government, and was made a matter of compulsion.[1] In order to realise the strength of the feeling that supported it, we must remember that the multitude firmly believed that the prosperity and adversity of the Empire depended chiefly upon the zeal or indifference that was shown in conciliating the national divinities, and also that the philosophers, as I have noticed in the last chapter, for the most part not only practised, but warmly defended, the official observances. The love of truth in many forms was exhibited among the Pagan philosophers to a degree which has never been surpassed; but there was one form in which it was absolutely unknown. The belief that it is wrong for a man in religious matters to act a lie, to sanction by his presence and by his example what he regards as baseless superstitions, had no place in the ethics of antiquity. The religious flexibility which polytheism had originally generated, the strong political feeling that pervaded all classes, and also the manifest impossibility of making philosophy the creed of the ignorant, had rendered nearly universal among philosophers a state of feeling which is often exhibited, but rarely openly professed, among ourselves.[2] The religious opinions of men had but

---

[1] Euseb. *Præp. Evang.* iv. 1. Fontenelle says very truly, 'Il y a lieu de croire que chez les payens la religion n'estoit qu'une pratique, dont la spéculation estoit indifférente. Faites comme les autres et croyez ce qu'il vous plaira.'—*Hist. des Oracles*, p. 95. It was a saying of Tiberius, that it is for the gods to care for the injuries done to them: 'Deorum injurias diis curæ.' —Tacit. *Annal.* i. 73.

[2] The most melancholy modern instance I remember is a letter of Hume to a young man who was thinking of taking orders but who, in the course of his studies, became a complete sceptic. Hume strongly advised him not to allow this consideration to interfere with his

little influence on their religious practices, and the sceptic considered it not merely lawful, but a duty, to attend the observances of his country.   No one did more to scatter the ancient superstitions than Cicero, who was himself an augur, and who strongly asserted the duty of complying with the national rites.[1]   Seneca, having recounted in the most derisive terms the absurdities of the popular worship, concludes his enumeration by declaring that 'the sage will observe all these things, not as pleasing to the Divinities, but as commanded by the law,' and that he should remember 'that his worship is due to custom, not to belief.'[2]   Epictetus, whose austere creed rises to the purest monotheism, teaches as a fundamental religious maxim that every man in his devotions should 'conform to the customs of his country.'[3]   The Jews and Christians, who alone refused to do so, were the representatives of a moral principle that was unknown to the Pagan world.

It should be remembered, too, that the Oriental custom of deifying emperors having been introduced into Rome, to burn incense before their statues had become a kind of test of loyalty.   This adoration does not, it is true, appear to have implied any particular article of belief, and it was probably regarded by most men as we regard the application of the term 'Sacred Majesty' to a sovereign, and the custom of kneeling in his presence ; but it was esteemed inconsistent with Christianity, and the conscientious refusal of the Christians to comply with it aroused a feeling resembling that which was long produced in Christendom by the refusal of Quakers to comply with the usages of courts.

---

career   (Burton, *Life of Hume,* vol. ii. pp. 187, 188.)   The utilitarian principles of the philosopher were doubtless at the root of his judgment.

[1] *De Divinat.* ii. 33; *De Nat. Deor.* ii. 3.

[2] 'Quæ omnia sapiens servabit tanquam legibus jussa non tanquam diis grata. . . . Meminerimus cultum ejus magis ad morem quam ad rem pertinere.'—St. Aug. *De Civ. Dei,* vi. 10.   St. Augustine denounces this view with great power. See, too, Lactantius. *Inst. Div.* ii. 3

[3] *Enchirid.* xxxi.

The obligation to perform the sacred rites of an idola-trous worship, if rigidly enforced, would have amounted, in the case of the Jews and the Christians, to a complete pro-scription. It does not, however, appear that the Jews were ever persecuted on this ground. They formed a large and influential colony in Rome. They retained undiminished, in the midst of the Pagan population, their exclusive habits, refusing not merely all religious communion, but most social intercourse with the idolaters, occupying a separate quarter of the city, and sedulously practising their distinctive rites. Tiberius, as we have seen, appears to have involved them in his proscription of Egyptian superstitions; but they were usually perfectly unmolested, or were molested only when their riotous conduct had attracted the attention of the rulers. The Government was so far from compelling them to perform acts contrary to their religion, that Augustus ex-pressly changed the day of the distribution of corn, in order that they might not be reduced to the alternative of forfeiting their share, or of breaking the Sabbath.[1]

It appears, then, that the old Republican intolerance had in the Empire been so modified as almost to have disappeared. The liberty of speculation and discussion was entirely un-checked. The liberty of practising foreign religious rites, though ostensibly limited by the law against unauthorised religions, was after Tiberius equally secure. The liberty of abstaining from the official national rites, though more pre-carious, was fully conceded to the Jews, whose jealousy of idolatry was in no degree inferior to that of the Christians It remains, then, to examine what were the causes of the very exceptional fanaticism and animosity that were directed against the latter.

The first cause of the persecution of the Christians was the religious notion to which I have already referred. The

---

[1] This is noticed by Philo.

ءelief that our world is governed by isolated acts of Divine intervention, and that, in consequence, every great calamity, whether physical, or military, or political, may be regarded as a punishment or a warning, was the basis of the whole religious system of antiquity.[1] In the days of the Republic every famine, pestilence, or drought was followed by a searching investigation of the sacred rites, to ascertain what irregularity or neglect had caused the Divine anger, and two instances are recorded in which vestal virgins were put to death because their unchastity was believed to have provoked a national calamity.[2] It might appear at first sight that the fanaticism which this belief would naturally produce would have been directed against the Jews as strongly as against the Christians; but a moment's reflection is sufficient to explain the difference. The Jewish religion was essentially conservative and unexpansive. Although, in the passion for Oriental religions, many of the Romans had begun to practise its ceremonies, there was no spirit of proselytism in the sect; and it is probable that almost all who followed this religion, to the exclusion of others, were of Hebrew nationality. The Christians, on the other hand, were ardent missionaries; they were, for the most part, Romans who had thrown off the allegiance of their old gods, and their activity was so great that from a very early period the temples were

---

[1] The ship in which the atheist Diagoras sailed was once nearly wrecked by a tempest, and the sailors declared that it was a just retribution from the gods because they had received the philosopher into their vessel. Diagoras, pointing to the other ships that were tossed by the same storm, asked whether they imagined there was a Diagoras in each. (Cic. *De Nat. Deor.* iii 37.)

[2] The vestal Oppia was put to death because the diviners attributed to her unchastity certain 'prodigies in the heavens,' that had alarmed the people at the beginning of the war with Veii. (Livy, ii. 42.) The vestal Urbinia was buried alive on account of a plague that had fallen upon the Roman women, which was attributed to her incontinence, and which is said to have ceased suddenly upon her execution. (Dion. Halicar. ix.)

in some districts almost deserted.[1] Besides this, the Jews simply abstained from and despised the religions around them. The Christians denounced them as the worship of dæmons, and lost no opportunity of insulting them. It is not, therefore, surprising that the populace should have been firmly convinced that every great catastrophe that occurred was due to the presence of the enemies of the gods. ' If the Tiber ascends to the walls,' says Tertullian, ' or if the Nile does not overflow the fields, if the heaven refuses its rain, if the earth quakes, if famine and pestilence desolate the land, immediately the cry is raised, "The Christians to the lions!"'[2] ' There is no rain—the Christians are the cause,' had become a popular proverb in Rome.[3] Earthquakes, which, on account of their peculiarly appalling, and, to ignorant men, mysterious nature, have played a very large part in the history of superstition, were frequent and terrible in the Asiatic provinces, and in three or four instances the persecution of the Christians may be distinctly traced to the fanaticism they produced.

There is no part of ecclesiastical history more curious than the effects of this belief in alternately assisting or impeding the progress of different Churches. In the first three centuries of Christian history, it was the cause of fearful sufferings to the faith; but even then the Christians usually accepted the theory of their adversaries, though they differed concerning its application. Tertullian and Cyprian strongly maintained, sometimes that the calamities were due to the anger of the Almighty against idolatry, sometimes that they were intended to avenge the persecution of the truth. A collection was early made of men who, having been hostile to the Christian faith, had died by some horrible

---

[1] Pliny, in his famous letter to Trajan about the Christians, notices that this had been the case in Bithynia.

[2] Tert. *Apol.* xl. See, too, Cyprian, *contra Demetrian.*, and Arnobius, *Apol.* lib. i.

[3] St. Aug. *De Civ. Dei,* ii. 3

death, and their deaths were pronounced to be Divine punishments.[1] The victory which established the power of the
first Christian emperor, and the sudden death of Arius,
were afterwards accepted as decisive proofs of the truth of
Christianity, and of the falsehood of Arianism.[2] But soon
the manifest signs of the dissolution of the Empire revived
the zeal of the Pagans, who began to reproach themselves
for their ingratitude to their old gods, and who recognised in
the calamities of their country the vengeance of an insulted
Heaven. When the altar of Victory was removed contemptuously from the Senate, when the sacred college of the
vestals was suppressed, when, above all, the armies of Alaric
encircled the Imperial city, angry murmurs arose which disturbed the Christians in their triumph. The standing-point
of the theologians was then somewhat altered. St. Ambrose
dissected with the most unsparing rationalism the theory
that ascribed the national decline to the suppression of the
vestals, traced it to all its consequences, and exposed all its
absurdities. Orosius wrote his history to prove that great
misfortunes had befallen the Empire before its conversion.
Salvian wrote his treatise on Providence to prove that the

---

[1] Instances of this kind are given
by Tertullian *Ad Scapulam*, and the
whole treatise *On the Deaths of the
Persecutors*, attributed to Lactantius, is a development of the same
theory. St. Cyprian's treatise against
Demetrianus throws much light on
the mode of thought of the Christians of his time. In the later historians. anecdotes of adversaries of
the Church dying horrible deaths
became very numerous. They were
said especially to have been eaten
by worms. Many examples of this
kind are collected by Jortin. (*Remarks on Eccles. Hist.* vol. i. p. 432.)

[2] 'It is remarkable, in all the
proclamations and documents which

Eusebius assigns to Constantine,
some even written by his own hand,
how, almost exclusively, he dwells
on this worldly superiority of the
God adored by the Christians over
those of the heathens, and the
visible temporal advantages which
attend on the worship of Christianity. His own victory, and the
disasters of his enemies, are his conclusive evidences of Christianity.'—
Milman, *Hist. of Early Christianity*
(ed. 1867), vol. ii. p. 327. 'It was
a standing argument of Athanasius,
that the death of Arius was a sufficient refutation of his heresy.'—
Ibid. p. 382.

barbarian invasions were a Divine judgment on the immorality of the Christians. St. Augustine concentrated all his genius on a great work, written under the impression of the invasion of Alaric, and intended to prove that 'the city of God' was not on earth, and that the downfall of the Empire need therefore cause no disquietude to the Christians. St. Gregory the Great continually represented the calamities of Italy as warnings foreboding the destruction of the world. When Rome sank finally before the barbarian hosts, it would seem as though the doctrine that temporal success was the proof of Divine favour must be finally abandoned. But the Christian clergy disengaged their cause from that of the ruined Empire, proclaimed its downfall to be a fulfilment of prophecy and a Divine judgment, confronted the barbarian conquerors in all the majesty of their sacred office, and overawed them in the very moment of their victory. In the conversion of the uncivilised tribes, the doctrine of special intervention occupied a commanding place. The Burgundians, when defeated by the Huns, resolved, as a last resource, to place themselves under the protection of the Roman God whom they vaguely believed to be the most powerful, and the whole nation in consequence embraced Christianity.[1] In a critical moment of a great battle, Clovis invoked the assistance of the God of his wife. The battle was won, and he, with many thousands of Franks, was converted to the faith.[2] In England, the conversion of Northumbria was partly, and the conversion of Mercia was mainly, due to the belief that the Divine interposition had secured the victory of a Christian king.[3] A Bulgarian prince was driven into the Church by the terror of a pestilence, and he speedily effected the conversion of his subjects.[4] The destruction of so many

---

Socrates, *Eccl. Hist.*, vii. 30.

[2] Greg. Tur. ii. 30. 31. Clovis wrote to St. Avitus, 'Your faith is our victory.'

[3] Milman's *Latin Christianity* (ed. 1867), vol. ii. pp. 236–245.

[4] Ibid. vol. iii. p. 248.

shrines, and the defeat of so many Christian armies, by
the followers of Mohamet; the disastrous and ignominious
overthrow of the Crusaders, who went forth protected by
all the blessings of the Church, were unable to impair the
belief. All through the middle ages, and for some centuries after the middle ages had passed, every startling cata
strophe was regarded as a punishment, or a warning, or a
sign of the approaching termination of the world Churches
and monasteries were built. Religious societies were
founded. Penances were performed. Jews were massacred,
and a long catalogue might be given of the theories by
which men attempted to connect every vicissitude of fortune,
and every convulsion of nature, with the wranglings of
theologians. Thus, to give but a few examples : St. Ambrose
confidently asserted that the death of Maximus was a consequence of the crime he had committed in compelling the
Christians to rebuild a Jewish synagogue they had destroyed.[1]
One of the laws in the Justinian code, directed against the
Jews, Samaritans, and Pagans, expressly attributes to them
the sterility of the soil, which in an earlier age the Pagans
had so often attributed to the Christians.[2] A volcanic eruption that broke out at the commencement of the iconoclastic
persecution was adduced as a clear proof that the Divine
anger was aroused, according to one party, by the hostility
of the emperor to the sacred images; according to the other
party, by his sinful hesitation in extirpating idolatry.[3] Bodin,
in a later age, considered that the early death of the sovereign

---

[1] *Ep.* xl.

[2] 'An diutius perferimus mutari
temporum vices, irata cœli tem-
perie? Quæ Paganorum exacerbata
perfidiâ nescit naturæ libramenta
servare. Unde enim ver solitam
gratiam abjuravit ? unde æstas,
messe jejuna, laboriosum agrico-
lam in spe destituit aristarum?

unde hyemis intemperata ferocitas
uberitatem terrarum penetrabili
frigore sterilitatis læsione damnavit? nisi quod ad impietatis vindictam transit lege sua naturæ
decretum.' — Novell. lii. Theodos.
De Judæis, Samaritanis, et Hæreticis.

[3] Milman's *Latin Christianity*
vol. ii. p. 354.

who commanded the massacre of St. Bartholomew was due to what he deemed the master crime of that sovereign's reign. He had spared the life of a famous sorcerer.[1] In the struggles that followed the Reformation, physical calamities were continually ascribed in one age to the toleration, in another to the endowment, of either heresy or Popery.[2] Sometimes, however, they were traced to the theatre, and sometimes to the writings of freethinkers. But gradually, and almost insensibly, these notions faded away. The old language is often heard, but it is no longer realised and operative, and the doctrine which played so large a part in the history of the world has ceased to exercise any appreciable influence upon the actions of mankind.

In addition to this religious motive, which acted chiefly upon the vulgar, there was a political motive which rendered Christianity obnoxious to the educated. The Church constituted a vast, highly organised, and in many respects secret society, and as such was not only distinctly illegal, but was also in the very highest degree calculated to excite the apprehensions of the Government. There was no principle in the Imperial policy more stubbornly upheld than the suppression of all corporations that might be made the nuclei of revolt. The extent to which this policy was carried is strikingly evinced by a letter from Trajan to Pliny, in which the emperor forbade the formation even of a guild of firemen, on the ground that they would constitute an association and hold meetings.[3] In such a state of feeling, the existence of a vast association, governed by countless functionaries, shrouding its meetings and some of its doctrines in impenetrable obscurity, evoking a degree of attachment and devotion

---

Démonomanie des Sorciers, p. 152.

[2] See a curious instance in Bayle's *Dictionary,* art. · Vergerius.'

[3] Pliny. *Ep.* x. 43. Trajan noticed

that Nicomedia was peculiarly turbulent. On the edict against the hetæriæ, or associations see *Ep.* x. 97.

greater than could be elicited by the State, ramifying through the whole extent of the empire, and restlessly extending its influence, would naturally arouse the strongest apprehension. That it did so is clearly recognised by the Christian apologists, who, however, justly retorted upon the objectors the impossi- bility of showing a single instance in which, in an age of con- tinual conspiracies, the numerous and persecuted Christians had proved disloyal. Whatever we may think of their doc- trine of passive obedience, it is impossible not to admire the constancy with which they clung to it, when all their interests were the other way. But yet the Pagans were not altogether wrong in regarding the new association as fatal to the great- ness of the Empire. It consisted of men who regarded the Roman Empire as a manifestation of Antichrist, and who looked forward with passionate longing to its destruction. It substituted a new enthusiasm for that patriotism which was the very life-blood of the national existence. Many of the Christians deemed it wrong to fight for their country. All of them aspired to a type of character, and were actuated by hopes and motives, wholly inconsistent with that proud martial ardour by which the triumphs of Rome had been won, and by which alone her impending ruin could be averted.

The aims and principles of this association were very imperfectly understood. The greatest and best of the Pagans spoke of it as a hateful superstition, and the phrase they most frequently reiterated, when speaking of its members, was 'enemies' or 'haters of the human race.' Such a charge, directed persistently against men whose main principle was the supreme excellence of love, and whose charity unques- tionably rose far above that of any other class, was probably due in the first place to the unsocial habits of the converts, who deemed it necessary to abstain from all the forms of public amusement, to refuse to illuminate their houses, or hang garlands from their portals in honour of the national

triumphs, and who somewhat ostentatiously exhibited themselves as separate and alien from their countrymen.   It may
also have arisen from a knowledge of the popular Christian
doctrine about the future destiny of Pagans.   When the
Roman learnt what fate the Christian assigned to the heroes
and sages of his nation, and to the immense mass of his living
fellow-countrymen, when he was told that the destruction of
the once glorious Empire to which he belonged was one of
the most fervent aspirations of the Church, his feelings were
very likely to clothe themselves in such language as I have
cited.

But, in addition to the general charges, specific accusations[1] of the grossest kind were directed against Christian
morals.   At a time when the moral standard was very low,
they were charged with deeds so atrocious as to scandalise the
most corrupt.   They were represented as habitually, in their
secret assemblies, celebrating the most licentious orgies,
feeding on human flesh, and then, the lights having been
extinguished, indulging in promiscuous, and especially in
incestuous, intercourse.   The persistence with which these
accusations were made is shown by the great prominence they
occupy, both in the writings of the apologists and in the
narrations of the persecutions.   That these charges were
absolutely false will now be questioned by no one.   The
Fathers were long able to challenge their adversaries to produce a single instance in which any other crime than his
faith was proved against a martyr, and they urged with a
just and noble pride that whatever doubt there might be of
the truth of the Christian doctrines, or of the Divine origin
of the Christian miracles, there was at least no doubt that
Christianity had transformed the characters of multitudes,
vivified the cold heart by a new enthusiasm, redeemed, re-

---

[1] All the apologists are full of
these charges.   The chief passages
have been collected in that very
useful and learned work, Korthold,
De Calumniis contra Christianos
(Cologne, 1683.)

generated, and emancipated the most depraved of mankind. Noble lives, crowned by heroic deaths, were the best arguments of the infant Church.[1] Their enemies themselves not unfrequently acknowledged it. The love shown by the early Christians to their suffering brethren has never been more emphatically attested than by Lucian,[2] or the beautiful simplicity of their worship than by Pliny,[3] or their ardent charity than by Julian.[4] There was, it is true, another side to the picture; but even when the moral standard of Christians was greatly lowered, it was lowered only to that of the community about them.

These calumnies were greatly encouraged by the ecclesiastical rule, which withheld from the unbaptised all knowledge of some of the more mysterious doctrines of the Church, and veiled, at least, one of its ceremonies in great obscurity. Vague rumours about the nature of that sacramental feast, to which none but the baptised Christian was suffered to penetrate, and which no ecclesiastic was permitted to explain either to the catechumens or to the world, were probably the origin of the charge of cannibalism; while the Agapæ or love feasts, the ceremony of the kiss of love, and the peculiar and, to the Pagans, perhaps unintelligible, language in which the Christians proclaimed themselves one body and fellow-members in Christ, may have suggested the other charges. The eager credulity with which equally baseless accusations against the Jews were for centuries believed, illustrates the readiness with which they were accepted, and the extremely imperfect system of police which rendered the verification of secret crimes very difficult, had no doubt greatly enlarged the sphere of calumny. But, in addition to these considerations, the orthodox were in some respects exceedingly unfortunate. In the eyes of the Pagans they

---

[1] Justin Martyr tells us it was the brave deaths of the Christians that converted him. (*Apol.* ii. 12.)

[2] Peregrinus.
[3] *Ep.* x. 97
[4] *Ep.* ii.

were regarded as a sect of Jews; and the Jews, on account
of their continual riots, their inextinguishable hatred of the
Gentile world,[1] and the atrocities that frequently accompanied their rebellions, had early excited the anger and the
contempt of the Pagans. On the other hand, the Jew, who
deemed the abandonment of the law the most heinous of
crimes, and whose patriotism only shone with a fiercer flame
amid the calamities of his nation, regarded the Christian
with an implacable hostility. Scorned or hated by those
around him, his temple levelled with the dust, and the last
vestige of his independence destroyed, he clung with a
desperate tenacity to the hopes and privileges of his ancient
creed. In his eyes the Christians were at once apostates
and traitors. He could not forget that in the last dark hour
of his country's agony, when the armies of the Gentile
encompassed Jerusalem, and when the hosts of the faithful
flocked to its defence, the Christian Jews had abandoned the
fortunes of their race, and refused to bear any part in the
heroism and the sufferings of the closing scene. They had
proclaimed that the promised Messiah, who was to restore
the faded glories of Israel, had already come; that the privileges which were so long the monopoly of a single people had
passed to the Gentile world; that the race which was once
supremely blest was for all future time to be accursed among
mankind. It is not, therefore, surprising that there should
have arisen between the two creeds an animosity which
Paganism could never rival. While the Christians viewed
with too much exultation the calamities that fell upon the
prostrate people,[2] whose cup of bitterness they were destined

---

[1] Juvenal describes the popular
estimate of the Jews:—
  'Tradidit arcano quodcunque
      volumine Moses;
  Non monstrare vias, eadem nisi
      sacra colenti,

Quæsitum ad fontem solos dedu
    cere verpos.'
              Sat. xix. 102–105.
It is not true that the Mosaic law
contains these precepts.
  [2] See Merivale's *Hist. of Rome*,
vol. viii. p. 176.

through long centuries to fill to the brim, the Jews laboured
with unwearied hatred to foment by calumnies the passions of the Pagan multitude.[1] On the other hand, the
Catholic Christians showed themselves extremely willing to
draw down the sword of the persecutor upon the heretical
sects. When the Pagans accused the Christians of indulging
in orgies of gross licentiousness, the first apologist, while repudiating the charge, was careful to add, of the heretics,
'Whether or not these people commit those shameful and
fabulous acts, the putting out the lights, indulging in promiscuous intercourse, and eating human flesh, I know not.'[2]
In a few years the language of doubt and insinuation was
exchanged for that of direct assertion ; and, if we may believe
St. Irenæus and St. Clement of Alexandria, the followers of
Carpocrates, the Marcionites, and some other Gnostic sects,
habitually indulged, in their secret meetings, in acts of
impurity and licentiousness as hideous and as monstrous as
can be conceived, and their conduct was one of the causes
of the persecution of the orthodox.[3] Even the most extravagant charges of the Pagan populace were reiterated by
the Fathers in their accusations of the Gnostics. St. Epiphanius, in the fourth century, assures us that some of their
sects were accustomed to kill, to dress with spices, and to eat
the children born of their promiscuous intercourse.[4] The

[1] See Justin Martyr, *Trypho*,
xvii.
[2] Justin Martyr, *Apol.* i. 26.
[3] Eusebius expressly notices
that the licentiousness of the sect
of Carpocrates occasioned calumnies
against the whole of the Christian
body. (iv. 7.) A number of passages
from the Fathers describing the
immorality of these heretics are
referred to by Cave, *Primitive
Christianity*, part ii. ch. v.
[4] Epiphanius, *Adv. Hær.* lib. i.
Hær. 26. The charge of murder-

ing children, and especially infants,
occupies a very prominent place
among the recriminations of religionists. The Pagans, as we have
seen, brought it against the Christians, and the orthodox against some
of the early heretics. The Christians accused Julian of murdering
infants for magical purposes, and
the bed of the Orontes was said to
have been choked with their bodies
The accusation was then commonly
directed against the Jews, against
the witches, and against the mid

heretics, in their turn, gladly accused the Catholics,[1] while the Roman judge, in whose eyes Judaism, orthodox Christianity, and heresy were but slightly differing modifications of one despicable superstition, doubtless found in this interchange of accusations a corroboration of his prejudices.

Another cause of the peculiar animosity felt against the Christians was the constant interference with domestic life, arising from the great number of female conversions. The Christian teacher was early noted for his unrivalled skill in playing on the chords of a woman's heart.[2] The graphic title of ' Earpicker of ladies,'[3] which was given to a seductive pontiff of a somewhat later period, might have been applied to many in the days of the persecution; and to the Roman, who regarded the supreme authority of the head of the family, in

---

wives, who were supposed to be in confederation with the witches.

[1] See an example in Eusebius, iii. 32. After the triumph of Christianity the Arian heretics appear to have been accustomed to bring accusations of immorality against the Catholics. They procured the deposition of St. Eustathius, Bishop of Antioch, by suborning a prostitute to accuse him of being the father of her child. The woman afterwards, on her deathbed, confessed the imposture. (Theodor. *Hist.* i. 21–22.) They also accused St. Athanasius of murder and unchastity, both of which charges he most triumphantly repelled. (Ibid. i. 30.)

[2] The great exertions and success of the Christians in making female converts is indignantly noticed by Celsus (*Origen*) and by the Pagan interlocutor in Minucius Felix (*Octavius*), and a more minute examination of ecclesiastical history amply confirms their statements.

I shall have in a future chapter to revert to this matter. Tertullian graphically describes the anger of a man he knew, at the conversion of his wife, and declares he would rather have had her 'a prostitute than a Christian.' (*Ad Nationes*, i. 4.) He also mentions a governor of Cappadocia, named Herminianus, whose motive for persecuting the Christians was his anger at the conversion of his wife, and who, in consequence of his having persecuted, was devoured by worms. (*Ad Scapul.* 3.)

[3] 'Matronarum Auriscalpius. The title was given to Pope St. Damasus. See Jortin's *Remarks on Ecclesiastical History*, vol. ii. p. 27. Ammianus Marcellinus notices (xxvii. 3) the great wealth the Roman bishops of his time had acquired through the gifts of women. Theodoret (*Hist. Eccl.* ii. 17) gives a curious account of the energetic proceedings of the Roman ladies upon the exile of Pope Liberius.

all religious matters, as the very foundation of domestic morality, no character could appear more infamous or more revolting. ' A wife,' said Plutarch, expressing the deepest conviction of the Pagan world, ' should have no friends but those of her husband ; and, as the gods are the first of friends, she should know no gods but those whom her husband a lores. Let her shut the door, then, against idle religions and foreign superstitions. No god can take pleasure in sacrifices offered by a wife without the knowledge of her husband.'[1] But these principles, upon which the whole social system of Paganism had rested, were now disregarded. Wives in multitudes deserted their homes to frequent the nocturnal meetings[2] of a sect which was looked upon with the deepest suspicion, and was placed under the ban of the law. Again and again, the husband, as he laid his head on the pillow by his wife, had the bitterness of thinking that all her sympathies were withdrawn from him ; that her affections belonged to an alien priesthood and to a foreign creed; that, though she might discharge her duties with a gentle and uncomplaining fidelity, he had for ever lost the power of touch-

---

[1] *Conj. Præcept.* This passage has been thought to refer to the Christians ; if so, it is the single example of its kind in the writings of Plutarch.

[2] Pliny, in his letter on the Christians, notices that their assemblies were before daybreak. Tertullian and Minucius Felix speak frequently of the 'nocturnes convocationes,' or 'nocturnes congregationes' of the Christians. The following passage, which the last of these writers puts into the mouth of a Pagan, describes forcibly the popular feeling about the Christians : ' Qui de ultima fæce collectis imperitioribus et mulieribus credulis sexus sui facilitate labentibus, plebem profanæ conjurationis instituunt : quæ nocturnis congregationibus et jejuniis solennibus et inhumanis cibis non sacro quodam sed piaculo fœderantur, latebrosa et lucifugax natio, in publico muta, in angulis garrula; templa ut busta despiciunt, deos despuunt, rident sacra.'— *Octavius.* Tertullian, in exhorting the Christian women not to intermarry with Pagans, gives as one reason that they would not permit them to attend this 'nightly convocation.' (*Ad Uxorem*, ii. 4.) This whole chapter is a graphic but deeply painful picture of the utter impossibility of a Christian woman having any real community of feeling with a 'servant of the devil.'

ing her heart—he was to her only as an outcast, as a brand prepared for the burning. Even to a Christian mind there is a deep pathos in the picture which St. Augustine has drawn of the broken-hearted husband imploring the assistance of the gods, and receiving from the oracle the bitter answer: 'You may more easily write in enduring characters on the wave, or fly with feathers through the air, than purge the mind of a woman when once tainted by the superstition.'[1]

I have already noticed the prominence which the practice of exorcism had acquired in the early Church, the contempt with which it was regarded by the more philosophic Pagans, and the law which had been directed against its professors. It is not, however, probable that this practice, though it lowered the Christians in the eyes of the educated as much as it elevated them in the eyes of the populace, had any appreciable influence in provoking persecution. In the crowd of superstitions that were invading the Roman Empire, exorcism had a prominent place; all such practices were popular with the masses; the only form of magic which under the Empire was seriously persecuted was political astrology or divination with a view to discovering the successors to the throne, and of this the Christians were never accused.[2] There was, however, another form of what was deemed superstition connected with the Church, which was regarded by Pagan philosophers with a much deeper feeling of aversion. To agitate the minds of men with religious terrorism, to fill the unknown world with hideous images of suffering, to govern the reason by alarming the imagination, was in the eyes of the Pagan world one of the most heinous of crimes.[3] These fears

---

[1] De Civ. Dei, xix. 23.

[2] The policy of the Romans with reference to magic has been minutely traced by Maury, Hist. de la Magie. Dr. Jeremie conjectures that the exorcisms of the Christians may have excited the antipathy of Marcus Aurelius, he, as I have already noticed, being a disbeliever on this subject. (Jeremie, Hist. of Church in the Second and Third Cent. p. 26.) But this is mere conjecture.

[3] See the picture of the senti

were to the ancients the very definition of superstition, anu their destruction was a main object both of the Epicurean and of the Stoic. To men holding such sentiments, it is easy to perceive how obnoxious must have appeared re'igious teachers who maintained that an eternity of torture was reserved for the entire human race then existing in the world, beyond the range of their own community, and who made the assertion of this doctrine one of their main instruments of success.[1] Enquiry, among the early theologians, was much less valued than belief,[2] and reason was less appealed to than fear. In philosophy the most comprehensive, but in theology the most intolerant, system is naturally the strongest. To weak women, to the young, the ignorant, and the timid, to all, in a word, who were doubtful of their own judgment, the doctrine of exclusive salvation must have come with an appalling power ; and, as no other religion professed it, it supplied the Church with an invaluable vantage-ground, and

ments of the Pagans on this matter, in Plutarch's noble *Treatise on Superstition.*

[1] Thus Justin Martyr: 'Since sensation remains in all men who have been in existence, and everlasting punishment is in store, do not hesitate to believe, and be convinced that what I say is true. . . This Gehenna is a place where all will be punished who live unrighteously, and who believe not that what God has taught through Christ will come to pass.'—*Apol.* l. 18–19. Arnobius has stated very forcibly the favourite argument of many later theologians: 'Cum ergo hæc sit conditio futurorum ut teneri et comprehendi nullius possiat anticipationis attactu: nonne prior ratio est, ex duobus incertis et in ambigua expectatione pendentibus, id potius credere quod

aliquas spes ferat, quam omnino quod nullas ? In illo enim periculi nihil est, si quod dicitur imminere cassum fiat et vacuum. In hoc damnum est maximum.'—*Adv. Gentes,* lib. i

[2] The continual enforcement of the duty of belief, and the credulity of the Christians, were perpetually dwelt on by Celsus and Julian. According to the first, it was usual for them to say, 'Do not examine, but believe only.' According to the latter, 'the sum of their wisdom was comprised in this single precept, believe.' The apologists frequently notice this charge of credulity as brought against the Christians, and some famous sentences of Tertullian go far to justify it. See Middleton's *Free Enquiry,* Introd. pp. xcii. xciii.

doubtless drove multitudes into its pale. To this doctrine we may also, in a great degree, ascribe the agony of terror that was so often displayed by the apostate, whose flesh shrank from the present torture, but who was convinced that the weakness he could not overcome would be expiated by an eternity of torment.[1] To the indignation excited by such teaching was probably due a law of Marcus Aurelius, which decreed that ' if any one shall do anything whereby the weak minds of any may be terrified by superstitious fear, the offender shall be exiled into an island.'[2]

There can, indeed, be little doubt that a chief cause of the hostility felt against the Christian Church was the intolerant aspect it at that time displayed. The Romans were prepared to tolerate almost any form of religion that would tolerate others. The Jews, though quite as obstinate as the Christians in refusing to sacrifice to the emperor, were rarely molested, except in the periods immediately following their insurrections, because Judaism, however exclusive and unsocial, was still an unaggressive national faith. But the Christian teachers taught that all religions, except their own and that of the Jews, were constructed by devils, and that all who dissented from their Church must be lost. It was impossible that men strung to the very highest pitch of religious excitement, and imagining they saw in every ceremony and oracle the direct working of a present dæmon, could restrain their zeal

---

[1] See the graphic picture of the agony of terror manifested by the apostates as they tottered to the altar at Alexandria, in the Decian persecution, in Dionysius apud Eusebius, vi. 41. Miraculous judgments (often, perhaps, the natural consequence of this extreme fear) were said to have frequently fallen upon the apostates. St. Cyprian has preserved a number of these in his treatise De Lapsis.

Persons, when excommunicated, were also said to have been sometimes visibly possessed by devils. See Church, On Miraculous Powers in the First Three Centuries, pp. 52–54.

[2] 'Si quis aliquid fecerit, quo leves hominum animi superstitione numinis terrerentur, Divus Marcus hujusmodi homines in insulam relegari rescripsit.' Dig. xlviii. tit. 19, l. 30.

or respect in any degree the feelings of others. Proselytising
with an untiring energy, pouring a fierce stream of invective
and ridicule upon the gods on whose favour the multitude
believed all national prosperity to depend, not unfrequently
insulting the worshippers, and defacing the idols,[1] they soon
stung the Pagan devotees to madness, and convinced them that
every calamity that fell upon the empire was the righteous
vengeance of the gods. Nor was the sceptical politician more
likely to regard with favour a religion whose development
was plainly incompatible with the whole religious policy of
the Empire. The new Church, as it was then organised,
must have appeared to him essentially, fundamentally, necessarily intolerant. To permit it to triumph was to permit the
extinction of religious liberty in an empire which comprised
all the leading nations of the world, and tolerated all their
creeds. It was indeed true that in the days of their distress
the apologists proclaimed, in high and eloquent language, the
iniquity of persecution, and the priceless value of a free
worship; but it needed no great sagacity to perceive that the
language of the dominant Church would be very different.
The Pagan philosopher could not foresee the ghastly histories
of the Inquisition, of the Albigenses, or of St. Bartholomew;
but he could scarcely doubt that the Christians, when in the
ascendant, would never tolerate rites which they believed to
be consecrated to devils, or restrain, in the season of their
power, a religious animosity which they scarcely bridled
when they were weak. It needed no prophetic inspiration

---

[1] A number of instances have
been recorded, in which the punishment of the Christians was due to
their having broken idols, over-
turned altars, or in other ways
insulted the Pagans at their worship. The reader may find many
examples of this collected in Cave's
Primitive Christianity, part i. c. v.;
Kortholt, *De Calumniis contra*
Christianos; Barbeyrac, *Morale des
Pères*, c. xvii.; Tillemont, *Mém.
ecclésiast.* tome vii. pp. 354–355;
Ceillier, *Hist. des Auteurs sacrés*,
tome iii. pp. 531-533. The Council
of Illiberis found it necessary to
make a canon refusing the title of
'martyr' to those who were executed for these offences.

to anticipate the time, that so speedily arrived, when, amid the wailings of the worshippers, the idols and the temples were shattered, and when all who practised the religious ceremonies of their forefathers were subject to the penalty of death.

There has probably never existed upon earth a community whose members were bound to one another by a deeper or a purer affection than the Christians, in the days of the persecution. There has probably never existed a community which exhibited in its dealings with crime a gentler or more judicious kindness, which combined more happily an unflinching opposition to sin with a boundless charity to the sinner, and which was in consequence more successful in reclaiming and transforming the most vicious of mankind. There has, however, also never existed a community which displayed more clearly the intolerance that would necessarily follow its triumph. Very early tradition has related three anecdotes of the apostle John which illustrate faithfully this triple aspect of the Church. It is said that when the assemblies of the Christians thronged around him to hear some exhortation from his lips, the only words he would utter were, 'My little children, love one another;' for in this, he said, is comprised the entire law. It is said that a young man he had once confided to the charge of a bishop, having fallen into the ways of vice, and become the captain of a band of robbers, the apostle, on hearing of it, bitterly reproached the negligence of the pastor, and, though in extreme old age, betook himself to the mountains till he had been captured by the robbers, when, falling with tears on the neck of the chief, he restored him to the path of virtue. It is said that the same apostle, once seeing the heretic Cerinthus in an establishment of baths into which he had entered, immediately rushed forth, fearing lest the roof should fall because a heretic was beneath it.[1]   All that fierce hatred

---

[1] The first of these anecdotes is told by St. Jerome, the second by St. Clement of Alexandria, the third by St. Irenæus.

which during the Arian and Donatist controversies convulsed
the Empire, and which in later times has deluged the world
with blood, may be traced in the Church long before the
conversion of Constantine. Already, in the second century.
it was the rule that the orthodox Christian should hold no
conversation, should interchange none of the most ordinary
courtesies of life, with the excommunicated or the heretic.[1]
Common sufferings were impotent to assuage the animosity,
and the purest and fondest relations of life were polluted by
the new intolerance.   The Decian persecution had scarcely
closed, when St. Cyprian wrote his treatise to maintain that
it is no more possible to be saved beyond the limits of the
Church, than it was during the deluge beyond the limits of the
ark; that martyrdom itself has no power to efface the guilt of
schism ; and that the heretic, who for his master's cause
expired in tortures upon the earth, passed at once, by that
master's decree, into an eternity of torment in hell![2]   Even

---

[1] The severe discipline of the
early Church on this point has
been amply treated in Marshall's
Penitential Discipline of the Primitive Church (first published in 1714,
but reprinted in the library of
Anglo-Catholic theology), and in
Bingham's *Antiquities of the Christian Church*, vol. vi. (Oxford, 1855).
The later saints continually dwelt
upon this duty of separation. Thus,
' St. Théodore de Phermé disoit,
que quand une personne dont nous
étions amis estoit tombée dans la
fornication, nous devions luy donner
la main et faire notre possible pour
le relever; mais que s'il estoit
tombé dans quelque erreur contre
la foi, et qu'il ne voulust pas s'en
corriger après les premières remonstrances, il falloit l'abandonner
promptement et rompre toute
amitié avec lu   de peur qu'en
nous amusant à le vouloir retirer
de ce gouffre il ne nous y entraînast

nous-mêmes.' — Tillemont, *Mém.
Ecclés.* tome xii. p. 367.
[2] ' Habere jam non potest Deum
patrem qui ecclesiam non habet
matrem. Si potuit evadere quisquam qui extra arcam Noe fuit,
et qui extra ecclesiam foris fuerit
evadit . . . hanc unitatem qui non
tenet . . . vitam non tenet et salutem . . . esse martyr non potest
qui in ecclesia non est. . . . Cum
Deo manere non possunt qui esse
in ecclesia Dei unanimes noluerunt.
Ardeant licet flammis et ignibus
traditi, vel objecti bestiis animas
suas ponunt, non erit illa fidei
corona, sed pœna perfidiæ, nec
religiosæ virtutis exitus gloriosus
sed desperationis interitus.   Occidi
talis potest, coronari non potest.
Sic se Christianum esse profitetur
quo modo et Christum diabolus
sæpe mentitur.'—Cyprian, *De Unit.
Eccles.*

in the arena the Catholic martyrs withdrew from the Montanists, lest they should be mingled with the heretics in death.[1]   At a later period St. Augustine relates that, when he was a Manichean, his mother for a time refused even to eat at the same table with her erring child.[2]   When St. Ambrose not only defended the act of a Christian bishop, who had burnt down a synagogue of the Jews, but denounced as a deadly crime the decree of the Government which ordered it to be rebuilt;[3] when the same saint, in advocating the plunder of the vestal virgins, maintained the doctrine that it is criminal for a Christian State to grant any endowment to the ministers of any religion but his own,[4] which it has needed all the efforts of modern liberalism to efface from legislation, he was but following in the traces of those earlier Christians, who would not even wear a laurel crown,[5] or join in the most innocent civic festival, lest they should appear in some indirect way to be acquiescing in the Pagan worship.   While the apologists were maintaining against the Pagan persecutors the duty of tolerance, the Sibylline books, which were the popular literature of the Christians, were filled with passionate anticipations of the violent destruction of the Pagan temples.[6]   And no sooner had Christianity mounted the throne than the policy they foreshadowed became ascendant.   The indifference or worldly sagacity of some of the rulers, and the imposing number of the Pagans, delayed, no doubt, the final consummation; but, from the time of Constantine, restrictive laws were put in force, the influence of the ecclesiastics was ceaselessly exerted in their favour, and no sagacious man could fail to anticipate the speedy and

---

[1] Eusebius, v. ' 6.
[2] *Confess.* iii. 11.   She was afterwards permitted by a special revelation to sit at the same table with her son!
[3] *Ep.* xl.
[4] *Ep.* xviii.

[5] Tertull. *De Corona.*
[6] Milman's *Hist. of Christianity*, vol. ii. pp. 116-125.   It is remarkable that the Serapeum of Alexandria was, in the Sibylline books, specially menaced with destruction.

absolute proscription of the Pagan worship. It is related of the philosopher Antoninus, the son of the Pagan prophetess Sospitra, that, standing one day with his disciples before that noble temple of Serapis, at Alexandria, which was one of the wonders of ancient art, and which was destined soon after to perish by the rude hands of the Christian monks, the prophetic spirit of his mother fell upon him. Like another prophet before another shrine, he appalled his hearers by the prediction of the approaching ruin. The time would come, he said, when the glorious edifice before them would be overthrown, the carved images would be defaced, the temples of the gods would be turned into the sepulchres of the dead, and a great darkness would fall upon mankind![1]

And, besides the liberty of worship, the liberty of thought and of expression, which was the supreme attainment of Roman civilisation, was in peril. The new religion, unlike that which was disappearing, claimed to dictate the opinions as well as the actions of men, and its teachers stigmatised as an atrocious crime the free expression of every opinion on religious matters diverging from their own. Of all the forms of liberty, it was this which lasted the longest, and was the most dearly prized. Even after Constantine, the Pagans Libanius, Themistius, Symmachus, and Sallust enforced their views with a freedom that contrasts remarkably with the restraints imposed upon their worship, and the beautiful friendships of St. Basil and Libanius, of Synesius and Hypatia, are among the most touching episodes of their time. But though the traditions of Pagan freedom, and the true catholicism of Justin Martyr and Origen, lingered long, it was inevitable that error, being deemed criminal, should be made penal.

---

[1] Eunapius, *Lives of the Sophists*. Eunapius gives an extremely pathetic account of the downfall of this temple. There is a Christian account in Theodoret (v. 22). Theophilus, Bishop of Alexandria, was the leader of the monks. The Pagans, under the guidance of a philosopher named Olympus, made a desperate effort to defend their temple. The whole story is very finely told by Dean Milman. (*Hist. of Christianity*, vol. iii. pp. 68–72.)

The dogmatism of Athanasius and Augustine, the increasing power of the clergy, and the fanaticism of the monks, hastened the end. The suppression of all religions but one by Theodosius, the murder of Hypatia at Alexandria by the monks of Cyril, and the closing by Justinian of the schools of Athens, are the three events which mark the decisive overthrow of intellectual freedom. A thousand years had rolled away before that freedom was in part restored.

The considerations I have briefly enumerated should not in the smallest degree detract from the admiration due to the surpassing courage, to the pure, touching, and sacred virtues of the Christian martyrs; but they in some degree palliate the conduct of the persecutors, among whom must be included one emperor, who was probably, on the whole, the best and most humane sovereign who has ever sat upon a throne, and at least two others, who were considerably above the average of virtue. When, combined with the indifference to human suffering, the thirst for blood, which the spectacles of the amphitheatre had engendered, they assuredly make the persecutions abundantly explicable. They show that if it can be proved that Christian persecutions sprang from the doctrine of exclusive salvation, the fact that the Roman Pagans, who did not hold that doctrine, also persecuted, need not cause the slightest perplexity. That the persecutions of Christianity by the Roman emperors, severe as they undoubtedly were, were not of such a continuous nature as wholly to counteract the vast moral, social, and intellectual agencies that were favourable to its spread, a few dates will show.

We have seen that when the Egyptian rites were introduced into Rome, they were met by prompt and energetic measures of repression; that these measures were again and again repeated, but that at last, when they proved ineffectual, the governors desisted from their opposition, and the new worship assumed a recognised place. The history of Christianity, in its relation to the Government, is the reverse of this. Its first introduction into Rome appears to have been altogether unopposed. Tertullian asserts that Tiberius, on the ground of a report from Pontius Pilate, desired to enrol Christ among the Roman gods, but that the Senate rejected the proposal; but this assertion, which is altogether unsupported by trustworthy evidence, and is, intrinsically, extremely improbable, is now generally recognised as false.[1] An isolated passage of Suetonius states that in the time of Claudius 'the Jews, being continually rioting, at the instigation of a certain Chrestus,'[2] were expelled from the city; but no Christian writer speaks of his co-religionists being disturbed in this reign, while all, with a perfect unanimity, and with great emphasis, describe Nero as the first persecutor. His persecution began at the close of A.D. 64.[3] It was directed against Christians, not ostensibly on the ground of their religion, but because they were falsely accused of having set fire to Rome, and it is very doubtful whether it extended beyond the city.[4] It had also this peculiarity, that, being

---

[1] *Apology*, v. The overwhelming difficulties attending this assertion are well stated by Gibbon, ch. xvi. Traces of this fable may be found in Justin Martyr. The freedom of the Christian worship at Rome appears not only from the unanimity with which Christian writers date their troubles from Nero, but also from the express statement in *Acts* xxviii. 31.

[2] 'Judæos, impulsore Chresto, assidue tumultuantes, Roma expulit.'—Sueton. *Claud.* xxv. This banishment of the Jews is mentioned in *Acts* xviii. 2, but is not there connected in any way with Christianity. A passage in Dion Cassius (lx. 6) is supposed to refer to the same transaction. Lactantius notices that the Pagans were accustomed to call Christus, *Chres-*

tus : 'Eum immutata litera Chrestum solent dicere.'—*Div. Inst.* iv. 7.

[3] This persecution is fully described by Tacitus (*Annal.* xv. 44), and briefly noticed by Suetonius (*Nero*, xvi.).

[4] This has been a matter of very great controversy. Looking at the question apart from direct testimony, it appears improbable that a persecution directed against the Christians on the charge of having burnt Rome, should have extended to Christians who did not live near Rome. On the other hand, it has been argued that Tacitus speaks of them as 'haud perinde in crimine incendii, quam odio humani generis convicti;' and it has been maintained that 'hatred of the human race' was treated as a crime, and punished in the pro

directed against the Christians not as Christians, but as incendiaries, it was impossible to escape from it by apostasy. Within
the walls of Rome it raged with great fury. The Christians, who
had been for many years [1] proselytising without restraint in the
great confluence of nations, and amid the disintegration of
old beliefs, had become a formidable body. They were, we
learn from Tacitus, profoundly unpopular; but the hideous
tortures to which Nero subjected them, and the conviction
that, whatever other crimes they might have committed, they
were not guilty of setting fire to the city, awoke general pity.
Some of them, clad in skins of wild beasts, were torn by
dogs. Others, arrayed in shirts of pitch, were burnt alive in

---

vinces. But this is, I think, extremely far-fetched; and it is evident from the sequel that the
Christians at Rome were burnt
as incendiaries, and that it was
the conviction that they were not
guilty of that crime that extorted
the pity which Tacitus notices.
There is also no reference in
Tacitus to any persecution beyond
the walls. If we pass to the
Christian evidence, a Spanish inscription referring to the Neronian
persecution, which was once appealed to as decisive, is now unanimously admitted to be a forgery.
In the fourth century, however,
Sulp. Severus (lib. ii.) and Orosius
(*Hist.* vii. 7) declared that general
laws condemnatory of Christianity
were promulgated by Nero; but
the testimony of credulous historians who wrote so long after
the event is not of much value.
Rossi, however, imagines that a
fragment of an inscription found
at Pompeii indicates a general
law against Christians. See his
Bulletino d'Archeologia Cristiana
(Roma, Dec. 1865), which, however,
should be compared with the very
remarkable *Compte rendu* of M.
Aubé, *Acad. des Inscrip. et Belles-
lettres,* Juin 1866. These two papers
contain an almost complete discussion of the persecutions of Nero
and Domitian. Gibbon thinks it
quite certain the persecution was
confined to the city; Mosheim
(*Eccl. Hist.* i. p. 71) adopts the
opposite view, and appeals to the
passage in Tertullian (*Ap.* v.), in
which he speaks of 'leges istæ . . .
quas Trajanus ex parte frustratus
est, vitando inquiri Christianos,' as
implying the existence of special
laws against the Christians. This
passage, however, may merely
refer to the general law against
unauthorised religions, which Tertullian notices in this very chapter;
and Pliny, in his famous letter,
does not show any knowledge of
the existence of special legislation
about the Christians.

[1] Ecclesiastical historians maintain, but not on very strong evidence, that the Church of Rome
was founded by St. Peter, A.D. 42
or 44. St. Paul came to Rome
A.D. 61.

Nero's garden.[1]   Others were affixed to crosses.   Great multitudes perished.   The deep impression the persecution made
on the Christian mind is shown in the whole literature of the
Sibyls, which arose soon after, in which Nero is usually the
central figure, and by the belief, that lingered for centuries,
that the tyrant was yet alive, and would return once more
as the immediate precursor of Antichrist, to inflict the last
great persecution upon the Church.[2]

Nero died A.D. 68.   From that time, for at least twenty-
seven years, the Church enjoyed absolute repose.   There is
no credible evidence whatever of the smallest interference
with its freedom till the last year of the reign of Domitian ;
and a striking illustration of the fearlessness with which it
exhibited itself to the world has been lately furnished in the
discovery, near Rome, of a large and handsome porch leading
to a Christian catacomb, built above ground between the
reigns of Nero and Domitian, in the immediate neighbourhood
of one of the principal highways.[3]   The long reign of Domitian,
though it may have been surpassed in ferocity, was never
surpassed in the Roman annals in the skilfulness and the
persistence of its tyranny.   The Stoics and literary classes,
who upheld the traditions of political freedom, and who had

---

[1] On this horrible punishment
see Juvenal, *Sat.* i. 155–157.

[2] Lactantius, in the fourth century, speaks of this opinion as
still held by some 'madmen' (*De
Mort. Persec.* cap. ii.) ; but Sulp.
Severus (*Hist.* lib. ii.) speaks of it
as a common notion, and he says
that St. Martin, when asked about
the end of the world, answered,
'Neronem et Antichristum prius
esse venturos : Neronem in occi-
dentali plaga regibus subactis
decem, imperaturum, persecutionem
autem ab eo hactenus exercendam
ut idola gentium coli cogat.'—
Dial. ii.   Among the Pagans, the

notion that Nero was yet alive
lingered long, and twenty years
after his death an adventurer pretending to be Nero was enthusiastically received by the Parthians.
(Sueton. *Nero*, lvii.)

[3] See the full description of it
in Rossi's *Bulletino d'Archeol.
Crist.* Dec. 1865. Eusebius (iii. 17)
and Tertullian (*Apol.* v.) have
expressly noticed the very remarkable fact that Vespasian, who was
a bitter enemy to the Jews, and
who exiled all the leading Stoical
philosophers except **Musonius**,
never troubled the Christians.

already suffered much at the hands of Vespasian, were persecuted with relentless animosity. Metius Modestus, Aru-
lenus Rusticus, Senecio, Helvidius, Dion Chrysostom, the
younger Priscus, Junius Mauricus, Artemidorus, Euphrates,
Epictetus, Arria, Fannia, and Gratilla were either killed or
banished.[1] No measures, however, appear to have been
taken against the Christians till A.D. 95, when a short and
apparently not very severe persecution, concerning which
our information is both scanty and conflicting, was directed
against them. Of the special cause that produced it we are
left in much doubt. Eusebius mentions, on the not very
trustworthy authority of Hegesippus, that the emperor,
having heard of the existence of the grandchildren of Judas,
the brother of Christ, ordered them to be brought before him,
as being of the family of David, and therefore possible pre-
tenders to the throne ; but on finding that they were simple
peasants, and that the promised kingdom of which they spoke
was a spiritual one, he dismissed them in peace, and arrested
the persecution he had begun.[2] A Pagan historian states
that, the finances of the Empire being exhausted by lavish
expenditure in public games, Domitian, in order to replenish
his exchequer, resorted to a severe and special taxation of the
Jews ; that some of these, in order to evade the impost,
concealed their worship, while others, who are supposed to
have been Christians, are described as following the Jewish
rites without being professed Jews.[3] Perhaps, however, the
simplest explanation is the truest, and the persecution may
be ascribed to the antipathy which a despot like Domitian

---

[1] See a pathetic letter of Pliny,
lib. iii. *Ep.* xi. and also lib. i. *Ep.*
v. and the *Agricola* of Tacitus.

[2] Euseb. iii. 20.

[3] 'Præter cæteros Judaicus
fiscus acerbissime actus est. Ad
quem deferebantur, qui vel impro-
fessi Judaicam intra urbem vive-
rent vitam, vel dissimulata origine
imposita genti tributa non pepen-
dissent.'—Sueton. *Domit.* xii. Suetonius adds that, when a young
man, he saw an old man of ninety
examined before a large assembly
to ascertain whether he was circumcised.

must necessarily have felt to an institution which, though it did not, like Stoicism, resist his policy, at least exercised a vast influence altogether removed from his control. St. John, who was then a very old man, is said to have been at this time exiled to Patmos. Flavius Clemens, a consul, and a relative of the emperor, was put to death. His wife, or, according to another account, his niece Domitilla, was banished, according to one account, to the island of Pontia, according to another, to the island of Pandataria, and many others were compelled to accompany her into exile.[1] Numbers, we are told, 'accused of conversion to impiety or Jewish rites,' were condemned. Some were killed, and others deprived of their offices.[2] Of the cessation of the persecution there are two different versions. Tertullian[3] and Eusebius[4] say that the tyrant speedily revoked his edict, and restored those who had been banished; but according to Lactantius these measures were not taken till after the death of Domitian,[5] and

---

[1] Euseb. iii. 18.

[2] See the accounts of these transactions in Xiphilin, the abbreviator of Dion Cassius (lxvii. 14); Euseb. iii. 17–18. Suetonius notices (*Domit.* xv.) that Flavius Clemens (whom he calls a man 'contemptissimæ inertiæ') was killed 'ex tenuissima suspicione.' The language of Xiphilin, who says he was killed for 'impiety and Jewish rites;' the express assertion of Eusebius, that it was for Christianity; and the declaration of Tertullian, that Christians were persecuted at the close of this reign, leave, I think, little doubt that this execution was connected with Christianity, though some writers have questioned it. At the same time, it is very probable, as Mr. Merivale thinks (*Hist. of Rome*, vol vii. pp. 381–384), that though the pretext of the execution might have been religious, the real

motive was political jealousy. Domitian had already put to death the brother of Flavius Clemens on the charge of treason. His sons had been recognised as successors to the throne, and at the time of his execution another leading noble named Glabrio was accused of having fought in the arena. Some ecclesiastical historians have imagined that there may have been two Domitillas—the wife and niece of Flavius Clemens. The islands of Pontia and Pandataria were close to one another.

[3] 'Tentaverat et Domitianus, portio Neronis de crudelitate; sed qua et homo facile cœptum repressit, restitutis etiam quos relegaverat.' (*Apol.* 5.) It will be observed that Tertullian makes no mention of any punishment more severe than exile.

[4] Euseb. iii. 20.

[5] *De Mort. Persec.* iii.

this latter statement is corroborated by the assertion of
Dion Cassius, that Nerva, upon his accession, 'absolved
those who were accused of impiety, and recalled the exiles.'[1]

When we consider the very short time during which this
persecution lasted, and the very slight notice that was taken
of it, we may fairly, I think, conclude that it was not of a
nature to check in any appreciable degree a strong religious
movement like that of Christianity. The assassination of
Domitian introduces us to the golden age of the Roman
Empire. In the eyes of the Pagan historian, the period
from the accession of Nerva, in A.D. 96, to the death of
Marcus Aurelius, in A.D. 180, is memorable as a period of
uniform good government, of rapidly advancing humanity,
of great legislative reforms, and of a peace which was very
rarely seriously broken. To the Christian historian it is
still more remarkable, as one of the most critical periods in
the history of his faith. The Church entered into it considerable indeed, as a sect, but not large enough to be reckoned
an important power in the Empire. It emerged from it so
increased in its numbers, and so extended in its ramifications,
that it might fairly defy the most formidable assaults. It
remains, therefore, to be seen whether the opposition against
which, during these eighty-four years, it had so successfully
struggled was of such a kind and intensity that the triumph
must be regarded as a miracle.

Nearly at the close of this period, during the persecution
of Marcus Aurelius, St. Melito, Bishop of Sardis, wrote a
letter of expostulation to the emperor, in which he explicitly
asserts that in Asia the persecution of the pious was an
event which 'had never before occurred,' and was the result
of 'new and strange decrees;' that the ancestors of the
emperor were accustomed to honour the Christian faith

---

[1] Xiphilin, lxviii. 1. An anno-
tator to Mosheim conjectures that
the edict may have been issued
just before the death of the
emperor, but not acted on till
after it.

'like other religions;' and that 'Nero and Domitian alone
had been hostile to it.[1] Rather more than twenty years
later, Tertullian asserted, in language equally distinct and
emphatic, that the two persecutors of the Christians were
Nero and Domitian, and that it would be impossible to name
a single good sovereign who had molested them. Marcus
Aurelius himself, Tertullian refuses to number among the
persecutors, and, even relying upon a letter which was falsely
imputed to him, enrols him among the protectors of the
Church.[2] About a century later, Lactantius, reviewing the
history of the persecutions, declared that the good sovereigns
who followed Domitian abstained from persecuting, and
passes at once from the persecution of Domitian to that of
Decius. Having noticed the measures of the former emperor, he proceeds: 'The acts of the tyrant being revoked,
the Church was not only restored to its former state, but
shone forth with a greater splendour and luxuriance; and a
period following in which many good sovereigns wielded the
Imperial sceptre, it suffered no assaults from its enemies, but
stretched out its hands to the east and to the west; . . .
but at last the long peace was broken. After many years,
that hateful monster Decius arose, who troubled the Church.'[3]

We have here three separate passages, from which we
may conclusively infer that the normal and habitual condition of the Christians during the eighty-four years we are
considering, and, if we accept the last two passages, during a
much longer period, was a condition of peace, but that peace
was not absolutely unbroken. The Christian Church, which
was at first regarded simply as a branch of Judaism, had
begun to be recognised as a separate body, and the Roman
law professedly tolerated only those religions which were

Euseb. iv. 26. The whole of
this apology has been recently
recovered, and translated into
Latin by M. Renan in the *Spici-
legium Solesmense.*
[2] *Apol.* 5.
[3] Lactant. *De Mort. Persec.* 3-4.

expressly authorised. It is indeed true that with the extension of the Empire, and especially of the city, the theory, or at least the practice, of religious legislation had been profoundly modified. First of all, certain religions, of which the Jewish was one, were officially recognised, and then many others, without being expressly authorised, were tolerated. In this manner, all attempts to resist the torrent of Oriental superstitions proving vain, the legislator had desisted from his efforts, and every form of wild superstition was practised with publicity and impunity. Still the laws forbidding them were unrevoked, although they were suffered to remain for the most part obsolete, or were at least only put in action on the occasion of some special scandal, or of some real or apprehended political danger. The municipal and provincial independence under the Empire was, however, so large, that very much depended on the character of the local governor; and it continually happened that in one province the Christians were unmolested or favoured, while in the adjoining province they were severely persecuted.

As we have already seen, the Christians had for many reasons become profoundly obnoxious to the people. They shared the unpopularity of the Jews, with whom they were confounded, while the general credence given to the calumnies about the crimes said to have been perpetrated at their secret meetings, their abstinence from public amusements, and the belief that their hostility to the gods was the cause of every physical calamity, were special causes of antipathy. The history of the period of the Antonines continually manifests the desire of the populace to persecute, restrained by the humanity of the rulers. In the short reign of Nerva there appears to have been no persecution, and our knowledge of the official proceedings with reference to the religion is comprised in two sentences of a Pagan historian, who tells us that the emperor 'absolved those who had been convicted of impiety,' and 'permitted no one to be convicted of impiety or Jewish rites.' Under Trajan, however, some serious though purely local disturbances took place. The emperor himself, though one of the most sagacious, and in most respects humane of Roman sovereigns, was nervously jealous of any societies or associations among his subjects, and had propounded a special edict against them; but the persecution of the Christians appears to have been not so much political as popular. If we may believe Eusebius, local persecutions, apparently of the nature of riots, but sometimes countenanced by provincial governors, broke out in several quarters of the Empire. In Bithynia, Pliny the Younger was the governor, and he wrote a very famous letter to Trajan, in which he professed himself absolutely ignorant of the proceedings to be taken against the Christians, who had already so multiplied that the temples were deserted, and who were arraigned in great numbers before his tribunal. He had, he says, released those who consented to burn incense before the image of the emperor, and to curse Christ, but had caused those to be executed who persisted in their refusal, and who were not Roman citizens, 'not doubting that a pertinacious obstinacy deserved punishment.' He had questioned the prisoners as to the nature of their faith, and had not hesitated to seek revelations by torturing two maid-servants, but had 'discovered nothing but a base and immoderate superstition.' He had asked the nature of their secret services, and had been told that they assembled on a certain day before dawn to sing a hymn to Christ as to a god; that they made a vow to abstain from every crime, and that they then, before parting, partook together of a harmless feast, which, however, they had given up since the decree against associations. To this letter Trajan answered that Christians, if brought before the tribunals and convicted, should be punished, but that they should not be sought for; that, if they consented to sacrifice, no inquisition should be made into their past lives, and that no anonymous accusations should be received against them.[1] In this reign there are two authentic instances of martyrdom.[2] Simeon, Bishop of Jerusalem, a man, it is said, one hundred and twenty years old, having been accused by the heretics, was tortured during several days, and at last crucified. Ignatius, the Bishop of Antioch, was arrested, brought to Rome, and, by the order of Trajan himself, thrown to wild beasts. Of the cause of this last act of severity we are left in ignorance, but it has been noticed that about this time Antioch had been the scene of one of those violent earthquakes which so frequently produced an outburst of religious excitement,[3] and the character of Ignatius, who was passionately desirous of martyrdom, may have very probably led him to some act of exceptional zeal. The letters of the martyr prove that at Rome the faith was openly and fearlessly professed ; the Government during the nineteen years of this reign never appears to have taken any initiative against the Christians, and, in spite of occasional local tumults, there was nothing resembling a general persecution.

During the two following reigns, the Government was more decidedly favourable to the Christians. Hadrian, having heard that the populace at the public games frequently called for their execution, issued an edict in which he commanded that none should be punished simply in obedience to the outcries against them, or without a formal trial and a conviction of some offence against the law, and he ordered that all false accusers should be punished.[4] His disposition towards the Christians was so pacific as to give rise to a legend that he intended to

---

[1] Pliny, *Ep.* x. 97–98.
[2] Euseb. lib. iii.
[3] There is a description of this earthquake in Merivale's *Hist. of the Romans,* vol viii. pp. 155–156.

Orosius (*Hist.* vii. 12) thought it was a judgment on account of the persecution of the Christians.
[4] Eusebius, iv. 8–9. See, too, Justin Martyr, *Apol.* i. 68–69.

enrol Christ among the gods;[1] but it is probable that,
although curious on religious matters, he regarded Christianity with the indifference of a Roman freethinker; and a
letter is ascribed to him in which he confounded it with the
worship of Serapis.[2] As far as the Government were concerned, the Christians appear to have been entirely unmolested; but many of them suffered dreadful tortures at the
hands of the Jewish insurgents, who in this reign, with a
desperate but ill-fated heroism, made one last effort to regain
their freedom.[3] The mutual hostility exhibited at this time
by the Jews and Christians contributed to separate them in
the eyes of the Pagans, and it is said that when Hadrian
forbade the Jews ever again to enter Jerusalem, he recognised the distinction by granting a full permission to the
Christians.[4]

Antoninus, who succeeded Hadrian, made new efforts to
restrain the passions of the people against the Christians.
He issued an edict commanding that they should not be
molested, and when, as a consequence of some earthquakes
in Asia Minor, the popular anger was fiercely roused, he
commanded that their accusers should be punished.[5] If we
except these riots, the twenty-three years of his reign appear
to have been years of absolute peace, which seems also to
have continued during several years of the reign of Marcus

---

[1] This is mentioned incidentally
by Lampridius in his *Life of A.
Severus.*

[2] See this very curious letter in
Vopiscus, *Saturninus.*

[3] Justin Mart. *Ap.* i. 31. Eusebius quotes a passage from Hegesippus to the same effect. (iv. 8.)

[4] 'Præcepitque ne cui Judæo
introeundi Hierosolymam esset licentia, Christianis tantum civitate
permissa.'—*Oros.* vii. 13.

[5] A letter which Eusebius gives
at full (iv. 13), and ascribes to

Antoninus Pius, has created a good
deal of controversy. Justin Mart.
(*Apol.* i. 71) and Tertullian (*Apol.*
5) ascribe it to Marcus Aurelius.
It is now generally believed to be
a forgery by a Christian hand, being
more like a Christian apology than
the letter of a Pagan emperor.
St. Melito, however, writing to
Marcus Aurelius, expressly states
that Antoninus had written a letter
forbidding the persecution of Christians. (Euseb. iv. 26.)

Aurelius ; but at last persecuting edicts, of the exact nature of which we have no knowledge, were issued. Of the reasons which induced one of the best men who have ever reigned to persecute the Christians, we know little or nothing. That it was not any ferocity of disposition or any impatience of resistance may be confidently asserted of one whose only fault was a somewhat excessive gentleness—who, on the death of his wife, asked the Senate, as a single favour, to console him by sparing the lives of those who had rebelled against him. That it was not, as has been strangely urged, a religious fanaticism resembling that which led St. Lewis to persecute, is equally plain. St. Lewis persecuted because he believed that to reject his religious opinions was a heinous crime, and that heresy was the path to hell. Marcus Aurelius had no such belief, and he, the first Roman emperor who made the Stoical philosophy his religion and his comfort, was also the first emperor who endowed the professors of the philosophies that were most hostile to his own. The fact that the Christian Church, existing as a State within a State, with government, ideals, enthusiasms, and hopes wholly different from those of the nation, was incompatible with the existing system of the Empire, had become more evident as the Church increased. The accusations of cannibalism and incestuous impurity had acquired a greater consistency, and the latter are said to have been justly applicable to the Carpocratian heretics, who had recently arisen. The Stoicism of Marcus Aurelius may have revolted from the practices of exorcism or the appeals to the terrors of another world, and the philosophers who surrounded him probably stimulated his hostility, for his master and friend Fronto had written a book against Christianity,[1] while Justin Martyr is said to have perished by the machinations of the Cynic Crescens.[2]   It must be added, too, that,

---

[1] It is alluded to by Minucius Felix.   [2] Eusebius, iv. 16.

while it is impossible to acquit the emperor of having issued
severe edicts against the Christians,[1] the atrocious details of
the persecutions in his reign were due to the ferocity of
the populace and the weakness of the governors in distant
provinces ; and it is inconceivable that, if he had been a very
bitter enemy of the Christians, Tertullian, writing little more
than twenty years later, should have been so ignorant of the
fact as to represent him as one of the most conspicuous of
their protectors.

But, whatever may be thought on these points, there can,
unhappily, be no question that in this reign Rome was
stained by the blood of Justin Martyr, the first philosopher,
and one of the purest and gentlest natures in the Church,
and that persecution was widely extended. In two far
distant quarters, at Smyrna and at Lyons, it far exceeded in
atrocity any that Christianity had endured since Nero, and
in each case a heroism of the most transcendent order was
displayed by the martyrs. The persecution at Smyrna, in
which St. Polycarp and many others most nobly died, took
place on the occasion of the public games, and we may trace
the influence of the Jews in stimulating it.[2] The persecution
at Lyons, which was one of the most atrocious in the whole
compass of ecclesiastical history, and which has supplied the
martyrology with some of its grandest and most pathetic
figures, derived its worst features from a combination of the
fury of the populace and of the subserviency of the governor.[3]
Certain servants of the Christians, terrified by the prospect
of torture, accused their masters of all the crimes which
popular report attributed to them, of incest, of infanticide,
of cannibalism, of hideous impurity. A fearful outburst of

---

[1] St. Melito expressly states
that the edicts of Marcus Aurelius
produced the Asiatic persecution.
[2] Eusebius, iv. 15.
[3] See the most touching and
horrible description of this perse
cution in a letter written by the
Christians of Lyons, in Eusebius
v. 1.

ferocity ensued. Tortures almost too horrible to recount were for hours and even days applied to the bodies of old men and of weak women, who displayed amid their agonies a nobler courage than has ever shone upon a battle-field, and whose memories are immortal among mankind. Blandina and Pothinus wrote in blood the first page of the glorious history of the Church of France.[1] But although, during the closing years of Marcus Aurelius, severe persecutions took place in three or four provinces, there was no general and organised effort to suppress Christianity throughout the Empire.[2]

We may next consider, as a single period, the space of time that elapsed from the death of Marcus Aurelius, in A.D. 180, to the accession of Decius, A.D. 249. During all this time Christianity was a great and powerful body, exercising an important influence, and during a great part of it Christians filled high civil and military positions. The hostility manifested towards them began now to assume a more political complexion than it had previously done,

---

[1] Sulpicius Severus (who was himself a Gaul) says of their martyrdom (*H. E.*, lib. ii.), 'Tum primum intra Gallias Martyria visa, serius trans Alpes Dei religione suscepta.' Tradition ascribes Gallic Christianity to the apostles, but the evidence of inscriptions appears to confirm the account of Severus. It is at least certain that Christianity did not acquire a great extension till later. The earliest Christian inscriptions found are (one in each year) of A.D. 334, 347, 377, 405, and 409. They do not become common till the middle of the fifth century. See a full discussion of this in the preface of M. Le Blant's admirable and indeed exhaustive work, *Inscriptions chrétiennes de la Gaule.*

[2] It was alleged among the Christians, that towards the close of his reign Marcus Aurelius issued an edict protecting the Christians, on account of a Christian legion having, in Germany, in a moment of great distress, procured a shower of rain by their prayers. (Tert. *Apol.* 5.) The shower is mentioned by Pagan as well as Christian writers, and is pourtrayed on the column of Antoninus. It was 'ascribed to the incantations of an Egyptian magician, to the prayers of a legion of Christians, or to the favour of Jove towards the best of mortals, according to the various prejudices of different observers. —Merivale's *Hist. of Rome*, vol. viii. p. 338.

except perhaps in the later years of Marcus Aurelius. The existence of a vast and rapidly increasing corporation, very alien to the system of the Empire, confronted every ruler. Emperors like Commodus or Heliogabalus were usually too immersed in selfish pleasures to have any distinct policy; but sagacious sovereigns, sincerely desiring the well-being of the Empire, either, like Marcus Aurelius and Diocletian, endeavoured to repress the rising creed, or, like Alexander Severus, and at last Constantine, actively encouraged it. The measures Marcus Aurelius had taken against Christianity were arrested under Commodus, whose favourite mistress, Marcia, supplies one of the very few recorded instances of female influence, which has been the cause of so much persecution, being exerted in behalf of toleration; [1] yet a Christian philosopher named Apollonius, and at the same time, by a curious retribution, his accuser, were in this reign executed at Rome.[2] During the sixty-nine years we are considering, the general peace of the Church was only twice broken. The first occasion was in the reign of Septimus Severus, who was for some time very favourable to the Christians, but who, in A.D. 202 or 203, issued an edict, forbidding any Pagan to join the Christian or Jewish faith; [3] and this edict was followed by a sanguinary persecu-

---

[1] Xiphilin, lxxii. 4. The most atrocious of the Pagan persecutions was attributed, as we shall see, to the mother of Galerius, and in Christian times the Spanish Inquisition was founded by Isabella the Catholic; the massacre of St. Bartholomew was chiefly due to Catherine of Medicis, and the most horrible English persecution to Mary Tudor.

[2] Euseb. v. 21. The accuser, we learn from St. Jerome, was a slave. On the law condemning slaves who accused their masters,

compare Pressensé, *Hist. des Trois premiers Siècles* (2ᵐᵉ série), tome i. pp. 182–183, and Jeremie's *Church History of Second and Third Centuries*, p. 29. Apollonius was of senatorial rank. It is said that some other martyrs died at the same time.

[3] 'Judæos fieri sub gravi pœna vetuit. Idem etiam de Christianis sanxit.'—Spartian. *S. Severus.* The persecution is described by Eusebius, lib. vi. Tertullian says Severus was favourable to the Christians, a Christian named Pro

tion in Africa and Syria, in which the father of Origen, and also St. Felicitas and St. Perpetua, perished. This persecution does not appear to have extended to the West, and was apparently rather the work of provincial governors, who interpreted the Imperial edict as a sign of hostility to the Christians, than the direct act of the emperor,[1] whose decree applied only to Christians actively proselytising. It is worthy of notice that Origen observed that previous to this time the number of Christian martyrs had been very small.[2] The second persecution was occasioned by the murder of Alexander Severus by Maximinus. The usurper pursued with great bitterness the leading courtiers of the deceased emperor, among whom were some Christian bishops,[3] and about the same time severe earthquakes in Pontus and Cappadocia produced the customary popular ebullitions. But with these exceptions the Christians were undisturbed. Caracalla, Macrinus, and Heliogabalus took no measures against them, while Alexander Severus, who reigned for thirteen years, warmly and steadily supported them. A Pagan historian assures us that this emperor intended to build temples in honour of Christ, but was dissuaded by the priests, who urged that all the other temples would be deserted. He venerated in his private oratory the statues of Apollonius of Tyana, Abraham, Orpheus, and Christ. He decreed that the provincial governors should not be appointed till the people had the opportunity of declaring any crime they had committed, borrowing this rule avowedly from the pro-

---

culus (whom he, in consequence, retained in the palace till his death) having cured him of an illness by the application of oil. (*Ad Scapul.* 4.)

[1] 'Of the persecution under Severus there are few, if any, traces in the West. It is confined to Syria, perhaps to Cappadocia, to Egypt, and to Africa, and in the latter provinces appears as the act of hostile governors proceeding upon the existing laws, rather than the consequence of any recent edict of the emperor.'—Milman's *Hist. of Christianity*, vol. ii. pp. 156–157.

[2] *Adv. Cels.* iii. See Gibbon ch. xvi.

[3] Eusebius, vi. 28.

cedure of the Jews and Christians in electing their clergy ; he
ordered the precept ' Do not unto others what you would not
that they should do unto you ' to be engraven on the palace
and other public buildings, and he decided a dispute con
cerning a piece of ground which the Christians had occupied,
and which the owners of certain eating-houses claimed, in
favour of the former, on the ground that the worship of a
god should be most considered.[1] Philip the Arab, who
reigned during the last five years of the period we are
considering, was so favourable to the Christians that he
was believed, though on no trustworthy evidence, to have
been baptised.

We have now reviewed the history of the persecutions to
the year A.D. 249, or about two hundred years after the
planting of Christianity in Rome. We have seen that, although during that period much suffering was occasionally
endured, and much heroism displayed, by the Christians, there
was, with the very doubtful exception of the Neronian persecution, no single attempt made to suppress Christianity
throughout the Empire. Local persecutions of great severity
had taken place at Smyrna and Lyons, under Marcus Aurelius ; in Africa and some Asiatic provinces, under Severus ;
popular tumults, arising in the excitement of the public
games, or produced by some earthquake or inundation, or by
some calumnious accusation, were not unfrequent ; but there
was at no time that continuous, organised, and universal persecution by which, in later periods, ecclesiastical tribunals
have again and again suppressed opinions repugnant to their
own ; and there was no part of the Empire in which whole
generations did not pass away absolutely undisturbed. No
martyr had fallen in Gaul or in great part of Asia Minor
till Marcus Aurelius. In Italy, after the death of Nero,

---

[1] Lampridius, A. Severus. The historian adds, ' Judæis privilegia.
reservavit. Christianos esse passus est.'

with the exception of some slight troubles under Domitian and Maximinus, probably due to causes altogether distinct from religion, there were, during the whole period we are considering, only a few isclated instances of martyrdom. The bishops, as the leaders of the Church, were the special objects of hostility, and several in different parts of the world had fallen; but it is extremely questionable whether any Roman bishop perished after the apostolic age, till Fabianus was martyred under Decius.[1] If Christianity was not formally authorised, it was, like many other religions in a similar position, generally acquiesced in, and, during a great part of the time we have reviewed, its professors appear to have found no obstacles to their preferment in the Court or in the army. The emperors were for the most part indifferent or favourable to them. The priests in the Pagan society had but little influence, and do not appear to have taken any prominent part in the persecution till near the time of Diocletian. With the single exception of the Jews, no class held that doctrine of the criminality of error which has been the parent of most modern persecutions; and although the belief that great calamities were the result of neglecting or insulting the gods furnished the Pagans with a religious motive for persecution, this motive only acted on the occasion of some rare and exceptional catastrophe.[2] In Christian times, the first objects

---

[1] Compare Milman's *History of Early Christianity* (1867), vol. ii. p. 188, and his *History of Latin Christianity* (1867), vol. i. pp. 26–59. There are only two cases of alleged martyrdom before this time that can excite any reasonable doubt. Irenæus distinctly asserts that Telesphorus was martyred; but his martyrdom is put in the beginning of the reign of Antoninus Pius (he had assumed the mitre near the end of the reign of Hadrian), and Antoninus is repre-

sented, by the general voice of the Church, as perfectly free from the stain of persecution. A tradition, which is in itself sufficiently probable, states that Pontianus, having been exiled by Maximinus, was killed in banishment.

[2] Tacitus has a very ingenicus remark on this subject, which illustrates happily the half scepticism of the Empire. After recounting a number of prodigies that were said to have taken place in the reign of Otho, he remarks that these

of the persecutor are to control education, to prevent the
publication of any heterodox works, to institute such a minute
police inspection as to render impossible the celebration of the
worship he desires to suppress. But nothing of this kind
was attempted, or indeed was possible, in the period we are
considering. With the exception of the body-guard of the
emperor, almost the whole army, which was of extremely
moderate dimensions, was massed along the vast frontier
of the Empire. The police force was of the scantiest kind,
sufficient only to keep common order in the streets. The
Government had done something to encourage, but absolutely nothing to control, education, and parents or societies
were at perfect liberty to educate the young as they pleased.
The expansion of literature, by reason of the facilities which
slavery gave to transcription, was very great, and it was
for the most part entirely uncontrolled.[1] Augustus, it is
true, had caused some volumes of forged prophecies to be
burnt,[2] and, under the tyranny of Tiberius and Domitian,
political writers and historians who eulogised tyrannicide, or
vehemently opposed the Empire, were persecuted; but the
extreme indignation these acts elicited attests their rarity,
and, on matters unconnected with politics, the liberty of

---

were things habitually noticed in
the ages of ignorance, but now only
noticed in periods of terror. ' Rudi-
bus sæculis etiam in pace observata,
quæ nunc tantum in metu audiun-
tur.'— *Hist*. i. 86.

[1] M. de Champagny has devoted
an extremely beautiful chapter (*Les
Antonins*, tome ii. pp. 179–200) to
the liberty of the Roman Empire.
See, too, the fifty-fourth chapter of
Mr. Merivale's *History*. It is the
custom of some of the apologists
for modern Cæsarism to defend it
by pointing to the Roman Empire
as the happiest period in human
history. No apology can be more

unfortunate. The first task of a
modern despot is to centralise to
the highest point, to bring every
department of thought and action
under a system of police regulation,
and, above all, to impose his shack-
ling tyranny upon the human mind.
The very perfection of the Roman
Empire was, that the municipal
and personal liberty it admitted
had never been surpassed, and the
intellectual liberty had never been
equalled.

[2] Sueton. *Aug*. xxxi. It appears
from a passage in Livy (xxxix. 16)
that books of oracles had been
sometimes burnt in the Republic.

literature was absolute.[1] In a word, the Church prosely·
tised in a society in which toleration was the rule, and at a
time when municipal, provincial, and personal independence
had reached the highest point, when the ruling classes were
for the most part absolutely indifferent to religious opinions,
and when an unprecedented concourse of influences facilitated
its progress.

When we reflect that these were the circumstances of the
Church till the middle of the third century, we may readily

---

[1] Tacitus has given us a very
remarkable account of the trial of
Cremutius Cordus, under Tiberius,
for having published a history
in which he had praised Brutus
and called Cassius the last o'
Romans. (*Annal.* iv. 34–35.) He
expressly terms this 'novo ac tunc
primum audito crimine.' and he
puts a speech in the mouth of the
accused, describing the liberty previously accorded to writers. Cordus
avoided execution by suicide. His
daughter, Marcia, preserved some
copies of his work, and published
it in the reign and with the approbation of Caligula. (Senec. *Ad
Marc.* 1; Suet. *Calig.* 16.) There are,
however, some traces of an earlier
persecution of letters. Under the
sanction of a law of the decemvirs
against libellers, Augustus exiled
the satiric writer Cassius Severus,
and he also destroyed the works of
an historian named Labienus, on
account of their seditious sentiments. These writings were republished with those of Cordus.
Generally, however, Augustus was
very magnanimous in his dealings
with his assailants. He refused
the request of Tiberius to punish
them (Suet. *Aug.* 51), and only excluded from his palace Timagenes,
who bitterly satirised both him and

the empress, and proclaimed himself everywhere the enemy of the
emperor. (Senec. *De Ira,* iii. 23.)
A similar magnanimity was shown
by most of the other emperors;
among others, by Nero. (Suet.
Nero, 39.) Under Vespasian, however, a poet, named Maternus, was
obliged to retouch a tragedy on
Cato (Tacit. *De Or.* 2–3), and
Domitian allowed no writings opposed to his policy. (Tacit. *Agric.*)
But no attempt appears to have
been made in the Empire to control religious writings till the
persecution of Diocletian, who
ordered the Scriptures to be burnt.
The example was speedily followed
by the Christian emperors. The
writings of Arius were burnt in
A D. 321, those of Porphyry in A D.
388. Pope Gelasius, in A.D. 496
drew up a list of books which
should not be read, and all liberty
of publication speedily became extinct. See on this subject Peignot,
*Essai historique sur la Liberté
d'Écrire;* Villemain, *Études de
Littér. ancienne;* Sir C. Lewis on
the *Credibility of Roman Hist.* vol.
i. p. 52; Nadal, *Mémoire sur la
liberté qu'avoient les soldats romains
de dire des vers satyriques contre
ceux qui triomphoient* (Paris, 1725)

perceive the absurdity of maintaining that Christianity was
propagated in the face of such a fierce and continuous persecution that no opinions could have survived it without a
miracle, or of arguing from the history of the early Church
that persecution never has any real efficacy in suppressing
truth. When, in addition to the circumstances under which
it operated, we consider the unexampled means both of attraction and of intimidation that were possessed by the
Church, we can have no difficulty in understanding that it
should have acquired a magnitude that would enable it to
defy the far more serious assaults it was still destined to
endure. That it had acquired this extension we have abundant evidence. The language I have quoted from Lactantius
is but a feeble echo of the emphatic statements of writers
before the Decian persecution.[1] 'There is no race of men,
whether Greek or barbarian,' said Justin Martyr, 'among
whom prayers and thanks are not offered up in the name of
the crucified.'[2] 'We are but of yesterday,' cried Tertullian,
'and we fill all your cities, islands, forts, councils, even the
camps themselves, the tribes, the decuries, the palaces, the
senate, and the forum.'[3] Eusebius has preserved a letter of
Cornelius, Bishop of Rome, containing a catalogue of the
officers of his Church at the time of the Decian persecution.
It consisted of one bishop, forty-six presbyters, seven deacons,
seven subdeacons, forty-two acolytes, fifty-two exorcists,
readers, and janitors. The Church also supported more
than fifteen hundred widows, and poor or suffering persons.[4]

The Decian persecution, which broke out in A.D. 249, and
was probably begun in hopes of restoring the Empire to
its ancient discipline, and eliminating from it all extraneous

---

[1] See a collection of passages.
on this point in Pressensé, *Hist.
des Trois premiers Siècles* (2me
série), tome i. pp. 3–4.

[2] *Trypho.*
[3] *Apol.* xxxvii.
[4] Euseb. vi. **43**

and unpatriotic influences,[1] is the first example of a deliberate
attempt, supported by the whole machinery of provincial
government, and extending over the entire surface of the
Empire, to extirpate Christianity from the world. It would
be difficult to find language too strong to paint its horrors
The ferocious instincts of the populace, that were long repressed, burst out anew, and they were not only permitted,
but encouraged by the rulers. Far worse than the deaths
which menaced those who shrank from the idolatrous sacrifices, were the hideous and prolonged tortures by which the
magistrates often sought to subdue the constancy of the
martyr, the nameless outrages that were sometimes inflicted
on the Christian virgin.[2] The Church, enervated by a long
peace, and deeply infected with the vices of the age, tottered
beneath the blow. It had long since arrived at the period
when men were Christians not by conviction, but through
family relationship; when the more opulent Christians vied
in luxury with the Pagans among whom they mixed, and
when even the bishops were, in many instances, worldly

---

[1] Eusebius, it is true, ascribes
this persecution (vi. 39) to the
hatred Decius bore to his predecessor Philip, who was very friendly
to the Christians. But although
such a motive might account for a
persecution like that of Maximin,
which was directed chiefly against
the bishops who had been about
the Court of Severus, it is insufficient to account for a persecution
so general and so severe as that of
Decius. It is remarkable that this
emperor is uniformly represented
by the Pagan historians as an eminently wise and humane sovereign.
See Dodwell, De Paucitate Martyrum, lii.
[2] St. Cyprian (Ep. vii.) and, at
a later period, St. Jerome (Vit.

Pauli), both notice that during this
persecution the desire of the persecutors was to subdue the constancy
of the Christians by torture, without gratifying their desire for
martyrdom. The consignment of
Christian virgins to houses of ill
fame was one of the most common
incidents in the later acts of martyrs which were invented in the
middle ages. Unhappily, however,
it must be acknowledged that there
are some undoubted traces of it at
an earlier date. Tertullian, in a
famous passage, speaks of the cry
'Ad Lenonem' as substituted for
that of 'Ad Leonem;' and St. Am
brose recounts some strange stories
on this subject in his treatise De
Virginibus.

aspirants after civil offices. It is not, therefore, surprising
that the defection was very large. The Pagans marked with
triumphant ridicule, and the Fathers with a burning indignation, the thousands who thronged to the altars at the very
commencement of persecution, the sudden collapse of the
most illustrious churches, the eagerness with which the offer
of provincial governors to furnish certificates of apostasy,
without exacting a compliance with the conditions which
those certificates attested, was accepted by multitudes.[1] The
question whether those who abandoned the faith should
afterwards be readmitted to communion, became the chief
question that divided the Novatians, and one of the questions
that divided the Montanists from the Catholics, while the
pretensions of the confessors to furnish indulgences, remitting
the penances imposed by the bishops, led to a conflict which
contributed very largely to establish the undisputed ascendancy of the episcopacy. But the Decian persecution, though
it exhibits the Church in a somewhat less noble attitude than
the persecutions which preceded and which followed it, was
adorned by many examples of extreme courage and devotion,
displayed in not a few cases by those who were physically
among the frailest of mankind. It was of a kind eminently
fitted to crush the Church. Had it taken place at an earlier
period, had it been continued for a long succession of years,
Christianity, without a miracle, must have perished. But
the Decian persecution fell upon a Church which had existed
for two centuries, and it lasted less than two years.[2] Its

---

[1] St. Cyprian has drawn a very
highly coloured picture of this general corruption, and of the apostasy
it produced, in his treatise *De
Lapsis*, a most interesting picture
of the society of his time   See,
too, the *Life of St. Gregory Thou-
maturgus*, by Greg. of Nyssa.

[2] 'La persécution de Dèce ne
dura qu'environ un an dans sa

grande violence. Car S. Cyprien,
dans les lettres écrites en 251, dès
devant Pasque, et mesme dans
quelques-unes écrites apparemment
dès la fin de 250, témoigne que son
église jouissoit déjà de quelque
paix, mais d'une paix encore peu
affermie, en sorte que le moindre
accident eust pu renouveler le
trouble et la persécution. Il semble

intensity varied much in different provinces. In Alexandria and the neighbouring towns, where a popular tumult had anticipated the menaces of the Government, it was extremely horrible.[1] In Carthage, at first, the proconsul being absent, no capital sentence was passed, but on the arrival of that functionary the penalty of death, accompanied by dreadful tortures, was substituted for that of exile or imprisonment.[2] The rage of the people was especially directed against the bishop St. Cyprian, who prudently retired till the storm had passed.[3] In general, it was observed that the object of the rulers was much less to slay than to vanquish the Christians.

---

mesme que l'on n'eust pas encore la liberté d'y tenir les assemblées, et néanmoins il paroist que tous les confesseurs prisonniers à Carthage y avoient esté mis en liberté dès ce temps-là.'—Tillemont, *Mém. d'Hist. ecclésiastique*, tome iii. p. 324.

[1] Dionysius the bishop wrote a full account of it, which Eusebius has preserved (vi. 41-42). In Alexandria, Dionysius says, the persecution produced by popular fanaticism preceded the edict of Decius by an entire year. He has preserved a particular catalogue of all who were put to death in Alexandria during the entire Decian persecution. They were seventeen persons. Several of these were killed by the mob, and their deaths were in nearly all cases accompanied by circumstances of extreme atrocity. Besides these, others (we know not how many) had been put to torture. Many, Dionysius says, perished in other cities or villages of Egypt.

[2] See St. Cyprian, *Ep.* viii.

[3] There was much controversy at this time as to the propriety of bishops evading persecution by flight. The Montanists maintained that such a conduct was equivalent to apostasy. Tertullian had written a book, *De Fuga in Persecutione*, maintaining this view; and among the orthodox the conduct of St. Cyprian (who afterwards nobly attested his courage by his death) did not escape animadversion. The more moderate opinion prevailed, but the leading bishops found it necessary to support their conduct by declaring that they had received special revelations exhorting them to fly. St. Cyprian, who constantly appealed to his dreams to justify him in his controversies (see some curious instances collected in Middleton's *Free Enquiry*, pp. 101-105), declared (*Ep.* ix.), and his biographer and friend Pontius reasserted (*Vit. Cyprianis*), that his flight was 'by the command of God.' Dionysius, the Bishop of Alexandria, asserts the same thing of his own flight, and attests it by an oath (see his own words in Euseb. vi. 40); and the same thing was afterwards related of St. Gregory Thaumaturgus. (See his *Life* by Gregory of Nyssa.)

Horrible tortures were continually employed to extort an apostasy, and, when those tortures proved vain, great numbers were ultimately released.

The Decian persecution is remarkable in Christian archæology as being, it is believed, the first occasion in which the Christian catacombs were violated. Those vast subterranean corridors, lined with tombs and expanding very frequently into small chapels adorned with paintings, often of no mean beauty, had for a long period been an inviolable asylum in seasons of persecution. The extreme sanctity which the Romans were accustomed to attach to the place of burial repelled the profane, and as early, it is said, as the very beginning of the third century, the catacombs were recognised as legal possessions of the Church.[1] The Roman legislators, however unfavourable to the formation of guilds or associations, made an exception in favour of burial societies, or associations of men subscribing a certain sum to ensure to each member a decent burial in ground which belonged to the corporation. The Church is believed to have availed itself of this privilege, and to have attained, in this capacity, a legal existence. The tombs, which were originally the properties of distinct families, became in this manner an ecclesiastical domain, and the catacombs were, from perhaps the first, made something more than places of burial.[2] The chapels with which they abound, and which are of the smallest dimensions and utterly unfit for general worship, were probably mortuary chapels, and may have also been employed in the services commemorating the martyrs, while the ordinary worship was probably at first conducted in

---

[1] ' E veramente che almeno fino dal secolo terzo i fedeli abbiano posseduto cimiteri a nome commune, e che il loro possesso sia stato riconosciuto dagl' imperatori, è cosa impossibile a negare.'— Rossi, *Roma Sotterranea*, tomo i.

p. 103.

[2] This is all fully discussed by Rossi, *Roma Sotterranea*, tomo i. pp. 101–108. Rossi thinks the Church, in its capacity of burial society, was known by the name of ' ecclesia fratrum.'

the private houses of the Christians. The decision of Alexander Severus, which I have already noticed, is the earliest notice we possess of the existence of buildings specially devoted to the Christian services; but we cannot tell how long before this time they may have existed in Rome.[1] In serious persecution, however, they would doubtless have to be abandoned; and, as a last resort, the catacombs proved a refuge from the persecutors.

The reign of Decius only lasted about two years, and before its close the persecution had almost ceased.[2] On the accession of his son Gallus, in the last month of A.D. 251, there was for a short time perfect peace; but Gallus resumed the persecution in the spring of the following year, and although apparently not very severe, or very general, it seems to have continued to his death, which took place a year after.[3] Two Roman bishops, Cornelius, who had succeeded the martyred Fabianus, and his successor Lucius, were at this time put to death.[4] Valerian, who ascended the throne

[1] See, on the history of early Christian Churches, Cave's *Primitive Christianity*, part i. c. vi.

[2] Dodwell (*De Paucit. Martyr.* lvii.) has collected evidence of the subsidence of the persecution in the last year of the reign of Decius.

[3] This persecution is not noticed by St. Jerome, Orosius, Sulpicius Severus, or Lactantius. The very little we know about it is derived from the letters of St. Cyprian, and from a short notice by Dionysius of Alexandria, in Eusebius, vii. 1. Dionysius says, Gallus began the persecution when his reign was advancing prosperously, and his affairs succeeding, which probably means, after he had procured the departure of the Goths from the Illyrian province, early in A.D. 252 (see Gibbon, chap. x.). The disastrous position into which

affairs had been thrown by the defeat of Decius appears, at first, to have engrossed his attention.

[4] Lucius was at first exiled and then permitted to return, on which occasion St. Cyprian wrote him a letter of congratulation (*Ep.* lvii.). He was, however, afterwards rearrested and slain, but it is not, I think, clear whether it was under Gallus or Valerian. St. Cyprian speaks (*Ep.* lxvi.) of both Cornelius and Lucius as martyred. The emperors were probably at this time beginning to realise the power the Bishops of Rome possessed. We know hardly anything of the Decian persecution at Rome except the execution of the bishop; and St. Cyprian says (*Ep.* li.) that Decius would have preferred a pretender to the throne to a Bishop of Rome.

A.D. 254, at first not only tolerated, but warmly patronised the Christians, and attracted so many to his Court that his house, in the language of a contemporary, appeared 'the Church of the Lord.'[1] But after rather more than four years his disposition changed. At the persuasion, it is said, of an Egyptian magician, named Macrianus, he signed in A.D. 258 an edict of persecution condemning Christian ecclesiastics and senators to death, and other Christians to exile, or to the forfeiture of their property, and prohibiting them from entering the catacombs.[2] A sanguinary and general persecution ensued. Among the victims were Sixtus, the Bishop of Rome, who perished in the catacombs,[3] and Cyprian, who was exiled, and afterwards beheaded, and was the first Bishop of Carthage who suffered martyrdom.[4] At last, Valerian, having been captured by the Persians, Gallienus, in A.D. 260, ascended the throne, and immediately proclaimed a perfect toleration of the Christians.[5]

The period from the accession of Decius, in A.D. 249, to the accession of Gallienus, in A.D. 260, which I have now very briefly noticed, was by far the most disastrous the Church had yet endured. With the exception of about five years in the reigns of Gallus and Valerian, the persecution was continuous, though it varied much in its intensity and its range. During the first portion, if measured, not by the number of deaths, but by the atrocity of the tortures inflicted, it was probably as severe as any upon record. It was subsequently directed chiefly against the leading clergy, and, as we have seen, four Roman bishops perished. In addition to the political reasons that inspired it, the popular fanaticism

---

[1] Dionysius, Archbishop of Alexandria; see Euseb. vii. 10.

[2] Eusebius, vii. 10–12; Cyprian, *Ep.* lxxxi. Lactantius says of Valerian, 'Multum quamvis brevi tempore justi sanguinis fudit.'

— *De Mort. Persec.* c. v.

[3] Cyprian *Ep.* lxxxi.

[4] See his *Life* by the deacon Pontius, which is reproduced by Gibbon.

[5] Eusebius, vii. 13.

caused by great calamities, which were ascribed to anger
of the gods at the neglect of their worship, had in this as in
former periods a great influence.   Political disasters, which
foreshadowed clearly the approaching downfall of the Empire,
were followed by fearful and general famines and plagues.
St. Cyprian, in a treatise addressed to one of the persecutors
who was most confident in ascribing these things to the
Christians, presents us with an extremely curious picture
both of the general despondency that had fallen upon the
Empire, and of the manner in which these calamities were
regarded by the Christians.   Like most of his co-religionists,
the saint was convinced that the closing scene of the earth
was at hand.   The decrepitude of the world, he said, had
arrived, the forces of nature were almost exhausted, the sun
had no longer its old lustre, or the soil its old fertility, the
spring time had grown less lovely, and the autumn less boun-
teous, the energy of man had decayed, and all things were
moving rapidly to the end.   Famines and plagues were the
precursors of the day of judgment.   They were sent to warn
and punish a rebellious world, which, still bowing down
before idols, persecuted the believers in the truth.   ' So true
is this, that the Christians are never persecuted without the
sky manifesting at once the Divine displeasure.'   The conception of a converted Empire never appears to have flashed
across the mind of the saint;[1] the only triumph he predicted
for the Church was that of another world ; and to the threats
of the persecutors he rejoined by fearful menaces.   ' A burning, scorching fire will for ever torment those who are
condemned ; there will be no respite or end to their torments.
We shall through eternity contemplate in their agonies those
who for a short time contemplated us in tortures, and for the

---

[1] Tertullian had before, in a
curious passage, spoken of the impossibility of Christian Cæsars.
' Sed et Cæsares credidissent super
Christo si aut Cæsares non essent
seculo necessarii aut si et Chris-
tiani potuissent esse Cæsares.'—
Apol. xxi.

brief pleasure which the barbarity of our persecutors took in feasting their eyes upon an inhuman spectacle, they will be themselves exposed as an eternal spectacle of agony.' As a last warning, calamity after calamity broke upon the world, and, with the solemnity of one on whom the shadow of death had already fallen, St. Cyprian adjured the persecutors to repent and to be saved.[1]

The accession of Gallienus introduced the Church to a new period of perfect peace, which, with a single inconsider-able exception, continued for no less than forty years. The exception was furnished by Aurelian, who during nearly the whole of his reign had been exceedingly favourable to the Christians, and had even been appealed to by the orthodox bishops, who desired him to expel from Antioch a prelate they had excommunicated for heresy,[2] but who, at the close of his reign, intended to persecute. He was assassinated, however, according to one account, when he was just about to sign the decrees ; according to another, before they had been sent through the provinces; and if any persecution actually took place, it was altogether inconsiderable.[3] Chris-tianity, during all this time, was not only perfectly free, it was greatly honoured. Christians were appointed governors of the provinces, and were expressly exonerated from the duty of sacrificing. The bishops were treated by the civil authorities with profound respect. The palaces of the em-peror were filled with Christian servants, who were authorised freely to profess their religion, and were greatly valued for their fidelity. The popular prejudice seems to have been lulled to rest; and it has been noticed that the rapid progress of the faith excited no tumult or hostility. Spacious churches

---

[1] *Contra Demetrianum.*

[2] Eusebius, vii. 30. Aurelian decided that the cathedral at Anti-och should be given up to whoever was appointed by the bishops of Italy.

[3] Compare the accounts in Eu-sebius, vii. 30, and Lactantius, *De Mort.* c. vi.

were erected in every quarter, and they could scarcely contain the multitude of worshippers.[1] In Rome itself, before the outburst of the Diocletian persecution, there were no less than forty churches.[2] The Christians may still have been outnumbered by the Pagans; but when we consider their organisation, their zeal, and their rapid progress, a speedy triumph appeared inevitable.

But before that triumph was achieved a last and a terrific ordeal was to be undergone. Diocletian, whose name has been somewhat unjustly associated with a persecution, the responsibility of which belongs far more to his colleague Galerius, having left the Christians in perfect peace for nearly eighteen years, suffered himself to be persuaded to make one more effort to eradicate the foreign creed. This emperor, who had risen by his merits from the humblest position, exhibited in all the other actions of his reign a moderate, placable, and conspicuously humane nature, and, although he greatly magnified the Imperial authority, the simplicity of his private life, his voluntary abdication, and, above all, his singularly noble conduct during many years of retirement, displayed a rare magnanimity of character. As a politician, he deserves, I think, to rank very high. Antoninus and Marcus Aurelius had been too fascinated by the traditions of the Republic, and by the austere teaching and retrospective spirit of the Stoics, to realise the necessity of adapting institutions to the wants of a luxurious and highly civilised people, and they therefore had little permanent influence upon the destinies of the Empire. But Diocletian invariably exhibited in his legislation a far-seeing and comprehensive mind, well aware of the condition of the society he ruled, and provident of distant events. Perceiving that Roman corruption was incurable, he attempted to regenerate

---

[1] See the forcible and very candid description of Eusebius, viii. 1.
[2] This is noticed by Optatus.

the Empire by creating new centres of political life in the great and comparatively unperverted capitals of the provinces; and Nicomedia, which was his habitual residence, Carthage, Milan, and Ravenna, all received abundant tokens of his favour. He swept away or disregarded the obsolete and inefficient institutions of Republican liberty that still remained, and indeed gave his government a somewhat Oriental character; but, at the same time, by the bold, and, it must be admitted, very perilous measure of dividing the Empire into four sections, he abridged the power of each ruler, ensured the better supervision and increased authority of the provinces, and devised the first effectual check to those military revolts which had for some time been threatening the Empire with anarchy. With the same energetic statesmanship, we find him reorganising the whole system of taxation, and attempting, less wisely, to regulate commercial transactions. To such an emperor, the problem presented by the rapid progress and the profoundly anti-national character of Christianity must have been a matter of serious consideration, and the weaknesses of his character were most unfavourable to the Church; for Diocletian, with many noble qualities of heart and head, was yet superstitious, tortuous, nervous, and vacillating, and was too readily swayed by the rude and ferocious soldier, who was impetuously inciting him against the Christians.

The extreme passion which Galerius displayed on this subject is ascribed, in the first instance, to the influence of his mother, who was ardently devoted to the Pagan worship. He is himself painted in dark colours by the Christian writers as a man of boundless and unbridled sensuality, of an imperiousness that rose to fury at opposition, and of a cruelty which had long passed the stage of callousness, and become a fiendish delight, in the infliction and contemplation of suffering.[1] His strong attachment to Paganism made him at

---

[1] See the vivid pictures in Lact. *De Mort. Persec.*

length the avowed representative of his party, which several causes had contributed to strengthen. The philosophy of the Empire had by this time fully passed into its Neoplatonic and Pythagorean phases, and was closely connected with religious observances. Hierocles and Porphyry, who were among its most eminent exponents, had both written books against Christianity, and the Oriental religions fostered much fanaticism among the people. Political interests united with superstition, for the Christians were now a very formidable body in the State. Their interests were supposed to be represented by the Cæsar Constantius Chlorus, and the religion was either adopted, or at least warmly favoured, by the wife and daughter of Diocletian (the latter of whom was married to Galerius[1]), and openly professed by some of the leading officials at the Court. A magnificent church crowned the hill facing the palace of the emperor at Nicomedia. The bishops were, in most cities, among the most active and influential citizens, and their influence was not always exercised for good. A few cases, in which an ill-considered zeal led Christians to insult the Pagan worship, one or two instances of Christians refusing to serve in the army, because they believed military life repugnant to their creed, a scandalous relaxation of morals, that had arisen during the long peace, and the fierce and notorious discord displayed by the leaders of the Church, contributed in different ways to accelerate the persecution.[2]

For a considerable time Diocletian resisted all the urgency of Galerius against the Christians, and the only measure taken was the dismissal by the latter sovereign of a number of Christian officers from the army. In A.D. 303, however, Diocletian yielded to the entreaties of his colleague, and a fearful persecution, which many circumstances conspired to stimulate, began. The priests, in one of the public ceremonies,

---

[1] Lactant. *De Mort. Persec.* 15.   [2] Eusebius, viii.

had declared that the presence of Christians prevented the entrails from showing the accustomed signs. The oracle of Apollo, at Miletus, being consulted by Diocletian, exhorted him to persecute the Christians. A fanatical Christian, who avowed his deed, and expiated it by a fearful death, tore down the first edict of persecution, and replaced it by a bitter taunt against the emperor. Twice, after the outburst of the persecution, the palace at Nicomedia, where Diocletian and Galerius were residing, was set on fire, and the act was ascribed, not without probability, to a Christian hand, as were also some slight disturbances that afterwards arose in Syria.[1] Edict after edict followed in rapid succession. The first ordered the destruction of all Christian churches and of all Bibles, menaced with death the Christians if they assembled in secret for Divine worship, and deprived them of all civil rights. A second edict ordered all ecclesiastics to be thrown into prison, while a third edict ordered that these prisoners, and a fourth edict that all Christians, should be compelled by torture to sacrifice. At first Diocletian refused to permit their lives to be taken, but after the fire at Nicomedia this restriction was removed. Many were burnt alive, and the tortures by which the persecutors sought to shake their resolution were so dreadful that even such a death seemed an act of mercy. The only province of the Empire where the Christians were at peace was Gaul, which had received its baptism of blood under Marcus Aurelius, but was now governed by Constantius Chlorus, who protected them from personal molestation, though he was compelled, in obedience to the emperor, to destroy their churches. In Spain, which was also under the government, but not under the direct inspection, of Constantius, the persecution was moderate, but in all other parts of the Empire it raged with

---

[1] These incidents are noticed by Eusebius in his *History*, and in his *Life of Constantine*, and by Lactantius, *De Mort. Persec.*

fierceness till the abdication of Diocletian in 305.   This
event almost immediately restored peace to the Western provinces,[1] but greatly aggravated the misfortunes of the Eastern
Christians, who passed under the absolute rule of Galerius.
Horrible, varied, and prolonged tortures were employed to
quell their fortitude, and their final resistance was crowned
by the most dreadful of all deaths, roasting over a slow fire.
It was not till A.D. 311, eight years after the commencement
of the general persecution, ten years after the first measure
against the Christians, that the Eastern persecution ceased.
Galerius, the arch-enemy of the Christians, was struck down
by a fearful disease.   His body, it is said, became a mass of
loathsome and fœtid sores—a living corpse, devoured by
countless worms, and exhaling the odour of the charnel-house.
He who had shed so much innocent blood, shrank himself
from a Roman death.   In his extreme anguish he appealed in
turn to physician after physician, and to temple after temple.
At last he relented towards the Christians.   He issued a
proclamation restoring them to liberty, permitting them to
rebuild their churches, and asking their prayers for his recovery.[2]   The era of persecution now closed.   One brief
spasm, indeed, due to the Cæsar Maximian, shot through the
long afflicted Church of Asia Minor;[3] but it was rapidly
allayed.   The accession of Constantine, the proclamation of
Milan, A.D. 313, the defeat of Licinius, and the conversion of

---

[1] 'Italy, Sicily, Gaul, and whatever parts extend towards the West,
—Spain, Mauritania, and Africa.'—
Euseb. *Mart. Palest.* ch. xiii. But
in Gaul, as I have said, the persecution had not extended beyond
the destruction of churches; in
these provinces the persecution,
Eusebius says, lasted not quite two
years.

[2] The history of this persecution
is given by Eusebius, *Hist.* lib.
viii., in his work on the *Martyrs*

of Palestine, and in Lactantius,
De Mort. Persec. The persecution
in Palestine was not quite continuous: in A.D. 308 it had almost
ceased; it then revived fiercely,
but at the close of A.D. 309, and in
the beginning of A.D. 310, there
was again a short lull, apparently
due to political causes.   See
Mosheim, *Eccles. Hist.* (edited by
Soames), vol. i. pp. 286–287.

[3] Eusebius.

the conqueror, speedily followed, and Christianity became the religion of the Empire.

Such, so far as we can trace it, is the outline of the last and most terrible persecution inflicted on the early Church. Unfortunately we can place little reliance on any information we possess about the number of its victims, the provocations that produced it, or the objects of its authors. The ecclesiastical account of these matters is absolutely unchecked by any Pagan statement, and it is derived almost exclusively from the history of Eusebius, and from the treatise 'On the Deaths of the Persecutors,' which is ascribed to Lactantius. Eusebius was a writer of great learning, and of critical abilities not below the very low level of his time, and he had personal knowledge of some of the events in Palestine which he has recorded; but he had no pretensions whatever to impartiality. He has frankly told us that his principle in writing history was to conceal the facts that were injurious to the reputation of the Church; [1] and although his practice was sometimes better than his principle, the portrait he has drawn of the saintly virtues of his patron Constantine, which we are able to correct from other sources, abundantly proves with how little scruple the courtly bishop could stray into the paths of fiction. The treatise of Lactantius, which has been well termed 'a party pamphlet,' is much more untrustworthy. It is a hymn of exultation over the disastrous ends of the persecutors, and especially of Galerius, written in a strain of the fiercest and most passionate invective, and bearing on every page unequivocal signs of inaccuracy and exaggeration. The whole history of the early persecution was soon enveloped in a thick cloud of falsehood. A notion, derived from prophecy, that ten great persecutions must precede the day of judgment, at an early period stimulated

---

[1] See two passages, which Gibbon justly calls remarkable. (*H. E.* viii. 2; *Martyrs of Palest.* ch. xii.)

the imagination of the Christians, who believed that day to be imminent; and it was natural that as time rolled on men should magnify the sufferings that had been endured, and that in credulous and uncritical ages a single real incident should be often multiplied, diversified, and exaggerated in many distinct narratives. Monstrous fictions, such as the crucifixion of ten thousand Christians upon Mount Ararat under Trajan, the letter of Tiberianus to Trajan, complaining that he was weary of ceaselessly killing Christians in Palestine, and the Theban legion of six thousand men, said to have been massacred by Maximilian, were boldly propagated and readily believed.[1] The virtue supposed to attach to the bones of martyrs, and the custom, and, after a decree of the second Council of Nice, in the eighth century, the obligation, of placing saintly remains under every altar, led to an immense multiplication of spurious relics, and a corresponding demand for legends.   Almost every hamlet soon required a patron martyr and a local legend, which the nearest monastery was usually ready to supply.   The monks occupied their time in composing and disseminating innumerable acts of martyrs, which purported to be strictly historical, but which were, in fact, deliberate, though it was thought edifying, forgeries; and pictures of hideous tortures, enlivened by fantastic miracles, soon became the favourite popular literature. To discriminate accurately the genuine acts of martyrs from the immense mass that were fabricated by the monks has been

---

[1] There is one instance of a wholesale massacre which appears to rest on good authority. Eusebius asserts that, during the Diocletian persecution, a village in Phrygia, the name of which he does not mention, being inhabited entirely by Christians who refused to sacrifice, was attacked and burnt with all that were in it by the Pagan soldiery. Lactantius (*Inst. Div.* v. 11) confines the conflagration to a church in which the entire population was burnt; and an early Latin translation of Eusebius states that the people were first summoned to withdraw, but refused to do so. Gibbon (ch. xvi.) thinks that this tragedy took place when the decree of Diocletian ordered the destruction of the churches.

attempted by Ruinart, but is perhaps impossible. Modern criticism has, however, done much to reduce the ancient persecutions to their true dimensions. The famous essay of Dodwell, which appeared towards the close of the seventeenth century, though written, I think, a little in the spirit of a special pleader, and not free from its own exaggerations, has had a great and abiding influence upon ecclesiastical history, and the still more famous chapter which Gibbon devoted to the subject rendered the conclusions of Dodwell familiar to the world.

Notwithstanding the great knowledge and critical acumen displayed in this chapter, few persons, I imagine, can rise from its perusal without a feeling both of repulsion and dissatisfaction. The complete absence of all sympathy with the heroic courage manifested by the martyrs, and the frigid and, in truth, most unphilosophical severity with which the historian has weighed the words and actions of men engaged in the agonies of a deadly struggle, must repel every generous nature, while the persistence with which he estimates persecutions by the number of deaths rather than by the amount of suffering, diverts the mind from the really distinctive atrocities of the Pagan persecutions. He has observed, that while the anger of the persecutors was at all times especially directed against the bishops, we know from Eusebius that only nine bishops were put to death in the entire Diocletian persecution, and that the particular enumeration, which the historian made on the spot, of all the martyrs who perished during this persecution in Palestine, which was under the government of Galerius, and was therefore exposed to the full fury of the storm, shows the entire number to have been ninety-two. Starting from this fact, Gibbon, by a well-known process of calculation, has estimated the probable number of martyrs in the whole Empire, during the Diocletian persecution, at about two thousand, which happens to be the number of persons burnt by the Spanish Inquisition during the

presidency of Torquemada alone,[1] and about one twenty-fifth
of the number who are said to have suffered for their religion
in the Netherlands in the reign of Charles V.[2] But although,
if measured by the number of martyrs, the persecutions inflicted by Pagans were less terrible than those inflicted by
Christians, there is one aspect in which the former appear by
far the more atrocious, and a truthful historian should suffer
no false delicacy to prevent him from unflinchingly stating it.
The conduct of the provincial governors, even when they
were compelled by the Imperial edicts to persecute, was
often conspicuously merciful. The Christian records contain
several examples of rulers who refused to search out the
Christians, who discountenanced or even punished their accusers, who suggested ingenious evasions of the law, who
tried by earnest and patient kindness to overcome what they
regarded as insane obstinacy, and who, when their efforts had
proved vain, mitigated by their own authority the sentence
they were compelled to pronounce. It was only on very rare
occasions that any, except conspicuous leaders of the Church,
and sometimes persons of a servile condition, were in danger;
the time that was conceded them before their trials gave
them great facilities for escaping, and, even when condemned,
Christian women had usually full permission to visit them in
their prisons, and to console them by their charity. But, on
the other hand, Christian writings, which it is impossible to
dispute, continually record barbarities inflicted upon converts,
so ghastly and so hideous that the worst horrors of the In-

---

[1] Mariana (*De Rebus Hispaniæ*, xxiv. 17). Llorente thought this number perished in the single year 1482; but the expressions of Mariana, though he speaks of 'this beginning,' do not necessarily im- ply this restriction. Besides these martyrs, 17,000 persons in Spain recanted, and endured punishments less than death, while great num-

bers fled. There does not appear to have been, in this case, either the provocation or the political danger which stimulated the Dio- cletian persecution.

[2] This is according to the cal- culation of Sarpi. Grotius esti- mates the victims at 100,000.— Gibbon, ch. xvi.

quisition pale before them. It is, indeed, true that burning
neretics by a slow fire was one of the accomplishments of the
Inquisitors, and that they were among the most consummate
masters of torture of their age. It is true that in one Catholic
country they introduced the atrocious custom of making the
spectacle of men burnt alive for their religious opinions an
element in the public festivities.[1] It is true, too, that the
immense majority of the acts of the martyrs are the transparent forgeries of lying monks; but it is also true that
among the authentic records of Pagan persecutions there are
histories which display, perhaps more vividly than any other,
both the depth of cruelty to which human nature may sink,
and the heroism of resistance it may attain. There was a time
when it was the just boast of the Romans, that no refinements of cruelty, no prolongations of torture, were admitted
in their stern but simple penal code. But all this was
changed. Those hateful games, which made the spectacle of
human suffering and death the delight of all classes, had
spread their brutalising influence wherever the Roman name
was known, had rendered millions absolutely indifferent to
the sight of human suffering, had produced in many, in the
very centre of an advanced civilisation, a relish and a passion
for torture, a rapture and an exultation in watching the
spasms of extreme agony, such as an African or an American
savage alone can equal. The most horrible recorded instances
of torture were usually inflicted, either by the populace, or in
their presence, in the arena.[2] We read of Christians bound
in chairs of red-hot iron, while the stench of their half-con-
sumec flesh rose in a suffocating cloud to heaven; of others
who were torn to the very bone by shells, or hooks of iron;

---

[1] See some curious information
on this in Ticknor's *Hist. of
Spanish Literature* (3rd American
edition), vol. iii. pp. 236–237.

[2] This was the case in the persecutions at Lyons and Smyrna,
under Marcus Aurelius. In the
Diocletian persecution at Alexandria the populace were allowed to
torture the Christians as they
pleased. (*Eusebius*, viii. 10.)

of holy virgins given over to the lust of the gladiator, or to
the mercies of the pander; of two hundred and twenty-se on
converts sent on one occasion to the mines, each with the
sinews of one leg severed by a red-hot iron, and with an eye
scooped from its socket; of fires so slow that the victims
writhed for hours in their agonies; of bodies torn limb from
limb, or sprinkled with burning lead; of mingled salt and
vinegar poured over the flesh that was bleeding from the
rack; of tortures prolonged and varied through entire days.
For the love of their Divine Master, for the cause they believed to be true, men, and even weak girls, endured these
things without flinching, when one word would have freed
them from their sufferings. No opinion we may form of the
proceedings of priests in a later age should impair the reverence with which we bend before the martyr's tomb.

END OF THE FIRST VOLUME.

VOLUME II

HISTORY OF
EUROPEAN MORALS.

CHAPTER IV.

FROM CONSTANTINE TO CHARLEMAGNE.

HAVING in the last chapter given a brief, but I trust not altogether indistinct, account of the causes that ensured the triumph of Christianity in Rome, and of the character of the opposition it overcame, I proceed to examine the nature of the moral ideal the new religion introduced, and also the methods by which it attempted to realise it. And at the very outset of this enquiry it is necessary to guard against a serious error. It is common with many persons to establish a comparison between Christianity and Paganism, by placing the teaching of the Christians in juxtaposition with corresponding passages from the writings of Marcus Aurelius or Seneca, and to regard the superiority of the Christian over the philosophical teaching as a complete measure of the moral advance that was effected by Christianity. But a moment's reflection is sufficient to display the injustice of such a conclusion. The ethics of Paganism were part of a philosophy. The ethics of Christianity were part of a religion. The first were the speculations of a few highly cultivated individuals, and neither had nor could have had any direct influence upon the masses of mankind. The second were indissolubly connected with the worship, hopes, and fears of a vast religious system, that acts at least as powerfully on the most ignorant as on the most educated. The chief objects of Pagan religions were to foretell the future, to explain the universe, to avert calamity, to obtain the assistance of the gods. They contained no instruments of moral teaching analogous to our institution of preaching, or to the moral preparation for the reception of the sacrament, or to confession, or to the reading of the Bible, or to religious education, or to united prayer for spiritual benefits. To make men virtuous was no more the function of the priest than of the physician. On the other hand, the philosophic expositions of duty were wholly unconnected with the religious ceremonies of the temple. To amalgamate these two spheres, to incorporate moral culture with religion, and thus to enlist in behalf of the former that desire to enter, by means of ceremonial observances, into direct communication with Heaven, which experience has shown to be one of the most universal and powerful passions of mankind, was among the most important achievements of Christianity. Something had, no doubt, been already attempted in this direction. Philosophy, in the hands of the rhetoricians, had become more popular. The Pythagoreans enjoined religious ceremonies for the purpose of purifying the mind, and expiatory rites were common, especially in the Oriental religions. But it was the distinguishing characteristic of Christianity that its moral influence was not indirect, casual, remote, or spasmodic. Unlike all Pagan religions, it made moral teaching a main function of its clergy, moral discipline the leading object of its services, moral dispositions the necessary condition of the due performance of its rites. By the pulpit, by its ceremonies, by all the agencies of power it possessed, it laboured systematically and perseveringly for the regeneration of mankind. Under its influence, doctrines concerning the nature of God, the immortality of the soul, and the duties of man, which the noblest intellects of antiquity could barely grasp, have become the truisms of the village school, the proverbs of the cottage and of the alley.

But neither the beauty of its sacred writings, nor the perfection of its religious services, could have achieved this great result without the introduction of new motives to virtue. These may be either interested or disinterested, and in both spheres the influence of Christianity was very great. In the first, it effected a complete revolution by its teaching concerning the future world and concerning the nature of sin. The doctrine of a future life was far too vague among the Pagans to exercise any powerful general influence, and among the philosophers who clung to it most ardently it was regarded solely in the light of a consolation. Christianity made it a deterrent influence of the strongest kind. In addition to the doctrines of eternal suffering, and the lost condition of the human race, the notion of a minute personal retribution must be regarded as profoundly original. That the commission of great crimes, or the omission of great duties, may be expiated hereafter, was indeed an idea familiar to the Pagans, though it exercised little influence over their lives, and seldom or never produced, even in the case of the worst criminals, those scenes of deathbed repentance which are so conspicuous in Christian biographies. But the Christian notion of the enormity of little sins, the belief that all the details of life will be scrutinised hereafter, that weaknesses of character and petty infractions of duty, of which the historian and the biographer take no note, which have no perceptible influence upon society, and which scarcely elicit a comment among mankind, may be made the grounds of eternal condemnation beyond the grave, was altogether unknown to the ancients, and, at a time when it possessed all the freshness of novelty, it was well fitted to transform the character. The eye of the Pagan philosopher was ever fixed

upon virtue, the eye of the Christian teacher upon sin. The
first sought to amend men by extolling the beauty of holi
ness ; the second by awakening the sentiment of remorse.
Each method had its excellences and its defects. Philosophy
was admirably fitted to dignify and ennoble, but altogether
impotent to regenerate, mankind. It did much to encourage
virtue, but little or nothing to restrain vice. A relish or
taste for virtue was formed and cultivated, which attracted
many to its practice; but in this, as in the case of all our
other higher tastes, a nature that was once thoroughly vitiated
became altogether incapable of appreciating it, and the transformation of such a nature, which was continually effected by
Christianity, was confessedly beyond the power of philosophy.[1]
Experience has abundantly shown that men who are wholly
insensible to the beauty and dignity of virtue, can be convulsed by the fear of judgment, can be even awakened to
such a genuine remorse for sin as to reverse the current of
their dispositions, detach them from the most inveterate
habits, and renew the whole tenor of their lives.

But the habit of dilating chiefly on the darker side of human
nature, while it has contributed much to the regenerating
efficacy of Christian teaching, has not been without its disadvantages. Habitually measuring character by its aberrations,
theologians, in their estimates of those strong and passionate
natures in which great virtues are balanced by great failings,
have usually fallen into a signal injustice, which is the more
inexcusable, because in their own writings the Psalms of
David are a conspicuous proof of what a noble, tender, and
passionate nature could survive, even in an adulterer and a
murderer. Partly, too, through this habit of operating
through the sense of sin, and partly from a desire to show
that man is in an abnormal and dislocated condition, they

---

[1] There is a remarkable passage
of Celsus, on the impossibility of
restoring a nature once thoroughly
depraved, quoted by Origen in his
answer to him.

have continually propounded distorted and degrading views of human nature, have represented it as altogether under the empire of evil, and have sometimes risen to such a height of extravagance as to pronounce the very virtues of the heathen to be of the nature of sin. But nothing can be more certain than that that which is exceptional and distinctive in human nature is not its vice, but its excellence. It is not the sensuality, cruelty, selfishness, passion, or envy, which are all displayed in equal or greater degrees in different departments of the animal world; it is that moral nature which enables man apparently, alone of all created beings, to classify his emotions, to oppose the current of his desires, and to aspire after moral perfection. Nor is it less certain that in civilised, and therefore developed man, the good greatly preponderates over the evil. Benevolence is more common than cruelty; the sight of suffering more readily produces pity than joy; gratitude, not ingratitude, is the normal result of a conferred benefit. The sympathies of man naturally follow heroism and goodness, and vice itself is usually but an exaggeration or distortion of tendencies that are in their own nature perfectly innocent.

But these exaggerations of human depravity, which have attained their extreme limits in some Protestant sects, do not appear in the Church of the first three centuries. The sense of sin was not yet accompanied by a denial of the goodness that exists in man. Christianity was regarded rather as a redemption from error than from sin,[1] and it is a significant fact that the epithet 'well deserving,' which the Pagans usually put upon their tombs, was also the favourite inscription in the Christian catacombs. The Pelagian controversy, the teaching of St. Augustine, and the progress of asceticism, gradually introduced the doctrine of the utter depravity of

---

[1] This is well shown by Pressensé in his *Hist. des Trois premiers Siècles.*

man, which has proved in later times the fertile source of degrading superstition.

In sustaining and defining the notion of sin, the early Church employed the machinery of an elaborate legislation. Constant communion with the Church was regarded as of the very highest importance. Participation in the Sacrament was believed to be essential to eternal life. At a very early period it was given to infants, and already in the time of St. Cyprian we find the practice universal in the Church, and pronounced by at least some of the Fathers to be ordinarily necessary to their salvation.[1] Among the adults it was customary to receive the Sacrament daily, in some churches four times a week.[2] Even in the days of persecution the only part of their service the Christians consented to omit was the half-secular agape.[3] The clergy had power to accord or withhold access to the ceremonies, and the reverence with which they were regarded was so great that they were able to dictate their own conditions of communion.

From these circumstances there very naturally arose a vast system of moral discipline. It was always acknowledged that men could only rightly approach the sacred table in certain moral dispositions, and it was very soon added that the commission of crimes should be expiated by a period of penance, before access to the communion was granted. A

---

[1] See a great deal of information on this subject in Bingham's *Antiquities of the Christian Church* (Oxford, 1853), vol. v. pp. 370–378. It is curious that those very noisy contemporary divines who profess to resuscitate the manners of the primitive Church, and who lay so much stress on the minutest ceremonial observances, have left unpractised what was undoubtedly one of the most universal, and was believed to be one of the most important, of the institutions of early Christianity. Bingham shows that the administration of the Eucharist to infants continued in France till the twelfth century.

[2] See Cave's *Primitive Christianity*, part i. ch. xi. At first the Sacrament was usually received every day; but this custom soon declined in the Eastern Church, and at last passed away in the West.

[3] Plin. *Ep.* x. 97.

multitude of offences, of very various degrees of magnitude, such as prolonged abstinence from religious services, prenuptial unchastity, prostitution, adultery, the adoption of the profession of gladiator or actor, idolatry, the betrayal of Christians to persecutors, and paiderastia or unnatural love, were specified, to each of which a definite spiritual penalty was annexed. The lowest penalty consisted of deprivation of the Eucharist for a few weeks. More serious offenders were deprived of it for a year, or for ten years, or until the hour of death, while in some cases the sentence amounted to the greater excommunication, or the deprivation of the Eucharist for ever. During the period of penance the penitent was compelled to abstain from the marriage-bed, and from all other pleasures, and to spend his time chiefly in religious exercises. Before he was readmitted to communion, he was accustomed publicly, before the assembled Christians, to appear clad in sackcloth, with ashes strewn upon his head, with his hair shaven off, and thus to throw himself at the feet of the minister, to confess aloud his sins, and to implore the favour of absolution. The excommunicated man was not only cut off for ever from the Christian rites; he was severed also from all intercourse with his former friends. No Christian, on pain of being himself excommunicated, might eat with him or speak with him. He must live hated and alone in this world, and be prepared for damnation in the next.[1]

This system of legislation, resting upon religious terrorism, forms one of the most important parts of early ecclesiastical history, and a leading object of the Councils was to develop or modify it. Although confession was not yet an habitual and universally obligatory rite, although it was only

---

[1] The whole subject of the penitential discipline is treated minutely in Marshall's *Penitential Discipline of the Primitive Church* (first published in 1714, and re- printed in the library of Anglo-Catholic Theology), and also in Bingham, vol. vii. Tertullian gives a graphic description of the public penances, *De Pudicit.* v. 13.

exacted in cases of notorious sins, it is manifest that we have in this system, not potentially or in germ, but in full developed activity, an ecclesiastical despotism of the most crushing order.   But although this recognition of the right of the clergy to withhold from men what was believed to be essential to their salvation, laid the foundation of the worst superstitions of Rome, it had, on the other hand, a very valuable moral effect.   Every system of law is a system of education, for it fixes in the minds of men certain conceptions of right and wrong, and of the proportionate enormity of different crimes; and no legislation was enforced with more solemnity, or appealed more directly to the religious feelings, than the penitential discipline of the Church.   More than, perhaps, any other single agency, it confirmed that conviction of the enormity of sin, and of the retribution that follows it, which was one of the two great levers by which Christianity acted upon mankind.

But if Christianity was remarkable for its appeals to the selfish or interested side of our nature, it was far more remarkable for the empire it attained over disinterested enthusiasm.   The Platonist exhorted men to imitate God; the Stoic, to follow reason; the Christian, to the love of Christ. The later Stoics had often united their notions of excellence in an ideal sage, and Epictetus had even urged his disciples to set before them some man of surpassing excellence, and to imagine him continually near them; but the utmost the Stoic ideal could become was a model for imitation, and the admiration it inspired could never deepen into affection.   It was reserved for Christianity to present to the world an ideal character, which through all the changes of eighteen centuries has inspired the hearts of men with an impassioned love; has shown itself capable of acting on all ages, nations, temperaments, and conditions; has been not only the highest pattern of virtue but the strongest incentive to its practice; and has exercised so deep an influence that it may be truly

said that the simple record of three short years of active life
has done more to regenerate and to soften mankind than all
the disquisitions of philosophers, and all the exhortations of
moralists. This has indeed been the well-spring of whatever
is best and purest in the Christian life. Amid all the sins
and failings, amid all the priestcraft and persecution and
fanaticism that have defaced the Church, it has preserved, in
the character and example of its Founder, an enduring
principle of regeneration. Perfect love knows no rights. It
creates a boundless, uncalculating self-abnegation that trans-
forms the character, and is the parent of every virtue. Side
by side with the terrorism and the superstitions of dogmatism, there have ever existed in Christianity those who
would echo the wish of St. Theresa, that she could blot out
both heaven and hell, to serve God for Himself alone; and
the power of the love of Christ has been displayed alike in the
most heroic pages of Christian martyrdom, in the most
pathetic pages of Christian resignation, in the tenderest pages
of Christian charity. It was shown by the martyrs who
sank beneath the fangs of wild beasts, extending to the last
moment their arms in the form of the cross they loved;[1]
who ordered their chains to be buried with them as the
insignia of their warfare;[2] who looked with joy upon their
ghastly wounds, because they had been received for Christ;[3]
who welcomed death as the bridegroom welcomes the bride,
because it would bring them near to Him. St. Felicitas was
seized with the pangs of childbirth as she lay in prison

---

[1] Eusebius. *H. E.* viii. 7.

[2] St. Chrysostom tells this of
St. Babylas. See Tillemont, *Mém.
pour servir à l'Hist. eccl.* tome iii.
p. 403.

[3] In the preface to a very
ancient Milanese missal it is said
of St. Agatha that as she lay in
the prison cell, torn by the instruments of torture, St. Peter came
to her in the form of a Christian
physician, and offered to dress her
wounds; but she refused, saying
that she wished for no physician
but Christ. St. Peter, in the name
of that Celestial Physician, commanded her wounds to close, and
her body became whole as before
(Tillemont, tome iii. p. 412.)

awaiting the hour of martyrdom, and as her sufferings ex
torted from her a cry, one who stood by said, 'If you now
suffer so much, what will it be when you are thrown to wild
beasts?' 'What I now suffer,' she answered, concerns myself alone; but then another will suffer for me, for I will
then suffer for Him.'[1] When St. Melania had lost both her
husband and her two sons, kneeling by the bed where the
remains of those she loved were laid, the childless widow
exclaimed, 'Lord, I shall serve Thee more humbly and
readily for being eased of the weight Thou hast taken from
me.'[2]

Christian virtue was described by St. Augustine as 'the
order of love.'[3] Those who know how imperfectly the
simple sense of duty can with most men resist the energy of
the passions; who have observed how barren Mahommedan-
ism has been in all the higher and more tender virtues,
because its noble morality and its pure theism have been
united with no living example; who, above all, have traced
through the history of the Christian Church the influence of
the love of Christ, will be at no loss to estimate the value of
this purest and most distinctive source of Christian enthusiasm. In one respect we can scarcely realise its effects upon
the early Church. The sense of the fixity of natural laws is
now so deeply implanted in the minds of men, that no truly
educated person, whatever may be his religious opinions,
seriously believes that all the more startling phenomena
around him—storms, earthquakes, invasions, or famines—
are results of isolated acts of supernatural power, and are
intended to affect some human interest. But by the early
Christians all these things were directly traced to the Master
they so dearly loved. The result of this conviction was a
state of feeling we can now barely understand. A great poet,

  See her acts in Ruinart.   tutis: ordo est amoris.'—De Civ.
[1] St. Jerome, Ep. xxxix.   Dei, xv. 22.
[3] 'Definitio brevis et vera vir-

in lines which are among the noblest in English literature,
has spoken of one who had died as united to the all-pervading soul of nature, the grandeur and the tenderness, the
beauty and the passion of his being blending with the kindred
elements of the universe, his voice heard in all its melodies,
his spirit a presence to be felt and known, a part of the one
plastic energy that permeates and animates the globe. Something of this kind, but of a far more vivid and real character,
was the belief of the early Christian world.   The universe,
to them, was transfigured by love.   All its phenomena, all
its catastrophes, were read in a new light, were endued with
a new significance, acquired a religious sanctity. Christianity
offered a deeper consolation than any prospect of endless life,
or of millennial glories.   It taught the weary, the sorrowing,
and the lonely, to look up to heaven and to say, ' Thou,
God, carest for me.'

It is not surprising that a religious system which made
it a main object to inculcate moral excellence, and which by
its doctrine of future retribution, by its organisation, and by
its capacity of producing a disinterested enthusiasm, acquired
an unexampled supremacy over the human mind, should
have raised its disciples to a very high condition of sanctity.
There can, indeed, be little doubt that, for nearly two hundred
years after its establishment in Europe, the Christian community exhibited a moral purity which, if it has been equalled,
has never for any long period been surpassed.   Completely
separated from the Roman world that was around them,
abstaining alike from political life, from appeals to the tribunals, and from military occupations ; looking forward
continually to the immediate advent of their Master, and
the destruction of the Empire in which they dwelt, and animated by all the fervour of a young religion, the Christians
found within themselves a whole order of ideas and feelings
sufficiently powerful to guard them from the contamination
of their age.   In their general bearing towards society, and

in the nature and minuteness of their scruples, they probably bore a greater resemblance to the Quakers than to any other existing sect.[1]   Some serious signs of moral decadence might, indeed, be detected even before the Decian persecution, and it was obvious that the triumph of the Church, by introducing numerous nominal Christians into its pale, by exposing it to the temptations of wealth and prosperity, and by forcing it into connection with secular politics, must have damped its zeal and impaired its purity; yet few persons, I think, who had contemplated Christianity as it existed in the first three centuries would have imagined it possible that it should completely supersede the Pagan worship around it; that its teachers should bend the mightiest monarchs to their will, and stamp their influence on every page of legislation, and direct the whole course of civilisation for a thousand years; and yet that the period in which they were so supreme should have been one of the most contemptible in history.

The leading features of that period may be shortly told. From the death of Marcus Aurelius, about which time Christianity assumed an important influence in the Roman world, the decadence of the Empire was rapid and almost uninterrupted.   The first Christian emperor transferred his capital to a new city, uncontaminated by the traditions and the glories of Paganism; and he there founded an Empire which derived all its ethics from Christian sources, and which continued in

---

[1] Besides the obvious points of resemblance in the common, though not universal, belief that Christians should abstain from all weapons and from all oaths, the whole teaching of the early Christians about the duty of simplicity, and the wickedness of ornaments in dress (see especially the writings of Tertullian, Clemens Alexandrinus, and Chrysostom, on this subject), is exceedingly like that of the Quakers.   The scruple of Tertullian (*De Coronâ*) about Christians wearing laurel wreaths in the festivals, because laurel was called after Daphne, the lover of Apollo, was much of the same kind as that which led the Quakers to refuse to speak of Tuesday or Wednesday, lest they should recognise the gods Tuesco or Woden.   On the other hand, the ecclesiastical aspects and the sacramental doctrines of the Church were the extreme opposites of Quakerism.

existence for about eleven hundred years. Of that Byzantine
Empire the universal verdict of history is that it constitutes,
with scarcely an exception, the most thoroughly base and
despicable form that civilisation has yet assumed. Though
very crue and very sensual, there have been times when
cruelty assumed more ruthless, and sensuality more extravagant, aspects; but there has been no other enduring civilisation so absolutely destitute of all the forms and elements of
greatness, and none to which the epithet *mean* may be so emphatically applied. The Byzantine Empire was pre-eminently
the age of treachery. Its vices were the vices of men who
had ceased to be brave without learning to be virtuous.
Without patriotism, without the fruition or desire of liberty,
after the first paroxysms of religious agitation, without genius
or intellectual activity; slaves, and willing slaves, in both
their actions and their thoughts, immersed in sensuality and
in the most frivolous pleasures, the people only emerged from
their listlessness when some theological subtilty, or some
rivalry in the chariot races, stimulated them into frantic
riots. They exhibited all the externals of advanced civilisation. They possessed knowledge; they had continually before
them the noble literature of ancient Greece, instinct with the
loftiest heroism; but that literature, which afterwards did so
much to revivify Europe, could fire the degenerate Greeks
with no spark or semblance of nobility. The history of the
Empire is a monotonous story of the intrigues of priests,
eunuchs, and women, of poisonings, of conspiracies, of uniform
ingratitude, of perpetual fratricides. After the conversion of
Constantine there was no prince in any section of the Roman
Empire altogether so depraved, or at least so shameless, as
Nero or Heliogabalus; but the Byzantine Empire can show
none bearing the faintest resemblance to Antonine or Marcus
Aurelius, while the nearest approximation to that character
at Rome was furnished by the Emperor Julian, who contemptuously abandoned the Christian faith. At last the

Mahommedan invasion terminated the long decrepitude of the Eastern Empire. Constantinople sank beneath the Crescent, its inhabitants wrangling about theological differences to the very moment of their fall.

The Asiatic Churches had already perished. The Christian faith, planted in the dissolute cities of Asia Minor, had produced many fanatical ascetics and a few illustrious theologians, but it had no renovating effect upon the people at large. It introduced among them a principle of interminable and implacable dissension, but it scarcely tempered in any appreciable degree their luxury or their sensuality. The frenzy of pleasure continued unabated, and in a great part of the Empire it seemed, indeed, only to have attained its climax after the triumph of Christianity.

The condition of the Western Empire was somewhat different. Not quite a century after the conversion of Constantine, the Imperial city was captured by Alaric, and a long series of barbarian invasions at last dissolved the whole framework of Roman society, while the barbarians themselves, having adopted the Christian faith and submitted absolutely to the Christian priests, the Church, which remained the guardian of all the treasures of antiquity, was left with a virgin soil to realise her ideal of human excellence. Nor did she fall short of what might have been expected. She exercised for many centuries an almost absolute empire over the thoughts and actions of mankind, and created a civilisation which was permeated in every part with ecclesiastical influence. And the dark ages, as the period of Catholic ascendancy is justly called, do undoubtedly display many features of great and genuine excellence. In active benevolence, in the spirit of reverence, in loyalty, in co-operative habits, they far transcend the noblest ages of Pagan antiquity, while in that humanity which shrinks from the infliction of suffering, they were superior to Roman, and in their respect for chastity, to Greek civilisation. On the other hand, they rank immeasurably below the best Pagan civilisations in civic and patriotic virtues, in the love of liberty, in the number and splendour of the great characters they produced, in the dignity and beauty of the type of character they formed. They had their full share of tumult, anarchy, injustice, and war, and they should probably be placed, in all intellectual virtues, lower than any other period in the history of mankind. A boundless intolerance of all divergence of opinion was united with an equally boundless toleration of all falsehood and deliberate fraud that could favour received opinions. Credulity being taught as a virtue, and all conclusions dictated by authority, a deadly torpor sank upon the human mind, which for many centuries almost suspended its action, and was only effectually broken by the scrutinising, innovating, and freethinking habits that accompanied the rise of the industrial republics in Italy. Few men who are not either priests or monks would not have preferred to live in the best days of the Athenian or of the Roman republics, in the age of Augustus or in the age of the Antonines, rather than in any period that elapsed between the triumph of Christianity and the fourteenth century.

It is, indeed, difficult to conceive any clearer proof than was furnished by the history of the twelve hundred years after the conversion of Constantine, that while theology has undoubtedly introduced into the world certain elements and principles of good, scarcely if at all known to antiquity, while its value as a tincture or modifying influence in society can hardly be overrated, it is by no means for the advantage of mankind that, in the form which the Greek and Catholic Churches present, it should become a controlling arbiter of civilisation. It is often said that the Roman world before Constantine was in a period of rapid decay; that the traditions and vitality of half-suppressed Paganism account for many of the aberrations of later times; that the influence of the Church was often rather nominal and superficial than supreme; and that, in judging the ignorance of the dark ages, we must make large allowance for the dislocations of society by the barbarians. In all this there is much truth; but when we remember that in the Byzantine Empire the renovating power of theology was tried in a new capital free from Pagan traditions, and for more than one thousand years un subdued by barbarians, and that in the West the Church, for at least seven hundred years after the shocks of the invasions had subsided, exercised a control more absolute than any other moral or intellectual agency has ever attained, it will appear, I think, that the experiment was very sufficiently tried. It is easy to make a catalogue of the glaring vices of antiquity, and to contrast them with the pure morality of Christian writings; but, if we desire to form a just estimate of the realised improvement, we must compare the classical and ecclesiastical civilisations as wholes, and must observe in each case not only the vices that were repressed, but also the degree and variety of positive excellence attained. In the first two centuries of the Christian Church the moral elevation was extremely high, and was continually appealed to as a proof of the divinity of the creed. In the century before the conversion of Constantine, a marked depression was already manifest. The two centuries after Constantine are uniformly represented by the Fathers as a period of general and scandalous vice. The ecclesiastical civilisation that followed, though not without its distinctive merits, assuredly supplies no justification of the common boast about the regeneration of society by the Church. That the civilisation of the last three centuries has risen in most respects to a higher level than any that had preceded it, I at least firmly believe; but theological ethics, though very important, form but one of the many and complex elements of its excellence. Mechanical inventions, the habits of industrial life, the discoveries of physical science, the improvements of government, the expansion of literature, the traditions of Pagan antiquity, have all a distinguished place, while, the more fully its history is investigated, the more clearly two capital truths are disclosed. The first is that the influence of theology having for centuries numbed and paralysed the whole intellect of Christian Europe, the revival, which forms the starting-point of our modern civilisation, was mainly due to the fact that two spheres of intellect still remained uncontrolled by the sceptre of Catholicism. The Pagan literature of antiquity, and the Mahommedan schools of science, were the chief agencies in resuscitating the dormant energies of Christendom. The second fact, which I have elsewhere endeavoured to establish in detail, is that during more than three centuries the decadence of theological influence has been one of the most invariable signs and measures of our progress.   In medicine, physical science, commercial interests, politics, and even ethics, the reformer has been confronted with theological affirmations which barred his way, which were all defended as of vital importance, and were all in turn compelled to yield before the secularising influence of civilisation.

We have here, then, a problem of deep interest and importance, which I propose to investigate in the present chapter. We have to enquire why it was that a religion which was not more remarkable for the beauty of its moral teaching than for the power with which it acted upon mankind, and which during the last few centuries has been the source of countless blessings to the world, should have proved itself for so long a period, and under such a variety of conditions, altogether unable to regenerate Europe. The question is not one of languid or imperfect action, but of conflicting agencies. In the vast and complex organism of Catholicity there were some parts which acted with admirable force in improving and elevating mankind. There were others which had a directly opposite effect.

The first aspect in which Christianity presented itself to the world was as a declaration of the fraternity of men in

Christ. Considered as immortal beings, destined for the
extremes of happiness or of misery, and united to one another
by a special community of redemption, the first and most
manifest duty of a Christian man was to look upon his fellow-
men as sacred beings, and from this notion grew up the
eminently Christian idea of the sanctity of all human life.
I have already endeavoured to show—and the fact is of such
capital importance in meeting the common objections to the
reality of natural moral perceptions, that I venture, at the
risk of tediousness, to recur to it—that nature does not tell
man that it is wrong to slay without provocation his fellow-
men. Not to dwell upon those early stages of barbarism in
which the higher faculties of human nature are still undeveloped, and almost in the condition of embryo, it is an historical fact beyond all dispute, that refined, and even moral
societies have existed, in which the slaughter of men of some
particular class or nation has been regarded with no more
compunction than the slaughter of animals in the chase. The
early Greeks, in their dealings with the barbarians ; the
Romans, in their dealings with gladiators, and in some periods
of their history, with slaves ; the Spaniards, in their dealings
with Indians ; nearly all colonists removed from European
supervision, in their dealings with an inferior race ; an immense proportion of the nations of antiquity, in their dealings
with new-born infants, display this complete and absolute
callousness, and we may discover traces of it even in our
own islands and within the last three hundred years.[1] And
difficult as it may be to realise it in our day, when the atrocity
of all wanton slaughter of men has become an essential part
of our moral feelings, it is nevertheless an incontestable fact

---

[1] See the masterly description
of the relations of the English to
the Irish in the reign of Queen
Elizabeth, in Froude's *History of
England*, ch. **xxiv.** ; and also Lord
Macaulay's description of the feelings of the Master of Stair towards
the Highlanders. (*History of Eng
land*, ch. **xviii.**)

that this callousness has been continually shown by good
men, by men who in all other respects would be regarded in
any age as conspicuous for their humanity.   In the days of
the Tudors, the best Englishmen delighted in what we should
now deem the most barbarous sports, and it is absolutely
certain that in antiquity men of genuine humanity—tender
relations, loving friends, charitable neighbours—men in
whose eyes the murder of a fellow-citizen would have appeared as atrocious as in our own, attended, instituted, and
applauded gladiatorial games, or counselled without a scruple
the exposition of infants.   But it is, as I conceive, a complete
confusion of thought to imagine, as is so commonly done,
that any accumulation of facts of this nature throws the
smallest doubt upon the reality of innate moral perceptions.
All that the intuitive moralist asserts is that we know by
nature that there is a distinction between humanity and
cruelty; that the first belongs to the higher or better part
of our nature, and that it is our duty to cultivate it.   The
standard of the age, which is itself determined by the general
condition of society, constitutes the natural line of duty; for
he who falls below it contributes to depress it.   Now, there
is no fact more absolutely certain than that nations and
ages which have differed most widely as to the standard have
been perfectly unanimous as to the excellence of humanity.
Plato, who recommended infanticide; Cato, who sold his
aged slaves; Pliny, who applauded the games of the arena;
the old generals, who made their prisoners slaves or gladiators, as well as the modern generals, who refuse to impose
upon them any degrading labour; the old legislators, who
filled their codes with sentences of torture, mutilation, and
hideous forms of death, as well as the modern legislators,
who are continually seeking to abridge the punishment of
the most guilty; the old disciplinarian, who governed by
force, as well as the modern instructor, who governs by sympathy; the Spanish girl, whose dark eye glows with rapture

as she watches the frantic bull, while the fire streams from
the explosive dart that quivers in its neck; as well as the
reformers we sometimes meet, who are scandalised by all
field sports, or by the sacrifice of animal life for food; or
who will eat only the larger animals, in order to reduce the
sacrifice of life to a minimum; or who are continually invent-
ing new methods of quickening animal death—all these
persons, widely as they differ in their acts and in their judgments of what things should be called 'brutal,' and of what
things should be called 'fantastic,' agree in believing humanity to be better than cruelty, and in attaching a definite
condemnation to acts that fall below the standard of their
country and their time. Now, it was one of the most important services of Christianity, that besides quickening greatly
our benevolent affections it definitely and dogmatically asserted the sinfulness of all destruction of human life as a
matter of amusement, or of simple convenience, and thereby
formed a new standard higher than any which then existed
in the world.

The influence of Christianity in this respect began with
the very earliest stage of human life. The practice of abortion was one to which few persons in antiquity attached any
deep feeling of condemnation. I have noticed in a former
chapter that the physiological theory that the fœtus did not
become a living creature till the hour of birth, had some
influence on the judgments passed upon this practice; and
even where this theory was not generally held, it is easy to
account for the prevalence of the act. The death of an
unborn child does not appeal very powerfully to the feeling
of compassion, and men who had not yet attained any strong
sense of the sanctity of human life, who believed that they
might regulate their conduct on these matters by utilitarian
views, according to the general interest of the community,
might very readily conclude that the prevention of birth was
in many cases an act of mercy. In Greece, Aristotle not

only countenanced the practice, but even desired that it should be enforced by law, when population had exceeded certain assigned limits.[1] No law in Greece, or in the Roman Republic, or during the greater part of the Empire, condemned it;[2] and if, as has been thought, some measure was adopted condemnatory of it before the close of the Pagan Empire, that measure was altogether inoperative. A long chain of writers, both Pagan and Christian, represent the practice as avowed and almost universal. They describe it as resulting, not simply from licentiousness or from poverty, but even from so slight a motive as vanity, which made mothers shrink from the disfigurement of childbirth. They speak of a mother who had never destroyed her unborn offspring as deserving of signal praise, and they assure us that the frequency of the crime was such that it gave rise to a regular profession. At the same time, while Ovid, Seneca, Favorinus the Stoic of Arles, Plutarch, and Juvenal, all speak of abortion as general and notorious, they all speak of it as unquestionably criminal.[3] It was probably regarded by the average Romans of the later days of Paganism much as

---

[1] See on the views of Aristotle, Labourt, *Recherches historiques sur les Enfans trouvés* (Paris, 1848), p. 9.

[2] See Gravina, *De Ortu et Progressu Juris Civilis*, lib. i. 44.

[3] ' Nunc uterum vitiat quæ vult formosa vide i,
Raraque in hoc ævo est, quæ velit esse parens.'
Ovid, *De Nuce*, 22-23.

The same writer has devoted one of his elegies (ii. 14) to reproaching his mistress Corinna with having been guilty of this act. It was not without danger, and Ovid says,

' Sæpe suos utero quæ necat ipsa perit.'

A niece of Domitian is said to have died in consequence of having, at the command of the emperor, practised it (Sueton. *Domit.* xxii.). Plutarch notices the custom (*De Sanitate tuenda*), and Seneca eulogises Helvia (*Ad Helv.* xvi.) for being exempt from vanity and having never destroyed her unborn offspring. Favorinus, in a remarkable passage (Aulus Gellius, *Noct. Att.* xii. 1), speaks of the act as 'publica detestatione communique odio dignum,' and proceeds to argue that it is only a degree less criminal for mothers to put out their children to nurse. Juvenal has some well-known and emphatic lines on the subject :—

Englishmen in the last century regarded convivial excesses, as certainly wrong, but so venial as scarcely to deserve censure.

The language of the Christians from the very beginning was widely different. With unwavering consistency and with the strongest emphasis, they denounced the practice, not simply as inhuman, but as definitely murder. In the penitential discipline of the Church, abortion was placed in the same category as infanticide, and the stern sentence to which the guilty person was subject imprinted on the minds of Christians, more deeply than any mere exhortations, a sense of the enormity of the crime. By the Council of Ancyra the guilty mother was excluded from the Sacrament till the very hour of death; and though this penalty was soon reduced, first to ten and afterwards to seven years' penitence,[1] the offence still ranked amongst the gravest in the legislation of the Church. In one very remarkable way the reforms of Christianity in this sphere were powerfully sustained by a doctrine which is perhaps the most revolting in the whole theology of the Fathers. To the Pagans, even when condemning abortion and infanticide, these crimes appeared comparatively trivial, because the victims seemed very insignificant and their sufferings very slight. The death of an adult man who is struck down in the midst of his enterprise and his hopes, who is united by ties of love or friendship to multitudes around him, and whose departure causes a perturbation and a pang to the society in which he

---

' Sed jacet aurato vix ulla puerpera lecto;
Tantum artes hujus, tantum medicamina possunt,
Quæ steriles facit, atque homines in ventre necandos
Conducit.

Sat. vi. 592–595.

There are also many allusions to it in the Christian writers. Thus

Minucius Felix (*Octavius*, xxx.): ' Vos enim video procreatos filios nunc feris et avibus exponere, nunc adstrangulatos misero mortis genere elidere. Sunt quæ in ipsis visceribus, medicaminibus epotis, originem futuri hominis extinguant, et parricidium faciant antequam pariant.'

[1] See Labourt, *Recherches sur les Enfans trouvés*, p. 25.

has moved, excites feelings very different from any produced
by the painless extinction of a new-born infant, which,
having scarcely touched the earth, has known none of its
cares and very little of its love.   But to the theologian this
infant life possessed a fearful significance.   The moment,
they taught, the fœtus in the womb acquired animation, it
became an immortal being, destined, even if it died unborn,
to be raised again on the last day, responsible for the sin of
Adam, and doomed, if it perished without baptism, to be
excluded for ever from heaven and to be cast, as the Greeks
taught, into a painless and joyless limbo, or, as the Latins
taught, into the abyss of hell.   It is probably, in a considerable degree, to this doctrine that we owe in the first instance
the healthy sense of the value and sanctity of infant life
which so broadly distinguishes Christian from Pagan societies, and which is now so thoroughly incorporated with our
moral feelings as to be independent of all doctrinal changes.
That which appealed so powerfully to the compassion of the
early and mediæval Christians, in the fate of the murdered
infants, was not that they died, but that they commonly
died unbaptised; and the criminality of abortion was immeasurably aggravated when it was believed to involve, not
only the extinction of a transient life, but also the damnation
of an immortal soul.[1]   In the 'Lives of the Saints' there is
a curious legend of a man who, being desirous of ascertaining

---

[1] Among the barbarian laws
there is a very curious one about
a daily compensation for children
who had been killed in the womb
on account of the daily suffering of those children in hell.
'Propterea diuturnam judicaverunt
antecessores nostri compositionem
et judices postquam religio Chris-
tianitatis inolevit in mundo. Quia
diuturnam postquam incarnationem
suscepit anima, quamvis ad nativi-
tatis lucem minime pervenissot,
patituc pœnam, quia sine sacra-
mento regenerationis abortivo modo
tradita est ad inferos.' — *Leges Ba-
juvariorum*, tit. vii. cap. xx. in
Canciani, *Leges Barbar*. vol. ii. p.
374.   The first foundling hospital
of which we have undoubted record
is that founded at Milan, by a man
named Datheus, in A.D. 789. Muratori has preserved (*Antich. Ital.*
Diss. xxxvii.) the charter embody-

the condition of a child before birth, slew a pregnant woman,
committing thereby a double murder, that of the mother and
of the child in her womb. Stung by remorse, the murderer
fled to the desert, and passed the remainder of his life in
constant penance and prayer. At last, after many years, the
voice of God told him that he had been forgiven the murder
of the woman. But yet his end was a clouded one. He
never could obtain an assurance that he had been forgiven
the death of the child.[1]

If we pass to the next stage of human life, that of the
new-born infant, we find ourselves in presence of that practice of infanticide which was one of the deepest stains of the
ancient civilisation. The natural history of this crime is
somewhat peculiar.[2] Among savages, whose feelings of
compassion are very faint, and whose warlike and nomadic

---

ing the motives of the founder, in
which the following sentences occur: ' Quia frequenter per luxu-
riam hominum genus decipitur, et
exinde malum homicidii generatur,
dum concipientes ex adulterio, ne
prodantur in publico, fetos teneros
necant, *et absque bapt smatis lavacro
parvulos ad Tartara mittunt*, quia
nullum reperiant locum, quo servare vivos valeant,' &c.   Henry
II. of France, 1556, made a long
law against women who, ' advenant
e temps de leur part et délivrance
de leur enfant, occultement s'en
délivrent, puis le suffoquent et au-
trement suppriment *sans leur avoir
fait empartir le Saint Sacrement
du Baptême*.'—Labourt, *Recherches
sur les Enfans trouvés*, p. 47. There
is a story told of a Queen of Portu-
gal (sister to Henry V. of England,
and mother of St. Ferdinand) that,
being in childbirth, her life was
despaired of unless she took a
medicine which would accelerate
the birth but probably sacrifice the

life of the child. She answered
that 'she would not purchase her
temporal life by sacrificing the
eternal salvation of her son.'—
Bollandists, *Act. Sanctor.*, June 5th.
    [1] Tillemont, *Mémoires pour ser-
vir à l'Histoire ecclésiastique* (Paris,
1701), tome x. p. 41. St. Clem.
Alexand. says that infants in the
womb and exposed infants have
guardian angels to watch over them.
(*Strom.* v.)
    [2] There is an extremely large
literature devoted to the subject
of infanticide, exposition, foundlings, &c. The books I have chiefly
followed are Terme et Monfalcon,
Histoire des Enfans trouvés (Paris,
1840); Remacle, *Des Hospices
d'Enfans trouvés* (1838); Labourt,
*Recherches historiques sur les Enfans
trouvés* (Paris, 1848); Kœnigswar-
ter, *Essai sur la Législation des
Peuples anciens et modernes relative
aux Enfans nés hors Mariage* (Paris
1842). There are also many details on the subject in Godefroy's

habits are eminently unfavourable to infant life, it is, as
might be expected, the usual custom for the parent to decide
whether he desires to preserve the child he has called into
existence, and if he does not, to expose or slay it. In nations
that have passed out of the stage of barbarism, but are still
rude and simple in their habits, the practice of infanticide is
usually rare; but, unlike other crimes of violence, it is not
naturally diminished by the progress of civilisation, for, after
the period of savage life is passed, its prevalence is influenced
much more by the sensuality than by the barbarity of a
people.[1] We may trace too, in many countries and ages, the
notion that children, as the fruit, representatives, and dearest
possessions of their parents, are acceptable sacrifices to the
gods.[2] Infanticide, as is well known, was almost universally

---

Commentary to the laws about
children in the Theodosian Code,
in Malthus, *On Population*, in
Edward's tract *On the State of
Slavery in the Early and Middle
Ages of Christianity*, and in most
ecclesiastical histories.

[1] It must not, however, be inferred from this that infanticide
increases in direct proportion to
the unchastity of a nation. Probably the condition of civilised
society in which it is most common, is where a large amount of
actual unchastity coexists with
very strong social condemnation of
the sinner, and where, in consequence, there is an intense anxiety
to conceal the fall. A recent writer
on Spain has noticed the almost
complete absence of infanticide in
that country, and has ascribed it
to the great leniency of public
opinion towards female frailty.
Foundling hospitals, also, greatly
influence the history of infanticide;
but the mortality in them was long
so great that it may be questioned

whether they have diminished the
number of the deaths, though they
have, as I believe, greatly diminished the number of the murders
of children. Lord Kames, writing
in the last half of the eighteenth
century, says: 'In Wales, even at
present, and in the Highlands of
Scotland, it is scarce a disgrace
for a young woman to have a bastard.   In the country last mentioned, the first instance known of
a bastard child being destroyed by
its mother through shame is a late
one. The virtue of chastity appears to be thus gaining ground, as
the only temptation a woman can
have to destroy her child is to conceal her frailty.'—*Sketches of the
History of Man—On the Progress
of the Female Sex.* The last clause
is clearly inaccurate, but there
seems reason for believing that
maternal affection is generally
stronger than want, but weaker
than shame.

[2] See Warburton's *Divine Lega
tion*, vii. 2

admitted among the Greeks, being sanctioned, and in some
cases enjoined, upon what we should now call ' the greatest
happiness principle,' by the ideal legislations of Plato and
Aristotle, and by the actual legislations of Lycurgus and
Solon.   Regarding the community as a whole, they clearly
saw that it is in the highest degree for the interest of society
that the increase of population should be very jealously restricted, and that the State should be as far as possible free
from helpless and unproductive members ; and they therefore
concluded that the painless destruction of infant life, and
especially of those infants who were so deformed or diseased
that their lives, if prolonged, would probably have been a
burden to themselves, was on the whole a benefit.   The very
sensual tone of Greek life rendered the modern notion of
prolonged continence wholly alien to their thoughts ; and the
extremely low social and intellectual condition of Greek
mothers, who exercised no appreciable influence over the
habits of thought of the nation should also, I think, be taken
into account, for it has always been observed that mothers
are much more distinguished than fathers for their affection
for infants that have not yet manifested the first dawning of
reason.   Even in Greece, however, infanticide and exposition
were not universally permitted.   In Thebes these offences
are said to have been punished by death.[1]

The power of life and death, which in Rome was originally conceded to the father over his children, would appear
to involve an unlimited permission of infanticide ; but a very
old law, popularly ascribed to Romulus, in this respect restricted the parental rights, enjoining the father to bring up

---

[1] Ælian, *Varia Hist.* ii. 7. Passages from the Greek imaginative
writers, representing exposition as
the avowed and habitual practice
of poor parents, are collected by
Terme et Monfalcon, *Hist. des Enfans trouvés*, pp. 39–45.   Tacitus
notices with praise (*Germania*, xix.)
that the Germans did not allow infanticide.   He also notices (*Hist.*
v. 5) the prohibition of infanticide
among the Jews, and ascribes it to
their desire to increase the population.

all his male children, and at least his eldest female child, forbidding him to destroy any well-formed child till it had completed its third year, when the affections of the parent might be supposed to be developed, but permitting the exposition of deformed or maimed children with the consent of their five nearest relations.[1] The Roman policy was always to encourage, while the Greek policy was rather to restrain, population, and infanticide never appears to have been common in Rome till the corrupt and sensual days of the Empire. The legislators then absolutely condemned it, and it was indirectly discouraged by laws which accorded special privileges to the fathers of many children, exempted poor parents from most of the burden of taxation, and in some degree provided for the security of exposed infants. Public opinion probably differed little from that of our own day as to the fact, though it differed from it much as to the degree, of its criminality.   It was, as will be remembered, one of the charges most frequently brought against the Christians, and it was one that never failed to arouse popular indignation. Pagan and Christian authorities are, however, united in speaking of infanticide as a crying vice of the Empire, and Tertullian observed that no laws were more easily or more constantly evaded than those which condemned it.[2] A broad distinction was popularly drawn between infanticide and exposition. The latter, though probably condemned, was certainly not punished by law;[3] it was practised on a

---

[1] Dion. Halic. ii.

[2] Ad Nat. i. 15.

[3] The well-known jurisconsult Paulus had laid down the proposition, ' Necare videtur non tantum is qui partum perfocat sed et is qui abjicit et qui alimonia denegat et qui publicis locis misericordiæ causa exponit quam ipse non habet.' (Dig. lib. xxv. tit. iii. l. 4.) These words have given rise to a famous controversy between two Dutch professors, named Noodt and Bynkershoek, conducted on both sides with great learning, and on the side of Noodt with great passion. Noodt maintained that these words are simply the expression of a moral truth, not a judicial decision, and that exposition was never illegal in Rome till some time after the establishment of Christianity.

gigantic scale and with absolute impunity, noticed by writers
with the most frigid indifference, and, at least in the case of
destitute parents, considered a very venial offence.[1] Often,
no doubt, the exposed children perished, but more frequently
the very extent of the practice saved the lives of the victims.
They were brought systematically to a column near the Vela-
brum, and there taken by speculators, who educated them as
slaves, or very frequently as prostitutes.[2]

His opponent argued that exposition was legally identical with infanticide, and became, therefore,
illegal when the power of life and
death was withdrawn from the
father. (See the works of Noodt
(Cologne, 1763) and of Bynkershoek (Cologne, 1761). It was at
least certain that exposition was
notorious and avowed, and the law
against it, if it existed, inoperative. Gibbon (*Decline and Fall*,
ch. xliv.) thinks the law censured
but did not punish exposition.
See, too, Troplong, *Influence du
Christianisme sur le Droit*, p. 271.

[1] Quintilian speaks in a tone of
apology, if not justification, of the
exposition of the children of destitute parents (*Decl.* cccvi.), and even
Plutarch speaks of it without censure. (*De Amor. Prolis.*) There
are several curious illustrations in
Latin literature of the different
feelings of fathers and mothers on
this matter. Terence (*Heauton.*
Act. iii. Scene 5) represents Chremes
as having, as a matter of course,
charged his pregnant wife to have
her child killed provided it was a
girl. The mother, overcome by
pity shrank from doing so, and
secretly gave it to an old woman
to expose it, in hopes that it might
be preserved. Chremes, on hearing what had been done, reproached
his wife for her womanly pity, and

told her she had been not only
disobedient but irrational, for she
was only consigning her daughter
to the life of a prostitute. In
Apuleius (*Metam.* lib. x.) we have a
similar picture of a father starting
for a journey, leaving his wife in
childbirth, and giving her his parting command to kill her child if it
should be a girl, which she could
not bring herself to do. The girl
was brought up secretly. In the
case of weak or deformed infants
infanticide seems to have been
habitual. 'Portentosos fœtus ex-
tinguimus, liberos quoque, si debiles
monstrosique editi sunt, mergimus.
Non ira, sed ratio est, a sanis inu-
tilia secernere.'—Seneca, *De Ira*, i.
15. Terence has introduced a
picture of the exposition of an infant into his *Andria*, Act. iv. Scene
5. See, too, Suet. *August.* lxv.
According to Suetonius (*Calig.* v.),
on the death of Germanicus, women
exposed their new-born children in
sign of grief. Ovid had dwelt with
much feeling on the barbarity of
these practices. It is a very
curious fact, which has been noticed by Warburton, that Chremes,
whose sentiments about infants we
have just seen, is the very personage
into whose mouth Terence has put
the famous sentiment, 'Homo sum,
humani nihil a me alienum puto.'

[2] That these were the usual

On the whole, what was demanded on this subject was
not any clearer moral teaching, but rather a stronger enforcement of the condemnation long since passed upon infanticide,
and an increased protection for exposed infants.   By the
penitential sentences, by the dogmatic considerations I have
enumerated, and by the earnest exhortations both of her
preachers and writers, the Church laboured to deepen the
sense of the enormity of the act, and especially to convince
men that the guilt of abandoning their children to the precarious and doubtful mercy of the stranger was scarcely
less than that of simple infanticide.[1]   In the civil law her
influence was also displayed, though not, I think, very
advantageously.   By the counsel, it is said, of Lactantius,
Constantine, in the very year of his conversion, in order to
diminish infanticide by destitute parents, issued a decree,
applicable in the first instance to Italy, but extended in A.D.
322 to Africa, in which he commanded that those children
whom their parents were unable to support should be clothed
and fed at the expense of the State,[2] a policy which had already
been pursued on a large scale under the Antonines.   In A.D.
331, a law intended to multiply the chances of the exposed
child being taken charge of by some charitable or interested
person, provided that the foundling should remain the absolute property of its saviour, whether he adopted it as a son

fates of exposed infants is noticed
by several writers. Some, too,
both Pagan and Christian (Quintilian, *Decl.* cccvi.; Lactantius, *Div.
Inst.* vi. 20, &c.), speak of the lia-
bility to incestuous marriages resulting from frequent exposition.
In the Greek poets there are
several allusions to rich childless
men adopting foundlings, and Juvenal says it was common for
Roman wives to palm off foundlings on their husbands for their
sons. (*Sat.* vi. 603.) There is an

extremely horrible declamation in
Seneca the Rhetorician (*Controvers.*
lib. v. 33) about exposed children
who were said to have been maimed
and mutilated, either to prevent
their recognition by their parents,
or that they might gain money as
beggars for their masters.
[1] See passages on this point
cited by Godefroy in his *Commentary to the Law 'De Expositis,' Codex
Theod.* lib. v. tit. 7.
[2] *Codex   Theod.* lib. xi. tit.
27.

or employed it as a slave, and that the parent should not have power at any future time to reclaim it.[1] By another law, which had been issued in A.D. 329, it had been provided that children who had been, not exposed, but sold, might be reclaimed upon payment by the father.[2]

The last two laws cannot be regarded with unmingled satisfaction. The law regulating the condition of exposed children, though undoubtedly enacted with the most benevolent intentions, was in some degree a retrograde step, the Pagan laws having provided that the father might always withdraw the child he had exposed, from servitude, by payment of the expenses incurred in supporting it,[3] while Trajan had even decided that the exposed child could not become under any circumstance a slave.[4] The law of Constantine, on the other hand, doomed it to an irrevocable servitude; and this law continued in force till A.D. 529, when Justinian, reverting to the principle of Trajan, decreed that not only the father lost all legitimate authority over his child by exposing it, but also that the person who had saved it could not by that act deprive it of its natural liberty. But this law applied only to the Eastern Empire; and in part at least of the West[5] the servitude of exposed infants continued for centuries, and appears only to have terminated with the general extinction of slavery in Europe. The law of Constantine concerning the sale of children was also a step, though perhaps a necessary step, of retrogression. A series of emperors, among whom Caracalla was conspicuous, had denounced and endeavoured to abolish, as 'shameful,' the traffic in free children, and Diocletian had expressly and absolutely condemned it.[6]

---

[1] *Codex Theod.* lib. v. tit. 7, lex. 1.

[2] *Ibid.* lib. v. tit. 8, lex 1.

[3] See Godefroy's *Commentary to the Law.*

[4] In a letter to the younger Pliny.

(*Ep.* x. 72.)

[5] See on this point **Muratori,** *Antich. Ital.* Diss. xxxvi.

[6] See on these laws, Wallon, *Hist. de l'Esc'avage,* tome iii. pp 52, 53.

The extreme misery, however, resulting from the civil wars under Constantine, had rendered it necessary to authorise the old practice of selling children in the case of absolute destitution, which, though it had been condemned, had probably never altogether ceased. Theodosius the Great attempted to take a step in advance, by decreeing that the children thus sold might regain their freedom without the repayment of the purchase-money, a temporary service being a sufficient compensation for the purchase; [1] but this measure was repealed by Valentinian III. The sale of children in case of great necessity, though denounced by the Fathers, [2] continued long after the time of Theodosius, nor does any Christian emperor appear to have enforced the humane enactment of Diocletian.

Together with these measures for the protection of exposed children, there were laws directly condemnatory of ـnfanticide. This branch of the subject is obscured by much ambiguity and controversy; but it appears most probable that the Pagan legislation reckoned infanticide as a form of homicide, though, being deemed less atrocious than other forms of homicide, it was punished, not by death, but by banishment. [3] A law of Constantine, intended principally, and perhaps exclusively, for Africa, where the sacrifices of children to Saturn were very common, assimilated to parricide the murder of a child by its father; [4] and finally, Valentinian, in A.D. 374, made all infanticide a capital offence, [5] and

---

[1] See *Cod. Theod.* lib. iii. tit. 3, lex 1, and the Commentary.

[2] On the very persistent denunciation of this practice by the Fathers, see many examples in Terme et Monfalcon.

[3] This is a mere question of definition, upon which lawyers have expended much learning and discussion. Cujas thought the Romans considered infanticide a crime, but a crime generically different from homicide. Godefroy maintains that it was classified as homicide, but that, being esteemed less heinous than the other forms of homicide, it was only punished by exile. See the Commentary to *Cod. Theod.* lib. ix. tit. 14, l. 1.

[4] *Cod. Theod.* lib. ix. tit. 15.

[5] *Ibid.* lib. ix. tit. 14, lex 1.

especially enjoined the punishment of exposition.[1] A law of
the Spanish Visigoths, in the seventh century, punished infanticide and abortion with death or blindness.[2] In the
Capitularies of Charlemagne the former crime was punished
as homicide.[3]

It is not possible to ascertain, with any degree of accuracy,
what diminution of infanticide resulted from these measures.
It may, however, be safely asserted that the publicity of the
trade in exposed children became impossible under the influence of Christianity, and that the sense of the serious nature
of the crime was very considerably increased. The extreme
destitution, which was one of its most fertile causes, was met
by Christian charity. Many exposed children appear to
have been educated by individual Christians.[4] Brephotrophia
and Orphanotrophia are among the earliest recorded charitable institutions of the Church ; but it is not certain that
exposed children were admitted into them, and we find no
trace for several centuries of Christian foundling hospitals.
This form of charity grew up gradually in the early part of
the middle ages. It is said that one existed at Trèves in the
sixth, and at Angers in the seventh century, and it is certain
that one existed at Milan in the eighth century.[5] The
Council of Rouen, in the ninth century, invited women who
had secretly borne children to place them at the door of the
church, and undertook to provide for them if they were not
reclaimed. It is probable that they were brought up among

---

[1] *Corp. Juris*, lib. viii. tit. 52,
lex 2.

[2] *Leges Wisigothorum* (lib. vi.
tit. 3, lex 7) and other laws (lib.
iv. tit. 4) condemned exposition.

[3] 'Si quis infantem necaverit
ut homicida teneatur.'—*Capit*. vii.
168.

[4] It appears, from a passage of
St. Augustine, that Christian virgins were accustomed to collect

exposed children and to have them
brought into the church.   See
Terme et Monfalcon, *Hist. des
Enfans trouvés*, p. 74.

[5] Compare Labourt, *Rech. sur
les Enfans trouvés*, pp. 32, 33;
Muratori, *Antichità Italiane*, Dissert. xxxvii. Muratori has also
briefly noticed the history of these
charities in his *Carità Christiana*,
cap. xxvii.

the numerous slaves or serfs attached to the ecclesiastical properties; for a decree of the Council of Arles, in the fifth century, and afterwards a law of Charlemagne, had echoed the enactment of Constantine, declaring that exposed children should be the slaves of their protectors. As slavery declined, the memorials of many sins, like many other of the discordant elements of mediæval society, were doubtless absorbed and consecrated in the monastic societies. The strong sense always evinced in the Church of the enormity of unchastity probably rendered the ecclesiastics more cautious in this than in other forms of charity, for institutions especially intended for deserted children advanced but slowly. Even Rome, the mother of many charities, could boast of none till the beginning of the thirteenth century.[1] About the middle of the twelfth century we find societies at Milan charged, among other functions, with seeking for exposed children. Towards the close of the same century, a monk of Montpellier, whose very name is doubtful, but who is commonly spoken of as Brother Guy, founded a confraternity called by the name of the Holy Ghost, and devoted to the protection and education of children; and this society in the two following centuries ramified over a great part of Europe.[2] Though principally and at first, perhaps, exclusively intended for the care of the orphans of legitimate marriages, though in the fifteenth

---

[1] The first seems to have been the hospital of Sta. Maria in Sassia, which had existed with various changes from the eighth century, but was made a foundling hospital and confided to the care of Guy of Montpellier in A.D. 1204. According to one tradition, Pope Innocent III. had been shocked at hearing of infants drawn in the nets of fishermen from the Tiber. According to another, he was inspired by an angel. Compare Remacle, *Hospices d'Enfans trouvés*, pp. 36–37, and Amydemus, *Pietas Romana* (a book written A.D. 1624, and translated in part into English in A.D. 1687), Eng. trans. pp. 2, 3.

[2] For the little that is known about this missionary of charity, compare Remacle, *Hospices d'Enfans trouvés*, pp. 34–44; and Labourt, *Recherches historiques sur les Enfans trouvés*, pp. 38–41.

century the Hospital of the Holy Ghost at Paris even refused to admit deserted children, yet the care of foundlings
soon passed in a great measure into its hands. At last, after
many complaints of the frequency of infanticide, St. Vincent
de Paul arose, and gave so great an impulse to that branch
of charity that he may be regarded as its second author, and
his influence was felt not only in private charities, but in
legislative enactments. Into the effects of these measures—
the encouragement of the vice of incontinence by institutions
that were designed to suppress the crime of infanticide, and
the serious moral controversies suggested by this apparent
conflict between the interests of humanity and of chastity—
it is not necessary for me to enter. We are at present concerned with the principles that actuated Christian charity,
not with the wisdom of its organisations. Whatever mistakes may have been made, the entire movement I have
traced displays an anxiety not only for the life, but also for
the moral well-being, of the castaways of society, such as the
most humane nations of antiquity had never reached. This
minute and scrupulous care for human life and human virtue
in the humblest forms, in the slave, the gladiator, the savage,
or the infant, was indeed wholly foreign to the genius of
Paganism. It was produced by the Christian doctrine of
the inestimable value of each immortal soul. It is the distinguishing and transcendent characteristic of every society
into which the spirit of Christianity has passed.

The influence of Christianity in the protection of infant
life, though very real, may be, and I think often has been,
exaggerated. It would be difficult to overrate its influence
in the sphere we have next to examine. There is scarcely
any other single reform so important in the moral history of
mankind as the suppression of the gladiatorial shows, and
this feat must be almost exclusively ascribed to the Christian
Church. When we remember how extremely few of the
best and greatest men of the Roman world had absolutely

condemned the games of the amphitheatre, it is impossible to
regard, without the deepest admiration, the unwavering and
uncompromising consistency of the patristic denunciations.
And even comparing the Fathers with the most enlightened
Pagan moralists in their treatment of this matter, we shall
usually find one most significant difference.   The Pagan, in
the spirit of philosophy, denounced these games as inhuman,
or demoralising, or degrading, or brutal.   The Christian, in
the spirit of the Church, represented them as a definite sin,
the sin of murder, for which the spectators as well as the
actors were directly responsible before Heaven.   In the very
latest days of the Pagan Empire, magnificent amphitheatres
were still arising,[1] and Constantine himself had condemned
numerous barbarian captives to combat with wild beasts.[2]
It was in A.D. 325, immediately after the convocation of the
Council of Nice, that the first Christian emperor issued the
first edict in the Roman Empire condemnatory of the gladiatorial games.[3]   It was issued in Berytus in Syria, and is
believed by some to have been only applicable to the province
of Phoenicia;[4] but even in this province it was suffered to
be inoperative, for, only four years later, Libanius speaks of
the shows as habitually celebrated at Antioch.[5]   In the
Western Empire their continuance was fully recognised,
though a few infinitesimal restrictions were imposed upon
them.   Constantine, in A.D. 357, prohibited the lanistæ, or

[1] E.g. the amphitheatre of
Verona was only built under Diocletian.

[2] 'Quid hoc triumpho pul-
chrius? . . . Tantam captivorum
multitudinem bestiis objicit ut in-
grati et perfidi non minus doloris
ex ludibrio sui quam ex ipsa morte
patiantur.'—Incerti Panegyricus
Constant. 'Puberes qui in manus
venerunt, quorum nec perfidia erat
apta militiæ, nec ferocia servituti

ad pœnas spectaculo dati sævientes
bestias multitudine sua fatiga-
runt.'—Eumenius, Paneg. Constant.
xi.

[3] Cod. Theod. lib. xv. tit. 12
lex 1.   Sozomen, i. 8.

[4] This, at least, is the opinion
of Godefroy, who has discussed the
subject very fully. (Cod. Theod.
lib. xv. tit. 12.)

[5] Libanius, De Vita Sua, 3.

purveyors of gladiators, from bribing servants of the palace to
enrol themselves as combatants.[1] Valentinian, in A.D. 365, forbade any Christian criminal,[2] and in A.D. 367, any one connected
with the Palatine,[3] being condemned to fight.   Honorius
prohibited any slave who had been a gladiator passing into
the service of a senator; but the real object of this last
measure was, I imagine, not so much to stigmatise the
gladiator, as to guard against the danger of an armed nobility.[4]
A much more important fact is that the spectacles were
never introduced into the new capital of Constantine.   At
Rome, though they became less numerous, they do not appear
to have been suspended until their final suppression.   The
passion for gladiators was the worst, while religious liberty
was probably the best, feature of the old Pagan society; and
it is a melancholy fact that of these two it was the nobler
part that in the Christian Empire was first destroyed.   Theodosius the Great, who suppressed all diversity of worship
throughout the Empire, and who showed himself on many
occasions the docile slave of the clergy, won the applause of
the Pagan Symmachus by compelling his barbarian prisoners
to fight as gladiators.[5]   Besides this occasion, we have special
knowledge of gladiatorial games that were celebrated in A.D.
385. in A.D. 391, and afterwards in the reign of Honorius,
and the practice of condemning criminals to the arena still
continued.[6]

But although the suppression of the gladiatorial shows
was not effected in the metropolis of the Empire till nearly
ninety years after Christianity had been the State religion,
the distinction between the teaching of the Christians and
Pagans on the subject remained unimpaired.   To the last,

---

[1] *Cod. Theod.* lib. xv. tit. 12, l. 2.

[2] Ibid. lib. ix. tit. 40, l. 8.

[3] Ibid. lib. ix. tit. 40, l. 11.

[4] Ibid. lib. xv. tit. 12, l. 3.

[5] Symmach. *Ex.* x. 61.

[6] M. Wallon has traced these
last shows with much learning.
(*Hist. de l'Esclavage*, tome iii. pp
421–429.)

the most estimable of the Pagans appear to have regarded them with favour or indifference. Julian, it is true, with a rare magnanimity, refused persistently, in his conflict with Christianity, to avail himself, as he might most easily have done, of the popular passion for games which the Church condemned; but Libanius has noticed them with some appro-bation,[1] and Symmachus, as we have already seen, both in-stituted and applauded them. But the Christians steadily refused to admit any professional gladiator to baptism till he had pledged himself to abandon his calling, and every Chris-tian who attended the games was excluded from communion. The preachers and writers of the Church denounced them with the most unqualified vehemence, and the poet Prudentius made a direct and earnest appeal to the emperor to suppress them. In the East, where they had never taken very firm root, they appear to have ceased about the time of Theodosius, and a passion for chariot races, which rose to the most extra-vagant height at Constantinople and in many other cities, took their place. In the West, the last gladiatorial show was celebrated at Rome, under Honorius, in A.D. 404, in honour of the triumph of Stilicho, when an Asiatic monk, named Telemachus, animated by the noblest heroism of philanthropy, rushed into the amphitheatre, and attempted to part the com-batants. He perished beneath a shower of stones flung by the angry spectators; but his death led to the final abolition of the games.[2] Combats of men with wild beasts continued, however, much later, and were especially popular in the East. The difficulty of procuring wild animals, amid the general poverty, contributed, with other causes, to their decline. They sank, at last, into games of cruelty to animals, but of little danger to men, and were finally condemned, at the end of the seventh century, by the Council of Trullo.[3] In Italy,

---

[1] He wavered, however, on the subject, and on one occasion condemned them. See Wallon,

tome iii. p. 423.

[2] Theodoret, v. 26.

[3] Muller, De Genio Ævi Theo-

the custom of sham fights, which continued through the whole
of the middle ages, and which Petrarch declares were in his
days sometimes attended with considerable bloodshed, may
perhaps be traced in some degree to the traditions of the
amphitheatre.[1]

The extinction of the gladiatorial spectacles is, of all the
results of early Christian influence, that upon which the
historian can look with the deepest and most unmingled
satisfaction. Horrible as was the bloodshed they directly
caused, these games were perhaps still more pernicious on
account of the callousness of feeling they diffused through all
classes, the fatal obstacle they presented to any general elevation of the standard of humanity.   Yet the attitude of the
Pagans decisively proves that no progress of philosophy or
social civilisation was likely, for a very long period, to have
extirpated them ; and it can hardly be doubted that, had they
been flourishing unchallenged as in the days of Trajan, when
the rude warriors of the North obtained the empire of Italy,
they would have been eagerly adopted by the conquerors,
would have taken deep root in mediæval life, and have indefinitely retarded the progress of humanity.   Christianity
alone was powerful enough to tear this evil plant from the
Roman soil.   The Christian custom of legacies for the relief
of the indigent and suffering replaced the Pagan custom of
bequeathing sums of money for games in honour of the dead ;
and the month of December, which was looked forward to
with eagerness through all the Roman world, as the special
season of the gladiatorial spectacles, was consecrated in the
Church by another festival commemorative of the advent of
Christ.

The notion of the sanctity of human life, which led the
early Christians to combat and at last to overthrow the

---

dosiani (1797), vol. ii. p. 88 ; Milman, *Hist. of Early Christianity,*
vol. iii. pp 343-347.

[1] See on these fights Ozanam's
Civilisation in the Fifth Century
(Eng. trans.), vol. i. p. 130.

gladiatorial games, was carried by some of them to an extent
altogether irreconcilable with national independence, and
with the prevailing penal system. Many of them taught
that no Christian might lawfully take away life, either as a
soldier, or by bringing a capital charge, or by acting as an
executioner. The first of these questions it will be convenient
to reserve for a later period of this chapter, when I propose
to examine the relations of Christianity to the military spirit,
and a very few words will be sufficient to dispose of the
others. The notion that there is something impure and defiling, even in a just execution, is one which may be traced
through many ages; and executioners, as the ministers of the
law, have been from very ancient times regarded as unholy.
In both Greece and Rome the law compelled them to live
outside the walls, and at Rhodes they were never permitted
even to enter the city.[1] Notions of this kind were very
strongly held in the early Church; and a decree of the penitential discipline which was enforced, even against emperors
and generals, forbade any one whose hands had been imbrued
in blood, even when that blood was shed in a righteous war,
approaching the altar without a preparatory period of penance.
The opinions of the Christians of the first three centuries
were usually formed without any regard to the necessities of
civil or political life; but when the Church obtained an
ascendancy, it was found necessary speedily to modify them;
and although Lactantius, in the fourth century, maintained
the unlawfulness of all bloodshed,[2] as strongly as Origen in
the third, and Tertullian in the second, the common doctrine
was simply that no priest or bishop must take any part in a
capital charge. From this exceptional position of the clergy
they speedily acquired the position of official intercessors for

---

[1] Nieupoort, *De Ritibus Romanorum*, p. 169.
[2] See a very unequivocal passage, *Inst. Div.* vi. 20. Several
earlier testimonies on the subject
are given by Barbeyrac, *Morale des
Pères*, and in many other books.

criminals, ambassadors of mercy, when, from some act of
sedition or other cause, their city or neighbourhood was
menaced with a bloody invasion. The right of sanctuary,
which was before possessed by the Imperial statues and by
the Pagan temples, was accorded to the churches. During
the holy seasons of Lent and Easter, no criminal trials could
be held, and no criminal could be tortured or executed.[1]
Miracles, it was said, were sometimes wrought to attest the
innocence of accused or condemned men, but were never
wrought to consign criminals to execution by the civil
power.[2]

All this had an importance much beyond its immediate
effect in tempering the administration of the law. It contributed largely to associate in the popular imagination the
ideas of sanctity and of mercy, and to increase the reverence
for human life. It had also another remarkable effect, to
which I have adverted in another work. The belief that it
was wrong for a priest to bring any charge that could give rise
to a capital sentence caused the leading clergy to shrink from
persecuting heresy to death, at a time when in all other
respects the theory of persecution had been fully matured.
When it was readily admitted that heresy was in the highest
degree criminal, and ought to be made penal, when laws ban-
ishing, fining, or imprisoning heretics filled the statute-book,
and when every vestige of religious liberty was suppressed at

[1] See two laws enacted in A.D.
380 (*Cod. Theod.* ix. tit. 35, l. 4)
and A.D. 389 (*Cod. Theod.* ix. tit.
35, l. 5). Theodosius the Younger
made a law (ix. tit. 35, l. 7) except-
ing the Isaurian robbers from the
privileges of those laws.

[2] There are, of course, innumerable miracles punishing guilty
men, but I know none assisting the
civil power in doing so. As an
example of the miracles in defence
of the innocent, I may cite one by
St. Macarius. An innocent man,
accused of a murder, fled to him.
He brought both the accused and
accusers to the tomb of the murdered man, and asked him whether
the prisoner was the murderer. The
corpse answered in the negative ;
the bystanders implored St. Macarius to ask it to reveal the real
culprit; but St. Macarius refused
to do so. (*Vitæ Patrum*, lib. ii.
cap. xxviii.)

the instigation of the clergy, these still shrank from the last
and inevitable step, not because it was an atrocious violation
of the rights of conscience, but because it was contrary to the
ecclesiastical discipline for a bishop, under any circumstances,
to countenance bloodshed. It was on this ground that St.
Augustine, while eagerly advocating the persecution of the
Donatists, more than once expressed a wish that they should
not be punished with death, and that St. Ambrose, and St.
Martin of Tours, who were both energetic persecutors, expressed their abhorrence of the Spanish bishops, who had
caused some Priscillianists to be executed. I have elsewhere
noticed the odious hypocrisy of the later inquisitors, who relegated the execution of the sentence to the civil power, with
a prayer that the heretics should be punished ' as mildly as
possible and without the effusion of blood,'[1] which came at
last to be interpreted, by the death of fire; but I may here
add, that this hideous mockery is not unique in the history of
religion. Plutarch suggests that one of the reasons for bury-
ing unchaste vestals alive was that they were so sacred that
it was unlawful to lay violent hands upon them,[2] and among
the Donatists the Circumcelliones were for a time accustomed
to abstain, in obedience to the evangelical command, from the
use of the sword, while they beat to death those who differed
from their theological opinions with massive clubs, to which
they gave the very significant name of Israelites.[3]

The time came when the Christian priests shed blood
enough. The extreme scrupulosity, however, which they at
first displayed, is not only exceedingly curious when contrasted with their later history; it was also, by the association
of ideas which it promoted, very favourable to humanity.

---

[1] ' Ut quam clementissime et
ultra sanguinis effusionem punire-
tur.'

[2] *Quæst. Romanæ*, xcvi.

Tillemont, *Mém. d' Hist. ecclés.*
tome vi. pp. 88–98. The Donatists
after a time, however, are said to
have overcome their scruples, and
used swords.

It is remarkable, however, that while some of the early Fathers were the undoubted precursors of Beccaria, their teaching, unlike that of the philosophers in the eighteenth century, had little or no appreciable influence in mitigating the severity of the penal code. Indeed, the more carefully the Christian legislation of the Empire is examined, and the more fully it is compared with what had been done under the influence of Stoicism by the Pagan legislators, the more evident, I think, it will appear that the golden age of Roman law was not Christian, but Pagan. Great works of codification were accomplished under the younger Theodosius, and under Justinian; but it was in the reign of Pagan emperors, and especially of Hadrian and Alexander Severus, that nearly all the most important measures were taken, redressing injustices, elevating oppressed classes, and making the doctrine of the natural equality and fraternity of mankind the basis of legal enactments. Receiving the heritage of these laws, the Christians, no doubt, added something; but a careful examination will show that it was surprisingly little. In no respect is the greatness of the Stoic philosophers more conspicuous than in the contrast between the gigantic steps of legal reform made in a few years under their influence, and the almost insignificant steps taken when Christianity had obtained an ascendancy in the Empire, not to speak of the long period of decrepitude that followed. In the way of mitigating the severity of punishments, Constantine made, it is true, three important laws prohibiting the custom of branding criminals upon the face, the condemnation of criminals as gladiators, and the continuance of the once degrading but now sacred punishment of crucifixion, which had been very commonly employed; but these measures were more than counterbalanced by the extreme severity with which the Christian emperors punished infanticide, adultery, seduction, rape, and several other crimes, and the number of capital offences became considerably greater

than before.[1] The most prominent evidence, indeed, of ecclesiastical influence in the Theodosian code is that which must
be most lamented.   It is the immense mass of legislation,
intended on the one hand to elevate the clergy into a
separate and sacred caste, and on the other to persecute in
every form, and with every degree of violence, all who
deviated from the fine line of Catholic orthodoxy.[2]

The last consequence of the Christian estimate of human
life was a very emphatic condemnation of suicide.   We have
already seen that the arguments of the Pagan moralists, who
were opposed to this act, were of four kinds.   The religious
argument of Pythagoras and Plato was, that we are all
soldiers of God, placed in an appointed post of duty, which it
is a rebellion against our Maker to desert.   The civic argument of Aristotle and the Greek legislators was that we owe
our services to the State, and that therefore voluntarily to
abandon life is to abandon our duty to our country.   The
argument which Plutarch and other writers derived from
human dignity was that true courage is shown in the
manful endurance of suffering, while suicide, being an act of
flight, is an act of cowardice, and therefore unworthy of man.
The mystical or Quietist argument of the Neoplatonists was
that all perturbation is a pollution of the soul; that the act
of suicide is accompanied by, and springs from, perturbation,

---

[1] Under the Christian kings, the
barbarians multiplied the number
of capital offences, but this has
usually been regarded as an improvement. The Abbè Mably says:
'Quoiqu'il nous reste peu d'ordon-
nances faites sous les premiers
Mérovingiens, nous voyons qu'avant
la fin du sixième siècle, les François avoient déjà adopté la doctrine
salutaire des Romains au sujet
de la prescription ; et que renon-
çant à cette humanité cruelle qui
les enhardissoit au mal, ils infli-
gèrent peine de mort contre l'inceste,

le vol et le meurtre qui jusques-là
n'avoient été punis que par l'exil,
ou dont on se rachetoit par une
composition. Les François, en ré-
formant quelques-unes de leurs lois
civiles, portèrent la sévérité aussi
loin que leurs pères avoient poussé
l'indulgence.'—Mably, *Observ. sur
l'Hist. des François*, liv. i. ch. iii.
See, too, Gibbon's *Decline and Fall*,
ch. xxxviii.

[2] The whole of the sixth volume
of Godefroy's edition (folio) of the
Theodosian code is taken up with
laws of these kinds.

and that therefore the perpetrator ends his days by a crime.
Of these four arguments, the last cannot, I think, be said to
have had any place among the Christian dissuasives from
suicide, and the influence of the second was almost imper-
ceptible. The notion of patriotism being a moral duty was
habitually discouraged in the early Church; and it was impossible to urge the civic argument against suicide without
at the same time condemning the hermit life, which in the
third century became the ideal of the Church. The duty a
man owes to his family, which a modern moralist would deem
the most obvious and, perhaps, the most conclusive proof of
the general criminality of suicide, and which may be said to
have replaced the civic argument, was scarcely noticed
either by the Pagans or the early Christians. The first
were accustomed to lay so much stress upon the authority,
that they scarcely recognised the duties, of the father; and
the latter were too anxious to attach all their ethics to the
interests of another world, to do much to supply the omission. The Christian estimate of the duty of humility, and
of the degradation of man, rendered appeals to human dignity somewhat uncongenial to the patristic writers; yet these
writers frequently dilated upon the true courage of patience,
in language to which their own heroism under persecution
gave a noble emphasis. To the example of Cato they opposed
those of Regulus and Job, the courage that endures suffering
to the courage that confronts death. The Platonic doctrine,
that we are servants of the Deity, placed upon earth to perform our allotted task in His sight, with His assistance, and
by His will, they continually enforced and most deeply
realised; and this doctrine was in itself, in most cases,
a sufficient preventive; for, as a great writer has said:
'Though there are many crimes of a deeper dye than suicide,
there is no other by which men appear so formally to renounce the protection of God.'[1]

[1] Mme. de Staël, *Réflexions sur le Suicide.*

But, in addition to this general teaching, the Christian theologians introduced into the sphere we are considering new elements both of terrorism and of persuasion, which have had a decisive influence upon the judgments of mankind. They carried their doctrine of the sanctity of human life to such a point that they maintained dogmatically that a man who destroys his own life has committed a crime similar both in kind and magnitude to that of an ordinary murderer,[1] and they at the same time gave a new character to death by their doctrines concerning its penal nature and concerning the future destinies of the soul. On the other hand, the high position assigned to resignation in the moral scale, the hope of future happiness, which casts a ray of light upon the darkest calamities of life, the deeper and more subtle consolations arising from the feeling of trust and from the outpouring of prayer, and, above all, the Christian doctrine of the remedial and providential character of suffering, have proved sufficient protection against despair. The Christian doctrine, that pain is a good, had in this respect an influence that was never attained by the Pagan doctrine, that pain is not an evil.

There were, however, two forms of suicide which were regarded in the early Church with some tolerance or hesitation. During the frenzy excited by persecution, and under the influence of the belief that martyrdom effaced in a moment the sins of a life, and introduced the sufferer at once into celestial joys, it was not uncommon for men, in a transport of enthusiasm, to rush before the Pagan judges, implor-

---

[1] The following became the theological doctrine on the subject: 'Est vere homicida et reus homicidii qui se interficiendo innocentem hominem interfecerit.'— Lisle, *Du Suicide*, p. 400. St. Augustine has much in this strain. Lucretia, he says, either consented to the act of Sextius, or she did not. In the first case she was an adulteress, and should therefore not be admired. In the second case she was a murderess, because in killing herself she killed an innocent and virtuous woman. (*De Civ. Dei*, i. 19.)

ing or provoking martyrdom; and some of the ecclesiastical writers have spoken of these men with considerable admiration,[1] though the general tone of the patristic writings and the councils of the Church condemned them. A more serious difficulty arose about Christian women who committed suicide to guard their chastity when menaced by the infamous sentences of their persecutors, or more frequently by the lust of emperors, or by barbarian invaders. St. Pelagia, a girl of only fifteen, who has been canonised by the Church, and who was warmly eulogised by St. Ambrose and St. Chrysostom, having been captured by the soldiery, obtained permission to retire to her room for the purpose of robing herself, mounted to the roof of the house, and, flinging herself down, perished by the fall.[2] A Christian lady of Antioch, named Domnina, had two daughters renowned alike for their beauty and their piety. Being captured during the Diocletian persecution, and fearing the loss of their chastity, they agreed by one bold act to free themselves from the danger, and, casting themselves into a river by the way, mother and daughters sank unsullied in the wave.[3] The tyrant Maxentius was fascinated by the beauty of a Christian lady, the wife of the Prefect of Rome. Having sought in vain to elude his addresses, having been dragged from her house by the minions of the tyrant, the faithful wife obtained permission, before yielding to her master's embraces, to retire for a moment into her chamber, and she there, with true Roman courage, stabbed herself to the heart.[4] Some Protestant

---

[1] Justin Martyr, Tertullian, and Cyprian are especially ardent in this respect; but their language is I think, in their circumstances, extremely excusable. Compare Barbeyrac, Morale des Pères, ch. ii. § 8; ch. viii. §§ 34-39. Donne's Biathanatos (ed. 1644), pp. 58-67. Cromaziano, Istoria critica e filoso-

fica del Suicidio ragionato (Venezia, 1788), pp. 135-140.

[2] Ambrose, De Virginibus, iii. 7.

[3] Eusebius, Eccles. Hist. viii. 12.

[4] Eusebius, Eccles. Hist. viii. 14. Bayle, in his article upon Sophronia, appears to be greatly scandalised at this act, and it seems that among the Catholics it is not

controversialists have been scandalised,[1] and some Catholic controversialists perplexed, by the undisguised admiration with which the early ecclesiastical writers narrate these histories. To those who have not suffered theological opinions to destroy all their natural sense of nobility it will need no defence.

This was the only form of avowed suicide which was in any degree permitted in the early Church. St. Ambrose rather timidly, and St. Jerome more strongly, commended it; but at the time when the capture of Rome by the soldiers of Alaric made the question one of pressing interest, St. Augustine devoted an elaborate examination to the subject, and while expressing his pitying admiration for the virgin suicides, decidedly condemned their act.[2] His opinion of the absolute sinfulness of suicide has since been generally adopted by the Catholic theologians, who pretend that Pelagia and Domnina acted under the impulse of a special revelation.[3] At the same time, by a glaring though very natural

---

considered right to admire this poor lady as much as her sister suicides. Tillemont remarks: 'Comme on ne voit pas que l'église romaine l'ait jamais honorée, nous n'avons pas le mesme droit de justifier son action.'—*Hist. ecclés.* tome v. pp. 404, 405.

[1] Especially Barbeyrac in his *Morale des Pères.* He was answered by Ceillier, Cromaziano, and others. Matthew of Westminster relates of Ebba, the abbess of a Yorkshire convent which was besieged by the Danes, that she and all the other nuns, to save their chastity, deformed themselves by cutting off their noses and upper lips. (A.D. 870.)

[2] *De Civ. Dei,* i. 22–7.

[3] This had been suggested by St. Augustine. In the case of Pelagia, Tillemont finds a strong argument in support of this view in the astounding, if not miraculous, fact that, having thrown herself from the top of the house, she was actually killed by the fall! 'Estant montée tout au haut de sa maison, fortifiée par le mouvement que J.-C. formoit dans son cœur et par le courage qu'il luy inspiroit, elle se précipita de là du hɑut en bas, et échapa ainsi à tous les piéges de ses ennemis. Son corps en tombant à terre frapa, dit S. Chrysostome, les yeux du démon plus vivement qu'un éclair. . . . . Ce qui marque encore que Dieu agissoit en tout ceci c'est qu'au lieu que ces chutes ne sont pas toujours mortelles, ou que souvent ne brisant que quelques membres, elles n'ostent la vie que longtemps

inconsistency, no characters were more enthusiastically extolled than those anchorites who habitually deprived their
bodies of the sustenance that was absolutely necessary to
health, and thus manifestly abridged their lives.   St. Jerome
has preserved a curious illustration of the feeling with which
these slow suicides were regarded by the outer world, in
his account of the life and death of a young nun named
Blesilla.   This lady had been guilty of what, according to
the religious notions of the fourth century, was, at least, the
frivolity of marrying, but was left a widow seven months
afterwards, having thus 'lost at once the crown of virginity
and the pleasure of marriage.'[1]   An attack of illness inspired
her with strong religious feelings.   At the age of twenty she
retired to a convent.   She attained such a height of devotion
that, according to the very characteristic eulogy of her biographer, 'she was more sorry for the loss of her virginity
than for the decease of her husband;'[2] and a long succession of atrocious penances preceded, if they did not produce,
her death.[3]   The conviction that she had been killed by fasting, and the spectacle of the uncontrollable grief of her mother,
filled the populace with indignation, and the funeral was
disturbed by tumultuous cries that the 'accursed race of
monks should be banished from the city, stoned, or drowned.'[4]
In the Church itself, however, we find very few traces of any
condemnation of the custom of undermining the constitution
by austerities,[5] and if we may believe but a small part of

---

après, n. l'un ni l'autre n'arriva en
cette rencontre; mais Dieu retira
aussitost l'âme de la sainte, en
sorte que sa mort parut autant
l'effet de la volonté divine que de
sa chute.'—*Hist. ecclés.* tome v.
pp. 401-402.

[1] 'Et virginitatis coronam et
nuptiarum perdidit voluptatem.'—
Ep. xxii.

[2] 'Quis enim siccis oculis re-
cordetur viginti annorum adoles-
centulam tam ardenti fide crucis
levasse vexillum ut magis amissam
virginitatem quam mariti doleret
interitum?'—*Ep.* xxxix.

[3] For a description of these
penances, see *Ep.* xxxviii.

[4] *Ep.* xxxix.

[5] St. Jerome gave some sensible
advice on this point to one of his
admirers. (*Ep.* cxxv.)

what is related of the habits of the early and mediæval monks, great numbers of them must have thus shortened their days. There is a touching story told by St. Bonaventura, of St. Francis Assisi, who was one of these victims to asceticism As the dying saint sank back exhausted with spitting blood, he avowed, as he looked upon his emaciated body, that 'he had sinned against his brother, the ass;' and then, the feeling of his mind taking, as was usual with him, the form of an hallucination, he imagined that, when at prayer during the night, he heard a voice saying : 'Francis, there is no sinner in the world whom, if he be converted, God will not pardon; but he who kills himself by hard penances will find no mercy in eternity.' He attributed the voice to the devil.[1]

Direct and deliberate suicide, which occupies so prominent a place in the moral history of antiquity, almost absolutely disappeared within the Church; but beyond its pale the Circumcelliones, in the fourth century, constituted themselves the apostles of death, and not only carried to the highest point the custom of provoking martyrdom, by challenging and insulting the assemblies of the Pagans, but even killed themselves in great numbers, imagining, it would seem, that this was a form of martyrdom, and would secure for them eternal salvation. Assembling in hundreds, St. Augustine says even in thousands, they leaped with paroxysms of frantic joy from the brows of overhanging cliffs, till the rocks below were reddened with their blood.[2] At a much later period, we find among the Albigenses a practice, known by the name of Endura, of accelerating death, in the case of dangerous illness, by fasting, and sometimes by bleeding.[3] The wretched Jews, stung to madness by the persecution of the Catholics, furnish

---

[1] Hase, *St. François d'Assise*, pp. 137–138. St. Palæmon is said to have died of his austerities. (*Vit. S. Pachomii.*)

[2] St. Augustine and St. Optatus

have given accounts of these suicides in their works against the Donatists.

[3] See Todd's *Life of St. Patrick* p. 462.

the most numerous examples of suicide during the middle ages. A multitude perished by their own hands, to avoid torture, in France, in 1095; five hundred, it is said, on a single occasion at York; five hundred in 1320, when besieged by the Shepherds. The old Pagan legislation on this subject remained unaltered in the Theodosian and Justinian codes; but a Council of Arles, in the fifth century, having pronounced suicide to be the effect of diabolical inspiration, a Council of Bragues, in the following century, ordained that no religious rites should be celebrated at the tomb of the culprit, and that no masses should be said for his soul; and these provisions, which were repeated by later Councils, were gradually introduced into the laws of the barbarians and of Charlemagne. St. Lewis originated the custom of confiscating the property of the dead man, and the corpse was soon subjected to gross and various outrages. In some countries it could only be removed from the house through a perforation specially made for the occasion in the wall; it was dragged upon a hurdle through the streets, hung up with the head downwards, and at last thrown into the public sewer, or burnt, or buried in the sand below high-water mark, or transfixed by a stake on the public highway.[1]

These singularly hideous and at the same time grotesque customs, and also the extreme injustice of reducing to beggary the unhappy relations of the dead, had the very natural effect of exciting, in the eighteenth century, a strong spirit of

---

[1] The whole history of suicide in the dark ages has been most minutely and carefully examined by M. Bourquelt, in a very interesting series of memoirs in the third and fourth volumes of the *Bibliothèque de l'École des Chartes.* I am much indebted to these memoirs in the following pages. See, too, Lisle, *Du Suicide, Statistique, Médecine, Histoire, et Législation.* (Paris, 1856.) The ferocious laws here recounted contrast remarkably with a law in the Capitularies (lib. vi. lex 70), which provides that though mass may not be celebrated for a suicide, any private person may, through charity, cause prayers to be offered up for his soul. ' Quia incomprehensibilia sunt judicia Dei, et profunditatem consilii ejus nemo potest investigare.'

reaction. Suicide is indeed one of those acts which may be condemned by moralists as a sin, but which, in modern times at least, cannot be regarded as within the legitimate sphere of law; for a society which accords to its members perfect liberty of emigration, cannot reasonably pronounce the simple renunciation of life to be an offence against itself. When, however, Beccaria and his followers went further, and maintained that the mediæval laws on the subject were as impotent as they were revolting, they fell, I think, into serious error. The outrages lavished upon the corpse of the suicide, though in the first instance an expression of the popular horror of his act, contributed, by the associations they formed, to strengthen the feeling that produced them, and they were also peculiarly fitted to scare the diseased, excited, and over-sensitive imaginations that are most prone to suicide. In the rare occasions when the act was deliberately contemplated, the knowledge that religious, legislative, and social influences would combine to aggravate to the utmost the agony of the surviving relatives, must have had great weight. The activity of the Legislature shows the continuance of the act; but we have every reason to believe that within the pale of Catholicism it was for many centuries extremely rare. It is said to have been somewhat prevalent in Spain in the last and most corrupt period of the Gothic kingdom,[1] and many instances occurred during a great pestilence which raged in England in the seventh century,[2] and also during the Black Death of the fourteenth century.[3] When the wives of priests were separated in vast numbers from their husbands by Hildebrand, and driven into the world blasted, heart-broken, and hopeless, not a few of them shortened

---

[1] See the very interesting work of the Abbé Bourret, *l'École chrétienne de Séville sous la monarchie des Visigoths* (Paris, 1855), p. 196.

[2] Roger of Wendover, A.D. 665
[3] Esquirol, *Maladies mentales,* tome i p. 591.

their agony by suicide.[1]   Among women it was in general
especially rare ; and a learned historian of suicide has even
asserted that a Spanish lady, who, being separated from her
husband, and finding herself unable to resist the energy of
her passions, killed herself rather than yield to temptation,
is the only instance of female suicide during several centuries.[2]
In the romances of chivalry, however, this mode of death is
frequently pourtrayed without horror,[3] and its criminality
was discussed at considerable length by Abelard and St.
Thomas Aquinas, while Dante has devoted some fine lines to
painting the condition of suicides in hell, where they are also
frequently represented in the bas-reliefs of cathedrals.   A
melancholy leading to desperation, and known to theologians
under the name of 'acedia,' was not uncommon in monasteries,
and most of the recorded instances of mediæval suicides in
Catholicism were by monks.   The frequent suicides of monks,
sometimes to escape the world, sometimes through despair at
their inability to quell the propensities of the body, sometimes
through insanity produced by their mode of life, and by their
dread of surrounding demons, were noticed in the early Church,[4]

---

[1] Lea's *History of Sacerdotal Celibacy* (Philadelphia, 1867), p. 248.

[2] 'Per lo corso di molti secoli abbiamo questo solo suicidio donnesco, e buona cosa è non averne più d'uno ; perchè io non credo che la impudicizia istessa sia peggiore di questa disperata castità.'—Cromaziano, *Ist. del. Suicidio*, p. 126. Mariana, who, under the frock of a Jesuit, bore the heart of an ancient Roman, treats the case in a very different manner.   'Ejus cxor Maria Coronelia cum mariti absentiam non ferret, ne pravis cupiditatibus cederet, vitam posuit, ardentem forte libidinem igne extinguens adacto per muliebria titione ; dignam meliori seculo fœminam, insigne studium castitatis.'—*De Rebus Hispan.* xvi. 17.

[3] A number of passages are cited by Bourquelot.

[4] This is noticed by St. Gregory Nazianzen in a little poem which is given in Migne's edition of *The Greek Fathers*, tome xxxvii. p. 1459.   St. Nilus and the biographer of St. Pachomius speak of these suicides, and St. Chrysostom wrote a letter of consolation to a young monk, named Stagirius, which is still extant, encouraging him to resist the temptation.   See Neander, *Ecclesiastical Hist* vol. iii. pp. 319, 320.

and a few examples have been gleaned, from the mediæval
chronicles,[1] of suicides produced by the bitterness of hopeless
love, or by the derangement that follows extreme austerity.
These are, however, but few ; and it is probable that the
monasteries, by providing a refuge for the disappointed and the
broken-hearted, have prevented more suicides than they have
caused, and that, during the whole period of Catholic ascendancy, the act was more rare than before or after.   The
influence of Catholicism was seconded by Mohammedanism,
which, on this as on many other points, borrowed its teaching
from the Christian Church, and even intensified it; for
suicide, which is never expressly condemned in the Bible, is
more than once forbidden in the Koran, and the Christian
duty of resignation was exaggerated by the Moslem into a
complete fatalism.   Under the empire of Catholicism and
Mohammedanism, suicide, during many centuries, almost
absolutely ceased in all the civilised, active, and progressive
part of mankind.   When we recollect how warmly it was
applauded, or how faintly it was condemned, in the civilisation of Greece and Rome; when we remember, too, that
there was scarcely a barbarous tribe, from Denmark to Spain,
who did not habitually practise it,[2] we may realise the com-

---

[1] Bourquelot.   Pinel notices
(*Traité médico-philosophique sur
l'Aliénation mentale* (2nd ed.), pp.
44–46) the numerous cases of insanity still produced by strong
religious feeling ; and the history of
the movements called 'revivals,' in
the present century, supplies much
evidence to the same effect.   Pinel
says, religious insanity tends peculiarly to suicide (p. 265)

[2] Orosius notices (*Hist.* v. 14)
that of all the Gauls conquered by
Q. Marcius, there were none who
did not prefer death to slavery.
The Spaniards were famous for
their suicides, to avoid old age as

well as slavery.   Odin, who, under
different names, was the supreme
divinity of most of the Northern
tribes, is said to have ended his
earthly life by suicide.   Boadicea,
the grandest figure of early British
history, and Cordeilla, or Cordelia,
the most pathetic figure of early
British romance, were both suicides.   (See on the first, Tacitus,
Ann. xiv. 35–37, and on the second
Geoffrey of Monmouth, ii. 15—a
version from which Shakspeare has
considerably diverged, but which is
faithfully followed by Spenser.
(*Faëry Queen*, book ii. canto 10.)

plete revolution which was effected in this sphere by the
influence of Christianity.

A few words may be added on the later phases of this
mournful history. The Reformation does not seem to have
had any immediate effect in multiplying suicide, for Protestants and Catholics held with equal intensity the religious
sentiments which are most fitted to prevent it, and in none of
the persecutions was impatience of life largely displayed.
The history at this period passes chiefly into the new world,
where the unhappy Indians, reduced to slavery, and treated
with atrocious cruelty by their conquerors, killed themselves
in great numbers; till the Spaniards, it is said, discovered an
ingenious method of deterring them, by declaring that the
master also would commit suicide, and would pursue his
victims into the world of spirits.[1] In Europe the act was very
common among the witches, who underwent all the sufferings with none of the consolations of martyrdom. Without
enthusiasm, without hope, without even the consciousness of
innocence, decrepit in body, and distracted in mind, compelled in this world to endure tortures, before which the
most impassioned heroism might quail, and doomed, as
they often believed, to eternal damnation in the next, they
not unfrequently killed themselves in the agony of their
despair. A French judge named Remy tells us that he knew
no less than fifteen witches commit suicide in a single year.[2]

[1] 'In our age, when the Spaniards extended that law which was
made only against the cannibals,
that they who would not accept
the Christian religion should incur
bondage, the Indians in infinite
numbers escaped this by killing
themselves, and never ceased till
the Spaniards, by some counter-
feitings, made them think that
they also would kill themselves,
and follow them with the same
severity into the next life. —
Donne's *Biathanatos*, p. 56 (ed.
1644). On the evidence of the
early travellers on this point, see
the essay on ' England's Forgotten
Worthies,' in Mr. Froude's *Short
Studies*.

[2] Lisle, pp. 427–434. Sprenger
has noticed the same tendency
among the witches he tried. See
Calmeil, *De la Folie* (Paris, 1845),
tome i. pp. 161, 303–305.

In these cases, fear and madness combined in urging the victims to the deed. Epidemics of purely insane suicide have also not unfrequently occurred. Both the women of Marseilles and the women of Lyons were afflicted with an epidemic not unlike that which, in antiquity, had been no ticed among the girls of Miletus.[1] In that strange mania which raged in the Neapolitan districts from the end of the fifteenth to the end of the seventeenth century, and which was attributed to the bite of the tarantula, the patients thronged in multitudes towards the sea, and often, as the blue waters opened to their view, they chanted a wild hymn of welcome, and rushed with passion into the waves.[2] But together with these cases, which belong rather to the history of medicine than to that of morals, we find many facts exhibiting a startling increase of deliberate suicide, and a no less startling modification of the sentiments with which it was regarded. The revival of classical learning, and the growing custom of regarding Greek and Roman heroes as ideals, necessarily brought the subject into prominence. The Catholic casuists, and at a later period philosophers of the school of Grotius and Puffendorf, began to distinguish certain cases of legitimate suicide, such as that committed to avoid dishonour or probable sin, or that of the soldier who fires a mine, knowing he must inevitably perish by the explosion, or that of a condemned person who saves himself from torture by anticipating an inevitable fate, or that of a man who offers himself to death for his friend.[3] The effect of the

---

[1] On modern suicides the reader may consult Winslow's *Anatomy of Suicide*; as well as the work of M. Lisle, and also Esquirol, *Maladies mentales* (Paris, 1838), tome i. pp. 526-676.

[2] Hecker's *Epidemics of the Middle Ages* (London, 1844), p. 121. Hecker in his very curious essay on this mania, has preserved

a verse of their song :

' Allu mari mi portati
Se voleti che mi sanati,
Allu mari, alla via,
Cosi m' ama la donna mia,
Allu mari, allu mari,
Mentre campo, t' aggio amari.

[3] Cromaziano, *Ist. del Suicidio*, caps. viii. ix.

Pagan examples may frequently be detected in the last words or writings of the suicides. Philip Strozzi, when accused of the assassination of Alexander I. of Tuscany, killed himself through fear that torture might extort from him revelations injurious to his friends, and he left behind him a paper in which, among other things, he commended his soul to God, with the prayer that, if no higher boon could be granted, he might at least be permitted to have his place with Cato of Utica and the other great suicides of antiquity.[1] In England, the act appears in the seventeenth century and in the first half of the eighteenth to have been more common than upon the Continent,[2] and several partial or even unqualified apologies for it were written.   Sir Thomas More, in his 'Utopia,' represented the priests and magistrates of his ideal republic permitting or even enjoining those who were afflicted with incurable disease to kill themselves, but depriving of burial those who had done so without authorisation.[3]   Dr. Donne, the learned and pious Dean of St.'Paul's, had in his youth written an extremely curious, subtle, and learned, but at the same time feeble and involved, work in defence of suicide, which on his deathbed he commanded his son neither to publish nor destroy, and which his son published in 1644.   Two or three English suicides left behind them elaborate defences, as did also a Swede named Robeck, who drowned himself in 1735, and whose treatise, published in the following year, acquired considerable celebrity.[4]   But

[1] Cromaziano, pp. 92–93.

[2] Montesquieu, and many Continental writers, have noticed this, and most English writers of the eighteenth century seem to admit the charge. There do not appear, however, to have been any accurate statistics, and the general statements are very untrustworthy. Suicides were supposed to be especially numerous under the depressing influence of English winter fogs. The statistics made in the present century prove beyond question that they are most numerous in summer.

[3] *Utopia*, book ii. ch. vi.

[4] A sketch of his life, which was rather curious, is given by Cromaziano, pp. 148–151. There is a long note on the early literature in defence of suicide, in Dumas, *Traité du Suicide* (Amsterdam, 1723), pp. 148–149. Dumas was

the most influential writings about suicide were those of the
French philosophers and revolutionists.   Montaigne, without
discussing its abstract lawfulness, recounts, with much admiration, many of the instances in antiquity.[1]   Montesquieu,
in a youthful work, defended it with ardent enthusiasm.[2]
Rousseau devoted to the subject two letters of a burning and
passionate eloquence,[3] in the first of which he presented with
matchless power the arguments in its favour, while in the
second he denounced those arguments as sophistical, dilated
upon the impiety of abandoning the post of duty, and upon the
cowardice of despair, and with a deep knowledge of the human
heart revealed the selfishness that lies at the root of most
suicide, exhorting all who felt impelled to it to set about
some work for the good of others, in which they would
assuredly find relief.   Voltaire, in the best-known couplet
he ever wrote, defends the act on occasions of extreme
necessity.[4]   Among the atheistical party it was warmly
eulogised, and Holbach and Deslandes were prominent as its
defenders.   The rapid decomposition of religious opinions
weakened the popular sense of its enormity, and at the same
time the humanity of the age, and also a clearer sense of the

---

a Protestant minister who wrote
against suicide.   Among   the
English apologists for suicide
(which he himself committed) was
Blount, the translator of the *Life
of Apollonius of Tyana*, and Creech,
an editor of Lucretius.   Concerning the former there is a note in
Bayle's *Dict.* art. 'Apollonius.'
The latter is noticed by Voltaire in
his *Lettres Philos.*   He wrote as a
memorandum on the margin of his
'Lucretius,' 'N.B. When I have
finished my Commentary I must
kill myself;' which he accordingly
did—Voltaire says to imitate his
favourite author.   (Voltaire, *Dict.
phil.* art. 'Caton.')

[1] *Essais*, liv. ii. ch. xiii.
[2] *Lettres persanes*, lxxvi.
[3] *Nouvelle Héloïse*, partie iii.
let. 21–22.   Esquirol gives a curious illustration of the way the
influence of Rousseau penetrated
through all classes.   A little child
of thirteen committed suicide,
leaving a writing beginning : 'Je
lègue mon âme à Rousseau, mon
corps à la terre.'—*Maladies mentales*, tome i. p. 588.
[4] In general, however, Voltaire
was extremely opposed to the philosophy of despair, but he certainly
approved of some forms of suicide.
See the articles 'Caton' and 'Suicide,' in his *Dict. philos.*

true limits of legislation, produced a reaction against the horrible laws on the subject. Grotius had defended them. Montesquieu at first denounced them with unqualified energy, but in his later years in some degree modified his opinions. Beccaria, who was, more than any other writer, the repre sentative of the opinions of the French school on such matters, condemned them partly as unjust to the innocent survivors, partly as incapable of deterring any man who was resolved upon the act. Even in 1749, in the full blaze of the philosophic movement, we find a suicide named Portier dragged through the streets of Paris with his face to the ground, hung from a gallows by his feet, and then thrown into the sewers;[1] and the laws were not abrogated till the Revolution, which, having founded so many other forms of freedom, accorded the liberty of death. Amid the dramatic vicissitudes, and the fierce enthusiasm of that period of convulsions, suicides immediately multiplied. 'The world,' it was said, had been 'empty since the Romans.'[2] For a brief period, and in this one country, the action of Christianity appeared suspended. Men seemed to be transported again into the age of Paganism, and the suicides, though more theatrical, were perpetrated with no less deliberation, and eulogised with no less enthusiasm, than among the Stoics. But the tide of revolution passed away, and with some qualifications the old opinions resumed their authority. The laws against suicide were, indeed, for the most part abolished. In France and several other lands there exists no legislation on the subject. In other countries the law simply enjoins burial without religious ceremonies. In England, the burial in a highway and the mutilation by a stake were abolished under George IV.; but the monstrous injustice of confiscating to the Crown the entire property of the deliberate suicide still

[1] Lisle, *Du Suicide*, pp. 411, 412.

'Romains.'—St.-Just, *Procès de Danton*.

[2] 'Le monde est vide depuis les

disgraces the statute-book, though the force of public opinion
and the charitable perjury of juries render it inoperative.

The common sentiment of Christendom has, however,
ratified the judgment which the Christian teachers pronounced
upon the act, though it has somewhat modified the severity of
the old censure, and has abandoned some of the old arguments. It was reserved for Madame de Staël, who, in a youthful work upon the Passions, had commended suicide, to reconstruct this department of ethics, which had been somewhat
disturbed by the Revolution, and she did so in a little treatise which is a model of calm, candid, and philosophic piety.
Frankly abandoning the old theological notions that the
deed is of the nature of murder, that it is the worst
of crimes, and that it is always, or even generally, the
offspring of cowardice; abandoning, too, all attempts to
scare men by religious terrorism, she proceeded, not so much
to meet in detail the isolated arguments of its defenders,
as to sketch the ideal of a truly virtuous man, and to show
how such a character would secure men against all temptation to suicide. In pages of the most tender beauty, she
traced the influence of suffering in softening, purifying, and
deepening the character, and showed how a frame of habitual and submissive resignation was not only the highest
duty, but also the source of the purest consolation, and at
the same time the appointed condition of moral amelioration. Having examined in detail the Biblical aspect of
the question, she proceeded to show how the true measure
of the dignity of man is his unselfishness. She contrasted
the martyr with the suicide—the death which spring from
devotion to duty with the death that springs from rebellion against circumstances. The suicide of Cato, which
had been absurdly denounced by a crowd of ecclesiastics as
an act of cowardice, and as absurdly alleged by many suicides
as a justification for flying from pain or poverty, she represented as an act of martyrdom—a death like that of

Curtius, accepted nobly for the benefit of Rome. The eye of the good man should be for ever fixed upon the interest of others. For them he should be prepared to relinquish life with all its blessings. For them he should be prepared to tolerate life, even when it seemed to him a curse.

Sentiments of this kind have, through the influence cf Christianity, thoroughly pervaded European society, and suicide, in modern times, is almost always found to have sprung either from absolute insanity; from diseases which, though not amounting to insanity, are yet sufficient to discolour our judgments; or from that last excess of sorrow, when resignation and hope are both extinct. Considering it in this light, I know few things more fitted to qualify the optimism we so often hear than the fact that statistics show it to be rapidly increasing, and to be peculiarly characteristic of those nations which rank most high in intellectual development and in general civilisation.[1] In one or two countries, strong religious feeling has counteracted the tendency; but the comparison of town and country, of different countries, of different provinces of the same country, and of different periods in history, proves conclusively its reality. Many reasons may be alleged to explain it. Mental occupations are peculiarly fitted to produce insanity,[2] and the blaze of publicity, which in modern time encircles an act of suicide, to draw weak minds to its imitation. If we put the condition of absolutely savage life, out of our calculation, it is probable that a highly developed civilisation, while it raises the average of well-being, is accompanied by more extreme misery and acute sufferings

---

[1] This fact has been often noticed. The reader may find many statistics on the subject in Lisle, *Du Suicide*, and Winslow's *Anatomy of Suicide*.

[2] 'There seems good reason to believe, that with the progress of mental development through the ages, there is, as in the case with other forms of organic development, a correlative degeneration going on, and that an increase of insanity is a penalty which an increase of our present civilisation necessarily pays.' — Maudsley's *Physiology of Mind*, p. 201.

than the simpler stages that had preceded it.   Nomadic
habits, the vast agglomeration of men in cities, the pressure
of a fierce competition, and the sudden fluctuations to which
manufactures are peculiarly liable, are the conditions of great
prosperity, but also the causes of the most profound misery.
Civilisation makes many of what once were superfluities,
necessaries of life, so that their loss inflicts a pang long after
their possession had ceased to be a pleasure.   It also, by
softening the character, renders it peculiarly sensitive to pain,
and it brings with it a long train of antipathies, passions,
and diseased imaginations, which rarely or never cross the
thoughts or torture the nerves of the simple peasant.   The
advance of religious scepticism, and the relaxation of religious
discipline, have weakened and sometimes destroyed the horror
of suicide; and the habits of self-assertion, the eager and
restless ambitions which political liberty, intellectual activity,
and manufacturing enterprise, all in their different ways
conspire to foster, while they are the very principles and
conditions of the progress of our age, render the virtue of
content in all its forms extremely rare, and are peculiarly
unpropitious to the formation of that spirit of humble and
submissive resignation which alone can mitigate the agony of
hopeless suffering.

From examining the effect of Christianity in promoting
a sense of the sanctity of human life, we may now pass to an
adjoining field, and examine its influence in promoting a fra-
ternal and philanthropic sentiment among mankind.   And
first of all we may notice its effects upon slavery.

The reader will remember the general position this institution occupied in the eyes of the Stoic moralists, and under
the legislation which they had in a great measure inspired.
The legitimacy of slavery was fully recognised; but Seneca
and other moralists had asserted, in the very strongest terms,
the natural equality of mankind, the superficial character of

the differences between the slave and his master, and the duty of the most scrupulous humanity to the former. Instances of a very warm sympathy between master and slave were of frequent occurrence; but they may unfortunately be paralleled by not a few examples of the most atrocious cruelty. To guard against such cruelty, a long series of enactments, 1 ased avowedly upon the Stoical principle of the essential equality of mankind, had been made under Hadrian, the Antonines, and Alexander Severus. Not to recapitulate at length what has been mentioned in a former chapter, it is sufficient to remind the reader that the right of life and death had been definitely withdrawn from the master, and that the murder of a slave was stigmatised and punished by the law. It had, however, been laid down, by the great lawyer Paul, that homicide implies an intention to kill, and that therefore the master was not guilty of that crime if his slave died under chastisement which was not administered with this intention. But the licence of punishment which this decision might give was checked by laws which forbade excessive cruelty to slaves, provided that, when it was proved, they should be sold to another master, suppressed the private prisons in which they had been immured, and appointed special officers to receive their complaints.

In the field of legislation, for about two hundred years after the conversion of Constantine, the progress was extremely slight. The Christian emperors, in A.D. 319 and 326, adverted in two elaborate laws to the subject of the murder of slaves,[1] but, beyond reiterating in very emphatic terms the previous enactments, it is not easy to see in what way they improved the condition of the class.[2]   They pro-

---

[1] *Cod. Theod.* lib. ix. tit. 12.

[2] Some commentators imagine (see Muratori, *Antich. Ital.* Diss. xiv.) that among the Pagans the murder of a man's own slave was only assimilated to the crime of murdering the slave of another man, while in the Christian law it was defined as homicide, equivalent to the murder of a freeman. I confess, however, this point does not appear to me at all clear.

vided that any master who applied to his slave certain
atrocious tortures, that are enumerated, with the object of
killing him, should be deemed a homicide, but if the slave
died under moderate punishment, or under any punishment
not intended to kill him, the master should be blameless; no
charge whatever, it was emphatically said, should be brought
against him.   It has been supposed, though I think without
evidence, by commentators [1] that this law accorded immunity
to the master only when the slave perished under the application of 'appropriate' or servile punishments—that is to
say, scourging, irons, or imprisonment; but the use of torture
not intended to kill was in no degree restricted, nor is there
anything in the law to make it appear either that the master
was liable to punishment, if contrary to his intention his
slave succumbed beneath torture, or that Constantine proposed any penalty for excessive cruelty which did not result
in death.   It is, perhaps, not out of place to observe, that this
law was in remarkable harmony with the well-known article
of the Jewish code, which provided that if a slave, wounded
to death by his master, linger for a day or two, the master
should not be punished, for the slave was his money.[2]

The two features that were most revolting in the slave
system, as it passed from the Pagan to the Christian emperors,
were the absolute want of legal recognition of slave marriage,
and the licence of torturing still conceded to the master.
The Christian emperors before Justinian took no serious
steps to remedy either of these evils, and the measures that
were taken against adultery still continued inapplicable to
slave unions, because 'the vileness of their condition makes
them unworthy of the observation of the law.'[3]   The abolition of the punishment of crucifixion had, however, a special

---

[1] See Godefroy's *Commentary* on
these laws.
[2] Exodus xxi. 21.
[3] 'Quas vilitates vitæ dignas
legum observatione non credidit.'—

Cod. Theod. lib. ix. tit. 7. See on
this law, Wallon, tome iii. pp. 417,
418.

Dean Milman observes. 'In the
old Roman society in the Eastern

value to the slave class, and a very merciful law of Constantine forbade the separation of the families of the slaves.[1] Another law, which in its effects was perhaps still more important, imparted a sacred character to manumission, ordaining that the ceremony should be celebrated in the Church,[2] and permitting it on Sundays. Some measures were also taken. providing for the freedom of the Christian slaves of Jewish masters, and, in two or three cases, freedom was offered as a bribe to slaves, to induce them to inform against criminals. Intermarriage between the free and slave classes was still strictly forbidden, and if a free woman had improper intercourse with her slave, Constantine ordered that the woman should be executed and the slave burnt alive.[3] By the Pagan law, the woman had been simply reduced to slavery. The laws against fugitive slaves were also rendered more severe.[4]

This legislation may on the whole be looked upon as a progress, but it certainly does not deserve the enthusiasm which ecclesiastical writers have sometimes bestowed upon it. For about two hundred years, there was an almost absolute pause in the legislation on this subject. Some slight restrictions were, however, imposed upon the use of torture in trials; some slight additional facilities of manumission were given, and some very atrocious enactments made to prevent slaves accusing their masters. According to that of Gratian, any slave who accused his master of any offence,

Empire this distinction between the marriage of the freeman and the concubinage of the slave was long recognised by Christianity itself. These unions were not blessed, as the marriages of their superiors had soon begun to be, by the Church. Basil the Macedonian (A.D. 867–886) first enacted that the priestly benediction should hallow the marriage of the slave; but the authority of the emperor was counteracted by the deep-rooted prejudices of centuries.'—*Hist. of Latin Christianity*, vol. ii. p. 15.

[1] *Cod. Theod.* lib. ii. tit. 25.
[2] Ibid. lib. iv. tit. 7.
[3] Ibid. lib. ix. tit. 9.
[4] *Corpus Juris*, vi. 1.

except high treason, should immediately be burnt alive, without any investigation of the justice of the charge.[1]

Under Justinian, however, new and very important measures were taken. In no other sphere were the laws of this emperor so indisputably an advance upon those of his predecessors. His measures may be comprised under three heads. In the first place, all the restrictions upon enfranchisement which had accumulated under the Pagan legislation were abolished; the legislator proclaimed in emphatic language, and by the provisions of many laws, his desire to encourage manumission, and free scope was thus given to the action of the Church. In the second place, the freedmen, considered as an intermediate class between the slave and the citizen, were virtually abolished, all or nearly all the privileges accorded to the citizen being granted to the emancipated slave. This was the most important contribution of the Christian emperors to that great amalgamation of nations and classes which had been advancing since the days of Augustus; and one of its effects was, that any person, even of senatorial rank, might marry a slave when he had first emancipated her. In the third place, a slave was permitted to marry a free woman with the authorisation of his master, and children born in slavery became the legal heirs of their emancipated father. The rape of a slave woman was also in this reign punished, like that of a free woman, by death.[2]

But, important as were these measures, it is not in the field of legislation that we must chiefly look for the influence of Christianity upon slavery. This influence was indeed very great, but it is necessary carefully to define its nature. The prohibition of all slavery, which was one of the peculiarities of the Jewish Essenes, and the illegitimacy of hereditary

---

[1] *Cod. Theod.* lib. vi. tit. 2.
[2] See on all this legislation,   Wallon, tome iii.; Champagny *Charité chrétienne*, pp. 214–224.

slavery, which was one of the speculations of the Stoic Dion
Chrysostom, had no place in the ecclesiastical teaching.
Slavery was distinctly and formally recognised by Christianity,[1] and no religion ever laboured more to encourage a
habit of docility and passive obedience.   Much was indeed
said by the Fathers about the natural equality of mankind,
about the duty of regarding slaves as brothers or companions,
and about the heinousness of cruelty to them ; but all this
had been said with at least equal force, though it had not been
disseminated over an equally wide area, by Seneca and Epictetus, and the principle of the original freedom of all men was
repeatedly averred by the Pagan lawyers.   The services of
Christianity in this sphere were of three kinds.   It supplied
a new order of relations, in which the distinction of classes
was unknown.   It imparted a moral dignity to the servile
classes, and it gave an unexampled impetus to the movement
of enfranchisement.

The first of these services was effected by the Church
ceremonies and the penitential discipline.   In these spheres,
from which the Christian mind derived its earliest, its
deepest, and its most enduring impressions, the difference
between the master and his slave was unknown.   They received the sacred elements together, they sat side by side at
the agape, they mingled in the public prayers.   In the penal
system of the Church, the distinction between wrongs done
to a freeman, and wrongs done to a slave, which lay at the
very root of the whole civil legislation, was repudiated.   At
a time when, by the civil law, a master, whose slave died as
a consequence of excessive scourging, was absolutely unpunished, the Council of Illiberis excluded that master for

---

[1] It is worthy of notice, too, that
the justice of slavery was frequently
based by the Fathers, as by modern
defenders of slavery, on the curse
of Ham. See a number of passages
noticed by Moehler, *Le Christianisme et l'Esclavage* (trad. franç.)
pp. 151–152.

ever from the communion.[1]   The chastity of female slaves,
for the protection of which the civil law made but little provision, was sedulously guarded by the legislation of the Church.
Slave birth, moreover, was no disqualification for entering
into the priesthood; and an emancipated slave, regarded as
the dispenser of spiritual life and death, often saw the
greatest and the most wealthy kneeling humbly at his feet
imploring his absolution or his benediction.[2]

In the next place, Christianity imparted a moral dignity
to the servile class.   It did this not only by associating
poverty and labour with that monastic life which was so profoundly revered, but also by introducing new modifications
into the ideal type of morals.   There is no fact more prominent in the Roman writers than the profound contempt with
which they regarded slaves, not so much on account of their
position, as on account of the character which that position
had formed. A servile character was a synonym for a vicious
one.   Cicero had declared that nothing great or noble could
exist in a slave, and the plays of Plautus exhibit the same estimate in every scene.   There were, it is true, some exceptions.
Epictetus had not only been, but had been recognised as one of
the noblest characters of Rome.   The fidelity of slaves to
their masters had been frequently extolled, and Seneca in
this, as in other respects, had been the defender of the op-

The penalty, however, appears
to have been reduced to two years'
exclusion from communion. Muratori says: 'In più consili si truova
decretato, " excommunicatione vel
pœnitentiæ biennii esse subjicien-
dum qui servum proprium sine con-
scientia judicis occiderit."'— Antich. Ital. Diss. xiv.

Besides the works which treat
generally of the penitential discipline, the reader may consult with
fruit Wright's letter On the Political Condition of the English Peasantry, and Moehler, p. 186.

[2] On the great multitude of
emancipated slaves who entered, and
at one time almost monopolised, the
ecclesiastical offices, compare Moehler, Le Christianisme et l'Esclavage,
pp. 177–178.   Leo the Great tried
to prevent slaves being raised to
the priestly office, because it would
degrade the latter.

pressed.   Still there can be no doubt that this contempt was
general, and also that in the Pagan world it was to a great
extent just.   Every age has its own moral ideal, to which all
virtuous men aspire.   Every sphere of life has also a tendency to produce a distinctive type being specially favourable
to some particular class of virtues, and specially unfavourable
to others.   The popular estimate, and even the real moral
condition, of each class depends chiefly upon the degree in
which the type of character its position naturally develops,
coincides with the ideal type of the age.   Now, if we remember that magnanimity, self-reliance, dignity, independence,
and, in a word, elevation of character, constituted the Roman
ideal of perfection, it will appear evident that this was pre-
eminently the type of freemen, and that the condition of
slavery was in the very highest degree unfavourable to its
development.   Christianity for the first time gave the servile
virtues the foremost place in the moral type.   Humility,
obedience, gentleness, patience, resignation, are all cardinal
or rudimentary virtues in the Christian character; they were
all neglected or underrated by the Pagans; they can all expand and flourish in a servile position.

The influence of Christianity upon slavery, by inclining the
moral type to the servile classes, though less obvious and less
discussed than some others, is, I believe, in the very highest degree important.   There is, probably, scarcely any other single
circumstance that exercises so profound an influence upon
the social and political relations of a religion, as the class
type with which it can most readily assimilate; or, in other
words, the group or variety of virtues to which it gives the
foremost place.   The virtues that are most suited to the
servile position were in general so little honoured by antiquity that they were not even cultivated in their appropriate
sphere.   The aspirations of good men were in a different
direction.   The virtue of the Stoic, which rose triumphantly
under adversity, nearly always withered under degradation

For the first time, under the influence of Christianity, a great moral movement passed through the servile class. The multitude of slaves who embraced the new faith was one of the reproaches of the Pagans; and the names of Blandina, Potamiæna, Eutyches, Victorinus, and Nereus, show how fully they shared in the sufferings and in the glory of martyrdom.[1] The first and grandest edifice of Byzantine architecture in Italy—the noble church of St. Vital, at Ravenna—was dedicated by Justinian to the memory of a martyred slave.

While Christianity thus broke down the contempt with which the master had regarded his slaves, and planted among the latter a principle of moral regeneration which expanded in no other sphere with an equal perfection, its action in procuring the freedom of the slave was unceasing. The law of Constantine, which placed the ceremony under the superintendence of the clergy, and the many laws that gave special facilities of manumission to those who desired to enter the monasteries or the priesthood, symbolised the religious character the act had assumed. It was celebrated on Church festivals, especially at Easter; and, although it was not proclaimed a matter of duty or necessity, it was always regarded as one of the most acceptable modes of expiating past sins. St. Melania was said to have emancipated 8,000 slaves; St. Ovidius, a rich martyr of Gaul, 5,000; Chromatius, a Roman prefect under Diocletian, 1,400; Hermes, a prefect in the reign of Trajan, 1,250.[2] Pope St. Gregory, many of the clergy at Hippo under the rule of St. Augustine, as well as great numbers of private individuals, freed their slaves as an act of piety.[3] It became customary to do so on occasions

---

[1] See a most admirable dissertation on this subject in Le Blant, *Inscriptions chrétiennes de la Gaule*, tome ii. pp. 284–299; Gibbon's *Decline and Fall*, ch. xxxviii.

[2] Champagny, *Charité chrétienne*, p. 210. These numbers are, no doubt, exaggerated; see Wallon, *Hist. de l'Esclavage*, tome iii. p. 38.

[3] See Schmidt, *La Société civile dans le Monde romain*, pp. 246–248.

of national or personal thanksgiving, on recovery from sickness, on the birth of a child, at the hour of death, and, above all, in testamentary bequests.[1] Numerous charters and epitaphs still record the gift of liberty to slaves throughout the middle ages, 'for the benefit of the soul' of the donor or testator. In the thirteenth century, when there were no slaves to emancipate in France, it was usual in many churches to release caged pigeons on the ecclesiastical festivals, in memory of the ancient charity, and that prisoners might still be freed in the name of Christ.[2]

Slavery, however, lasted in Europe for about 800 years after Constantine, and during the period with which alone this volume is concerned, although its character was changed and mitigated, the number of men who were subject to it was probably greater than in the Pagan Empire. In the West the barbarian conquests modified the conditions of labour in two directions. The cessation of the stream of barbarian captives, the impoverishment of great families, who had been surrounded by vast retinues of slaves, the general diminution of town life, and the barbarian habits of personal independence, checked the old form of slavery, while the misery and the precarious condition of the free peasants induced them in great numbers to barter their liberty for protection by the neighbouring lord.[3] In the East, the de-

---

[1] Muratori has devoted two valuable dissertations (*Antich. Ital.* xiv. xv.) to mediæval slavery.

[2] Ozanam's *Hist. of Civilisation in the Fifth Century* (Eng. trans.), vol. ii. p. 43. St. Adelbert, Archbishop of Prague at the end of the tenth century, was especially famous for his opposition to the slave trade. In Sweden, the abolition of slavery in the thirteenth century was avowedly accomplished in obedience to Christian principles. (Moehler, *Le Christianisme et l'Esclavage*, pp.

194–196; Ryan's *History of the Effects of Religion upon Mankind*, pp. 142. 143.)

[3] Salvian, in a famous passage (*De Gubernatione Dei*, lib. v.), notices the multitudes of poor who voluntarily became 'coloni' for the sake of protection and a livelihood. The coloni, who were attached to the soil, were much the same as the mediæval serfs. We have already noticed them coming into being, apparently when the Roman emperors settled barbarian prisoners to cul-

struction of great fortunes through excessive taxation diminished the number of superfluous slaves; and the fiscal system of the Byzantine Empire, by which agricultural slaves were taxed according to their employments,[1] as well as the desire of emperors to encourage agriculture, led the legislators to attach the slaves permanently to the soil. In the course of time, almost the entire free peasantry, and the greater number of the old slaves, had sunk or risen into the qualified slavery called serfdom, which formed the basis of the great edifice of feudalism. Towards the end of the eighth century, the sale of slaves beyond their native provinces was in most countries prohibited.[2] The creation of the free cities of Italy, the custom of emancipating slaves who were enrolled in the army, and economical changes which made free labour more profitable than slave labour, conspired with religious motives in effecting the ultimate freedom of labour. The practice of manumitting, as an act of devotion, continued to the end; but the ecclesiastics, probably through the feeling that they had no right to alienate corporate property, in which they had only a life interest, were among the last to follow the counsels they so liberally bestowed upon the laity.[3] In the twelfth century, however, slaves in Europe were very rare. In the fourteenth century, slavery was almost unknown.[4]

---

tivate the desert lands of Italy; and before the barbarian invasions their numbers seem to have much increased. M. Guizot has devoted two chapters to this subject. (*Hist. de la Civilisation en France*, vii. viii.)

[1] See Finlay's *Hist. of Greece*, vol. i. p. 241.

[2] Moehler, p. 181.

[3] 'Non v'era anticamente signor secolare, vescovo, abbate, capitolo di canonici e monistero che non avesse al suo servigio molti servi. Molto frequentemente solevano i secolari manometterli. Non così le chiese, e i monisteri, non per altra cagione, a mio credere, se non perchè la manumissione è una spezie di alienazione, ed era dai canoni proibito l'alienare i beni delle chiese.' — Muratori, *Dissert.* xv. Some Councils, however, recognised the right of bishops to emancipate Church slaves. Moehler, *Le Christianisme et l'Esclavage*, p. 187. Many peasants placed themselves under the dominion of the monks, as being the best masters, and also to obtain the benefit of their prayers.

[4] Muratori; Hallam's *Middle Ages*, ch. ii. part ii.

Closely connected with the influence of the Church in de
stroying hereditary slavery, was its influence in redeeming
captives from servitude. In no other form of charity was its
beneficial character more continually and more splendidly
displayed. During the long and dreary trials of the barbarian
invasions, when the whole structure of society was dislocated, when vast districts and mighty cities were in a few
months almost depopulated, and when the flower of the youth
of Italy were mown down by the sword, or carried away
into captivity, the bishops never desisted from their efforts to
alleviate the sufferings of the prisoners. St. Ambrose, disre-
garding the outcries of the Arians, who denounced his act as
atrocious sacrilege, sold the rich church ornaments of Milan
to rescue some captives who had fallen into the hands of the
Goths, and this practice—which was afterwards formally
sanctioned by St. Gregory the Great—became speedily general.
When the Roman army had captured, but refused to support,
seven thousand Persian prisoners, Acacius, Bishop of Amida,
undeterred by the bitter hostility of the Persians to Christianity, and declaring that 'God had no need of plates or
dishes,' sold all the rich church ornaments of his diocese,
rescued the unbelieving prisoners, and sent them back unharmed to their king. During the horrors of the Vandal
invasion, Deogratias, Bishop of Carthage, took a similar step
to ransom the Roman prisoners. St. Augustine, St. Gregory
the Great, St. Cæsarius of Arles, St. Exuperius of Toulouse,
St. Hilary, St. Remi, all melted down or sold their church
vases to free prisoners. St. Cyprian sent a large sum for the
same purpose to the Bishop of Nicomedia. St. Epiphanius
and St. Avitus, in conjunction with a rich Gaulish lady
named Syagria, are said to have rescued thousands. St.
Eligius devoted to this object his entire fortune. St. Paulinus
of Nola displayed a similar generosity, and the legends even
assert, though untruly, that he, like St. Peter Teleonarius
and St. Serapion, having exhausted all other forms of charity,

as a last gift sold himself to slavery.   When, long afterwards, the Mohammedan conquests in a measure reproduced
the calamities of the barbarian invasions, the same unwearied
charity was displayed. The Trinitarian monks, founded by John
of Matha in the twelfth century, were devoted to the release
of Christian captives, and another society was founded with
the same object by Peter Nolasco, in the following century.[1]

The different branches of the subject I am examining are
so closely intertwined that it is difficult to investigate one
without in a measure anticipating the others.   While discussing the influence of the Church in protecting infancy, in
raising the estimate of human life, and in alleviating slavery,
I have trenched largely upon the last application of the
doctrine of Christian fraternity I must examine—I mean the
foundation of charity. The difference between Pagan and
Christian societies in this matter is very profound; but a
great part of it must be ascribed to causes other than
religious opinions.   Charity finds an extended scope for
action only, where there exists a large class of men at once
independent and impoverished.   In the ancient societies,
slavery in a great measure replaced pauperism, and, by
securing the subsistence of a very large proportion of the
poor, contracted the sphere of charity.   And what slavery
did at Rome for the very poor, the system of clientage did
for those of a somewhat higher rank. The existence of these
two institutions is sufficient to show the injustice of judging
the two societies by a mere comparison of their charitable
institutions, and we must also remember that among the
ancients the relief of the indigent was one of the most important functions of the State.   Not to dwell upon the many
measures taken with this object in ancient Greece, in considering the condition of the Roman poor we are at once met

---

[1] See on this subject, Ryan, pp.
151–152; Cibrario, *Economica politica del Medio Evo*, lib. iii. cap. ii.,
and especially Le Blant, *Inscriptions chrétiennes de la Gaule*, tome
ii. pp. 284–299.

by the simple fact that for several centuries the immense
majority of these were habitually supported by gratuitous
distributions of corn.   In a very early period of Roman
history we find occasional instances of distribution; but it
was not till A.U.C. 630 that Caius Gracchus caused a law to
be made, supplying the poorer classes with corn at a price
that was little more than nominal; and although, two years
after, the nobles succeeded in revoking this law, it was after
several fluctuations finally re-enacted in A.U.C. 679.   The
Cassia-Terentia law, as it was called from the consuls under
whom it was at last established, was largely extended in its
operation, or, as some think, revived from neglect in A.U.C.
691, by Cato of Utica, who desired by this means to divert
popularity from the cause of Cæsar, under whom multitudes
of the poor were enrolling themselves.   Four years later,
Clodius Pulcher, abolishing the small payment which had
been demanded, made the distribution entirely gratuitous.
It took place once a month, and consisted of five modii[1] a
head.   In the time of Julius Cæsar no less than 320,000
persons were inscribed as recipients; but Cæsar reduced the
number by one half.   Under Augustus it had risen to
200,000.   This emperor desired to restrict the distribution
of corn to three or four times a year, but, yielding to the
popular wish, he at last consented that it should continue
monthly.   It soon became the leading fact of Roman life.
Numerous officers were appointed to provide it.   A severe
legislation controlled their acts, and to secure a regular and
abundant supply of corn for the capital became the principal
object of the provincial governors.   Under the Antonines the
number of the recipients had considerably increased, having
sometimes, it is said, exceeded 500,000.   Septimus Severus
added to the corn a ration of oil.   Aurelian replaced the

---

[1] About ⅝ths of a bushel.   See Hume's *Essay on the Populousness
of Ancient Nations.*

monthly distribution of unground corn by a daily distribution of bread, and added, moreover, a portion of pork. Gratuitous distributions were afterwards extended to Constantinople, Alexandria, and Antioch, and were probably not altogether unknown in smaller towns.[1]

We have already seen that this gratuitous distribution of corn ranked, with the institution of slavery and the gladiatorial exhibitions, as one of the chief demoralising influences of the Empire. The most injudicious charity, however pernicious to the classes it is intended to relieve, has commonly a beneficial and softening influence upon the donor, and through him upon society at large. But the Roman distribution of corn, being merely a political device, had no humanising influence upon the people, while, being regulated only by the indigence, and not at all by the infirmities or character, of the recipient, it was a direct and overwhelming encouragement to idleness. With a provision of the necessaries of life, and with an abundant supply of amusements, the poor Romans readily gave up honourable labour, all trades in the city languished, every interruption in the distribution of corn was followed by fearful sufferings, free gifts of land were often insufficient to attract the citizens to honest labour, and the multiplication of children, which rendered the public relief inadequate, was checked by abortion, exposition, or infanticide.

When we remember that the population of Rome probably never exceeded a million and a half, that a large proportion of the indigent were provided for as slaves, and that more than 200,000 freemen were habitually supplied

---

[1] The history of these distributions is traced with admirable learning by M. Naudet in his *Mémoire sur les Secours publics dans l'Antiquité* (*Mém. de l'Académie des Inscrip. et Belles-lettres,* tome xiii.), an essay to which I am much indebted. See, too, Monnier, *Hist. de l'Assistance publique*; B. Dumas, *Des Secours publics chez les Anciens*; and Schmidt, *Essai sur la Société civile dans le Monde romain et sur sa Transformation par le Christianisme.*

with the first necessary of life, we cannot, I think, charge the Pagan society of the metropolis, at least, with an excessive parsimony in relieving poverty. But besides the distribution of corn, several other measures were taken. Salt, which was very largely used by the Roman poor, had during the Republic been made a monopoly of the State, and was sold by it at a price that was little more than nominal.[1] The distribution of land, which was the subject of the agrarian laws, was, under a new form, practised by Julius Cæsar,[2] Nerva,[3] and Septimus Severus,[4] who bought land to divide it among the poor citizens. Large legacies were left to the people by Julius Cæsar, Augustus, and others, and considerable, though irregular, donations made on occasions of great rejoicings. Numerous public baths were established, to which, when they were not absolutely gratuitous, the smallest coin in use gave admission, and which were in consequence habitually employed by the poor. Vespasian instituted, and the Antonines extended, a system of popular education, and the movement I have already noticed, for the support of the children of poor parents, acquired very considerable proportions. The first trace of it at Rome may be found under Augustus, who gave money and corn for the support of young children, who had previously not been included in the public distributions.[5] This appears, however, to have been but an act of isolated benevolence, and the honour of first instituting a systematic effort in this direction belongs to Nerva, who enjoined the support of poor children, not only in Rome, but in all the cities of Italy.[6] Trajan greatly extended the system. In

[1] Livy, ii. 9; Pliny, *Hist. Nat.* xxxi. 41.
[2] Dion Cassius, xxxviii. 1–7.
[3] Xiphilin, lxviii. 2; Pliny, *Ep.* vii. 31.
[4] Spartian. *Sept. Severus.*
[5] Suet. *August.* 41; Dion Cassius, li. 21.
[6] 'Afflictos civitatis relevavit;

puellas puerosque natos parentibus egestosis sumptu publico per Italiæ oppida ali jussit.'—Sext. Aurelius Victor, *Epitome,* 'Nerva.' This measure of Nerva, though not mentioned by any other writer, is confirmed by the evidence of medals. (Naudet, p. 75.)

his reign 5,000 poor children were supported by the Government in Rome alone,[1] and similar measures, though we know not on what scale, were taken in the other Italian and even African cities. At the little town of Velleia, we find a charity instituted by Trajan, for the partial support of 270 children.[2] Private benevolence followed in the same direction, and several inscriptions which still remain, though they do not enable us to write its history, sufficiently attest its activity. The younger Pliny, besides warmly encouraging schools, devoted a small property to the support of poor children in his native city of Como.[3] The name of Cælia Macrina is preserved as the foundress of a charity for 100 children at Terracina.[4] Hadrian increased the supplies of corn allotted to these charities, and he was also distinguished for his bounty to poor women.[5] Antoninus was accustomed to lend money to the poor at four per cent., which was much below the normal rate of interest,[6] and both he and Marcus Aurelius dedicated to the memory of their wives institutions for the support of girls.[7] Alexander Severus in like manner dedicated an institution for the support of children to the memory of his mother.[8] Public hospitals were probably unknown in Europe before Christianity; but there are traces of the distribution of medicine to the sick poor;[9] there were private infirmaries for slaves, and also, it is believed, military hospitals.[10] Provincial towns were occasionally assisted by

---

[1] Plin. *Panegyr.* xxvi. xxviii.

[2] We know of this charity from an extant bronze tablet. See Schmidt, *Essai historique sur la Société romaine,* p. 428.

[3] Plin. *Ep.* i. 8; iv. 13.

[4] Schmidt, p. 428.

[5] Spartianus, *Hadrian.*

[6] Capitolinus, *Antoninus.*

[7] Capitolinus, *Anton., Marc. Aurel.*

[8] Lampridius, *A. Severus.*

[9] See Friedlænder, *Hist. des Mœurs romaines,* iii. p. 157.

[10] Seneca (*De Ira,* lib. i. cap. 16) speaks of institutions called valetudinaria, which most writers think were private infirmaries in rich men's houses. The opinion that the Romans had public hospitals is maintained in a very learned and valuable, but little-known work, called *Collections relative to the Systematic Relief of the Poor.* (London, 1815.)

the Government in seasons of great distress, and there are some recorded instances of private legacies for their benefit.[1]

These various measures are by no means inconsiderable, and it is nct unreasonable to suppose that many similar steps were taken, of which all record has been lost. The history of charity presents so few salient features, so little that can strike the imagination or arrest the attention, that it is usually almost wholly neglected by historians; and it is easy to conceive what inadequate notions of our existing charities could be gleaned from the casual allusions in plays or poems, in political histories or court memoirs. There can, however, be no question that neither in practice nor in theory, neither in the institutions that were founded nor in the place that was assigned to it in the scale of duties, did charity in antiquity occupy a position at all comparable to that which it has obtained by Christianity. Nearly all relief was a State measure, dictated much more by policy than by benevolence; and the habit of selling young children, the innumerable expositions, the readiness of the poor to enrol themselves as gladiators, and the frequent famines, show how large was the measure of unrelieved distress. A very few Pagan examples of charity have, indeed, descended to us. Among the Greeks we find Epaminondas ransoming captives, and collecting dowers for poor girls;[2] Cimon, feeding the hungry and clothing the naked;[3] Bias, purchasing, emancipating, and furnishing with dowers some captive girls of Messina.[4] Tacitus has described with enthusiasm how, after a catastrophe near Rome, the rich threw open their houses and taxed all their resources to relieve the sufferers.[5] There existed, too, among the poor, both of Greece and Rome, mutual insurance societies, which undertook to pro-

---

[1] See Tacit. *Annal.* xii. 58; Pliny, v. 7; x. 79.
[2] Cornelius Nepos, *Epaminondas*, cap. iii.
[3] Plutarch, *Cimon.*
[4] Diog. Laërt. *Bias.*
[5] Tac. *Annal.* iv. 63.

vide for their sick and infirm members.[1]　The very frequent
reference to mendicancy in the Latin writers shows that
beggars, and therefore those who relieved beggars, were
numerous.　The duty of hospitality was also strongly enjoined, and was placed under the special protection of the
supreme Deity.　But the active, habitual, and detailed
charity of private persons, which is so conspicuous a feature
in all Christian societies, was scarcely known in antiquity,
and there are not more than two or three moralists who
have even noticed it.　Of these, the chief rank belongs to
Cicero, who devoted two very judicious but somewhat cold
chapters to the subject.　Nothing, he said, is more suitable
to the nature of man than beneficence or liberality, but there
are many cautions to be urged in practising it.　We must
take care that our bounty is a real blessing to the person we
relieve ; that it does not exceed our own means ; that it is
not, as was the case with Sylla and Cæsar, derived from the
spoliation of others ; that it springs from the heart and not
from ostentation ; that the claims of gratitude are preferred
to the mere impulses of compassion, and that due regard is
paid both to the character and to the wants of the recipient.[2]

Christianity for the first time made charity a rudimentary
virtue, giving it a leading place in the moral type, and in the
exhortations of its teachers.　Besides its general influence in
stimulating the affections, it effected a complete revolution
in this sphere, by regarding the poor as the special representatives of the Christian Founder, and thus making the
love of Christ, rather than the love of man, the principle of
charity.　Even in the days of persecution, collections for the
relief of the poor were made at the Sunday meetings.
The agapæ or feasts of love were intended mainly for the
poor, and food that was saved by the fasts was devoted to
their benefit.　A vast organisation of charity, presided over

---

[1] See Pliny, *Ep.* x. 94, and the remarks of Naudet, pp. 38, 39.
[2] *De Offic.* i. 14, 15.

by the bishops, and actively directed by the deacons, soon ramified over Christendom, till the bond of charity became the bond of unity, and the most distant sections of the Christian Church corresponded by the interchange of mercy. Long before the era of Constantine, it was observed that the charities of the Christians were so extensive—it may, perhaps, be said so excessive— that they drew very many impostors to the Church;[1] and when the victory of Christianity was achieved, the enthusiasm for charity displayed itself in the erection of numerous institutions that were altogether unknown to the Pagan world. A Roman lady, named Fabiola, in the fourth century, founded at Rome, as an act of penance, the first public hospital, and the charity p'anted by that woman's hand overspread the world, and will alleviate, to the end of time, the darkest anguish of humanity. Another hospital was soon after founded by St. Pammachus; another of great celebrity by St. Basil, at Cæsarea. St. Basil also erected at Cæsarea what was probably the first asylum for lepers. Xenodochia, or refuges for strangers, speedily rose, especially along the paths of the pilgrims. St. Pammachus founded one at Ostia ; Paula and Melania founded others at Jerusalem. The Council of Nice ordered that one should be erected in every city. In the time of St. Chrysostom the church of Antioch supported 3,000 widows and virgins, besides strangers and sick. Legacies for the poor became common ; and it was not unfrequent for men and women who desired to live a life of peculiar sanctity, and especially for priests who attained the episcopacy

---

[1] Lucian describes this in his famous picture of Peregrinus; and Julian, much later, accused the Christians of drawing men into the Church by their charities. Socrates (*Hist. Eccl.* vii. 17) tells a story of a Jew who, pretending to be a convert to Christianity, had been often baptised in different sects, and had amassed a considerable fortune by the gifts he received on those occasions. He was at last miraculously detected by the Novatian bishop Paul. There are several instances in the *Lives of the Saints* of judgments falling on those who duped benevolent Christians.

to bestow their entire properties in charity.   Even the early
Oriental monks, who for the most part were extremely
removed from the active and social virtues, supplied many
noble examples of charity.   St. Ephrem, in a time of pestilence, emerged from his solitude to found and superintend a
hospital at Edessa.   A monk named Thalasius collected
blind beggars in an asylum on the banks of the Euphrates.
A merchant named Apollonius founded on Mount Nitria a
gratuitous dispensary for the monks.   The monks often
assisted by their labours provinces that were suffering from
pestilence or famine.   We may trace the remains of the
pure socialism that marked the first phase of the Christian
community, in the emphatic language with which some of
the Fathers proclaimed charity to be a matter not of mercy but
of justice, maintaining that all property is based on usurpation, that the earth by right is common to all men, and
that no man can claim a superabundant supply of its goods
except as an administrator for others.   A Christian, it was
maintained, should devote at least one-tenth of his profits to
the poor.[1]

The enthusiasm of charity, thus manifested in the Church,
speedily attracted the attention of the Pagans.   The ridicule
of Lucian, and the vain efforts of Julian to produce a rival
system of charity within the limits of Paganism,[2] emphatically
attested both its pre-eminence and its catholicity.   During

---

[1] See on this subject Chastel,
Études historiques sur la Charité
(Paris, 1853); Martin Doisy, Hist.
de la Charité pendant les quatre
premiers Siècles (Paris, 1848);
Champagny, Charité chrétienne;
Tollemer, Origines de la Charité
catholique (Paris, 1863); Ryan,
History of the Effects of Religion
upon Mankind (Dublin, 1820);
and the works of Bingham and of
Cave.   I am also indebted, in this
part of my subject, to Dean Milman's

histories, Neander's Ecclesiastical
History, and Private Life of the
Early Christians, and to Migne's
Encyclopédie.
[2] See the famous epistle of
Julian to Arsacius, where he
declares that it is shameful that
'the Galileans' should support
not only their own, but also the
heathen poor; and also the comments of Sozomen, Hist. eccl. v
16.

the pestilences that desolated Carthage in A.D. 326, and
Alexandria in the reigns of Gallienus and of Maximian, while
the Pagans fled panic-stricken from the contagion, the
Christians extorted the admiration of their fellow-countrymen
by the courage with which they rallied around their bishops,
consoled the last hours of the sufferers, and buried the abandoned dead.[1] In the rapid increase of pauperism arising
from the emancipation of numerous slaves, their charity
found free scope for action, and its resources were soon taxed
to the utmost by the horrors of the barbarian invasions.
The conquest of Africa by Genseric deprived Italy of the
supply of corn upon which it almost wholly depended,
arrested the gratuitous distribution by which the Roman
poor were mainly supported, and produced all over the land
the most appalling calamities.[2] The history of Italy became
one monotonous tale of famine and pestilence, of starving
populations and ruined cities. But everywhere amid this
chaos of dissolution we may detect the majestic form of the
Christian priest mediating between the hostile forces, straining every nerve to lighten the calamities around him. When
the Imperial city was captured and plundered by the hosts
of Alaric, a Christian church remained a secure sanctuary,
which neither the passions nor the avarice of the Goths
transgressed. When a fiercer than Alaric had marked out
Rome for his prey, the Pope St. Leo, arrayed in his sacerdotal robes, confronted the victorious Hun, as the ambas-

[1] The conduct of the Christians,
on the first of these occasions, is
described by Pontius, *Vit. Cypriani*,
ix. 19. St. Cyprian organised
their efforts. On the Alexandrian
famines and pestilences, see Eusebius, *H. E.* vii. 22 ; ix. 8.

[2] The effects of this conquest
have been well described by Sismondi, *Hist. de la Chute de l'Empire
Romain*, tome i. pp. 258-260.

Theodoric afterwards made some
efforts to re-establish the distribution, but it never regained its
former proportions. The pictures
of the starvation and depopulation
of Italy at this time are appalling.
Some fearful facts on the subject
are collected by Gibbon, *Decline
and Fall*, ch. xxxvi.; Chateaubriand,
vime *Disc.* 2de partie.

sador of his fellow countrymen, and Attila, overpowered by
religious awe, turned aside in his course.   When, two years
later, Rome lay at the mercy of Genseric, the same Pope
interposed with the Vandal conqueror, and obtained from
him a partial cessation of the massacre.   The Archdeacon
Pelagius interceded with similar humanity and similar
success, when Rome had been captured by Totila.   In Gaul,
Troyes is said to have been saved from destruction by the
influence of St. Lupus, and Orleans by the influence of St.
Agnan.   In Britain an invasion of the Picts was averted by
St. Germain of Auxerre.   The relations of rulers to their
subjects, and of tribunals to the poor, were modified by the
same intervention.   When Antioch was threatened with
destruction on account of its rebellion against Theodosius,
the anchorites poured forth from the neighbouring deserts to
intercede with the ministers of the emperor, while the Archbishop Flavian went himself as a suppliant to Constantinople.
St. Ambrose imposed public penance on Theodosius, on
account of the massacre of Thessalonica.   Synesius excommunicated for his oppressions a governor named Andronicus;
and two French Councils, in the sixth century, imposed the
same penalty on all great men who arbitrarily ejected the
poor.   Special laws were found necessary to restrain the
turbulent charity of some priests and monks, who impeded
the course of justice, and even snatched criminals from the
hands of the law.[1]   St. Abraham, St. Epiphanius, and St.
Basil are all said to have obtained the remission or reduction
of oppressive imposts.   To provide for the interests of widows
and orphans was part of the official ecclesiastical duty, and
a Council of Macon anathematised any ruler who brought
them to trial without first apprising the bishop of the diocese.
A Council of Toledo, in the fifth century, threatened with
excommunication all who robbed priests, monks, or poor

---

[1] *Cod. Theod.* ix. xl. 15–16.   by Theodosius, A.D. 392; the second
The first of these laws was made   by Honorius, A.D. 398.

men, or refused to listen to their expostulations.   One of the
chief causes of the inordinate power acquired by the clergy
was their mediatorial office, and their gigantic wealth was
in a great degree due to the legacies of those who regarded
them as the trustees of the poor.   As time rolled on, charity
assumed many forms, and every monastery became a centre
from which it radiated.   By the monks the nobles were
overawed, the poor protected, the sick tended, travellers
sheltered, prisoners ransomed, the remotest spheres of suffering explored.   During the darkest period of the middle ages,
monks founded a refuge for pilgrims amid the horrors of the
Alpine snows.   A solitary hermit often planted himself,
with his little boat, by a bridgeless stream, and the charity
of his life was to ferry over the traveller.[1]   When the
hideous disease of leprosy extended its ravages over Europe,
when the minds of men were filled with terror, not only by
its loathsomeness and its contagion, but also by the notion
that it was in a peculiar sense supernatural,[2] new hospitals
and refuges overspread Europe, and monks flocked in multitudes to serve in them.[3]   Sometimes, the legends say, the
leper's form was in a moment transfigured, and he who
came to tend the most loathsome of mankind received his
reward, for he found himself in the presence of his Lord.

There is no fact of which an historian becomes more

---

[1] Cibrario, *Economica politica del Medio Evo*, lib. ii. cap. iii. The most remarkable of these saints was St. Julien l'Hospitalier, who having under a mistake killed his father and mother, as a penance became a ferryman of a great river, and having embarked on a very stormy and dangerous night at the voice of a traveller in dis-tress, received Christ into his boat. His story is painted on a window of the thirteenth century, in Rouen Cathedral.   See Langlois, *Essai historique sur la Peinture sur verre*, pp. 32-37.

[2] The fact of leprosy being taken as the image of sin gave rise to some curious notions of its supernatural character, and to many legends of saints curing leprosy by baptism.   See Maury, *Légendes pieuses du Moyen-Age*, pp. 64-65.

[3] See on these hospitals Cibrario, *Econ. Politica del Medio Evo*, lib. iii. cap. ii.

speedily or more painfully conscious than the great difference between the importance and the dramatic interest of the subjects he treats.   Wars or massacres, the horrors of martyrdom or the splendours of individual prowess, are susceptible of such brilliant colouring, that with but little literary skill they can be so pourtrayed that their importance is adequately realised, and they appeal powerfully to the emotions of the reader.   But this vast and unostentatious movement of charity, operating in the village hamlet and in the lonely hospital, staunching the widow's tears, and following all the windings of the poor man's griefs, presents few features the imagination can grasp, and leaves no deep impression upon the mind.   The greatest things are often those which are most imperfectly realised; and surely no achievements of the Christian Church are more truly great than those which it has effected in the sphere of charity.   For the first time in the history of mankind, it has inspired many thousands of men and women, at the sacrifice of all worldly interests, and often under circumstances of extreme discomfort or danger, to devote their entire lives to the single object of assuaging the sufferings of humanity.   It has covered the globe with countless institutions of mercy, absolutely unknown to the whole Pagan world.   It has indissolubly united, in the minds of men, the idea of supreme goodness with that of active and constant benevolence.   It has placed in every parish a religious minister, who, whatever may be his other functions, has at least been officially charged with the superintendence of an organisation of charity, and who finds in this office one of the most important as well as one of the most legitimate sources of his power.

There are, however, two important qualifications to the admiration with which we regard the history of Christian charity—one relating to a particular form of suffering, and the other of a more general kind.   A strong, ill-defined notion of the supernatural character of insanity had existed from the earliest times; but there were special circumstances which rendered the action of the Church peculiarly unfavourable to those who were either predisposed to or afflicted with this calamity. The reality both of witchcraft and diabolical possession had been distinctly recognised in the Jewish writings. The received opinions about eternal torture, and ever-present dæmons, and the continued strain upon the imagination, in dwelling upon an unseen world, were pre-eminently fitted to produce madness in those who were at all predisposed to it, and, where insanity had actually appeared. to determine the form and complexion of the hallucinations of the maniac.[1] Theology supplying all the images that acted most powerfully upon the imagination, most madness, for many centuries, took a theological cast. One important department of it appears chiefly in the lives of the saints. Men of lively imaginations and absolute ignorance, living apart from all their fellows, amid the horrors of a savage wilderness, practising austerities by which their physical system was thoroughly deranged, and firmly persuaded that innumerable devils were continually hovering about their cells and interfering with their devotions, speedily and very naturally became subject to constant hallucinations, which probably form the nucleus of truth in the legends of their lives. But it was impossible that insanity should confine itself to the orthodox forms of celestial visions, or of the apparitions and the defeats of devils. Very frequently it led the unhappy maniac to some delusion, which called down

---

[1] Calmeil observes: 'On a souvent constaté depuis un demi-siècle que la folie est sujette à prendre la teinte des croyances religieuses, des idées philosophiques ou superstitieuses, des préjugés sociaux qui ont cours, qui sont actuellement en vogue parmi les peuples ou les nations; que cette teinte varie dans un même pays suivant le caractère des événements relatifs à la politique extérieure, le caractère des événements civils, la nature des productions littéraires. des représentations théâtrales, suivant la tournure, la direction, le genre d'élan qu'y prennent l'industrie, les arts et les sciences.'—*De la Folie,* tome i. pp. 122–123.

upon him the speedy sentence of the Church. Thus, in the year 1300, the corpse of a Bohemian, or, according to another version, an English girl, who imagined herself to be the Holy Ghost incarnate for the redemption of women, was dug up and burnt; and two women who believed in her perished at the stake.[1] In the year 1359, a Spaniard declared himself to be the brother of the archangel Michael, and to be destined for the place in heaven which Satan had lost; and he added that he was accustomed every day both to mount into heaven and descend into hell, that the end of the world was at hand, and that it was reserved for him to enter into single combat with Antichrist. The poor lunatic fell into the hands of the Archbishop of Toledo, and was burnt alive.[2] In some cases the hallucination took the form of an irregular inspiration. On this charge, Joan of Arc, and another girl, who had been fired by her example, and had endeavoured, apparently under a genuine hallucination, to follow her career,[3] were burnt alive. A famous Spanish physician and scholar, named Torralba, who lived in the sixteenth century, and who imagined that he had an attendant angel continually about him, escaped with public penance and confession;[4] but a

---

[1] Milman's *History of Latin Christianity*, vol. vii., p. 353-354. 'Venit de Anglia virgo decora valde, pariterque facunda, dicens, Spiritum Sanctum incarnatum in redemptionem mulierum, et baptisavit mulieres in nomine Patris, Filii et sui. Quæ mortua ducta fuit in Mediolanum, ibi et cremata.' —*Annales Dominicanorum Colmariensium* (in the 'Rerum Germanic. Scriptores').

[2] 'Martin Gonçalez, du diocèse de Cuenca, disoit qu'il étoit frère de l'archange S Michel, la première vérité et l'échelle du ciel; que c'étoit pour lui que Dieu réservoit la place que Lucifer avoit perdue;

que tous les jours il s'élevoit au plus haut de l'Empirée et descendoit ensuite au plus profond des enfers; qu'à la fin du monde, qui étoit proche, il iroit au devant de l'Antichrist et qu'il le terrasseroit, ayant à sa main la croix de Jésus-Christ et sa couronne d'épines. L'archevêque de Tolède, n'ayant pu convertir ce fanatique obstiné, ni l'empêcher de dogmatiser, l'avoit enfin livré au bras séculier.—Touron, *Hist. des Hommes illustres de l'ordre de St. Dominique*, Paris, 1745 (*Vie d'Eyméricus*), tome ii. p. 635.

[3] Calmeil, *De la Folie*, tome i. p. 134.

[4] Ibid. tome i. pp. 242–247.

professor of theology in Lima, who laboured under the same
delusion, and added to it some wild notions about his spiritual
dignities, was less fortunate. He was burnt by the Inquisition of Peru.[1]   Most commonly, however, the theological
notions about witchcraft either produced madness or determined its form, and, through the influence of the clergy of
the different sections of the Christian Church, many thousands
of unhappy women, who, from their age, their loneliness, and
their infirmity, were most deserving of pity, were devoted to
the hatred of mankind, and, having been tortured with
horrible and ingenious cruelty, were at last burnt alive.

The existence, however, of some forms of natural madness
was generally admitted ; but the measures for the relief of
the unhappy victims were very few, and very ill judged.
Among the ancients, they were brought to the temples, and
subjected to imposing ceremonies, which were believed
supernaturally to relieve them, and which probably had a
favourable influence through their action upon the imagination.   The great Greek physicians had devoted considerable
attention to this malady, and some of their precepts anticipated modern discoveries ; but no lunatic asylum appears
to have existed in antiquity.[2]   In the first period of the
hermit life, when many anchorites became insane through
their penances, a refuge is said to have been opened for them
at Jerusalem.[3]   This appears, however, to be a solitary
instance, arising from the exigencies of a single class, and no
lunatic asylum existed in Christian Europe till the fifteenth
century.   The Mohammedans, in this form of charity, seem
to have preceded the Christians.   Benjamin of Tudela, who
visited Bagdad in the twelfth century, describes a palace in
that city, called 'the House of Mercy,' in which all mad
persons found in the country were confined and bound with

Calmeil, tome i. p. 247.   [3] Gibbon, *Decline and Fall*, ch.
[1] See Esquirol, *Maladies men-*   xxxvii.
tales.

iron chains. They were carefully examined every month
and released as soon as they recovered.[1] The asylum of
Cairo is said to have been founded in A.D. 1304.[2] Leo
Africanus notices the existence of a similar institution at Fez,
in the beginning of the sixteenth century, and mentions that
the patients were restrained by chains,[3] and it is probable
that the care of the insane was a general form of charity
in Mohammedan countries. Among the Christians it first
appeared in quarters contiguous to the Mohammedans; but
there is, I think, no real evidence that it was derived from
Mohammedan example. The Knights of Malta were famous
as the one order who admitted lunatics into their hospitals;
but no Christian asylum expressly for their benefit existed
till 1409. The honour of instituting this form of charity in
Christendom belongs to Spain. A monk named Juan Gila-
berto Joffre, filled with compassion at the sight of the
maniacs who were hooted by crowds through the streets of
Valencia, founded an asylum in that city, and his example
was speedily followed in other provinces. The new charity
was introduced into Saragossa in A.D. 1425, into Seville and
Valladolid in A.D. 1436, into Toledo in A.D. 1483. All these
institutions existed before a single lunatic asylum had been
founded in any other part of Christendom.[4] Two other very
honourable facts may be mentioned, establishing the pre-
eminence of Spanish charity in this field. The first is, that
the oldest lunatic asylum in the metropolis of Catholicism
was that erected by Spaniards, in A.D. 1548.[5] The second is,

[1] Purchas's *Pilgrims*, ii. 1452.
[2] Desmaisons' *Asiles d'Aliénés
en Espagne*, p. 53.
[3] Leo Africanus, *Description of
Africa*, book iii.
[4] I have taken these facts from
a very interesting little work, Desmaisons, *Des Asiles d'Aliénés en
Espagne; Recherches historiques et
médicales* (Paris, 1859). Dr. Desmaisons conjectures that the

Spaniards took their asylums from
the Mohammedans; but, as it
seems to me, he altogether fails to
prove his point. His work, however, contains some curious information on the history of lunatic
asylums.
[5] Amydemus, *Pietas Romana*
(Oxford, 1687), p. 21; Desmaisons,
p. 108.

that when, at the close of the last century, Pinel began his great labours in this sphere, he pronounced Spain to be the country in which lunatics were treated with most wisdom and most humanity.[1]

In most countries their condition was indeed truly deplorable. While many thousands were burnt as witches, those who were recognised as insane were compelled to endure all the horrors of the harshest imprisonment. Blows, bleeding, and chains were their usual treatment, and horrible accounts were given of madmen who had spent decades bound in dark cells.[2] Such treatment naturally aggravated their malady, and that malady in many cases rendered impossible the resignation and ultimate torpor which alleviate the sufferings of ordinary prisoners. Not until the eighteenth century was the condition of this unhappy class seriously improved. The combined progress of theological scepticism and scientific knowledge relegated witchcraft to the world of phantoms, and the exertions of Morgagni in Italy, of Cullen in Scotland, and of Pinel in France, renovated the whole treatment of acknowledged lunatics.

The second qualification to the admiration with which we regard the history of Christian charity arises from the undoubted fact that a large proportion of charitable institutions have directly increased the poverty they were intended to relieve. The question of the utility and nature of charity is one which, since the modern discoveries of political economy, has elicited much discussion, and in many cases, I think, much exaggeration. What political economy has effected on the subject may be comprised under two heads. It has elucidated more clearly, and in greater detail than had before been done, the effect of provident self-interest in determining the

---

[1] Pinel, *Traité médico-philosophique*, pp. 241, 242.

[2] See the dreadful description in Pinel, pp. 200–202.

welfare of societies, and it has established a broad distinction between productive and unproductive expenditure. It has shown that, where idleness is supported, idleness will become common; that, where systematic public provision is made for old age, the parsimony of foresight will be neglected; and that therefore these forms of charity, by encouraging habits of idleness and improvidence, ultimately increase the wretchedness they were intended to alleviate. It has also shown that, while unproductive expenditure, such as that which is devoted to amusements or luxury, is undoubtedly beneficial to those who provide it, the fruit perishes in the usage; while productive expenditure, such as the manufacture of machines, or the improvement of the soil, or the extension of commercial enterprise, gives a new impulse to the creation of wealth. It has proved that the first condition of the rapid accumulation of capital is the diversion of money from unproductive to productive channels, and that the amount of accumulated capital is one of the two regulating influences of the wages of the labourer. From these positions some persons have inferred that charity should be condemned as a form of unproductive expenditure. But, in the first place, all charities that foster habits of forethought and develop new capacities in the poorer classes, such as popular education, or the formation of savings banks, or insurance companies, or, in many cases, small and discriminating loans, or measures directed to the suppression of dissipation, are in the strictest sense productive; and the same may be said of many forms of employment, given in exceptional crises through charitable motives; and, in the next place, it is only necessary to remember that the happiness of mankind, to which the accumulation of wealth should only be regarded as a means, is the real object of charity, and it will appear that many forms which are not strictly productive, in the commercial sense, are in the highest degree conducive to this end, and have no serious counteracting evil. In the alleviation of those sufferings that do not spring either from improvidence or from vice, the warmest as well as the most enlightened charity will find an ample sphere for its exertions.[1]   Blindness, and other exceptional calamities, against the effects of which prudence does not and cannot provide, the miseries resulting from epidemics, from war, from famine, from the first sudden collapse of industry, produced by new inventions or changes in the channels of commerce ; hospitals, which, besides other advantages, are the greatest schools of medical science, and withdraw from the crowded alley multitudes who would otherwise form centres of contagion—these, and such as these, will long tax to the utmost the generosity of the wealthy ; while, even in the spheres upon which the political economist looks with the most unfavourable eye, exceptional cases will justify exceptional assistance.   The charity which is pernicious is commonly not the highest but the lowest kind.   The rich man, prodigal of money, which is to him of little value, but altogether incapable of devoting any personal attention to the object of his alms, often injures society by his donations; but this is rarely the case with that far nobler charity which makes men familiar with the haunts of wretchedness, and follows the object of its care through all the phases of his life.   The question of the utility of charity is merely a question of ultimate consequences.   Political economy has, no doubt, laid down some general rules of great value on the subject ; but yet the pages which Cicero devoted to it nearly two thousand years ago might have been written by the most enlightened modern economist ; and it will be continually found that the Protestant lady, working in her parish, by the simple force of

---

[1] Malthus, who is sometimes, though most unjustly, described as an enemy to all charity, has devoted an admirable chapter (*On Population*, book iv. ch. ix.) to the 'direc- tion of our charity;' but the fullest examination of this subject with which I am acquainted is the very interesting work of Duchâtel, *Sur la Charité.*

common sense and by a scrupulous and minute attention to the condition and character of those whom she relieves, is unconsciously illustrating with perfect accuracy the en lightened charity of Malthus.

But in order that charity should be useful, it is essential that the benefit of the sufferer should be a real object to the donor; and a very large proportion of the evils that have arisen from Catholic charity may be traced to the absence of this condition. The first substitution of devotion for philanthropy, as the motive of benevolence, gave so powerful a stimulus to the affections, that it may on the whole be regarded as a benefit, though, by making compassion operate solely through a theological medium, it often produced among theologians a more than common indifference to the sufferings of all who were external to their religious community. But the new principle speedily degenerated into a belief in the expiatory nature of the gifts. A form of what may be termed selfish charity arose, which acquired at last gigantic proportions, and exercised a most pernicious influence upon Christendom. Men gave money to the poor, simply and exclusively for their own spiritual benefit, and the welfare of the sufferer was altogether foreign to their thoughts.[1]

The evil which thus arose from some forms of Catholic charity may be traced from a very early period, but it only acquired its full magnitude after some centuries. The Roman system of gratuitous distribution was, in the eyes of the political economist, about the worst that could be conceived, and the charity of the Church being, in at least a measure, discriminating, was at first a very great, though even then not an unmingled, good. Labour was also not unfrequently en-

---

[1] This is very tersely expressed by a great Protestant writer: 'I give no alms to satisfy the hunger of my brother, but to fulfil and accomplish the will and command of my God.' — Sir T. Brown, *Religio Medici*, part ii. § 2. A saying almost exactly similar is, if I remember right, ascribed to St. Elizabeth of Hungary.

joined as a duty by the Fathers, and at a later period the services of the Benedictine monks, in destroying by their example the stigma which slavery had attached to it, were very great. Still, one of the first consequences of the exuberant charity of the Church was to multiply impostors and mendicants, and the idleness of the monks was one of the earliest complaints. Valentinian made a severe law, condemning robust beggars to perpetual slavery. As the monastic system was increased, and especially after the mendicant orders had consecrated mendicancy, the evil assumed gigantic dimensions. Many thousands of strong men, absolutely without private means, were in every country withdrawn from productive labour, and supported by charity. The notion of the meritorious nature of simple almsgiving immeasurably multiplied beggars. The stigma, which it is the highest interest of society to attach to mendicancy, it became a main object of theologians to remove. Saints wandered through the world begging money, that they might give to beggars, or depriving themselves of their garments, that they might clothe the naked, and the result of their teaching was speedily apparent. In all Catholic countries where ecclesiastical influences have been permitted to develop unmolested, the monastic organisations have proved a deadly canker, corroding the prosperity of the nation. Withdrawing multitudes from all production, encouraging a blind and pernicious almsgiving, diffusing habits of improvidence through the poorer classes, fostering an ignorant admiration for saintly poverty, and an equally ignorant antipathy to the habits and aims of an industrial civilisation, they have paralysed all energy, and proved an insuperable barrier to material progress. The poverty they have relieved has been insignificant compared with the poverty they have caused. In no case was the abolition of monasteries effected in a more indefensible manner than in England; but the transfer of property, that was once employed in a great measure in charity, to the courtiers of King Henry, was ultimately a benefit to the English poor; for no misapplication of this property by private persons could produce as much evil as an unrestrained monasticism. The value of Catholic services in alleviating pain and sickness, and the more exceptional forms of suffering, can never be overrated. The noble heroism of her servants, who have devoted themselves to charity, has never been surpassed, and the perfection of their organisation has, I think, never been equalled; but in the sphere of simple poverty it can hardly be doubted that the Catholic Church has created more misery than it has cured.

Still, even in this field, we must not forget the benefits resulting, if not to the sufferer, at least to the donor. Charitable habits, even when formed in the first instance from selfish motives, even when so misdirected as to be positively injurious to the recipient, rarely fail to exercise a softening and purifying influence on the character. All through the darkest period of the middle ages, amid ferocity and fanaticism and brutality, we may trace the subduing influence of Catholic charity, blending strangely with every excess of violence and every outburst of persecution. It would be difficult to conceive a more frightful picture of society than is presented by the history of Gregory of Tours; but that long series of atrocious crimes, narrated with an almost appalling tranquillity, is continually interspersed with accounts of kings, queens, or prelates, who, in the midst of the disorganised society, made the relief of the poor the main object of their lives. No period of history exhibits a larger amount of cruelty, licentiousness, and fanaticism than the Crusades; but side by side with the military enthusiasm, and with the almost universal corruption, there expanded a vast movement of charity, which covered Christendom with hospitals for the relief of leprosy, and which grappled nobly, though ineffectually, with the many forms of suffering that were generated. St. Peter Nolasco, whose great labours in ransoming captive Christians I have already noticed, was an active participator

in the atrocious massacre of the Albigenses.[1] Of Shane
O'Neale, one of the ablest, but also one of the most ferocious,
Irish chieftains who ever defied the English power, it is related, amid a crowd of crimes, that, 'sitting at meat, before
he put one morsel into his mouth he used to slice a portion
above the daily alms, and send it to some beggar at his gate,
saying it was meet to serve Christ first.'[2]

The great evils produced by the encouragement of mendicancy which has always accompanied the uncontrolled development of Catholicity, have naturally given rise to much
discussion and legislation. The fierce denunciations of the
mendicant orders by William of St. Amour in the thirteenth
century were not on account of their encouragement of mischievous charity;[3] but one of the disciples of Wycliffe, named
Nicholas of Hereford, was conspicuous for his opposition to
indiscriminate gifts to beggars;[4] and a few measures of an
extended order appear to have been taken even before the
Reformation.[5] In England laws of the most savage cruelty
were then passed, in hopes of eradicating mendicancy. A
parliament of Henry VIII., before the suppression of the
monasteries, issued a law providing a system of organised
charity, and imposing on any one who gave anything to a
beggar a fine of ten times the value of his gift. A sturdy
beggar was to be punished with whipping for the first offence,
with whipping and the loss of the tip of his ear for the second,

---

[1] See Butler's *Lives of the
Saints.*

[2] Campion's *Historie of Ireland,*
book ii. chap. x.

[3] He wrote his *Perils of the Last
Times* in the interest of the University of Paris, of which he was
a Professor, and which was at war
with the mendicant orders. See
Milman's *Latin Christianity,* vol.
vi. pp. 348-356; Fleury, *Eccl.
Hist.* lxxxiv. 57.

[4] Henry de Knyghton, *De
Eventibus Angliæ.*

[5] There was some severe legis-
tion in England on the subject
after the Black Death. Eden's
History of the Working Classes,
vol. i. p. 34. In France, too, a
royal ordinance of 1350 ordered
men who had been convicted of
begging three times to be branded
with a hot iron. Monteil, *Hist.
des Français,* tome i. p. 434.

and with death for the third.[1]   Under Edward VI., an atrocious law, which, however, was repealed in the same reign,
enacted that every sturdy beggar who refused to work should
be branded, and adjudged for two years as a slave to the
person who gave information against him ; and if he took
flight during his period of servitude, he was condemned for
the first offence to perpetual slavery, and for the second to
death.   The master was authorised to put a ring of iron
round the neck of his slave, to chain him, and to scourge him.
Any one might take the children of a sturdy beggar for ap-
prentices, till the boys were twenty-four and the girls twenty.[2]
Another law, made under Elizabeth, punished with death any
strong man under the age of eighteen who was convicted for
the third time of begging; but the penalty in this reign was
afterwards reduced to a life-long service in the galleys, or to
banishment, with a penalty of death to the returned convict.[3]
Under the same queen the poor-law system was elaborated,
and Malthus long afterwards showed that its effects in dis-
couraging parsimony rendered it scarcely less pernicious than
the monastic system that had preceded it.   In many Catholic
countries, severe, though less atrocious, measures were taken
to grapple with the evil of mendicancy.   That shrewd and
sagacious pontiff, Sixtus V., who, though not the greatest
man, was by far the greatest statesman who has ever sat on
the papal throne, made praiseworthy efforts to check it at
Rome, where ecclesiastical influence had always made it peculiarly prevalent.[4]   Charles V., in 1531, issued a severe enactment against beggars in the Netherlands, but excepted
from its operation mendicant friars and pilgrims.[5]   Under
Lewis XIV., equally severe measures were taken in France.
But though the practical evil was fully felt, there was little

---

Eden, vol. i. pp. 83-87.
[2] Ibid. pp. 101-103.
[3] Ibid. pp. 127-130.
[4] Morighini, *Institutions pieuses*

de Rome.
    [5] Eden, *History of the Labour-
ing Classes*, i. 83.

philosophical investigation of its causes before the eighteenth
century.   Locke in England,[1] and Berkeley in Ireland,[2]
briefly glanced at the subject ; and in 1704 Defoe published a
very remarkable tract, called, ' Giving Alms no Charity,' in
which he noticed the extent to which mendicancy existed in
England, though wages were higher than in any Continental
country.[3] A still more remarkable book, written by an author
named Ricci, appeared at Modena in 1787, and excited considerable attention.   The author pointed out with much force
the gigantic development of mendicancy in Italy, traced it to
the excessive charity of the people, and appears to have regarded as an evil all charity which sprang from religious
motives and was greater than would spring from the unaided
instincts of men.[4] The freethinker Mandeville had long before
assailed charity schools, and the whole system of endeavouring
to elevate the poor,[5] and Magdalen asylums and foundling
hospitals have had fierce, though I believe much mistaken,
adversaries.[6] The reforms of the poor-laws, and the writings

[1] Locke discussed the great increase of poverty, and a bill was
brought in suggesting some remedies, but did not pass. (Eden, vol.
i. pp. 243-248.)

[2] In a very forcible letter addressed to the Irish Catholic clergy.

[3] This tract, which is extremely
valuable for the light it throws
upon the social condition of England at the time, was written in
opposition to a bill providing that
the poor in the poor-houses should
do wool, hemp, iron, and other
works. Defoe says that wages in
England were higher than anywhere on the Continent, though the
amount of mendicancy was enormous. ' The reason why so many pretend to want work is, that they can
live so well with the pretence of
wanting work. . .I affirm of my own

knowledge, when I have wanted
a man for labouring work, and
offered nine shillings per week to
strolling fellows at my door, they
have frequently told me to my face
they could get more a-begging.'

[4] *Reforma degl' Instituti pii di
Modena* (published first anonymously at Modena). It has been
reprinted in the library of the
Italian economists.

[5] *Essay on Charity Schools.*

[6] Magdalen asylums have been
very vehemently assailed by M.
Charles Comte, in his *Traité de
Législation*. On the subject of
Foundling Hospitals there is a
whole literature. They were violently attacked by I believe, Lord
Brougham, in the *Edinburgh Review* in the early part of this century. Writers of this stamp, and

of Malthus, gave a new impulse to discussion on the subject; but, with the qualifications I have stated, no new discoveries have, I conceive, thrown any just cloud upon the essential principle of Christian charity.

The last method by which Christianity has laboured to soften the characters of men has been by accustoming the imagination to expatiate continually upon images of tenderness and of pathos. Our imaginations, though less influential than our occupations, probably affect our moral characters more deeply than our judgments, and, in the case of the poorer classes especially, the cultivation of this part of our nature is of inestimable importance. Rooted, for the most part, during their entire lives, to a single spot, excluded by their ignorance and their circumstances from most of the varieties of interest that animate the minds of other men, condemned to constant and plodding labour, and engrossed for ever with the minute cares of an immediate and an anxious present, their whole natures would have been hopelessly contracted, were there no sphere in which their imaginations could expand. Religion is the one romance of the poor. It alone extends the narrow horizon of their thoughts, supplies the images of their dreams, allures them to the supersensual and the ideal. The graceful beings with which the creative fancy of Paganism peopled the universe shed a poetic glow on the peasant's toil. Every stage of agriculture was presided over by a divinity, and the world grew bright by the companionship of the gods. But it is the peculiarity of the Christian types, that, while they have fascinated the imagination, they have also purified the heart. The tender, winning, and almost feminine beauty of the Christian

---

indeed most political economists, greatly exaggerate the forethought of men and women, especially in matters where the passions are concerned. It may be questioned whether one woman in a hundred, who plunges into a career of vice, is in the smallest degree influenced by a consideration of whether or not charitable institutions are provided for the support of aged penitents.

Founder, the Virgin mother, the agonies of Gethsemane or
of Calvary, the many scenes of compassion and suffering that
fil' the sacred writings, are the pictures which, for eighteen
hundred years, have governed the imaginations of the rudest
and most ignorant of mankind. Associated with the fondest
recollections of childhood, with the music of the church bells,
with the clustered lights and the tinsel splendour, that seem
to the peasant the very ideal of majesty; painted over the
altar where he received the companion of his life, around the
cemetery where so many whom he had loved were laid, on
the stations of the mountain, on the portal of the vineyard,
on the chapel where the storm-tossed mariner fulfils his
grateful vow; keeping guard over his cottage door, and looking down upon his humble bed, forms of tender beauty and
gentle pathos for ever haunt the poor man's fancy, and
silently win their way into the very depths of his being.
More than any spoken eloquence, more than any dogmatic
teaching, they transform and subdue his character, till he
learns to realise the sanctity of weakness and suffering, the
supreme majesty of compassion and gentleness.

Imperfect and inadequate as is the sketch I have drawn,
it will be sufficient to show how great and multiform have
been the influences of Christian philanthropy. The shadows
that rest upon the picture, I have not concealed; but, when
all due allowance has been made for them, enough will
remain to claim our deepest admiration. The high conception that has been formed of the sanctity of human life, the
protection of infancy, the elevation and final emancipation of
the slave classes, the suppression of barbarous games, the
creation of a vast and multifarious organisation of charity,
and the education of the imagination by the Christian type,
constitute together a movement of philanthropy which has
never been paralleled or approached in the Pagan world. The
effects of this movement in promoting happiness have been
very great. Its effect in determining character has probably

been still greater. In that proportion or disposition of
qualities which constitutes the ideal character, the gentler
and more benevolent virtues have obtained, through Christianity, the foremost place. In the first and purest period
they were especially supreme; but in the third century a great
ascetic movement arose, which gradually brought a new type
of character into the ascendant, and diverted the enthusiasm
of the Church into new channels.

Tertullian, writing in the second century, contrasts, in a
well-known passage, the Christians of his day with the gymnosophists or hermits of India, declaring that, unlike these,
the Christians did not fly from the world, but mixed with
Pagans in the forum, in the market-places, in the public
baths, in the ordinary business of life.[1] But although the
life of the hermit or the monk was unknown in the Church
for more than two hundred years after its foundation, we
may detect, almost from the earliest time, a tone of feeling
which produces it. The central conceptions of the monastic
system are the meritoriousness of complete abstinence from
all sexual intercourse, and of complete renunciation of the
world. The first of these notions appeared in the very
earliest period, in the respect attached to the condition of
virginity, which was always regarded as sacred, and especially
esteemed in the clergy, though for a long time it was not
imposed as an obligation. The second was shown in the
numerous efforts that were made to separate the Christian
community as far as possible from the society in which it
existed. Nothing could be more natural than that, when
the increase and triumph of the Church had thrown the bulk
of the Christians into active political or military labour,
some should, as an exercise of piety, have endeavoured
to imitate the separation from the world which was once

---

[1] *Apol.* ch. xlii.

the common condition of all. Besides this, a movement of asceticism had long been raging like a mental epidemic through the world. Among the Jews—whose law, from the great stress it laid upon marriage, the excellence of the rapid multiplication of population, and the hope of being the ancestor of the Messiah, was peculiarly repugnant to monastic conceptions—the Essenes had constituted a complete monastic society, abstaining from marriage and separating themselves wholly from the world. In Rome, whose practical genius was, if possible, even more opposed than that of the Jews to an inactive monasticism, and even among those philosophers who most represented its active and practical spirit, the same tendency was shown. The Cynics of the later Empire recommended a complete renunciation of domestic ties, and a life spent mainly in the contemplation of wisdom. The Egyptian philosophy, that soon after acquired an ascendancy in Europe, anticipated still more closely the monastic ideal. On the outskirts of the Church, the many sects of Gnostics and Manicheans all held under different forms the essential evil of matter. The Docetæ, following the same notion, denied the reality of the body of Christ. The Montanists and the Novatians surpassed and stimulated the private penances of the orthodox.[1] The soil was thus thoroughly prepared for a great outburst of asceticism, whenever the first seed was sown. This was done during the Decian persecution. Paul, the hermit, who fled to the desert during that

---

[1] On these penances, see Bingham, *Antiq.* book vii. Bingham, I think, justly divides the history of asceticism into three periods. During the first, which extends from the foundation of the Church to A.D. 250, there were men and women who, with a view to spiritual perfection, abstained from marriage, relinquished amusements, accustomed themselves to severe fasts, and gave up their property to works of charity; but did this in the middle of society and without leading the life of either a hermit or a monk. During the second period, which extended from the Decian persecution, anchorites were numerous, but the custom of a common or cœnobitic life was unknown. It was originated in the time of Constantine by Pachomius

persecution, is said to have been the first of the tribe. Antony, who speedily followed, greatly extended the movement, and in a few years the hermits ha l become a mighty nation. Persecution, which in the first instance drove great numbers as fugitives to the deserts, soon aroused a passionate religious enthusiasm that showed itself in an ardent desire for those sufferings which were believed to lead directly to heaven; and this enthusiasm, after the peace of Constantine, found its natural vent and sphere in the macerations of the desert life. The imaginations of men were fascinated by the poetic circumstances of that life which St. Jerome most eloquently embellished. Women were pre-eminent in recruiting for it. The same spirit that had formerly led the wife of the Pagan official to entertain secret relations with the Christian priests, now led the wife of the Christian to become the active agent of the monks. While the father designed his son for the army, or for some civil post, the mother was often straining every nerve to induce him to become a hermit. The monks secretly corresponded with her, they skilfully assumed the functions of education, in order that they might influence the young; and sometimes, to evade the precautions or the anger of the father, they concealed their profession, and assumed the garb of lay pedagogues.[2] The pulpit, which had almost superseded, and immeasurably transcended in influence, the chairs of the rhetoricians, and which was filled by such men as Ambrose, Augustine, Chrysostom, Basil, and the Gregories, was continually exerted in the same cause, and the extreme luxury of the great cities produced a violent, but not unnatural, reaction of asceticism. The dignity of the monastic position, which sometimes brought men who had been simple

---

[1] This is expressly stated by St. Jerome (*Vit. Pauli*).

[2] See on this subject some curious evidence in Neander's *Life of Chrysostom*. St. Chrysostom wrote a long work to console fathers whose sons were thus seduced to the desert.

peasants into connection with the emperors, the security it
furnished to fugitive slaves and criminals, the desire of
escaping from those fiscal burdens which, in the corrupt and
oppressive administration of the Empire, had acquired an
intolerable weight, and especially the barbarian invasions,
which produced every variety of panic and wretchedness,
conspired with the new religious teaching in peopling the
desert. A theology of asceticism was speedily formed. The
examples of Elijah and Elisha, to the first of whom, by a
bold flight of imagination, some later Carmelites ascribed
the origin of their order, and the more recent instance of the
Baptist, were at once adduced. To an ordinary layman the
life of an anchorite might appear in the highest degree opposed
to that of the Teacher who began His mission at a marriage
feast; who was continually reproached by His enemies for
the readiness with which He mixed with the world, and who
selected from the female sex some of His purest and most
devoted followers; but the monkish theologians, avoiding,
for the most part, these topics, dilated chiefly on His immaculate birth, His virgin mother, His life of celibacy, His exhortation to the rich young man. The fact that St. Peter, to
whom a general primacy was already ascribed, was unquestionably married was a difficulty which was in a measure
met by a tradition that both he, and the other married
apostles, abstained from intercourse with their wives after
their conversion.[1] St. Paul, however, was probably un
married, and his writings showed a decided preference for
the unmarried state, which the ingenuity of theologians also
discovered in some quarters where it might be least expected.
Thus, St. Jerome assures us that when the clean animals
entered the ark by sevens, and the unclean ones by pairs, the
odd number typified the celibate, and the even the married
condition. Even of the unclean animals but one pair of each

---

[1] On this tradition see Champagny, *Les Antonins*, tome i. p. 193.

kind was admitted, lest they should perpetrate the enormity of second marriage.[1] Ecclesiastical tradition sustained the tendency, and St. James, as he has been portrayed by Hegesippus, became a kind of ideal saint, a faithful picture of what, according to the notions of theologians, was the true type of human nobility. He 'was consecrated,' it was said, 'from his mother's womb. He drank neither wine nor fermented liquors, and abstained from animal food. A razor never came upon his head. He never anointed himself with oil, or used a bath. He alone was allowed to enter the sanctuary. He never wore woollen, but linen, garments. He was in the habit of entering the temple alone, and was often found upon his bended knees, and interceding for the forgiveness of the people, so that his knees became as hard as a camel's.' [2]

The progress of the monastic movement, as has been truly said, 'was not less rapid or universal than that of Christianity itself.' [3] Of the actual number of the anchorites, those who are acquainted with the extreme unveracity of the first historians of the movement will hesitate to speak with confidence. It is said that St. Pachomius, who, early in the fourth century, founded the coenobitic mode of life, enlisted under his jurisdiction 7,000 monks;[4] that in the days of St. Jerome nearly 50,000 monks were sometimes assembled at the Easter festivals;[5] that in the desert of Nitria alone there were, in the fourth century, 5,000 monks under a single abbot;[6] that an Egyptian city named Oxyrynchus devoted itself almost exclusively to the ascetic life, and included 20,000 virgins and 10,000 monks;[7] that St. Serapion presided over 10,000 monks;[8] and that, towards the close of the fourth century, the monastic population in a great part of Egypt

[1] *Ep.* cxxiii.
[2] Euseb. *Eccl. Hist.* ii. 23.
[3] Gibbon, *Decline and Fall*, ch. xxxvii.; a brief but masterly sketch of the progress of the movement.
[4] Palladius *Hist. Laus.* xxxviii.

[5] Jerome, Preface to the Rule of St. Pachomius, § 7.
[6] Cassian, *De Coenob. Inst.* iv. 1
[7] Rufinus, *Hist. Monach.* ch. v Rufinus visited it himself.
[8] Palladius, *Hist. Laus.* lxxvi.

was nearly equal to the population of the cities.[1] Egypt was the parent of monachism, and it was there that it attained both its extreme development and its most austere severity; but there was very soon scarcely any Christian country in which a similar movement was not ardently propagated. St. Athanasius and St. Zeno are said to have introduced it into Italy,[2] where it soon afterwards received a great stimulus from St. Jerome. St. Hilarion instituted the first monks in Palestine, and he lived to see many thousands subject to his rule, and towards the close of his life to plant monachism in Cyprus. Eustathius, Bishop of Sebastia, spread it through Armenia, Paphlagonia, and Pontus. St. Basil laboured along the wild shores of the Euxine. St. Martin of Tours founded the first monastery in Gaul, and 2,000 monks attended his funeral. Unrecorded missionaries planted the new institution in the heart of Æthiopia, amid the little islands that stud the Mediterranean, in the secluded valleys of Wales and Ireland.[3] But even more wonderful than the many thousands who thus abandoned the world is the reverence with which they were regarded by those who, by their attainments or their character, would seem most opposed to the monastic ideal. No one had more reason than Augustine to know the danger of enforced celibacy, but St. Augustine exerted all his energies to spread monasticism through his diocese. St. Ambrose, who was by nature an acute statesman; St. Jerome and St. Basil, who were ambitious scholars;

---

[1] Rufinus, *Hist. Mon.* vii.

[2] There is a good deal of doubt and controversy about this. See a note in Mosheim's *Eccl. Hist.* (Soame's edition), vol. i. p. 354.

[3] Most of the passages remaining on the subject of the foundation of monachism are given by Thomassin, *Discipline de l'Église,* part i. livre iii. ch. xii. This work contains also much general information about monachism. A curious collection of statistics of the numbers of the monks in different localities, additional to those I have given and gleaned from the *Lives of the Saints,* may be found in Pitra (*Vie de St. Léger,* Introd. p. lix.); 2,100, or, according to another account, 3,000 monks, lived in the monastery of Banchor.

St. Chrysostom, who was pre-eminently formed to sway the refined throngs of a metropolis—all exerted their powers in favour of the life of solitude, and the last three practised it themselves. St. Arsenius, who was surpassed by no one in the extravagance of his penances, had held a high office at the court of the Emperor Arcadius. Pilgrims wandered among the deserts, collecting accounts of the miracles and the austerities of the saints, which filled Christendom with admiration; and the strange biographies which were thus formed, wild and grotesque as they are, enable us to realise very vividly the general features of the anchorite life which became the new ideal of the Christian world.[1]

There is, perhaps, no phase in the moral history of mankind of a deeper or more painful interest than this ascetic epidemic. A hideous, sordid, and emaciated maniac, without knowledge, without patriotism, without natural affection, passing his life in a long routine of useless and atrocious self-torture, and quailing before the ghastly phantoms of his delirious brain, had become the ideal of the nations which had known the writings of Plato and Cicero and the lives of Socrates and Cato. For about two centuries, the hideous maceration of the body was regarded as the highest proof of excellence. St. Jerome declares, with a thrill of admiration,

---

[1] The three principal are the *Historia Monachorum* of Rufinus, who visited Egypt A.D. 373, about seventeen years after the death of St. Antony; the *Institutiones* of Cassian, who, having visited the Eastern monks about A.D. 394, founded vast monasteries containing, it is said, 5,000 monks, at Marseilles, and died at a great age about A.D. 448; and the *Historia Lausiaca* (so called from Lausus, Governor of Cappadocia) of Palladius, who was himself a hermit on Mount Nitria, in A.D. 388. The first and last, as well as many minor works of the same period, are given in Rosweyde's invaluable collection of the lives of the Fathers, one of the most fascinating volumes in the whole range of literature.

The hospitality of the monks was not without drawbacks. In a church on Mount Nitria three whips were hung on a palm-tree— one for chastising monks, another for chastising thieves, and a third for chastising guests. (Palladius *Hist. Laus.* vii.)

how he had seen a monk, who for thirty years had lived exclusively on a small portion of barley bread and of muddy water; another, who lived in a hole and never ate more than five figs for his daily repast;[1] a third, who cut his hair only on Easter Sunday, who never washed his clothes, who never changed his tunic till it fell to pieces, who starved himself till his eyes grew dim, and his skin 'like a pumice stone,' and whose merits, shown by these austerities, Homer himself would be unable to recount.[2] For six months, it is said, St. Macarius of Alexandria slept in a marsh, and exposed his body naked to the stings of venomous flies. He was accustomed to carry about with him eighty pounds of iron. His disciple, St. Eusebius, carried one hundred and fifty pounds of iron, and lived for three years in a dried-up well. St. Sabinus would only eat corn that had become rotten by remaining for a month in water. St. Besarion spent forty days and nights in the middle of thorn-bushes, and for forty years never lay down when he slept,[3] which last penance was also during fifteen years practised by St. Pachomius.[4] Some saints, like St. Marcian, restricted themselves to one meal a day, so small that they continually suffered the pangs of hunger.[5] Of one of them it is related that his daily food was six ounces of bread and a few herbs; that he was never seen to recline on a mat or bed, or even to place his limbs easily for sleep; but that sometimes, from excess of weariness, his eyes would close at his meals, and the food would drop from his mouth.[6] Other saints, however, ate only every second day;[7] while many, if we could believe the

---

[1] *Vita Pauli.* St. Jerome adds, that some will not believe this, because they have no faith, but that all things are possible for those that believe.

[2] *Vita St. Hilarion.*

[3] See a long list of these penances in Tillemont, *Mém. pour servir à l'Hist. ecclés.* tome viii.

[4] *Vitæ Patrum* (Pachomius). He used to lean against a wall when overcome by drowsiness.

[5] *Vitæ Patrum*, ix. 3.

[6] Sozomen, vi. 29.

[7] E.g. St. Antony, according to his biographer St. Athanasius.

monkish historian, abstained for whole weeks from all
nourishment.[1] St. Macarius of Alexandria is said during
an entire week to have never lain down, or eaten anything but a few uncooked herbs on Sunday.[2] Of another
famous saint, named John, it is asserted that for three
whole years he stood in prayer, leaning upon a rock; that
during all that time he never sat or lay down, and that
his only nourishment was the Sacrament, which was brought
him on Sundays.[3] Some of the hermits lived in deserted
dens of wild beasts, others in dried-up wells, while others
found a congenial resting-place among the tombs.[4] Some
disdained all clothes, and craw'ed abroad like the wild beasts,
covered only by their matted hair. In Mesopotamia, and
part of Syria, there existed a sect known by the name of
'Grazers,' who never lived under a roof, who ate neither
flesh nor bread, but who spent their time for ever on the
mountain side, and ate grass like cattle.[5] The cleanliness
cf the body was regarded as a pollution of the soul, and
the saints who were most admired had become one hideous
mass of clotted filth. St. Athanasius relates with enthu-

[1] 'Il y eut dans le désert de
Scété des solitaires d'une éminente
perfection. . . . On prétend que
pour l'ordinaire ils passoient des
semaines entières sans manger,
mais apparemment cela ne se faisoit que dans des occasions parti-
culières.'—Tillemont, *Mém. pour
servir à l'Hist. eccl.* tome viii. p.
580. Even this, however, was admirable!

[2] Palladius, *Hist. Laus.* cap. xx.

[3] 'Primum cum accessisset ad
eremum tribus continuis annis sub
cujusdam saxi rupe stans, semper
oravit, ita ut nunquam omnino re-
cederit neque Jacuerit. Somni autem tantum caperet, quantum stans
capere potuit; cibum vero nunquam sumpserat nisi die Dominica.

Presbyter enim tunc veniebat ad
eum et offerebat pro eo sacrificium
idque ei solum sacramentum erat
et victus.'—Rufinus, *Hist. Monach.*
cap. xv.

[4] Thus St. Antony used to live
in a tomb, where he was beaten by
the devil. (St. Athanasius, *Life of
Antony.*)

[5] βοσκοί. See on these monks
Sozomen, vi. 33; Evagrius, i. 21.
It is mentioned of a certain St.
Marc of Athens, that, having lived
for thirty years naked in the desert, his body was covered with
hair like that of a wild beast.
(Bollandists, March 29.) St. Mary
of Egypt, during part of her period
of penance, lived upon grass
(*Vitæ Patrum.*)

siasm how St. Antony, the patriarch of monachism, had never, to extreme old age, been guilty of washing his feet.[1] The less constant St. Pœmen fell into this habit for the first time when a very old man, and, with a glimmering of common sense, defended himself against the astonished monks by saying that he had 'learnt to kill not his body, but his passions.'[2]   St. Abraham the hermit, however, who lived for fifty years after his conversion, rigidly refused from that date to wash either his face or his feet.[3]   He was, it is said, a person of singular beauty, and his biographer somewhat strangely remarks that 'his face reflected the purity of his soul.'[4]   St. Ammon had never seen himself naked.[5]   A famous virgin named Silvia, though she was sixty years old and though bodily sickness was a consequence of her habits, resolutely refused, on religious principles, to wash any part of her body except her fingers.[6]   St. Euphraxia joined a convent of one hundred and thirty nuns, who never washed their feet, and who shuddered at the mention of a bath.[7]   An anchorite once imagined that he was mocked by an illusion of the devil, as he saw gliding before him through the desert a naked creature black with filth and years of exposure, and with white hair floating to the wind.   It was a once beautiful woman, St. Mary of Egypt, who had thus, during forty-seven

---

[1] *Life of Antony.*

[2] 'Il ne faisoit pas aussi difficulté dans sa vieillesse de se laver quelquefois les piez.   Et comme on témoignoit s'en étonner et trouver que cela ne répondoit pas à la vie austère des anciens, il se justifioit par ces paroles: Nous avons appris à tuer, non pas notre corps mais nos passions.'—Tillemont, *Mém. Hist. eccl.* tome xv. p. 148.   This saint was so very virtuous, that he sometimes remained without eating for whole weeks.

[3] 'Non appropinquavit oleum corpusculo ejus.   Facies vel etiam

pedes a die conversionis suæ nunquam diluti sunt.'—*Vitæ Patrum,* c. xvii.

[4] 'In facie ejus puritas animi noscebatur.'—Ibid. c. xviii.

[5] Socrates, iv. 23.

[6] Heraclidis Paradisus (Rosweyde), c. xlii.

[7] 'Nulla earum pedes suos abluebat; aliquantæ vero audientes de balneo loqui, irridentes, confusionem et magnam abominationem se audire judicabant, quæ neque auditum suum hoc audire patiebantur.' —*Vit. S. Euphrax.* c. vi.   (Rosweyde.)

years, been expiating her sins.[1] The occasional decadence
of the monks into habits of decency was a subject of much
reproach. 'Our fathers,' said the abbot Alexander, looking
mournfully back to the past, 'never washed their faces, but
we frequent the public baths.'[2] It was related of one monastery in the desert, that the monks suffered greatly from
want of water to drink; but at the prayer of the abbot
Theodosius a copious stream was produced. But soon some
monks, tempted by the abundant supply, diverged from their
old austerity, and persuaded the abbot to avail himself of
the stream for the construction of a bath. The bath was
made. Once, and once only, did the monks enjoy their
ablutions, when the stream ceased to flow. Prayers, tears,
and fastings were in vain. A whole year passed. At last
the abbot destroyed the bath, which was the object of the
Divine displeasure, and the waters flowed afresh.[3] But of
all the evidences of the loathsome excesses to which this
spirit was carried, the life of St. Simeon Stylites is probably
the most remarkable. It would be difficult to conceive a
more horrible or disgusting picture than is given of the
penances by which that saint commenced his ascetic career.
He had bound a rope around him so that it became im-

---

[1] See her acts, Bollandists, April
2, and in the *Vitæ Patrum*.

[2] 'Patres nostri nunquam facies
suas lavabant, nos autem lavacra
publica balneaque frequentamus.'
—Moschus, *Pratum Spirituale*,
clxviii.

[3] *Pratum Spirituale*, lxxx.

An Irish saint, named Coem-
genus, is said to have shown his
devotion in a way which was directly opposite to that of the other
saints I have mentioned—by his
special use of cold water—but the
principle in each case was the same
—to mortify nature. St. Coem-

genus was accustomed to pray for
an hour every night in a pool of
cold water, while the devil sent a
horrible beast to swim round him.
An angel, however, was sent to him
for three purposes. 'Tribus de
causis à Domino missus est angelus
ibi ad S. Coemgenum. Prima ut a
diversis suis gravibus laboribus
levius viveret paulisper; secunda
ut horridam bestiam sancto infes-
tam repelleret; tertia *ut frigidi-
tatem aquæ calefaceret*.'—Bollandists, June 3. The editors say these
acts are of doubtful authenticity.

bedded in his flesh, which putrefied around it. 'A horrible stench, intolerable to the bystanders, exhaled from his body, and worms dropped from him whenever he moved, and they filled his bed.   Sometimes he left the monastery and slept in a dry well, inhabited, it is said, by dæmons.   He built successively three pillars, the last being sixty feet high and scarcely two cubits in circumference, and on this pillar, during thirty years, he remained exposed to every change of climate, ceaselessly and rapidly bending his body in prayer almost to the level of his feet.   A spectator attempted to number these rapid motions, but desisted from weariness when he had counted 1,244.   For a whole year, we are told, St. Simeon stood upon one leg, the other being covered with hideous ulcers, while his biographer was commissioned to stand by his side, to pick up the worms that fell from his body, and to replace them in the sores, the saint saying to the worm, 'Eat what God has given you.'   From every quarter pilgrims of every degree thronged to do him homage. A crowd of prelates followed him to the grave.   A brilliant star is said to have shone miraculously over his pillar ; the general voice of mankind pronounced him to be the highest model of a Christian saint ; and several other anchorites imitated or emulated his penances.[1]

There is, if I mistake not, no department of literature the importance of which is more inadequately realised than the lives of the saints.   Even where they have no direct historical value, they have a moral value of the very highest order. They may not tell us with accuracy what men did at particular epochs ; but they display with the utmost vividness what they thought and felt, their measure of probability, and their ideal of excellence.   Decrees of councils, elaborate treatises of theologians, creeds, liturgies, and canons, are all but

---

[1] See his Life by his disciple Antony, in the *Vitæ Patrum*, Eva- grius, i. 13, 14.   Theodoret, *Philo theos*, cap. xxvi.

the husks of religious history. They reveal what was professed and argued before the world, but not that which was realised in the imagination or enshrined in the heart. The history of art, which in its ruder day reflected with delicate fidelity the fleeting images of an anthropomorphic age, is in this respect invaluable; but still more important is that vast Christian mythology, which grew up spontaneously from the intellectual condition of the time, included all its dearest hopes, wishes, ideals, and imaginings, and constituted, during many centuries, the popular literature of Christendom. In the case of the saints of the deserts, there can be no question that the picture—which is drawn chiefly by eye-witnesses—however grotesque may be some of its details, is in its leading features historically true. It is true that self-torture was for some centuries regarded as the chief measure of human excellence, that tens of thousands of the most devoted men fled to the desert to reduce themselves by maceration nearly to the condition of the brute, and that this odious superstition had acquired an almost absolute ascendancy in the ethics of the age. The examples of asceticism I have cited are but a few out of many hundreds, and volumes might be written, and have been written, detailing them. Till the reform of St. Benedict, the ideal was on the whole unchanged. The Western monks, from the conditions of their climate, were constitutionally incapable of rivalling the abstinence of the Egyptian anchorites; but their conception of supreme excellence was much the same, and they laboured to compensate for their inferiority in penances by claiming some superiority in miracles. From the time of St. Pachomius, the cœnobitic life was adopted by most monks; but the Eastern monasteries, with the important exception of a vow of obedience, differed little from a collection of hermitages. They were in the deserts; the monks commonly lived in separate cells; they kept silence at their repasts; they rivalled one another in the extravagance of their penances. A few feeble efforts were indeed made by

St. Jerome and others to moderate austerities, which frequently led to insanity and suicide, to check the turbulence of certain wandering monks, who were accustomed to defy the ecclesiastical authorities, and especially to suppress monastic mendicancy, which had appeared prominently among some heretical sects. The orthodox monks commonly employed themselves in weaving mats of palm-leaves; but, living in the deserts, with no wants, they speedily sank into a listless apathy; and the most admired were those who, like Simeon Stylites, and the hermit John, of whom I have already spoken, were most exclusively devoted to their superstition. Diversities of individual character were, however, vividly displayed. Many anchorites, without knowledge, passions, or imagination, having fled from servile toil to the calm of the wilderness, passed the long hours in sleep or in a mechanical routine of prayer, and their inert and languid existences, prolonged to the extreme of old age, closed at last by a tranquil and almost animal death. Others made their cells by the clear fountains and clustering palm-trees of some oasis in the desert, and a blooming garden arose beneath their toil. The numerous monks who followed St. Serapion devoted themselves largely to agriculture, and sent shiploads of corn for the benefit of the poor.[1] Of one old hermit it is related that, such was the cheerfulness of his mind, that every sorrow was dispelled by his presence, and the weary and the heartbroken were consoled by a few words from his lips.[2] More commonly, however, the hermit's cell was the scene of perpetual mourning. Tears and sobs, and frantic strugglings with imaginary dæmons, and paroxysms of religious despair, were the texture of his life, and the dread of spiritual enemies, and of that death which his superstition had rendered so terrible, embittered every hour of his existence.[3] The solace of intellectual occupations was rarely

---

[1] Palladius. *Hist. Laus.* lxxvi.
[2] Rufinus, *Hist. Monach.* xxxiii.
[3] We have a striking illustration of this in St. Arsenius. His

resorted to. 'The duty,' said St. Jerome, 'of a monk is not to teach, but to weep.'[1] A cultivated and disciplined mind was the least subject to those hallucinations, which were regarded as the highest evidence of Divine favour;[2] and although in an age when the passion for asceticism was general, many scholars became ascetics, the great majority of the early monks appear to have been men who were not only absolutely ignorant themselves, but who also looked upon learning with positive disfavour. St. Antony, the true founder of mona-chism, refused when a boy to learn letters, because it would bring him into too great intercourse with other boys.[3] At a time when St. Jerome had suffered himself to feel a deep ad-miration for the genius of Cicero, he was, as he himself tells us, borne in the night before the tribunal of Christ, accused of being rather a Ciceronian than a Christian, and severely flagellated by the angels.[4] This saint, however, afterwards modified his opinions about the Pagan writings, and he was

---

eyelashes are said to have fallen off through continual weeping, and he had always, when at work, to put a cloth on his breast to receive his tears. As he felt his death approaching, his terror rose to the point of agony. The monks who were about him said, ' "Quid fles, pater? numquid et tu times?" Ille respondit, "In veritate timeo et iste timor qui nunc mecum est, semper in me fuit, ex quo factus sum monachus." '—*Verba Senio-rum*, Prol. § 163. It was said of St. Abraham that no day passed after his conversion without his shedding tears. (*Vit. Patrum.*) St. John the dwarf once saw a monk laughing immoderately at dinner, and was so horrified that he at once began to cry. (Tille-mont, *Mém. de l'Hist. ecclés.* tome x. p. 430.) St. Basil (*Regulæ*, in-terrog. xvii.) gives a remarkable

disquisition on the wickedness of laughing, and he observes that this was the one bodily affection which Christ does not seem to have known. Mr. Buckle has collected a series of passages to precisely the same effect from the writings of the Scotch divines. (*Hist. of Civili-sation*, vol. ii. pp. 385–386.)

[1] 'Monachus autem non doctoris habet sed plangentis officium.'— *Contr. Vigilant.* xv.

[2] As Tillemont puts it: 'Il se trouva très-peu de saints en qui Dieu ait joint les talens extérieurs de l'éloquence et de la science avec la grâce de la prophétie et des miracles. Ce sont des dons que sa Providence a presque toujours séparés.'—*Mém. Hist. ecclés.* tome iv. p. 315.

[3] St. Athanasius, *Vit. Anton.*

[4] *Ep.* xxii. He says his shoul-ders were bruised when he awoke.

116   HISTORY OF EUROPEAN MORALS.

compelled to defend himself at length against his more jealous brethren, who accused him of defiling his writings with quotations from Pagan authors, of employing some monks in copying Cicero, and of explaining Virgil to some children at Bethlehem.[1] Of one monk it is related that, being especially famous as a linguist, he made it his penance to remain perfectly silent for thirty years;[2] of another, that having discovered a few books in the cell of a brother hermit, he reproached the student with having thus defrauded of their property the widow and the orphan;[3] of others, that their only books were copies of the New Testament, which they sold to relieve the poor.[4]

With such men, living such a life, visions and miracles were necessarily habitual. All the elements of hallucination were there. Ignorant and superstitious, believing as a matter of religious conviction that countless dæmons filled the air, attributing every fluctuation of his temperament, and every exceptional phenomenon in surrounding nature, to spiritual agency; delirious, too, from solitude and long continued austerities, the hermit soon mistook for palpable realities the phantoms of his brain. In the ghastly gloom of the sepulchre, where, amid mouldering corpses, he took up his abode; in the long hours of the night of penance, when the desert wind sobbed around his lonely cell, and the cries of wild

[1] Ep. lxx.; Adv. Rufinum, lib. i. ch. xxx. He there speaks of his vision as a mere dream, not binding. He elsewhere (Ep. cxxv.) speaks very sensibly of the advantage of hermits occupying themselves, and says he learnt Hebrew to keep away unholy thoughts.
[2] Sozomen, vi. 28; Rufinus, Hist. Monach. ch. vi. Socrates tells rather a touching story of one of these illiterate saints, named Pambos. Being unable to read, he came to some one to be taught a psalm. Having learnt the single verse, 'I said I will take heed to my ways, that I offend not with my tongue,' he went away, saying that was enough if it were practically acquired. When asked, six months, and again many years, after, why he did not come to learn another verse, he answered that he had never been able truly to master this. (H. E. iv. 23.)
[3] Tillemont, x. p. 61.
[4] Ibid. viii. 490; Socrates, H E. iv. 23.

beasts were borne upon his ear, visible forms of lust or terror
appeared to haunt him, and strange dramas were enacted by
those who were contending for his soul.   An imagination
strained to the utmost limit, acting upon a frame attenuated
and diseased by macerations, produced bewildering psychological phenomena, paroxysms of conflicting passions, sudden
alternations of joy and anguish, which he regarded as manifestly supernatural.   Sometimes, in the very ecstasy of his
devotion, the memory of old scenes would crowd upon his
mind.   The shady groves and soft voluptuous gardens of his
native city would arise, and, kneeling alone upon the burning
sand, he seemed to see around him the fair groups of dancing-
girls, on whose warm, undulating limbs and wanton smiles
his youthful eyes had too fondly dwelt.   Sometimes his temptation sprang from remembered sounds.   The sweet, licentious songs of other days came floating on his ear, and his
heart was thrilled with the passions of the past.   And then
the scene would change.   As his lips were murmuring the
psalter, his imagination, fired perhaps by the music of some
martial psalm, depicted the crowded amphitheatre.   The
throng and passion and mingled cries of eager thousands were
present to his mind, and the fierce joy of the gladiators
passed through the tumult of his dream.[1]   The simplest incident came at last to suggest diabolical influence.   An old
hermit, weary and fainting upon his journey, once thought
how refreshing would be a draught of the honey of wild bees

---

[1] I have combined in this passage
incidents from three distinct lives.
St. Jerome, in a very famous and
very beautiful passage of his letter
to Eustochium (*Ep.* xxii.) describes
the manner in which the forms of
dancing-girls appeared to surround
him as he knelt upon the desert
sands.   St. Mary of Egypt (*Vitæ
Patrum,* ch. xix.) was especially
tortured by the recollection of the
songs she had sung when young,
which continually haunted her
mind.   St. Hilarion (see his *Life*
by St. Jerome) thought he saw a
gladiatorial show while he was repeating the psalms.   The manner
in which the different visions faded
into one another like dissolving
views is repeatedly described in the
biographies.

of the desert. At that moment his eye fell upon a rock on which they had built a hive. He passed on with a shudder and an exorcism, for he believed it to be a temptation of the devil.[1] But most terrible of all were the struggles of young and ardent men, through whose veins the hot blood of passion continually flowed, physically incapable of a life of celibacy, and with all that proneness to hallucination which a southern sun engenders, who were borne on the wave of enthusiasm to the desert life. In the arms of Syrian or African brides, whose soft eyes answered love with love, they might have sunk to rest, but in the lonely wilderness no peace could ever visit their souls. The Lives of the Saints paint with an appalling vividness the agonies of their struggle. Multiplying with frantic energy the macerations of the body, beating their breasts with anguish, the tears for ever streaming from their eyes, imagining themselves continually haunted by ever-changing forms of deadly beauty. which acquired a greater vividness from the very passion with which they resisted them, their struggles not unfrequently ended in insanity and in suicide. It is related that when St. Pachomius and St. Palæmon were conversing together in the desert, a young monk, with his countenance distracted with madness, rushed into their presence, and, in a voice broken with convulsive sobs, poured out his tale of sorrows. A woman, he said, had entered his cell, had seduced him by her artifices, and then vanished miraculously in the air, leaving him half dead upon the ground;—and then with a wild shriek the monk broke away from the saintly listeners. Impelled, as they imagined, by an evil spirit, he rushed across the desert, till he arrived at the next village, and there, leaping into the open furnace of the public baths, he perished in the flames.[2] Strange stories were told

---

[1] Rufinus, *Hist. Monach.*, ch. xi. This saint was St. Helenus.   [2] Life of St. Pachomius (*Vit. Patrum*), cap. ix.

among the monks of revulsions of passion even in the most advanced. Of one monk especially, who had long been regarded as a pattern of asceticism, but who had suffered himself to fall into that self-complacency which was very common among the anchorites, it was told that one evening a fainting woman appeared at the door of his cell, and implored him to give her shelter, and not permit her to be devoured by the wild beasts. In an evil hour he yielded to her prayer. With all the aspect of profound reverence she won his regards, and at last ventured to lay her hand upon him. But that touch convulsed his frame. Passions long slumbering and forgotten rushed with impetuous fury through his veins. In a paroxysm of fierce love, he sought to clasp the woman to his heart, but she vanished from his sight, and a chorus of dæmons, with peals of laughter, exulted over his fall. The sequel of the story, as it is told by the monkish writer, is, I think, of a very high order of artistic merit. The fallen hermit did not seek, as might have been expected, by penance and prayers to renew his purity. That moment of passion and of shame had revealed in him a new nature, and severed him irrevocably from the hopes and feelings of the ascetic life. The fair form that had arisen upon his dream, though he knew it to be a deception luring him to destruction, still governed his heart. He fled from the desert, plunged anew into the world, avoided all intercourse with the monks, and followed the light of that ideal beauty even into the jaws of hell.[1]

---

[1] Rufinus, *Hist. Monach.* cap. i. This story was told to Rufinus by St. John the hermit. The same saint described his own visions very graphically. ' Denique etiam me frequenter dæmones noctibus seduxerunt, et neque orare neque requiescere permiserunt, phantasias quasdam per noctem totam sensibus meis et cogitationes suggerentes. Mane vero velut cum quadam illusione prosternebant se ante me dicentes, Indulge nobis, abbas, quia laborem tibi incussimus tota nocte.'—Ibid. St. Benedict in the desert is said to have been tortured by the recollection of a beautiful girl he had once seen, and only regained his composure by rolling in thorns. (St. Greg. *Dial.* ii. 2.)

Anecdotes of this kind, circulated among the monks, contributed to heighten the feelings of terror with which they regarded all communication with the other sex. But to avoid such communication was sometimes very difficult. Few things are more striking, in the early historians of the movement we are considering, than the manner in which narratives of the deepest tragical interest alternate with extremely whimsical accounts of the profound admiration with which the female devotees regarded the most austere anchorites, and the unwearied perseverance with which they endeavoured to force themselves upon their notice. Some women seem in this respect to have been peculiarly fortunate. St. Melania, who devoted a great portion of her fortune to the monks, accompanied by the historian Rufinus, made, near the end of the fourth century, a long pilgrimage through the Syrian and Egyptian hermitages.[1] But with many of the hermits it was a rule never to look upon the face of any woman, and the number of years they had escaped this contamination was commonly stated as a conspicuous proof of their excellence. St. Basil would only speak to a woman under extreme necessity.[2] St. John of Lycopolis had not seen a woman for forty-eight years.[3] A tribune was sent by his wife on a pilgrimage to St. John the hermit to implore him to allow her to visit him, her desire being so intense that she would probably, in the opinion of her husband, die if it were ungratified. At last the hermit told his suppliant that he would that night visit his wife when she was in bed in her house. The tribune brought this strange message to his wife, who

---

[1] She lived also for some time in a convent at Jerusalem, which she had founded. Melania (who was one of St. Jerome's friends) was a lady of rank and fortune, who devoted her property to the monks. See her journey in Ros-weyde, lib. ii.

[2] See his *Life* in Tillemont.

[3] Ibid. x. p. 14. A certain Didymus lived entirely alone till his death, which took place when he was ninety. (Socrates, *H.E.* iv. 23.)

that night saw the hermit in a dream.[1]   A young Roman
girl made a pilgrimage from Italy to Alexandria, to look
upon the face and obtain the prayers of St. Arsenius,
into whose presence she forced herself.   Quailing beneath
his rebuffs, she flung herself at his feet, imploring him
with tears to grant her only request — to remember her,
and to pray for her.   ' Remember you !' cried the indignant
saint; ' it shall be the prayer of my life that I may forget
you.'   The poor girl sought consolation from the Archbishop
of Alexandria, who comforted her by assuring her that,
though she belonged to the sex by which dæmons commonly
tempt saints, he doubted not the hermit would pray for her
soul, though he would try to forget her face.[2]   Sometimes
this female enthusiasm took another and a more subtle form,
and on more than one occasion women were known to attire
themselves as men, and to pass their lives undisturbed as
anchorites.   Among others, St. Pelagia, who had been the
most beautiful, and one of the most dangerously seductive
actresses of Antioch, having been somewhat strangely converted, was appointed by the bishops to live in penance with
an elderly virgin of irreproachable piety ; but, impelled, we
are told, by her desire for a more austere life, she fled from
her companion, assumed a male attire, took refuge among the
monks on the Mount of Olives, and, with something of the
skill of her old profession, supported her feigned character so
consistently that she acquired great renown, and it was only
(it is said) after her death that the saints discovered who had
been living among them.[3]

---

[1] Rufinus, *Hist. Monachorum*,
cap. i.
[2] *Verba Seniorum*, § 65.
[3] Pelagia was very pretty, and,
according to her own account, ' her
sins were heavier than the sand.'
The people of Antioch, who were
very fond of her, called her Marga-
rita, or the pearl.   'Il arriva un
jour que divers évesques, appelez
par celui d'Antioche pour quelques
affaires, estant ensemble à la porte
de l'église de S.-Julien, Pélagie
passa devant eux dans tout l'éclat
des pompes du diable, n'ayant pas
seulement une coeffe sur sa teste ni

The foregoing anecdotes and observations will, I hope, have given a sufficiently clear idea of the general nature of the monastic life in its earliest phase, and also of the writings it produced. We may now proceed to examine the ways in which this mode of life affected both the ideal type and the realised condition of Christian morals. And in the first place, it is manifest that the proportion of virtues was altered. If an impartial person were to glance over the ethics of the New Testament, and were asked what was the central and distinctive virtue to which the sacred writers most continually referred, he would doubtless answer that it was that which is described as love, charity, or philanthropy. If he were to apply a similar scrutiny to the writings of the fourth and fifth centuries, he would answer that the cardinal virtue of the religious type was not love, but chastity. And this chastity, which was regarded as the ideal state, was not the purity of an undefiled marriage. It was the absolute suppression of the whole sensual side of our nature. The chief form of virtue, the central conception of the saintly life, was a perpetual struggle against all carnal impulses, by men who altogether refused the compromise of marriage. From this fact, if I mistake not, some interesting and important consequences may be deduced.

In the first place, religion gradually assumed a very sombre hue. The business of the saint was to eradicate a natural appetite, to attain a condition which was emphatically abnormal. The depravity of human nature, especially

---

un mouchoir sur ses épaules, ce qu'on remarqua comme le comble de son impudence. Tous les évesques baissèrent les yeux en gémissant pour ne pas voir ce dangereux objet de péché, hors Nonne, très-saint évesque d'Héliople, qui la regarda avec une attention qui fit peine aux autres.' However, this bishop im-

mediately began crying a great deal, and reassured his brethren, and a sermon which he preached led to the conversion of the actress. (Tillemont, *Mém. d'Hist. ecclés.* tome xii. pp. 378–380. See, too, on women, 'under pretence of religion,' attiring themselves as men, Sozomen, iii. 14.)

the essential evil of the body, was felt with a degree of intensity that could never have been attained by moralists who were occupied mainly with transient or exceptional vices, such as envy, anger, or cruelty. And in addition to the extreme inveteracy of the appetite which it was desired to eradicate, it should be remembered that a somewhat luxurious and indulgent life, even when that indulgence is not itself distinctly evil, even when it has a tendency to mollify the character, has naturally the effect of strengthening the animal passions, and is therefore directly opposed to the ascetic ideal. The consequence of this was first of all a very deep sense of the habitual and innate depravity of human nature; and, in the next place, a very strong association of the idea of pleasure with that of vice. All this necessarily flowed from the supreme value placed upon virginity. The tone of calm and joyousness that characterises Greek philosophy, the almost complete absence of all sense of struggle and innate sin that it displays, is probably in a very large degree to be ascribed to the fact that, in the department of morals we are considering, Greek moralists made no serious efforts to improve our nature, and Greek public opinion acquiesced, without scandal, in an almost boundless indulgence of illicit pleasures.

But while the great prominence at this time given to the conflicts of the ascetic life threw a dark shade upon the popular estimate of human nature, it contributed, I think, very largely to sustain and deepen that strong conviction of the freedom of the human will which the Catholic Church has always so strenuously upheld; for there is, probably, no other form of moral conflict in which men are so habitually and so keenly sensible of that distinction between our will and our desires, upon the reality of which all moral freedom ultimately depends. It had also, I imagine, another result, which it is difficult to describe with the same precision. What may be called a strong animal nature—a nature, that is, in which the passions are in vigorous, and at the same time healthy, action—is that in which we should most natu rally expect to find several moral qualities. Good humour, frankness, generosity, active courage, sanguine energy, buoyancy of temper, are the usual and appropriate accompaniments of a vigorous animal temperament, and they are much more rarely found either in natures that are essentially feeble and effeminate, or in natures which have been artificially emasculated by penances, distorted from their original tendency, and habitually held under severe control. The ideal type of Catholicism being, on account of the supreme value placed upon virginity, of the latter kind, the qualities I have mentioned have always ranked very low in the Catholic conceptions of excellence, and the steady tendency of Protestant and industrial civilisation has been to elevate them.

I do not know whether the reader will regard these speculations—which I advance with some diffidence—as farfetched and fanciful. Our knowledge of the physical antecedents of different moral qualities is so scanty that it is difficult to speak on these matters with much confidence; but few persons, I think, can have failed to observe that the physical temperaments I have described differ not simply in the one great fact of the intensity of the animal passions, but also in the aptitude of each to produce a distinct moral type, or, in other words, in the harmony of each with several qualities, both good and evil. A doctrine, therefore, which connects one of these two temperaments indissolubly with the moral ideal, affects the appreciation of a large number of moral qualities. But whatever may be thought of the moral results springing from the physical temperament which asceticism produced, there can be little controversy as to the effects springing from the condition of life which it enjoined. Severance from the interests and affections of all around him was the chief object of the anchorite, and the first conse-

quence of the prominence of asceticism was a profound discredit thrown upon the domestic virtues.

The extent to which this discredit was carried, the
intense hardness of heart and ingratitude manifested by the
saints towards those who were bound to them by the closest
of earthly ties, is known to few who have not studied the
original literature on the subject. These things are commonly
thrown into the shade by those modern sentimentalists who
delight in idealising the devotees of the past. To break by
his ingratitude the heart of the mother who had borne him,
to persuade the wife who adored him that it was her duty to
separate from him for ever, to abandon his children, uncared
for and beggars, to the mercies of the world, was regarded by
the true hermit as the most acceptable offering he could make
to his God. His business was to save his own soul. The
serenity of his devotion would be impaired by the discharge
of the simplest duties to his family. Evagrius, when a
hermit in the desert, received, after a long interval, letters
from his father and mother. He could not bear that the
equable tenor of his thoughts should be disturbed by the
recollection of those who loved him, so he cast the letters
unread into the fire.[1] A man named Mutius, accompanied
by his only child, a little boy of eight years old, abandoned his possessions and demanded admission into a
monastery. The monks received him, but they proceeded to
discipline his heart. 'He had already forgotten that he was
rich; he must next be taught to forget that he was a father.'[2]

---

[1] Tillemont, tome x. pp. 376,
377. Apart from family affections,
there are some curious instances
recorded of the anxiety of the
saints to avoid distractions. One
monk used to cover his face when
he went into his garden, lest the
sight of the trees should disturb
his mind. (*Verb. Seniorum.*) St.
Arsenius could not bear the rust-
ling of the reeds (ibid.); and a

saint named Boniface struck dead
a man who went about with an ape
and a cymbal, because he had (apparently quite unintentionally) disturbed him at his prayers. (St.
Greg. *Dial.* i. 9.)

[2] 'Quemadmodum se jam divi-
tem non esse sciebat, ita etiam
patrem se esse nesciret.'—Cassian.
De Cœnobiorum Institutis, iv. 27.

His little child was separated from him, clothed in dirty rags, subjected to every form of gross and wanton hardship, beaten, spurned, and ill treated.   Day after day the father was compelled to look upon his boy wasting away with sorrow, his once happy countenance for ever stained with tears, distorted by sobs of anguish.   But yet, says the admiring biographer, 'though he saw this day by day, such was his love for Christ, and for the virtue of obedience, that the father's heart was rigid and unmoved.   He thought little of the tears of his child.   He was anxious only for his own humility and perfection in virtue.'[1]   At last the abbot told him to take his child and throw it into the river.   He proceeded, without a murmur or apparent pang, to obey, and it was only at the last moment that the monks interposed, and on the very brink of the river saved the child.   Mutius afterwards rose to a high position among the ascetics, and was justly regarded as having displayed in great perfection the temper of a saint.[2] An inhabitant of Thebes once came to the abbot Sisoes, and asked to be made a monk.   The abbot asked if he had any one belonging to him.   He answered, 'A son.'   'Take your son,' rejoined the old man, 'and throw him into the river, and then you may become a monk.'   The father hastened to fulfil the command, and the deed was almost consummated when a messenger sent by Sisoes revoked the order.[3]

Sometimes the same lesson was taught under the form of a miracle.   A man had once deserted his three children to become a monk.   Three years after, he determined to bring them into the monastery, but, on returning to his home, found that the two eldest had died during his absence.   He came to his abbot, bearing in his arms his youngest child,

---

[1] 'Cumque taliter infans sub oculis ejus per dies singulos ageretur, pro amore nihilominus Christi et obedientiæ virtute, rigida semper atque immobilia patris viscera permanserunt . . . . parum cogitans de lacrymis ejus, sed de propria humilitate ac perfectione sollicitus.'—Ibid.

[2] Ibid.

[3] Bollandists, July 6; *Verba Seniorum*, xiv.

who was still little more than an infant. The abbot turned
to him and said, 'Do you love this child?' The father
answered, 'Yes.' Again the abbot said, 'Do you love it
dearly?' The father answered as before. 'Then take the
child,' said the abbot, 'and throw it into the fire upon yonder
hearth.' The father did as he was commanded, and the child
remained unharmed amid the flames.[1]   But it was especially
in their dealings with their female relations that this aspect
of the monastic character was vividly displayed. In this
case the motive was not simply to mortify family affections—
it was also to guard against the possible danger resulting
from the presence of a woman. The fine flower of that
saintly purity might have been disturbed by the sight of a
mother's or a sister's face. The ideal of one age appears
sometimes too grotesque for the caricature of another; and it
is curious to observe how pale and weak is the picture
which Molière drew of the affected prudery of Tartuffe,[2]
when compared with the narratives that are gravely propounded in the Lives of the Saints. When the abbot Sisoes
had become a very old, feeble, and decrepit man, his disciples
exhorted him to leave the desert for an inhabited country.
Sisoes seemed to yield; but he stipulated, as a necessary
condition, that in his new abode he should never be compelled to encounter the peril and perturbation of looking on
a woman's face. To such a nature, of course, the desert alone
was suitable, and the old man was suffered to die in peace.[3]
A monk was once travelling with his mother—in itself a

---

[1] *Verba Seniorum*, xiv.
[2] Tartuffe (*tirant un mouchoir de sa poche*).

'Ah, mon Dieu, je vous prie,
Avant que de parler, prenez-moi ce
mouchoir.

Dorine.

Comment!

Tartuffe.
Couvrez ce sein que je ne
saurois voir;
Par de pareils objets des âmes sont
blessées,
Et cela fait venir de coupables
pensées.'
Tartuffe, Acte iii. scène 2.
[3] Bollandists, July 6.

most unusual circumstance—and, having arrived at a bridgeless stream, it became necessary for him to carry her across.
To her surprise, he began carefully wrapping up his hands
in cloths; and upon her asking the reason, he explained that
he was alarmed lest he should be unfortunate enough to
touch her, and thereby disturb the equilibrium of his nature.[1]
The sister of St. John of Calama loved him dearly, and
earnestly implored him that she might look upon his face
once more before she died. On his persistent refusal, she
declared that she would make a pilgrimage to him in the
desert. The alarmed and perplexed saint at last wrote
to her, promising to visit her if she would engage to relinquish her design. He went to her in disguise, received a
cup of water from her hands, and came away without being
discovered. She wrote to him, reproaching him with not
having fulfilled his promise. He answered her that he
had indeed visited her, that 'by the mercy of Jesus
Christ he had not been recognised,' and that she must
never see him again.[2] The mother of St. Theodorus came
armed with letters from the bishops to see her son, but
he implored his abbot, St. Pachomius, to permit him to
decline the interview; and, finding all her efforts in vain,
the poor woman retired into a convent, together with her
daughter, who had made a similar expedition with similar
results.[3] The mother of St. Marcus persuaded his abbot to
command the saint to go out to her. Placed in a dilemma
between the sin of disobedience and the perils of seeing his
mother, St. Marcus extricated himself by an ingenious device.
He went to his mother with his face disguised and his eyes

---

[1] *Verba Seniorum*, iv. The
poor woman, being startled and
perplexed at the proceedings of her
son, said, 'Quid sic operuisti manus
tuas, fili? Ille autem dixit: Quia
corpus mulieris ignis est, et ex eo
ipso quo te contingebam veniebat

mihi commemoratio aliarum femi-
narum in animo.'

[2] Tillemont, *Mém de l'Hist
ecclés.* tome x. pp. 444, 445.

[3] *Vit. S. Pachomius*, ch. xxxi.;
Verba Seniorum.

shut. The mother did not recognise her son. The son did not see his mother.[1] The sister of St. Pior in like manner induced the abbot of that saint to command him to admit her to his presence. The command was obeyed, but St. Pior resolutely kept his eyes shut during the interview.[2] St. Pœmen and his six brothers had all deserted their mother to cultivate the perfections of an ascetic life. But ingratitude can seldom quench the love of a mother's heart, and the old woman, now bent by infirmities, went alone into the Egyptian desert to see once more the children she so dearly loved. She caught sight of them as they were about to leave their cell for the church, but they immediately ran back into the cell, and, before her tottering steps could reach it, one of her sons rushed forward and closed the door in her face. She remained outside weeping bitterly. St. Pœmen then, coming to the door, but without opening it, said, ‘ Why do you, who are already stricken with age, pour forth such cries and lamentations ? ’ But she, recognising the voice of her son, answered, ‘ It is because I long to see you, my sons. What harm could it do you that I should see you ? Am I not your mother ? did I not give you suck ? I am now an old and wrinkled woman, and my heart is troubled at the sound of your voices.’ [3] The saintly brothers, however, refused to

---

[1] *Verba Senorium,* xiv.

[2] Palladius, *Hist. Laus.* cap. lxxxvii.

[3] Bollandists, June 6. I avail myself again of the version of Tillemont. ‘ Lorsque S Pemen demeuroit en Egypte avec ses frères, leur mère, qui avoit un extrême désir de les voir, venoit souvent au lieu où ils estoient, sans pouvoir jamais avoir cette satisfaction. Une fois enfin elle prit si bien son temps qu'elle les rencontra qui alloient à l'église, mais dès qu'ils la virent ils s'en retournèrent en haste dans leur cellule et fermèrent la porte sur eux. Elle les suivit, et trouvant la porte, elle les appeloit avec des larmes et des cris capables de les toucher de compassion. . . . . Pemen s'y leva et s'y en alla, et l'entendant pleurer il luy dit, tenant toujours la porte fermée, ‘ Pourquoi vous lassez-vous inutilement à pleurer et crier ? N'êtes-vous pas déjà assez abattue par la vieillesse ? ’ Elle reconnut la voix de Pemen, et s'efforçant encore davantage, elle s'écria, ‘ Hé, mes enfans, c'est que je voudrais bien vous voir: et quel mal y a-t-il que je vous voie ? Ne suis-je pas votre mère, et ne

open their door. They told their mother that she would see
them after death ; and the biographer says she at last went
away contented with the prospect. St. Simeon Stylites, in
this as in other respects, stands in the first line. He had
been passionately loved by his parents, and, if we may believe
his eulogist and biographer, he began his saintly career by
breaking the heart of his father, who died of grief at his
flight. His mother, however, lingered on. Twenty-seven
years after his disappearance, at a period when his austerities
had made him famous, she heard for the first time where he
was, and hastened to visit him. But all her labour was in
vain. No woman was admitted within the precincts of his
dwelling, and he refused to permit her even to look upon his
face. Her entreaties and tears were mingled with words of
bitter and eloquent reproach.[1] ‘ My son,’ she is represented
as having said, ‘ why have you done this ? I bore you in my
womb, and you have wrung my soul with grief. I gave you
milk from my breast, you have filled my eyes with tears.
For the kisses I gave you, you have given me the anguish of
a broken heart ; for all that I have done and suffered for you,
you have repaid me by the most cruel wrongs.’ At last the
saint sent a message to tell her that she would soon see him.
Three days and three nights she had wept and entreated in
vain, and now, exhausted with grief and age and privation,
she sank feebly to the ground and breathed her last sigh before that inhospitable door. Then for the first time the saint,
accompanied by his followers, came out. He shed some pious

vous ai-je pas nourri du lait de mes
mammelles ? Je suis déjà toute
pleine de rides, et lorsque je vous
ay entendu, l’extrême envie que
j’ay de vous voir m’a tellement
émue que je suis presque tombée
en défaillance.” ’ — *Mémoires de
l'Hist. ecclès.* tome xv. pp. 157,
158.

[1] The original is much more eloquent than my translation. ‘ Fili,
quare hoc fecisti? Pro utero quo
te portavi, satiasti me luctu, pro
lactatione qua te lactavi dedisti
mihi lacrymas, pro osculo quo te
osculata sum, dedisti mihi amaras
cordis angustias ; pro dolore et
labore quem passa sum, imposuisti
mihi sævissimas plagas.’ — *Vita
Simeonis* (in Rosweyde).

tears over the corpse of his murdered mother, and offered up
a prayer consigning her soul to heaven.   Perhaps it was but
fancy, perhaps life was not yet wholly extinct, perhaps the
story is but the invention of the biographer; but a faint
motion—which appears to have been regarded as miraculous
—is said to have passed over her prostrate form.   Simeon
once more commended her soul to heaven, and then, amid the
admiring murmurs of his disciples, the saintly matricide
returned to his devotions.

The glaring mendacity that characterises the Lives of the
Catholic Saints, probably to a greater extent than any other
important branch of existing literature, makes it not unreasonable to hope that many of the foregoing anecdotes represent
much less events that actually took place than ideal pictures
generated by the enthusiasm of the chroniclers.   They are
not, however, on that account the less significant of the moral
conceptions which the ascetic period had created.   The ablest
men in the Christian community vied with one another in
inculcating as the highest form of duty the abandonment of
social ties and the mortification of domestic affections.   A
few faint restrictions were indeed occasionally made.   Much
—on which I shall hereafter touch—was written on the
liberty of husbands and wives deserting one another; and
something was written on the cases of children forsaking or
abandoning their parents.   At first, those who, when children,
were devoted to the monasteries by their parents, without
their own consent, were permitted, when of mature age, to
return to the world; and this liberty was taken from them
for the first time by the fourth Council of Toledo, in A.D. 633.[1]
The Council of Gangra condemned the heretic Eustathius for
teaching that children might, through religious motives, for-
sake their parents, and St. Basil wrote in the same strain;[2]
but cases of this kind of rebellion against parental authority
were continually recounted with admiration in the Lives of the

---

Bingham, *Antiquities*, book vii. ch. iii.   [2] Ibid.

Saints, applauded by some of the leading Fathers, and virtually
sanctioned by a law of Justinian, which deprived parents of
the power of either restraining their children from entering
monasteries, or disinheriting them if they had done so without
their consent.[1]   St. Chrysostom relates with enthusiasm the
case of a young man who had been designed by his father for
the army, and who was lured away to a monastery.[2]   The
eloquence of St. Ambrose is said to have been so seductive,
that mothers were accustomed to shut up their daughters to
guard them against his fascinations.[3]   The position of affectionate parents was at this time extremely painful.   The
touching language is still preserved, in which the mother of
Chrysostom—who had a distinguished part in the conversion
of her son—implored him, if he thought it his duty to fly to
the desert life, at least to postpone the act till she had died.[4]
St. Ambrose devoted a chapter to proving that, while those
are worthy of commendation who enter the monasteries
with the approbation, those are still more worthy of praise
who do so against the wishes, of their parents; and he proceeded to show how small were the penalties the latter could
inflict when compared with the blessings asceticism could
bestow.[5]   Even before the law of Justinian, the invectives of
the clergy were directed against those who endeavoured to
prevent their children flying to the desert.   St. Chrysostom
explained to them that they would certainly be damned.[6]   St.
Ambrose showed that, even in this world, they might not be
unpunished.   A girl, he tells us, had resolved to enter into a
convent, and as her relations were expostulating with her on
her intention, one of those present tried to move her by the
memory of her dead father, asking whether, if he were still

---

[1] Bingham, *Antiquities*, book
vii chap. 3.
[2] Milman's *Early Christianity*
(ed. 1867), vol. iii. p. 122.
[3] Ibid. vol. iii. p. 153.

[4] Ibid. vol. iii. p. 120.
[5] *De Virginibus*, i. 11.
[6] See Milman's *Early Christianity*, vol. iii. p. 121.

alive, he would have suffered her to remain unmarried.
'Perhaps,' she calmly answered, 'it was for this very purpose
he died, that he should not throw any obstacle in my way.'
Her words were more than an answer; they were an oracle.
The indiscreet questioner almost immediately died, and the
relations, shocked by the manifest providence, desisted from
their opposition, and even implored the young saint to accomplish her design.[1] St. Jerome tells with rapturous enthusiasm
of a little girl, named Asella, who, when only twelve years
old, devoted herself to the religious life and refused to look
on the face of any man, and whose knees, by constant prayer,
became at last like those of a camel.[2] A famous widow,
named Paula, upon the death of her husband, deserted her
family, listened with 'dry eyes' to her children, who were
imploring her to stay, fled to the society of the monks at
Jerusalem, made it her desire that 'she might die a beggar,
and leave not one piece of money to her son,' and, having dissipated the whole of her fortune in charities, bequeathed to
her children only the embarrassment of her debts.[3] It was
carefully inculcated that all money given or bequeathed to the
poor, or to the monks, produced spiritual benefit to the donors
or testators, but that no spiritual benefit sprang from money
bestowed upon relations; and the more pious minds recoiled

---

[1] *De Virginibus,* i. 11.

[2] *Epist.* xxiv.

[3] St. Jerome describes the scene
at her departure with admiring
eloquence. 'Descendit ad portum
fratre, cognatis, affinibus et quod
majus est liberis prosequentibus,
et clementissimam matrem pietate
vincere cupientibus. Jam carbasa
tendebantur, et remorum ductu
navis in altum protrahebatur.
Parvus Toxotius supplices manus
tendebat in littore, Ruffina jam
nubilis ut suas expectaret nuptias
tacens fletibus obsecrabat. Et
tamen illa siccos tendebat ad cælum
oculos, pietatem in filios pietate in
Deum superans. Nesciebat se
matrem ut Christi probaret ancil-
lam.'—*Ep.* cviii. In another place
he says of her: 'Testis est Jesus,
ne unum quidem nummum ab ea
filiæ derelictum sed, ut ante jam
dixi, derelictum magnum æs alienum.'—Ibid. And again: 'Vis,
lector, ejus breviter scire virtutes?
Omnes suos pauperes, pauperior
ipsa dimisit.'—Ibid.

from disposing of their property in a manner that would not
redound to the advantage of their souls.   Sometimes parents
made it a dying request to their children that they would
preserve none of their property, but would bestow it all
among the poor.[1]   It was one of the most honourable incidents of the life of St. Augustine, that he, like Aurelius,
Bishop of Carthage, refused to receive legacies or donations
which unjustly spoliated the relatives of the benefactor.[2]
Usually, however, to outrage the affections of the nearest and
dearest relations was not only regarded as innocent, but proposed as the highest virtue.   'A young man,' it was acutely
said, 'who has learnt to despise a mother's grief, will easily
bear any other labour that is imposed upon him.'[3]   St.
Jerome, when exhorting Heliodorus to desert his family and
become a hermit, expatiated with a fond minuteness on every
form of natural affection he desired him to violate.   'Though
your little nephew twine his arms around your neck; though
your mother, with dishevelled hair and tearing her robe asunder, point to the breast with which she suckled you; though
your father fall down on the threshold before you, pass on
over your father's body.   Fly with tearless eyes to the banner of the cross.   In this matter cruelty is the only piety
. . . Your widowed sister may throw her gentle arms around
you. . . . Your father may implore you to wait but a short
time to bury those near to you, who will soon be no more;
your weeping mother may recall your childish days, and may
point to her shrunken breast and to her wrinkled brow.
Those around you may tell you that all the household rests
upon you.   Such chains as these, the love of God and the

---

[1] See Chastel, *Etudes historiques
sur la Charité*, p. 231. The parents
of St. Gregory Nazianzen had made
this request, which was faithfully
observed.

[2] Chastel, p. 232.

[3] See a characteristic passage

from the *Life of St. Fulgentius*,
quoted by Dean Milman. 'Facile
potest juvenis tolerare quemcunque
imposuerit laborem qui poterit
maternum jam despicere dolorem.'
—*Hist. of Latin Christianity*, vol.
ii. p. 82.

fear of hell can easily break.   You say that Scripture orders
you to obey your parents, but he who loves them more than
Christ loses his soul.   The enemy brandishes a sword to slay
me.   Shall I think of a mother's tears ? '[1]

The sentiment manifested in these cases continued to be
displayed in later ages.   Thus, St. Gregory the Great assures us that a certain young boy, though he had enrolled
himself as a monk, was unable to repress his love for his
parents, and one night stole out secretly to visit them.   But
the judgment of God soon marked the enormity of the offence.
On coming back to the monastery, he died that very day, and
when he was buried, the earth refused to receive so heinous a
criminal.   His body was repeatedly thrown up from the
grave, and it was only suffered to rest in peace when St.
Benedict had laid the Sacrament upon its breast.[2]   One nun
revealed, it is said, after death, that she had been condemned
for three days to the fires of purgatory, because she had loved
her mother too much.[3]   Of another saint it is recorded that
his benevolence was such that he was never known to be
hard or inhuman to any one except his relations.[4]   St.
Romuald, the founder of the Camaldolites, counted his father
among his spiritual children, and on one occasion punished
him by flagellation.[5]   The first nun whom St. Francis of
Assisi enrolled was a beautiful girl of Assisi named Clara
Scifi, with whom he had for some time carried on a clandestine correspondence, and whose flight from her father's home
he both counselled and planned.[6]   As the first enthusiasm
of asceticism died away, what was lost in influence by
the father was gained by the priest.   The confessional made

---

[1] *Ep.* xiv. (*Ad Heliodorum*).

[2] St. Greg. *Dial.* ii. 24.

[3] Bollandists, May 3 (vol. vii.
p. 561).

[4] 'Hospitibus omni loco ac tempore liberalissimus fuit. . . Solis
consanguineis durus erat et inhu-
manus, tamquam ignotos illos re-
spiciens.'— Bollandists, May 29.

[5] See Helyot, *Dict. des Ordres
religieux*, art. ' Camaldules.'

[6] See the charming sketch in the
Life of St. Francis, by Hase.

this personage the confidant in the most delicate secrets of domestic life. The supremacy of authority, of sympathy, and sometimes even of affection, passed away beyond the domestic circle, and, by establishing an absolute authority over the most secret thoughts and feelings of nervous and credulous women, the priests laid the foundation of the empire of the world.

The picture I have drawn of the inroads made in the first period of asceticism upon the domestic affections, tells, I think, its own story, and I shall only add a very few words of comment. That it is necessary for many men who are pursuing a truly heroic course to break loose from the trammels which those about them would cast over their actions or their opinions, and that this severance often constitutes at once one of the noblest and one of the most painful incidents in their career, are unquestionable truths ; but the examples of such occasional and exceptional sacrifices, endured for some great unselfish end, cannot be compared with the conduct of those who regarded the mortification of domestic love as in itself a form of virtue, and whose ends were mainly or exclusively selfish. The sufferings endured by the ascetic who fled from his relations were often, no doubt, very great. Many anecdotes remain to show that warm and affectionate hearts sometimes beat under the cold exterior of the monk ;[1] and St. Jerome, in one of his letters, remarked, with much complacency and congratulation, that the very bitterest pang of captivity is simply this irrevocable

---

[1] The legend of St. Scholastica, the sister of St. Benedict, has been often quoted. He had visited her, and was about to leave in the evening, when she implored him to stay. He refused, and she then prayed to God, who sent so violent a tempest that the saint was unable to depart. (St. Greg. *Dial.* ii. 33.) Cassian speaks of a monk who thought it his duty never to see his mother, but who laboured for a whole year to pay off a debt she had incurred. (Cœnob. *Inst.* v. 38.) St. Jerome mentions the strong natural affection of Paula, though she considered it a virtue to mortify it. (*Ep.* cviii.)

separation which the superstition he preached induced multitudes to inflict upon themselves.   But if, putting aside the intrinsic excellence of an act, we attempt to estimate the nobility of the agent, we must consider not only the cost of what he did, but also the motive which induced him to do it. It is this last consideration which renders it impossible for us to place the heroism of the ascetic on the same level with that of the great patriots of Greece or Rome.   A man may be as truly selfish about the next world as about this.   Where an overpowering dread of future torments, or an intense realisation of future happiness, is the leading motive of action, the theological virtue of faith may be present, but the ennobling quality of disinterestedness is assuredly absent.   In our day, when pictures of rewards and punishments beyond the grave act but feebly upon the imagination, a religious motive is commonly an unselfish motive ; but it has not always been so, and it was undoubtedly not so in the first period of asceticism.   The terrors of a future judgment drove the monk into the desert, and the whole tenor of the ascetic life, while isolating him from human sympathies, fostered an intense, though it may be termed a religious, selfishness.

The effect of the mortification of the domestic affections upon the general character was probably very pernicious. The family circle is the appointed sphere, not only for the performance of manifest duties, but also for the cultivation of the affections ; and the extreme ferocity which so often characterised the ascetic was the natural consequence of the discipline he imposed upon himself.   Severed from all other ties, the monks clung with a desperate tenacity to their opinions and to their Church, and hated those who dissented from them with all the intensity of men whose whole lives were concentrated on a single subject, whose ignorance and bigotry prevented them from conceiving the possibility of any good thing in opposition to themselves, and who had made it a main object of their discipline to eradicate all

natural sympathies and affections. We may reasonably attri
bute to the fierce biographer the words of burning hatred of
all heretics which St. Athanasius puts in the mouth of the
dying patriarch of the hermits ;[1] but ecclesiastical history,
and especially the writings of the later Pagans, abundantly
prove that the sentiment was a general one. To the Chris
tian bishops it is mainly due that the wide and general,
though not perfect, recognition of religious liberty in the
Roman legislation was replaced by laws of the most minute
and stringent intolerance. To the monks, acting as the exe-
cutive of an omnipresent, intolerant, and aggressive clergy,
is due an administrative change, perhaps even more important than the legislative change that had preceded it. The
system of conniving at, neglecting, or despising forms of
worship that were formally prohibited, which had been so
largely practised by the sceptical Pagans, and under the lax
police system of the Empire, and which is so important a fact
in the history of the rise of Christianity, was absolutely destroyed. Wandering in bands through the country, the
monks were accustomed to burn the temples, to break the
idols, to overthrow the altars, to engage in fierce conflicts
with the peasants, who often defended with desperate courage
the shrines of their gods. It would be impossible to conceive
men more fitted for the task. Their fierce fanaticism, their
persuasion that every idol was tenanted by a literal dæmon,
and their belief that death incurred in this iconoclastic
crusade was a form of martyrdom, made them careless of all
consequences to themselves, while the reverence that attached
to their profession rendered it scarcely possible for the civil
power to arrest them. Men who had learnt to look with indifference on the tears of a broken-hearted mother, and whose
ideal was indissolubly connected with the degradation of the

---

[1] *Life of Antony.* See, too, the sentiments of St. Pachomius, *Vit.*
cap. xxvii.

body, were but little likely to be moved either by the pathos
of old associations, and of reverent, though mistaken, worship,
or by the grandeur of the Serapeum, or of the noble statues of
Phidias and Praxiteles.   Sometimes the civil power ordered
the reconstruction of Jewish synagogues or heretical churches
which had been illegally destroyed ; but the doctrine was
early maintained that such a reconstruction was a deadly sin.
Under Julian some Christians suffered martyrdom sooner
than be parties to it ; and St. Ambrose from the pulpit
of Milan, and Simeon Stylites from his desert pillar, united
in denouncing Theodosius, who had been guilty of issuing
this command.

Another very important moral result to which asceticism
largely contributed was the depression and sometimes almost
the extinction of the civic virtues.   A candid examination
will show that the Christian civilisations have been as inferior to the Pagan ones in civic and intellectual virtues as they
have been superior to them in the virtues of humanity and
of chastity.   We have already seen that one remarkable feature of the intellectual movement that preceded Christianity
was the gradual decadence of patriotism.   In the early days
both of Greece and Rome, the first duty enforced was that of
a man to his country.   This was the rudimentary or cardinal
virtue of the moral type.   It gave the tone to the whole
system of ethics, and different moral qualities were valued
chiefly in proportion to their tendency to form illustrious
citizens.   The destruction of this spirit in the Roman Empire
was due, as we have seen, to two causes—one of them being
political and the other intellectual.   The political cause
was the amalgamation of the different nations in one great
despotism, which gave indeed an ample field for personal
and intellectual freedom, but extinguished the sentiment
of nationality and closed almost every sphere of political
activity.   The intellectual cause, which was by no means
unconnected with the political one, was the growing ascend

ancy of Oriental philosophies, which dethroned the active
Stoicism of the early Empire, and placed its ideal of excellence in contemplative virtues and in elaborate puri·
fications.   By this decline of the patriotic sentiment the
progress of the new faith was greatly aided.   In all matters
of religion the opinions of men are governed much more by
their sympathies than by their judgments; and it rarely or
never happens that a religion which is opposed to a strong
national sentiment, as Christianity was in Judea, as Catholicism and Episcopalian Protestantism have been in Scotland,
and as Anglicanism is even now in Ireland, can win the acceptance of the people.

The relations of Christianity to the sentiment of patriot·
ism were from the first very unfortunate.   While the Chris
tians were, for obvious reasons, completely separated from
the national spirit of Judea, they found themselves equally
at variance with the lingering remnants of Roman patriotism.   Rome was to them the power of Antichrist, and its
overthrow the necessary prelude to the millennial reign.
They formed an illegal organisation, directly opposed to the
genius of the Empire, anticipating its speedy destruction,
looking back with something more than despondency to
the fate of the heroes who adorned its past, and refusing
resolutely to participate in those national spectacles which
were the symbols and the expressions of patriotic feeling.
Though scrupulously averse to all rebellion, they rarely concealed their sentiments, and the whole tendency of their
teaching was to withdraw men as far as possible both from
the functions and the enthusiasm of public life.   It was at
once their confession and their boast, that no interests were
more indifferent to them than those of their country.[1]   They
regarded the lawfulness of taking arms as very questionable,

---

[1] 'Nec alla res aliena magis quam publica.'—Tertullian, *Apol.*
ch. xxxviii.

and all those proud and aspiring qualities that constitute the distinctive beauty of the soldier's character as emphatically unchristian. Their home and their interests were in another world, and, provided only they were unmolested in their worship, they avowed with frankness, long after the Empire had become Christian, that it was a matter of indifference to them under what rule they lived.[1] Asceticism, drawing all the enthusiasm of Christendom to the desert life, and elevating as an ideal the extreme and absolute abnegation of all patriotism,[2] formed the culmination of the movement, and was undoubtedly one cause of the downfall of the Roman Empire.

There are, probably, few subjects on which popular judgments are commonly more erroneous than upon the relations

[1] 'Quid interest sub cujus imperio vivat homo moriturus, si illi qui imperant, ad impia et iniqua non cogant.'—St. Aug. *De Civ. Dei,* v. 17.

[2] St. Jerome declares that 'Monachum in patria sua perfectum esse non posse, perfectum autem esse nolle delinquere est.' — *Ep.* xiv. Dean Milman well says of a later period : 'According to the monastic view of Christianity, the total abandonment of the world, with all its ties and duties, as well as its treasures, its enjoyments, and objects of ambition, advanced rather than diminished the hopes of salvation. Why should they fight for a perishing world, from which it was better to be estranged ? . . . It is singular, indeed, that while we have seen the Eastern monks turned into fierce undisciplined soldiers, periling their own lives and shedding the blood of others without remorse, in assertion of some shadowy shade of orthodox expression, hardly anywhere do we find them asserting their liberties or their religion with intrepid resistance. Hatred of heresy was a more stirring motive than the dread or the danger of Islamism. After the first defeats the Christian mind was still further prostrated by the common notion that the invasion was a just and heaven-commissioned visitation ; . . . resistance a vain, almost an impious struggle to avert inevitable punishment.' — Milman's *Latin Christianity,* vol. ii. p. 206. Compare Massillon's famous *Discours au Régiment de Catinat :*—'Ce qu'il y a ici de plus déplorable, c'est que dans une vie rude et pénible, dans des emplois dont les devoirs passent quelquefois la rigueur des cloîtres les plus austères, vous souffrez toujours en vain pour l'autre vie. . . . Dix ans de services ont plus usé votre corps qu'une vie entière de pénitence . . . . un seul jour de ces souffrances, consacré au Seigneur, vous aurait peut-être valu un bonheur éternel.

between positive religions and moral enthusiasm. Religions have, no doubt, a most real power of evoking a latent energy which, without their existence, would never have been called into action; but their influence is on the whole probably more attractive than creative. They supply the channel in which moral enthusiasm flows, the banner under which it is enlisted, the mould in which it is cast, the ideal to which it tends. The first idea which the phrase 'a very good man' would have suggested to an early Roman would probably have been that of great and distinguished patriotism, and the passion and interest of such a man in his country's cause were in direct proportion to his moral elevation. Ascetic Christianity decisively diverted moral enthusiasm into another channel, and the civic virtues, in consequence, necessarily declined. The extinction of all public spirit, the base treachery and corruption pervading every department of the Government, the cowardice of the army, the despicable frivolity of character that led the people of Treves, when fresh from their burning city, to call for theatres and circuses, and the people of Roman Carthage to plunge wildly into the excitement of the chariot races, on the very day when their city succumbed beneath the Vandal;[1] all these things coexisted with extraordinary displays of ascetic and of missionary devotion. The genius and the virtue that might have defended the Empire were engaged in fierce disputes about the Pelagian controversy, at the very time when Alaric was encircling Rome with his armies,[2] and there was no subtlety of theological metaphysics which did not kindle a deeper interest in the Christian leaders than the throes of their expiring country. The moral enthusiasm that in other days would have fired the armies of Rome with

[1] See a very striking passage in Salvian, *De Gubern. Div.* lib. vi.

[2] Chateaubriand very truly says, 'qu'Orose et saint Augustin étoient plus occupés du schisme de Pélage que de la désolation de l'Afrique et des Gaules.'—*Études histor.* vime discours, 2de partie. The remark might certainly be extended much further.

an invincible valour, impelled thousands to abandon their country and their homes, and consume the weary hours in a long routine of useless and horrible macerations.   When the Goths had captured Rome, St. Augustine, as we have seen, pointed with a just pride to the Christian Church, which remained an unviolated sanctuary during the horrors of the sack, as a proof that a new spirit of sanctity and of reverence had descended upon the world.   The Pagan, in his turn, pointed to what he deemed a not less significant fact—the golden statues of Valour and of Fortune were melted down to pay the ransom to the conquerors.[1]   Many of the Christians contemplated with an indifference that almost amounted to complacency what they regarded as the predicted ruin of the city of the fallen gods.[2]   When the Vandals swept over Africa, the Donatists, maddened by the persecution of the orthodox, received them with open arms, and contributed their share to that deadly blow.[3]   The immortal pass of Thermopylæ was surrendered without a struggle to the Goths.   A Pagan writer accused the monks of having betrayed it.[4]   It is more probable that they had absorbed or diverted the heroism that in other days would have defended it.   The conquest, at a later date, of Egypt, by the Mohammedans, was in a great measure due to an invitation from the persecuted Monophysites.[5]   Subsequent religious wars

[1] Zosimus, *Hist.* v. 41. This was on the first occasion when Rome was menaced by Alaric.

[2] See Merivale's *Conversion of the Northern Nations*, pp. 207–210.

[3] See Sismondi, *Hist. de la Chute de l'Empire romain*, tome i. p. 230.

[4] Eunapius.   There is no other authority for the story of the treachery, which is not believed by Gibbon.

[5] Sismondi, *Hist. de la Chute de l'Empire romain*, tome ii. pp. 52–54; Milman, *Hist. of Latin Christianity*, vol. ii. p. 213.   The Monophysites were greatly afflicted because, after the conquest, the Mohammedans tolerated the orthodox believers as well as themselves, and were unable to appreciate the distinction between them.   In Gaul, the orthodox clergy favoured the invasions of the Franks, who, alone of the barbarian conquerors

have again and again exhibited the same phenomenon. The treachery of a religionist to his country no longer argued an absence of all moral feeling. It had become compatible with the deepest religious enthusiasm, and with all the courage of a martyr.

It is somewhat difficult to form a just estimate of how far the attitude assumed by the Church towards the barbarian invaders has on the whole proved beneficial to mankind. The Empire, as we have seen, had long been, both morally and politically, in a condition of manifest decline; its fall, though it might have been retarded, could scarcely have been averted, and the new religion, even in its most superstitious form, while it did much to displace, did also much to elicit moral enthusiasm. It is impossible to deny that the Christian priesthood contributed very materially, both by their charity and by their arbitration, to mitigate the calamities that accompanied the dissolution of the Empire;[1] and it is equally impossible to doubt that their political attitude greatly increased their power for good. Standing between the conflicting forces, almost indifferent to the issue, and notoriously exempt from the passions of the combat, they obtained with the conqueror, and used for the benefit of the conquered, a degree of influence they would never have possessed, had they been regarded as Roman patriots. Their attitude, however, marked a complete, and, as it has proved, a permanent, change in the position assigned to patriotism in the moral scale. It

---

of Gaul, were Catholics, and St. Aprunculus was obliged to fly, the Burgundians desiring to kill him on account of his suspected connivance with the invaders. (Greg. *Tur.* ii. 23.)

[1] Dean Milman says of the Church, 'if treacherous to the interests of the Roman Empire, it was true to those of mankind.'— *Hist. of Christianity*, vol. iii. p. 48. So Gibbon: 'If the decline of the Roman Empire was hastened by the conversion of Constantine, the victorious religion broke the violence of the fall and mollified the ferocious temper of the conquerors.' —Ch. xxxviii.

has occasionally happened in later times, that churches have found it for their interest to appeal to this sentiment in their conflict with opposing creeds, or that patriots have found the objects of churchmen in harmony with their own; and in these cases a fusion of theological and patriotic feeling has taken place, in which each has intensified the other.   Such has been the effect of the conflict between the Spaniards and the Moors, between the Poles and the Russians, between the Scotch Puritans and the English Episcopalians, between the Irish Catholics and the English Protestants.   But patriotism itself, as a duty, has never found any place in Christian ethics, and strong theological feeling has usually been directly hostile to its growth.   Ecclesiastics have, no doubt, taken a very large share in political affairs, but this has been in most cases solely with the object of wresting them into conformity with ecclesiastical designs; and no other body of men have so uniformly sacrificed the interests of their country to the interests of their class.   For the repugnance between the theological and the patriotic spirit, three reasons may, I think, be assigned.   The first is that tendency of strong religious feeling to divert the mind from all terrestrial cares and passions, of which the ascetic life was the extreme expression, but which has always, under different forms, been manifested in the Church.   The second arises from the fact that each form of theological opinion embodies itself in a visible and organised church, with a government, interest, and policy of its own, and a frontier often intersecting rather than following national boundaries; and these churches attract to themselves the attachment and devotion that would naturally be bestowed upon the country and its rulers.   The third reason is, that the saintly and the heroic characters, which represent the ideals of religion and of patriotism, are generically different; for although they have no doubt many common elements of virtue, the distinctive excellence of each is derived from a proportion or disposition of qualities altogether different from that of the other.[1]

Before dismissing this very important revolution in moral history, I may add two remarks. In the first place, we may observe that the relation of the two great schools of morals to active and political life has been completely changed. Among the ancients, the Stoics, who regarded virtue and vice as generically different from all other things, participated actively in public life, and made this participation one of the first of duties; while the Epicureans, who resolved virtue into utility, and esteemed happiness its supreme motive, abstained from public life, and taught their disciples to neglect it. Asceticism followed the Stoical school in teaching that virtue and happiness are generically different things; but it was at the same time eminently unfavourable to civic virtue. On the other hand, that great industrial movement which has arisen since the abolition of slavery, and which has always been essentially utilitarian in its spirit, has been one of the most active and influential elements of political progress. This change, though, as far as I know, entirely unnoticed by historians, constitutes, I believe, one of the great landmarks of moral history.

The second observation I would make relates to the estimate we form of the value of patriotic actions. However

---

[1] Observe with what a fine perception St. Augustine notices the essentially unchristian character of the moral dispositions to which the greatness of Rome was due. He quotes the sentence of Sallust: 'Civitas, incredibile memoratu est, adeptâ libertate quantum brevi creverit, tanta cupido gloriæ incesserat; and adds: 'Ista ergo laudis aviditas et cupido gloriæ multa illa miranda fecit, laudabil'a scilicet atque gloriosa secundum homi-

num existimationem . . . causa honoris, laudis et gloriæ consuluerunt patriæ, in qua ipsam gloriam requirebant, salutemque ejus saluti suæ præponere non dubitaverunt, pro isto uno vitio, id est, amore laudis, pecuniæ cupiditatem et multa alia vitia comprimentes. . . Quid aliud amarent quam gloriam, qua volebant etiam post mortem tanquam vivere in ore laudantium? —De Civ. Dei, v. 12–13.

mucn historians may desire to extend their researches to the private and domestic virtues of a people, civic virtues are always those which must appear most prominently in their pages. History is concerned only with large bodies of men. The systems of philosophy or religion which produce splendid results on the great theatre of public life are fully and easily appreciated, and readers and writers are both liable to give them very undue advantages over those systems which do not favour civic virtues, but exercise their beneficial influence in the more obscure fields of individual self-culture, domestic morals, or private charity. If valued by the self-sacrifice they imply, or by their effects upon human happiness, these last rank very high, but they scarcely appear in history, and they therefore seldom obtain their due weight in historical comparisons. Christianity has, I think, suffered peculiarly from this cause. Its moral action has always been much more powerful upon individuals than upon societies, and the spheres in which its superiority over other religions is most incontestable, are precisely those which history is least capable of realising.

In attempting to estimate the moral condition of the Roman and Byzantine Empires during the Christian period, and before the old civilisation had been dissolved by the barbarian or Mohammedan invasions, we must continually bear this last consideration in mind. We must remember, too, that Christianity had acquired an ascendancy among nations which were already deeply tainted by the inveterate vices of a corrupt and decaying civilisation, and also that many of the censors from whose pages we are obliged to form our estimate of the age were men who judged human frailties with all the fastidiousness of ascetics, and who expressed their judgments with all the declamatory exaggeration of the pulpit. Modern critics will probably not lay much stress upon the relapse of the Christians into the ordinary dress and usages of the luxurious society about them, upon

the ridicule thrown by Christians on those who still adhered
to the primitive austerity of the sect, or upon the fact that
multitudes who were once mere nominal Pagans had become
mere nominal Christians.   We find, too, a frequent disposition on the part of moralists to single out some new form of
luxury, or some trivial custom which they regarded as indeco-
rous, for the most extravagant denunciation, and to magnify
its importance in a manner which in a later age it is difficult
even to understand.   Examples of this kind may be found
both in Pagan and in Christian writings, and they form an
extremely curious page in the history of morals.   Thus
Juvenal exhausts his vocabulary of invective in denouncing
the atrocious criminality of a certain noble, who in the very
year of his consulship did not hesitate—not, it is true, by
day, but at least in the sight of the moon and of the stars—
with his own hand to drive his own chariot along the public
road.[1]   Seneca was scarcely less scandalised by the atrocious
and, as he thought, unnatural luxury of those who had
adopted the custom of cooling different beverages by mixing
them with snow.[2]   Pliny assures us that the most monstrous
of all criminals was the man who first devised the luxurious
custom of wearing golden rings.[3]   Apuleius was compelled
to defend himself for having eulogised tooth-powder, and he
did so, among other ways, by arguing that nature has justified
this form of propriety, for crocodiles were known periodically
to leave the waters of the Nile, and to lie with open jaws

---

[1] 'Præter majorum cineres atque
    ossa, volucri
Carpento rapitur pinguis Dama-
    sippus et ipse,
Ipse rotam stringit multo suffla-
    mine consul;
Nocte quidem; sed luna videt,
    sed sidera testes
Intendunt oculos.   Finitum tem-
    pus honoris

Quum fuerit, clara Damasippus
    luce flagellum
Sumet.'—Juvenal, *Sat.* viii. 146.

[2] *Nat. Quæst.* iv. 13.   *Ep.* 78.
[3] 'Pessimum vitæ scelus fecit,
qui id [aurum] primus induit di
gitis. . . . quisquis primus instituit
cunctanter id fecit, lævisque mani-
bus, latentibusque induit.'—Plin.
Hist. Nat. xxxiii. 4.

upon the banks, while a certain bird proceeds with its beak
to clean their teeth.[1]   If we were to measure the criminality
of different customs by the vehemence of the patristic denunciations, we might almost conclude that the most atrocious
offence of their day was the custom of wearing false hair,
or dyeing natural hair.   Clement of Alexandria questioned
whether the validity of certain ecclesiastical ceremonies
might not be affected by wigs; for, he asked, when the priest
is placing his hand on the head of the person who kneels
before him, if that hand is resting upon false hair, who is it
he is really blessing?   Tertullian shuddered at the thought
that Christians might have the hair of those who were in hell,
upon their heads, and he found in the tiers of false hair that
were in use a distinct rebellion against the assertion that no
one can add to his stature, and, in the custom of dyeing the
hair, a contravention of the declaration that man cannot
make one hair white or black.   Centuries rolled away.   The
Roman Empire tottered to its fall, and floods of vice and
sorrow overspread the world; but still the denunciations of
the Fathers were unabated.   St. Ambrose, St. Jerome, and
St. Gregory Nazianzen continued with uncompromising vehemence the war against false hair, which Tertullian and
Clement of Alexandria had begun.[2]

But although the vehemence of the Fathers on such trivial
matters might appear at first sight to imply the existence of
a society in which grave corruption was rare, such a conclusion would be totally untrue.   After every legitimate allowance has been made, the pictures of Roman society by Ammianus Marcellinus, of the society of Marseilles, by Salvian,
of the society of Asia Minor, and of Constantinople, by
Chrysostom, as well as the whole tenor of the history, and

---

[1] See a curious passage in his
Apologia.   It should be said that
we have only his own account of
the charges brought against him.

[2] The history of false hair has
been written with much learning
by M. Guerle in his *Éloge des Per-
ruques.*

innumerable incidental notices in the writers, of the time, exhibit a condition of depravity, and especially of degradation, which has seldom been surpassed.[1] The corruption had reached classes and institutions that appeared the most holy. The Agapæ, or love feasts, which formed one of the most touching symbols of Christian unity, had become scenes of drunkenness and of riot. Denounced by the Fathers, condemned by the Council of Laodicea in the fourth century, and afterwards by the Council of Carthage, they lingered as a scandal and an offence till they were finally suppressed by the Council of Trullo, at the end of the seventh century.[2] The commemoration of the martyrs soon degenerated into scandalous dissipation. Fairs were held on the occasion, gross breaches of chastity were frequent, and the annual festival was suppressed on account of the immorality it produced.[3] The ambiguous position of the clergy with reference to marriage already led to grave disorder. In the time of St. Cyprian, before the outbreak of the Decian persecution, it had been common to find clergy professing celibacy, but keeping, under various pretexts, their mistresses in their houses ;[4] and, after Constantine, the complaints on this subject became loud and general.[5] Virgins and monks often lived together in the same house, professing sometimes to share in

---

[1] The fullest view of this age is given in a very learned little work by Peter Erasmus Müller (1797), *De Genio Ævi Theodosiani.* Montfaucon has also devoted two essays to the moral condition of the Eastern world, one of which is given in Jortin's *Remarks on Ecclesiastical History.*

[2] See on these abuses Mosheim, *Eccl. Hist.* (Soame's ed.), vol. i. p. 463; Cave's *Primitive Christianity,* part i. ch. xi.

[3] Cave's *Primitive Christianity,* part i. ch. vii.

[4] *Ep.* lxi.

[5] Evagrius describes with much admiration how certain monks of Palestine, by 'a life wholly excellent and divine,' had so overcome their passions that they were accustomed to bathe with women ; for 'neither sight nor touch, nor a woman's embrace, could make them relapse into their natural condition. Among men they desired to be men, and among women, women.' (*H. E.* i. 21.)

chastity the same bed.[1] Rich widows were surrounded by
swarms of clerical sycophants, who addressed them in tender
diminutives, studied and consulted their every foible, and,
under the guise of piety, lay in wait for their gifts or bequests.[2] The evil attained such a point that a law was
made under Valentinian depriving the Christian priests
and monks of that power of receiving legacies which was
possessed by every other class of the community; and St.
Jerome has mournfully acknowledged that the prohibition
was necessary.[3] Great multitudes entered the Church to
avoid municipal offices;[4] the deserts were crowded with men
whose sole object was to escape from honest labour, and even
soldiers used to desert their colours for the monasteries.[5]

---

[1] These 'mulieres subintro-
ductæ,' as they were called, are
continually noticed by Cyprian,
Jerome, and Chrysostom. See
Müller, *De Genio Ævi Theodosiani*,
and also the *Codex Theod.* xvi. tit.
ii lex 44, with the Comments. Dr.
Todd, in his learned *Life of St.
Patrick* (p. 91), quotes (I shall not
venture to do so) from the *Lives of
the Irish Saints* an extremely curious legend of a kind of contest of
sanctity between St. Scuthinus and
St. Brendan, in which it was clearly
proved that the former had mas-
tered his passions more completely
than the latter. An enthusiast
named Robert d'Arbrisselles is said
in the twelfth century to have revived the custom. (Jortin's *Remarks*, A.D. 1106.)

[2] St. Jerome gives (*Ep.* lii.) an
extremely curious picture of these
clerical flatterers, and several examples of the terms of endearment
they were accustomed to employ.
The tone of flattery which St. Jerome himself, though doubtless
with the purest motives, employs

in his copious correspondence with
his female admirers, is to a modern
layman peculiarly repulsive, and
sometimes verges upon blasphemy.
In his letter to Eustochium, whose
daughter as a nun had become the
'bride of Christ,' he calls the
mother 'Socrus Dei,' the mother-
in-law of God. See, too, the extravagant flatteries of Chrysostom
in his correspondence with Olym-
pias.

[3] 'Pudet dicere sacerdotes ido-
lorum, mimi et aurigæ et scorta
hæreditates capiunt; solis clericis et monachis hoc lege prohibetur, et prohibetur non a perse-
cutoribus, sed a principibus Christianis. Nec de lege conqueror sed
doleo cur meruerimus hanc legem.'
Ep. lii.

[4] See Milman's *Hist. of Early
Christianity*, vol. ii. p. 314.

[5] This was one cause of the
disputes between St. Gregory the
Great and the Emperor Eustace.
St. Chrysostom frequently notices
the opposition of the military and
the monastic spirits.

Noble ladies, pretending a desire to lead a higher life, aban-doned their husbands to live with low-born lovers.[1] Pales-tine, which was soon crowded with pilgrims, had become, in the time of St. Gregory of Nyssa, a hotbed of debauchery.[2] The evil reputation of pilgrimages long continued; and in the eighth century we find St. Boniface writing to the Arch-bishop of Canterbury, imploring the bishops to take some measures to restrain or regulate the pilgrimages of their fellow-countrywomen; for there were few towns in central Europe, on the way to Rome, where English ladies, who started as pilgrims, were not living in open prostitution.[3] The luxury and ambition of the higher prelates, and the pas-sion for amusements of the inferior priests,[4] were bitterly acknowledged. St. Jerome complained that the banquets of many bishops eclipsed in splendour those of the provincial governors, and the intrigues by which they obtained offices, and the fierce partisanship of their supporters, appear in every page of ecclesiastical history.

In the lay world, perhaps the chief characteristic was ex-treme childishness. The moral enthusiasm was greater than it had been in most periods of Paganism, but, being drawn away to the desert, it had little influence upon society. The

---

[1] Hieron. *Ep.* cxxviii.

[2] St. Greg. Nyss. *Ad eund. Hieros.* Some Catholic writers have attempted to throw doubt upon the genuineness of this epistle, but, Dean Milman thinks, with no sufficient reason. Its account of Jerusalem is to some extent corro-borated by St. Jerome. (*Ad Pauli-num, Ep.* xxix.)

[3] 'Præterea non taceo charitati vestræ, quia omnibus servis Dei qui hic vel in Scriptura vel in timore Dei probatissimi esse videntur, displicet quod bonum et honestas et pudici-tia vestræ ecclesiæ illuditur; et aliquod levamentum turpitudinis esset, si prohiberet synodus et principes vestri mulieribus et ve-latis feminis illud iter et frequen-tiam, quam ad Romanam civitatem veniendo et redeundo faciunt, quia magna ex parte pereunt, paucis remeantibus integris. Perpaucæ enim sunt civitates in Longobardia vel in Francia aut in Gallia in qua non sit adultera vel meretrix gene-ris Anglorum, quod scandalum est et turpitudo totius ecclesiæ ves træ.'—(A.D. 745) *Ep.* lxiii.

[4] See Milman's *Latin Chris-tianity,* vol. ii. p. 8.

simple fact that the quarrels between the factions of the chariot races for a long period eclipsed all political, intellectual, and even religious differences, filled the streets again and again with bloodshed, and more than once determined great revolutions in the State, is sufficient to show the extent of the decadence.   Patriotism and courage had almost disappeared, and, notwithstanding the rise of a Belisarius or a Narses, the level of public men was extremely depressed. The luxury of the court, the servility of the courtiers, and the prevailing splendour of dress and of ornament, had attained an extravagant height.   The world grew accustomed to a dangerous alternation of extreme asceticism and gross vice, and sometimes, as in the case of Antioch,[1] the most vicious and luxurious cities produced the most numerous anchorites. There existed a combination of vice and superstition which is eminently prejudicial to the nobility, though not equally detrimental to the happiness, of man.   Public opinion was so low, that very many forms of vice attracted little condemnation and punishment, while undoubted belief in the absolving efficacy of superstitious rites calmed the imagination and allayed the terrors of conscience.   There was more falsehood and treachery than under the Cæsars, but there was much less cruelty, violence, and shamelessness.   There was also less public spirit, less independence of character, less intellectual freedom.

In some respects, however, Christianity had already effected a great improvement.   The gladiatorial games had disappeared from the West, and had not been introduced into Constantinople.   The vast schools of prostitution which had grown up under the name of temples of Venus were suppressed.   Religion, however deformed and debased, was at least no longer a seedplot of depravity, and under the influence of Christianity the effrontery of vice had in a great

---

[1] Tillemont, *Hist. eccl.* tome xi. p. 547.

measure disappeared. The gross and extravagant indecency
of representation, of which we have still examples in the
paintings on the walls, and the signs on many of the portals
of Pompeii; the banquets of rich patricians, served by naked
girls; the hideous excesses of unnatural lust, in which some
of the Pagan emperors had indulged with so much publicity,
were no longer tolerated. Although sensuality was very
general, it was less obtrusive, and unnatural and eccentric
forms had become rare. The presence of a great Church,
which, amid much superstition and fanaticism, still taught a
pure morality, and enforced it by the strongest motives, was
everywhere felt—controlling, strengthening, or overawing.
The ecclesiastics were a great body in the State. The cause
of virtue was strongly organised; it drew to itself the best
men, determined the course of vacillating but amiable natures, and placed some restraint upon the vicious. A bad
man might be insensible to the moral beauties of religion,
but he was still haunted by the recollection of its threaten-
ings. If he emancipated himself from its influence in health
and prosperity, its power returned in periods of sickness or
danger, or on the eve of the commission of some great crime.
If he had nerved himself against all its terrors, he was at least
checked and governed at every turn by the public opinion
which it had created. That total absence of all restraint,
all decency, and all fear and remorse, which had been evinced
by some of the monsters of crime who occupied the Pagan
throne, and which proves most strikingly the decay of the
Pagan religion, was no longer possible. The virtue of the
best Pagans was perhaps of as high an order as that of the
best Christians, though it was of a somewhat different type,
but the vice of the worst Pagans certainly far exceeded that
of the worst Christians. The pulpit had become a powerful
centre of attraction, and charities of many kinds were actively
developed.

The moral effects of the first great outburst of asceticism

so far as we have yet traced them, appear almost unmingled evils. In addition to the essentially distorted ideal of perfection it produced, the simple withdrawal from active life of that moral enthusiasm, which is the leaven of society, was extremely pernicious, and there can be little doubt that to this cause we must in a great degree attribute the conspicuous failure of the Church, for some centuries, to effect any more considerable amelioration in the moral condition of Europe. There were, however, some distinctive excellences springing even from the first phase of asceticism, which, although they do not, as I conceive, suffice to counterbalance these evils, may justly qualify our censure.

The first condition of all really great moral excellence is a spirit of genuine self-sacrifice and self-renunciation. The habits of compromise, moderation, reciprocal self-restraint, gentleness, courtesy, and refinement, which are appropriate to luxurious or utilitarian civilisations, are very favourable to the development of many secondary virtues; but there is in human nature a capacity for a higher and more heroic reach of excellence; which demands very different spheres for its display, accustoms men to far nobler aims, and exercises a far greater attractive influence upon mankind. Imperfect and distorted as was the ideal of the anchorite; deeply, too, as it was perverted by the admixture of a spiritual selfishness, still the example of many thousands, who, in obedience to what they believed to be right, voluntarily gave up every thing that men hold dear, cast to the winds every compromise with enjoyment, and made extreme self-abnegation the very principle of their lives, was not wholly lost upon the world. At a time when increasing riches had profoundly tainted the Church, they taught men 'to love labour more than rest, and ignominy more than glory, and to give more than to receive.'[1] At a time when the passion for ecclesiastical

---

[1] This was enjoined in the rule of St. Paphnutius. See Tillemont, tome x. p. 45.

dignities had become the scandal of the Empire, they systematically abstained from them, teaching, in their quaint but energetic language, that 'there are two classes a monk should especially avoid—bishops and women.'[1]   The very eccentricities of their lives, their uncouth forms, their horrible penances, won the admiration of rude men, and the superstitious reverence thus excited gradually passed to the charity and the self-denial which formed the higher elements of the monastic character. Multitudes of barbarians were converted to Christianity at the sight of St. Simeon Stylites. The hermit, too, was speedily idealised by the popular imagination. The more repulsive features of his life and appearance were forgotten.   He was thought of only as an old man with long white beard and gentle aspect, weaving his mats beneath the palm-trees, while dæmons vainly tried to distract him by their stratagems, and the wild beasts grew tame in his presence, and every disease and every sorrow vanished at his word. The imagination of Christendom, fascinated by this ideal, made it the centre of countless legends, usually very childish, and occasionally, as we have seen, worse than childish, yet full of beautiful touches of human nature, and often conveying admirable moral lessons.[2]   Nursery tales, which first determine the course of the infant imagination, play no inconsiderable part in the history of humanity. In the fable of Psyche—

---

[1] 'Omnimodis monachum fugere debere mulieres et episcopos.' --Cassian, *De Cœnob. Inst.* xi. 17.

[2] We also find now and then, though I think very rarely, intellectual flashes of some brilliancy. Two of them strike me as especially noteworthy. St. Arsenius refused to separate young criminals from communion though he had no hesitation about old men; for he had observed that young men speedily get accustomed and in-different to the state of excommunication, while old men feel continually, and acutely, the separation. (Socrates, iv. 23.   St. Apollonius explained the Egyptian idolatry with the most intelligent rationalism. The ox, he thought, was in the first instance worshipped for its domestic uses; the Nile, because it was the chief cause of the fertility of the soil, &c. (Rufinus, *Hist. Mon.* cap. vii.)

that bright tale of passionate love with which the Greek
mother lulled her child to rest—Pagan antiquity has bequeathed us a single specimen of transcendent beauty, and the
lives of the saints of the desert often exhibit an imagination
different indeed in kind, but scarcely less brilliant in its display. St. Antony, we are told, was thinking one night that
he was the best man in the desert, when it was revealed to
him that there was another hermit far holier than himself. In
the morning he started across the desert to visit this unknown
saint. He met first of all a centaur, and afterwards a little
man with horns and goat's feet, who said that he was a faun;
and these, having pointed out the way, he arrived at last at
his destination. St. Paul the hermit, at whose cell he stopped,
was one hundred and thirteen years old, and, having been
living for a very long period in absolute solitude, he at first
refused to admit the visitor, but at last consented, embraced
him, and began, with a very pardonable curiosity, to question
him minutely about the world he had left; 'whether there
was much new building in the towns, what empire ruled the
world, whether there were any idolaters remaining?' The
colloquy was interrupted by a crow, which came with a loaf
of bread, and St. Paul, observing that during the last sixty
years his daily allowance had been only half a loaf, declared
that this was a proof that he had done right in admitting
Antony. The hermits returned thanks, and sat down together by the margin of a glassy stream. But now a difficulty arose. Neither could bring himself to break the loaf
before the other. St. Paul alleged that St. Antony, being
his guest, should take the precedence; but St. Antony, who
was only ninety years old, dwelt upon the greater age of St.
Paul. So scrupulously polite were these old men, that they
passed the entire afternoon disputing on this weighty question, till at last, when the evening was drawing in, a happy
thought struck them, and, each holding one end of the loaf,
they pulled together. To abridge the story, St. Paul soon

died, and his companion, being a weak old man, was unable
to bury him, when two lions came from the desert and dug
the grave with their paws, deposited the body in it, raised a
loud howl of lamentation, and then knelt down submissively
before St. Antony, to beg a blessing. The authority for this
history is no less a person than St. Jerome, who relates it as
literally true, and intersperses his narrative with severe
reflections on all who might question his accuracy.

The historian Palladius assures us that he heard from
the lips of St. Macarius of Alexandria an account of a pilgrimage which that saint had made, under the impulse of
curiosity, to visit the enchanted garden of Jannes and Jam-
bres, tenanted by dæmons. For nine days Macarius traversed
the desert, directing his course by the stars, and, from time
to time, fixing reeds in the ground, as landmarks for his
return; but this precaution proved useless, for the devils
tore up the reeds, and placed them during the night by the
head of the sleeping saint. As he drew near the garden,
seventy dæmons of various forms came forth to meet him,
and reproached him for disturbing them in their home. St.
Macarius promised simply to walk round and inspect the
wonders of the garden, and then depart without doing it
any injury. He fulfilled his promise, and a journey of twenty
days brought him again to his cell.[1] Other legends are,
however, of a less fantastic nature; and many of them
display, though sometimes in very whimsical forms, a spirit
of courtesy which seems to foreshadow the later chivalry,
and some of them contain striking protests against the very
superstitions that were most prevalent. When St. Macarius
was sick, a bunch of grapes was once given to him; but his
charity impelled him to give them to another hermit, who in
his turn refused to keep them, and at last, having made the
circuit of the entire desert, they were returned to the saint.[2]

---

[1] Palladius, *Hist. Laus.* cap.
xix.

[2] Rufinus, *Hist. Monach.* cap.
xxix.

The same saint, whose usual beverage was putrid water,
never failed to drink wine when set before him by the
hermits he visited, atoning privately for this relaxation,
which he thought the laws of courtesy required, by ab
staining from water for as many days as he had drunk
glasses of wine.[1]   One of his disciples once meeting an
idolatrous priest running in great haste across the desert,
with a great stick in his hand, cried out in a loud voice,
'Where are you going, dæmon?'   The priest, naturally
indignant, beat the Christian severely, and was proceeding
on his way, when he met St. Macarius, who accosted him
so courteously and so tenderly that the Pagan's heart was
touched, he became a convert, and his first act of charity
was to tend the Christian whom he had beaten.[2]   St. Avitus
being on a visit to St. Marcian, this latter saint placed before
him some bread, which Avitus refused to eat, saying that
it was his custom never to touch food till after sunset.   St.
Marcian, professing his own inability to defer his repast,
implored his guest for once to break this custom, and being
refused, exclaimed, 'Alas! I am filled with anguish that you
have come here to see a wise man and a saint, and you see
only a glutton.'   St. Avitus was grieved, and said, 'he
would rather even eat flesh than hear such words,' and
he sat down as desired.   St. Marcian then confessed that his
own custom was the same as that of his brother saint; 'but,'
he added, 'we know that charity is better than fasting; for
charity is enjoined by the Divine law, but fasting is left in
our own power and will.'[3]   St. Epiphanius having invited
St. Hilarius to his cell, placed before him a dish of fowl.
'Pardon me, father,' said St. Hilarius, 'but since I have
become a monk I have never eaten flesh.'   'And I,' said St.
Epiphanius, 'since I have become a monk have never suffered

---

[1] Tillemont, *Hist. eccl.* tome   [2] Ibid. p. 589.
viii. pp. 583, 584.   [3] Theodoret, *Philoth.* cap. iii.

the sun to go down upon my wrath.' 'Your rule,' rejoined
the other, 'is more excellent than mine.'[1] While a rich lady
was courteously fulfilling the duties of hospitality to a monk,
her child, whom she had for this purpose left, fell into a well.
It lay unharmed upon the surface of the water, and afterwards told its mother that it had seen the arms of the saint
sustaining it below.[2]   At a time when it was the custom to
look upon the marriage state with profound contempt, it was
revealed to St. Macarius of Egypt that two married women
in a neighbouring city were more holy than he was. The
saint immediately visited them, and asked their mode of
life, but they utterly repudiated the notion of their sanctity.
'Holy father,' they said, 'suffer us to tell you frankly the
truth. Even this very night we did not shrink from sleeping
with our husbands, and what good works, then, can you
expect from us?' The saint, however, persisted in his in-
quiries, and they then told him their stories. 'We are,' they
said, 'in no way related, but we married two brothers. We
have lived together for fifteen years, without one licentious
or angry word. We have entreated our husbands to let us
leave them, to join the societies of holy virgins, but they
refused to permit us, and we then promised before Heaven
that no worldly word should sully our lips.' 'Of a truth,'
cried St. Macarius, 'I see that God regards not whether one
is virgin or married, whether one is in a monastery or in the
world. He considers only the disposition of the heart, and
gives the Spirit to all who desire to serve Him, whatever
their condition may be.'[3]

I have multiplied these illustrations to an extent that
must, I fear, have already somewhat taxed the patience of
my readers; but the fact that, during a long period of history,
these saintly legends formed the ideals guiding the imagina-

---

[1] *Verba Seniorum.*   [3] Tillemont, tome viii. pp. 594,
[2] Theodoret, *Philoth.* cap. ii.   595.

tion and reflecting the moral sentiment of the Christian
world, gives them an importance far beyond their intrinsic
value.   Before dismissing the saints of the desert, there is
one other class of legends to which I desire to advert.   I
mean those which describe the connection between saints
and the animal world.   These legends are, I think, worthy of
special notice in moral history, as representing the first,
and at the same time one of the most striking efforts ever
made in Christendom to inculcate a feeling of kindness and
pity towards the brute creation.   In Pagan antiquity, considerable steps had been made to raise this form of humanity
to a recognised branch of ethics.   The way had been prepared by numerous anecdotes growing for the most part
out of simple ignorance of natural history, which all tended
to diminish the chasm between men and animals, by representing the latter as possessing to a very high degree both
moral and rational qualities.   Elephants, it was believed,
were endowed not only with reason and benevolence, but
also with reverential feelings.   They worshipped the sun and
moon, and in the forests of Mauritania they were accustomed
to assemble every new moon, at a certain river, to perform
religious rites.[1]   The hippopotamus taught men the medicinal
value of bleeding, being accustomed, when affected by ple-
thory, to bleed itself with a thorn, and afterwards close the
wound with slime.[2]   Pelicans committed suicide to feed their
young; and bees, when they had broken the laws of their
sovereign.[3]   A temple was erected at Sestos to commemorate
the affection of an eagle which loved a young girl, and upon
her death cast itself in despair into the flames by which her
body was consumed.[4]   Numerous anecdotes are related of

[1] Pliny, *Hist. Nat.* viii. 1.
Many anecdotes of elephants are
collected viii. 1–12.   See, too,
Dion Cassius, xxxix. 38.
[2] Pliny, viii. 40.
[3] Donne's *Biathanatos*, p. 22.

This habit of bees is mentioned by
St. Ambrose.   The pelican, as is
well known, afterwards became an
emblem of Christ.
[4] Plin. *Hist. Nat.* x. 6.

faithful dogs which refused to survive their masters, and one of these had, it was said, been transformed into the dog-star.[1] The dolphin, especially, became the subject of many beautiful legends, and its affection for its young, for music, and above all for little children, excited the admiration not only of the populace, but of the most distinguished naturalists.[2]   Many philosophers ascribed to animals a rational soul, like that of man.   According to the Pythagoreans, human souls transmigrate after death into animals.   According to the Stoics and others, the souls of men and animals were alike parts of the all-pervading Divine Spirit that animates the world.[3]

We may even find traces from an early period of a certain measure of legislative protection for animals.   By a very natural process, the ox, as a principal agent in agriculture, and therefore a kind of symbol of civilisation, was in many different countries regarded with a peculiar reverence.   The sanctity attached to it in Egypt is well known.   That tenderness to animals, which is one of the most beautiful features in the Old Testament writings, shows itself, among other ways, in the command not to muzzle the ox that treadeth out the corn, or to yoke together the ox and the ass.[4]   Among the early Romans the same feeling was carried so far, that for a long time it was actually a capital offence to slaughter an ox, that animal being pronounced, in a special sense, the

---

[1] A long list of legends about dogs is given by Legendre, in the very curious chapter on animals, in his *Traité de l'Opinion*, tome i. pp. 308–327.

[2] Pliny tells some extremely pretty stories of this kind. (*Hist. Nat.* ix. 8–9.)   See, too, Aulus Gellius, xvi. 19.   The dolphin, on account of its love for its young, became a common symbol of Christ among the early Christians.

[3] A very full account of the opinions, both of ancient and modern philosophers, concerning the souls of animals, is given by Bayle, *Dict.* arts. 'Pereira E,' 'Rorarius K.'

[4] The Jewish law did not confine its care to oxen.   The reader will remember the touching provision, 'Thou shalt not seethe a kid in his mother's milk' (Deut. xiv. 21) ; and the law forbidding men to take a parent bird that was sitting on its young or on its eggs (Deut. xxii. 6, 7.)

fellow-labourer of man.[1] A similar law is said to have in early times existed in Greece.[2] The beautiful passage in which the Psalmist describes how the sparrow could find a shelter and a home in the altar of the temple, was as applicable to Greece as to Jerusalem. The sentiment of Xenocrates who, when a bird pursued by a hawk took refuge in his breast, caressed and finally released it, saying to his disciples, that a good man should never give up a suppliant,[3] was believed to be shared by the gods, and it was regarded as an act of impiety to disturb the birds who had built their nests beneath the porticoes of the temple.[4] A case is related of a child who was even put to death on account of an act of aggravated cruelty to birds.[5]

The general tendency of nations, as they advance from a rude and warlike to a refined and peaceful condition, from the stage in which the realising powers are faint and dull, to that in which they are sensitive and vivid, is undoubtedly to become more gentle and humane in their actions; but this, like all other general tendencies in history, may be counteracted or modified by many special circumstances. The law I

[1] 'Cujus tanta fuit apud antiquos veneratio, ut tam capital esset bovem necuisse quam civem.'—Columella, lib. vi. in proœm.' 'Hic socius hominum in rustico opere et Cereris minister. Ab hoc antiqui manus ita abstinere voluerunt ut capite sanxerint si quis occidisset.—Varro, De Re Rustic. lib. ii. cap. v.

[2] See Legendre, tome ii. p. 338. The sword with which the priest sacrificed the ox was afterwards pronounced accursed. (Ælian, Hist. Var. lib. viii. cap. iii.)

[3] Diog. Laërt. Xenocrates.

[4] There is a story told by Herodotus (i. 157–159) of an ambassador who was sent by his fellow-countrymen to consult an oracle at Miletus about a suppliant who had taken refuge with the Cymæans and was demanded with menace by his enemies. The oracle, being bribed, enjoined the surrender. The ambassador on leaving, with seeming carelessness disturbed the sparrows under the portico of the temple, when the voice from behind the altar denounced his impiety for disturbing the guests of the gods. The ambassador replied with an obvious and withering retort. Ælian says (Hist. Var.) that the Athenians condemned to death a boy for killing a sparrow that had taken refuge in the temple of Æsculapius.

[5] Quintilian, Inst. v. 9.

have mentioned about oxen was obviously one of those that belong to a very early stage of progress, when legislators are labouring to form agricultural habits among a warlike and nomadic people.[1]   The games in which the slaughter of animals bore so large a part, having been introduced but a little before the extinction of the republic, did very much to arrest or retard the natural progress of humane sentiments. In ancient Greece, besides the bull-fights of Thessaly, the combats of quails and cocks[2] were favourite amusements, and were much encouraged by the legislators, as furnishing examples of valour to the soldiers.   The colossal dimensions of the Roman games, the circumstances that favoured them, and the overwhelming interest they speedily excited, I have described in a former chapter. We have seen, however, that, notwithstanding the gladiatorial shows, the standard of humanity towards men was considerably raised during the Empire. It is also well worthy of notice that, notwithstanding

---

[1] In the same way we find several chapters in the *Zendavesta* about the criminality of injuring dogs ; which is explained by the great importance of shepherd's dogs to a pastoral people.

[2] On the origin of Greek cock-fighting, see Ælian, *Hist. Var.* ii. 28. Many particulars about it are given by Athenæus. Chrysippus maintained that cock-fighting was the final cause of cocks, these birds being made by Providence in order to inspire us by the example of their courage. (Plutarch, *De Repug. Stoic.*) The Greeks do not. however, appear to have known 'cock-throwing,' the favourite English game of throwing a stick called a 'cock-stick' at cocks.   It was a very ancient and very popular amusement, and was practised especially on Shrove Tuesday, and by school-boys. Sir Thomas More

had been famous for his skill in it. (Strutt's *Sports and Pastimes*, p. 283.) Three origins of it have been given :—1st, that in the Danish wars the Saxons failed to surprise a certain city in consequence of the crowing of cocks, and had in consequence a great hatred of that bird ; 2nd, that the cocks (*galli*) were special representatives of Frenchmen, with whom the English were constantly at war : and 3rd, that they were connected with the denial of St. Peter.   As Sir Charles Sedley said :—

'Mayst thou be punished for St.
    Peter's crime,
And on Shrove Tuesday perish in
    thy prime.'
Knight's *Old England*, vol. ii. p 126.

the passion for the combats of wild beasts, Roman literature
and the later literature of the nations subject to Rome abound
in delicate touches displaying in a very high degree a sensitiveness to the feelings of the animal world.   This tender
interest in animal life is one of the most distinctive features
of the poetry of Virgil.   Lucretius, who rarely struck the
chords of pathos, had at a still earlier period drawn a very
beautiful picture of the sorrows of the bereaved cow, whose
calf had been sacrificed upon the altar.[1]   Plutarch mentions,
incidentally, that he could never bring himself to sell, in its
old age, the ox which had served him faithfully in the time
of its strength.[2]   Ovid expressed a similar sentiment with an
almost equal emphasis.[3]   Juvenal speaks of a Roman lady
with her eyes filled with tears on account of the death of a
sparrow.[4]   Apollonius of Tyana, on the ground of humanity,
refused, even when invited by a king, to participate in the
chase.[5]   Arrian, the friend of Epictetus, in his book upon

---

[1] *De Natura Rerum*, lib. ii.
[2] *Life of Marc. Cato.*
[3] ' Quid meruere boves, animal sine
      fraude dolisque,
    Innocuum, simplex, natum tole-
      rare labores ?
    Immemor est demum nec fru-
      gum munere dignus.
    Qui potuit curvi dempto modo
      pondere aratri
    Ruricolam   mactare   suum.'—
        Metamorph. xv. 120–124.
      ' Cujus
    Turbavit nitidos extinctus pas-
      ser ocellos.'
                 Juvenal, *Sat.* vi. 7–8.

There is a little poem in Catullus
(iii.) to console his mistress upon
the death of her favourite sparrow ;
and Martial more than once alludes to the pets of the Roman
ladies.

Compare the charming de-
scription of the Prioress, in Chau-
cer :—

'She was so charitable and so
  pitous,
She wolde wepe if that she saw a
  mous
Caught in a trappe, if it were ded
  or bledde.
Of smale houndes had she that
  she fedde
With rosted flesh and milke and
  wastel brede,
But sore wept she if one of them
  were dede,
Or if men smote it with a yerde
  smert :
And all was conscience and tendre
  herte.'
Prologue to the ' Canterbury Tales.

[5] Philost. *Apol.* i. 38.

coursing, anticipated the beautiful picture which Addison has drawn of the huntsman refusing to sacrifice the life of the captured hare which had given him so much pleasure in its flight.[1]

These touches of feeling, slight as they may appear, indi cate, I think, a vein of sentiment such as we should scarcely have expected to find coexisting with the gigantic slaughter of the amphitheatre. The progress, however, was not only one of sentiment—it was also shown in distinct and definite teaching. Pythagoras and Empedocles were quoted as the founders of this branch of ethics. The moral duty of kindness to animals was in the first instance based upon a dogmatic assertion of the transmigration of souls, and, the doctrine that animals are within the circle of human duty being thus laid down, subsidiary considerations of humanity were alleged. The rapid growth of the Pythagorean school, in the latter days of the Empire, made these considerations familiar to the people.[2] Porphyry elaborately advocated, and even Seneca for a time practised, abstinence from flesh. But the most remarkable figure in this movement is unquestionably Plutarch. Casting aside the dogma of transmigration, or at least speaking of it only as a doubtful conjecture, he places the duty of kindness to animals on the broad ground of the affections, and he urges that duty with an emphasis and a detail to which no adequate parallel can, I believe, be found in the Christian writings for at least seventeen hundred years. He condemns absolutely the games of the amphitheatre,

---

[1] See the curious chapter in his Κυνηγετικός, xvi. and compare it with No. 116 in the Spectator.

[2] In his De Abstinentia Carnis. The controversy between Origen and Celsus furnishes us with a very curious illustration of the extravagances into which some Pagans of the third century fell about animals. Celsus objected to the Christian doctrine about the position of men in the universe, that many of the animals were at least the equals of men both in reason, religious feeling, and know ledge. (Orig. Cont. Cels. lib. iv.)

dwells with great force upon the effect of such spectacles in hardening the character, enumerates in detail, and denounces with unqualified energy, the refined cruelties which gastronomic fancies had produced, and asserts in the strongest language that every man has duties to the animal world as truly as to his fellow-men.[1]

If we now pass to the Christian Church, we shall find that little or no progress was at first made in this sphere. Among the Manicheans, it is true, the mixture of Oriental notions was shown in an absolute prohibition of animal food, and abstinence from this food was also frequently practised upon totally different grounds by the orthodox. One or two of the Fathers have also mentioned with approbation the humane counsels of the Pythagoreans.[2] But, on the other hand, the doctrine of transmigration was emphatically repudiated by the Catholics; the human race was isolated, by the scheme of redemption, more than ever from all other races; and in the range and circle of duties inculcated by the early Fathers those to animals had no place. This is indeed the one form of humanity which appears more prominently in the Old Testament than in the New. The many beautiful traces of it in the former, which indicate a sentiment,[3] even where they do not very strictly define a duty, gave way before an

---

[1] These views are chiefly defended in his two tracts on eating flesh. Plutarch has also recurred to the subject, incidentally, in several other works, especially in a very beautiful passage in his *Life of Marcus Cato*.

[2] See, for example, a striking passage in Clem. Alex. *Strom.* lib. ii. St. Clement imagines Pythagoras had borrowed his sentiments on this subject from Moses.

[3] There is, I believe, no record of any wild beast combats existing among the Jews, and the rabbinical

writers have been remarkable for the great emphasis with which they inculcated the duty of kindness to animals. See some passages from them, cited in Wollaston, *Religion of Nature*, sec. ii., note. Maimonides believed in a future life for animals, to recompense them for their sufferings here. (Bayle, *Dict.* art, 'Rorarius D.') There is a curious collection of the opinions of different writers on this last point in a little book called the *Rights of Animals*, by William Drummond (London, 1838), pp. 197-205.

ardent philanthropy which regarded human interests as the one end, and the relations of man to his Creator as the one question, of life, and dismissed somewhat contemptuously, as an idle sentimentalism, notions of duty to animals.[1] A refined and subtle sympathy with animal feeling is indeed rarely found among those who are engaged very actively in the affairs of life, and it was not without a meaning or a reason that Shakespeare placed that exquisitely pathetic analysis of the sufferings of the wounded stag, which is perhaps its most perfect poetical expression, in the midst of the morbid dreamings of the diseased and melancholy Jacques.

But while what are called the rights of animals had no place in the ethics of the Church, a feeling of sympathy with the irrational creation was in some degree inculcated indirectly by the incidents of the hagiology. It was very natural that the hermit, living in the lonely deserts of the East, or in the vast forests of Europe, should come into an intimate connection with the animal world, and it was no less natural that the popular imagination, when depicting the hermit life, should make this connection the centre of many picturesque and sometimes touching legends. The birds, it was said, stooped in their flight at the old man's call; the lion and the hyena crouched submissively at his feet; his heart, which was closed to all human interests, expanded freely at the sight of some suffering animal; and something of his own sanctity descended to the companions of his solitude and the objects of his miracles. The wild beasts attended St. Theon when he walked abroad, and the saint rewarded them by giving them drink out of his well. An Egyptian hermit had made a beautiful garden in the desert, and used to sit beneath the palm-trees while a lion ate fruit from his hand. When

---

[1] Thus St. Paul (1 Cor. ix. 9) turned aside the precept, 'Thou shalt not muzzle the mouth of the ox that treadeth out the corn,' from its natural meaning, with the contemptuous question. 'Doth God take care for oxen?'

St. Pœmen was shivering in a winter night, a lion crouched beside him, and became his covering. Lions buried St. Paul the hermit and St. Mary of Egypt. They appear in the legends of St. Jerome, St. Gerasimus, St. John the Silent, St. Simeon, and many others. When an old and feeble monk, named Zosimas, was on his journey to Cæsarea, with an ass which bore his possessions, a lion seized and devoured the ass, but, at the command of the saint, the lion itself carried the burden to the city gates. St. Helenus called a wild ass from its herd to bear his burden through the wilderness. The same saint, as well as St. Pachomius, crossed the Nile on the back of a crocodile, as St. Scuthinus did the Irish Channel on a sea monster. Stags continually accompanied saints upon their journeys, bore their burdens, ploughed their fields, revealed their relics. The hunted stag was especially the theme of many picturesque legends. A Pagan, named Branchion, was once pursuing an exhausted stag, when it took refuge in a cavern, whose threshold no inducement could persuade the hounds to cross. The astonished hunter entered, and found himself in presence of an old hermit, who at once protected the fugitive and converted the pursuer. In the legends of St. Eustachius and St. Hubert, Christ is represented as having assumed the form of a hunted stag, which turned upon its pursuer, with a crucifix glittering on its brow, and, addressing him with a human voice, converted him to Christianity. In the full frenzy of a chase, hounds and stag stopped and knelt down together to venerate the relics of St. Fingar. On the festival of St. Regulus, the wild stags assembled at the tomb of the saint, as the ravens used to do at that of St. Apollinar of Ravenna. St. Erasmus was the special protector of oxen, and they knelt down voluntarily before his shrine. St. Antony was the protector of hogs, who were usually introduced into his pictures. St. Bridget kept pigs, and a wild boar came from the forest to subject itself to her rule. A horse foreshadowed by its lamentations the death of St. Columba. The three companions of St. Colman were a cock, a mouse, and a fly. The cock announced the hour of devotion, the mouse bit the ear of the drowsy saint till he got up, and if in the course of his studies he was afflicted by any wandering thoughts, or called away to other business, the fly alighted on the line where he had left off, and kept the place. Legends, not without a certain whimsical beauty, described the moral qualities existing in animals. A hermit was accustomed to share his supper with a wolf, which, one evening entering the cell before the return of the master, stole a loaf of bread. Struck with remorse, it was a week before it ventured again to visit the cell, and when it did so, its head hung down, and its whole demeanour manifested the most profound contrition. The hermit 'stroked with a gentle hand its bowed down head,' and gave it a double portion as a token of forgiveness. A lioness knelt down with lamentations before another saint, and then led him to its cub, which was blind, but which received its sight at the prayer of the saint. Next day the lioness returned, bearing the skin of a wild beast as a mark of its gratitude. Nearly the same thing happened to St. Macarius of Alexandria; a hyena knocked at his door, brought its young, which was blind, and which the saint restored to sight, and repaid the obligation soon afterwards by bringing a fleece of wool. 'O hyena!' said the saint, 'how did you obtain this fleece? you must have stolen and eaten a sheep.' Full of shame, the hyena hung its head down, but persisted in offering its gift, which, however, the holy man refused to receive till the hyena 'had sworn' to cease for the future to rob. The hyena bowed its head in token of its acceptance of the oath, and St. Macarius afterwards gave the fleece to St. Melania. Other legends simply speak of the sympathy between saints and the irrational world. The birds came at the call of St. Cuthbert, and a dead bird was resuscitated by his prayer. When St. Aengussius, in felling wood, had cut his hand, the birds gathered round, and with loud cries lamented his misfortune. A little bird, struck down and mortally wounded by a hawk, fell at the feet of St. Kieranus, who shed tears as he looked upon its torn breast, and offered up a prayer, upon which the bird was instantly healed.[1]

Many hundreds, I should perhaps hardly exaggerate were I to say many thousands, of legends of this kind exist in the lives of the saints. Suggested in the first instance by that desert life which was at once the earliest phase of monachism and one of the earliest sources of Christian mythology, strengthened by the symbolism which represented different virtues and vices under the forms of animals, and by the reminiscences of the rites and the superstitions of Paganism, the connection between men and animals became the key-note of an infinite variety of fantastic tales. In our eyes they may appear extravagantly puerile, yet it will scarcely, I hope, be necessary to apologise for introducing them into what purports to be a grave work, when it is remembered that for many centuries they were universally accepted by mankind, and were so interwoven with all local traditions, and with all the associations of education, that they at once determined and reflected the inmost feelings of the heart. Their tendency to create a certain feeling of sympathy towards animals is manifest, and this is probably the utmost

---

[1] I have taken these illustrations from the collection of hermit literature in Rosweyde, from different volumes of the Bollandists, from the *Dialogues* of Sulpicius Severus, and from what is perhaps the most interesting of all collections of saintly legends, Colgan's *Acta Sanctorum Hiberniæ.* M. Alfred Maury, in his most valuable work, *Légendes pieuses du Moyen Age,* has examined minutely the part played by animals in symbolising virtues and vices, and has shown the way in which the same incidents were repeated, with slight variations, in different legends. M. de Montalembert has devoted what is probably the most beautiful chapter of his *Moines d'Occident* ('Les Moines et la Nature') to the relations of monks to the animal world; but the numerous legends he cites are all, with one or two exceptions, different from those I have given.

the Catholic Church has done in that direction.[1] A very few authentic instances may, indeed, be cited of saints whose natural gentleness of disposition was displayed in kindness to the animal world. Of St. James of Venice—an obscure saint of the thirteenth century—it is told that he was accustomed to buy and release the birds with which Italian boys used to play by attaching them to strings, saying that 'he pitied the little birds of the Lord,' and that his 'tender charity recoiled from all cruelty, even to the most diminutive of animals.'[2] St. Francis of Assisi was a more conspicuous example of the same spirit. 'If I could only be presented to the emperor,' he used to say, 'I would pray him, for the love of God, and of me, to issue an edict prohibiting any one from catching or imprisoning my sisters the larks, and ordering that all who have oxen or asses should at Christmas feed them particularly well.' A crowd of legends turning upon this theme were related of him. A wolf, near Gubbio, being adjured by him, promised to abstain from eating sheep, placed its paw in the hand of the saint to ratify the promise, and was afterwards fed from house to house by the inhabitants of the city. A crowd of birds, on another occasion, came to hear the saint preach, as fish did to hear St. Antony of Padua. A falcon awoke him at his hour of prayer. A grasshopper encouraged him by her melody to sing praises to God. The noisy swallows kept silence when he began to teach.[3]

[1] Chateaubriand speaks, however (*Études historiques*, étude vime, 1re partie), of an old Gallic law, forbidding to throw a stone at an ox attached to the plough, or to make its yoke too tight.

[2] Bollandists, May 31. Leonardo da Vinci is said to have had the same fondness for buying and releasing caged birds, and (to go back a long way) Pythagoras to have purchased one day, near Metapontus, from some fishermen all the fish in their net, that he might have the pleasure of releasing them. (Apuleius, *Apologia*.)

[3] See these legends collected by Hase (*St. Francis. Assisi*). It is said of Cardinal Bellarmine that he used to allow vermin to bite him, saying, 'We shall have heaven to reward us for our sufferings, but these poor creatures have nothing but the enjoyment of this present life.' (Bayle, *Dict. philos.* art. Bellarmine.')

On the whole, however, Catholicism has done very little
to inculcate humanity to animals. The fatal vice of theologians, who have always looked upon others solely through
the medium of their own special dogmatic views, has been
an obstacle to all advance in this direction. The animal
world, being altogether external to the scheme of redemption,
was regarded as beyond the range of duty, and the belief
that we have any kind of obligation to its members has never
been inculcated—has never, I believe, been even admitted—by
Catholic theologians. In the popular legends, and in the
recorded traits of individual amiability, it is curious to observe how constantly those who have sought to inculcate
kindness to animals have done so by endeavouring to associate them with something distinctively Christian. The
legends I have noticed glorified them as the companions of
the saints. The stag was honoured as especially commissioned to reveal the relics of saints, and as the deadly enemy
of the serpent. In the feast of asses, that animal was led
with veneration into the churches, and a rude hymn proclaimed its dignity, because it had borne Christ in His flight
to Egypt, and in His entry into Jerusalem. St. Francis
always treated lambs with a peculiar tenderness, as being
symbols of his Master. Luther grew sad and thoughtful
at a hare hunt, for it seemed to him to represent the pursuit
of souls by the devil. Many popular legends exist, associating some bird or animal with some incident in the evangelical narrative, and securing for them in consequence an
unmolested life. But such influences have never extended
far. There are two distinct objects which may be considered
by moralists in this sphere. They may regard the character
of the men, or they may regard the sufferings of the animals.
The amount of callousness or of conscious cruelty displayed
or elicited by amusements or practices that inflict suffering
on animals, bears no kind of proportion to the intensity of
that suffering. Could we follow with adequate realisation

the pangs of the wounded birds that are struck down in our sports, or of the timid hare in the long course of its flight, we should probably conclude that they were not really less than those caused by the Spanish bull-fight, or by the English pastimes of the last century. But the excitement of the chase refracts the imagination, and owing to the diminutive size of the victim, and the undemonstrative character of its suffering, these sports do not exercise that prejudicial influence upon character which they would exercise if the sufferings of the animals were vividly realised, and were at the same time accepted as an element of the enjoyment. The class of amusements of which the ancient combats of wild beasts form the type, have no doubt nearly disappeared from Christendom, and it is possible that the softening power of Christian teaching may have had some indirect influence in abolishing them ; but a candid judgment will confess that it has been very little. During the periods, and in the countries, in which theological influence was supreme, they were unchallenged.[1] They disappeared[2] at last, because a luxurious and industrial civilisation involved a refinement of manners; because a fastidious taste recoiled with a sensation of disgust from pleasures that an uncultivated taste would keenly relish; because the drama, at once reflecting

---

[1] I have noticed, in my *History of Rationalism,* that, although some Popes did undoubtedly try to suppress Spanish bull-fights, this was solely on account of the destruction of human life they caused. Full details on this subject will be found in Concina, *De Spectaculis* (Romæ, 1752). Bayle says, ' Il n'y a point de casuiste qui croie qu'on pèche en faisant combattre des taureaux contre des dogues,' &c. (*Dict. philos.* 'Rorarius, C.')

[2] On the ancient amusements of England the reader may consult

Seymour's *Survey of London* (1734), vol. i. pp. 227–235 ; Strutt's *Sports and Pastimes of the English People.* Cock-fighting was a favourite children's amusement in England as early as the twelfth century. (Hampson's *Medii Ævi Kalendarii,* vol. i. p. 160.) It was, with foot-ball and several other amusements, for a time suppressed by Edward III., on the ground that they were diverting the people from archery, which was necessary to the military greatness of England.

and accelerating the change, gave a new form to popular amusements, and because, in consequence of this revolution, the old pastimes, being left to the dregs of society, became the occasions of scandalous disorders.[1]   In Protestant

---

[1] The decline of these amusements in England began with the great development of the theatre under Elizabeth. An order of the Privy Council in July, 1591, prohibits the exhibition of plays on Thursday, because on Thursdays bear-baiting and suchlike pastimes had been usually practised, and an injunction to the same effect was sent to the Lord Mayor, wherein it was stated that, 'in divers places the players do use to recite their plays, to the great hurt and destruction of the game of bear-baiting and like pastimes, which are maintained for Her Majesty's pleasure.'—Nichols, *Progresses of Queen Elizabeth* (ed. 1823), vol. i. p. 438. The reader will remember the picture in *Kenilworth* of the Earl of Sussex petitioning Elizabeth against Shakespeare, on the ground of his plays distracting men from bear-baiting. Elizabeth (see Nichols) was extremely fond of bear-baiting. James I. especially delighted in cock-fighting, and in 1610 was present at a great fight between a lion and a bear. (Hone, *Every Day Book*, vol. i. pp. 255-299.) The theatres, however, rapidly multiplied, and a writer who lived about 1629 said, 'that no less than seventeen playhouses had been built in or about London within threescore years.' (Seymour's *Survey*, vol. i. p. 229.) The Rebellion suppressed all public amusements, and when they were re-established after the Restoration, it was found that the tastes of the better classes no longer sympathised with the bear-garden. Pepys (*Diary*, August 14, 1666) speaks of bull-baiting as 'a very rude and nasty pleasure,' and says he had not been in the bear-garden for many years. Evelyn (*Diary*, June 16, 1670), having been present at these shows, describes them as 'butcherly sports, or rather barbarous cruelties,' and says he had not visited them before for twenty years. A paper in the *Spectator* (No. 141, written in 1711) talks of those who 'seek their diversion at the bear-garden, . . . where reason and good manners have no right to disturb them.' In 1751, however, Lord Kames was able to say, 'The bear garden, which is one of the chief entertainments of the English, is held in abhorrence by the French and other polite nations.'—*Essay on Morals* (1st ed.), p. 7; and he warmly defends (p. 30) the English taste. During the latter half of the last century there was constant controversy on the subject (which may be traced in the pages of the *Annual Register*), and several forgotten clergymen published sermons upon it, and the frequent riots resulting from the fact that the bear-gardens had become the resort of the worst classes assisted the movement. The London magistrates took measures to suppress cock-throwing in 1769 (Hampson's *Med. Æv. Kalend.* p. 160); but bull-baiting continued far into the

countries the clergy have, on the whole, sustained this movement.   In Catholic countries it has been much more faithfully
represented by the school of Voltaire and Beccaria.   A
judicious moralist may, however, reasonably question whether
amusements which derive their zest from a display of the
natural ferocious instincts of animals, and which substitute
death endured in the frenzy of combat for death in the
remote slaughter-house or by the slow process of decay, have
added in any appreciable degree to the sum of animal
misery, and in these cases he will dwell less upon the suffering inflicted than upon the injurious influence the spectacle
may sometimes exercise on the character of the spectator.
But there are forms of cruelty which must be regarded in a
different light.   The horrors of vivisection, often so wantonly,
so needlessly practised,[1] the prolonged and atrocious tortures,

---

present century.   Windham and
Canning strongly defended it; Dr.
Parr is said to have been fond of it
(*Southey's Commonplace Book*, vol.
iv. p. 585); and as late as 1824,
Sir Robert (then Mr) Peel argued
strongly against its prohibition.
(*Parliamentary Debates*, vol. x.
pp. 132-133, 491-495.)

  [1] Bacon, in an account of the
deficiencies of medicine, recommends vivisection in terms that
seem to imply that it was not
practised in his time.   'As for the
passages and pores, it is true, which
was anciently noted, that the more
subtle of them appear not in anato-
mies, because they are shut and
latent in dead bodies, though they
be open and manifest in live;
which being supposed, though the
inhumanity of *anatomia vivorum*
was by Celsus justly reproved, yet,
in regard of the great use of this
observation, the enquiry needed
not by him so slightly to have been

relinquished altogether, or referred
to the casual practices of surgery;
but might have been well diverted
upon the dissection of beasts alive,
which, notwithstanding the dis-
similitude of their parts, may
sufficiently satisfy this enquiry.'—
Advancement of Learning, x. 4.
Harvey speaks of vivisections as
having contributed to lead him to
the discovery of the circulation of the
blood. (Acland's *Harveian Oration*
(1865), p. 55.) Bayle, describing
the treatment of animals by men,
says, 'Nous fouillons dans leurs
entrailles pendant leur vie afin de
satisfaire notre curiosité.'—*Dict.
philos.* art. 'Rorarius, C.' Public
opinion in England was very
strongly directed to the subject in
the present century, by the atrocious cruelties perpetrated by Ma-
jendie at his lectures. See a most
frightful account of them in a
speech by Mr. Martin (an eccentric
Irish member, who was generally

sometimes inflicted in order to procure some gastronomic delicacy, are so far removed from the public gaze that they exercise little influence on the character of men. Yet no humane man can reflect upon them without a shudder. To bring these things within the range of ethics, to create the notion of duties towards the animal world, has, so far as Christian countries are concerned, been one of the peculiar merits of the last century, and, for the most part, of Protestant nations. However fully we may recognise the humane spirit transmitted to the world in the form of legends from the saints of the desert, it must not be forgotten that the inculcation of humanity to animals on a wide scale is mainly the work of a recent and a secular age; that the Mohammedans and the Brahmins have in this sphere considerably surpassed the Christians, and that Spain and Southern Italy, in which Catholicism has most deeply planted its roots, are even now, probably beyond all other countries in Europe, those in which inhumanity to animals is most wanton and most unrebuked.

The influence the first form of monachism has exercised upon the world, so far as it has been beneficial, has been chiefly through the imagination, which has been fascinated by its legends. In the great periods of theological controversy, the Eastern monks had furnished some leading theologians; but in general, in Oriental lands, the hermit life predominated, and extreme maceration was the chief merit of the saint. But in the West, monachism assumed very different forms, and exercised far higher functions. At first the Oriental saints were the ideals of Western monks. The Eastern St. Athanasius had been the founder of Italian monachism. St.

ridiculed during his life, and has been almost forgotten since his death, but to whose untiring exertions the legislative protection of animals in England is due). *Parliament. Hist.* vol. xii. p. 652. Mandeville. in his day, was a very strong advocate of kindness to animals.—*Commentary on the Fable of the Bees.*

Martin of Tours excluded labour from the discipline of his monks, and he and they, like the Eastern saints, were accustomed to wander abroad, destroying the idols of the temples.[1] But three great causes conspired to direct the monastic spirit in the West into practical channels. Conditions of race and climate have ever impelled the inhabitants of these lands to active life, and have at the same time rendered them constitutionally incapable of enduring the austerities or enjoying the hallucinations of the sedentary Oriental. There arose, too, in the sixth century, a great legislator, whose form may be dimly traced through a cloud of fantastic legends, and the order of St. Benedict, with that of St. Columba and some others, founded on substantially the same principle, soon ramified through the greater part of Europe, tempered the wild excesses of useless penances, and, making labour an essential part of the monastic system, directed the movement to the purposes of general civilisation. In the last place, the barbarian invasions, and the dissolution of the Western Empire, dislocating the whole system of government and almost re- solving society into its primitive elements, naturally threw upon the monastic corporations social, political, and intellectual functions of the deepest importance.

It has been observed that the capture of Rome by Alaric, involving as it did the destruction of the grandest religious monuments of Paganism, in fact established in that city the supreme authority of Christianity.[2] A similar remark may be extended to the general downfall of the Western civilisation. In that civilisation Christianity had indeed been legally enthroned; but the philosophies and traditions of Paganism, and the ingrained habits of an ancient, and at the same time an effete society, continually paralysed its energies. What Europe would have been without the barbarian invasions, we may partly divine from the history of

---

[1] See his *Life* by Sulpicius Severus.   [2] Milman.

the Lower Empire, which represented, in fact, the old Roman civilisation prolonged and Christianised. The barbarian conquests, breaking up the old organisation, provided the Church with a virgin soil, and made it, for a long period, the supreme and indeed sole centre of civilisation.

It would be difficult to exaggerate the skill and courage displayed by the ecclesiastics in this most trying period. We have already seen the noble daring with which they interfered between the conqueror and the vanquished, and the unwearied charity with which they sought to alleviate the unparalleled sufferings of Italy, when the colonial supplies of corn were cut off. and when the fairest plains were desolated by the barbarians. Still more wonderful is the rapid conversion of the barbarian tribes. Unfortunately this, which is one of the most important, is also one of the most obscure pages in the history of the Church. Of whole tribes or nations it may be truly said that we are absolutely ignorant of the cause of their change. The Goths had already been converted by Ulphilas, before the downfall of the Empire, and the conversion of the Germans and of several northern nations was long posterior to it; but the great work of Christianising the barbarian world was accomplished almost in the hour when that world became supreme. Rude tribes, accustomed in their own lands to pay absolute obedience to their priests, found themselves in a foreign country, confronted by a priesthood far more civilised and imposing than that which they had left, by gorgeous ceremonies, well fitted to entice, and by threats of coming judgment, well fitted to scare their imaginations. Disconnected from all their old associations, they bowed before the majesty of civilisation, and the Latin religion, like the Latin language, though with many adulterations, reigned over the new society. The doctrine of exclusive salvation, and the doctrine of dæmons, had an admirable missionary power. The first produced an ardour of proselytising which the polytheist could never rival; while the Pagan, who was easily led to recognise the Christian God, was menaced with eternal fire if he did not take the further step of breaking off from his old divinities.   The second dispensed the con vert from the perhaps impossible task of disbelieving his former religion, for it was only necessary for him to degrade it, attributing its prodigies to infernal beings.   The priests, in addition to their noble devotion, carried into their mis- sionary efforts the most masterly judgment.   The barbarian tribes usually followed without enquiry the religion of their sovereign; and it was to the conversion of the king, and still more to the conversion of the queen, that the Christians devoted all their energies.   Clotilda, the wife of Clovis, Bertha, the wife of Ethelbert, and Theodolinda, the wife of Lothaire, were the chief instruments in converting their husbands and their nations.   Nothing that could affect the imagination was neglected.   It is related of Clotilda, that she was careful to attract her husband by the rich draperies of the ecclesiastical ceremonies.[1]   In another case, the first work of proselytising was confided to an artist, who painted before the terrified Pagans the last judgment and the tor- ments of hell.[2]   But especially the belief, which was sincerely held, and sedulously inculcated, that temporal success fol- lowed in the train of Christianity, and that every pestilence, famine, or military disaster was the penalty of idolatry, heresy, sacrilege, or vice, assisted the movement.   The theory was so wide, that it met every variety of fortune, and being taught with consummate skill, to barbarians who were totally destitute of all critical power, and strongly predis- posed to accept it, it proved extremely efficacious; and hope, fear, gratitude, and remorse drew multitudes into the Church.

---

[1] Greg. Turon. ii. 29.
[2] This was the first step towards the conversion of the Bulgarians.—

Milman's *Latin Christianity*, vol iii. p. 249.

The transition was softened by the substitution of Christian ceremonies and saints for the festivals and the divinities of the Pagans.[1] Besides the professed missionaries, the Christian captives zealously diffused their faith among their Pagan masters. When the chieftain had been converted, and the army had followed his profession, an elaborate monastic and ecclesiastical organisation grew up to consolidate the conquest, and repressive laws soon crushed all opposition to the faith.

In these ways the victory of Christianity over the barbarian world was achieved. But that victory, though very great, was less decisive than might appear. A religion which professed to be Christianity, and which contained many of the ingredients of pure Christianity, had risen into the ascendant, but it had undergone a profound modification through the struggle. Religions, as well as worshippers, had been baptised. The festivals, images, and names of saints had been substituted for those of the idols, and the habits of thought and feeling of the ancient faith reappeared in new forms and a new language. The tendency to a material, idolatrous, and polytheistic faith, which had long been encouraged by the monks, and which the heretics Jovinian, Vigilantius, and Aerius had vainly resisted, was fatally strengthened by the infusion of a barbarian element into the Church, by the general depression of intellect in Europe, and by the many accommodations that were made to facilitate conversion. Though apparently defeated and crushed, the old gods still retained, under a new faith, no small part of their influence over the world.

To this tendency the leaders of the Church made in genera, no resistance, though in another form they were

---

[1] A remarkable collection of instances of this kind is given by Ozanam, *Civilisation in the Fifth* *Century* (Eng. trans.), vol. i. pp 124–127.

deeply persuaded of the vitality of the old gods. Many curious and picturesque legends attest the popular belief that the old Roman and the old barbarian divinities, in their capacity of dæmons, were still waging an unrelenting war against the triumphant faith. A great Pope of the sixth century relates how a Jew, being once benighted on his journey, and finding no other shelter for the night, lay down to rest in an abandoned temple of Apollo. Shuddering at the loneliness of the building, and fearing the dæmons who were said to haunt it, he determined, though not a Christian, to protect himself by the sign of the cross, which he had often heard possessed a mighty power against spirits. To that sign he owed his safety. For at midnight the temple was filled with dark and threatening forms. The god Apollo was holding his court at his deserted shrine, and his attendant dæmons were recounting the temptations they had devised against the Christians.[1] A newly married Roman, when one day playing ball, took off his wedding-ring, which he found an impediment in the game, and he gaily put it on the finger of a statue of Venus, that was standing near. When he returned, the marble finger had bent so that it was impossible to withdraw the ring, and that night the goddess appeared to him in a dream, and told him that she was now his wedded wife, and that she would abide with him for ever.[2] When the Irish missionary St. Gall was fishing one night upon a Swiss lake, near which he had planted a monastery, he heard strange voices sweeping over the lonely deep. The Spirit of the Water and the Spirit of the Mountains were consulting

---

[1] St. Gregory, *Dial.* iii. 7. The particular temptation the Jew heard discussed was that of the bishop of the diocese, who, under the instigation of one of the dæmons, was rapidly falling in love with a nun, and had proceeded so far as jocosely to stroke her on the back. The Jew, having related the vision to the bishop, the latter reformed his manners, the Jew became a Christian, and the temple was turned into a church.

[2] William of Malmesbury, ii. 13.

together how they could expel the intruder who had disturbed their ancient reign.[1]

The details of the rapid propagation of Western monachism have been amply treated by many historians, and the causes of its success are sufficiently manifest. Some of the reasons I have assigned for the first spread of asceticism continued to operate, while others of a still more powerful kind had arisen. The rapid decomposition of the entire Roman Empire by continuous invasions of barbarians rendered the existence of an inviolable asylum and centre of peaceful labour a matter of transcendent importance, and the monastery as organised by St. Benedict soon combined the most heterogeneous elements of attraction. It was at once eminently aristocratic and intensely democratic. The power and princely position of the abbot were coveted, and usually obtained, by members of the most illustrious families ; while emancipated serfs, or peasants who had lost their all in the invasions, or were harassed by savage nobles, or had fled from military service, or desired to lead a more secure and easy life, found in the monastery an unfailing refuge. The institution exercised all the influence of great wealth, expended for the most part with great charity, while the monk himself was invested with the aureole of a sacred poverty. To ardent and philanthropic natures, the profession opened boundless vistas of missionary, charitable, and civilising activity. To the superstitious it was the plain road to heaven. To the ambitious it was the portal to bishoprics, and, after the monk St. Gregory, not unfrequently to the Popedom. To the studious it offered the only opportunity then existing in the world of seeing many books and passing a life of study. To the timid and retiring it afforded the most secure, and probably the least laborious life a poor peasant could hope to find. Vast as were the multitudes that thronged the monasteries, the means for their support

---

[1] See Milman's *Hist. of Latin Christianity*, vol. ii. p. 293.

were never wanting. The belief that gifts or legacies to a monastery opened the doors of heaven was in a superstitious age sufficient to secure for the community an almost boundless wealth, which was still further increased by the skill and perseverance with which the monks tilled the waste lands, by the exemption of their domains from all taxation, and by the tranquillity which in the most turbulent ages they usually enjoyed. In France, the Low Countries, and Germany they were pre-eminently agriculturists. Gigantic forests were felled, inhospitable marshes reclaimed, barren plains cultivated by their hands. The monastery often became the nucleus of a city. It was the centre of civilisation and industry, the symbol of moral power in an age of turbulence and war.

It must be observed, however, that the beneficial influence of the monastic system was necessarily transitional, and the subsequent corruption the normal and inevitable result of its constitution. Vast societies living in enforced celibacy, exercising an unbounded influence, and possessing enormous wealth, must necessarily have become hotbeds of corruption when the enthusiasm that had created them expired. The services they rendered as the centres of agriculture, the refuge of travellers, the sanctuaries in war, the counterpoise of the baronial castle, were no longer required when the convulsions of invasion had ceased and when civil society was definitely organised. And a similar observation may be extended even to their moral type. Thus, while it is undoubtedly true that the Benedictine monks, by making labour an essential element of their discipline, did very much to efface the stigma which slavery had affixed upon it, it is also true that, when industry had passed out of its initial stage, the monastic theories of the sanctity of poverty, and the evil of wealth, were its most deadly opponents. The dogmatic condemnation by theologians of loans at interest, which are the basis of industrial enterprise, was the expression of a far deeper antagonism of tendencies and ideals.

In one important respect, the transition from the eremite to the monastic life involved not only a change of circumstances, but also a change of character. The habit of obedience, and the virtue of humility, assumed a position which they had never previously occupied. The conditions of the hermit life contributed to develop to a very high degree a spirit of independence and spiritual pride, which was still further increased by a curious habit that existed in the Church of regarding each eminent hermit as the special model or professor of some particular virtue, and making pilgrimages to him, in order to study this aspect of his character.[1] These pilgrimages, combined with the usually solitary and self-sufficing life of the hermit, and also with the habit of measuring progress almost entirely by the suppression of a physical appetite, which it is quite possible wholly to destroy, very naturally produced an extreme arrogance.[2] But in the highly organised and disciplined monasteries of the West, passive obedience and humility were the very first things that were inculcated. The monastery, beyond all other institutions, was the school for their exercise; and as the monk represented the highest moral ideal of the age, obedience and humility acquired a new value in the minds of men. Nearly

---

[1] Cassian. *Cœnob. Instit.* v. 4. See, too, some striking instances of this in the life of St. Antony.

[2] This spiritual pride is well noticed by Neander, *Ecclesiastical History* (Bohn's ed.), vol. iii. pp. 321–323. It appears in many traits scattered through the lives of these saints. I have already cited the visions telling St. Antony and St. Macarius that they were not the best of living people; and also the case of the hermit, who was deceived by a devil in the form of a woman, because he had been exalted by pride. Another hermit, being very holy, received pure white bread every day from heaven, but, being extravagantly elated, the bread got worse and worse till it became perfectly black. (Tillemont. tome x. pp. 27–28.) A certain Isidore affirmed that he had not been conscious of sin, even in thought, for forty years. (Socrates, iv. 23.) It was a saying of St. Antony, that a solitary man in the desert is free from three wars—of sight, speech, and hearing: he has to combat only fornication. (*Apothegmata Patrum.*)

all the feudal and other organisations that arose out of the chaos that followed the destruction of the Roman Empire were intimately related to the Church, not simply because the Church was the strongest power in Christendom, and supplied in itself an admirable model of an organised body, but also because it had done much to educate men in habits of obedience. The special value of this education depended upon the peculiar circumstances of the time. The ancient civilisations, and especially that of Rome, had been by no means deficient in those habits; but it was in the midst of the dissolution of an old society, and of the ascendancy of barbarians, who exaggerated to the highest degree their personal independence, that the Church proposed to the reverence of mankind a life of passive obedience as the highest ideal of virtue.

The habit of obedience was no new thing in the world, but the disposition of humility was pre-eminently and almost exclusively a Christian virtue; and there has probably never been any sphere in which it has been so largely and so successfully inculcated as in the monastery. The whole penitential discipline, the entire mode or tenor of the monastic life, was designed to tame every sentiment of pride, and to give humility a foremost place in the hierarchy of virtues. We have here one great source of the mollifying influence of Catholicism. The gentler virtues—benevolence and amiability—may, and in an advanced civilisation often do, subsist in natures that are completely devoid of genuine humility; but, on the other hand, it is scarcely possible for a nature to be pervaded by a deep sentiment of humility without this sentiment exercising a softening influence over the whole character. To transform a fierce warlike nature into a character of a gentler type, the first essential is to awaken this feeling. In the monasteries, the extinction of social and domestic feelings, the narrow corporate spirit, and, still more, the atrocious opinions that were prevalent concerning the guilt of heresy, produced in many minds an extreme and most active ferocity; but the practice of charity, and the ideal of humility, never failed to exercise some softening influence upon Christendom.

But, however advantageous the temporary pre-eminence of this moral type may have been, it was obviously unsuited for a later stage of civilisation. Political liberty is almost impossible where the monastic system is supreme, not merely because the monasteries divert the energies of the nation from civic to ecclesiastical channels, but also because the monastic ideal is the very apotheosis of servitude. Catholicism has been admirably fitted at once to mitigate and to perpetuate despotism. When men have learnt to reverence a life of passive, unreasoning obedience as the highest type of perfection, the enthusiasm and passion of freedom necessarily decline. In this respect there is an analogy between the monastic and the military spirit, both of which promote and glorify passive obedience, and therefore prepare the minds of men for despotic rule; but, on the whole, the monastic spirit is probably more hostile to freedom than the military spirit, for the obedience of the monk is based upon humility, while the obedience of the soldier coexists with pride. Now, a considerable measure of pride, or self-assertion, is an invariable characteristic of free communities.

The ascendancy which the monastic system gave to the virtue of humility has not continued. This virtue is indeed the crowning grace and beauty of the most perfect characters of the saintly type; but experience has shown that among common men humility is more apt to degenerate into servility than pride into arrogance; and modern moralists have appealed more successfully to the sense of dignity than to the opposite feeling. Two of the most important steps of later moral history have consisted of the creation of a sentiment of pride as the parent and the guardian of many virtues. The first of these encroachments on the monastic spirit was chivalry, which called into being a proud and jealous military honour that has never since been extinguished. The second was the creation of that feeling of self-respect which is one of the most remarkable characteristics that distinguish Protestant from the most Catholic populations, and which has proved among the former an invaluable moral agent, forming frank and independent natures, and checking every servile habit and all mean and degrading vice.[1] The peculiar vigour with which it has been developed in Protestant countries may be attributed to the suppression of monastic institutions and habits; to the stigma Protestantism has attached to mendicancy, which Catholicism has usually glorified and encouraged; to the high place Protestantism has accorded to private judgment and personal responsibility; and lastly, to the action of free political institutions, which have taken deepest root where the principles of the Reformation have been accepted.

The relation of the monasteries to the intellectual virtues, which we have next to examine, opens out a wide field of

---

[1] 'Pride, under such training [that of modern rationalistic philosophy], instead of running to waste, is turned to account. It gets a new name; it is called self-respect. . . . It is directed into the channel of industry, frugality, honesty, and obedience, and it becomes the very staple of the religion and morality held in honour in a day like our own. It becomes the safeguard of chastity, the guarantee of veracity, in high and low; it is the very household god of the Protestant, inspiring neatness and decency in the servant-girl, propriety of carriage and refined manners in her mistress, uprightness, manliness, and generosity in the head of the family. . . . It is the stimulating principle of providence on the one hand, and of free expenditure on the other; of an honourable ambition and of elegant enjoyment.'—Newman, *On University Education*, Discourse ix. In the same lecture (which is, perhaps, the most beautiful of the many beautiful productions of its illustrious author), Dr. Newman describes, with admirable eloquence, the manner in which modesty has supplanted humility in the modern type of excellence. It is scarcely necessary to say that the lecturer strongly disapproves of the movement he describes.

discussion; and, in order to appreciate it, it will be necessary
to revert briefly to a somewhat earlier stage of ecclesiastical
history. And in the first place, it may be observed, that the
phrase intellectual virtue, which is often used in a metaphorical sense, is susceptible of a strictly literal interpretation.
If a sincere and active desire for truth be a moral duty, the
discipline and the dispositions that are plainly involved in
every honest search fall rigidly within the range of ethics.
To love truth sincerely means to pursue it with an earnest,
conscientious, unflagging zeal. It means to be prepared to
follow the light of evidence even to the most unwelcome
conclusions; to labour earnestly to emancipate the mind from
early prejudices; to resist the current of the desires, and the
refracting influence of the passions; to proportion on all occasions conviction to evidence, and to be ready, if need be, to
exchange the calm of assurance for all the suffering of a perplexed and disturbed mind. To do this is very difficult and
very painful; but it is clearly involved in the notion of
earnest love of truth. If, then, any system stigmatises as
criminal the state of doubt, denounces the examination of
some one class of arguments or facts, seeks to introduce the
bias of the affections into the enquiries of the reason, or
regards the honest conclusion of an upright investigator as
involving moral guilt, that system is subversive of intellectual honesty.

Among the ancients, although the methods of enquiry
were often very faulty, and generalisations very hasty, a respect for the honest search after truth was widely diffused.[1]
There were, as we have already seen, instances in which
certain religious practices which were regarded as attestations
of loyalty, or as necessary to propitiate the gods in favour of

---

[1] Thus 'indagatio veri' was
reckoned among the leading virtues,
and the high place given to σοφία
and 'prudentia' in ethical writings
preserved the notion of the moral
duties connected with the discipline
of the intellect.

the State, were enforced by law; there were even a few instances of philosophies, which were believed to lead directly to immoral results or social convulsions, being suppressed; but, as a general rule, speculation was untrammelled, the notion of there being any necessary guilt in erroneous opinion was unknown, and the boldest enquirers were regarded with honour and admiration. The religious theory of Paganism had in this respect some influence. Polytheism, with many faults, had three great merits. It was eminently poetical, eminently patriotic, and eminently tolerant. The conception of a vast hierarchy of beings more glorious than, but not wholly unlike, men, presiding over all the developments of nature, and filling the universe with their deeds, supplied the chief nutriment of the Greek imagination. The national religions, interweaving religious ceremonies and associations with all civic life, concentrated and intensified the sentiment of patriotism, and the notion of many distinct groups of gods led men to tolerate many forms of worship and great variety of creeds. In that colossal amalgam of nations of which Rome became the metropolis, intellectual liberty still further advanced; the vast variety of philosophies and beliefs expatiated unmolested; the search for truth was regarded as an important element of virtue, and the relent-less and most sceptical criticism which Socrates had applied in turn to all the fundamental propositions of popular belief remained as an example to his successors.

We have already seen that one leading cause of the rapid progress of the Church was that its teachers enforced their distinctive tenets as absolutely essential to salvation, and thus assailed at a great advantage the supporters of all other creeds which did not claim this exclusive authority. We have seen, too, that in an age of great and growing credulity they had been conspicuous for their assertion of the duty of absolute, unqualified, and unquestioning belief. The notion of the guilt both of error and of doubt grew rapidly, and, being

soon regarded as a fundamental tenet, it determined the
vhole course and policy of the Church.

And here, I think, it will not be unadvisable to pause for
a moment, and endeavour to ascertain what misconceived
truth lay at the root of this fatal tenet. Considered abstractedly and by the light of nature, it is as unmeaning to
speak of the immorality of an intellectual mistake as it
would be to talk of the colour of a sound. If a man has
sincerely persuaded himself that it is possible for parallel
lines to meet, or for two straight lines to enclose a space, we
pronounce his judgment to be absurd; but it is free from all
tincture of immorality.   And if, instead of failing to appreciate a demonstrable truth, his error consisted in a false estimate of the conflicting arguments of an historical problem,
this mistake—assuming always that the enquiry was an upright one—is still simply external to the sphere of morals.
It is possible that his conclusion, by weakening some barrier
against vice, may produce vicious consequences, like those
which might ensue from some ill-advised modification of the
police force ; but it in no degree follows from this that the
judgment is in itself criminal.   If a student applies himself
with the same dispositions to Roman and Jewish histories,
the mistakes he may make in the latter are no more
immoral than those which he may make in the former.

There are, however, two cases in which an intellectual
error may be justly said to involve, or at least to represent,
guilt. In the first place, error very frequently springs from
the partial or complete absence of that mental disposition
which is implied in a real love of truth. Hypocrites, or men
who through interested motives profess opinions which they
do not really believe, are probably rarer than is usually supposed ; but it would be difficult to over-estimate the number
of those whose genuine convictions are due to the unresisted
bias of their interests. By the term interests, 1 mean not
only material well-being, but also all those mental luxuries,

all those grooves or channels for thought, which it is easy and
pleasing to follow, and painful and difficult to abandon.
Such are the love of ease, the love of certainty, the love of
system, the bias of the passions, the associations of the
imagination, as well as the coarser influences of social
position, domestic happiness, professional interest, party
feeling, or ambition. In most men, the love of truth is so
languid, and the reluctance to encounter mental suffering is
so great, that they yield their judgments without an effort to
the current, withdraw their minds from all opinions or
arguments opposed to their own, and thus speedily convince
themselves of the truth of what they wish to believe. He
who really loves truth is bound at least to endeavour to
resist these distorting influences, and in as far as his opinions
are the result of his not having done so, in so far they represent a moral failing.

In the next place, it must be observed that every moral
disposition brings with it an intellectual bias which exercises
a great and often a controlling and decisive influence even
upon the most earnest enquirer. If we know the character
or disposition of a man, we can usually predict with
tolerable accuracy many of his opinions. We can tell to
what side of politics, to what canons of taste, to what theory
of morals he will naturally incline. Stern, heroic, and
haughty natures tend to systems in which these qualities
occupy the foremost position in the moral type, while gentle
natures will as naturally lean towards systems in which the
amiable virtues are supreme. Impelled by a species of moral
gravitation, the enquirer will glide insensibly to the system
which is congruous to his disposition, and intellectual difficulties will seldom arrest him. He can have observed
human nature with but little fruit who has not remarked
how constant is this connection, and how very rarely men
change fundamentally the principles they had deliberately
adopted on religious, moral, or even political questions,

without the change being preceded, accompanied, or very speedily followed, by a serious modification of character So, too, a vicious and depraved nature, or a nature which is hard, narrow, and unsympathetic, will tend, much less by calculation or indolence than by natural affinity, to low and degrading views of human nature. Those who have never felt the higher emotions will scarcely appreciate them. The materials with which the intellect builds are often derived from the heart, and a moral disease is therefore not unfrequently at the root of an erroneous judgment.

Of these two truths the first cannot, I think, be said to have had any influence in the formation of the theological notion of the guilt of error. An elaborate process of mental discipline, with a view to strengthening the critical powers of the mind, is utterly remote from the spirit of theology; and this is one of the great reasons why the growth of an inductive and scientific spirit is invariably hostile to theological interests. To raise the requisite standard of proof, to inculcate hardness and slowness of belief, is the first task of the inductive reasoner. He looks with great favour upon the condition of a suspended judgment; he encourages men rather to prolong than to abridge it; he regards the tendency of the human mind to rapid and premature generalisations as one of its most fatal vices; he desires especially that that which is believed should not be so cherished that the mind should be indisposed to admit doubt, or, on the appearance of new arguments, to revise with impartiality its conclusions. Nearly all the greatest intellectual achievements of the last three centuries have been preceded and prepared by the growth of scepticism. The historic scepticism which Vico, Beaufort, Pouilly, and Voltaire in the last century, and Niebuhr and Lewis in the present century, applied to ancient history, lies at the root of all the great modern efforts to reconstruct the history of mankind. The splendid discoveries of physical science would have been impossible but for the

scientific scepticism of the school of Bacon, which dissipated
the old theories of the universe, and led men to demand a
severity of proof altogether unknown to the ancients. The
philosophic scepticism with which the system of Hume
ended and the system of Kant began, has given the greatest
modern impulse to metaphysics and ethics. Exactly in proportion, therefore, as men are educated in the inductive
school, they are alienated from those theological systems
which represent a condition of doubt as sinful, seek to govern
the reason by the interests and the affections, and make it a
main object to destroy the impartiality of the judgment.

But although it is difficult to look upon Catholicism in
any other light than as the most deadly enemy of the
scientific spirit, it has always cordially recognised the most
important truth, that character in a very great measure
determines opinions. To cultivate the moral type that is
most congenial to the opinions it desires to recommend has
always been its effort, and the conviction that a deviation
from that type has often been the predisposing cause of intellectual heresy, had doubtless a large share in the first persuasion of the guilt of error. But priestly and other influences
soon conspired to enlarge this doctrine. A crowd of speculative, historical, and administrative propositions were
asserted as essential to salvation, and all who rejected them
were wholly external to the bond of Christian sympathy.

If, indeed, we put aside the pure teaching of the Christian
founders, and consider the actual history of the Church since
Constantine, we shall find no justification for the popular
theory that beneath its influence the narrow spirit of patriotism faded into a wide and cosmopolitan philanthropy. A
real though somewhat languid feeling of universal brotherhood had already been created in the world by the universality of the Roman Empire. In the new faith the range of
genuine sympathy was strictly limited by the creed. According to the popular belief, all who differed from the

teaching of the orthodox lived under the hatred of the
Almighty, and were destined after death for an eternity of
anguish. Very naturally, therefore, they were wholly
alienated from the true believers, and no moral or intellectual
excellence could atone for their crime in propagating error.
The eighty or ninety sects,[1] into which Christianity speedily
divided, hated one another with an intensity that extorted
the wonder of Julian and the ridicule of the Pagans of
Alexandria, and the fierce riots and persecutions that hatred
produced appear in every page of ecclesiastical history.
There is, indeed, something at once grotesque and ghastly in
the spectacle. The Donatists, having separated from the
orthodox simply on the question of the validity of the consecration of a certain bishop, declared that all who adopted
the orthodox view must be damned, refused to perform their
rites in the orthodox churches which they had seized, till they
had burnt the altar and scraped the wood, beat multitudes to
death with clubs, blinded others by anointing their eyes with
lime, filled Africa, during nearly two centuries, with war and
desolation, and contributed largely to its final ruin.[2] The
childish and almost unintelligible quarrels between the
Homoiousians and the Homoousians, between those who
maintained that the nature of Christ was like that of the
Father and those who maintained that it was the same,
filled the world with riot and hatred. The Catholics tell
how an Arian Emperor caused eighty orthodox priests to be
drowned on a single occasion;[3] how three thousand persons
perished in the riots that convulsed Constantinople when the
Arian Bishop Macedonius superseded the Athanasian Paul;[4]
how George of Cappadocia, the Arian Bishop of Alexandria,

---

[1] St. Augustine reckoned eighty-
eight sects as existing in his time.

[2] See a full account of these
persecutions in Tillemont, *Mém.
d' Histoire ecclés.* tome vi.

[3] Socrates, *H. E.*, iv. 16. This
anecdote is much doubted by
modern historians.

[4] Milman's *Hist. of Christianity*
(ed. 1867), vol. ii. p. 422.

caused the widows of the Athanasian party to be scourged on the soles of their feet, the holy virgins to be stripped naked, to be flogged with the prickly branches of palm-trees or to be slowly scorched over fires till they abjured their creed.[1] The triumph of the Catholics in Egypt was accompanied (if we may believe the solemn assertions of eighty Arian Bishops) by every variety of plunder, murder, sacrilege, and outrage,[2] and Arius himself was probably poisoned by Catholic hands.[3] The followers of St. Cyril of Alexandria, who were chiefly monks, filled their city with riot and bloodshed, wounded the prefect Orestes, dragged the pure and gifted Hypatia into one of their churches, murdered her, tore the flesh from her bones with sharp shells, and, having stripped her body naked, flung her mangled remains into the flames.[4] In Ephesus, during the contest between St. Cyril and the Nestorians, the cathedral itself was the theatre of a fierce and bloody conflict.[5] Constantinople, on the occasion of the deposition of St. Chrysostom, was for several days in a condition of absolute anarchy.[6] After the Council of Chalcedon, Jerusalem and Alexandria were again convulsed, and the bishop of the latter city was murdered in his baptistery.[7] About fifty years later, when the Monophysite controversy was at its height, the palace of the emperor at Constantinople was blockaded, the churches were besieged, and the streets commanded by furious bands of contending monks.[8] Repressed for a time, the riots broke

---

[1] St. Athanasius, *Historical Treatises* (Library of the Fathers), pp. 192, 284.

[2] Milman, *Hist. of Christianity*, ii. pp. 436-437.

[3] The death of Arius, as is well known, took place suddenly (his bowels, it is said, coming out) when he was just about to make his triumphal entry into the Cathedral of Constantinople. The death (though possibly natural) never

seems to have been regarded as such, but it was a matter of controversy whether it was a miracle or a murder.

[4] Socrates, *H. E.*, vii. 13-15.

[5] Milman, *Hist. of Latin Christianity*, vol. i. pp. 214-215.

[6] Milman, *Hist. of Christianity* vol. iii. p. 145.

[7] Milman, *Hist. of Latin Chris-tianity*, vol. i. pp. 290-291.

[8] Ibid. vol. i. pp. 310-311.

out two years after with an increased ferocity, and almost
every leading city of the East was filled by the monks with
bloodshed and with outrage.[1] St. Augustine himself is accused
of having excited every kind of popular persecution against
the Semi-Pelagians.[2] The Councils, animated by an almost
frantic hatred, urged on by their anathemas the rival sects.[3]
In the 'Robber Council' of Ephesus, Flavianus, the Bishop
of Constantinople, was kicked and beaten by the Bishop of
Alexandria, or at least by his followers, and a few days later
died from the effect of the blows.[4] In the contested election
that resulted in the election of St. Damasus as Pope of Rome,
though no theological question appears to have been at issue,
the riots were so fierce that one hundred and thirty-seven
corpses were found in one of the churches.[5] The precedent

---

[1] Milman, *Hist. of Latin Christianity*, vol. i. pp. 314–318.
Dean Milman thus sums up the
history: 'Monks in Alexandria,
monks in Antioch, monks in Jerusalem, monks in Constantinople,
decide peremptorily on orthodoxy
and heterodoxy. The bishops
themselves cower before them.
Macedonius in Constantinople, Flavianus in Antioch, Elias in Jerusalem, condemn themselves and
abdicate, or are driven from their
sees. Persecution is universal—
persecution by every means of vio
lence and cruelty; the only question
is, in whose hands is the power to
persecute. . . . Bloodshed, murder,
treachery, assassination, even during the public worship of God—
these are the frightful means by
which each party strives to maintain its opinions and to defeat its
adversary.'
[2] See a striking passage from
Julianus of Eclana, cited by Milman, *Hist. of Latin Christianity*,
vol. i. p. 164.
'Nowhere is Christianity less

attractive than in the Councils of
the Church. . . . Intrigue, injustice, violence, decisions on authority
alone, and that the authority of a
turbulent majority, . . . detract
from the reverence and impugn the
judgments of at least the later
Councils. The close is almost invariably a terrible anathema, in
which it is impossible not to dis-
cern the tones of human hatred, of
arrogant triumph, of rejoicing at
the damnation imprecated against
the humiliated adversary.'—Ibid.
vol. i. p. 202.
[4] See the account of this scene in
Gibbon, *Decline and Fall*, ch. xlvii.;
Milman, *Hist. of Latin Christianity*,
vol. i. p. 263.   There is a conflict of authorities as to whether
the Bishop of Alexandria himself
kicked his adversary, or, to speak
more correctly, the act which is
charged against him by some contemporary writers is not charged
against him by others. The violence was certainly done by his
followers and in his presence.

[5] Ammianus Marcellinus, xxvii. 3.

45

of the Jewish persecutions of idolatry having been adduced
by St. Cyprian, in the third century, in favour of excommunication,[1] was urged by Optatus, in the reign of Constantine, in favour of persecuting the Donatists;[2] in the next
reign we find a large body of Christians presenting to the
emperor a petition, based upon this precedent, imploring
him to destroy by force the Pagan worship.[3] About fifteen
years later, the whole Christian Church was prepared, on the
same grounds, to support the persecuting policy of St.
Ambrose,[4] the contending sects having found, in the duty of
crushing religious liberty, the solitary tenet on which they
were agreed. The most unaggressive and unobtrusive forms
of Paganism were persecuted with the same ferocity.[5] To
offer a sacrifice was to commit a capital offence; to hang up
a simple chaplet was to incur the forfeiture of an estate.
The noblest works of Asiatic architecture and of Greek
sculpture perished by the same iconoclasm that shattered the
humble temple at which the peasant loved to pray, or the
household gods which consecrated his home. There were no
varieties of belief too minute for the new intolerance to
embitter. The question of the proper time of celebrating
Easter was believed to involve the issue of salvation or
damnation;[6] and when, long after, in the fourteenth century,

---

[1] Cyprian, *Ep.* lxi.

[2] Milman, *Hist. of Christianity*,
vol. ii. p. 306.

[3] Ibid. iii. 10.

[4] 'By this time the Old Testament language and sentiment with
regard to idolatry were completely
incorporated with the Christian
feeling; and when Ambrose enforced on a Christian Emperor the
sacred duty of intolerance against
opinions and practices which
scarcely a century before had been
the established religion of the
Empire, his zeal was supported by

almost the unanimous applause of
the Christian world.'—Milman's
Hist. of Christianity, vol. iii. p. 159.

[5] See the Theodosian laws of
Paganism.

[6] This appears from the whole
history of the controversy; but the
prevailing feeling is, I think, expressed with peculiar vividness in
the following passage:—'Eadmer
says (following the words of Bede)
in Colman's times there was a sharp
controversy about the observing of
Easter, and other rules of life for
churchmen; therefore, this ques

the question of the nature of the light at the transfigura-
tion was discussed at Constantinople, those who refused to
admit that that light was uncreated, were deprived of the
honours of Christian burial.[1]

Together with these legislative and ecclesiastical measures,
a literature arose surpassing in its mendacious ferocity any
other the world had known. The polemical writers habitually
painted as dæmons those who diverged from the orthodox
belief, gloated with a vindictive piety over the sufferings of
the heretic upon earth, as upon a Divine punishment, and
sometimes, with an almost superhuman malice, passing in
imagination beyond the threshold of the grave, exulted in
no ambiguous terms on the tortures which they believed to
be reserved for him for ever. A few men, such as Synesius,
Basil, or Salvian, might still find some excellence in Pagans
or heretics, but their candour was altogether exceptional;
and he who will compare the beautiful pictures the Greek
poets gave of their Trojan adversaries, or the Roman historians
of the enemies of their country, with those which ecclesiastical
writers, for many centuries, almost invariably gave of all
who were opposed to their Church, may easily estimate the
extent to which cosmopolitan sympathy had retrograded.

At the period, however, when the Western monasteries
began to discharge their intellectual functions, the supremacy
of Catholicism was nearly established, and polemical ardour
had begun to wane. The literary zeal of the Church took
other forms, but all were deeply tinged by the monastic
spirit. It is difficult or impossible to conceive what would
have been the intellectual future of the world had Catholicism
never arisen—what principles or impulses would have guided
the course of the human mind, or what new institutions

tion deservedly excited the minds
and feeling of many people, fearing
lest perhaps, after having received
the name of Christians, they should

run, or had run in vain.—King's
Hist. of the Church of Ireland, book
ii. ch. vi.

[1] Gibbon, chap. lxiii.

would have been created for its culture.   Under the influence of Catholicism, the monastery became the one sphere of intellectual labour, and it continued during many centuries to occupy that position.   Without entering into anything resembling a literary history, which would be foreign to the objects of the present work, I shall endeavour briefly to estimate the manner in which it discharged its functions.

The first idea that is naturally suggested by the mention of the intellectual services of monasteries is the preservation of the writings of the Pagans.   I have already observed that among the early Christians there was a marked difference on the subject of their writings.   The school which was represented by Tertullian regarded them with abhorrence; while the Platonists, who were represented by Justin Martyr, Clement of Alexandria, and Origen, not merely recognised with great cordiality their beauties, but even imagined that they could detect in them both the traces of an original Divine inspiration, and plagiarisms from the Jewish writings. While avoiding, for the most part, these extremes, St. Augustine, the great organiser of Western Christianity, treats the Pagan writings with appreciative respect.   He had himself ascribed his first conversion from a course of vice to the 'Hortensius' of Cicero, and his works are full of discriminating, and often very beautiful, applications of the old Roman literature.   The attempt of Julian to prevent the Christians from teaching the classics, and the extreme resentment which that attempt elicited, show how highly the Christian leaders of that period valued this form of education; and it was naturally the more cherished on account of the contest.   The influence of Neoplatonism, the baptism of multitudes of nominal Christians after Constantine, and the decline of zeal which necessarily accompanied prosperity, had all in different ways the same tendency.   In Synesius we have the curious phenomenon of a bishop who, not content with proclaiming himself the admiring friend of the

Pagan Hypatia, openly declared his complete disbelief in the resurrection of the body, and his firm adhesion to the Platonic doctrine of the pre-existence of souls.[1]   Had the ecclesiastical theory prevailed which gave such latitude even to the leaders of the Church, the course of Christianity would have been very different. A reactionary spirit, however, arose at Rome. The doctrine of exclusive salvation supplied its intellectual basis; the political and organising genius of the Roman ecclesiastics impelled them to reduce belief into a rigid form; the genius of St. Gregory guided the movement,[2] and a series of historical events, of which the ecclesiastical and political separation of the Western empire from the speculative Greeks, and the invasion and conversion of the barbarians, were the most important, definitely established the ascendancy of the Catholic type. In the convulsions that followed the barbarian invasions, intellectual energy of a secular kind almost absolutely ceased. A parting gleam issued, indeed, in the sixth century, from the Court of Theodoric, at Ravenna, which was adorned by the genius of

---

[1] An interesting sketch of this very interesting prelate has lately been written by M. Druon, *Étude sur la Vie et les Œuvres de Synésius* (Paris, 1859).

[2] Tradition has pronounced Gregory the Great to have been the destroyer of the Palatine library, and to have been especially zealous in burning the writings of Livy, because they described the achievements of the Pagan gods. For these charges, however (which I am sorry to find repeated by so eminent a writer as Dr. Draper), there is no real evidence, for they are not found in any writer earlier than the twelfth century. (See Bayle, *Dict.* art. ' Greg.') The extreme contempt of Gregory for Pagan literature is, however, suffi-ciently manifested in his famous and very curious letter to Desiderius, Bishop of Vienne, rebuking him for having taught certain persons Pagan literature, and thus mingled ' the praises of Jupiter with the praises of Christ;' doing what would be impious even for a religious layman, 'polluting the mind with the blasphemous praises of the wicked.' Some curious evidence of the feelings of the Christians of the fourth, fifth, and sixth centuries, about Pagan literature, is given in Guinguené, *Hist. littéraire de l'Italie*, tome i. p. 29–31, and some legends of a later period are candidly related by one of the most enthusiastic English advocates of the Middle Ages. (Maitland, *Dark Ages.*)

Boëthius, and the talent of Cassiodorus and Symmachus; but after this time, for a long period, literature consisted almost exclusively of sermons and lives of saints, which were composed in the monasteries.[1] Gregory of Tours was succeeded as an annalist by the still feebler Frede garius, and there was then a long and absolute blank. A few outlying countries showed some faint animation. St. Leander and St. Isidore planted at Seville a school, which flourished in the seventh century, and the distant monasteries of Ireland continued somewhat later to be the receptacles of learning; but the rest of Europe sank into an almost absolute torpor, till the rationalism of Abelard, and the events that followed the crusades, began the revival of learning. The principal service which Catholicism rendered during this period to Pagan literature was probably the perpetuation of Latin as a sacred language. The complete absence of all curiosity about that literature is shown by the fact that Greek was suffered to become almost absolutely extinct, though there was no time when the Western nations had not some relations with the Greek empire, or when pilgrimages to the Holy Land altogether ceased. The study of the Latin classics was for the most part positively discouraged. The writers, it was believed, were burning in hell; the monks were too inflated with their imaginary knowledge to regard with any respect a Pagan writer, and periodical panics about the approaching termination of the

---

[1] Probably the best account of the intellectual history of these times is still to be found in the admirable introductory chapters with which the Benedictines prefaced each century of their *Hist. littéraire de la France*. The Benedictines think (with Hallam) that the eighth century was, on the whole, the darkest on the continent, though England attained its lowest point somewhat later. Of the great protectors of learning Theodoric was unable to write (see Guinguené, tome i. p. 31), and Charlemagne (Eginhard) only began to learn when advanced in life, and was never quite able to master the accomplishment. Alfred, however, was distinguished in literature

world continually checked any desire for secular learning.[1]
It was the custom among some monks, when they were under
the discipline of silence, and desired to ask for Virgil, Horace,
or any other Gentile work, to indicate their wish by scratching
their ears like a dog, to which animal it was thought the
Pagans might be reasonably compared.[2] The monasteries
contained, it is said, during some time, the only libraries in
Europe, and were therefore the sole receptacles of the Pagan
manuscripts; but we cannot infer from this that, if the
monasteries had not existed, similar libraries would not have
been called into being in their place. To the occasional
industry of the monks, in copying the works of antiquity,
we must oppose the industry they displayed, though chiefly
at a somewhat later period, in scraping the ancient parch-
ments, in order that, having obliterated the writing of the
Pagans, they might cover them with their own legends.[3]

There are some aspects, however, in which the monastic
period of literature appears eminently beautiful. The fret-

---

[1] The belief that the world was
just about to end was, as is well
known, very general among the
early Christians, and greatly
affected their lives. It appears in
the New Testament, and very
clearly in the epistle ascribed to
Barnabas in the first century. The
persecutions of the second and
third centuries revived it, and both
Tertullian and Cyprian (in Demetrianum) strongly assert it. With
the triumph of Christianity the
apprehension for a time subsided;
but it reappeared with great force
when the dissolution of the Empire
was manifestly impending, when it
was accomplished, and in the prolonged anarchy and suffering that
ensued. Gregory of Tours, writing
in the latter part of the sixth century, speaks of it as very prevalent
(Prologue to the First Book); and
St. Gregory the Great, about the
same time, constantly expresses it.
The panic that filled Europe at the
end of the tenth century has been
often described.

[2] Maitland's Dark Ages, p. 403.

[3] This passion for scraping
MSS. became common, according to
Montfaucon, after the twelfth century. (Maitland, p. 40.) According
to Hallam, however (Middle Ages,
ch. ix. part i.), it must have begun
earlier, being chiefly caused by the
cessation or great diminution of
the supply of Egyptian papyrus,
in consequence of the capture of
Alexandria by the Saracens, early
in the seventh century.

fulness and impatience and extreme tension of modern literary life, the many anxieties that paralyse, and the feverish craving for applause that perverts, so many noble intellects, were then unknown. Severed from all the cares of active life, in the deep calm of the monastery, where the turmoil of the outer world could never come, the monkish scholar pursued his studies in a spirit which has now almost faded from the world. No doubt had ever disturbed his mind. To him the problem of the universe seemed solved. Expatiating for ever with unfaltering faith upon the unseen world, he had learnt to live for it alone. His hopes were not fixed upon human greatness or fame, but upon the pardon of his sins, and the rewards of a happier world. A crowd of quaint and often beautiful legends illustrate the deep union that subsisted between literature and religion. It is related of Cædmon, the first great poet of the Anglo-Saxons, that he found in the secular life no vent for his hidden genius. When the warriors assembled at their banquets, sang in turn the praises of war or beauty, as the instrument passed to him, he rose and went out with a sad heart, for he alone was unable to weave his thoughts in verse. Wearied and desponding he lay down to rest, when a figure appeared to him in his dream and commanded him to sing the Creation of the World. A transport of religious fervour thrilled his brain, his imprisoned intellect was unlocked, and he soon became the foremost poet of his land.[1] A Spanish boy, having long tried in vain to master his task, and driven to despair by the severity of his teacher, ran away from his father's home. Tired with wandering, and full of anxious thoughts, he sat down to rest by the margin of a well, when his eye was caught by the deep furrow in the stone. He asked a girl who was drawing water to explain it, and she told him that it had been worn by the constant attrition of the rope. The poor boy, who

---

[1] Bede, *H. E.* iv. 24.

was already full of remorse for what he had done, recognised
in the reply a Divine intimation. 'If,' he thought, 'by daily
use the soft rope could thus penetrate the hard stone, surely
a long perseverance could overcome the dulness of my
brain.' He returned to his father's house; he laboured with
redoubled earnestness, and he lived to be the great St. Isidore
of Spain.[1] A monk who had led a vicious life was saved, it
is said, from hell, because it was found that his sins, though
very numerous, were just outnumbered by the letters of a
ponderous and devout book he had written.[2] The Holy
Spirit, in the shape of a dove, had been seen to inspire St.
Gregory; and the writings of St. Thomas Aquinas, and of
several other theologians, had been expressly applauded by
Christ or by his saints. When, twenty years after death, the
tomb of a certain monkish writer was opened, it was found
that, although the remainder of the body had crumbled into
dust, the hand that had held the pen remained flexible and
undecayed.[3] A young and nameless scholar was once buried
near a convent at Bonn. The night after his funeral, a nun
whose cell overlooked the cemetery was awakened by a brilliant light that filled the room. She started up, imagining
that the day had dawned, but on looking out she found that
it was still night, though a dazzling splendour was around.
A female form of matchless loveliness was bending over the
scholar's grave. The effluence of her beauty filled the air
with light, and she clasped to her heart a snow-white dove
that rose to meet her from the tomb. It was the Mother of

---

[1] Mariana, *De Rebus Hispaniæ*,
vi. 7. Mariana says the stone was
in his time preserved as a relic.

[2] Odericus Vitalis, quoted by
Maitland (*Dark Ages*, pp. 268–269).
The monk was restored to life that
he might have an opportunity of
reformation. The escape was a
narrow one, for there was only one
letter against which no sin could

be adduced—a remarkable instance
of the advantages of a diffuse style.

[3] Digby, *Mores Catholici*, book
x. p. 246. Matthew of Westminster tells of a certain king who was
very charitable, and whose right
hand (which had assuaged many
sorrows) remained undecayed after
death (A.D. 644).

God come to receive the soul of the martyred scholar; 'for scholars too,' adds the old chronicler, 'are martyrs if they live in purity and labour with courage.'[1]

But legends of this kind, though not without a very real beauty, must not blind us to the fact that the period of Catholic ascendancy was on the whole one of the most deplorable in the history of the human mind. The energies of Christendom were diverted from all useful and progressive studies, and were wholly expended on theological disquisitions. A crowd of superstitions, attributed to infallible wisdom, barred the path of knowledge, and the charge of magic, or the charge of heresy, crushed every bold enquiry in the sphere of physical nature or of opinions. Above all, the conditions of true enquiry had been cursed by the Church. A blind unquestioning credulity was inculcated as the first of duties, and the habit of doubt, the impartiality of a suspended judgment, the desire to hear both sides of a disputed question, and to emancipate the judgment from unreasoning prejudice, were all in consequence condemned. The belief in the guilt of error and doubt became universal, and that belief may be confidently pronounced to be the most pernicious superstition that has ever been accredited among mankind. Mistaken facts are rectified by enquiry. Mistaken methods of research, though far more inveterate, are gradually altered; but the spirit that shrinks from enquiry as sinful, and deems a state of doubt a state of guilt, is the most enduring disease that can afflict the mind of man. Not till the education of Europe passed from the monasteries to the universities, not till Mohammedan science, and classical freethought, and industrial independence broke the sceptre of the Church, did the intellectual revival of Europe begin.

I am aware that so strong a statement of the intellectual darkness of the middle ages is likely to encounter opposition

[1] See Hauréau, *Hist de la Philosophie scolastique*, tome i. pp. 24–25.

from many quarters. The blindness which the philosophers of the eighteenth century manifested to their better side has produced a reaction which has led many to an opposite, and, I believe, far more erroneous extreme. Some have become eulogists of the period, through love of its distinctive theological doctrines, and others through archæological enthusiasm, while a very pretentious and dogmatic, but, I think, sometimes superficial, school of writers, who loudly boast themselves the regenerators of history, and treat with supreme contempt all the varieties of theological opinion, are accustomed, partly through a very shallow historical optimism which scarcely admits the possibility of retrogression, and partly through sympathy with the despotic character of Catholicism, to extol the mediæval society in the most extravagant terms. Without entering into a lengthy examination of this subject, I may be permitted to indicate shortly two or three fallacies which are continually displayed in their appreciations.

It is an undoubted truth that, for a considerable period, almost all the knowledge of Europe was included in the monasteries, and from this it is continually inferred that, had these institutions not existed, knowledge would have been absolutely extinguished. But such a conclusion I conceive to be altogether untrue. During the period of the Pagan empire, intellectual life had been diffused over a vast portion of the globe. Egypt and Asia Minor had become great centres of civilisation. Greece was still a land of learning. Spain, Gaul, and even Britain,[1] were full of libraries and teachers. The schools of Narbonne, Arles, Bordeaux, Toulouse, Lyons, Marseilles, Poitiers, and Trèves were already famous. The Christian emperor Gratian, in A D. 376, carried out in Gaul a system similar to that which

---

[1] On the progress of Roman civilisation in Britain, see Tacitus, *Agricola*, xxi.

had already, under the Antonines, been pursued in Italy, ordaining that teachers should be supported by the State in every leading city.[1]   To suppose that Latin literature, having been so widely diffused, could have totally perished, or that all interest in it could have permanently ceased, even under the extremely unfavourable circumstances that followed the downfall of the Roman Empire and the Mohammedan invasions, is, I conceive, absurd.   If Catholicism had never existed, the human mind would have sought other spheres for its development, and at least a part of the treasures of antiquity would have been preserved in other ways.   The monasteries, as corporations of peaceful men protected from the incursions of the barbarians, became very naturally the reservoirs to which the streams of literature flowed; but much of what they are represented as creating, they had in reality only attracted.   The inviolable sanctity which they secured rendered them invaluable receptacles of ancient learning in a period of anarchy and perpetual war, and the industry of the monks in transcribing, probably more than counterbalanced their industry in effacing, the classical writings.   The ecclesiastical unity of Christendom was also of extreme importance in rendering possible a general interchange of ideas.   Whether these services outweighed the intellectual evils resulting from the complete diversion of the human mind from all secular learning, and from the persistent inculcation, as a matter of duty, of that habit of abject credulity which it is the first task of the intellectual reformer to eradicate, may be reasonably doubted.

It is not unfrequent, again, to hear the preceding fallacy stated in a somewhat different form.   We are reminded that almost all the men of genius during several centuries were great theologians, and we are asked to conceive the more than Egyptian darkness that would have prevailed had the

---

[1] See the Benedictine *Hist. littér. de la France*, tome i. part ii. p. 9.

Catholic theology which produced them not existed. This judgment resembles that of the prisoner in a famous passage of Cicero, who, having spent his entire life in a dark dungeon, and knowing the light of day only from a single ray which passed through a fissure in the wall, inferred that if the wall were removed, as the fissure would no longer exist, all light would be excluded. Mediæval Catholicism discouraged and suppressed in every way secular studies, while it conferred a monopoly of wealth and honour and power upon the distinguished theologian. Very naturally, therefore, it attracted into the path of theology the genius that would have existed without it, but would under other circumstances have been displayed in other forms.

It is not to be inferred, however, from this, that mediæval Catholicism had not, in the sphere of intellect, any real creative power. A great moral or religious enthusiasm always evokes a certain amount of genius that would not otherwise have existed, or at least been displayed, and the monasteries were peculiarly fitted to develop certain casts of mind, which in no other sphere could have so perfectly expanded. The great writings of St. Thomas Aquinas[1] and his followers, and, in more modern times, the massive and conscientious erudition of the Benedictines, will always make certain periods of the monastic history venerable to the scholar. But, when we remember that during many centuries nearly every one possessing any literary taste or talents became a monk, when we recollect that these monks were familiar with the language, and might easily have been familiar with the noble literature, of ancient Rome, and when

---

[1] A biographer of St. Thomas Aquinas modestly observes:— 'L'opinion généralement répandue parmi les théologiens c'est que la *Somme de Théologie* de St. Thomas est non-seulement son chef-d'œuvre mais aussi celui de l'esprit humain.' (!!)—Carle, *Hist. de St.-Thomas d'Aquin*, p. 140.

we also consider the mode of their life, which would seem, from its freedom from care, and from the very monotony of its routine, peculiarly calculated to impel them to study we can hardly fail to wonder how very little of any real value they added, for so long a period, to the knowledge of man kind.   It is indeed a remarkable fact that, even in the ages when the Catholic ascendancy was most perfect, some of the greatest achievements were either opposed or simply external to ecclesiastical influence.   Roger Bacon, having been a monk, is frequently spoken of as a creature of Catholic teaching. But there never was a more striking instance of the force of a great genius in resisting the tendencies of his age.   At a time when physical science was continually neglected, discouraged, or condemned, at a time when all the great prizes of the world were open to men who pursued a very different course, Bacon applied himself with transcendent genius to the study of nature.   Fourteen years of his life were spent in prison, and when he died his name was blasted as a magician.   The mediæval laboratories were chiefly due to the pursuit of alchemy, or to Mohammedan encouragement. The inventions of the mariner's compass, of gunpowder, and of rag paper were all, indeed, of extreme importance; but no part of the credit of them belongs to the monks.   Their origin is involved in much obscurity, but it is almost certain that the last two, at all events, were first employed in Europe by the Mohammedans of Spain.   Cotton paper was in use among these as early as 1009.   Among the Christian nations it appears to have been unknown till late in the thirteenth century.   The first instance of the employment of artillery among Christian nations was at the battle of Crecy, but the knowledge of gunpowder among them has been traced back as far as 1338.   There is abundant evidence, however, of its employment in Spain by Mohammedans in several sieges in the thirteenth century, and even in a battle between the Moors of Seville and those of Tunis at the end of the eleventh century.[1] In invention, indeed, as well as in original research, the mediæval monasteries were singularly barren. They cultivated formal logic to great perfection. They produced many patient and laborious, though, for the most part, wholly uncritical scholars, and many philosophers who, having assumed their premises with unfaltering faith, reasoned from them with admirable subtlety; but they taught men to regard the sacrifice of secular learning as a noble thing; they impressed upon them a theory of the habitual government of the universe, which is absolutely untrue; and they diffused, wherever their influence extended, habits of credulity and intolerance that are the most deadly poisons to the human mind.

It is, again, very frequently observed among the more philosophic eulogists of the mediæval period, that although the Catholic Church is a trammel and an obstacle to the progress of civilised nations, although it would be scarcely possible to exaggerate the misery her persecuting spirit caused, when the human mind had outstripped her teaching; yet there was a time when she was greatly in advance of the age, and the complete and absolute ascendancy she then exercised was intellectually eminently beneficial. That there is much truth in this view, I have myself repeatedly maintained. But when men proceed to isolate the former period, and to make it the theme of unqualified eulogy, they fall, I think, into a grave error. The evils that sprang from the later period of Catholic ascendancy were not an accident or a perversion, but a normal and necessary consequence of the previous despotism. The principles which were imposed on the mediæval world, and which were the conditions of so

[1] See Viardot, *Hist. des Arabes m Espagne*, ii. 142–166. Prescott's *Ferdinand and Isabella*, ch. viii. Viardot contends that the compass —which appears to have been long known in China—was first introduced into Europe by the Mohammedans; but the evidence of this appears inconclusive.

much of its distinctive excellence, were of such a nature that
they claimed to be final, and could not possibly be discarded
without a struggle and a convulsion.   We must estimate
the influence of these principles considered as a whole, and
during the entire period of their operation.   There are some
poisons which, before they kill men, allay pain and diffuse
a soothing sensation through the frame.   We may recognise
the hour of enjoyment they procure, but we must not separate
it from the price at which it is purchased.

The extremely unfavourable influence the Catholic
Church long exercised upon intellectual development had
important moral consequences.   Although moral progress
does not necessarily depend upon intellectual progress it is
materially affected by it, intellectual activity being the most
important element in the growth of that great and complex organism which we call civilisation.   The mediæval
credulity had also a more direct moral influence in producing that indifference to truth, which is the most repulsive feature of so many Catholic writings.   The very large
part that must be assigned to deliberate forgeries in the early
apologetic literature of the Church we have already seen; and
no impartial reader can, I think, investigate the innumerable
grotesque and lying legends that, during the whole course of
the Middle Ages, were deliberately palmed upon mankind as
undoubted facts, can follow the histories of the false decretals,
and the discussions that were connected with them, or can
observe the complete and absolute incapacity most Catholic
historians have displayed, of conceiving any good thing in the
ranks of their opponents, or of stating with common fairness
any consideration that can tell against their cause, without
acknowledging how serious and how inveterate has been the
evil.   There have, no doubt, been many noble individual ex
ceptions.   Yet it is, I believe, difficult to exaggerate the
extent to which this moral defect exists in most of the ancient
and very much of the modern literature of Catholicism.   It

is this which makes it so unspeakably repulsive to all independent and impartial thinkers, and has led a great German
historian[1] to declare, with much bitterness, that the phrase
Christian veracity deserves to rank with the phrase Punic
faith. But this absolute indifference to truth whenever
falsehood could subserve the interests of the Church is perfectly explicable, and was found in multitudes who, in other
respects, exhibited the noblest virtue. An age which has
ceased to value impartiality of judgment will soon cease to
value accuracy of statement; and when credulity is inculcated
as a virtue, falsehood will not long be stigmatised as a vice.
When, too, men are firmly convinced that salvation can only
be found within their Church, and that their Church can absolve from all guilt, they will speedily conclude that nothing
can possibly be wrong which is beneficial to it. They exchange the love of truth for what they call the love of *the*
truth. They regard morals as derived from and subordinate
to theology, and they regulate all their statements, not by the
standard of veracity, but by the interests of their creed.

Another important moral consequence of the monastic
system was the great prominence given to pecuniary com-
pensations for crime. It had been at first one of the broad
distinctions between Paganism and Christianity, that, while
the rites of the former were for the most part unconnected
with moral dispositions, Christianity made purity of heart an
essential element of all its worship. Among the Pagans a
few faint efforts had, it is true, been made in this direction.
An old precept or law, which is referred to by Cicero, and
which was strongly reiterated by Apollonius of Tyana, and
the Pythagoreans, declared that 'no impious man should
dare to appease the anger of the divinities by gifts;'[2] and
oracles are said to have more than once proclaimed that the

---

[1] Herder.

[2] 'Impius ne audeto placare
ionis iram Deorum.'—Cicero, *De*
Leg. ii. 9. See, too, Philost.
Apoll. Tyan. i. 11.

hecatombs of noble oxen with gilded horns that were offered up ostentatiously by the rich, were less pleasing to the gods than the wreaths of flowers and the modest and reverential worship of the poor.[1] In general, however, in the Pagan world, the service of the temple had little or no connection with morals, and the change which Christianity effected in this respect was one of its most important benefits to mankind. It was natural, however, and perhaps inevitable, that in the course of time, and under the action of very various causes, the old Pagan sentiment should revive, and even with an increased intensity. In no respect had the Christians been more nob'y distinguished than by their charity. It was not surprising that the Fathers, while exerting all their eloquence to stimulate this virtue—especially during the calamities that accompanied the dissolution of the Empire—should have dilated in extremely strong terms upon the spiritual benefits the donor would receive for his gift. It is also not surprising that this selfish calculation should gradually, and among hard and ignorant men, have absorbed all other motives. A curious legend, which is related by a writer of the seventh century, illustrates the kind of feeling that had arisen. The Christian bishop Synesius succeeded in converting a Pagan named Evagrius, who for a long time, however, felt doubts about the passage, 'He who giveth to the poor lendeth to the Lord.' On his conversion, and in obedience to this verse, he gave Synesius three hundred pieces of gold to be distributed among the poor; but he exacted from the bishop, as the representative of Christ, a promissory note, engaging that he should be repaid in the future world. Many years later, Evagrius, being on his death-bed, commanded his sons, when they buried him, to place the note in his hand, and to do so without informing Synesius. His

---

[1] There are three or four instances of this related by Porphyry *De Abstin. Carnis*, lib. ii.

lying injunction was observed, and three days afterwards he appeared to Synesius in a dream, told him that the debt had been paid, and ordered him to go to the tomb, where he would find a written receipt. Synesius did as he was commanded, and, the grave being opened, the promissory note was found in the hand of the dead man, with an endorsement declaring that the debt had been paid by Christ. The note, it was said, was long after preserved as a relic in the church of Cyrene.[1]

The kind of feeling which this legend displays was soon turned with tenfold force into the channel of monastic life. A law of Constantine accorded, and several later laws enlarged, the power of bequests to ecclesiastics. Ecclesiastical property was at the same time exonerated from the public burdens, and this measure not only directly assisted its increase, but had also an important indirect influence; for, when taxation was heavy, many laymen ceded the ownership of their estates to the monasteries, with a secret condition that they should, as vassals, receive the revenues unburdened by taxation, and subject only to a slight payment to the monks as to their feudal lords.[2] The monks were regarded as the trustees of the poor, and also as themselves typical poor, and all the promises that applied to those who gave to the poor applied, it was said, to the benefactors of the monasteries. The monastic chapel also contained the relics of saints or sacred images of miraculous power, and throngs of worship-

[1] Moschus, *Pratum Spirituale* (Rosweyde), cap. cxcv. M. Wallon quotes from the *Life of St.-Jean l'Aumônier* an even stranger event which happened to St. Peter Telonearius. 'Pour repousser les importunités des pauvres, il leur jetait des pierres. Un jour, n'en trouvant pas sous la main. il leur jeta un pain à la tête. Il tomba malade et eut une vision. Ses mérites étaient comptés: d'un côté étaient tous ses crimes, de l'autre ce pain jeté comme une insulte aux pauvres et accepté comme une aumône par Jésus Christ.'—*Hist. de l'Esclavage,* tome iii. p. 397.

I may mention here that the ancient Gauls were said to have been accustomed to lend money on the condition of its being repaid to the lender in the next life.—(Val. Maximus, lib. ii. cap. vi. § 10.)

[2] Muratori, *Antich. Italiane,* diss. lxvii.

pers were attracted by the miracles, and desired to place them selves under the protection, of the saint.   It is no exaggeration to say that to give money to the priests was for several centuries the first article of the moral code.   Political minds may have felt the importance of aggrandising a pacific and industrious class in the centre of a disorganised society, and family affection may have predisposed many in favour of institutions which contained at least one member of most families; but in the overwhelming majority of cases the motive was simple superstition.   In seasons of sickness, of danger, of sorrow, or of remorse, whenever the fear or the conscience of the worshipper was awakened, he hastened to purchase with money the favour of a saint.   Above all, in the hour of death, when the terrors of the future world loomed darkly upon his mind, he saw in a gift or legacy to the monks a sure means of effacing the most monstrous crimes, and securing his ultimate happiness.   A rich man was soon scarcely deemed a Christian if he did not leave a portion of his property to the Church, and the charters of innumerable monasteries in every part of Europe attest the vast tracts of land that were ceded by will to the monks, 'for the benefit of the soul' of the testator.[1]

It has been observed by a great historian that we may trace three distinct phases in the early history of the Church. In the first period religion was a question of morals; in the second period, which culminated in the fifth century, it had become a question of orthodoxy; in the third period, which dates from the seventh century, it was a question of munificence to monasteries.[2]   The despotism of Catholicism, and

---

[1] See, on the causes of the wealth of the monasteries, two admirable dissertations by Muratori, *Antich. Italiane,* lxvii., lxviii.; Hallam's *Middle Ages,* ch. vii. part i.

[2] 'Lors de l'établissement du christianisme la religion avoit essentiellement consisté dans l'enseignement moral; elle avoit exercé les cœurs et les âmes par la recherche de ce qui étoit vraiment beau, vraiment honnête. Au cinquième siècle on l'avoit surtout attachée à l'orthodoxie, au septième on l'avoit ré-

the ignorance that followed the barbarian invasions, had repressed the struggles of heresy, and in the period of almost absolute darkness that continued from the sixth to the twelfth century, the theological ideal of unquestioning faith and of perfect unanimity was all but realised in the West. All the energy that in previous ages had been expended in combating heresy was now expended in acquiring wealth. The people compounded for the most atrocious crimes by gifts to shrines of those saints whose intercession was supposed to be unfailing. The monks, partly by the natural cessation of their old enthusiasm, partly by the absence of any hostile criticism of their acts, and partly too by the very wealth they had acquired, sank into gross and general immorality. The great majority of them had probably at no time been either saints actuated by a strong religious motive, nor yet diseased and desponding minds seeking a refuge from the world; they had been simply peasants, of no extraordinary devotion or sensitiveness, who preferred an ensured subsistence, with no care, little labour, a much higher social position than they could otherwise acquire, and the certainty, as they believed, of going to heaven, to the laborious and precarious existence of the serf, relieved, indeed, by the privilege of marriage, but exposed to military service, to extreme hardships, and to constant oppression. Very naturally, when they could do so with impunity, they broke their vows of chastity. Very naturally, too, they availed themselves to the full of the condition of affairs, to draw as much wealth as possible into their community.[1] The belief in the approaching

---

duite à la bienfaisance envers les couvens.' — Sismondi, *Hist. des Français*, tome ii. p. 50.

[1] Mr. Hallam, speaking of the legends of the miracles of saints, says: 'It must not be supposed that these absurdities were produced as well as nourished by ignorance. In most cases they were the work of deliberate imposture. Every cathedral or monastery had its tutelar saint, and every saint his legend, fabricated in order to enrich the churches under his protection, by exaggerating his virtues, his miracles, and consequently his

end of the world, especially at the close of the tenth century, the crusades, which gave rise to a profitable traffic in the form of a pecuniary commutation of vows, and the black death, which produced a paroxysm of religious fanaticism, stimulated the movement. In the monkish chronicles, the merits of sovereigns are almost exclusively judged by their bounty to the Church, and in some cases this is the sole part of their policy which has been preserved.[1]

There were, no doubt, a few redeeming points in this dark period. The Irish monks are said to have been honourably distinguished for their reluctance to accept the lavish donations of their admirers,[2] and some missionary monasteries of a high order of excellence were scattered through Europe. A few legends, too, may be cited censuring the facility with which money acquired by crime was accepted as an atonement for crime.[3] But these cases were very rare, and the religious history of several centuries is little more than a history of the rapacity of priests and of the credulity of laymen. In

---

power of serving those who paid liberally for his patronage.'—*Middle Ages*, ch. ix. part i. I do not think this passage makes sufficient allowance for the unconscious formation of many saintly myths, but no impartial person can doubt its substantial truth.

[1] Sismondi, *Hist. des Français*, tome ii. pp. 54, 62-63.

[2] Milman's *Hist. of Latin Christianity*, vol. ii. p. 257.

[3] Durandus, a French bishop of the thirteenth century, tells how, 'when a certain bishop was consecrating a church built out of the fruits of usury and pillage, he saw behind the altar the devil in a pontifical vestment, standing at the bishop's throne, who said unto the bishop, "Cease from consecrating the church; for it pertaineth to my jurisdiction, since it is built from the fruits of usuries and robberies." Then the bishop and the clergy having fled thence in fear, immediately the devil destroyed that church with a great noise.'— *Rationale Divinorum*, i. 6 (translated for the Camden Society).

A certain St. Launomar is said to have refused a gift for his monastery from a rapacious noble, because he was sure it was derived from pillage. (Montalembert's *Moines d'Occident*, tome ii. pp. 350-351.) When prostitutes were converted in the early Church, it was the rule that the money of which they had become possessed should never be applied to ecclesiastical purposes, but should be distributed among the poor.

England, the perpetual demands of the Pope excited a fierce resentment; and we may trace with remarkable clearness, in every page of Matthew Paris, the alienation of sympathy arising from this cause, which prepared and foreshadowed the final rupture of England from the Church. Ireland, on the other hand, had been given over by two Popes to the English invader, on the condition of the payment of Peter's pence. The outrageous and notorious immorality of the monasteries, during the century before the Reformation, was chiefly due to their great wealth; and that immorality, as the writings of Erasmus and Ulric von Hutten show, gave a powerful impulse to the new movement, while the abuses of the indulgences were the immediate cause of the revolt of Luther. But these things arrived only after many centuries of successful fraud. The religious terrorism that was unscrupulously employed had done its work, and the chief riches of Christendom had passed into the coffers of the Church.

It is, indeed, probable that religious terrorism played a more important part in the monastic phase of Christianity than it had done even in the great work of the conversion of the Pagans. Although two or three amiable theologians had made faint and altogether abortive attempts to question the eternity of punishment; although there had been some slight difference of opinion concerning the future of some Pagan philosophers who had lived before the introduction of Christianity, and also upon the question whether infants who died unbaptised were only deprived of all joy, or were actually subjected to never-ending agony, there was no question as to the main features of the Catholic doctrine. According to the patristic theologians, it was part of the gospel revelation that the misery and suffering the human race endures upon earth is but a feeble image of that which awaits it in the future world; that all its members beyond the Church, as well as a very large proportion of those who are within its pale, are doomed to an eternity of agony in a

literal and undying fire. The monastic legends took up this
doctrine, which in itself is sufficiently revolting, and they
developed it with an appalling vividness and minuteness.
St. Macarius, it is said, when walking one day through the
desert, saw a skull upon the ground. He struck it with his
staff and it began to speak. It told him that it was the
skull of a Pagan priest who had lived before the introduction
of Christianity into the world, and who had accordingly been
doomed to hell. As high as the heaven is above the earth,
so high does the fire of hell mount in waves above the souls
that are plunged into it. The damned souls were pressed
together back to back, and the lost priest made it his single
entreaty to the saint that he would pray that they might
be turned face to face, for he believed that the sight of a
brother's face might afford him some faint consolation in the
eternity of agony that was before him.[1]   The story is well
known of how St. Gregory, seeing on a bas-relief a representation of the goodness of Trajan to a poor widow, pitied the
Pagan emperor, whom he knew to be in hell, and prayed
that he might be released. He was told that his prayer was
altogether unprecedented; but at last, on his promising that
he would never offer such a prayer again, it was partially
granted. Trajan was not withdrawn from hell, but he was
freed from the torments which the remainder of the Pagan
world endured.[2]

An entire literature of visions depicting the torments of

---

[1] *Verba Seniorum*, Prol. § 172.
[2] This vision is not related by
St. Gregory himself, and some
Catholics are perplexed about it, on
account of the vision of another
saint, who afterwards asked whether
Trajan was saved, and received
for answer, 'I wish men to rest in
ignorance of this subject, that the
Catholics may become stronger.
For this emperor, though he had

great virtues, was an unbaptised
infidel.' The whole subject of the
vision of St. Gregory is discussed
by Champagny, *Les Antonins*, tome
i. pp. 372-373. This devout writer
says, 'Cette légende fut acceptée
par tout le moyen-âge, *indulgent
pour les païens illustres* et tout dis-
posé à les supposer chrétiens et
sauvés.'

hell was soon produced by the industry of the monks. The apocryphal Gospel of Nicodemus, which purported to describe the descent of Christ into the lower world, contributed to foster it; and St. Gregory the Great has related many visions in a more famous work, which professed to be compiled with scrupulous veracity from the most authentic sources,[1] and of which it may be confidently averred that it scarcely contains a single page which is not tainted with grotesque and deliberate falsehood. Men, it was said, passed into a trance or temporary death, and were then carried for a time to hell. Among others, a certain man named Stephen, from whose lips the saint declares that he had heard the tale, had died by mistake. When his soul was borne to the gates of hell, the Judge declared that it was another Stephen who was wanted; the disembodied spirit, after inspecting hell, was restored to its former body, and the next day it was known that another Stephen had died.[2] Volcanoes were the portals of hell, and a hermit had seen the soul of the Arian emperor Theodoric, as St. Eucherius afterwards did the soul of Charles Martel, carried down that in the Island of Lipari.[3] The craters in Sicily, it was remarked, were continually agitated, and continually increasing, and this, as St. Gregory observes, was probably due to the impending ruin of the world, when the great press of lost souls would render it necessary to enlarge the approaches to their prisons.[4]

But the glimpses of hell that are furnished in the ' Dialogues' of St. Gregory appear meagre and unimaginative, compared with those of some later monks. A long series of monastic visions, of which that of St. Fursey, in the seventh century, was one of the first, and which followed

---

[1] See the solemn asseveration of the care which he took in going only to the most credible and authorised sources for his materials, in the Preface to the First Book of *Dialogues*.
[2] *Dial.* iv. 36.
[3] Ibid. iv. 30.
[4] Ibid. iv. 35.

in rapid succession, till that of Tundale, in the twelfth century, professed to describe with the most detailed accuracy the condition of the lost.[1]   It is impossible to conceive more ghastly, grotesque, and material conceptions of the future world than they evince, or more hideous calumnies against that Being who was supposed to inflict upon His creatures such unspeakable misery.   The devil was represented bound by red-hot chains, on a burning gridiron in the centre of hell.   The screams of his never-ending agony made its rafters to resound ; but his hands were free, and with these he seized the lost souls, crushed them like grapes against his teeth, and then drew them by his breath down the fiery cavern of his throat.   Dæmons with hooks of red-hot iron plunged souls alternately into fire and ice.   Some of the lost were hung up by their tongues, others were sawn asunder, others gnawed by serpents, others beaten together on an anvil and welded into a single mass, others boiled and then strained through a cloth, others twined in the embraces of dæmons whose limbs were of flame.   The fire of earth, it was said, was but a picture of that of hell.   The latter was so immeasurably more intense that it alone could be called real.   Sulphur was mixed with it, partly to increase its heat, and partly, too, in order that an insufferable stench might be added to the misery of the lost, while, unlike other flames, it emitted, according to some visions, no light,

---

[1] The fullest collection of these visions with which I am acquainted is that made for the Philobiblion Society (vol. ix.), by M. Delepierre, called *L'Enfer décrit par ceux qui l'ont vu,* of which I have largely availed myself.   See, too, Rusca *De Inferno* Wright's *Purgatory of St. Patrick,* and an interesting collection of visions given by Mr. Longfellow, in his translation of Dante. The Irish saints were, I am sorry to say, pro-minent in producing this branch of literature.   St. Fursey, whose vision is one of the earliest, and Tondale, or Tundale, whose vision is one of the most detailed, were both Irish. The English historians contain several of these visions.   Bede relates two or three—William of Malmesbury that of Charles the Fat ; Matthew Paris three visions of purgatory.

that the horror of darkness might be added to the horror of pain. A narrow bridge spanned the abyss, and from it the souls of sinners were plunged into the darkness that was below.[1]

Such catalogues of horrors, though they now awake in an educated man a sentiment of mingled disgust, weariness, and contempt, were able for many centuries to create a degree of panic and of misery we can scarcely realise. With the exception of the heretic Pelagius, whose noble genius, anticipating the discoveries of modern science, had repudiated the theological notion of death having been introduced into the world on account of the act of Adam, it was universally held among Christians that all the forms of suffering and dissolution that are manifested on earth were penal inflictions. The destruction of the world was generally believed to be at hand. The minds of men were filled with images of the approaching catastrophe, and innumerable legends of visible dæmons were industriously circulated. It was the custom then, as it is the custom now, for Catholic priests to stain the imaginations of young children by ghastly pictures of future misery, to imprint upon the virgin mind atrocious images which they hoped, not unreasonably, might prove indelible.[2]   In hours of weakness and of sickness their

---

[1] The narrow bridge over hell (in some visions covered with spikes), which is a conspicuous feature in the Mohammedan pictures of the future world, appears very often in Catholic visions. See Greg. Tur. iv. 33 ; St. Greg. *Dial.* iv. 36 ; and the vision of Tundale, in Delepierre.

[2] Few Englishmen, I imagine, are aware of the infamous publications written with this object, that are circulated by the Catholic priests among the poor. I have before me a tract 'for children and young persons,' called *The Sight of Hell*, by the Rev. J. Furniss, C.S.S.R., published 'permissu superiorum,' by Duffy (Dublin and London). It is a detailed description of the dungeons of hell, and a few sentences may serve as a sample. 'See! on the middle of that red-hot floor stands a girl; she looks about sixteen years old. Her feet are bare. She has neither shoes nor stockings. . . . Listen! she speaks. She says, I have been standing on this red-hot floor for years. Day and night my only standing-place has

overwrought fancy seemed to see hideous beings hovering around, and hell itself yawning to receive its victim. St. Gregory describes how a monk, who, though apparently a man of exemplary and even saintly piety, had been accustomed secretly to eat meat, saw on his deathbed a fearful dragon twining its tail round his body, and, with open jaws, sucking his breath;[1] and how a little boy of five years old, who had learnt from his father to repeat blasphemous words, saw, as he lay dying, exulting dæmons who were waiting to carry him to hell.[2] To the jaundiced eye of the theologian, all nature seemed stricken and forlorn, and its brightness and beauty suggested no ideas but those of deception and of sin. The redbreast, according to one popular legend, was commissioned by the Deity to carry a drop of water to the souls of unbaptised infants in hell, and its breast was singed in piercing the flames.[3] In the calm, still hour of evening,

---

been this red-hot floor. . . . Look at my burnt and bleeding feet. Let me go off this burning floor for one moment, only for one single short moment . . . The fourth dungeon is the boiling kettle . . . in the middle of it there is a boy. . . . His eyes are burning like two burning coals. Two long flames come out of his ears. . . . Sometimes he opens his mouth, and blazing fire rolls out. But listen! there is a sound like a kettle boiling. . . . The blood is boiling in the scalded veins of that boy. The brain is boiling and bubbling in his head. The marrow is boiling in his bones. . . . The fifth dungeon is the red-hot oven. . . . The little child is in this red hot oven. Hear how it screams to come out. See how it turns and twists itself about in the fire. It beats its head against the roof of the oven. It stamps its little feet on the floor. . . . God

was very good to this child. Very likely God saw it would get worse and worse, and would never repent, and so it would have to be punished much more in hell. So God in His mercy called it out of the world in its early childhood.' If the reader desires to follow this subject further, he may glance over a companion tract by the same reverend gentleman, called *A Terrible Judgment on a Little Child*; and also a book on *Hell*, translated from the Italian of Pinamonti, and with illustrations depicting the various tortures.

[1] St. Greg. *Dial.* iv. 38.

[2] Ibid. iv. 18.

[3] Alger's *History of the Doctrine of a Future Life* (New York. 1866), p. 414. The ignis fatuus was sometimes supposed to be the soul of an unbaptised child. There is, I believe, another Catholic legend about the redbreast, of a very

when the peasant boy asked why the sinking sun, as it dipped beneath the horizon, flushed with such a glorious red, he was answered, in the words of an old Saxon catechism, because it is then looking into hell.[1]

It is related in the vision of Tundale, that as he gazed upon the burning plains of hell, and listened to the screams of ceaseless and hopeless agony that were wrung from the sufferers, the cry broke from his lips, ' Alas, Lord ! what truth is there in what I have so often heard—the earth is filled with the mercy of God?'[2] It is, indeed, one of the most curious things in moral history, to observe how men who were sincerely indignant with Pagan writers for attributing to their divinities the frailties of an occasional jealousy or an occasional sensuality—for representing them, in a word, like men of mingled characters and passions—have nevertheless unscrupulously attributed to their own Divinity a degree of cruelty which may be confidently said to transcend the utmost barbarity of which human nature is capable. Neither Nero nor Phalaris could have looked complacently for ever on millions enduring the torture of fire—most of them because of a crime which was committed, not by themselves, but by their ancestors, or because they had adopted some mistaken conclusion on intricate questions of history or metaphysics.[3]

---

different kind—that its breast was stained with blood when it was trying to pull out the thorns from the crown of Christ.

[1] Wright's *Purgatory of St. Patrick*, p. 26. M. Delepierre quotes a curious theory of Father Hardouin (who is chiefly known for his suggestion that the classics were composed by the mediæval monks) that the rotation of the earth is caused by the lost souls trying to escape from the fire that is at the centre of the globe, climbing, in consequence, on the inner

crust of the earth, which is the wall of hell, and thus making the whole revolve, as the squirrel by climbing turns its cage! (*L'Enfer décrit par ceux qui l'ont vu*, p. 151.)

[2] Delepierre, p. 70.

[3] Thus, in a book which was attributed (it is said erroneously) to Jeremy Taylor, we find two singularly unrhetorical and unimpassioned chapters, deliberately enumerating the most atrocious acts of cruelty in human history, and maintaining that they are surpassed by the tortures inflicted by the

To those who do not regard such teaching as true, it must appear without exception the most odious in the religious history of the world, subversive of the very foundations of morals, and well fitted to transform the man who at once realised it, and accepted it with pleasure, into a monster of barbarity. Of the writers of the mediæval period, certainly one of the two or three most eminent was Peter Lombard, whose 'Sentences,' though now, I believe, but little read, were for a long time the basis of all theological literature in Europe. More than four thousand theologians are said to have written commentaries upon them [1] — among others, Albert the Great, St. Bonaventura, and St. Thomas Aquinas. Nor is the work unworthy of its former reputation. Calm, clear, logical, subtle, and concise, the author professes to ex-

---

Deity. A few instances will suffice. Certain persons ' put rings of iron, stuck full of sharp points of needles, about their arms and feet, in such a manner as the prisoners could not move without wounding themselves; then they compassed them about with fire, to the end that, standing still, they might be burnt alive, and if they stirred the sharp points pierced their flesh. . . . . What, then, shall be the torment of the damned where they shall burn eternally without dying, and without possibility of removing? . . . Alexander, the son of Hyrcanus, caused eight hundred to be crucified, and whilst they were yet alive caused their wives and children to be murdered before their eyes, that so they might not die once, but many deaths. This rigour shall not be wanting in hell. . . . Mezentius tied a living body to a dead until the putrefied exhalations of the dead had killed the living. . . . What is this in respect of hell, when each body of the damned is more loathsome and unsavoury than a million of dead dogs? . . . Bonaventure says, if one of the damned were brought into this world it were sufficient to infect the whole earth. . . . We are amazed to think of the inhumanity of Phalaris, who roasted men alive in his brazen bull. That was a joy in respect of that fire of hell. . . . This torment . . . comprises as many torments as the body of man has joints, sinews, arteries, &c., being caused by that penetrating and real fire, of which this temporal fire is but a painted fire. . . . What comparison will there be between burning for a hundred years' space, and to be burning without interruption as long as God is God?'—*Contemplations on the State of Man,* book ii. ch. 6–7, in Heber's Edition of the works of Taylor.

[1] Perrone, *Historiæ Theologiæ cum Philosophia comparata Synopsis,* p. 29. Peter Lombard's work was published in A.D. 1160.

pound the whole system of Catholic theology and ethics, and to reveal the interdependence of their various parts. Having explained the position and the duties, he proceeds to examine the prospects, of man. He maintains that until the day of judgment the inhabitants of heaven and hell will continually see one another; but that, in the succeeding eternity, the inhabitants of heaven alone will see those of the opposite world; and he concludes his great work by this most impressive passage : ' In the last place, we must enquire whether the sight of the punishment of the condemned will impair the glory of the blest, or whether it will augment their beatitude.   Concerning this, Gregory says the sight of the punishment of the lost will not obscure the beatitude of the just; for when it is accompanied by no compassion it can be no diminution of happiness. And although their own joys might suffice to the just, yet to their greater glory they will see the pains of the evil, which by grace they have escaped. . . . . The elect will go forth, not indeed locally, but by intelligence, and by a clear vision, to behold the torture of the impious, and as they see them they will not grieve. Their minds will be sated with joy as they gaze on the unspeakable anguish of the impious, returning thanks for their own freedom. Thus Esaias, describing the torments of the impious, and the joy of the righteous in witnessing it, says : " The elect in truth will go out and will see the corpses of men who have prevaricated against Him ; their worm will not die, and they will be to the satiety of vision to all flesh, that is to the elect. The just man will rejoice when he shall see the vengeance." ' [1]

---

[1] 'Postremo quæritur, An pœna reproborum visa decoloret gloriam beatorum? an eorum beatitudini proficiat? De hoc ita Gregorius ait, Apud animum justorum non obfuscat beatitudinem aspecta pœna reproborum; quia ubi jam com-passio miseriæ non erit, minuere beatorum lætitiam non valebit. Et licet justis sua gaudia sufficiant, ad majorem gloriam vident pœnas malorum quas per gratiam evaserunt. . . . Egredientur ergo electi, non loco, sed intelligentia vel visione

This passion for visions of heaven and hell was, in fact, a natural continuation of the passion for dogmatic definition, which had raged during the fifth century. It was natural that men, whose curiosity had left no conceivable question of theology undefined, should have endeavoured to describe with corresponding precision the condition of the dead. Much, however, was due to the hallucinations of solitary and ascetic life, and much more to deliberate imposture. It is impossible for men to continue long in a condition of extreme panic, and superstition speedily discovered remedies to allay the fears it had created. If a malicious dæmon was hovering around the believer, and if the jaws of hell were opening to receive him, he was defended, on the other hand by countless angels; a lavish gift to a church or monastery could always enlist a saint in his behalf, and priestly power could protect him against the dangers which priestly sagacity had revealed. When the angels were weighing the good and evil deeds of a dead man, the latter were found by far to preponderate; but a priest of St. Lawrence came in, and turned the scale by throwing down among the former a heavy gold chalice, which the deceased had given to the altar.[1] Dagobert was snatched from the very arms of dæmons by St. Denis, St. Maurice, and St. Martin.[2] Charlemagne was saved, because the monasteries he had built outweighed

---

manifesta ad videndum impiorum cruciatus; quos videntes non dolore afficientur sed lætitia satiabuntur, agentes gratias de sua liberatione visa impiorum ineffabili calamitate. Unde Esaias impiorum tormenta describens et ex eorum visione lætitiam bonorum exprimens, ait, Egredientur electi scilicet et videbunt cadavera virorum qui prævaricati sunt in me. Vermis eorum non morietur et ignis non extinguetur, et erunt usque ad satietatem visionis omni carni, id est electis.

Lætabitur justus cum viderit vindictam.'—Peter Lombard, *Senten.* lib. iv. finis. These amiable views have often been expressed both by Catholic and by Puritan divines. See Alger's *Doctrine of a Future Life*, p. 541.

[1] *Legenda Aurea.* There is a curious fresco representing this transaction, on the portal of the church of St. Lorenzo, near Rome.

[2] Aimoni, *De Gestis Francorum Hist.* iv. 34.

nis evil deeds.[1]   Others, who died in mortal sin, were raised from the dead at the desire of their patron saint, to expiate their guilt.   To amass relics, to acquire the patronage of saints, to endow monasteries, to build churches, became the chief part of religion, and the more the terrors of the unseen world were unfolded, the more men sought tranquillity by the consolations of superstition.[2]

The extent to which the custom of materialising religion was carried, can only be adequately realised by those who have examined the mediæval literature itself.   That which strikes a student in perusing this literature, is not so much the existence of these superstitions, as their extraordinary multiplication, the many thousands of grotesque miracles wrought by saints, monasteries, or relics, that were deliberately asserted and universally believed.   Christianity had assumed a form that was quite as polytheistic and quite as idolatrous as the ancient Paganism.   The low level of intellectual cultivation, the religious feelings of half-converted barbarians, the interests of the clergy, the great social importance of the monasteries, and perhaps also the custom of compounding for nearly all crimes by pecuniary fines, which was so general in the penal system of the barbarian tribes, combined in their different ways, with the panic created by the fear of hell, in driving men in the same direction, and the wealth and power of the clergy rose to a point that enabled them to overshadow all other classes.   They had found, as has been well said, in another world, the standing-

---

[1] Turpin's *Chronicle*, ch. 32. In the vision of Watlin, however (A.D. 824), Charlemagne was seen tortured in purgatory on account of his excessive love of women. (Delepierre, *L'Enfer décrit par ceux qui l'ont vu*, pp. 27-28.)

[2] As the Abbé Mably observes : 'On croyoit en quelque sorte dans ces siècles grossiers que l'avarice étoit le premier attribut de Dieu, et que les saints faisoient un commerce de leur crédit et de leur protection.   De-là les richesses immenses données aux églises par des hommes dont les mœurs déshonoroient la religion.' — *Observations sur l'Hist. de France.* i. 4.

point of Archimedes from which they could move this. No ɔther system had ever appeared so admirably fitted to endure for ever. The Church had crushed or silenced every opponent in Christendom. It had an absolute control over education in all its branches and in all its stages. It had absorbed all the speculative knowledge and art of Europe. It possessed or commanded wealth, rank, and military power. It had so directed its teaching, that everything which terrified or distressed mankind drove men speedily into its arms, and it had covered Europe with a vast network of institutions, admirably adapted to extend and perpetuate its power. In addition to all this, it had guarded with consummate skill all the approaches to its citadel. Every doubt was branded as a sin, and a long course of doubt must necessarily have preceded the rejection of its tenets. All the avenues of enquiry were painted with images of appalling suffering, and of malicious dæmons. No sooner did the worshipper begin to question any article of faith, or to lose his confidence in the virtue of the ceremonies of his Church, than he was threatened with a doom that no human heroism could brave, that no imagination could contemplate undismayed.

Of all the suffering that was undergone by those brave men who in ages of ignorance and superstition dared to break loose from the trammels of their Church, and who laid the foundation of the liberty we now enjoy, it is this which was probably the most poignant, and which is the least realised. Our imaginations can reproduce with much vividness gigantic massacres like those of the Albigenses or of St. Bartholomew. We can conceive, too, the tortures of the rack and of the boots, the dungeon, the scaffold, and the slow fire. We can estimate, though less perfectly, the anguish which the bold enquirer must have undergone from the desertion of those he most dearly loved, from the hatred of mankind, from the malignant calumnies that were heaped

upon his name.   But in the chamber of his own soul, in the
hours of his solitary meditation, he must have found elements
of a suffering that was still more acute.   Taught from his
earliest childhood to regard the abandonment of his hereditary opinions as the most deadly of crimes, and to ascribe
it to the instigation of deceiving dæmons, persuaded that
if he died in a condition of doubt he must pass into a state
of everlasting torture, his imagination saturated with images
of the most hideous and appalling anguish, he found himself
alone in the world, struggling with his difficulties and his
doubts.   There existed no rival sect in which he could take
refuge, and where, in the professed agreement of many minds,
he could forget the anathemas of the Church.   Physical
science, that has disproved the theological theories which
attribute death to human sin, and suffering to Divine vengeance, and all natural phenomena to isolated acts of Divine
intervention—historical criticism, which has dispelled so
many imposing fabrics of belief, traced so many elaborate
superstitions to the normal action of the undisciplined imagination, and explained and defined the successive phases of
religious progress, were both unknown.   Every comet that
blazed in the sky, every pestilence that swept over the land,
appeared a confirmation of the dark threats of the theologian.
A spirit of blind and abject credulity, inculcated as the first
of duties, and exhibited on all subjects and in all forms,
pervaded the atmosphere he breathed.   Who can estimate
aright the obstacles against which a sincere enquirer in such
an age must have struggled?   Who can conceive the secret
anguish he must have endured in the long months or years
during which rival arguments gained an alternate sway
over his judgment, while all doubt was still regarded as
damnable?   And even when his mind was convinced, his
imagination would still often revert to his old belief.   Our
thoughts in after years flow spontaneously, and even unconsciously, in the channels that are formed in youth.   In

moments when the controlling judgment has relaxed its grasp, old intellectual habits reassume their sway, and images painted on the imagination will live, when the intellectual propositions on which they rested have been wholly abandoned. In hours of weakness, of sickness, and of drowsiness, in the feverish and anxious moments that are known to all, when the mind floats passively upon the stream, the phantoms which reason had exorcised must have often reappeared, and the bitterness of an ancient tyranny must have entered into his soul.

It is one of the greatest of the many services that were rendered to mankind by the Troubadours, that they cast such a flood of ridicule upon the visions of hell, by which the monks had been accustomed to terrify mankind, that they completely discredited and almost suppressed them.[1] Whether, however, the Catholic mind, if unassisted by the literature of Paganism and by the independent thinkers who grew up under the shelter of Mohammedanism, could have ever unwound the chains that had bound it, may well be questioned. The growth of towns, which multiplied secular interests and feelings, the revival of learning, the depression of the ecclesiastical classes that followed the crusades, and, at last, the dislocation of Christendom by the Reformation, gradually impaired the ecclesiastical doctrine, which ceased to be realised before it ceased to be believed. There was, however, another doctrine which exercised a still greater influence in augmenting the riches of the clergy, and in making donations to the Church the chief part of religion. I allude, of course, to the doctrine of purgatory.

A distinguished modern apologist for the middle ages has made this doctrine the object of his special and very characteristic eulogy, because, as he says, by providing a

---

[1] Many curious examples of the way in which the Troubadours burlesqued the monkish visions of hell are given by Delepierre, p. 144.— Wright's *Purgatory of St. Patrick*, 47–52.

finite punishment graduated to every variety of guilt, and
adapted for those who, without being sufficiently virtuous
to pass at once into heaven, did not appear sufficiently
vicious to pass into hell, it formed an indispensable corrective to the extreme terrorism of the doctrine of eternal
punishment.[1] This is one of those theories which, though
exceedingly popular with a class of writers who are not without
influence in our day, must appear, I think, almost grotesque
to those who have examined the actual operation of the
doctrine during the middle ages.   According to the practical
teaching of the Church, the expiatory powers at the disposal
of its clergy were so great, that those who died believing its
doctrines, and fortified in their last hours by its rites, had no
cause whatever to dread the terrors of hell.   On the other
hand, those who died external to the Church had no prospect
of entering into purgatory.   This latter was designed altogether for true believers ; it was chiefly preached at a time
when no one was in the least disposed to question the powers
of the Church to absolve any crime, however heinous, or to
free the worst men from hell, and it was assuredly never
regarded in the light of a consolation.   Indeed, the popular
pictures of purgatory were so terrific that it may be doubted
whether the imagination could ever fully realise, though the
reason could easily recognise, the difference between this state
and that of the lost.   The fire of purgatory, according to the
most eminent theologians, was like the fire of hell—a literal
fire, prolonged, it was sometimes said, for ages.   The de-
clamations of the pulpit described the sufferings of the saved
souls in purgatory as incalculably greater than any that were
endured by the most wretched mortals upon earth.[2] The rude

---

[1] Comte *Philosophie positive*,
tome v. p. 269.

[2] 'Saint-Bernard, dans son sermon *De obitu Humberti*, affirme que
tous les tourments de cette vie sont
joies si on les compare à une se-
conde des peines du purgatoire.
" Imaginez - vous donc, délicates
dames," dit le père Valladier (1613)
dans son sermon du 3me dimanche

artists of mediævalism exhausted their efforts in depicting
the writhings of the dead in the flames that encircled them.
Innumerable visions detailed with a ghastly minuteness the
various kinds of torture they underwent,[1] and the monk,
who described what he professed to have seen, usually ended
by the characteristic moral, that could men only realise those
sufferings, they would shrink from no sacrifice to rescue their
friends from such a state.   A special place, it was said, was
reserved in purgatory for those who had been slow in paying
their tithes.[2]   St. Gregory tells a curious story of a man
who was, in other respects, of admirable virtue; but who,

---

de l'Avent, "d'estre au travers de
vos chenets, sur vostre petit feu
pour une centaine d'ans : ce n'est
rien au respect d'un moment de purgatoire. Mais si vous vistes jamais
tirer quelqu'un à quatre chevaux,
quelqu'un brusler à petit feu, en-
rager de faim ou de soif, une heure de
purgatoire est pire que tout cela.'')
—Meray, *Les Libres Prêcheurs*
(Paris, 1860), pp. 130-131 (an extremely curious and suggestive
book). I now take up the first
contemporary book of popular Catholic devotion on this subject which
is at hand, and read: 'Compared
with the pains of purgatory, then,
all those wounds and dark prisons,
all those wild beasts, hooks of iron,
red-hot plates, &c., which the holy
martyrs suffered, are nothing.'
'They (souls in purgatory) are in
a real, though miraculous manner,
tortured by fire, which is of the
same kind (says Bellarmine) as our
element fire.' 'The Angelic Doctor
affirms "that the fire which torments the damned is like the fire
which purges the elect."' 'What
agony will not those holy souls
suffer when tied and bound with
the most tormenting chains of a

living fire like to that of hell! and
we, while able to make them free
and happy, shall we stand like un-
interested spectators?' 'St. Austin
is of opinion that the pains of a
soul in purgatory during the time
required to open and shut one's
eye is more severe than what St.
Lawrence suffered on the gridiron;'
and much more to the same effect.
(*Purgatory opened to the Piety of
the Faithful.* Richardson, London.)
[1] See Delepierre, Wright, and
Alger.
[2] This appears from the vision
of Thurcill. (Wright's *Purgatory
of St. Patrick*, p. 42.) Brompton
(*Chronicon*) tells of an English landlord who had refused to pay tithes.
St. Augustine, having vainly reasoned with him, at last convinced
him by a miracle. Before celebrating mass he ordered all excommunicated persons to leave the church,
whereupon a corpse got out of a
grave and walked away. The corpse,
on being questioned, said it was the
body of an ancient Briton who refused to pay tithes, and had in consequence been excommunicated and
damned.

in a contested election for the popedom, supported the wrong candidate, and without, as it would appear, in any degree refusing to obey the successful candidate when elected, continued secretly of opinion that the choice was an unwise one. He was accordingly placed for some time after death in boiling water.[1] Whatever may be thought of its other aspects, it is impossible to avoid recognising in this teaching a masterly skill in the adaptation of means to ends, which almost rises to artistic beauty. A system which deputed its minister to go to the unhappy widow in the first dark hour of her anguish and her desolation, to tell her that he who was dearer to her than all the world besides was now burning in a fire, and that he could only be relieved by a gift of money to the priests, was assuredly of its own kind not without an extraordinary merit.

If we attempt to realise the moral condition of the society of Western Europe in the period that elapsed between the downfall of the Roman Empire and Charlemagne, during which the religious transformations I have noticed chiefly arose, we shall be met by some formidable difficulties. In the first place, our materials are very scanty. From the year A.D. 642, when the meagre chronicle of Fredigarius closes, to the biography of Charlemagne by Eginhard, a century later, there is an almost complete blank in trustworthy history, and we are reduced to a few scanty and very doubtful notices in the chronicles of monasteries, the lives of saints, and the decrees of Councils. All secular literature had almost disappeared, and the thought of posterity seems to have vanished from the world.[2] Of the first half of the seventh century, however, and of the two centuries that preceded it, we have much information from

---

[1] Greg. *Dial.* iv. 40.

[2] As Sismondi says: 'Pendant quatre-vingts ans, tout au moins, il n'y eut pas un Franc qui songeât à transmettre à la postérité la mémoire des événements contemporains, et pendant le même espace de temps il n'y eut pas un personnage puissant qui ne bâtit des temples pour la postérité la plus reculée.'—*Hist. des Français*, tome ii. p. 46.

Gregory of Tours, and Fredigarius, whose tedious and repulsive pages illustrate with considerable clearness the conflict of races and the dislocation of governments that for centuries existed. In Italy, the traditions and habits of the old Empire had in some degree reasserted their sway; but in Gaul the Church subsisted in the midst of barbarians, whose native vigour had never been emasculated by civilisation and refined by knowledge. The picture which Gregory of Tours gives us is that of a society which was almost absolutely anarchical. The mind is fatigued by the monotonous account of acts of violence and of fraud springing from no fixed policy, tending to no end, leaving no lasting impress upon the world.[1] The two queens Frédégonde and Brunehaut rise conspicuous above other figures for their fierce and undaunted ambition, for the fascination they exercised over the minds of multitudes, and for the number and atrocity of their crimes. All classes seem to have been almost equally tainted with vice. We read of a bishop named Cautinus, who had to be carried, when intoxicated, by four men from the table;[2] who, upon

[1] Gibbon says of the period during which the Merovingian dynasty reigned, that 'it would be difficult to find anywhere more vice or less virtue.' Hallam reproduces this observation, and adds: 'The facts of these times are of little other importance than as they impress on the mind a thorough notion of the extreme wickedness of almost every person concerned in them, and consequently of the state to which society was reduced.'—*Hist. of the Middle Ages*, ch. i. Dean Milman is equally unfavourable and emphatic in his judgment. 'It is difficult to conceive a more dark and odious state of society than that of France under her Merovingian kings, the descendants of Clovis, as described by Gregory of Tours. In the conflict of barbarism with Roman Christianity, barbarism has introduced into Christianity all its ferocity with none of its generosity and magnanimity; its energy shows itself in atrocity of cruelty, and even of sensuality. Christianity has given to barbarism hardly more than its superstition and its hatred of heretics and unbelievers. Throughout, assassinations, parricides, and fratricides intermingle with adulteries and rapes.'—*History of Latin Christianity*, vol. i. p. 365.

[2] Greg. Tur. iv. 12. Gregory mentions (v. 41) another bishop who used to become so intoxicated as to be unable to stand; and St. Boniface, after describing the extreme sensuality of the clergy of his time

the refusal of one of his priests to surrender some private property, deliberately ordered that priest to be buried alive, and who, when the victim, escaping by a happy chance from the sepulchre in which he had been immured, revealed the crime, received no greater punishment than a censure.[1] The worst sovereigns found flatterers or agents in ecclesiastics. Frédégonde deputed two clerks to murder Childebert,[2] and another clerk to murder Brunehaut ;[3] she caused a bishop of Rouen to be assassinated at the altar—a bishop and an archdeacon being her accomplices ;[4] and she found in another bishop, named Ægidius, one of her most devoted instruments and friends.[5] The pope, St. Gregory the Great, was an ardent flatterer of Brunehaut.[6] Gundebald, having murdered his three brothers, was consoled by St. Avitus, the bishop of Vienne, who, without intimating the slightest disapprobation of the act, assured him that by removing his rivals he had been a providential agent in preserving the happiness of his people.[7] The bishoprics were filled by men of notorious debauchery, or by grasping misers.[8] The priests sometimes celebrated the sacred mysteries ' gorged with food and dull with wine.'[9] They had already begun to carry arms, and Gregory tells of two bishops of the sixth century

adds that there are some bishops ' qui licet dicant se fornicarios vel adulteros non esse, sed sunt ebriosi et injuriosi,' &c. —*Ep.* xlix.

[1] Greg. Tur. iv. 12.

[2] Ibid. viii. 29. She gave them knives with hollow grooves, filled with poison, in the blades.

[3] Ibid. vii. 20.

[4] Ibid. viii. 31-41.

[5] Ibid. v. 19.

[6] See his very curious correspondence with her. — *Ep.* vi. 5, 50, 59 ; ix. 11, 117 ; xi. 62–63.

[7] Avitus, *Ep.* v. He adds : ' Mi-

nuebat regni felicitas numerum regalium personarum.'

[8] See the emphatic testimony of St. Boniface in the eighth century. ' Modo autem maxima ex parte per civitates episcopales sedes traditæ sunt laicis cupidis ad possidendum, vel adulteratis clericis, scortatoribus et publicanis sæculariter ad perfruendum.'—*Epist.* xlix. ' ad Zachariam.' The whole epistle contains an appalling picture of the clerical vices of the times.

[9] More than one Council made decrees about this. See the *Vie de St. Léger*, by Dom Pitra, pp 172–177.

who had killed many enemies with their own hands.[1]   There
was scarcely a reign that was not marked by some atrocious
domestic tragedy.   There were few sovereigns who were not
guilty of at least one deliberate murder.   Never, perhaps,
was the infliction of mutilation, and prolonged and agonising
forms of death, more common.   We read, among other atrocities, of a bishop being driven to a distant place of exile
upon a bed of thorns;[2] of a king burning together his rebellious son, his daughter-in-law, and their daughters;[3] of a
queen condemning a daughter she had had by a former marriage to be drowned, lest her beauty should excite the passions
of her husband;[4] of another queen endeavouring to strangle
her daughter with her own hands;[5] of an abbot, compelling
a poor man to abandon his house, that he might commit
adultery with his wife, and being murdered, together with his
partner, in the act;[6] of a prince who made it an habitual
amusement to torture his slaves with fire, and who buried
two of them alive, because they had married without his
permission;[7] of a bishop's wife, who, besides other crimes,
was accustomed to mutilate men and to torture women, by
applying red-hot irons to the most sensitive parts of their
bodies;[8] of great numbers who were deprived of their ears

---

[1] Greg. Tur. iv. 43.   St. Boniface, at a much later period (A.D.
742), talks of bishops 'Qui pug-
nant in exercitu armati et effun-
dunt propria manu sanguinem hominum.'—*Ep.* xlix.

[2] Greg. Tur. iv. 26.

[3] Ibid. iv. 20.

[4] Ibid. iii. 26.   [5] Ibid. ix. 34.

[6] Ibid. viii. 19.   Gregory says
this story should warn clergymen not to meddle with the
wives of other people, but 'content
themselves with those that they may
possess without crime.' The abbot
had previously tried to seduce the

husband within the precincts of
the monastery, that he might murder him.

[7] Ibid v. 3.

[8] Ibid. viii. 39. She was guilty
of many other crimes, which the
historian says 'it is better to pass in
silence.' The bishop himself had
been guilty of outrageous and violent tyranny. The marriage of
ecclesiastics appears at this time
to have been common in Gaul,
though the best men commonly deserted their wives when they were
ordained. Another bishop's wife (iv.
36) was notorious for her tyranny

and noses, tortured through several days, and at last burnt alive or broken slowly on the wheel. Brunehaut, at the close of her long and in some respects great though guilty career, fell into the hands of Clotaire, and the old queen, having been subjected for three days to various kinds of torture, was led out on a camel for the derision of the army, and at last bound to the tail of a furious horse, and dashed to pieces in its course.[1]

And yet this age was, in a certain sense, eminently religious. All literature had become sacred. Heresy of every kind was rapidly expiring. The priests and monks had acquired enormous power, and their wealth was inordinately increasing.[2] Several sovereigns voluntarily abandoned their thrones for the monastic life.[3] The seventh century, which, together with the eighth, forms the darkest period of the dark ages, is famous in the hagiology as having produced more saints than any other century, except that of the martyrs.[4]

The manner in which events were regarded by historians was also exceedingly characteristic. Our principal authority,

---

[1] Fredigarius, xlii. The historian describes Clotaire as a perfect paragon of Christian graces.

[2] 'Au sixième siècle on compte 214 établissements religieux des Pyrénées à la Loire et des bouches du Rhône aux Vosges.'—Ozanam, *Études germaniques*, tome ii. p. 93. In the two following centuries the ecclesiastical wealth was enormously increased.

[3] Matthew of Westminster (A.D. 757) speaks of no less than eight Saxon kings having done this.

[4] 'Le septième siècle est celui peut-être qui a donné le plus de saints au calendrier.'—Sismondi, *Hist. de France*, tome ii. p. 50. 'Le plus beau titre du septième siècle à une réhabilitation c'est le nombre considérable de saints qu'il a produits. . . . Aucun siècle n'a été ainsi glorifié sauf l'âge des martyrs dont Dieu s'est réservé de compter le nombre. Chaque année fournit sa moisson, chaque jour a sa gerbe. . . . Si donc il plaît à Dieu et au Christ de répandre à pleines mains sur un siècle les splendeurs des saints, qu'importe que l'histoire et la gloire humaine en tiennent peu compte ?'—Pitra, *Vie de St. Léger*, Introd. p. x.-xi. This learned and very credulous writer (who is now a cardinal) afterwards says that we have the record of more than eight hundred saints of the seventh century. (Introd. p. lxxx.)

Gregory of Tours, was a bishop of great eminence, and a man of the most genuine piety, and of very strong affections.[1] He describes his work as a record 'of the virtues of saints, and the disasters of nations;'[2] and the student who turns to his pages from those of the Pagan historians, is not more struck by the extreme prominence he gives to ecclesiastical events, than by the uniform manner in which he views all secular events in their religious aspect, as governed and directed by a special Providence. Yet, in questions where the difference between orthodoxy and heterodoxy is concerned, his ethics sometimes exhibit the most singular distortion. Of this, probably the most impressive example is the manner in which he has described the career of Clovis, the great representative of orthodoxy.[3] Having recounted the circumstances of his conversion, Gregory proceeds to tell us, with undisguised admiration, how that chieftain, as the first-fruits of his doctrine, professed to be grieved at seeing that part of Gaul was held by an Arian sovereign; how he accordingly resolved to invade and appropriate that territory; how, with admirable piety, he commanded his soldiers to abstain from all devastations when traversing the territory of St. Martin, and how several miracles attested the Divine approbation of the expedition. The war—which is the first of the long series of professedly religious wars that have been undertaken by Christians—was fully successful, and Clovis proceeded to direct his ambition to new fields. In his expedition against the Arians, he had found a faithful ally in his relative Sighebert, the old and infirm king of the Ripuarian Franks. Clovis now proceeded artfully to suggest to the son of Sighebert the advantages that son might obtain by his father's death. The hint was taken. Sighebert was murdered, and Clovis

---

[1] See, e.g., the very touching passage about the death of his children, v. 35.

[2] Lib. ii. Prologue.

[3] Greg. Tur. ii. 27–43.

sent ambassadors to the parricide, professing a warm friendship, but with secret orders on the first opportunity to kill
him. This being done, and the kingdom being left entirely
without a head, Clovis proceeded to Cologne, the capital of
Sighebert; he assembled the people, professed with much
solemnity his horror of the tragedies that had taken place,
and his complete innocence of all connection with them ;[1]
but suggested that, as they were now without a ruler, they
should place themselves under his protection. The proposition was received with acclamation. The warriors elected
him as their king, and thus, says the episcopal historian,
'Clovis received the treasures and dominions of Sighebert,
and added them to his own. Every day God caused his
enemies to fall beneath his hand, and enlarged his kingdom,
because he walked with a right heart before the Lord, and
did the things that were pleasing in His sight.'[2] His
ambition was, however, still unsated. He proceeded, in a
succession of expeditions, to unite the whole of Gaul under
his sceptre, invading, defeating, capturing, and slaying the
lawful sovereigns, who were for the most part his own
relations. Having secured himself against dangers from
without, by killing all his relations, with the exception of
his wife and children, he is reported to have lamented
before his courtiers his isolation, declaring that he had no
relations remaining in the world to assist him in his
adversity ; but this speech, Gregory assures us, was a strata-
gem ; for the king desired to discover whether any possible
pretender to the throne had escaped his knowledge and his

---

[1] He observes how impossible it
was that he could be guilty of shedding the blood of a relation : ' Sed
in his ego nequaquam conscius
sum. Nec enim possum sanguinem
parentum mecrum effundere.'—
Greg. Tur ii. 40

[2] ' Prosternebat enim quotidie
Deus hostes ejus sub manu ipsius,
et augebat regnum ejus eo quod
ambularet recto corde coram eo, et
faceret quæ placita erant in oculis
ejus.'—Greg. Tur. ii. 40.

sword. Soon after, he died, full of years and honours, and was buried in a cathedral which he had built.

Having recounted all these things with unmoved composure, Gregory of Tours requests his reader to permit him to pause, to draw the moral of the history. It is the admirable manner in which Providence guides all things for the benefit of those whose opinions concerning the Trinity are strictly orthodox. Having briefly referred to Abraham, Jacob, Moses, Aaron, and David, all of whom are said to have intimated the correct doctrine on this subject, and all of whom were exceedingly prosperous, he passes to more modern times. 'Arius, the impious founder of the impious sect, his entrails having fallen out, passed into the flames of hell; but Hilary, the blessed defender of the undivided Trinity, though exiled on that account, found his country in Paradise. The King Clovis, who confessed the Trinity, and by its assistance crushed the heretics, extended his dominions through all Gaul. Alaric, who denied the Trinity, was deprived of his kingdom and his subjects, and, what was far worse, was punished in the future world.' [1]

It would be easy to cite other, though perhaps not quite such striking, instances of the degree in which the moral judgments of this unhappy age were distorted by superstition.[2] Questions of orthodoxy, or questions of fasting, appeared to the popular mind immeasurably more important than what

---

[1] Lib. iii. Prologue. St. Avitus enumerates in glowing terms the Christian virtues of Clovis (*Ep.* xli.), but, as this was in a letter addressed to the king himself, the eulogy may easily be explained.

[2] Thus Hallam says: 'There are continual proofs of immorality in the monkish historians. In the history of Rumsey Abbey, one of our best documents for Anglo-Saxon times, we have an anecdote of a bishop who made a Danish nobleman drunk, that he might cheat him out of an estate, which is told with much approbation. Walter de Hemingford records, with excessive delight, the well-known story of the Jews who were persuaded by the captain of their vessel to walk on the sands at low water till the rising tide drowned them.'—Hallam's *Middle Ages* (12th ed.), iii. p. 306.

we should now call the fundamental principles of right
and wrong. A law of Charlemagne, and also a law of the
Saxons, condemned to death any one who ate meat in Lent,[1]
unless the priest was satisfied that it was a matter of absolute
necessity. The moral enthusiasm of the age chiefly drove
men to abandon their civic or domestic duties, to immure
themselves in monasteries, and to waste their strength by
prolonged and extravagant maceration.[2] Yet, in the midst
of all this superstition, there can be no question that in
some respects the religious agencies were operating for good.
The monastic bodies that everywhere arose, formed secure
asylums for the multitudes who had been persecuted by
their enemies, constituted an invaluable counterpoise to the
rude military forces of the time, familiarised the imagination
of men with religious types that could hardly fail in some
degree to soften the character, and led the way in most
forms of peaceful labour. When men, filled with admiration
at the reports of the sanctity and the miracles of some
illustrious saint, made pilgrimages to behold him, and found
him attired in the rude garb of a peasant, with thick shoes,
and with a scythe on his shoulder, superintending the labours
of the farmers,[3] or sitting in a small attic mending lamps,[4]
whatever other benefit they might derive from the interview,
they could scarcely fail to return with an increased sense of

---

[1] Canciani, *Leges Barbarorum*,
vol. iii. p. 64. Canciani notices,
that among the Poles the teeth of
the offending persons were pulled
out. The following passage, from
Bodin, is, I think, very remarkable:
'Les loix et canons veulent qu'on
pardonne aux hérétiques repentis
(combien que les magistrats en
quelques lieux par cy-devant, y ont
eu tel esgard, que celui qui avoit
mangé de la chair au Vendredy
estoit bruslé tout vif, comme il fut
faict en la ville d'Angers l'an mil

cinq cens trente-neuf, s'il ne s'en
repentoit: et jaçoit qu'il se repen-
tist si estoit-il pendu par compassion).'—*Démonomanie des Sorciers*,
p. 216.

[2] A long list of examples of extreme maceration, from lives of the
saints of the seventh and eighth
centuries is given by Pitra, *Vie de
St. Léger*, Introd. pp. cv.-cvii.

[3] This was related of St. Equi-
tius.—Greg. *Dialog.* i. 4.

[4] Ibid. i. 5. This saint was
named Constantius.

the dignity of labour. It was probably at this time as much for the benefit of the world as of the Church, that the ecclesiastical sanctuaries and estates should remain inviolate, and the numerous legends of Divine punishment having overtaken those who transgressed them,[1] attest the zeal with which the clergy sought to establish that inviolability. The great sanctity that was attached to holidays was also an important boon to the servile classes. The celebration of the first day of the week, in commemoration of the resurrection, and as a period of religious exercises, dates from the earliest age of the Church. The Christian festival was carefully distinguished from the Jewish Sabbath, with which it never appears to have been confounded till the close of the six-teenth century; but some Jewish converts, who considered the Jewish law to be still in force, observed both days. In general, however, the Christian festival alone was observed, and the Jewish Sabbatical obligation, as St. Paul most explicitly affirms, no longer rested upon the Christians. The grounds of the observance of Sunday were the manifest propriety and expediency of devoting a certain portion of time to devout exercises, the tradition which traced the sanctification of Sunday to apostolic times, and the right of the Church to appoint certain seasons to be kept holy by its members. When Christianity acquired an ascendancy in the Empire, its policy on this subject was manifested in one of the laws of Constantine, which, without making any direct reference to religious motives, ordered that, ' on the day of the sun,' no servile work should be performed except

---

[1] A vast number of miracles of this kind are recorded. See, e.g., Greg. Tur. *De Miraculis*, i. 61–66; *Hist.* iv. 49. Perhaps the most singular instance of the violation of the sanctity of the church was that by the nuns of a convent founded by St. Radegunda. They, having broken into rebellion, four bishops, with their attendant clergy, went to compose the dispute, and having failed, excommunicated the rebels, whereupon the nuns almost beat them to death in the church. —Greg. Tur. ix. 41.

agriculture, which, being dependent on the weather, could not, it was thought, be reasonably postponed. Theodosius took a step further, and suppressed the public spectacles on that day. During the centuries that immediately followed the dissolution of the Roman Empire, the clergy devoted themselves with great and praiseworthy zeal to the suppression of labour both on Sundays and on the other leading Church holidays. More than one law was made, forbidding all Sunday labour, and this prohibition was reiterated by Charlemagne in his Capitularies.[1] Several Councils made decrees on the subject,[2] and several legends were circulated, of men who had been afflicted miraculously with disease or with death, for having been guilty of this sin.[3] Although the moral side of religion was greatly degraded or forgotten, there was, as I have already intimated, one important exception. Charity was so interwoven with the superstitious parts of ecclesiastical teaching, that it continued to grow and flourish in the darkest period. Of the acts of Queen Bathilda, it is said we know nothing except her donations to the monasteries, and the charity with which she purchased slaves and captives, and released them or converted them into monks.[4] While many of the bishops were men of gross and scandalous vice, there were always some who laboured assiduously in the old episcopal vocation of protecting the oppressed, interceding for the captives, and opening their sanctuaries to the fugitives. St. Germanus, a bishop of Paris,

---

[1] See Canciani, *Leges Barbarorum*, vol. iii. pp. 19, 151.

[2] Much information about these measures is given by Dr. Hessey, in his *Bampton Lectures on Sunday*. See especially, lect. 3. See, too, Moehler, *Le Christianisme et l'Esclavage*, pp. 186-187.

[3] Gregory of Tours enumerates some instances of this in his extravagant book *De Miraculis*, ii. 11;

iv. 57; v. 7. One of these cases, however, was for having worked on the day of St. John the Baptist. Some other miracles of the same nature, taken, I believe, from English sources, are given in Hessey's *Sunday* (3rd edition), p. 321.

[4] Compare Pitra, *Vie de St.-Léger*, p. 137. Sismondi, *Hist. des Français*, tome ii. pp. 62-63.

near the close of the sixth century, was especially famous for his zeal in ransoming captives.[1] The fame he acquired was so great, that prisoners are said to have called upon him to assist them, in the interval between his death and his burial; and the body of the saint becoming miraculously heavy, it was found impossible to carry it to the grave till the captives had been released.[2] In the midst of the complete eclipse of all secular learning, in the midst of a reign of ignorance, imposture, and credulity which cannot be paralleled in history, there grew up a vast legendary literature, clustering around the form of the ascetic; and the lives of the saints, among very much that is grotesque, childish, and even immoral, contain some fragments of the purest and most touching religious poetry.[3]

But the chief title of the period we are considering, to the indulgence of posterity, lies in its missionary labours. The stream of missionaries which had at first flowed from Palestine and Italy began to flow from the West. The Irish monasteries furnished the earliest, and probably the most numerous, labourers in the field. A great portion of the north of England was converted by the Irish monks of Lindisfarne. The fame of St. Columbanus in Gaul, in Germany, and in Italy, for a time even balanced that of St. Benedict himself, and the school which he founded at Luxeuil became the great seminary for mediæval missionaries, while

---

[1] See a remarkable passage from his life, cited by Guizot, *Hist. de la Civilisation en France*, xviime leçon. The English historians contain several instances of the activity of charity in the darkest period. Alfred and Edward the Confessor were conspicuous for it. Ethelwolf is said to have provided, 'for the good of his soul,' that, till the day of judgment, one poor man in ten should be provided with meat, drink, and clothing. (Asser's *Life of Alfred*.) There was a popular legend that a poor man having in vain asked alms of some sailors, all the bread in their vessel was turned into stone. (Roger of Wendover, A.D. 606.) See, too, another legend of charity in Matthew of Westminster, A.D. 611.

[2] Greg. Tur. *Hist.* v. 8.

[3] M. Guizot has given several specimens of this (*Hist. de la Civilis.* xviime leçon).

the monastery he planted at Bobbio continued to the present century. The Irish missionary, St. Gall, gave his name to a portion of Switzerland he had converted, and a crowd of other Irish missionaries penetrated to the remotest forests of Germany. The movement which began with St. Columba in the middle of the sixth century, was communicated to England and Gaul about a century later. Early in the eighth century it found a great leader in the Anglo-Saxon St. Boniface, who spread Christianity far and wide through Germany, and at once excited and disciplined an ardent enthusiasm, which appears to have attracted all that was morally best in the Church. During about three centuries, and while Europe had sunk into the most extreme moral, intellectual, and political degradation, a constant stream of missionaries poured forth from the monasteries, who spread the knowledge of the Cross and the seeds of a future civilisation through every land, from Lombardy to Sweden.[1]

On the whole, however, it would be difficult to exaggerate the superstition and the vice of the period between the dissolution of the Empire and the reign of Charlemagne. But in the midst of the chaos the elements of a new society may be detected, and we may already observe in embryo the movement which ultimately issued in the crusades, the feudal system, and chivalry. It is exclusively with the moral aspect of this movement that the present work is concerned, and I shall endeavour, in the remainder of this chapter, to describe and explain its incipient stages. It consisted of two parts—a fusion of Christianity with the

---

[1] This portion of mediæval history has lately been well traced by Mr. Maclear, in his *History of Christian Missions in the Middle Ages* (1863). See, too, Montalembert's *Moines d' Occident*; Ozanam's *Études germaniques.* The original materials are to be found in Bede, and in the *Lives of the Saints*—especially that of St. Columba, by Adamnan. On the French missionaries, see the Benedictine *Hist. lit. de la France,* tome iv. p. 5 ; and on the English missionaries, Sharon Turner's *Hist. of England,* book x. ch. ii.

military spirit, and an increasing reverence for secular
rank.

It had been an ancient maxim of the Greeks, that no
more acceptable gifts can be offered in the temples of the
gods than the trophies won from an enemy in battle.[1] Of
this military religion Christianity had been at first the
extreme negation. I have already had occasion to observe
that it had been one of its earliest rules that no arms should
be introduced within the church, and that soldiers returning
even from the most righteous war should not be admitted to
communion until after a period of penance and purification.
A powerful party, which counted among its leaders Clement
of Alexandria, Tertullian, Origen, Lactantius, and Basil,
maintained that all warfare was unlawful for those who had
been converted ; and this opinion had its martyr in the celebrated Maximilianus, who suffered death under Diocletian
solely because, having been enrolled as a soldier, he declared
that he was a Christian, and that therefore he could not
fight. The extent to which this doctrine was disseminated
has been suggested with much plausibility as one of the
causes of the Diocletian persecution.[2] It was the subject of
one of the reproaches of Celsus ; and Origen, in reply, frankly
accepted the accusation that Christianity was incompatible
with military service, though he maintained that the prayers
of the Christians were more efficacious than the swords of
the legions.[3] At the same time, there can be no question
that many Christians, from a very early date, did enlist in
the army, and that they were not cut off from the Church.
The legend of the thundering legion, under Marcus Aurelius,
whatever we may think of the pretended miracle, attested
the fact, and it is expressly asserted by Tertullian.[4] The

---

[1] Dion Chrysostom, *Or.* ii. (*De Regno*).

[2] Gibbon, ch. **xvi.**

[3] Origen, *Cels.* lib. viii.

[4] 'Navigamus et nos vobiscum
et militamus.' — Tert. *Apol.* xlii
See, too, Grotius *De Jure*, i. cap. ii.

first fury of the Diocletian persecution fell upon Christian
soldiers, and by the time of Constantine the army appears
to have become, in a great degree, Christian. A Council of
Arles, under Constantine, condemned soldiers who, through
religious motives, deserted their colours; and St. Augustine
threw his great influence into the same scale. But even
where the calling was not regarded as sinful, it was strongly
discouraged. The ideal or type of supreme excellence conceived by the imagination of the Pagan world and to which
all their purest moral enthusiasm naturally aspired, was the
patriot and soldier. The ideal of the Catholic legends was
the ascetic, whose first duty was to abandon all secular
feelings and ties. In most family circles the conflict between
the two principles appeared, and in the moral atmosphere of
the fourth and fifth centuries it was almost certain that
every young man who was animated by any pure or genuine
enthusiasm would turn from the army to the monks. St.
Martin, St. Ferreol, St. Tarrachus, and St. Victricius, were
among those who through religious motives abandoned the
army.[1] When Ulphilas translated the Bible into Gothic, he
is said to have excepted the four books of Kings, through
fear that they might encourage the martial disposition of the
barbarians.[2]

The first influence that contributed to bring the military
profession into friendly connection with religion was the
received doctrine concerning the Providential government
of affairs. It was generally taught that all national catastrophes were penal inflictions, resulting, for the most part,
from the vices or the religious errors of the leading men, and
that temporal prosperity was the reward of orthodoxy and

---

[1] See an admirable dissertation
on the opinions of the early Chris-
tians about military service, in Le
Blant, *Inscriptions chrétiennes de la
Gaule*, tome i. pp. 81–87. The
subject is frequently referred to by
Barbeyrac, *Morale des Pères*, and
Grotius, *De Jure*, lib. i. cap. ii.

[2] Philostorgius, ii. 5.

virtue. A great battle, on the issue of which the fortunes of
a people or of a monarch depended, was therefore supposed
to be the special occasion of Providential interposition, and
the hope of obtaining military success became one of the
most frequent motives of conversion. The conversion of
Constantine was professedly, and the conversion of Clovis
was perhaps really, due to the persuasion that the Divine
interposition had in a critical moment given them the
victory; and I have already noticed how large a part must
be assigned to this order of ideas in facilitating the progress
of Christianity among the barbarians. When a cross was
said to have appeared miraculously to Constantine, with an
inscription announcing the victory of the Milvian bridge;
when the same holy sign, adorned with the sacred mono-
gram, was carried in the forefront of the Roman armies;
when the nails of the cross, which Helena had brought
from Jerusalem, were converted by the emperor into a
helmet, and into bits for his war-horse, it was evident that
a great change was passing over the once pacific spirit of the
Church.[1]

Many circumstances conspired to accelerate it. Northern
tribes, who had been taught that the gates of the Walhalla
were ever open to the warrior who presented himself stained
with the blood of his vanquished enemies, were converted to
Christianity; but they carried their old feelings into their
new creed. The conflict of many races, and the paralysis of
all government that followed the fall of the Empire, made
force everywhere dominant, and petty wars incessant. The
military obligations attached to the ' benefices ' which the
sovereigns gave to their leading chiefs, connected the idea
of military service with that of rank still more closely than
it had been connected before, and rendered it doubly honour-

---

[1] See some excellent remarks on   *of Christianity*, vol. ii. pp. 287
this change, in Milman's *History*   288.

able in the eyes of men. Many bishops and abbots, partly
from the turbulence of their times and characters, and partly,
at a later period, from their position as great feudal lords,
were accustomed to lead their followers in battle; and this
custom, though prohibited by Charlemagne, may be traced
to so late a period as the battle of Agincourt.[1]

The stigma which Christianity had attached to war was
thus gradually effaced. At the same time, the Church
remained, on the whole, a pacific influence. War was
rather condoned than consecrated, and, whatever might be
the case with a few isolated prelates, the Church did nothing
to increase or encourage it. The transition from the almost
Quaker tenets of the primitive Church to the essentially
military Christianity of the Crusades was chiefly due to
another cause—to the terrors and to the example of Mohammedanism.

This great religion, which so long rivalled the influence
of Christianity, had indeed spread the deepest and most
justifiable panic through Christendom. Without any of
those aids to the imagination which pictures and images
can furnish, without any elaborate sacerdotal organisation,
preaching the purest Monotheism among ignorant and barbarous men, and inculcating, on the whole, an extremely
high and noble system of morals, it spread with a rapidity
and it acquired a hold over the minds of its votaries, which
it is probable that no other religion has altogether equalled.
It borrowed from Christianity that doctrine of salvation by
belief, which is perhaps the most powerful impulse that can
be applied to the characters of masses of men, and it elaborated so minutely the charms of its sensual heaven, and the
terrors of its material hell, as to cause the alternative to
appeal with unrivalled force to the gross imaginations of the

---

[1] Mably, *Observations sur l'Histoire de France*, i. 6; Hallam's *Middle Ages*, ch. ii. part ii.

people. It possessed a book which, however inferior to that
of the opposing religion, has nevertheless been the consolation
and the support of millions in many ages. It taught a fatalism
which in its first age nerved its adherents with a matchless
military courage, and which, though in later days it has
often paralysed their active energies, has also rarely failed to
support them under the pressure of inevitable calamity.
But, above all, it discovered the great, the fatal secret of
uniting indissolubly the passion of the soldier with the
passion of the devotee. Making the conquest of the infidel
the first of duties, and proposing heaven as the certain
reward of the valiant soldier, it created a blended enthusiasm that soon overpowered the divided counsels and the
voluptuous governments of the East, and, within a century
of the death of Mohammed, his followers had almost extirpated
Christianity from its original home, founded great monarchies in Asia and Africa, planted a noble, though
transient and exotic, civilisation in Spain, menaced the
capital of the Eastern empire, and, but for the issue of a
single battle, they would probably have extended their
sceptre over the energetic and progressive races of Central
Europe. The wave was broken by Charles Martel, at the
battle of Poitiers, and it is now useless to speculate what
might have been the consequences had Mohammedanism
unfurled its triumphant banner among those Teutonic tribes
who have so often changed their creed, and on whom the
course of civilisation has so largely depended. But one
great change was in fact achieved. The spirit of Mohammedanism slowly passed into Christianity, and transformed
it into its image. The spectacle of an essentially military
religion fascinated men who were at once very warlike and
very superstitious. The panic that had palsied Europe was after
a long interval succeeded by a fierce reaction of resentment.
Pride and religion conspired to urge the Christian warriors
against those who had so often defeated the armies and
wasted the territory of Christendom, who had shorn the

empire of the Cross of many of its fairest provinces, and profaned that holy city which was venerated not only for its past associations, but also for the spiritual blessings it could still bestow upon the pilgrim. The papal indulgences proved not less efficacious in stimulating the military spirit than the promises of Mohammed, and for about two centuries every pulpit in Christendom proclaimed the duty of war with the unbeliever, and represented the battle-field as the sure path to heaven. The religious orders which arose united the character of the priest with that of the warrior, and when, at the hour of sunset, the soldier knelt down to pray before his cross, that cross was the handle of his sword.

It would be impossible to conceive a more complete transformation than Christianity had thus undergone, and it is melancholy to contrast with its aspect during the crusades the impression it had once most justly made upon the world, as the spirit of gentleness and of peace encountering the spirit of violence and war. Among the many curious habits of the Pagan Irish, one of the most significant was that of perpendicular burial. With a feeling something like that which induced Vespasian to declare that a Roman emperor should die standing, the Pagan warriors shrank from the notion of being prostrate even in death, and they appear to have regarded this martial burial as a special symbol of Paganism. An old Irish manuscript tells how, when Christianity had been introduced into Ireland, a king of Ulster on his deathbed charged his son never to become a Christian, but to be buried standing upright like a man in battle, with his face for ever turned to the south, defying the men of Leinster.[1] As late as the sixteenth century, it is said that in some parts of Ireland children were baptised by

---

[1] Wakeman's *Archæologia Hibernica*, p. 21. However, Giraldus Cambrensis observes that the Irish saints were peculiarly vindictive, and St. Columba and St. Comgall are said to have been leaders in a sanguinary conflict about a church near Coleraine. See Reeve's edition of Adamnan's *Life of St. Columba*, pp. lxxvii. 253.

immersion; but the right arms of the males were carefully held above the water, in order that, not having been dipped in the sacred stream, they might strike the more deadly blow.[1]

It had been boldly predicted by some of the early Christians that the conversion of the world would lead to the establishment of perpetual peace. In looking back, with our present experience, we are driven to the melancholy conclusion that, instead of diminishing the number of wars, ecclesiastical influence has actually and very seriously increased it. We may look in vain for any period since Constantine, in which the clergy, as a body, exerted themselves to repress the military spirit, or to prevent or abridge a particular war, with an energy at all comparable to that which they displayed in stimulating the fanaticism of the crusaders, in producing the atrocious massacre of the Albigenses, in embittering the religious contests that followed the Reformation. Private wars were, no doubt, in some degree repressed by their influence; for the institution of the 'Truce of God' was for a time of much value, and when, towards the close of the middle ages, the custom of duels arose, it was strenuously condemned by the clergy; but we can hardly place any great value on their exertions in this field, when we remember that duels were almost or altogether unknown to the Pagan world; that, having arisen in a period of great superstition, the anathemas of the Church were almost impotent to discourage them; and that in our own century they are rapidly disappearing before the simple censure of an industrial society. It is possible—though it would, I imagine, be difficult to prove it—that the mediatorial office, so often exercised by bishops, may sometimes have prevented wars; and it is certain that during the period of the religious wars, so much military spirit existed in Europe that it must necessarily have found a vent, and

---

Campion's *Historie of Ireland* (1571), book i. ch. vi.

ander no circumstances could the period have been one of perfect peace. But when all these qualifications have been fully admitted, the broad fact will remain, that, with the exception of Mohammedanism, no other religion has done so much to produce war as was done by the religious teachers of Christendom during several centuries. The military fanaticism evoked by the indulgences of the popes, by the exhortations of the pulpit, by the religious importance attached to the relics at Jerusalem, and by the prevailing hatred of misbelievers, has scarcely ever been equalled in its intensity, and it has caused the effusion of oceans of blood, and has been productive of incalculable misery to the world. Religious fanaticism was a main cause of the earlier wars, and an important ingredient in the later ones. The peace principles, that were so common before Constantine, have found scarcely any echo except from Erasmus, the Anabaptists, and the Quakers; [1] and although some very important pacific agencies have arisen out of the industrial progress of modern times, these have been, for the most part, wholly unconnected with, and have in some cases been directly opposed to, theological interests.

But although theological influences cannot reasonably be said to have diminished the number of wars, they have had a very real and beneficial effect in diminishing their atrocity. On few subjects have the moral opinions of different ages exhibited so marked a variation as in their judgments of what punishment may justly be imposed on a conquered enemy, and these variations have often been cited as an argument against those who believe in the existence of natural moral perceptions. To those, however, who accept

---

[1] It seems curious to find in so calm and unfanatical a writer as Justus Lipsius the following passage: 'Jam et invasio quædam legitima videtur etiam sine injuria, ut in barbaros et moribus aut *religione* prorsum a nobis abhorrentes.' —*Politicorum sive Civilis Doctrina libri* (Paris, 1594), lib. iv. ch. ii, cap. iv.

that doctrine, with the limitations that have been stated in the first chapter, they can cause no perplexity. In the first dawning of the human intelligence (as I have said) the notion of duty, as distinguished from that of interest, appears, and the mind, in reviewing the various emotions by which it is influenced, recognises the unselfish and benevolent motives as essentially and generically superior to the selfish and the cruel. But it is the general condition of society alone that determines the standard of benevolence—the classes towards which every good man will exercise it. At first, the range of duty is the family, the tribe, the state, the confederation. Within these limits every man feels himself under moral obligations to those about him; but he regards the outer world as we regard wild animals, as beings upon whom he may justifiably prey. Hence, we may explain the curious fact that the terms brigand or corsair conveyed in the early stages of society no notion of moral guilt.[1] Such men were looked upon simply as we look upon huntsmen, and if they displayed courage and skill in their pursuit, they were deemed fit subjects for admiration. Even in the writings of the most enlightened philosophers of Greece, war with barbarians is represented as a form of chase, and the simple desire of obtaining the barbarians as slaves was considered a sufficient reason for invading them. The right of the conqueror to kill his captives

---

[1] ' Con l'occasione di queste cose Plutarco nel *Teseo* dice che gli eroi si recavano a grande onore e si reputavano in pregio d'armi con l'esser chiamati ladroni; siccome a' tempi barbari ritornati quello di Corsale era titolo riputato di signoria; d'intorno a' quali tempi venuto Solone, si dice aver permesso nelle sue leggi le società per cagion di prede; tanto Solone ben intese questa nostra compiuta Umanità, nella quale costoro non godono del diritto natural delle genti   Ma quel che fa più maraviglia è che Platone ed Aristotile posero il ladroneccio fralle spezie della caccia e con tali e tanti filosofi d'una gente umanissima convengono con la loro barbarie i Germani antichi: appo i quali al referire di Cesare i ladronecci non solo non eran infami, ma si tenevano tra gli esercizi della virtù siccome **tra** quelli che per costume non applicando ad arte alcuna così fuggivano l' ozio.'—Vico, *Scienza Nuova*, ii. 6. See, too, Whewell's *Elements of Morality,* book vi. ch. ii.

was generally recognised, nor was it at first restricted by any considerations of age or sex. Several instances are recorded of Greek and other cities being deliberately destroyed by Greeks or by Romans, and the entire populations ruthlessly massacred.[1] The whole career of the early republic of Rome, though much idealised and transfigured by later historians, was probably governed by these principles.[2] The normal fate of the captive, which, among barbarians, had been death, was, in civilised antiquity, slavery; but many thousands were condemned to the gladiatorial shows, and the vanquished general was commonly slain in the Mamertine prison, while his conqueror ascended in triumph to the Capitol.

A few traces of a more humane spirit may, it is true, be discovered. Plato had advocated the liberation of all Greek prisoners upon payment of a fixed ransom,[3] and the Spartan general Callicratidas had nobly acted upon this principle;[4] but his example never appears to have been generally followed. In Rome, the notion of international obligation was

---

[1] The ancient right of war is fully discussed by Grotius, *De Jure*, lib. iii. See, especially, the horrible catalogue of tragedies in cap. 4. The military feeling that regards capture as disgraceful, had probably some, though only a very subordinate, influence in producing cruelty to the prisoners.

[2] 'Le jour où Athènes décréta que tous les Mityléniens, sans distinction de sexe ni d'âge, seraient exterminés, elle ne croyait pas dépasser son droit; quand le lendemain elle revint sur son décret et se contenta de mettre à mort mille citoyens et de confisquer toutes les terres, elle se crut humaine et indulgente. Après la prise de Platée les hommes furent égorgés, les femmes vendues, et personne n'ac-cusa les vainqueurs d'avoir violé le droit. . . . . C'est en vertu de ce droit de la guerre que Rome a étendu la solitude autour d'elle; du territoire où les Volsques avaient vingt-trois cités elle a fait les marais pontins; les cinquante-trois villes du Latium ont disparu; dans le Samnium on put longtemps reconnaître les lieux où les armées romaines avaient passé, moins aux vestiges de leurs camps qu'à la solitude qui règnait aux environs.' —Fustel de Coulanges, *La Cité antique*, pp. 263–264.

[3] Plato, *Republic*, lib. v.; Bodin, *République*, liv. i. cap. 5.

[4] Grote, *Hist. of Greece*, vol. viii. p. 224. Agesilaus was also very humane to captives. — Ibid. pp 365–6.

very strongly felt. No war was considered just which had not been officially declared ; and even in the case of wars with barbarians, the Roman historians often discuss the suffi ciency or insufficiency of the motives, with a conscientious severity a modern historian could hardly surpass.[1] The latei Greek and Latin writings occasionally contain maxims which exhibit a considerable progress in this sphere. The sole legitimate object of war, both Cicero and Sallust declared to be an assured peace. That war, according to Tacitus, ends well which ends with a pardon. Pliny refused to apply the epithet great to Cæsar, on account of the torrents of human blood he had shed. Two Roman conquerors[2] are credited with the saying that it is better to save the life of one citizen than to destroy a thousand enemies. Marcus Aurelius mournfully assimilated the career of a conqueror to that of a simple robber. Nations or armies which voluntarily submitted to Rome were habitually treated with great leniency, and numerous acts of individual magnanimity are recorded. The violation of the chastity of conquered women by soldiers in a siege was denounced as a rare and atrocious crime.[3] The extreme atrocities of ancient war appear at last to have been practically, though not legally, restricted to two classes.[4] Cities where Roman ambassadors had been insulted, or where some special act of ill faith or cruelty had taken place, were razed to the ground, and their populations massacred or delivered into slavery. Barbarian prisoners were regarded almost as wild beasts, and sent in thousands to fill the slave market or to combat in the arena.

---

[1] This appears continually in Livy, but most of all, I think, in the Gaulish historian, Florus.

[2] Scipio and Trajan.

[3] See some very remarkable passages in Grotius, *De Jure Bell.* lib. iii. cap. 4, § 19.

[4] These mitigations are fully enumerated by Ayala, *De Jure et Officiis Bellicis* (Antwerp, 1597), Grotius, *De Jure.* It is remarkable that both Ayala and Grotius base their attempts to mitigate the severity of war chiefly upon the writings and examples of the Pagans. The limits of the right of conquerors and the just causes of war are discussed by Cicero, *De Offic.* lib. i.

The changes Christianity effected in the rights of war were very important, and they may, I think, be comprised under three heads.   In the first place, it suppressed the gladiatorial shows, and thereby saved thousands of captives from a bloody death.   In the next place, it steadily discou-raged the practice of enslaving prisoners, ransomed immense multitudes with charitable contributions, and by slow and insensible gradations proceeded on its path of mercy till it became a recognised principle of international law, that no Christian prisoners should be reduced to slavery.[1]   In the third place, it had a more indirect but very powerful influ-ence by the creation of a new warlike ideal.   The ideal knight of the Crusades and of chivalry, uniting all the force and fire of the ancient warrior, with something of the tender-ness and humility of the Christian saint, sprang from the conjunction of the two streams of religious and of military

---

[1] In England the change seems to have immediately followed con-version. 'The evangelical precepts of peace and love,' says a very learned historian, 'did not put an end to war, they did not put an end to aggressive conquests, but they distinctly humanised the way in which war was carried on. From this time forth the never-ending wars with the Welsh cease to be wars of extermination. The heathen English had been satisfied with nothing short of the destruc-tion and expulsion of their enemies; the Christian English thought it enough to reduce them to political subjection. . . . The Christian Welsh could now sit down as sub-jects of the Christian Saxon. The Welshman was acknowledged as a man and a citizen, and was put under the protection of the law.'— Freeman's *Hist. of the Norman Conquest*, vol. i. pp. 33–34. Chris-tians who assisted infidels in wars were *ipso facto* excommunicated, and might therefore be enslaved, but all others were free from sla-very.   'Et quidem inter Chris-tianos laudabili et antiqua consue-tudine introductum est, ut capti hinc inde, utcunque justo bello, non fierent servi, sed liberi servarentur donec solvant precium redemptio-nis.'—Ayala, lib. i. cap. 5.   'This rule, at least,' says Grotius, '(though but a small matter) the reverence for the Christian law has enforced, which Socrates vainly sought to have established among the Greeks.' The Mohammedans also made it a rule not to enslave their co-religionists.—Grotius, *De Jure*, iii. 7, § 9.   Pagan and bar-barian prisoners were, however, sold as slaves (especially by the Spaniards) till very recently.

feeling; and although this ideal, like all others, was a creation of the imagination not often perfectly realised in
life, yet it remained the type and model of warlike excellence, to which many generations aspired; and its softening
influence may even now be largely traced in the character of
the modern gentleman.

Together with the gradual fusion of the military spirit
with Christianity, we may dimly descry, in the period before
Charlemagne, the first stages of that consecration of secular
rank which at a later period, in the forms of chivalry, the
divine right of kings, and the reverence for aristocracies,
played so large a part both in moral and in political history.

We have already seen that the course of events in the
Roman Empire had been towards the continual aggrandisement of the imperial power. The representative despotism
of Augustus was at last succeeded by the oriental despotism
of Diocletian. The senate sank into a powerless assembly of
imperial nominees, and the spirit of Roman freedom wholly
perished with the extinction of Stoicism.

It would probably be a needless refinement to seek any
deeper causes for this change than may be found in the ordinary principles of human nature. Despotism is the normal
and legitimate government of an early society in which
knowledge has not yet developed the powers of the people;
but when it is introduced into a civilised community, it is of
the nature of a disease, and a disease which, unless it be
checked, has a continual tendency to spread. When free
nations abdicate their political functions, they gradually lose
both the capacity and the desire for freedom. Political talent
and ambition, having no sphere for action, steadily decay,
and servile, enervating, and vicious habits proportionately
increase. Nations are organic beings in a constant process
of expansion or decay, and where they do not exhibit a progress of liberty they usually exhibit a progress of servitude.

It can hardly be asserted that Christianity had much in

fluence upon this change. By accelerating in some degree
that withdrawal of the virtuous energies of the people from
the sphere of government which had long been in process, it
prevented the great improvement of morals, which it undoubtedly effected, from appearing perceptibly in public
affairs. It taught a doctrine of passive obedience, which its
disciples nobly observed in the worst periods of persecution.
On the other hand, the Christians emphatically repudiated
the ascription of Divine honours to the sovereign, and they
asserted with heroic constancy their independent worship, in
defiance of the law. After the time of Constantine, however,
their zeal became far less pure, and sectarian interests wholly
governed their principles.   Much misapplied learning has
been employed in endeavouring to extract from the Fathers
a consistent doctrine concerning the relations of subjects
to their sovereigns; but every impartial observer may
discover that the principle upon which they acted was exceedingly simple.   When a sovereign was sufficiently orthodox in his opinions, and sufficiently zealous in patronising
the Church and in persecuting the heretics, he was extolled
as an angel. When his policy was opposed to the Church,
he was represented as a dæmon. The estimate which Gregory
of Tours has given of the character of Clovis, though far
more frank, is not a more striking instance of moral perversion than the fulsome and indeed blasphemous adulation
which Eusebius poured upon Constantine—a sovereign whose
character was at all times of the most mingled description,
and who, shortly after his conversion, put to a violent death
his son, his nephew, and his wife. If we were to estimate
the attitude of ecclesiastics to sovereigns by the language of
Eusebius, we should suppose that they ascribed to them a
direct Divine inspiration, and exalted the Imperial dignity
to an extent that was before unknown.[1]   But when Julian

[1] The character of Constantine, *Lectures on the Eastern Church*
and the estimate of it in Eusebius, (Lect. **vi.**).
are well treated by Dean Stanley.

mounted the throne, the whole aspect of the Church was changed. This great and virtuous, though misguided sovereign, whose private life was a model of purity, who carried to the throne the manners, tastes, and friendships of a philosophic life, and who proclaimed and, with very slight exceptions, acted with the largest and most generous toleration, was an enemy of the Church, and all the vocabulary of invective was in consequence habitually lavished upon him. Ecclesiastics and laymen combined in insulting him, and when, after a brief but glorious reign of less than two years, he met an honourable death on the battle-field, neither the disaster that had befallen the Roman arms, nor the present dangers of the army, nor the heroic courage which the fallen emperor had displayed, nor the majestic tranquillity of his end, nor the tears of his faithful friends, could shame the Christian community into the decency of silence. A peal of brutal merriment filled the land. In Antioch the Christians assembled in the theatres and in the churches, to celebrate with rejoicing the death which their emperor had met in fighting against the enemies of his country.[1] A crowd of vindictive legends expressed the exultation of the Church,[2] and St. Gregory Nazianzen devoted his eloquence to immortalising it. His brother had at one time been a high official in the Empire, and had fearlessly owned his Christianity under Julian; but that emperor not only did not remove him from his post, but even honoured him with his warm friendship.[3] The body of Julian had been laid but a short time in the grave, when St. Gregory delivered two fierce invectives against his memory, collected the grotesque calumnies that had been heaped upon his character, expressed a regret that his remains had not been flung after death into the common sewer, and regaled the hearers by an

---

[1] Theodoret, iii. 28.
[2] They are collected by Chateaubriand, *Études hist.* 2ᵐᵉ disc.

2ᵐᵉ partie.
[3] See St. Gregory's oration on *Cesairius.*

emphatic assertion of the tortures that were awaiting him in
hell. Among the Pagans a charge of the gravest kind was
brought against the Christians. It was said that Julian died
by the spear, not of an enemy, but of one of his own Christian
soldiers. When we remember that he was at once an em·
peror and a general, that he fell when bravely and confidently
leading his army in the field, and in the critical moment of a
battle on which the fortunes of the Empire largely depended,
this charge, which Libanius has made, appears to involve as
large an amount of base treachery as any that can be conceived. It was probably a perfectly groundless calumny;
but the manner in which it was regarded among the
Christians is singularly characteristic. 'Libanius,' says
one of the ecclesiastical historians, 'clearly states that
the emperor fell by the hand of a Christian; and this, probably, was the truth. It is not unlikely that some of the
soldiers who then served in the Roman army might have
conceived the idea of acting like the ancient slayers of
tyrants who exposed themselves to death in the cause of
liberty, and fought in defence of their country, their families,
and their friends, and whose names are held in universal
admiration. Still less is he deserving of blame who, for the
sake of God and of religion, performed so bold a deed.'[1]

It may be asserted, I think, without exaggeration, that
the complete subordination of all other principles to their
theological interests, which characterised the ecclesiastics
under Julian, continued for many centuries. No language
of invective was too extreme to be applied to a sovereign
who opposed their interests. No language of adulation was too
extravagant for a sovereign who sustained them. Of all the
emperors who disgraced the throne of Constantinople, the
most odious and ferocious was probably Phocas. An obscure
centurion, he rose by a military revolt to the supreme power,

---

[1] Sozomen, vi. 2.

and the Emperor Maurice, with his family, fell into his hands.
He resolved to put the captive emperor to death; but, first of
all, he ordered his five children to be brought out and to
be successively murdered before the eyes of their father, who
bore the awful sight with a fine mixture of antique heroism
and of Christian piety, murmuring, as each child fell beneath
the knife of the assassin, 'Thou art just, O Lord, and
righteous are Thy judgments,' and even interposing, at the
last moment, to reveal the heroic fraud of the nurse who
desired to save his youngest child by substituting for it her
own.   But Maurice—who had been a weak and avaricious
rather than a vicious sovereign—had shown himself jealous
of the influence of the Pope, had forbidden the soldiers,
during the extreme danger of their country, deserting their
colours to enrol themselves as monks, and had even encouraged the pretensions of the Archbishop of Constantinople to
the title of Universal Bishop; and, in the eyes of the Roman
priests, the recollection of these crimes was sufficient to
excuse the most brutal of murders.   In two letters, full of
passages from Scripture, and replete with fulsome and
blasphemous flattery, the Pope, St. Gregory the Great, wrote
to congratulate Phocas and his wife upon their triumph; he
called heaven and earth to rejoice over them; he placed their
images to be venerated in the Lateran, and he adroitly insinuated that it was impossible that, with their well-know   piety,
they could fail to be very favourable to the See of Pe   r.[1]

The course of events in relation to the monarchical power
was for some time different in the East and the West.
Constantine had himself assumed more of the pomp and

<hr/>

[1] *Ep.* xiii. 31–39. In the second of these letters (which is addressed to Leontia), he says: 'Rogare fositan debui ut ecclesiam bea i Petri apostoli quæ nunc usque gravibus insidiis laboravit, haberet Vestra Tranquillitas specialiter commendatam. Sed qui scio quia omnipotentem Deum diligitis, non debeo petere quod sponte ex benignitate vestræ pietatis exhibetis.'

manner of an oriental sovereign than any preceding emperor, and the court of Constantinople was soon characterised by an extravagance of magnificence on the part of the monarch, and of adulation on the part of the subjects, which has probably never been exceeded.[1] The imperial power in the East overshadowed the ecclesiastical, and the priests, notwith-standing their fierce outbreak during the iconoclastic controversy, and a few minor paroxysms of revolt, gradually sank into that contented subservience which has usually characterised the Eastern Church. In the West, however, the Roman bishops were in a great degree independent of the sovereigns, and in some degree opposed to their interests. The transfer of the imperial power to Constantinople, by leaving the Roman bishops the chief personages in a city which long association as well as actual power rendered the foremost in the world, was one of the great causes of the aggrandisement of the Papacy and the Arianism of many sovereigns, the jealousy which others exhibited of ecclesias-tical encroachments, and the lukewarmness of a few in persecuting heretics, were all causes of dissension. On the severance of the Empire, the Western Church came in contact with rulers of another type. The barbarian kings were little more than military chiefs, elected for the most part by the people, surrounded by little or no special sanctity, and maintaining their precarious and very restricted authority by their courage or their skill. A few feebly imitated the pomp of the Roman emperors, but their claims had no great weight with the world. The aureole which the genius of Theodoric cast around his throne passed away upon his death, and the Arianism of that great sovereign sufficiently debarred him from the sympathies of the Church. In Gaul, under a few bold and unscrupulous men, the Merovingian dynasty emerged from a host of petty kings, and consolidated the

---

See the graphic description in Gibbon, ch. liii,

whole country into one kingdom; but after a short period it degenerated, the kings became mere puppets in the hands of the mayors of the palace, and these latter, whose office had become hereditary, who were the chiefs of the great landed proprietors, and who had acquired by their position a personal ascendancy over the sovereigns, became the virtual rulers of the nation.

It was out of these somewhat unpromising conditions that the mediæval doctrine of the Divine right of kings, and the general reverence for rank, that formed the essence of chivalry, were slowly evolved. Political and moral causes conspired in producing them. The chief political causes— which are well known—may be summed up in a few words.

When Leo the Isaurian attempted, in the eighth century, to repress the worship of images, the resistance which he met at Constantinople, though violent, was speedily allayed; but the Pope, assuming a far higher position than any Byzantine ecclesiastic could attain, boldly excommunicated the emperor, and led a revolt against his authority, which resulted in the virtual independence of Italy. His position was at this time singularly grand. He represented a religious cause to which the great mass of the Christian world were passionately attached. He was venerated as the emancipator of Italy. He exhibited in the hour of his triumph a moderation which conciliated many enemies, and prevented the anarchy that might naturally have been expected. He presided, at the same time, over a vast monastic organisation, which ramified over all Christendom, propagated his authority among many barbarous nations, and, by its special attachment to the Papacy, as distinguished from the Episcopacy, contri-buted very much to transform Christianity into a spiritual despotism. One great danger, however, still menaced his power. The barbarous Lombards were continually invading his territory, and threatening the independence of Rome. The Lombard monarch, Luitprand, had quailed in the very hour of his triumph before the menace of eternal torture; but his successor, Astolphus, was proof against every fear, and it seemed as though the Papal city must have inevitably succumbed before his arms.

In their complete military impotence, the Popes looked abroad for some foreign succour, and they naturally turned to the Franks, whose martial tastes and triumphs were universally renowned. Charles Martel, though simply a mayor of the palace, had saved Europe from the Mohammedans, and the Pope expected that he would unsheath his sword for the defence of the Vatican. Charles, however, was deaf to all entreaties; and, although he had done more than any ruler since Constantine for the Church, his attention seems to have been engrossed by the interests of his own country, and he was much alienated from the sympathies of the clergy. An ancient legend tells how a saint saw his soul carried by dæmons into hell, because he had secularised Church property, and a more modern historian[1] has ascribed his death to his having hesitated to defend the Pope. His son, Pepin, however, actuated probably in different degrees by personal ambition, a desire for military adventure, and religious zeal, listened readily to the prayer of the Pope, and a compact was entered into between the parties, which proved one of the most important events in history. Pepin agreed to secure the Pope from the danger by which he was threatened. The Pope agreed to give his religious sanction to the ambition of Pepin, who designed to depose the Merovingian dynasty, and to become in name, as he was already in fact, the sovereign of Gaul.

It is not necessary for me to recount at length the details of these negotiations, which are described by many historians. It is sufficient to say, that the compact was religiously observed. Pepin made two expeditions to Italy, and com

---

[1] Baronius.

pletely shattered the power of the Lombards, wresting from them the rich exarchate of Ravenna, which he ceded to the Pope, who still retained his nominal allegiance to the Byzantine emperor, but who became, by this donation, for the first time avowedly an independent temporal prince. On the other hand, the deposition of Childeric was peaceably effected; the last of the Merovingians was immured in a monastery, and the Carlovingian dynasty ascended the throne under the special benediction of the Pope, who performed on the occasion the ceremony of consecration, which had not previously been in general use,[1] placed the crown with his own hands on the head of Pepin, and delivered a solemn anathema against all who should rebel against the new king or against his successors.

The extreme importance of these events was probably not fully realised by any of the parties concerned in them. It was evident, indeed, that the Pope had been freed from a pressing danger, and had acquired a great accession of temporal power, and also that a new dynasty had arisen in Gaul under circumstances that were singularly favourable and imposing. But, much more important than these facts was the permanent consecration of the royal authority that had been effected. The Pope had successfully asserted his power of deposing and elevating kings, and had thus acquired a position which influenced the whole subsequent course of European history. The monarch, if he had become in some degree subservient to the priest, had become in a great degree independent of his people; the Divine origin of his power was regarded as a dogma of religion, and a sanctity surrounded him which immeasurably aggrandised his power. The ascription, by the Pagans, of divinity to kings had had no appreciable effect in increasing their authority or restraining the limits of criticism or of rebellion. The ascription of

---

[1] Mably, ii. 1; Gibbon, ch. xlix.

a Divine right to kings, independent of the wishes of the people, has been one of the most enduring and most potent of superstitions, and it has even now not wholly vanished from the world.[1]

Mere isolated political events have, however, rarely or never this profound influence, unless they have been preceded and prepared by other agencies. The first predisposing cause of the ready reception of the doctrine of the Divine character of authority, may probably be found in the prominence of the monastic system. I have already observed that this system represents in its extreme form that exaltation of the virtues of humility and of obedience which so broadly distinguishes the Christian from the Pagan type of excellence. I have also noticed that, owing to the concurrence of many causes, it had acquired such dimensions and influence as to supply the guiding ideal of the Christian world. Controlling or monopolising all education and literature, furnishing most of the legislators and many of the statesmen of the age, attracting to themselves all moral enthusiasm and most intellectual ability, the monks soon left their impress on the character of nations. Habits of obedience and dispositions of humility were diffused, revered, and idealised, and a Church which rested mainly on tradition fostered a deep sense of the sanctity of antiquity, and a natural disposition to observe traditional customs. In this

---

[1] There are some good remarks upon the way in which, among the free Franks, the bishops taught the duty of passive obedience, in Mably, *Obs. sur l'Histoire de France*, livre i. ch. iii. Gregory of Tours, in his address to Chilperic, had said: 'If any of us, O king, transgress the boundaries of justice, thou art at hand to correct us; but if thou shouldest exceed them, who is to condemn thee? We address thee, and if it please thee thou listenest to us; but if it please thee not, who is to condemn thee save He who has proclaimed Himself Justice.' — Greg. Tur. v. 19. On the other hand, Hincmar, Archbishop of Rheims, strongly asserted the obligation of kings to observe the law, and denounced as diabolical the doctrine that they are subject to none but God. (Allen, *On the Royal Prerogative* (1849), pp. 171–172.)

manner a tone of feeling was gradually formed that assimilated with the monarchical and aristocratical institutions of
feudalism, which flourished chiefly because they corresponded
with the moral feelings of the time.

In the next place, a series of social and political causes
diminished the personal independence for which the barbarians had been noted. The king had at first been, not the
sovereign of a country, but the chief of a tribe.[1] Gradually,
however, with more settled habits, the sovereignty assumed a
territorial character, and we may soon discover the rudiments
of a territorial aristocracy. The kings gave their leading
chiefs portions of conquered land or of the royal domains,
under the name of benefices. The obligation of military
service was attached to these benefices, and by slow and
perhaps insensible stages, each of which has been the subject
of fierce controversy, they were made irrevocable, and
ultimately hereditary. While society was still disorganised,
small landlords purchased the protection of the Church, or of
some important chief, by surrendering their estates, which
they received back as tenants, subject to the condition of the
payment of rent, or of military service. Others, without
making such surrender, placed themselves under the care of
a neighbouring lord, and offered, in return, homage or military aid. At the same time, through causes to which I have
already adverted, the free peasants for the most part sank
into serfs, subject to and protected by the landowners. In
this manner a hierarchy of ranks was gradually formed, of
which the sovereign was the apex and the serf the basis.
The complete legal organisation of this hierarchy belongs to

---

[1] The exact degree of the authority of the barbarian kings, and the
different stages by which their
power was increased, are matters
of great controversy. The reader
may consult Thierry's *Lettres sur*
l'Hist. de France (let. 9), Guizot's
Hist. de la Civilisation; Mably,
Observ. sur l'Hist. de France; Freeman's *Hist. of the Norman Conquest*, vol. i.

the period of feudalism, which is not within the scope of the
present volume; but the chief elements of feudalism existed
before Charlemagne, and the moral results flowing from them
may be already discerned. Each rank, except the very
highest, was continually brought into contact with a superior,
and a feeling of constant dependence and subordination was
accordingly fostered. To the serf, who depended for all
things upon the neighbouring noble, to the noble, who held
all his dignities on the condition of frequent military service
under his sovereign, the idea of secular rank became indissolubly connected with that of supreme greatness.

It will appear evident, from the foregoing observations,
that in the period before Charlemagne the moral and political causes were already in action, which at a much later
period produced the organisation of chivalry—an organisation which was founded on the combination and the glorification of secular rank and military prowess. But, in order
that the tendencies I have described should acquire their full
force, it was necessary that they should be represented or
illustrated in some great personage, who, by the splendour
and the beauty of his career, could fascinate the imaginations
of men. It is much easier to govern great masses of men
through their imagination than through their reason. Moral
principles rarely act powerfully upon the world, except by
way of example or ideals. When the course of events has
been to glorify the ascetic or monarchical or military spirit, a
great saint, or sovereign, or soldier will arise, who will concentrate in one dazzling focus the blind tendencies of his
time, kindle the enthusiasm and fascinate the imagination of
the people. But for the prevailing tendency, the great man
would not have arisen, or would not have exercised his great
influence. But for the great man, whose career appealed
vividly to the imagination, the prevailing tendency would
never have acquired its full intensity.

This typical figure appeared in Charlemagne, whose

colossal form towers with a majestic grandeur both in history
and in romance. Of all the great rulers of men, there has
probably been no other who was so truly many-sided, whose
influence pervaded so completely all the religious, intellectual,
and political modes of thought existing in his time. Rising
in one of the darkest periods of European history, this great
emperor resuscitated, with a brief but dazzling splendour, the
faded glories of the Empire of the West, conducted, for the
most part in person, numerous expeditions against the barbarous nations around him, promulgated a vast system of
legislation, reformed the discipline of every order of the
Church, and reduced all classes of the clergy to subservience
to his will, while, by legalising tithes, he greatly increased
their material prosperity. He at the same time contributed,
in a measure, to check the intellectual decadence by founding
schools and libraries, and drawing around him all the scattered learning of Europe. He reformed the coinage, extended
commerce, influenced religious controversies, and convoked
great legislative assemblies, which ultimately contributed
largely to the organisation of feudalism. In all these
spheres the traces of his vast, organising, and far-seeing
genius may be detected, and the influence which he exercised
over the imaginations of men is shown by the numerous
legends of which he is the hero. In the preceding ages the
supreme ideal had been the ascetic. When the popular
imagination embodied in legends its conception of humanity
in its noblest and most attractive form, it instinctively
painted some hermit-saint of many penances and many
miracles. In the Romances of Charlemagne and of Arthur
we may trace the dawning of a new type of greatness. The
hero of the imagination of Europe was no longer a hermit,
but a king, a warrior, a knight. The long train of influences
I have reviewed, culminating in Charlemagne, had done
their work. The age of the ascetics began to fade. The age
of the crusades and of chivalry succeeded it.

It is curious to observe the manner in which, under the influence of the prevailing tendency, the career of Charlemagne was transfigured by the popular imagination. His military enterprises had been chiefly directed against the Saxons, against whom he had made not less than thirty-two expeditions. With the Mohammedans he had but little contact. It was Charles Martel, not his grandson, who, by the great battle of Poitiers, had checked their career. Charlemagne made, in person, but a single expedition against them in Spain, and that expedition was on a small scale, and was disastrous in its issue. But in the Carlovingian romances, which arose at a time when the enthusiasm of the Crusades was permeating Christendom, events were represented in a wholly different light. Charles Martel has no place among the ideal combatants of the Church. He had appeared too early, his figure was not sufficiently great to fascinate the popular imagination, and by confiscating ecclesiastical property, and refusing to assist the Pope against the Lombards, he had fallen under the ban of the clergy. Charlemagne, on the other hand, was represented as the first and greatest of the crusaders. His wars with the Saxons were scarcely noticed. His whole life was said to have been spent in heroic and triumphant combats with the followers of Mohammed.[1] Among the achievements attributed to him was an expedition to rescue Nismes and Carcassonne from their grasp, which was, in fact, a dim tradition of the victories of Charles Martel.[2] He is even said to have carried his victorious arms into the heart of Palestine, and he is the hero of what are probably the three earliest extant romances of the Crusades.[3] In fiction, as in history, his reign forms the

---

[1] Fauriel, *Hist. de la Poésie provençale*, tome ii. p. 252.
[2] Ibid, p. 258.
[3] Le Grand D'Aussy, *Fabliaux*, préf. p. xxiv. These romances were accounts of his expeditions to Spain, to Languedoc, and to Palestine.

great landmark separating the early period of the middle ages from the age of military Christianity.

On the verge of this great change I draw this history to a close. In pursuing our long and chequered course, from Augustus to Charlemagne, we have seen the rise and fall of many types of character, and of many forms of enthusiasm. We have seen the influence of universal empire expanding, and the influence of Greek civilisation intensifying, the sympathies of Europe. We have surveyed the successive progress of Stoicism, Platonism, and Egyptian philosophies, at once reflecting and guiding the moral tendencies of society. We have traced the course of progress or retrogression in many fields of social, political, and legislative life, have watched the cradle of European Christianity, examined the causes of its triumph, the difficulties it encountered, and the priceless blessings its philanthropic spirit bestowed upon mankind. We have also pursued step by step the mournful history of its corruption, its asceticism, and its intolerance, the various transformations it produced or underwent when the turbid waters of the barbarian invasions had inundated the civilisations of Europe. It remains for me, before concluding this work, to investigate one class of subjects to which I have, as yet, but briefly adverted—to examine the effects of the changes I have described upon the character and position of woman, and upon the grave moral question concerning the relations of the sexes.

CHAPTER V.

THE POSITION OF WOMEN.

IN the long series of moral revolutions that have been described in the foregoing chapters, I have more than once had occasion to refer to the position that was assigned to woman in the community, and to the virtues and vices that spring directly from the relations of the sexes. I have not, however, as yet discussed these questions with a fulness at all corresponding to their historical importance, and I propose, in consequence, before concluding this volume, to devote a few pages to their examination. Of all the many questions that are treated in this work, there is none which I approach with so much hesitation, for there is probably none which it is so difficult to treat with clearness and impartiality, and at the same time without exciting any scandal or offence. The complexity of the problem, arising from the very large place which exceptional institutions or circumstances, and especially the influence of climate and race, have had on the chastity of nations, I have already noticed, and the extreme delicacy of the matters with which this branch of ethics is connected must be palpable to all. The first duty of an historian, however, is to truth; and it is absolutely impossible to present a true picture of the moral condition of different ages, and to form a true estimate of the moral effects of different religions, without adverting to the department of morals, which has exhibited most change, and has probably exercised most influence.

It is natural that, in the period when men are still perfect barbarians, when their habits of life are still nomadic, and when, war and the chase, being their sole pursuits, the qualities that are required in these form their chief measure of excellence, the inferiority of women to men should be regarded as undoubted, and their position should be extremely degraded. In all those qualities which are then most prized, women are indisputably inferior. The social qualities in which they are especially fitted to excel have no sphere for their display. The ascendancy of beauty is very faint, and, even if it were otherwise, few traces of female beauty could survive the hardships of the savage life. Woman is looked upon merely as the slave of man, and as the minister to his passions. In the first capacity, her life is one of continual, abject, and unrequited toil. In the second capacity, she is exposed to all the violent revulsions of feeling that follow, among rude men, the gratification of the animal passions.

Even in this early stage, however, we may trace some rudiments of those moral sentiments which are destined at a later period to expand. The institution of marriage exists. The value of chastity is commonly in some degree felt, and appears in the indignation which is displayed against the adulterer. The duty of restraining the passions is largely recognised in the female, though the males are only restricted by the prohibition of adultery.

The first two steps which are taken towards the elevation of woman are probably the abandonment of the custom of purchasing wives, and the construction of the family on the basis of monogamy. In the earliest periods of civilisation, the marriage contract was arranged between the bridegroom and the father of the bride, on the condition of a sum of money being paid by the former to the latter. This sum, which is known in the laws of the barbarians as the 'mundium,' [1]

---

[1] The ἔδνα of the Greeks.

was in fact a payment to the father for the cession of his
daughter, who thus became the bought slave of her husband.
It is one of the most remarkable features of the ancient laws
of India, that they forbade this gift, on the ground that the
parent should not sell his child;[1] but there can be little
doubt that this sale was at one time the ordinary type of
marriage.   In the Jewish writings we find Jacob purchasing
Leah and Rachel by certain services to their father; and
this custom, which seems to have been at one time
general in Judea,[2] appears in the age of Homer to have
been general in Greece.   At an early period, however, of
Greek history, the purchase-money was replaced by the
dowry, or sum of money paid by the father of the bride for
the use of his daughter;[3] and this, although it passed into the
hands of the husband, contributed to elevate the wife, in the
first place, by the dignity it gave her, and, in the next place,
by special laws, which both in Greece and Rome secured it
to her in most cases of separation.[4]   The wife thus possessed
a guarantee against ill-usage by her husband.   She ceased to
be his slave, and became in some degree a contracting party.

---

[1] Legouvé, *Histoire morale des
Femmes*, pp. 95–96.

[2] Gen. xxix., xxxiv. 12; Deut.
xxii. 29; 1 Sam. xviii. 25.

[3] The history of dowries is
briefly noticed by Grote, *Hist. of
Greece*, vol. ii. pp. 112–113; and
more fully by Lord Kames, in the
admirable chapter 'On the Progress of the Female Sex,' in his
Sketches of the History of Man, a
book less read than it deserves to
be. M. Legouvé has also devoted
a chapter to it in his *Hist. morale
des Femmes*. See, too, Legendre,
Traité de l'Opinion, tome ii. pp.
329–330. We find traces of the
dowry, as well as of the ἕδνα, in
Homer. Penelope had received a
dowry from Icarus, her father.
M. Michelet, in one of those fanciful books which he has recently
published, maintains a view of the
object of the ἕδνα which I do not
remember to have seen elsewhere,
and which I do not believe. He
says: 'Ce prix n'est point un achat
de la femme, mais une indemnité
qui dédommage la famille du père
pour les enfants futurs, qui ne
profiteront pas à cette famille mais
à celle où la femme va entrer.'—
La Femme, p. 166.

[4] In Rome, when the separation
was due to the misconduct of the
wife, the dowry belonged to her
husband.

Among the early Germans, a different and very remarkable custom existed. The bride did not bring any dowry to her husband, nor did the bridegroom give anything to the father of the bride; but he gave his gift to the bride herself, on the morning after the first night of marriage, and this, which was called the 'Morgengab,' or morning gift, was the origin of the jointure.[1]

Still more important than the foregoing was the institution of monogamy, by which, from its earliest days, the Greek civilisation proclaimed its superiority to the Asiatic civilisations that had preceded it. We may regard monogamy either in the light of our intuitive moral sentiment on the subject of purity, or in the light of the interests of society. In its Oriental or polygamous stage, marriage is regarded almost exclusively, in its lowest aspect, as a gratification of the passions; while in European marriages the mutual attachment and respect of the contracting parties, the formation of a household, and the long train of domestic feelings and duties that accompany it, have all their distinguished place among the motives of the contract, and the lower element has comparatively little prominence. In this way it may be intelligibly said, without any reference to utilitarian considerations, that monogamy is a higher state than polygamy. The utilitarian arguments in its defence are also extremely powerful, and may be summed up in three sentences. Nature, by making the number of males and females nearly equal, indicates it as natural. In no other form of marriage can the government of the family, which is one of the chief ends of marriage, be so happily sustained,

---

[1] ' Dotem non uxor marito sed uxori maritus offert.'—Tac. Germ. xviii. On the Morgengab, see Canciani, Leges Barbarorum (Venetiis, 1781), vol. i. pp. 102–104; ii. pp. 230–231. Muratori, Antich. Ital. diss. xx. Luitprand enacted that no Longobard should give more than one-fourth of his substance as a Morgengab. In Gregory of Tours (ix. 20) we have an example of the gift of some cities as a Morgengab.

and in no other does woman assume the position of the equal of man.

Monogamy was the general system in Greece, though there are said to have been slight and temporary deviations into the earlier system, after some great disasters, when an increase of population was ardently desired.[1] A broad line must, however, be drawn between the legendary or poetical period, as reflected in Homer and perpetuated in the trage-dians, and the later historical period. It is one of the most remarkable, and to some writers one of the most perplexing, facts in the moral history of Greece, that in the former and ruder period women had undoubtedly the highest place, and their type exhibited the highest perfection. Moral ideas, in a thousand forms, have been sublimated, enlarged, and changed, by advancing civilisation; but it may be fearlessly asserted that the types of female excellence which are contained in the Greek poems, while they are among the earliest, are also among the most perfect in the literature of mankind. The conjugal tenderness of Hector and Andro-mache; the unwearied fidelity of Penelope, awaiting through the long revolving years the return of her storm-tossed husband, who looked forward to her as to the crown of all his labours; the heroic love of Alcestis, voluntarily dying that her husband might live; the filial piety of Antigone; the majestic grandeur of the death of Polyxena; the more subdued and saintly resignation of Iphigenia, excusing with her last breath the father who had condemned her; the joyous, modest, and loving Nausicaa, whose figure shines like a perfect idyll among the tragedies of the Odyssey—all these are pictures of perennial beauty, which Rome and Christen-dom, chivalry and modern civilisation, have neither eclipsed nor transcended. Virgin modesty and conjugal fidelity, the

---

[1] See, on this point, Aul. Gellius, *Noct. Att.* xv. 20. Euripides is said to have had two wives.

graces as well as the virtues of the most perfect womanhood, have never been more exquisitely pourtrayed. The female figures stand out in the canvas almost as prominently as the male ones, and are surrounded by an almost equal reverence The whole history of the Siege of Troy is a history of the catastrophes that followed a violation of the nuptial tie. Yet, at the same time, the position of women was in some respects a degraded one. The custom of purchase-money given to the father of the bride was general. The husbands appear to have indulged largely, and with little or no censure, in concubines.[1] Female captives of the highest rank were treated with great harshness. The inferiority of women to men was strongly asserted, and it was illustrated and defended by a very curious physiological notion, that the generative power belonged exclusively to men, women having only a very subordinate part in the production of their children.[2] The woman Pandora was said to have been the author of all human ills.

In the historical age of Greece, the legal position of women had in some respects slightly improved, but their moral condition had undergone a marked deterioration. Virtuous women lived a life of perfect seclusion. The foremost and most dazzling type of Ionic womanhood was the

---

[1] Aristotle said that Homer never gives a concubine to Menelaus, in order to intimate his respect for Helen—though false. (*Athenæus*, xiii. 3.)

[2] Æschylus has put this curious notion into the mouth of Apollo, in a speech in the *Eumenides*. It has, however, been very widely diffused, and may be found in Indian, Greek, Roman, and even Christian writers. M. Legouvé, who has devoted a very curious chapter to the subject, quotes a passage from St. Thomas Aquinas, accepting it, and arguing from it, that a father should be more loved than a mother. M. Legouvé says that when the male of one animal and the female of another are crossed, the type of the female usually predominates in the offspring. See Legouvé, *Hist. morale des Femmes*, pp. 216-228 ; Fustel de Coulanges, *La Cité antique*, pp. 39-40 ; and also a curious note by Boswell, in Croker's edition of Boswell's *Life of Johnson* (1847), p. 472.

courtesan, while, among the men, the latitude accorded by
public opinion was almost unrestricted.

The facts in moral history, which it is at once most
important and most difficult to appreciate, are what may be
called the facts of feeling. It is much easier to show what
men did or taught than to realise the state of mind that rendered possible such actions or teaching; and in the case before
us we have to deal with a condition of feeling so extremel·
remote from that of our own day, that the difficulty is pr
eminently great. Very sensual, and at the same time very
brilliant societies, have indeed repeatedly existed, and the
histories of both France and Italy afford many examples of
an artistic and intellectual enthusiasm encircling those who
were morally most frail; but the peculiarity of Greek sensuality is, that it grew up, for the most part, uncensured,
and indeed even encouraged, under the eyes of some of the
most illustrious of moralists. If we can imagine Ninon de
l'Enclos at a time when the rank and splendour of Parisian
society thronged her drawing-rooms, reckoning a Bossuet
or a Fénelon among her followers—if we can imagine these
prelates publicly advising her about the duties of her profession, and the means of attaching the affections of her
lovers—we shall have conceived a relation scarcely more
strange than that which existed between Socrates and the
courtesan Theodota.

In order to reconstruct, as far as possible, the modes of
feeling of the Greek moralists, it will be necessary in the
first place to say a few words concerning one of the most
delicate, but at the same time most important, problems
with which the legislator and the moralist have to deal.

It was a favourite doctrine of the Christian Fathers, that
concupiscence, or the sensual passion, was 'the original sin'
of human nature; and it must be owned that the progress of
knowledge, which is usually extremely opposed to the ascetic
theory of life, concurs with the theological view, in showing

the natural force of this appetite to be far greater than the
well-being of man requires.   The writings of Malthus have
proved, what the Greek moralists appear in a considerable
degree to have seen, that its normal and temperate exercise
in the form of marriage, would produce, if universal, the
utmost calamities to the world, and that, while nature seems
in the most unequivocal manner to urge the human race to
early marriages, the first condition of an advancing civilisation in populous countries is to restrain or diminish them.
In no highly civilised society is marriage general on the first
development of the passions, and the continual tendency of
increasing knowledge is to render such marriages more rare.
It is also an undoubted truth that, however much moralists
may enforce the obligation of extra-matrimonial purity, this
obligation has never been even approximately regarded ; and
in all nations, ages, and religions a vast mass of irregular
indulgence has appeared, which has probably contributed
more than any other single cause to the misery and the degradation of man.

There are two ends which a moralist, in dealing with this
question, will especially regard — the natural duty of every
man doing something for the support of the child he has
called into existence, and the preservation of the domestic
circle unassailed and unpolluted.   The family is the centre
and the archetype of the State, and the happiness and goodness of society are always in a very great degree dependent
upon the purity of domestic life.   The essentially exclusive
nature of marital affection, and the natural desire of every
man to be certain of the paternity of the child he supports,
render the incursions of irregular passions within the domestic
circle a cause of extreme suffering.   Yet it would appear as
if the excessive force of these passions would render such
incursions both frequent and inevitable.

Under these circumstances, there has arisen in society a
figure which is certainly the most mournful, and in some

respects the most awful, upon which the eye of the moralist can dwell. That unhappy being whose very name is a shame to speak; who counterfeits with a cold heart the transports of affection, and submits herself as the passive instrument of lust; who is scorned and insulted as the vilest of her sex, and doomed, for the most part, to disease and abject wretchedness and an early death, appears in every age as the perpetual symbol of the degradation and the sinfulness of man. Herself the supreme type of vice, she is ultimately the most efficient guardian of virtue. But for her, the un-challenged purity of countless happy homes would be polluted, and not a few who, in the pride of their untempted chastity, think of her with an indignant shudder, would have known the agony of remorse and of despair. On that one degraded and ignoble form are concentrated the passions that might have filled the world with shame. She remains, while creeds and civilisations rise and fall, the eternal priestess of humanity, blasted for the sins of the people.

In dealing with this unhappy being, and with all of her sex who have violated the law of chastity, the public opinion of most Christian countries pronounces a sentence of extreme severity. In the Anglo-Saxon nations especially, a single fault of this kind is sufficient, at least in the upper and middle classes, to affix an indelible brand which no time, no virtues, no penitence can wholly efface. This sentence is probably, in the first instance, simply the expression of the religious feeling on the subject, but it is also sometimes defended by powerful arguments drawn from the interests of society. It is said that the preservation of domestic purity is a matter of such transcendent importance that it is right that the most crushing penalties should be attached to an act which the imagination can easily transfigure, which legal enactments can never efficiently control, and to which the most violent passions may prompt. It is said, too, that an anathema which drives into obscurity all evidences of sensual passions is peculiarly fitted to restrict their operation; for, more than any other passions, they are dependent on the imagination, which is readily fired by the sight of evil. It is added, that the emphasis with which the vice is stigmatised produces a corresponding admiration for the opposite virtue, and that a feeling of the most delicate and scrupulous honour is thus formed among the female population, which not only preserves from gross sin, but also dignifies and ennobles the whole character.

In opposition to these views, several considerations of much weight have been urged. It is argued that, however persistently society may ignore this form of vice, it exists nevertheless, and on the most gigantic scale, and that evil rarely assumes such inveterate and perverting forms as when it is shrouded in obscurity and veiled by an hypocritical appearance of unconsciousness. The existence in England of certainly not less than fifty thousand unhappy women,[1] sunk in the very lowest depths of vice and misery, shows sufficiently what an appalling amount of moral evil is festering uncontrolled, undiscussed, and unalleviated, under the fair surface of a decorous society. In the eyes of every physician, and indeed in the eyes of most continental writers who have adverted to the subject, no other feature of English life appears so infamous as the fact that an epidemic, which is one of the most dreadful now existing among mankind, which communicates itself from the guilty husband to the innocent wife, and even transmits its taint to her offspring, and which the experience of other nations conclusively proves may be vastly diminished, should be suffered to rage unchecked

---

[1] Dr. Vintras, in a remarkable pamphlet (London, 1867) *On the Repression of Prostitution*, shows from the police statistics that the number of prostitutes *known to the police* in England and Wales, in 1864, was 49,370; and this is certainly much below the entire number. These, it will be observed, comprise only the habitual, professional prostitutes

because the Legislature refuses to take official cognisance **of** **its** existence, or proper sanitary measures for its repression.[1] **If** the terrible censure which English public opinion passes upon every instance of female frailty in some degree dimi- nishes the number, it does not prevent such instances from being extremely numerous, and it immeasurably aggravates the suffering they produce. Acts which in other European countries would excite only a slight and transient emotion, spread in England, over a wide circle, all the bitterness **of** unmitigated anguish. Acts which naturally neither imply nor produce a total subversion of the moral feelings, and which, in other countries, are often followed by happy, virtuous, and affectionate lives, in England almost invari- ably lead to absolute ruin. Infanticide is greatly multiplied, and a vast proportion of those whose reputations and lives have been blasted by one momentary sin, are hurled into the abyss of habitual prostitution—a condition which, owing **to** the sentence of public opinion and the neglect of legislators, is in no other European country so hopelessly vicious or so irrevocable.[2]

It is added, too, that the immense multitude who are thus doomed to the extremity of life-long wretchedness are not always, perhaps not generally, of those whose disposi- tions seem naturally incapable of virtue. The victims of

---

[1] Some measures have recently been taken in a few garrison towns. The moral sentiment of the com- munity, it appears, would be shocked if Liverpool were treated on the same principles as Ports- mouth. This very painful and revolting, but most important, sub- ject has been treated with great knowledge, impartiality, and ability, by Parent-Duchâtelet, in his famous work, *La Prosti- tution dans la ville de Paris.* The third edition contains very copious supplementary accounts, furnished by different doctors in different countries.

[2] Parent Duchâtelet has given many statistics, showing the very large extent to which the French system of supervision deters those who were about to enter into prostitution, and reclaims those who had entered into it. He and Dr. Vintras concur in representing English prostitution as about the most degraded, and at the same time the most irrevocable.

seduction are often led aside quite as much by the ardour of
their affections, and by the vivacity of their intelligence, as
by any vicious propensities.[1] Even in the lowest grades, the
most dispassionate observers have detected remains of higher
feelings, which, in a different moral atmosphere, and under
different moral husbandry, would have undoubtedly been
developed.[2] The statistics of prostitution show that a great
proportion of those who have fallen into it have been impelled by the most extreme poverty, in many instances
verging upon starvation.[3]

These opposing considerations, which I have very briefly
indicated, and which I do not propose to discuss or to

---

[1] Miss Mulock, in her amiable but rather feeble book, called *A Woman's Thoughts about Women*, has some good remarks on this point (pp. 291–293), which are all the more valuable, as the authoress has not the faintest sympathy with any opinions concerning the character and position of women which are not strictly conventional. She notices the experience of Sunday school mistresses, that, of their pupils who are seduced, an extremely large proportion are 'of the very best, refined, intelligent, truthful, and affectionate.'

[2] See the very singular and painful chapter in Parent-Duchâtelet, called 'Mœurs et Habitudes des Prostituées.' He observes that they are remarkable for their kindness to one another in sickness or in distress; that they are not unfrequently charitable to poor people who do not belong to their class; that when one of them has a child, it becomes the object of very general interest and affection; that most of them have lovers, to whom they are sincerely attached; that they rarely fail to show in the hospitals a very real sense of shame; and that many of them entered into their mode of life for the purpose of supporting aged parents. One anecdote is worth giving in the words of the author: 'Un médecin n'entrant jamais dans leurs salles sans ôter légèrement son chapeau, par cette seule politesse il sut tellement conquérir leur confiance qu'il leur faisait faire tout ce qu'il voulait.' This writer, I may observe, is not a romance writer or a theorist of any description. He is simply a physician who describes the results of a very large official experience.

[3] 'Parent-Duchâtelet atteste que sur trois mille créatures perdues trente cinq seulement avaient un état qui pouvait les nourrir, et que quatorze cents avaient été précipitées dans cette horrible vie par la misère. Une d'elles, quand elle s'y résolut, n'avait pas mangé depuis trois jours.'—Legouvé, *Hist morale des Femmes*, pp. 322–323.

estimate, will be sufficient to exhibit the magnitude of the problem. In the Greek civilisation, legislators and moralists endeavoured to meet it by the cordial recognition of two distinct orders of womanhood [1]—the wife, whose first duty was fidelity to her husband; the hetæra, or mistress, who subsisted by her fugitive attachments. The wives of the Greeks lived in almost absolute seclusion. They were usually married when very young. Their occupations were to weave, to spin, to embroider, to superintend the household, to care for their sick slaves. They lived in a special and retired part of the house. The more wealthy seldom went abroad, and never except when accompanied by a female slave; never attended the public spectacles; received no male visitors except in the presence of their husbands, and had not even a seat at their own tables when male guests were there. Their pre-eminent virtue was fidelity, and it is probable that this was very strictly and very generally observed. Their remarkable freedom from temptations, the public opinion which strongly discouraged any attempt to seduce them, and the ample sphere for illicit pleasures that was accorded to the other sex, all contributed to protect it. On the other hand, living, as they did, almost exclusively among their female slaves, being deprived of all the educating influence of male society, and having no place at those public spectacles which were the chief means of Athenian culture, their minds must necessarily have been exceedingly contracted. Thucydides doubtless expressed the prevailing sentiment of his countrymen when he said that the highest merit of woman is not to be spoken of either for good or for

---

[1] Concerning the position and character of Greek women, the reader may obtain ample information by consulting Becker's *Chari-* *cles* (translated by Metcalfe, 1845); Rainneville, *La Femme dans l'Antiquité* (Paris, 1865); and an article 'On Female Society in Greece,' in the twenty-second volume of the *Quarterly Review*.

evil; and Phidias illustrated the same feeling when he represented the heavenly Aphrodite standing on a tortoise, typi-
fying thereby the secluded life of a virtuous woman.[1]

In their own restricted sphere their lives were probably
not unhappy. Education and custom rendered the purely
domestic life that was assigned to them a second nature, and
it must in most instances have reconciled them to the extra-
matrimonial connections in which their husbands too frequently indulged. The prevailing manners were very gentle.
Domestic oppression is scarcely ever spoken of; the husband
lived chiefly in the public place; causes of jealousy and of
dissension could seldom occur; and a feeling of warm affection,
though not a feeling of equality, must doubtless have in most
cases spontaneously arisen. In the writings of Xenophon
we have a charming picture of a husband who had received
into his arms his young wife of fifteen, absolutely ignorant of
the world and of its ways. He speaks to her with extreme
kindness, but in the language that would be used to a little
child. Her task, he tells her, is to be like a queen bee,
dwelling continually at home and superintending the work of
her slaves. She must distribute to each their tasks, must
economise the family income, and must take especial care
that the house is strictly orderly—the shoes, the pots, and
the clothes always in their places. It is also, he tells her, a
part of her duty to tend her sick slaves; but here his wife
interrupted him, exclaiming, ' Nay, but that will indeed be
the most agreeable of my offices, if such as I treat with kindness are likely to be grateful, and to love me more than
before.' With a very tender and delicate care to avoid
everything resembling a reproach, the husband persuades
his wife to give up the habits of wearing high-heeled boots,
in order to appear tall, and of colouring her face with ver-
milion and white lead. He promises her that if she faith-

---

[1] Plutarch, *Conj. Præc.*

fully performs her duties he will himself be the first and
most devoted of her slaves. He assured Socrates that when
any domestic dispute arose he could extricate himself admirably, if he was in the right; but that, whenever he was
in the wrong, he found it impossible to convince his wife
that it was otherwise.[1]

We have another picture of Greek married life in the
writings of Plutarch, but it represents the condition of the
Greek mind at a later period than that of Xenophon. In
Plutarch the wife is represented not as the mere housekeeper,
or as the chief slave of her husband, but as his equal and
his companion. He enforces, in the strongest terms,
reciprocity of obligations, and desires that the minds of
women should be cultivated to the highest point.[2] His
precepts of marriage, indeed, fall little if at all below any
that have appeared in modern days. His letter of consolation to his wife, on the death of their child, breathes a spirit
of the tenderest affection. It is recorded of him that,
having had some dispute with the relations of his wife, she
feared that it might impair their domestic happiness, and she
accordingly persuaded her husband to accompany her on a
pilgrimage to Mount Helicon, where they offered up together
a sacrifice to Love, and prayed that their affection for one
another might never be diminished.

In general, however, the position of the virtuous Greek
woman was a very low one. She was under a perpetual
tutelage : first of all to her parents, who disposed of her hand,
then to her husband, and in her days of widowhood to her
sons. In cases of inheritance her male relations were
preferred to her. The privilege of divorce, which, in Athens,
at least, she possessed as well as her husband, appears to
have been practically almost nugatory, on account of the

---

[1] Xenophon, *Econ.* ii.
[2] Plut. *Conj. Præc.* There is
also an extremely beautiful picture

of the character of a good wife in
Aristotle. (*Economics*, book i. cap
vii.)

shock which public declarations in the law court gave to the habits which education and public opinion had formed. She brought with her, however, a dowry, and the recognised necessity of endowing daughters was one of the causes of those frequent expositions which were perpetrated with so little blame. The Athenian law was also peculiarly careful and tender in dealing with the interests of female orphans.[1] Plato had argued that women were equal to men; but the habits of the people were totally opposed to this theory. Marriage was regarded chiefly in a civic light, as the means of producing citizens, and in Sparta it was ordered that old or infirm husbands should cede their young wives to stronger men, who could produce vigorous soldiers for the State. The Lacedæmonian treatment of women, which differed in many respects from that which prevailed in the other Greek States, while it was utterly destructive of all delicacy of feeling or action, had undoubtedly the effect of producing a fierce and masculine patriotism; and many fine examples are recorded of Spartan mothers devoting their sons on the altar of their country, rejoicing over their deaths when nobly won, and infusing their own heroic spirit into the armies of the people. For the most part, however, the names of virtuous women seldom appear in Greek history. The simple modesty which was evinced by Phocion's wife, in the period when her husband occupied the foremost position in Athens,[2] and a few instances of conjugal and filial affection, have been recorded; but in general the only women who attracted the notice of the people were the hetæræ, or courtesans.[3]

---

[1] See Alexander's *History of Women* (London, 1783), vol. i. p. 201.

[2] Plutarch, *Phocion.*

[3] Our information concerning the Greek courtesans is chiefly derived from the thirteenth book of the *Deipnosophists* of Athenæus, from the *Letters* of Alciphron, from the *Dialogues* of Lucian on courtesans, and from the oration of Demosthenes against Neæra. See, too, Xenophon, *Memorabilia*, iii. 11; and among modern books, Becker's *Charicles*. Athenæus was an Egyptian, whose exact date is unknown, but who appears to have

In order to understand the position which these last assumed in Greek life, we must transport ourselves in thought into a moral latitude totally different from our own The Greek conception of excellence was the full and perfect development of humanity in all its organs and functions, and without any tinge of asceticism. Some parts of human nature were recognised as higher than others; and to suffer any of the lower appetites to obscure the mind, restrain the will and engross the energies of life, was acknowledged to be disgraceful; but the systematic repression of a natural appetite was totally foreign to Greek modes of thought. Legislators, moralists, and the general voice of the people, appear to have applied these principles almost unreservedly to intercourse between the sexes, and the most virtuous men habitually and openly entered into relations which would now be almost universally censured.

The experience, however, of many societies has shown that a public opinion may accord, in this respect, almost unlimited licence to one sex, without showing any corresponding indulgence to the other. But, in Greece, a concurrence of causes had conspired to bring a certain section of courtesans into a position they have in no other society attained. The voluptuous worship of Aphrodite gave a kind of religious sanction to their profession. Courtesans were the priestesses in her temples, and those of Corinth were believed by their prayers to have averted calamities from their city. Prostitution is said to have entered into the religious rites of Babylon, Biblis, Cyprus, and Corinth, and these as well as Miletus, Tenedos, Lesbos, and Abydos became famous for their schools of vice, which grew up under the shadow of the temples.[1]

---

survived Ulpian, who died in A.D. 228. He had access to, and gave extracts from, many works on this subject, which have now perished.

Alciphron is believed to have lived near the time of Lucian.

[1] According to some writers the word 'venerari' comes from 'Vene-

In the next place, the intense æsthetic enthusiasm that prevailed was eminently fitted to raise the most beautiful to honour. In a land and beneath a sky where natural beauty developed to the highest point, there arose a school of matchless artists both in painting and in sculpture, and public games and contests were celebrated, in which supreme physical perfection was crowned by an assembled people. In no other period of the world's history was the admiration of beauty in all its forms so passionate or so universal. It coloured the whole moral teaching of the time, and led the chief moralists to regard virtue simply as the highest kind of supersensual beauty. It appeared in all literature, where the beauty of form and style was the first of studies. It supplied at once the inspiration and the rule of all Greek art. It led the Greek wife to pray, before all other prayers, for the beauty of her children. It surrounded the most beautiful with an aureole of admiring reverence. The courtesan was often the queen of beauty. She was the model of the statues of Aphrodite, that commanded the admiration of Greece. Praxiteles was accustomed to reproduce the form of Phryne, and her statue, carved in gold, stood in the temple of Apollo at Delphi; and when she was accused of corrupting the youth of Athens, her advocate, Hyperides, procured her acquittal by suddenly unveiling her charms before the dazzled eyes of the assembled judges. Apelles was at once the painter and the lover of Laïs, and Alexander gave him, as the choicest gift, his own favourite concubine, of whom the painter had become enamoured while pourtraying her. The chief flower-painter of antiquity acquired his skill through his love of the flower-girl Glycera, whom he was accustomed to paint among her garlands. Pindar and Simonides sang the praises of courtesans, and

---

rem exercere,' on account of the devotions in the temple of Venus. See Vossius, *Etymologicon Linguæ* *Latinæ*, 'veneror;' also La Mothe le Vayer, *Lettre* xc.

grave philosophers made pilgrimages to visit them, and their names were known in every city.[1]

It is not surprising that, in such a state of thought and feeling, many of the more ambitious and accomplished women should have betaken themselves to this career, nor yet that they should have attained the social position which the secluded existence and the enforced ignorance of the Greek wives had left vacant. The courtesan was the one free woman of Athens, and she often availed herself of her freedom to acquire a degree of knowledge which enabled her to add to her other charms an intense intellectual fascination. Gathering around her the most brilliant artists, poets, historians, and philosophers, she flung herself unreservedly into the intellectual and æsthetic enthusiasms of her time, and soon became the centre of a literary society of matchless splendour. Aspasia, who was as famous for her genius as for her beauty, won the passionate love of Pericles. She is said to have instructed him in eloquence, and to have composed some of his most famous orations; she was continually consulted on affairs of state; and Socrates, like other philosophers, attended her assemblies. Socrates himself has owned his deep obligations to the instructions of a courtesan named Diotima. The courtesan Leontium was among the most ardent disciples of Epicurus.[2]

Another cause probably contributed indirectly to the elevation of this class, to which it is extremely difficult to allude in an English book, but which it is impossible alto-

---

[1] On the connection of the courtesans with the artistic enthusiasm, see Raoul Rochette, *Cours d'Archéologie*, pp. 278 279. See, too, Athenæus, xiii. 59; Pliny, *Hist. Nat.* xxxv. 40.

[2] See the very curious little work of Ménage, *Historia Mulierum Philosopharum* (Lugduni, MDXC.); also Rainneville, *La Femme dans l'Antiquité*, p. 244. At a much later date Lucian described the beauty, accomplishments, generosity, and even modesty, of Panthea of Smyrna, the favourite mistress of Lucius Verus.

gether to omit, even in the most cursory survey of Greek
morals. Irregular female connections were looked upon as
ordinary and not disgraceful incidents in the life of a good
man, for they were compared with that lower abyss of
unnatural love, which was the deepest and strangest taint of
Greek civilisation. This vice, which never appears in the
writings of Homer and Hesiod, doubtless arose under the
influence of the public games, which, accustoming men to the
contemplation of absolutely nude figures,[1] awoke an unnatural
passion,[2] totally remote from all modern feelings, but which
in Greece it was regarded as heroic to resist.[3] The popular
religion in this, as in other cases, was made to bend to the
new vice. Hebe, the cup-bearer of the gods, was replaced
by Ganymede, and the worst vices of earth were transported
to Olympus.[4] Artists sought to reflect the passion in their

[1] The ζῶμα, which was at first in
use, was discarded by the Lacedæ-
monians, and afterwards by the
other Greeks. There are three
curious memoirs tracing the history
of the change, by M. Burette, in
the Hist. de l'Académie royale des
Inscriptions, tome i.

[2] On the causes of paiderastia
in Greece, see the remarks of Mr.
Grote in the review of the Sympo-
sium, in his great work on Plato.
The whole subject is very ably
treated by M. Maury, Hist. des
Religions de la Grèce antique, tome
iii. pp. 35–39. Many facts connected with it are collected by Döllinger, in his Jew and Gentile, and
by Chateaubriand, in his Études
historiques. The chief original
authority is the thirteenth book of
Athenæus, a book of very painful
interest in the history of morals.

[3] Plutarch, in his Life of Agesilaus, dwells on the intense self-
control manifested by that great

man, in refraining from gratifying
a passion he had conceived for a
boy named Megabetes, and Maximus Tyrius says it deserved greater
praise than the heroism of Leonidas.
(Diss. xxv.) Diogenes Laërtius, in
his Life of Zeno, the founder of
Stoicism, the most austere of all
ancient sects, praises that philosopher for being but little addicted
to this vice. Sophocles is said to
have been much addicted to it.

[4] Some examples of the ascription of this vice to the divinities
are given by Clem. Alex. Admonitio
ad Gentes. Socrates is said to have
maintained that Jupiter loved
Ganymede for his wisdom, as his
name is derived from γάνυμαι and
μῆδος, to be delighted with prudence. (Xenophon, Banquet.) The
disaster of Cannæ was ascribed to
the jealousy of Juno because a
beautiful boy was introduced into
the temple of Jupiter. (Lactantius,
Inst. Div. ii. 17.)

Statute of the Hermaphrodite, of Bacchus, and the more effeminate Apollo; moralists were known to praise it as the bond of friendship, and it was spoken of as the inspiring enthusiasm of the heroic Theban legion of Epaminondas.[1] In general, however, it was stigmatised as unquestionably a vice, but it was treated with a levity we can now hardly conceive. We can scarcely have a better illustration of the extent to which moral ideas and feelings have changed, than the fact that the first two Greeks who were considered worthy of statues by their fellow-countrymen are said to have been Harmodius and Aristogeiton, who were united by an impure love, and who were glorified for a political assassination.[2]

It is probable that this cause conspired with the others to dissociate the class of courtesans from the idea of supreme depravity with which they have usually been connected. The great majority, however, were sunk in this, as in all other ages, in abject degradation;[3] comparatively few attained the condition of hetærææ, and even of these it is probable that the greater number exhibited the characteristics which in all ages have attached to their class. Faithlessness, extreme rapacity, and extravagant luxury, were common among them; but yet it is unquestionable that there were many exceptions. The excommunication of society did not press upon or degrade them; and though they were never regarded with the same honour as married women, it seems generally to have been believed that the wife and the courtesan had each her place and her function in the world, and her own peculiar type of excellence. The courtesan Leæna, who was a friend of Harmodius, died in torture rather than reveal

---

[1] Athenæus, xiii. 78. See, too, the very revolting book on different kinds of love, ascribed (it is said falsely) to Lucian.

[2] Pliny, *Hist. Nat.* xxxiv. 9.

[3] There is ample evidence of this in Athenæus, and in the Dialogues of Lucian on the courtesans. See, too, Terence, *The Eunuch,* act v. scene 4, which is copied from the Greek. The majority of the class were not called hetæræ, but πόρναι.

the conspiracy of her friend, and the Athenians, in allusion to her name, caused the statue of a tongueless lioness to be erected to commemorate her constancy.[1]   The gentle manners an1 disinterested affection of a courtesan named Bacchis were especially recorded, and a very touching letter paints her character, and describes the regret that followed her to the tomb.[2]   In one of the most remarkable of his pictures of Greek life, Xenophon describes how Socrates, having heard of the beauty of the courtesan Theodota, went with his disciples to ascertain for himself whether the report was true; how with a quiet humour he questioned her about the sources of the luxury of her dwelling, and how he proceeded to sketch for her the qualities she should cultivate in order to attach her lovers. She ought, he tells her, to shut the door against the insolent, to watch her lovers in sickness, to rejoice greatly when they succeed in anything honourable, to love tenderly those who love her. Having carried on a cheerful and perfectly unembarrassed conversation with her, with no kind of reproach on his part, either expressed or implied, and with no trace either of the timidity or effrontery of conscious guilt upon hers, the best and wisest of the Greeks left his hostess with a graceful compliment to her beauty.[3]

My task in describing this aspect of Greek life has been an eminently unpleasing one, and I should certainly not have entered upon even the baldest and most guarded disquisition on a subject so difficult, painful, and delicate, had it not been absolutely indispensable to a history of morals to give at least an outline of the progress that has

---

[1] Plutarch, *De Garrulitate;* Plin. *Hist. Nat.* xxxiv. 19. The feat of biting out their tongues rather than reveal secrets, or yield to passion, is ascribed to a suspiciously large number of persons. Ménage cites five besides Leæna. (*Hist. Mulier. Philos.* pp. 104–108.)

[2] See, upon Bacchis, several of the letters of Alciphron, especially the very touching letter (x.) on her death, describing her kindness and disinterestedness. Athenæus (xiii. 66) relates a curious anecdote illustrating these aspects of her character.

[3] Xenophon, *Memorab.* iii. 11.

been effected in this sphere. What I have written will sufficiently explain why Greece, which was fertile, beyond all other lands, in great men, was so remarkably barren of great women. It will show, too, that while the Greek moralists recognised, like ourselves, the distinction between the higher and the lower sides of our nature, they differed very widely from modern public opinion in the standard of morals they enforced. The Christian doctrine, that it is criminal to gratify a powerful and a transient physical appetite, except under the condition of a lifelong contract, was altogether unknown. Strict duties were imposed upon Greek wives. Duties were imposed at a later period, though less strictly, upon the husband. Unnatural love was stigmatised, but with a levity of censure which to a modern mind appears inexpressibly revolting. Some slight legal disqualifications rested upon the whole class of hetæræ, and, though more admired, they were less respected than women who had adopted a domestic life ; but a combination of circumstances had raised them, in actual worth and in popular estimation, to an unexampled elevation, and an aversion to marriage became very general, and extra-matrimonial connections were formed with the most perfect frankness and publicity.

If we now turn to the Roman civilisation, we shall find that some important advances had been made in the condition of women. The virtue of chastity has, as I have shown, been regarded in two different ways. The utilitarian view, which commonly prevails in countries where a political spirit is more powerful than a religious spirit, regards marriage as the ideal state, and to promote the happiness, sanctity, and security of this state is the main object of all its precepts. The mystical view which rests upon the natural feeling of shame, and which, as history proves, has prevailed especially where political sentiment is very low, and religious sentiment very strong, regards virginity as its supreme type, nd marriage as simply the most pardonable declension from

ideal purity. It is, I think, a very remarkable fact, that at
the head of the religious system of Rome we find two sacerdotal bodies which appear respectively to typify these ideas.
The Flamens of Jupiter and the Vestal Virgins were the two
most sacred orders in Rome. The ministrations of each were
believed to be vitally important to the State. Each could
officiate only within the walls of Rome. Each was appointed
with the most imposing ceremonies. Each was honoured with
the most profound reverence. But in one important respect
they differed. The Vestal was the type of virginity, and
her purity was guarded by the most terrific penalties. The
Flamen, on the other hand, was the representative of Roman
marriage in its strictest and holiest form. He was necessarily
married. His marriage was celebrated with the most solemn
rites. It could only be dissolved by death. If his wife died,
he was degraded from his office.[1]

Of these two orders, there can be no question that the
Flamen was the most faithful expression of the Roman sentiments. The Roman religion was essentially domestic, and
it was a main object of the legislator to surround marriage
with every circumstance of dignity and solemnity. Monogamy
was, from the earliest times, strictly enjoined ; and it was
one of the great benefits that have resulted from the
expansion of Roman power, that it made this type dominant
in Europe. In the legends of early Rome we have ample
evidence both of the high moral estimate of women, and
of their prominence in Roman life. The tragedies of Lucretia
and of Virginia display a delicacy of honour, a sense of the
supreme excellence of unsullied purity, which no Christian
nation could surpass. The legends of the Sabine women
interceding between their parents and their husbands, and
thus saving the infant republic, and of the mother of Coriolanus

---

[1] On the Flamens, see Aulus Gell. *Noct.* **x. 15.**

averting by her prayers the ruin impending over her country, entitled women to claim their share in the patriotic glories of Rome. A temple of Venus Calva was associated with the legend of Roman ladies, who, in an hour of danger, cut off their long tresses to make bowstrings for the soldiers.[1] Another temple preserved to all posterity the memory of the filial piety of that Roman woman who, when her mother was condemned to be starved to death, obtained permission to visit her in her prison, and was discovered feeding her from her breast.[2]

The legal position, however, of the Roman wife was for a long period extremely low. The Roman family was constituted on the principle of the uncontrolled authority of its head, both over his wife and over his children, and he could repudiate the former at will. Neither the custom of gifts to the father of the bride, nor the custom of dowries, appears to have existed in the earliest period of Roman history; but the father disposed absolutely of the hand of his daughter, and sometimes even possessed the power of breaking off marriages that had been actually contracted.[3] In the forms of marriage, however, which were usual in the earlier periods of Rome, the absolute power passed into the hands of the husband, and he had the right, in some cases, of putting her to death.[4] Law and public opinion combined in making matrimonial purity most strict. For

---

[1] Capitolinus, *Maximinus Junior*.
[2] Pliny, *Hist. Nat.* vii. 36. There is (as is well known) a similar legend of a daughter thus feeding her father. Val. Max. Lib. v. cap. 4.
[3] This appears from the first act of the *Stichus* of Plautus. The power appears to have become quite obsolete during the Empire; but the first legal act (which was rather of the nature of an exhortation than of a command) against it was issued by Antoninus Pius, and it was only definitely abolished under Diocletian. (Laboulaye, *Recherches sur la condition civile et politique des femmes*, pp. 16–17.)
[4] Aul. Gell. *Noct.* x. 23.

five hundred and twenty years, it was said, there was no such thing as a divorce in Rome.[1] Manners were so severe, that a senator was censured for indecency because he had kissed his wife in the presence of their daughter.[2] It was considered in a high degree disgraceful for a Roman mother to delegate to a nurse the duty of suckling her child.[3] Sumptuary laws regulated with the most minute severity all the details of domestic economy.[4] The courtesan class, though probably numerous and certainly uncontrolled, were regarded with much contempt. The disgrace of publicly professing themselves members of it was believed to be a sufficient punishment;[5] and an old law, which was probably intended to teach in symbol the duties of married life, enjoined that no such person should touch the altar of Juno.[6] It was related of a certain aedile, that he failed to obtain redress for an assault which had been made upon him, because it had occurred in a house of ill-fame, in which it was disgraceful for a Roman magistrate to be found.[7] The sanctity of female purity was believed to be attested by all nature. The most savage animals became tame before a virgin.[8] When a woman walked naked round a field, caterpillars and all loathsome insects fell dead before her.[9] It was said that drowned men floated on their backs, and drowned women on their faces; and this, in the opinion of Roman naturalists, was due to the superior purity of the latter.[10]

---

[1] Val. Maximus, ii. 1, § 4; Aul. Gellius, *Noct.* iv. 3.

[2] Ammianus Marcellinus, xxviii. 4

[3] Tacitus, *De Oratoribus*, xxviii.

[4] See Aulus Gellius, *Noct.* ii. 24.

[5] 'More inter veteres recepto, qui satis poenarum adversum impudicas in ipsa professione flagitii credebant.'—Tacitus, *Annal.* ii. 85.

[6] Aul. Gell. iv. 3. Juno was the goddess of marriage.

[7] Ibid. iv. 14.

[8] The well-known superstition about the lion, &c., becoming docile before a virgin is, I believe, as old as Roman times. St. Isidore mentions that rhinoceroses were said to be captured by young girls being put in their way to fascinate them. (Legendre, *Traité de l'Opinion*, tome ii. p. 35.)

[9] Pliny, *Hist. Nat.* xxviii. 23.

[10] Ibid. vii. 18.

It was a remark of Aristotle, that the superiority of the Greeks to the barbarians was shown, among other things, in the fact that the Greeks did not, like other nations, regard their wives as slaves, but treated them as helpmates and companions. A Roman writer has appealed, on the whole with greater justice, to the treatment of wives by his fellow countrymen, as a proof of the superiority of Roman to Greek civilisation. He has observed that while the Greeks kept their wives in a special quarter in the interior of their houses, and never permitted them to sit at banquets except with their relatives, or to see any male except in the presence of a relative, no Roman ever hesitated to lead his wife with him to the feast, or to place the mother of the family at the head of his table.[1] Whether, in the period when wives were completely subject to the rule of their husbands, much domestic oppression occurred, it is now impossible to say. A temple dedicated to a goddess named Viriplaca, whose mission was to appease husbands, was worshipped by Roman women on the Palatine;[2] and a strange and improbable, if not incredible story, is related by Livy, of the discovery during the Republic, of a vast conspiracy by Roman wives to poison their husbands.[3] On the whole, however, it is probable that the Roman matron was from the earliest period a name of honour;[4] that the beautiful sentence of a jurisconsult of the Empire, who defined marriage as a lifelong fellowship of all divine and human rights,[5] expressed most faithfully the

---

[1] 'Quem enim Romanorum pudet uxorem ducere in convivium? aut cujus materfamilias non primum locum tenet ædium, atque in celebritate versatur? quod multo fit aliter in Græcia. Nam neque in convivium adhibetur, nisi propinquorum, neque sedet nisi in interiore parte ædium quæ *gynæcontis* appellatur ouo nemo accedit, nisi propinqua cognatione conjunctus.'— Corn. Nepos. præfat.

[2] Val. Max. ii. 1, § 6.

[3] Liv. viii. 18.

[4] See Val. Max. ii. 1.

[5] 'Nuptiæ sunt conjunctio maris et feminæ, et consortium omnis vitæ, divini et humani juris communicatio.'—Modestinus

feelings of the people, and that female virtue had in every age a considerable place in Roman biographies.[1]

I have already enumerated the chief çauses of that complete dissolution of Roman morals which began shortly after the Punic wars, which contributed very largely to the destruction of the Republic, and which attained its climax under the Cæsars. There are few examples in history of a revolution pervading so completely every sphere of religious, domestic, social, and political life. Philosophical scepticism corroded the ancient religions. An inundation of Eastern luxury and Eastern morals submerged all the old habits of austere simplicity. The civil wars and the Empire degraded the character of the people, and the exaggerated prudery of republican manners only served to make the rebound into vice the more irresistible. In the fierce outburst of ungovernable and almost frantic depravity that marked this evil period, the violations of female virtue were infamously prominent. The vast multiplication of slaves, which is in every age peculiarly fatal to moral purity ; the fact that a great proportion of those slaves were chosen from the most voluptuous provinces of the Empire ; the games of Flora, in which races of naked courtesans were exhibited ; the pantomimes, which derived their charms chiefly from the audacious indecencies of the actors ; the influx of the Greek and Asiatic hetæræ who were attracted by the wealth of the metropolis ; the licentious paintings which began to adorn every house ; the rise of Baiæ, which rivalled the luxury and surpassed the beauty of the chief centres of Asiatic vice, combining with the intoxication of great wealth suddenly acquired, with the disruption, through many causes, of all the ancient habits and beliefs, and with the tendency to pleasure which the closing of the paths of honourable political ambition by the imperial

[1] Livy, xxxiv. 5. There is a fine collection of legends or histories of heroic women (but chiefly Greek) in Clem. Alexand. *Strom.* iv. 19.

despotism, naturally produced, had all their part in preparing those orgies of vice which the writers of the Empire reveal. Most scholars will, I suppose, retain a vivid recollection of the new insight into the extent and wildness of human guilt which they obtained when they first opened the pages of Suetonius or Lampridius; and the sixth Satire of Juvenal paints with a fierce energy, though probably with the natural exaggeration of a satirist, the extent to which corruption had spread among the women. It was found necessary, under Tiberius, to make a special law prohibiting members of noble houses from enrolling themselves as prostitutes.[1] The extreme coarseness of the Roman disposition prevented sensuality from assuming that æsthetic character which had made it in Greece the parent of Art, and had very profoundly modified its influence, while the passion for gladiatorial shows often allied it somewhat unnaturally with cruelty. There have certainly been many periods in history when virtue was more rare than under the Cæsars; but there has probably never been a period when vice was more extravagant or uncontrolled. Young emperors especially, who were surrounded by swarms of sycophants and panders, and who often lived in continual dread of assassination, plunged with the most reckless and feverish excitement into every variety of abnormal lust. The reticence which has always more or less characterised modern society and modern writers was unknown, and the unblushing, undisguised obscenity of the Epigrams of Martial, of the Romances of Apuleius and Petronius, and of some of the Dialogues of Lucian, reflected but too faithfully the spirit of their time.

There had arisen, too, partly through vicious causes, and partly, I suppose, through the unfavourable influence which the attraction of the public institutions exercised on domestic

---

[1] Tacitus, *Annal.* ii. 85. This decree was on account of a patrician lady named Vistilia having so enrolled herself.

life, a great and general indisposition towards marriage, which Augustus attempted in vain to arrest by his laws against celibacy, and by conferring many privileges on the fathers of three children.[1] A singularly curious speech is preserved, which is said to have been delivered on this subject, shortly before the close of the Republic, by Metellus Numidicus, in order, if possible, to overcome this indisposition. 'If, Romans,' he said, 'we could live without wives, we should all keep free from that source of trouble; but since nature has ordained that men can neither live sufficiently agreeably with wives, nor at all without them, let us consider the perpetual endurance of our race rather than our own brief enjoyment.'[2]

In the midst of this torrent of corruption a great change was passing over the legal position of Roman women. They had at first been in a condition of absolute subjection or subordination to their relations. They arrived, during the Empire, at a point of freedom and dignity which they subsequently lost, and have never altogether regained. The Romans recognised two distinct classes of marriages: the stricter, and, in the eyes of the law, more honourable, forms, which placed the woman 'in the hand' of her husband and gave him an almost absolute authority over her person and her property; and a less strict form, which left her

[1] Dion Cassius, liv. 16, lvi. 10.

[2] 'Si sine uxore possemus, Quirites, esse, omnes ea molestia careremus; sed quoniam ita natura tradidit, ut nec cum illis satis commode nec sine illis ullo modo vivi possit, saluti perpetuæ potius quam brevi voluptati consulendum.'—Aulus Gellius, *Noct.* i. 6. Some of the audience, we are told, thought that, in exhorting to matrimony, the speaker should have concealed its undoubted evils. It was decided, however, that it was more honourable to tell the whole truth. Stobæus (*Sententiæ*) has preserved a number of harsh and often heartless sayings about wives, that were popular among the Greeks. It was a saying of a Greek poet, that 'marriage brings only two happy days—the day when the husband first clasps his wife to his breast, and the day when he lays her in the tomb;' and in Rome it became a proverbial saying, that a wife was only good 'in thalamo vel in tumulo.'

legal position unchanged. The former, which were general during the Republic, were of three kinds—the 'confarreatio,' which was celebrated and could only be dissolved by the most solemn religious ceremonies, and was jealously restricted to patricians; the 'coemptio,' which was purely civil, and derived its name from a symbolical sale; and the 'usus,' which was effected by the mere cohabitation of a woman with a man without interruption for the space of a year. Under the Empire, however, these kinds of marriage became almost wholly obsolete; a laxer form, resting upon a simple mutual agreement, without any religious or civil ceremony, was general, and it had this very important consequence, that the woman so married remained, in the eyes of the law, in the family of her father, and was under his guardianship, not under the guardianship of her husband. But the old *patria potestas* had become completely obsolete, and the practical effect of the general adoption of this form of marriage was the absolute legal independence of the wife. With the exception of her dowry, which passed into the hands of her husband, she held her property in her own right; she inherited her share of the wealth of her father, and she retained it altogether independently of her husband. A very considerable portion of Roman wealth thus passed into the uncontrolled possession of women. The private man of business of the wife was a favourite character with the comedians, and the tyranny exercised by rich wives over their husbands—to whom it is said they sometimes lent money at high interest—a continual theme of satirists.[1]

A complete revolution had thus passed over the consti-

---

[1] Friedländer, *Hist. des Mœurs romaines*, tome i. pp. 360–364. On the great influence exercised by Roman ladies on political affairs some remarkable passages are collected in Denis, *Hist. des Idées Morales*, tome ii. pp. 98–99. This author is particularly valuable in all that relates to the history of domestic morals. The *Asinaria* of Plautus, and some of the epigrams of Martial, throw much light upon this subject.

tution of the family. Instead of being constructed on the
principle of autocracy, it was constructed on the principle of
coequal partnership. The legal position of the wife had
become one of complete independence, while her social
position was one of great dignity. The more conservative
spirits were naturally alarmed at the change, and two
measures were taken to arrest it. The Oppian law was
designed to restrain the luxury of women ; but, in spite of
the strenuous exertions of Cato, this law was speedily repealed.[1] A more important measure was the Voconian law,
which restricted within very narrow limits the property
which women might inherit; but public opinion never fully
acquiesced in it, and by several legal subterfuges its operation
was partially evaded.[2]

Another and a still more important consequence resulted
from the changed form of marriage. Being looked upon
merely as a civil contract, entered into for the happiness of
the contracting parties, its continuance depended upon
mutual consent. Either party might dissolve it at will, and
the dissolution gave both parties a right to remarry. There
can be no question that under this system the obligations of
marriage were treated with extreme levity. We find Cicero
repudiating his wife Terentia, because he desired a new
dowry ;[3] Augustus compelling the husband of Livia to repudiate her when she was already pregnant, that he might
marry her himself ;[4] Cato ceding his wife, with the consent
of her father, to his friend Hortensius, and resuming her

---

[1] See the very remarkable discussion about this repeal in Livy,
lib. xxxiv. cap. 1–8.

[2] Legouvé, *Hist. Morale des
Femmes*, pp. 23–26. St. Augustine
denounced this law as the most unjust that could be mentioned or
even conceived. ' Qua lege quid
iniquius dici aut cogitari possit,

ignoro.'—St. Aug. *De Civ. Dei*, iii.
21 — a curious illustration of the
difference between the habits of
thought of his time and those of
the middle ages, when daughters
were habitually sacrificed, without
a protest, by the feudal laws.

[3] Plutarch, *Cicero*.

[4] Tacit. *Ann.* i. 10.

after his death;[1] Mæcenas continually changing his wife;[2]
Sempronius Sophus repudiating his wife, because she had
once been to the public games without his knowledge;[3]
Paulus Æmilius taking the same step without assigning any
reason, and defending himself by saying, 'My shoes are new
and well made, but no one knows where they pinch me.'[4]
Nor did women show less alacrity in repudiating their
husbands. Seneca denounced this evil with especial
vehemence, declaring that divorce in Rome no longer brought
with it any shame, and that there were women who reckoned
their years rather by their husbands than by the consuls.[5]
Christians and Pagans echoed the same complaint. According to Tertullian, 'divorce is the fruit of marriage.'[6]
Martial speaks of a woman who had already arrived at her
tenth husband;[7] Juvenal, of a woman having eight husbands
in five years.[8] But the most extraordinary recorded instance
of this kind is related by St. Jerome, who assures us that
there existed at Rome a wife who was married to her twenty-
third husband, she herself being his twenty-first wife.[9]

These are, no doubt, extreme cases; but it is unquestionable that the stability of married life was very seriously
impaired. It would be easy, however, to exaggerate the
influence of legal changes in affecting it. In a purer state of
public opinion a very wide latitude of divorce might probably
have been allowed to both parties, without any serious consequence. The right of repudiation, which the husband had
always possessed, was, as we have seen, in the Republic
never or very rarely exercised. Of those who scandalised
good men by the rapid recurrence of their marriages, probably

[1] Plutarch, *Cato*; Lucan, *Pharsal.* ii.
[2] Senec. *Ep.* cxiv.
[3] Val. Max. vi. 3.
[4] Plutarch, *Paul. Æmil.* It is
not quite clear whether this remark
was made by Paulus himself.
[5] Sen. *De Benef.* iii. 16. & e
too, *Ep.* xcv. *Ad Helv.* xvi.
[6] Apol. 6.
[7] *Epig.* vi. 7.
[8] Juv. *Sat.* vi. 230.
[9] *Ep.* 2.

most, if marriage had been indissoluble, would have refrained from entering into it, and would have contented themselves with many informal connections, or, if they had married, would have gratified their love of change by simple adultery. A vast wave of corruption had flowed in upon Rome, and under any system of law it would have penetrated into domestic life.   Laws prohibiting all divorce have never secured the purity of married life in ages of great corruption, nor did the latitude which was accorded in imperial Rome prevent the existence of a very large amount of female virtue.

I have observed, in a former chapter, that the moral contrasts shown in ancient life surpass those of modern societies, in which we very rarely find clusters of heroic or illustrious men arising in nations that are in general very ignorant or very corrupt.   I have endeavoured to account for this fact by showing that the moral agencies of antiquity were in general much more fitted to develop virtue than to repress vice, and that they raised noble natures to almost the highest conceivable point of excellence, while they entirely failed to coerce or to attenuate the corruption of the depraved. In the female life of Imperial Rome we find these contrasts vividly displayed.   There can be no question that the moral tone of the sex was extremely low—lower, probably, than in France under the Regency, or in England under the Restoration—and it is also certain that frightful excesses of unnatural passion, of which the most corrupt of modern courts present no parallel, were perpetrated with but little concealment on the Palatine.   Yet there is probably no period in which examples of conjugal heroism and fidelity appear more frequently than in this very age, in which marriage was most free and in which corruption was so general.   Much simplicity of manners continued to co-exist with the excesses of an almost unbridled luxury.   Augustus, we are told, used to make his daughters and granddaughters weave and spin, and his wife and sister made most of the clothes he wore.[1] The skill of wives in domestic economy, and especially in spinning, was frequently noticed in their epitaphs.[2] Intellectual culture was much diffused among them,[3] and we meet with several noble specimens, in the sex, of large and accomplished minds united with all the gracefulness of intense womanhood, and all the fidelity of the truest love. Such were Cornelia, the brilliant and devoted wife of Pompey,[4] Marcia, the friend, and Helvia, the mother of Seneca. The Northern Italian cities had in a great degree escaped the contamination of the times, and Padua and Brescia were especially noted for the virtue of their women.[5] In an age of extravagant sensuality a noble lady, named Mallonia, plunged her dagger in her heart rather than yield to the embraces of Tiberius.[6] To the period when the legal bond of marriage was most relaxed must be assigned most of those noble examples of the constancy of Roman wives, which have been for so many generations household tales among mankind. Who has not read with emotion of the tenderness and heroism of Porcia, claiming her right to share in the trouble which clouded her husband's brow; how, doubting her own courage, she did not venture to ask Brutus to reveal to her his enterprise till she had secretly tried her power of endurance by piercing her thigh with a knife; how once, and but once in his presence, her noble spirit failed, when, as she was about to separate from him for the last time, her eye chanced to fall upon a picture of the parting interview of Hector and Andromache?[7] Paulina,

---

[1] Sueton. *Aug.* Charlemagne, in like manner, made his daughters work in wool. (Eginhardus, *Vit. Car. Mag.* xix.)

[2] Friedländer, *Mœurs romaines du règne d'Auguste à la fin des Antonins* (trad. franç.), tome i. p. 14.

[3] Much evidence of this is collected by Friedländer, tome i. pp. 387–395.

[4] Plutarch, *Pompeius.*

[5] Martial, xi. 16. Pliny, *Ep.* i. 14.

[6] Suet. *Tiberius,* xlv.

[7] Plutarch, *Brutus.*

the wife of Seneca, opened her own veins in order to accompany her husband to the grave; when much blood had already flowed, her slaves and freedmen bound her wounds, and thus compelled her to live; but the Romans ever after observed with reverence the sacred pallor of her countenance—the memorial of her act.[1] When Pætus was condemned to die by his own hand, those who knew the love which his wife Arria bore him, and the heroic fervour of her character, predicted that she would not long survive him. Thrasea, who had married her daughter, endeavoured to dissuade her from suicide by saying, 'If I am ever called upon to perish, would you wish your daughter to die with me?' She answered, 'Yes, if she will have then lived with you as long and as happily as I with Pætus.' Her friends attempted, by carefully watching her, to secure her safety, but she dashed her head against the wall with such force that she fell upon the ground, and then, rising up, she said, 'I told you I would find a hard way to death if you refuse me an easy way.' All attempts to restrain her were then abandoned, and her death was perhaps the most majestic in antiquity. Pætus for a moment hesitated to strike the fatal blow; but his wife, taking the dagger, plunged it deeply into her own breast, and then, drawing it out, gave it, all reeking as it was, to her husband, exclaiming, with her dying breath, 'My Pætus, it does not pain.'[2]

The form of the elder Arria towers grandly above her fellows, but many other Roman wives in the days of the early Cæsars and of Domitian exhibited a very similar fidelity. Over the dark waters of the Euxine, into those unknown and inhospitable regions from which the Roman imagination recoiled with a peculiar horror, many noble ladies freely followed their husbands, and there were some wives who

---

[1] Tacit. *Annal.* xv. 63, 64.   iii. 16; Martial, *Ep.* i. 14.
[2] 'Pæte, non dolet.'--Plin. *Ep.*

refused to survive them.[1] The younger Arria was the faithful companion of Thrasea during his heroic life, and when he died she was only persuaded to live that she might bring up their daughters.[2] She spent the closing days of her life with Domitian in exile;[3] while her daughter, who was as remarkable for the gentleness as for the dignity of her character,[4] went twice into exile with her husband Helvidius, and was once banished, after his death, for defending his memory.[5] Incidental notices in historians, and a few inscriptions which have happened to remain, show us that such instances were not uncommon, and in Roman epitaphs no feature is more remarkable than the deep and passionate expressions of conjugal love that continually occur.[6] It would be difficult to find a more touching image of that love, than the medallion which is so common on the Roman sarcophagi, in which husband and wife are represented together, each with an arm thrown fondly over the shoulder of the other, united in death as they had been in life, and meeting it with an aspect of perfect calm, because they were companions in the tomb.

In the latter days of the Pagan Empire some measures were taken to repress the profligacy that was so prevalent. Domitian enforced the old Scantinian law against unnatural love.[7] Vespasian moderated the luxury of the court; Macrinus caused those who had committed adultery to be bound together and burnt alive.[8] A practice of men and women bathing together was condemned by Hadrian, and afterwards by Alexander Severus, but was only finally sup-

---

[1] Tacit. *Annal.* xvi. 10–11; *Hist.* i. 3. See, too, Friedländer, tome i. p. 406.

[2] Tacit. *Ann.* xvi. 34.

[3] Pliny mentions her return after the death of the tyrant (*Ep.* iii. 11).

[4] 'Quod paucis datum est, non minus amabilis quam veneranda.' —Plin. *Ep.* vii. 19.

[5] See Plin. *Ep.* vii. 19. Dion Cassius and Tacitus relate the exiles of Helvidius, who appears to have been rather intemperate and unreasonable.

[6] Friedländer gives many and most touching examples, tome i. pp 410-414.

[7] Suet. *Dom.* viii.

[8] Capitolinus, *Macrinus*

pressed by Constantine.   Alexander Severus and Philip
waged an energetic war against panders.[1]   The extreme
excesses of this, as of most forms of vice, were probably
much diminished after the accession of the Antonines; but
Rome continued to be a centre of very great corruption till
the influence of Christianity, the removal of the court to
Constantinople, and the impoverishment that followed the
barbarian conquests, in a measure corrected the evil.

Among the moralists, however, some important steps
were taken.   One of the most important was a very clear
assertion of the reciprocity of that obligation to fidelity in
marriage which in the early stages of society had been imposed almost exclusively upon wives.[2]   The legends of
Clytemnestra and of Medea reveal the feelings of fierce
resentment which were sometimes produced among Greek
wives by the almost unlimited indulgence that was accorded
to their husbands;[3] and it is told of Andromache, as the
supreme instance of her love of Hector, that she cared for his
illegitimate children as much as for her own.[4]   In early
Rome, the obligations of husbands were never, I imagine,
altogether unfelt; but they were rarely or never enforced,
nor were they ever regarded as bearing any kind of equality
to those imposed upon the wife.   The term adultery, and all
the legal penalties connected with it, were restricted to the
infractions by a wife of the nuptial tie.   Among the many
instances of magnanimity recorded of Roman wives, few are
more touching than that of Tertia Æmilia, the faithful wife
of Scipio.   She discovered that her husband had become

---

[1] Lampridius, *A. Severus.*

[2] In the oration against Neæra,
which is ascribed to Demosthenes,
but is of doubtful genuineness, the
licence accorded to husbands is
spoken of as a matter of course:
'We keep mistresses for our pleasures, concubines for constant attendance, and wives to bear us

legitimate children, and to be our
faithful housekeepers.'

[3] There is a remarkable passage
on the feelings of wives, in different nations, upon this point, in
Athenæus, xiii. 3.   See, too, Plutarch, *Conj. Præc.*

[4] Euripid. *Andromache.*

enamoured of one of her slaves; but she bore her pain in silence, and when he died she gave liberty to her captive, for she could not bear that she should remain in servitude whom her dear lord had loved.[1]

Aristotle had clearly asserted the duty of husbands to observe in marriage the same fidelity as they expected from their wives,[2] and at a later period both Plutarch and Seneca enforced this duty in the strongest and most unequivocal manner.[3] The degree to which, in theory at least, it won its way in Roman life is shown by its recognition as a legal maxim by Ulpian,[4] and by its appearance in a formal judgment of Antoninus Pius, who, while issuing, at the request of a husband, a condemnation for adultery against a guilty wife, appended to it this remarkable condition : 'Provided always it is established that by your life you gave her an example of fidelity. It would be unjust that a husband should exact a fidelity he does not himself keep.'[5]

---

[1] Valer. Max. vi. 7, § 1. Some very scandalous instances of cynicism on the part of Roman husbands are recorded. Thus, Augustus had many mistresses, 'Quæ [virgines] sibi undique etiam *ab uxore* conquirerentur.'—Sueton. *Aug.*lxxi. When the wife of Verus, the colleague of Marcus Aurelius, complained of the tastes of her husband, he answered, 'Uxor enim dignitatis nomen est, non voluptatis.'—Spartian. *Verus.*

[2] Aristotle, *Econom.* i. 4–8–9.

[3] Plutarch enforces the duty at length, in his very beautiful work on marriage. In case husbands are guilty of infidelity, he recommends their wives to preserve a prudent blindness, reflecting that it is out of respect for them that they choose another woman as the companion of their intemperance. Seneca touches briefly, but unequivocally,

on the subject: 'Scis improbum esse qui ab uxore pudicitiam exigit, ipse alienarum corruptor uxorum. Scis ut illi nil cum adultero, sic nihil tibi esse debere cum pellice.' —*Ep.* xciv. 'Sciet in uxorem gravissimum esse genus injuriæ, habere pellicem.'—*Ep.* xcv.

[4] 'Periniquum enim videtur esse, ut pudicitiam vir ab uxore exigat, quam ipse non exhibeat.'— *Cod. Just. Dig.* xlviii. 5–13.

[5] Quoted by St. Augustine, *De Conj. Adult.* ii. 19. Plautus, long before, had made one of his characters complain of the injustice of the laws which punished unchaste wives but not unchaste husbands, and ask why, since every honest woman is contented with one husband, every honest man should not be contented with one wife? (*Mercator*, Act iv. scene 5.)

Another change, which may be dimly descried in the later Pagan society, was a tendency to regard purity rather in a mystical point of view, as essentially good, than in the utilitarian point of view. This change resulted chiefly from the rise of the Neoplatonic and Pythagorean philosophies, which concurred in regarding the body, with its passions, as essentially evil, and in representing all virtue as a purification from its taint. Its most important consequence was a somewhat stricter view of pre-nuptial unchastity, which in the case of men, and when it was not excessive, and did not take the form of adultery, had previously been uncensured, or was looked upon with a disapprobation so slight as scarcely to amount to censure. The elder Cato had expressly justified it;[1] and Cicero has left us an extremely curious judgment on the subject, which shows at a glance the feelings of the people, and the vast revolution that, under the influence of Christianity, has been effected in, at least, the professions of mankind. 'If there be any one,' he says, 'who thinks that young men should be altogether restrained from the love of courtesans, he is indeed very severe. I am not prepared to deny his position; but he differs not only from the licence of our age, but also from the customs and allowances of our ancestors. When, indeed, was this not done? When was it blamed? When was it not allowed? When was that which is now lawful not lawful?'[2] Epictetus, who on most subjects was among the most austere of the Stoics, recommends his disciples to ab-

---

[1] Horace, *Sat.* i. 2.

[2] 'Verum si quis est qui etiam meretriciis amoribus interdictum juventuti putet, est ille quidem valde severus; negare non possum; sed abhorret non modo ab hujus sæculi licentia, verum etiam a majorum consuetudine atque concessis. Quando enim hoc factum non est? Quando reprehensum? Quando non permissum? Quando denique fuit ut quod licet non liceret?'—Cicero, *Pro Cælio*, cap. xx. The whole speech is well worthy of the attention of those who would understand Roman feelings on these matters; but it should be remembered that it is the speech of a lawyer defending a dissolute client.

stain, 'as far as possible, from pre-nuptial connections, and
at least from those which were adulterous and unlawful, but
not to blame those who were less strict.[1] The feeling of the
Romans is curiously exemplified in the life of Alexander
Severus, who, of all the emperors, was probably the most
energetic in legislating against vice. When appointing a
provincial governor, he was accustomed to provide him with
horses and servants, and, if he was unmarried, with a concubine, 'because,' as the historian very gravely observes, 'it
was impossible that he could exist without one.'[2]

What was written among the Pagans in opposition to
these views was not much, but it is worthy of notice, as
illustrating the tendency that had arisen. Musonius Rufus
distinctly and emphatically asserted that no union of the
sexes other than marriage was permissible.[3] Dion Chrysostom desired prostitution to be suppressed by law. The
ascetic notion of the impurity even of marriage may be
faintly traced. Apollonius of Tyana lived, on this ground,
a life of celibacy.[4] Zenobia refused to cohabit with her
husband except so far as was necessary for the production of
an heir. Hypatia is said, like many Christian saints, to
have maintained the position of a virgin wife.[5] The belief

---

[1] Π. ρ̀ ἀφροδίσια, εἰς δύναμιν πρὸ
γάμου ι.ἀ/αρευτέον. ἁπτομένῳ δέ,
ὃν νομιμόν ἐστι, μεταληπτέον, μὴ
μέν τοι ἐπαχθῆς γίνου τοῖς χρωμένοις,
μηδὲ ἐλεγκτικός, μηδὲ πολλαχοῦ τό,
Ὅτι αὐτὸς οὐ χρῇ, παράφερε.—Enchir. xxxiii.

[2] 'Et si uxores non haberent,
singulas concubinas, quod sine his
esse non possent.'—Lampridius, A.
Severus. We have an amusing
picture of the common tone of
people of the world on this matter,
in the speech Apuleius puts into
the mouth of the gods, remonstrat-
ing with Venus for being angry

because her son formed a connection with Psyche. (Metam. lib. v.)

[3] Preserved by Stobæus. See
Denis, Hist. des Idées morales dans
l'Antiquité, tome ii. pp. 134–136,
149–150.

[4] Philos. Apol. i. 13. When a
saying of Pythagoras, 'that a man
should only have commerce with
his own wife,' was quoted, he said
that this concerned others.

[5] Trebellius Pollio, Zenobia.

[6] This is asserted by an anonymous writer quoted by Suidas. See
Ménage, Hist. Mulierum Philose-
pharum, p. 58.

in the impurity of all corporeal things, and in the **duty** of rising above them, was in the third century strenuously enforced.[1]   Marcus Aurelius and Julian were both admirable representatives of the best Pagan spirit of their time.   Each of them lost his wife early, each was eulogised by his biographer for the virtue he manifested after her death; but there is a curious and characteristic difference in the forms which that virtue assumed.   Marcus Aurelius, we are told, did not wish to bring into his house a stepmother **to** rule over his children, and accordingly took a concubine.[2] Julian ever after lived in perfect continence.[3]

The foregoing facts, which I have given in the most condensed form, and almost unaccompanied by criticism or by comment, will be sufficient, I hope, to exhibit the state of feeling of the Romans on this subject, and also the direction in which that feeling was being modified.   Those who are familiar with this order of studies will readily understand that it is impossible to mark out with precision the chronology of a moral sentiment; but there can be no question that in the latter days of the Roman Empire the perceptions of men on this subject became more subtle and more refined than they had previously been, and it is equally certain that the Oriental philosophies which had superseded Stoicism largely influenced the change.   Christianity soon constituted itself the representative of the new tendency.   It regarded purity as the most important of all virtues, and it strained to the utmost all the vast agencies it possessed, to enforce it. In the legislation of the first Christian emperors we find many traces of a fiery zeal.   Panders were condemned to have molten lead poured down their throats.   In the case of rape, not only the ravisher, but even the injured person, if she consented to the act, was put to death.[4]   A great service

---

[1] See, e.g., Plotinus, 1st Enn. vi. 6.

[2] Capitolinus, *M. Aurelius.*

[3] Amm. Marcell. xxv. 4.

[4] *Cod. Theod.* lib. ix. tit. **24.**

was done to the cause both of purity and of philanthropy, by
a law which permitted actresses, on receiving baptism, to
abandon their profession, which had been made a form of
slavery, and was virtually a slavery to vice.[1] Certain
musical girls, who were accustomed to sing or play at the
banquets of the rich, and who were regarded with extreme
horror by the Fathers, were suppressed, and a very stringent
law forbade the revival of the class.[2]

Side by side with the civil legislation, the penitential
legislation of the Church was exerted in the same direction.
Sins of unchastity probably occupy a larger place than any
others in its enactments. The cases of unnatural love, and of
mothers who had made their daughters courtesans, were
punished by perpetual exclusion from communion, and a
crowd of minor offences were severely visited. The ascetic
passion increased the prominence of this branch of ethics,
and the imaginations of men were soon fascinated by the
pure and noble figures of the virgin martyrs of the Church,
who on more than one occasion fully equalled the courage of
men, while they sometimes mingled with their heroism traits
of the most exquisite feminine gentleness. For the patient
endurance of excruciating physical suffering, Christianity
produced no more sublime figure than Blandina, the poor
servant-girl who was martyred at Lyons; and it would be
difficult to find in all history a more touching picture of
natural purity than is contained in one simple incident of
the martyrdom of St. Perpetua. It is related of that saint
that she was condemned to be slaughtered by a wild bull,
and, as she fell half dead from its horns upon the sand of the

---

[1] *Cod. Theod.* lib. xv. tit. 7.

[2] 'Fidicinam nulli liceat vel
emere vel docere vel vendere, vel
conviviis aut spectaculis adhibere.
Nec cuiquam aut delectationis de-
siderio erudita feminea aut musicæ
artis studio liceat habere mancipia.'

—*Cod. Theod.* xv. 7, 10. This curious law was issued in A.D. 385. St.
Jerome said these musicians were
the chorus of the devil, and quite
as dangerous as the sirens. See
the comments on the law.

arena, it was observed that even in that awful moment her
virgin modesty was supreme, and her first instinctive movement was to draw together her dress, which had been torn
in the assault.[1]

A crowd of very curious popular legends also arose,
which, though they are for the most part without much
intrinsic excellence, have their importance in history, as
showing the force with which the imaginations of men were
turned in this direction, and the manner in which Christianity
was regarded as the great enemy of the passions of the flesh.
Thus, St. Jerome relates an incredible story of a young
Christian, being, in the Diocletian persecution, bound with
ribands of silk in the midst of a lovely garden, surrounded
by everything that could charm the ear and the eye, while a
beautiful courtesan assailed him with her blandishments,
against which he protected himself by biting out his tongue
and spitting it in her face.[2] Legends are recounted of young

---

[1] Ruinart, *Act. S. Perpetuæ.*
These acts, are, I believe, generally
regarded as authentic. There is
nothing more instructive in history
than to trace the same moral feelings through different ages and religions; and I am able in this case
to present the reader with an illustration of their permanence, which
I think somewhat remarkable. The
younger Pliny gives in one of his
letters a pathetic account of the
execution of Cornelia, a vestal
virgin, by the order of Domitian.
She was buried alive for incest;
but her innocence appears to have
been generally believed; and she
had been condemned unheard, and
in her absence. As she was being
lowered into the subterranean cell
her dress was caught and deranged
in the descent. She turned round
and drew it to her, and when the
executioner stretched out his hand

to assist her, she started back lest
he should touch her, for this, according to the received opinion, was
a pollution; and even in the supreme moment of her agony her
vestal purity shrank from the unholy contact. (Plin. *Ep.* iv. 11.)
If we now pass back several centuries, we find Euripides attributing to Polyxena a trait precisely
similar to that which was attributed to Perpetua. As she fell
beneath the sword of the executioner, it was observed that her
last care was that she might fall
with decency.

ἡ δὲ καὶ θνήσκουσ᾽ ὅμως
πολλὴν πρόνοιαν εἶχεν εὐσχήμως
πεσεῖν,
κρύπτουσ᾽ ἃ κρύπτειν ὄμματ᾽ ἀρσέ-
νων χρεών.

Euripides, *Hec.* 566-68.

[2] *Vita Pauli.*

Christian men assuming the garb and manners of libertines, that they might obtain access to maidens who had been condemned to vice, exchanging dresses with them, and thus enabling them to escape.[1] St. Agnes was said to have been stripped naked before the people, who all turned away their eyes except one young man, who instantly became blind.[2] The sister of St. Gregory of Nyssa was afflicted with a cancer in her breast, but could not bear that a surgeon should see it, and was rewarded for her modesty by a miraculous cure.[3] To the fabled zone of beauty the Christian saints opposed their zones of chastity, which extinguished the passion of the wearer, or would only meet around the pure.[4] Dæmons were said not unfrequently to have entered into the profligate. The garment of a girl who was possessed was brought to St. Pachomius, and he discovered from it that she had a lover.[5] A courtesan accused St. Gregory Thaumaturgus of having been her lover, and having refused to pay her what he had promised. He paid the required sum, but she was immediately possessed by a dæmon.[6] The efforts of the saints to reclaim courtesans from the path of vice created

---

[1] St. Ambrose relates an instance of this, which he says occurred at Antioch (*De Virginibus*, lib. ii. cap. iv.). When the Christian youth was being led to execution, the girl whom he had saved reappeared and died with him. Eusebius tells a very similar story, but places the scene at Alexandria.

[2] See Ceillier, *Hist. des Auteurs ecclés.* tome iii. p. 523.

[3] Ibid. tome viii. pp. 204–207.

[4] Among the Irish saints St. Colman is said to have had a girdle which would only meet around the chaste, and which was long preserved in Ireland as a relic (Colgan, *Acta Sanctorum Hiberniæ*, Louvain, 1645, vol. i. p. 246); and St.

Fursæus a girdle that extinguished lust. (Ibid. p. 292.) The girdle of St. Thomas Aquinas seems to have had some miraculous pro perties of this kind. (See his *Life* in the Bollandists, Sept. 29.) Among both the Greeks and Romans it was customary for the bride to be girt with a girdle which the bridegroom unloosed in the nuptial bed, and hence 'zonam solvere' became a proverbial expression for 'pudicitiam mulieris imminuere.' (Nieupoort, *De Ritibus Romanorum*, p. 479; Alexander's *History of Women*, vol. ii. p. 300.)

[5] *Vit. St. Pachom.* (Rosweyde).

[6] See his *Life*, by Gregory of Nyssa.

a large class of legends. St. Mary Magdalene, St. Mary cf Egypt, St. Afra, St. Pelagia, St. Thais, and St. Theodota, in the early Church, as well as St. Marguerite of Cortona, and Clara of Rimini, in the middle ages, had been courtesans.[1] St. Vitalius, it is said, was accustomed every night to visit the dens of vice in his neighbourhood, to give the inmates money to remain without sin for that night, and to offer up prayers for their conversion.[2] It is related of St. Serapion, that, as he was passing through a village in Egypt, a courtesan beckoned to him. He promised at a certain hour to visit her. He kept his appointment, but declared that there was a duty which his order imposed on him. He fell down on his knees and began repeating the Psalter, concluding every psalm with a prayer for his hostess. The strangeness of the scene, and the solemnity of his tone and manner, overawed and fascinated her. Gradually her tears began to flow. She knelt beside him and began to join in his prayers. He heeded her not, but hour after hour continued in the same stern and solemn voice, without rest and without interruption, to repeat his alternate prayers and psalms, till her repentance rose to a paroxysm of terror, and, as the grey morning streaks began to illumine the horizon, she fell half dead at his feet, imploring him with broken sobs to lead her anywhere where she might expiate the sins of her past.[3]

But the services rendered by the ascetics in imprinting on the minds of men a profound and enduring conviction of the importance of chastity, though extremely great, were

---

[1] A little book has been written on these legends by M. Charles de Bussy, called *Les Courtisanes saintes.* There is said to be some doubt about St. Afra, for, while her acts represent her as a reformed courtesan, St. Fortunatus, in two lines he has devoted to her, calls her a virgin. (Ozanam, *Études*

german. tome ii. p. 8.)

[2] See the *Vit. Sancti Joannis Eleemosynarii* (Rosweyde).

[3] Tillemont, tome x. pp. 61–62. There is also a very picturesque legend of the manner in which St. Paphnutius converted the courtesan Thais.

seriously counterbalanced by their noxious influence upon marriage. Two or three beautiful descriptions of this institution have been culled out of the immense mass of the patristic writings;[1] but, in general, it would be difficult to conceive anything more coarse or more repulsive than the manner in which they regarded it.[2] The relation which nature has designed for the noble purpose of repairing the ravages of death, and which, as Linnæus has shown, extends even through the world of flowers, was invariably treated as a consequence of the fall of Adam, and marriage was regarded almost exclusively in its lowest aspect. The tender love which it elicits, the holy and beautiful domestic qualities that follow in its train, were almost absolutely omitted from consideration.[3] The object of the ascetic was to attract men to a life of virginity, and, as a necessary consequence, marriage was treated as an inferior state. It was regarded as being necessary, indeed, and therefore justifiable, for the propagation of the species, and to free men from greater evils; but still as a condition of degradation from which all who aspired to real sanctity should fly. To 'cut down by the axe of Virginity the wood of Marriage,' was, in the energetic language of St. Jerome, the end of the saint;[4] and if he

---

[1] See especially, Tertullian, *Ad Uxorem*. It was beautifully said, at a later period, that woman was not taken from the head of man, for she was not intended to be his ruler, nor from his feet, for she was not intended to be his slave, but from his side, for she was to be his companion and his comfort. (Peter Lombard, *Senten.* lib. ii. dis. 18.)

[2] The reader may find many passages on this subject in Barbeyrac, *Morale des Pères*, ii. § 7; iii. § 8; iv. § 31–35; vi. § 31; xiii. § 2–8.

[3] 'It is remarkable how rarely,

if ever (I cannot call to mind an instance), in the discussions of the comparative merits of marriage and celibacy, the social advantages appear to have occurred to the mind. . . . . It is always argued with relation to the interests and the perfection of the individual soul; and, even with regard to that, the writers seem almost unconscious of the softening and humanising effect of the natural affections, the beauty of parental tenderness and filial love.' — Milman's *Hist. of Christianity*, vol. iii. p. 196.

[4] 'Tempus breve est, et jam securis ad radices arborum posita

consented to praise marriage, it was merely because it produced virgins.[1] Even when the bond had been formed, the ascetic passion retained its sting. We have already seen how it embittered other relations of domestic life. Into this, the holiest of all, it infused a tenfold bitterness. Whenever any strong religious fervour fell upon a husband or a wife, its first effect was to make a happy union impossible. The more religious partner immediately desired to live a life of solitary asceticism, or at least, if no ostensible separation took place, an unnatural life of separation in marriage. The immense place this order of ideas occupies in the hortatory writings of the Fathers, and in the legends of the saints, must be familiar to all who have any knowledge of this department of literature. Thus—to give but a very few examples—St. Nilus, when he had already two children, was seized with a longing for the prevailing asceticism, and his wife was persuaded, after many tears, to consent to their separation.[2] St. Ammon, on the night of his marriage, proceeded to greet his bride with an harangue upon the evils of the married state, and they agreed, in consequence, at once to separate.[3] St. Melania laboured long and earnestly to induce her husband to allow her to desert his bed, before he would consent.[4] St. Abraham ran away from his wife on the night of his marriage.[5] St. Alexis, according to a somewhat later legend, took the same step, but many years after returned from Jerusalem to his father's house, in which his wife was still lamenting her desertion, begged and received a lodging as an act of charity, and lived there unrecognised and unknown till his death.[6] St. Gregory of Nyssa—who was

---

est, quæ silvam legis et nuptiarum evangelica castitate succidat.'—*Ep.* cxxiii.

[1] 'Laudo nuptias, laudo conjugium, sed quia mihi virgines generant.'—*Ep.* xxii.

[2] See Ceillier, *Auteurs ecclés.*

xiii. p. 147.

[3] Socrates, iv. 23.

[4] Palladius, *Hist. Laus.* cxix.

[5] *Vit. S. Abr.* (Rosweyde), cap. 1.

[6] I do not know when this legend first appeared. M. Littré mentions having found it in a French MS. of

so unfortunate as to be married—wrote a glowing eulogy of virginity, in the course of which he mournfully observed that this privileged state could never be his. He resembled, he assures us, an ox that was ploughing a field, the fruit of which he must never enjoy; or a thirsty man, who was gazing on a stream of which he never can drink; or a poor man, whose poverty seems the more bitter as he contemplates the wealth of his neighbours; and he proceeded to descant in feeling terms upon the troubles of matrimony.[1] Nominal marriages, in which the partners agreed to shun the marriage bed, became not uncommon. The emperor Henry II., Edward the Confessor, of England, and Alphonso II., of Spain, gave examples of it. A very famous and rather picturesque history of this kind is related by Gregory of Tours. A rich young Gaul, named Injuriosus, led to his home a young bride to whom he was passionately attached. That night, she confessed to him, with tears, that she had vowed to keep her virginity, and that she regretted bitterly the marriage into which her love for him had betrayed her. He told her that they should remain united, but that she should still observe her vow; and he fulfilled his promise. When, after several years, she died, her husband, in laying her in the tomb, declared, with great solemnity, that he restored her to God as immaculate as he had received her; and then a smile lit up the face of the dead woman, and she said, 'Why do you tell that which no one asked you?' The husband soon afterwards died, and his corpse, which had been laid in a distinct compartment from that of his wife in the tomb, was placed side by side with it by the angels.[2]

---

the eleventh century (Littré, *Les Barbares*, pp. 123–124); and it also forms the subject of a very curious fresco, I imagine of a somewhat earlier date, which was discovered, within the last few years, in the subterranean church of St. Clement at Rome. An account of it is given by Father Mullooly, in his interesting little book about that Church.

[1] *De Virgin.* cap. iii.
[2] Greg. Tur. i. 42.

The extreme disorders which such teaching produced in domestic life, and also the extravagances which grew up among some heretics, naturally alarmed the more judicious leaders of the Church, and it was ordained that married persons should not enter into an ascetic life, except by mutual consent.[1] The ascetic ideal, however, remained unchanged. To abstain from marriage, or in marriage to abstain from a perfect union, was regarded as a proof of sanctity, and marriage was viewed in its coarsest and most degraded form. The notion of its impurity took many forms, and exercised for some centuries an extremely wide influence over the Church. Thus, it was the custom during the middle ages to abstain from the marriage bed during the night after the ceremony, in honour of the sacrament.[2] It was expressly enjoined that no married persons should participate in any of the great Church festivals if the night before they had lain together, and St. Gregory the Great tells of a young wife who was possessed by a dæmon, because she had taken part in a procession of St. Sebastian, without fulfilling this condition.[3] The extent to which the feeling on the subject was carried is shown by the famous vision of Alberic in the twelfth century, in which a special place of torture, consisting of a lake of mingled lead, pitch, and resin is represented as existing in hell for the punishment of married people who had lain together on Church festivals or fast days.[4]

Two other consequences of this way of regarding marriage were a very strong disapproval of second marriages, and a very strong desire to secure celibacy in the clergy. The first of these notions had existed, though in a very different form, and connected with very different motives, among the early Romans, who were accustomed, we are told, to honour with

---

[1] The regulations on this point are given at length in Bingham.

[2] Muratori, *Antich. Ital.* diss. xx.

[3] St. Greg. *Dial.* i. 10.

[4] Delepierre, *L'Enfer décrit par ceux qui l'ont vu*, pp. 44–56.

the crown of modesty those who were content with one marriage, and to regard many marriages as a sign of illegitimate intemperance.[1] This opinion appears to have chiefly grown out of a very delicate and touching feeling which had taken deep root in the Roman mind, that the affection a wife owes her husband is so profound and so pure that it must not cease even with his death; that it should guide and consecrate all her subsequent life, and that it never can be transferred to another object. Virgil, in very beautiful lines, puts this sentiment into the mouth of Dido;[2] and several examples are recorded of Roman wives, sometimes in the prime of youth and beauty, upon the death of their husbands, devoting the remainder of their lives to retirement and to the memory of the dead.[3] Tacitus held up the Germans as in this respect a model to his countrymen,[4] and the epithet 'univiræ' inscribed on many Roman tombs shows how this devotion was practised and valued.[5] The family of Camillus was especially honoured for the absence of second marriages among its members.[6] 'To love a wife when living,' said one of the latest Roman poets, 'is a pleasure; to love her when dead is an act of religion.'[7] In the case of men, the propriety of abstaining from second marriages was probably not felt so strongly as in the case of women, and what feeling on the subject existed was chiefly due to another motive—affection for the children, whose interests, it was thought, might be injured by a stepmother.[8]

---

[1] Val. Max. ii. 1. § 3.

[2] 'Ille meos, primus qui me sibi junxit, amores
    Abstulit; ille habeat secum, servetque sepulchro.'
    Æn. iv. 28.

[3] E.g., the wives of Lucan, Drusus, and Pompey.

[4] Tacit. *German.* xix.

[5] Friedländer, tome i. p. 411.

[6] Hieron. *Ep.* liv.

[7] 'Uxorem vivam amare voluptas;
    Defunctam religio.'
    Statius. *Sylv.* v. in proœmio.

[8] By one of the laws of Charondas it was ordained that those who cared so little for the happiness of their children as to place a stepmother over them. should be excluded from the councils of the State. (Diod. Sic. xii. 12.)

The sentiment which thus recoiled from second marriages
passed with a vastly increased strength into ascetic Christianity, but it was based upon altogether different grounds.
We find, in the first place, that an affectionate remembrance
of the husband had altogether vanished from the motives of the
abstinence. In the next place, we may remark that the ecclesiastical writers, in perfect conformity with the extreme coarseness of their views about the sexes, almost invariably assumed
that the motive to second or third marriages must be simply
the force of the animal passions. The Montanists and the
Novatians absolutely condemned second marriages.[1] The
orthodox pronounced them lawful, on account of the weakness of human nature, but they viewed them with the most
emphatic disapproval,[2] partly because they considered them
manifest signs of incontinence, and partly because they regarded them as inconsistent with their doctrine that marriage is an emblem of the union of Christ with the Church.
The language of the Fathers on this subject appears to a
modern mind most extraordinary, and, but for their distinct
and reiterated assertion that they considered these marriages
permissible,[3] would appear to amount to a peremptory condemnation. Thus—to give but a few samples—digamy, or
second marriage, is described by Athenagoras as 'a decent
adultery.'[4] 'Fornication,' according to Clement of Alexandria, ' is a lapse from one marriage into many.'[5] 'The first
Adam,' said St. Jerome, 'had one wife; the second Adam

---

[1] Tertullian expounded the
Montanist view in his treatise,
De Monogamia.

[2] A full collection of the statements of the Fathers on this subject is given by Perrone, *De Matrimonio,* lib. iii. Sect. I.; and by
Natalis Alexander, *Hist. Eccles.*
Sæc. II. dissert. 18.

[3] Thus, to give but a single instance, St. Jerome, who was one of

their strongest opponents, says :
'Quid igitur? damnamus secunda
matrimonia? Minime, sed prima
laudamus. Abjicimus de ecclesia
digamos? absit; sed monogamos
ad continentiam provocamus. In
arca Noe non solum munda sed et
immunda fuerunt animalia.'—*Ep.*
cxxiii.

[4] *In Legat.*

[5] *Strom.* lib. iii.

had no wife. They who approve of digamy hold forth a third Adam, who was twice married, whom they follow.'[1] 'Consider,' he again says, 'that she who has been twice married, though she be an old, and decrepit, and poor woman, is not deemed worthy to receive the charity of the Church. But if the bread of charity is taken from her, how much more that bread which descends from heaven!'[2] 'Digamists,' according to Origen, 'are saved in the name of Christ, but are by no means crowned by him.'[3] 'By this text,' said St. Gregory Nazianzen, speaking of St. Paul's comparison of marriage to the union of Christ with the Church, 'second marriages seem to me to be reproved. If there are two Christs there may be two husbands or two wives. If there is but one Christ, one Head of the Church, there is but one flesh—a second is repelled. But if he forbids a second, what is to be said of third marriages? The first is law, the second is pardon and indulgence, the third is iniquity; but he who exceeds this number is manifestly bestial.'[4] The collective judgment of the ecclesiastical authorities on this subject is shown by the rigid exclusion of digamists from the priesthood, and from all claim to the charity of the Church, and by the decrees of more than one Council, which imposed a period of penance upon all who married a second time, before they were admitted to communion.[5] One of the canons of the Council of Illiberis, in the beginning of the fourth century, while in general condemning baptism by laymen, permitted it in case of extreme necessity; but provided that even then it was indispensable that the officiating layman should not have been twice married.[6]

---

[1] *Contra Jovin.* i.
[2] Ibid. See, too, *Ep.* cxxiii.
[3] Hom. xvii. in Luc.
[4] *Orat.* xxxi.
[5] Perrone, *De Matr.* iii. § 1, art. 1; Natalis Alexander, *Hist. Eccles.* II. dissert. 18. The penances are

said not to imply that the second marriage was a sin, but that the moral condition that made it necessary was a bad one.
[6] Conc. Illib. can. xxxviii. Bingham thinks the feeling of the Council to have been, that if bap-

Among the Greeks fourth marriages were at one time deemed absolutely unlawful, and much controversy was excited by the Emperor Leo the Wise, who, having had three wives, had taken a mistress, but afterwards, in defiance of the religious feelings of his people, determined to raise her to the position of a wife.[1]

The subject of the celibacy of the clergy, in which the ecclesiastical feelings about marriage were also shown, is an extremely large one, and I shall not attempt to deal with it, except in a most cursory manner.[2] There are two facts connected with it which every candid student must admit. The first is, that in the earliest period of the Church, the privilege of marriage was accorded to the clergy. The second is, that a notion of the impurity of marriage existed, and that it was felt that the clergy, as pre-eminently the holy class, should have less licence than laymen. The first form this feeling took appears in the strong conviction that a second marriage of a priest, or the marriage of a priest with a widow, was unlawful and criminal.[3] This belief seems to

---

tism was not administered by a priest, it should at all events be administered by one who might have been a priest.

[1] Perrone, *De Matrimonio*, tome iii. p. 102.

[2] This subject has recently been treated with very great learning and with admirable impartiality by an American author, Mr. Henry C. Lea, in his *History of Sacerdotal Celibacy* (Philadelphia, 1867), which is certainly one of the most valuable works that America has produced. Since the great history of Dean Milman, I know no work in English which has thrown more light on the moral condition of the middle ages, and none which is more fitted to dispel the gross illusions concerning that period which

High Church writers, and writers of the positive school, have conspired to sustain.

[3] See Lea, p. 36. The command of St. Paul, that a bishop or deacon should be the husband of *one* wife (1 Tim. iii. 2-12) was believed by all ancient and by many modern commentators to be prohibitory of second marriages; and this view is somewhat confirmed by the widows who were to be honoured and supported by the Church, being only those who had been but once married (1 Tim. v. 9). See Pressensé, *Hist. des trois-premiers Siècles* (1re série), tome ii. p. 233. Among the Jews it was ordained that the high priest should not marry a widow (Levit. xxi. 13-14.)

have existed from the earliest period of the Church, and was retained with great tenacity and unanimity through many centuries. In the next place, we find from an extremely early date an opinion, that it was an act of virtue, at a later period that it was an act of duty, for priests after ordination to abstain from cohabiting with their wives. The Council of Nice refrained, by the advice of Paphnutius, who was himself a scrupulous celibate, from imposing this last rule as a matter of necessity ;[1] but in the course of the fourth century it was a recognised principle that clerical marriages were criminal. They were celebrated, however, habitually, and usually with the greatest openness. The various attitudes assumed by the ecclesiastical authorities in dealing with this subject form an extremely curious page of the history of morals, and supply the most crushing evidence of the evils which have been produced by the system of celibacy. I can at present, however, only refer to the vast mass of evidence which has been collected on the subject, derived from the writings of Catholic divines and from the decrees of Catholic Councils during the space of many centuries. It is a popular illusion, which is especially common among writers who have little direct knowledge of the middle ages, that the atrocious immorality of monasteries, in the century before the Reformation, was a new fact, and that the ages when the faith of men was undisturbed, were ages of great moral purity. In fact, it appears, from the uniform testimony of the ecclesiastical writers, that ecclesiastical immorality in the eighth and three following centuries was little if at all less outrageous than in any other period, while the Papacy, during almost the whole of the tenth century, was held by men of

---

[1] Socrates, *H. E.* i. 11. The Council of Illiberis (can. xxxiii.) had ordained this, but both the precepts and the practice of divines varied greatly. A brilliant summary of the chief facts is given in Milman's *History of Early Christianity*, vol. iii. pp. 277-282.

infamous lives. Simony was nearly universal.[1] Barbarian chieftains married at an early age, and totally incapable of restraint, occupied the leading positions in the Church, and gross irregularities speedily became general. An Italian bishop of the tenth century epigrammatically described the morals of his time, when he declared, that if he were to enforce the canons against unchaste people administering ecclesiastical rites, no one would be left in the Church except the boys; and if he were to observe the canons against bastards, these also must be excluded.[2] The evil acquired such magnitude that a great feudal clergy, bequeathing the ecclesiastical benefices from father to son, appeared more than once likely to arise.[3] A tax called 'Culagium,' which was in fact a licence to clergymen to keep concubines, was during several centuries systematically levied by princes.[4] Sometimes the evil, by its very extension, corrected itself. Priestly marriages were looked upon as normal events not implying any guilt, and in the eleventh century several instances are recorded in which they were not regarded as any impediment to the power of working miracles.[5] But this was a rare exception. From the earliest period a long succession of Councils as well as such men as St. Boniface, St. Gregory the Great, St. Peter Damiani, St. Dunstan, St. Anselm, Hildebrand and his successors in the Popedom, denounced priestly marriage or concubinage as an atrocious crime, and the habitual life of the priests was, in theory at least, generally recognised as a life of sin.

It is not surprising that, having once broken their vows and begun to live what they deemed a life of habitual sin,

---

[1] See, on the state of things in the tenth and eleventh centuries, Lea, pp. 162–192.

[2] Ratherius, quoted by Lea, p. 151.

[3] See some curious evidence of the extent to which the practice of the hereditary transmission of ecclesiastical offices was carried, in Lea, pp. 149, 150, 266, 299, 339.

[4] Lea, pp. 271, 292, 422.

[5] Ibid. pp. 186–187.

the clergy should soon have sunk far below the level of the laity. We may not lay much stress on such isolated instances of depravity as that of Pope John XXIII., who was condemned among many other crimes for incest, and for adultery;[1] or the abbot-elect of St. Augustine, at Canterbury, who in 1171 was found, on investigation, to have seventeen illegitimate children in a single village;[2] or an abbot of St. Pelayo, in Spain, who in 1130 was proved to have kept no less than seventy concubines;[3] or Henry III., Bishop of Liége, who was deposed in 1274 for having sixty-five illegitimate children;[4] but it is impossible to resist the evidence of a long chain of Councils and ecclesiastical writers, who conspire in depicting far greater evils than simple concubinage. It was observed that when the priests actually took wives the knowledge that these connections were illegal was peculiarly fatal to their fidelity, and bigamy and extreme mobility of attachments were especially common among them. The writers of the middle ages are full of accounts of nunneries that were like brothels, of the vast multitude of infanticides within their walls, and of that inveterate prevalence of incest among the clergy, which rendered it necessary again and again to issue the most stringent enactments that priests should not be permitted to live with their mothers or sisters. Unnatural love, which it had been one of the great services of Christianity almost to eradicate from the world, is more than once spoken of as lingering in the monasteries; and, shortly before the Reformation, complaints became loud and frequent of the employment of the confessional for the purposes of debauchery.[5] The measures taken on the subject were very numerous and severe. At first, the evil chiefly complained of was the clandestine

---

[1] Lea, p. 358.
[2] Ibid. p. 296.
[3] Ibid. p. 322.
[4] Ibid. p. 349.

[5] The reader may find the most ample evidence of these positions in Lea. See especially pp. 138, 141, 153, 155, 260, 344.

marriage of priests, and especially their intercourse with wives whom they had married previous to their ordination. Several Councils issued their anathemas against priests ' who had improper relations with their wives;' and rules were made that priests should always sleep in the presence of a subordinate clerk; and that they should only meet their wives in the open air and before at least two witnesses. Men were, however, by no means unanimous in their way of regarding this matter. Synesius, when elected to a bishopric, at first declined, boldly alleging as one of his reasons, that he had a wife whom he loved dearly, and who, he hoped, would bear him many sons, and that he did not mean to separate from her or visit her secretly as an adulterer.[1]   A Bishop of Laon, at a later date, who was married to a niece of St. Rémy, and who remained with his wife till after he had a son and a daughter, quaintly expressed his penitence by naming them respectively Latro and Vulpecula.[2]   St. Gregory the Great describes the virtue of a priest, who, through motives of piety, had discarded his wife. As he lay dying, she hastened to him to watch the bed which for forty years she had not been allowed to share, and, bending over what seemed the inanimate form of her husband, she tried to ascertain whether any breath still remained, when the dying saint, collecting his last energies, exclaimed, ' Woman, begone; take away the straw; there is fire yet.'[3]   The destruction of priestly marriage is chiefly due to Hildebrand, who pursued this object with the most untiring resolution. Finding that his appeals to the ecclesiastical authorities and to the civil rulers were insufficient, he boldly turned to the people, exhorted them, in defiance of all Church traditions, to withdraw their obedience from married priests, and

---

[1] Synesius, *Ep.* cv.
[2] Lea, p. 122. St. Augustine had named *his* illegitimate son Adeodatus, or the Gift of God, and had made him a principal inter locutor in one of his religious dia logues.
[3] *Dialog.* iv. 11.

kindled among them a fierce fanaticism of asceticism, which
speedily produced a fierce persecution of the offending pastors.
Their wives, in immense numbers, were driven forth with
hatred and with scorn; and many crimes, and much intolerable suffering, followed the disruption. The priests
sometimes strenuously resisted. At Cambrai, in A.D. 1077,
they burnt alive as a heretic a zealot who was maintaining
the doctrines of Hildebrand. In England, half a century
later, they succeeded in surprising a Papal legate in the arms
of a courtesan, a few hours after he had delivered a fierce
denunciation of clerical unchastity.[1] But Papal resolution
supported by popular fanaticism won the victory. Pope
Urban II. gave licence to the nobles to reduce to slavery
the wives whom priests had obstinately refused to abandon,
and after a few more acts of severity priestly marriage became obsolete. The extent, however, of the disorders that
still existed, is shown by the mournful confessions of
ecclesiastical writers, by the uniform and indignant testimony of the poets and prose satirists who preceded the
Reformation, by the atrocious immoralities disclosed in the
monasteries at the time of their suppression, and by the
significant prudence of many lay Catholics, who were accustomed to insist that their priest should take a concubine
for the protection of the families of his parishioners.[2]

[1] This is mentioned by Henry
of Huntingdon, who was a contemporary. (Lea, p. 293.)

[2] The first notice of this very
remarkable precaution is in a canon
of the Council of Palencia (in
Spain) held in 1322, which anathe-
matises laymen who compel their
pastors to take concubines. (Lea,
p. 324.) Sleidan mentions that it
was customary in some of the Swiss
cantons for the parishioners to
oblige the priest to select a concubine as a necessary precaution for

the protection of his female parishioners. (Ibid. p. 355.) Sarpi, in
his *Hist. of the Council of Trent*,
mentions (on the authority of
Zuinglius) this Swiss custom.
Nicolas of Clemangis, a leading
member of the Council of Con-
stance, declared that this custom
had become very common, that
the laity were firmly persuaded
that priests *never* lived a life of
real celibacy, and that, where
no proofs of concubinage were
found, they always assumed the

It is scarcely possible to conceive a more demoralising influence than a priesthood living such a life as I have described.   In Protestant countries, where the marriage of the clergy is fully recognised, it has, indeed, been productive of the greatest and the most unequivocal benefits.   Nowhere, it may be confidently asserted, does Christianity assume a more beneficial or a more winning form than in those gentle clerical households which stud our land, constituting, as Coleridge said, 'the one idyll of modern life,' the most perfect type of domestic peace, the centre of civilisation in the remotest village.   Notwithstanding some class narrowness and professional bigotry, notwithstanding some unworthy, but half unconscious mannerism, which is often most unjustly stigmatised as hypocrisy, it would be difficult to find in any other quarter so much happiness at once diffused and enjoyed, or so much virtue attained with so little tension or struggle.   Combining with his sacred calling a warm sympathy with the intellectual, social, and political movements of his time, possessing the enlarged practical knowledge of a father of a family, and entering with a keen zest into the occupations and the amusements of his parishioners, a good clergyman will rarely obtrude his religious convictions into secular spheres, but yet will make them apparent in all.   They will be revealed by a higher and deeper moral tone, by a more scrupulous purity in word and action, by an all-pervasive gentleness, which refines, and softens, and mellows, and adds as much to the charm as to the excellence of the character

existence of more serious vice. The passage (which is quoted by Bayle) is too remarkable to be omitted. 'Taceo de fornicationibus et adulteriis a quibus qui alieni sunt probro cæteris ac ludibrio esse solent, spadonesque aut sodomitæ appellantur; denique laici usque adeo persuasum habent nullos cælibes esse, ut in plerisque parochiis non aliter velint presbyterum tolerare nisi concubinam habeat, quo vel sic suis sit consultum uxoribus, quæ nec sic quidem usquequaque sunt extra periculum.' Nic. de Clem. *De Præsul. Simoniaa* (Lea, p. 386.)

in which it is displayed. In visiting the sick, relieving the poor, instructing the young, and discharging a thousand delicate offices for which a woman's tact is especially needed, his wife finds a sphere of labour which is at once intensely active and intensely feminine, and her example is not less beneficial than her ministrations.

Among the Catholic priesthood, on the other hand, where the vow of celibacy is faithfully observed, a character of a different type is formed, which with very grave and deadly faults combines some of the noblest excellences to which humanity can attain. Separated from most of the ties and affections of earth, viewing life chiefly through the distorted medium of the casuist or the confessional, and deprived of those relationships which more than any others soften and expand the character, the Catholic priests have been but too often conspicuous for their fierce and sanguinary fanaticism, and for their indifference to all interests except those of their Church; while the narrow range of their sympathies, and the intellectual servitude they have accepted, render them peculiarly unfitted for the office of educating the young, which they so persistently claim, and which, to the great misfortune of the world, they were long permitted to monopolise. But, on the other hand, no other body of men have ever exhibited a more single minded and unworldly zeal, refracted by no personal interests, sacrificing to duty the dearest of earthly objects, and confronting with undaunted heroism every form of hardship, of suffering, and of death.

That the middle ages, even in their darkest periods, produced many good and great men of the latter type it would be unjust and absurd to deny. It can hardly, however, be questioned that the extreme frequency of illicit connections among the clergy tended during many centuries most actively to lower the moral tone of the laity, and to counteract the great services in the cause of purity which Christian teaching had undoubtedly effected.   The priestly connections were rarely so fully recognised as to enable the mistress to fill a position like that which is now occupied by the wife of a clergyman, and the spectacle of the chief teachers and exemplars of morals living habitually in an intercourse which was acknowledged to be ambiguous or wrong, must have acted most injuriously upon every class of the community.   Asceticism, proclaiming war upon human nature, produced a revulsion towards its extreme opposite, and even when it was observed it was frequently detrimental to purity of mind.   The habit of continually looking upon marriage in its coarsest light, and of regarding the propagation of the species as its one legitimate end, exercised a peculiarly perverting influence upon the imagination.   The exuberant piety of wives who desired to live apart from their husbands often drove the latter into serious irregularities.[1] The notion of sin was introduced into the dearest of relationships,[2] and the whole subject was distorted and degraded.   It is one of the great benefits of Protestantism that it did much to banish these modes of thought and feeling from the world, and to restore marriage to its simplicity and its dignity.   We have a gratifying illustration

---

[1] This was energetically noticed by Luther, in his famous sermon ' De Matrimonio,' and some of the Catholic preachers of an earlier period had made the same complaint.   See a curious passage from a contemporary of Boccaccio, quoted by Meray, *Les Libres prêcheurs*, p. 155.   ' Vast numbers of laymen separated from their wives under the influence of the ascetic enthusiasm which Hildebrand created.'—Lea, p. 254.

[2] ' Quando enim servata fide thori causa prolis conjuges conveniunt sic excusatur coitus ut culpam non habeat.   Quando vero deficiente bono prolis fide tamen servata conveniunt causa incontinentiæ non sic excusatur ut non habeat culpam, sed venialem. . . . Item hoc quod conjugati victi con cupiscentia utuntur invicem, ultra necessitatem liberos procreandi, ponam in his pro quibus quotidie dicimus Dimitte nobis debita nostra. . . . Unde in sententiolis Sexti Pythagorici legitur "omnis ardentior amator propriæ uxoris adulter est." '—Peter Lombard, *Sentent.* lib. iv. dist. 31.

of the extent to which an old superstition has declined, in the fact that when Goldsmith, in his great romance, desired to depict the harmless eccentricities of his simple-minded and unworldly vicar, he represented him as maintaining that opinion concerning the sinfulness of the second marriage of a clergyman which was for many centuries universal in the Church.

Another injurious consequence, resulting, in a great measure, from asceticism, was a tendency to depreciate extremely the character and the position of women. In this tendency we may detect in part the influence of the earlier Jewish writings, in which an impartial observer may find evident traces of the common Oriental depreciation of women. The custom of purchase-money to the father of the bride was admitted. Polygamy was authorised,[1] and practised by the wisest man on an enormous scale. A woman was regarded as the origin of human ills. A period of purification was appointed after the birth of every child; but. by a very significant provision, it was twice as long in the case of a female as of a male child.[2] 'The badness of men,' a Jewish writer emphatically declared, 'is better than the goodness of women.'[3] The types of female excellence exhibited in the early period of Jewish history are in general of a low order, and certainly far inferior to those of Roman history or Greek poetry; and the warmest eulogy of a woman in the Old Testament is probably that which was bestowed upon her who, with circumstances of the most aggravated treachery, had murdered the sleeping fugitive who had taken refuge under her roof.

---

[1] Many wives, however, were forbidden. (Deut. xvii. 17.) Polygamy is said to have ceased among the Jews after the return from the Babylonish captivity.— Whewell's *Elements of Morality*, book iv. ch. v.

[2] Levit. xii. 1–5.
[3] Ecclesiasticus, xlii. 14. I believe, however, the passage has been translated 'Better the badness of a man than the blandishments of a woman.'

The combined influence of the Jewish writings, and of that ascetic feeling which treated women as the chief source of temptation to man, was shown in those fierce invectives, which form so conspicuous and so grotesque a portion of the writings of the Fathers, and which contrast so curiously with the adulation bestowed upon particular members of the sex. Woman was represented as the door of hell, as the mother of all human ills. She should be ashamed at the very thought that she is a woman. She should live in continual penance, on account of the curses she has brought upon the world. She should be ashamed of her dress, for it is the memorial of her fall. She should be especially ashamed of her beauty, for it is the most potent instrument of the dæmon. Physical beauty was indeed perpetually the theme of ecclesiastical denunciations, though one singular exception seems to have been made, for it has been observed that in the middle ages the personal beauty of bishops was continually noticed upon their tombs.[1] Women were even forbidden by a provincial Council, in the sixth century, on account of their impurity, to receive the Eucharist into their naked hands.[2] Their essentially subordinate position was continually maintained.

It is probable that this teaching had its part in determining the principles of legislation concerning the sex. The Pagan laws during the Empire had been continually repealing the old disabilities of women, and the legislative movement in their favour continued with unabated force from Constantine to Justinian, and appeared also in some of the early laws of the barbarians.[3] But in the whole feudal legislation

[1] This curious fact is noticed by Le Blant, *Inscriptions chrétiennes de la Gaule*, pp. xcvii.-xcviii.

[2] See the decree of a Council of Auxerre (A.D. 578), can. 36.

See the last two chapters of Troplong, *Influences du Christianisme sur le Droit* (a work, however, which is written much more in the spirit of an apologist than in that of an historian), and Legouvé, pp. 27-29.

women were placed in a much lower legal position than in the Pagan Empire.[1] In addition to the personal restrictions which grew necessarily out of the Catholic doctrines concerning divorce, and concerning the subordination of the weaker sex, we find numerous and stringent enactments, which rendered it impossible for women to succeed to any considerable amount of property, and which almost reduced them to the alternative of marriage or a nunnery.[2] The complete inferiority of the sex was continually maintained by the law; and that generous public opinion which in Rome had frequently revolted against the injustice done to girls, in depriving them of the greater part of the inheritance of their fathers, totally disappeared. Wherever the canon law has been the basis of legislation, we find laws of succession sacrificing the interests of daughters and of wives,[3] and a state of public opinion which has been formed and regulated by these laws; nor was any serious attempt made to abolish them till the

---

[1] Even in matters not relating to property, the position of women in feudalism was a low one. 'Tout mari,' says Beaumanoir, 'peut battre sa femme quand elle ne veut pas obéir à son commandement, ou quand elle le maudit, ou quand elle le dément, pourvu que ce soit modérément et sans que mort s'ensuive,' quoted by Legouvé, p. 148. Contrast with this the saying of the elder Cato: 'A man who beats his wife or his children lays impious hands on that which is most holy and most sacred in the world.' — Plutarch, *Marcus Cato*.

[2] See Legouvé, pp. 29–38; Maine's *Ancient Law*, pp. 154–159.

[3] 'No society which preserves any tincture of Christian institutions is likely to restore to married women the personal liberty conferred on them by the middle Roman law: but the proprietary disabilities of married females stand on quite a different basis from their personal incapacities, and it is by keeping alive and consolidating the former that the expositors of the canon law have deeply injured civilisation. There are many vestiges of a struggle between the secular and ecclesiastical principles; but the canon law nearly everywhere prevailed.'— Maine's *Ancient Law*, p. 158. I may observe that the Russian law was early very favourable to the proprietary rights of married women. See a remarkable letter in the *Memoirs of the Princess Daschkaw* (edited by Mrs. Bradford: London, 1840), vol. ii. p. 404.

close of the last century. The French revolutionists, though rejecting the proposal of Siéyès and Condorcet to accord political emancipation to women, established at least an equal succession of sons and daughters, and thus initiated a great reformation of both law and opinion, which sooner or later must traverse the world.

In their efforts to raise the standard of purity, the Christian teachers derived much assistance from the incursions and the conquests of the barbarians. The dissolution of vast retinues of slaves, the suspension of most public games, and the general impoverishment that followed the invasions, were all favourable to female virtue; and in this respect the various tribes of barbarians, however violent and lawless, were far superior to the more civilised community. Tacitus, in a very famous work, had long before pourtrayed in the most flattering colours the purity of the Germans. Adultery, he said, was very rare among them. The adulteress was driven from the house with shaven hair, and beaten ignominiously through the village. Neither youth, nor beauty, nor wealth could enable a woman who was known to have sinned to secure a husband. Polygamy was restricted to the princes, who looked upon a plurality of wives rather as a badge of dignity than as a gratification of the passions. Mothers invariably gave suck to their own children. Infanticide was forbidden. Widows were not allowed to re-marry. The men feared captivity, much more for their wives than for themselves; they believed that a sacred and prophetic gift resided in women; they consulted them as oracles, and followed their counsels.[1]

It is generally believed, and it is not improbable, that Tacitus in this work intended to reprove the dissolute habits of his fellow-countrymen, and considerably over-coloured the virtue of the barbarians. Of the substantial justice, however,

---

[1] *Germania*, cap. ix. xviii.-xx.

of his picture we have much evidence.   Salvian, who, about
three centuries later, witnessed and described the manners of
the barbarians who had triumphed over the Empire, attested
in the strongest language the contrast which their chastity
presented to the vice of those whom they had subdued.[1]   The
Scandinavian mythology abounds in legends exhibiting the
clear sentiment of the heathen tribes on the subject of purity,
and the awful penalties threatened in the next world against
the seducers.[2]   The barbarian women were accustomed to practise medicine and to interpret dreams, and they also very
frequently accompanied their husbands to battle, rallied their
broken forces, and even themselves took part in the fight.[3]
Augustus had discovered that it was useless to keep barbarian chiefs as hostages, and that the one way of securing
the fidelity of traitors was by taking their wives, for these,
at least, were never sacrificed.   Instances of female heroism
are said to have occurred among the conquered nations which
might rival the most splendid in Roman annals.   When Marius had vanquished an army of the Teutons, their wives
besought the conqueror to permit them to become the servants of the Vestal Virgins, in order that their honour, at
least, might be secure in slavery.   Their request was refused,
and that night they all perished by their own hands.[4]   A
powerful noble once solicited the hand of a Galatian lady
named Camma, who, faithful to her husband, resisted all his
entreaties.   Resolved at any hazard to succeed, he caused her
husband to be assassinated, and when she took refuge in the
temple of Diana, and enrolled herself among the priestesses,
he sent noble after noble to induce her to relent.   After
a time, he ventured himself into her presence.   She feigned

---

[1] *De Gubernatione Dei.*
[2] See, for these legends, Mal-
let's *Northern Antiquities.*
[3] Tacitus, *Germ.* 9; *Hist.* iv.
18; Xiphilin. lxxi. 3; Amm.

Marcellinus, xv. 12; Vopiscus,
Aurelianus; Florus, iii. 3.
[4] Valer. Max. vi. 1; Hieron.
Ep. cxxiii.

a willingness to yield, but told him it was first necessary to make a libation to the goddess. She appeared as a priestess before the altar, bearing in her hand a cup of wine, which she had poisoned. She drank half of it herself, handed the remainder to her guilty lover, and when he had drained the cup to the dregs, burst into a fierce thanksgiving, that she had been permitted to avenge, and was soon to rejoin her murdered husband.[1] Another and still more remarkable instance of conjugal fidelity was furnished by a Gaulish woman named Epponina. Her husband, Julius Sabinus, had rebelled against Vespasian; he was conquered, and might easily have escaped to Germany, but could not bear to abandon his young wife. He retired to a villa of his own, concealed himself in subterranean cellars that were below it, and instructed a freedman to spread the report that he had committed suicide, while, to account for the disappearance of his body, he set fire to the villa. Epponina, hearing of the suicide, for three days lay prostrate on the ground without eating. At length the freedman came to her, and told her that the suicide was feigned. She continued her lamentations by day, but visited her husband by night. She became with child, but owing, it is said, to an ointment, she succeeded in concealing her state from her friends. When the hour of parturition was at hand, she went alone into the cellar, and without any assistance or attendance was delivered of twins, whom she brought up underground. For nine years she fulfilled her task, when Sabinus was discovered, and, to the lasting disgrace of Vespasian, was executed, in spite of the supplications of his wife, who made it her last request that she might be permitted to die with him.[2]

The moral purity of the barbarians was of a kind alto

---

[1] Plutarch, *De Mulier. Virt.*

[2] Plutarch, *Amatorius*; Xiphi-nn. lxvi. 16; Tacit. *Hist.* iv. 67.

The name of this heroic wife is given in three different forms.

gether different from that which the ascetic movement
inculcated. It was concentrated exclusively upon marriage.
It showed itself in a noble conjugal fidelity; but it was
little fitted for a life of celibacy, and did not, as we have
seen, prevent excessive disorders among the priesthood. The
practice of polygamy among the barbarian kings was also
for some centuries unchecked, or at least unsuppressed, by
Christianity. The kings Caribert and Chilperic had both
many wives at the same time.[1] Clotaire married the sister
of his first wife during the lifetime of the latter, who, on the
intention of the king being announced, is reported to have
said, 'Let my lord do what seemeth good in his sight, only
let thy servant live in thy favour.'[2] Theodebert, whose
general goodness of character is warmly extolled by the
episcopal historian, abandoned his first wife on account of an
atrocious crime which she had committed; took, during her
lifetime, another, to whom he had previously been betrothed;
and upon the death of this second wife, and while the first
was still living, took a third, whom, however, at a later
period he murdered.[3] St. Columbanus was expelled from
Gaul chiefly on account of his denunciations of the polygamy
of King Thierry.[4] Dagobert had three wives, as well as a
multitude of concubines.[5] Charlemagne himself had at the
same time two wives, and he indulged largely in concubines.[6] After this period examples of this nature became
rare. The Popes and the bishops exercised a strict supervision over domestic morals, and strenuously, and in most
cases successfully, opposed the attempts of kings and nobles
to repudiate their wives.

---

[1] On the polygamy of the first,
see Greg. Tur. iv. 26; on the
polygamy of Chilperic, Greg. Tur.
iv. 28; v. 14.
[2] Greg. Tur. iv. 3.
[3] Ibid. iii. 25–27, 36.
[4] Fredegarius, xxxvi.

[5] Ibid. lx.
[6] Eginhardus, *Vit. Kar. Mag.*
xviii. Charlemagne had, according to Eginhard, four wives, but, as
far as I can understand, only two
at the same time.

But, notwithstanding these startling facts, there can be
no doubt that the general purity of the barbarians was from
the first superior to that of the later Romans, and it appears
in many of their laws. It has been very happily observed,[1]
that the high value placed on this virtue is well illustrated
by the fact that in the Salic code, while a charge of cowardice
falsely brought against a man was only punished by a fine
of three solidi, a charge of unchastity falsely brought against
a woman was punished by a fine of forty-five. The Teutonic
sentiment was shown in a very stern legislation against
adultery and rape,[2] and curiously minute precautions were
sometimes taken to guard against them. A law of the
Spanish Visigoths prohibited surgeons from bleeding any
free woman except in the presence of her husband, of her
nearest relative, or at least of some properly appointed
witness, and a Salic law imposed a fine of fifteen pieces of
gold upon any one who improperly pressed her hand.[3]

Under the influence of Christianity, assisted by the barbarians, a vast change passed gradually over the world. The
vice we are considering was probably more rare; it certainly
assumed less extravagant forms, and it was screened from
observation with a new modesty. The theory of morals had
become clearer, and the practice was somewhat improved.
The extreme grossness of literature had disappeared, and the
more glaring violations of marriage were always censured
and often repressed. The penitential discipline, and the
exhortations of the pulpit, diffused abroad an immeasurably
higher sense of the importance of purity than Pagan antiquity had known. St. Gregory the Great, following in the
steps of some Pagan philosophers,[4] strenuously urged upon

---

[1] Smyth's *Lectures on Modern History*, vol. i. pp. 61–62.

[2] Milman's *Hist. of Latin Christianity*, vol. i. p. 363; Legouvé, *Hist. Morale des Femmes*, p. 57.

[3] See, on these laws. Lord Kames *On Women*; Legouvé, p. 57.

[4] Favorinus had strongly urged it. (Aul. Gell. *Noct.* xii. 1.)

mothers the duty of themselves suckling their children; and many minute and stringent precepts were made against extravagances of dress and manners. The religious institutions of Greece and Asia Minor, which had almost conse crated prostitution, were for ever abolished, and the courtesan sank into a lower stage of degradation.

Besides these changes, the duty of reciprocal fidelity in marriage was enforced with a new earnestness. The contrast between the levity with which the frailty of men has in most ages been regarded, and the extreme severity with which women who have been guilty of the same offence have generally been treated, forms one of the most singular anomalies in moral history, and appears the more remarkable when we remember that the temptation usually springs from the sex which is so readily pardoned; that the sex which is visited with such crushing penalties is proverbially the most weak; and that, in the case of women, but not in the case of men, the vice is very commonly the result of the most abject misery and poverty. For this disparity of censure several reasons have been assigned. The offence can be more surely and easily detected, and therefore more certainly punished, in the case of women than of men; and, as the duty of providing for his children falls upon the father, the introduction into the family of children who are not his own is a special injury to him, while illegitimate children who do not spring from adultery will probably, on account of their father having entered into no compact to support them, ultimately become criminals or paupers, and therefore a burden to society.[1] It may be added, I think, that several causes render the observance of this virtue more difficult for one sex than for the other; that its violation, when every allowance has been made for the moral degradation which is a result of

---

[1] These are the reasons given by Malthus, *On Population*, book iii. ch. ii.

the existing condition of public opinion, is naturally more profoundly prejudicial to the character of women than of men; and also that much of our feeling on these subjects is due to laws and moral systems which were formed by men, and were in the first instance intended for their own protection.

The passages in the Fathers, asserting the equality of the obligation imposed upon both sexes, are exceedingly unequivocal; [1] and although the doctrine itself had been anticipated by Seneca and Plutarch, it had probably never before, and it has never since, been so fully realised as in the early Church. It cannot, however, be said that the conquest has been retained. At the present day, although the standard of morals is far higher than in Pagan Rome, it may be questioned whether the inequality of the censure which is bestowed upon the two sexes is not as great as in the days of Paganism, and that inequality is continually the cause of the most shameful and the most pitiable injustice. In one respect, indeed, a great retrogression resulted from chivalry, and long survived its decay. The character of the seducer, and especially of the passionless seducer who pursues his career simply as a kind of sport, and under the influence of no stronger motive than vanity or a spirit of adventure, has been glorified and idealised in the popular literature of Christendom in a manner to which we can find no parallel in antiquity. When we reflect that the object of such a man is by the coldest and most deliberate treachery to blast the

---

[1] St. Augustine (*De Conj. Adult.* ii. 19) maintains that adultery is even more criminal in the man than in the woman. St. Jerome has an impressive passage on the subject: 'Aliæ sunt leges Cæsarum, aliæ Christi; aliud Papianus, aliud Paulus nostri præcepit. Apud illos viris impudicitiæ fræna laxantur et solo stupro atque adulterio condemnato passim per lupanaria et ancillulas libido permittitur, quasi culpam dignitas faciat non voluntas. Apud nos quod non licet feminis æque non licet viris; et eadem servitus pari conditione censetur.'—*Ep.* lxxvii. St. Chrysostom writes in a similar strain.

lives of innocent women; when we compare the levity of his motive with the irreparable injury he inflicts; and when we remember that he can only deceive his victim by persuading her to love him, and can only ruin her by persuading her to trust him, it must be owned that it would be difficult to conceive a cruelty more wanton and more heartless, or a character combining more numerous elements of infamy and of dishonour. That such a character should for many centuries have been the popular ideal of a considerable section of literature, and the boast of numbers who most plume themselves upon their honour, is assuredly one of the most mournful facts in history, and it represents a moral deflection certainly not less than was revealed in ancient Greece by the position that was assigned to the courtesan.

The fundamental truth, that the same act can never be at once venial for a man to demand, and infamous for a woman to accord, though nobly enforced by the early Christians, has not passed into the popular sentiment of Christendom. The mystical character, however, which the Church imparted to marriage has been extremely influential. Partly by raising it into a sacrament, and partly by representing it as, in some mysterious and not very definable sense, an image of the union of Christ with His Church, a feeling was fostered that a lifelong union of one man and one woman is, under all circumstances, the single form of intercourse between the sexes which is not illegitimate; and this conviction has acquired the force of a primal moral intuition.

There can, I think, be little doubt that, in the stringency with which it is usually laid down, it rests not upon the law of nature, but upon positive law, although unassisted nature is sufficient to lead men many steps in its direction. Considering the subject simply in the light of unaided reason, two rules comprise the whole duty of man. He must abstain from whatever injures happiness or degrades character

Under the first head, he must include the more remote as well as the immediate consequences of his act. He must consider how his partner will be affected by the union, the light in which society will view the connection, the probable position of the children to be born, the effect of these births, and also the effect of his example upon the well-being of society at large. Some of the elements of this calculation vary in different stages of society. Thus, public opinion in one age will reprobate, and therefore punish, connections which, in another age, are fully sanctioned; and the probable position of the children, as well as the effect of the births upon society, will depend greatly upon particular and national circumstances.

Under the second head is comprised the influence of this intercourse in clouding or developing the moral feelings, lowering or elevating the tone of character, exciting or allaying the aberrations of the imagination, incapacitating men for pure affections or extending their range, making the animal part of our nature more or less predominant. We know, by the intuition of our moral nature, that this predominance is always a degraded, though it is not always an unhappy, condition. We also know that it is a law of our being, that powerful and beautiful affections, which had before been latent, are evoked in some particular forms of union, while other forms of union are peculiarly fitted to deaden the affections and to pervert the character.

In these considerations we have ample grounds for maintaining that the lifelong union of one man and of one woman should be the normal or dominant type of intercourse between the sexes. We can prove that it is on the whole most conducive to the happiness, and also to the moral elevation, of all parties. But beyond this point it would, I conceive, be impossible to advance, except by the assistance of a special revelation. It by no means follows that because this should be the dominant type it should be the only one, or that the interests of society demand that all connections should be forced into the same die. Connections, which were confessedly only for a few years, have always subsisted side by side with permanent marriages; and in periods when pub-lic opinion, acquiescing in their propriety, inflicts no excom-munication on one or both of the partners, when these partners are not living the demoralising and degrading life which accompanies the consciousness of guilt, and when proper provision is made for the children who are born, it would be, I believe, impossible to prove, by the light of simple and unassisted reason, that such connections should be invariably condemned. It is extremely important, both for the happiness and for the moral well-being of men, that life-long unions should not be effected simply under the imperious prompting of a blind appetite. There are always multitudes who, in the period of their lives when their passions are most strong, are incapable of supporting children in their own social rank, and who would therefore injure society by marrying in it, but are nevertheless perfectly capable of securing an honourable career for their illegitimate children in the lower social sphere to which these would naturally belong. Under the conditions I have mentioned, these connections are not injurious, but beneficial, to the weaker partner; they soften the differences of rank, they stimulate social habits, and they do not produce upon character the degrading effect of promiscuous intercourse, or upon society the injurious effects of imprudent marriages, one or other of which will multiply in their absence. In the immense variety of circumstances and characters, cases will always appear in which, on utilitarian grounds, they might seem advisable.

It is necessary to dwell upon such considerations as these, if we would understand the legislation of the Pagan Empire or the changes that were effected by Christianity. The legislators of the Empire distinctly recognised these connections, and made it a main object to authorise, dignify, and regulate them. The unlimited licence of divorce practically included them under the name of marriage, while that name sheltered them from stigma, and prevented many of the gravest evils of unauthorised unions. The word concubine also, which in the Republic had the same signification as among ourselves, represented in the Empire a strictly legal union—an innovation which was chiefly due to Augustus, and was doubtless intended as part of the legislation against celibacy, and also, it may be, as a corrective of the licentious habits that were general. This union was in essentials merely a form of marriage, for he who, having a concubine, took to himself either a wife or another concubine, was legally guilty of adultery. Like the commonest form of marriage, it was consummated without any ceremony, and was dissoluble at will. Its peculiarities were that it was contracted between men of patrician rank and freedwomen, who were forbidden by law to intermarry; that the concubine, though her position was perfectly recognised and honourable, did not share the rank of her partner, that she brought no dowry, and that her children followed her rank, and were excluded from the rank and the inheritance of their father.[1]

Against these notions Christianity declared a direct and implacable warfare, which was imperfectly reflected in the civil legislation, but appeared unequivocally in the writings of the Fathers, and in most of the decrees of the Councils.[2]

---

[1] See Troplong, *Influence du Christianisme sur le Droit*, pp. 239–251.

[2] We find, however, traces of a toleration of the Roman type of concubine in Christianity for some time. Thus, a Council of Toledo decreed: 'Si quis habens uxorem fidelis concubinam habeat non com-municet. Cæterum is qui non habet uxorem et pro uxore concubinam habet a communione non repellatur, tantum ut unius mulieris, aut uxoris aut concubinæ ut ei placuerit, sit conjunctione contentus.'— 1 *Can.* 17. St. Isidore said: 'Christiano non dicam plurimas sed nec duas simul habere licitum est, nisi unam

It taught, as a religious dogma, invariable, inflexible, and independent of all utilitarian calculations, that all forms of intercourse of the sexes, other than lifelong unions, were criminal. By teaching men to regard this doctrine as axiomatic, and therefore inflicting severe social penalties and deep degradation on transient connections, it has profoundly modified even their utilitarian aspect, and has rendered them in most countries furtive and disguised. There is probably no other branch of ethics which has been so largely determined by special dogmatic theology, and there is none which would be so deeply affected by its decay.

As a part of the same movement, the purely civil marriage of the later Pagan Empire was gradually replaced by religious marriages. There is a manifest propriety in invoking a divine benediction upon an act which forms so important an epoch in life, and the mingling of a religious ceremony impresses a deeper sense of the solemnity of the contract. The essentially religious and even mystical character imparted by Christianity to marriage rendered the consecration peculiarly natural, but it was only very gradually that it came to be looked upon as absolutely necessary. As I have already noticed, it was long dispensed with in the marriage of slaves; and even in the case of freemen, though generally performed, it was not made compulsory till the tenth century.[1] In addition to its primary object of sanctifying marriage, it became in time a powerful

---

tantum aut uxorem, aut certo loco uxoris, si conjux deest, concubinam.' —*Apud Gratianum*, diss. 4. Quoted by Natalis Alexander, *Hist. Eccles.* Sæc. I. diss. 29. Mr. Lea (*Hist. of Sacerdotal Celibacy*, pp. 203–205) has devoted an extremely interesting note to tracing the history of the word concubine through the middle ages. He shows that even up to the thirteenth century a concubine was not necessarily an abandoned woman. The term was applied to marriages that were real, but not officially recognised. Coleridge notices a remarkable instance of the revival of this custom in German history.—*Notes on English Divines* (ed. 1853), vol. i. p. 221.

[1] Legouvé, p. 199.

instrument in securing the authority of the priesthood, who were able to compel men to submit to the conditions they imposed in the formation of the most important contract of life; and the modern authorisation of civil marriages, by diminishing greatly the power of the Catholic priesthood over domestic life, has been one of the most severe blows ecclesiastical influence has undergone.

The absolute sinfulness of divorce was at the same time strenuously maintained by the Councils, which in this, as in many other points, differed widely from the civil law. Constantine restricted it to three cases of crime on the part of the husband, and three on the part of the wife; but the habits of the people were too strong for his enactments, and, after one or two changes in the law, the full latitude of divorce reappeared in the Justinian Code. The Fathers, on the other hand, though they hesitated a little about the case of a divorce which followed an act of adultery on the part of the wife,[1] had no hesitation whatever in pronouncing all other divorces to be criminal, and periods of penitential discipline were imposed upon Christians who availed themselves of the privileges of the civil law.[2] For many centuries this duality of legislation continued. The barbarian laws restricted divorce by imposing severe fines on those who repudiated their wives. Charlemagne pronounced divorce to be criminal, but did not venture to make it penal, and he practised it himself. On the other hand, the Church threatened with excommunication, and in some cases actually launched its thunders against, those who were guilty of it. It was only in the twelfth century that the victory was

---

[1] See some curious passages in Troplong, pp. 222–223. The Fathers seem to have thought dissolution of marriage was not lawful on account of the adultery of the husband, but that it was not absolutely unlawful, though not commendable, for a husband whose wife had committed adultery to re-marry.

[2] Some of the great charities of Fabiola were performed as penances, on account of her crime in availing herself of the legislative permission of divorce.

definitely achieved, and the civil law, adopting the principle of the canon law, prohibited all divorce.[1]

I do not propose in the present work to examine how far this total prohibition has been for the happiness or the moral well-being of men. I will simply observe that, though it is now often defended, it was not originally imposed in Christian nations, upon utilitarian grounds, but was based upon the sacramental character of marriage, upon the belief that marriage is the special symbol of the perpetual union of Christ with His Church, and upon a well-known passage in the Gospels. The stringency of the Catholic doctrine, which forbids the dissolution of marriage even in the case of adultery, has been considerably relaxed by modern legislation, and there can, I think, be little doubt that further steps will yet be taken in the same direction; but the vast change that was effected in both practice and theory since the unlimited licence of the Pagan Empire must be manifest to all.

It was essential, or at least very important, that a union which was so solemn and so irrevocable should be freely contracted. The sentiment of the Roman patriots towards the close of the Republic was that marriage should be regarded as a means of providing children for the State, and should be entered into as a matter of duty with that view, and the laws of Augustus had imposed many disqualifications on those who abstained from it. Both of these inducements to marriage passed away under the influence of Christianity. The popular sentiment disappeared with the decline of civic virtues. The laws were rescinded under the influence of the ascetic enthusiasm which made men regard the state of celibacy as pre-eminently holy.

There was still one other important condition to be attained by theologians in order to realise their ideal type of

[1] Laboulaye, *Recherches sur la Condition civile et politique des Femmes*, pp. 152–158.

marriage. It was to prevent the members of the Chuicn from intermarrying with those whose religious opinions differed from their own. Mixed marriages, it has been truly said, may do more than almost any other influence to assuage the rancour and the asperity of sects, but it must be added that a considerable measure of tolerance must have been already attained before they become possible. In a union in which each partner believes and realises that the other is doomed to an eternity of misery there can be no real happiness, no sympathy, no trust; and a domestic agreement that some of the children should be educated in one religion and some in the other would be impossible when each parent believed it to be an agreement that some children should be doomed to hell.

The domestic unhappiness arising from differences of belief was probably almost or altogether unknown in the world before the introduction of Christianity; for, although differences of opinion may have before existed, the same momentous consequences were not attached to them. It has been the especial bane of periods of great religious change, such as the conversion of the Roman Empire, or the Reformation, or our own day when far more serious questions than those which agitated the sixteenth century are occupying the attention of a large proportion of thinkers and scholars, and when the deep and widening chasm between the religious opinions of most highly educated men, and of the immense majority of women, is painfully apparent. While a multitude of scientific discoveries, critical and historical researches, and educational reforms have brought thinking men face to face with religious problems of extreme importance, women have been almost absolutely excluded from their influence. Their minds are usually by nature less capable than those of men of impartiality and suspense, and the almost complete omission from female education of those studies which most discipline and strengthen the intellect increases the difference, while at the same time it has been usually made a main object to imbue them with a passionate faith in traditional opinions, and to preserve them from all contact with opposing views. But contracted knowledge and imperfect sympathy are not the sole fruits of this education. It has always been the peculiarity of a certain kind of theological teaching that it inverts all the normal principles of judgment, and absolutely destroys intellectual diffidence. On other subjects we find, if not a respect for honest conviction, at least some sense of the amount of knowledge that is requisite to entitle men to express an opinion on grave controversies. A complete ignorance of the subject-matter of a dispute restrains the confidence of dogmatism; and an ignorant person, who is aware that, by much reading and thinking in spheres of which he has himself no knowledge, his educated neighbour has modified or rejected opinions which that ignorant person had been taught, will, at least if he is a man of sense or modesty, abstain from compassionating the benighted condition of his more instructed friend. But on theological questions this has never been so. Unfaltering belief being taught as the first of duties, and all doubt being usually stigmatised as criminal or damnable, a state of mind is formed to which we find no parallel in other fields. Many men and most women, though completely ignorant of the very rudiments of biblical criticism, historical research, or scientific discoveries, though they have never read a single page, or understood a single proposition of the writings of those whom they condemn, and have absolutely no rational knowledge either of the arguments by which their faith is defended, or of those by which it has been impugned, will nevertheless adjudicate with the utmost confidence upon every polemical question; denounce, hate, pity, or pray for the conversion of all who dissent from what they have been taught; assume, as a matter beyond the faintest possibility of doubt, that the opinions they have received without enquiry must be true, and that the opinions which others have arrived at by enquiry must be false, and make it a main object of their lives to assail what they call heresy in every way in their power, except by examining the grounds on which it rests. It is probable that the great majority of voices that swell the clamour against every book which is regarded as heretical are the voices of those who would deem it criminal even to open that book, or to enter into any real, searching, and impartial investigation of the subject to which it relates. Innumerable pulpits support this tone of thought, and represent, with a fervid rhetoric well fitted to excite the nerves and imaginations of women, the deplorable condition of all who deviate from a certain type of opinions or of emotions; a blind propagandism or a secret wretchedness penetrates into countless households, poisoning the peace of families, chilling the mutual confidence of husband and wife, adding immeasurably to the difficulties which every searcher into truth has to encounter, and diffusing far and wide intellectual timidity, disingenuousness, and hypocrisy.

These domestic divisions became very apparent in the period of the conversion of the Roman Empire; and a natural desire to guard intact the orthodoxy and zeal of the converts, and to prevent a continual discordance, stimulated the Fathers in their very vehement denunciations of all mixed marriages. We may also trace in these denunciations the outline of a very singular doctrine, which was afterwards suffered to fall into obscurity, but was revived in the last century in England in a curious and learned work of the nonjuror Dodwell.[1]   The union of Christ and His Church

---

[1] 'A discourse concerning the obligation to marry within the true communion, following from their style (*sic*) of being called a holy seed.' This rare discourse is appended to a sermon against mixed marriages by Leslie. (London, 1702.) The reader may find something about Dodwell in Macaulay's *Hist. of England*, ch. xiv.; but Macaulay, who does not appear to have known Dodwell's masterpiece—his dissertation *De Paucitate Martyrum*, which is one of the finest

had been represented as a marriage; and this image was not regarded as a mere metaphor or comparison, but as intimating a mysterious unity, which, though not susceptible of any very clear definition, was not on that account the less real. Christians were the 'limbs of Christ,' and for them to join themselves in marriage with those who were not of the Christian fold was literally, it was said, a species of adultery or fornication. The intermarriage of the Israelites, the chosen seed of the ancient world, with the Gentiles, had been described in the Old Testament as an act of impurity; [1] and in the opinion of some, at least, of the Fathers, the Christian community occupied towards the unbelievers a position analogous to that which the Jews had occupied towards the Gentiles. St. Cyprian denounced the crime of those 'who prostitute the limbs of Christ in marriage with the Gentiles.' [2] Tertullian described the intermarriage as fornication; [3] and after the triumph of the Church, the intermarriage of Jews and Christians was made a capital offence, and was stigmatised by the law as adultery. [4] The civil law did not prohibit the orthodox from intermarrying with heretics, but many councils in strong terms denounced such marriages as criminal.

The extreme sanctity attributed to virginity, the absolute condemnation of all forms of sexual connection other than marriage, and the formation and gradual realisation of the Christian conception of marriage as a permanent union of a

---

specimens of criticism of his time— and who only knew the discourse on marriages by extracts, has, I think, done him considerable injustice.

[1] Dodwell relies mainly upon this fact, and especially upon Ezra's having treated these marriages as essentially null.

[2] 'Jungere cum infidelibus vinculum matrimonii, prostituere gentilibus membra Christi.'—Cyprian,

De Lapsis.

[3] 'Hæc cum ita sint, fideles Gentilium matrimonia subeuntes stupri reos esse constat, et arcendos ab omni communicatione fraternitatis.'—Tert. *Ad Uxor.* ii. 3.

[4] See on this law, and on the many councils which condemned the marriage of orthodox with heretics, Bingham, *Antiq.* xxii. 2, §§ 1–2.

man and woman of the same religious opinions, consecrated by solemn religious services, carrying with it a deep religious signification, and dissoluble only by death, were the most obvious signs of Christian influence in the sphere of ethics we are examining. Another very impcrtant result of the new religion was to raise to a far greater honour than they had previously possessed, the qualities in which women peculiarly excel.

There are few more curious subjects of enquiry than the distinctive differences between the sexes, and the manner in which those differences have affected the ideal types of different ages, nations, philosophies, and religions. Physically, men have the indisputable superiority in strength, and women in beauty. Intellectually, a certain inferiority of the female sex can hardly be denied when we remember how almost exclusively the foremost places in every department of science, literature, and art have been occupied by men, how infinitesimally small is the number of women who have shown in any form the very highest order of genius, how many of the greatest men have achieved their greatness in defiance of the most adverse circumstances, and how completely women have failed in obtaining the first position, even in music or painting, for the cultivation of which their circumstances would appear most propitious. It is as impossible to find a female Raphael, or a female Handel, as a female Shakspeare or Newton. Women are intellectually more desultory and volatile than men; they are more occupied with particular instances than with general principles; they judge rather by intuitive perceptions than by deliberate reasoning or past experience. They are, however, usually superior to men in nimbleness and rapidity of thought, and in the gift of tact or the power of seizing speedily and faithfully the finer inflexions of feeling, and they have therefore often attained very great eminence in conversation, as letter-writers, as actresses, and as novelists.

Morally, the general superiority of women over men, is, I think, unquestionable. If we take the somewhat coarse and inadequate criterion of police statistics, we find that, while the male and female populations are nearly the same in number, the crimes committed by men are usually rather more than five times as numerous as those committed by women;[1] and although it may be justly observed that men, as the stronger sex, and the sex upon whom the burden of supporting the family is thrown, have more temptations than women, it must be remembered, on the other hand, that extreme poverty which verges upon starvation is most common among women, whose means of livelihood are most restricted, and whose earnings are smallest and most precarious. Self-sacrifice is the most conspicuous element of a virtuous and religious character, and it is certainly far less common among men than among women, whose whole lives are usually spent in yielding to the will and consulting the pleasures of another. There are two great departments of virtue : the impulsive, or that which springs spontaneously from the emotions; and the deliberative, or that which is performed in obedience to the sense of duty ; and in both of these I imagine women are superior to men. Their sensibility is greater, they are more chaste both in thought and act, more tender to the erring, more compassionate to the suffering, more affectionate to all about them. On the other hand, those who have traced the course of the wives of the poor, and of many who, though in narrow circumstances,

---

[1] Many curious statistics illustrating this fact are given by M. Bonneville de Marsangy—a Portuguese writer who was counsellor of the Imperial Court at Paris—in his *Étude sur la Moralité comparée de la Femme et de l'Homme.* (Paris, 1862.) The writer would have done better if he had not maintained, in lawyer fashion, that the statistics of crime are absolutely decisive on the question of the comparative morality of the sexes, and also, if he had not thought it due to his official position to talk in a rather grotesque strain about the regeneration and glorification of the sex in the person of the Empress Eugénie.

can hardly be called poor, will probably admit that in no
other class do we so often find entire lives spent in daily persistent self-denial, in the patient endurance of countless trials,
in the ceaseless and deliberate sacrifice of their own enjoyments to the well-being or the prospects of others. Women,
however, though less prone than men to intemperance and
brutality, are in general more addicted to the petty forms of
vanity, jealousy, spitefulness, and ambition, and they are
also inferior to men in active courage. In the courage of
endurance they are commonly superior; but their passive
courage is not so much fortitude which bears and defies, as
resignation which bears and bends. In the ethics of intellect
they are decidedly inferior. To repeat an expression I have
already employed, women very rarely love truth, though
they love passionately what they call 'the truth,' or opinions
they have received from others, and hate vehemently those
who differ from them. They are little capable of impartiality
or of doubt; their thinking is chiefly a mode of feeling;
though very generous in their acts, they are rarely generous
in their opinions or in their judgments. They persuade
rather than convince, and value belief rather as a source of
consolation than as a faithful expression of the reality of
things. They are less capable than men of perceiving qualifying circumstances, of admitting the existence of elements
of good in systems to which they are opposed, of distinguishing the personal character of an opponent from the opinions
he maintains. Men lean most to justice and women to
mercy. Men excel in energy, self-reliance, perseverance, and
magnanimity; women in humility, gentleness, modesty, and
endurance. The realising imagination which causes us to
pity and to love is more sensitive in women than in men,
and it is especially more capable of dwelling on the unseen.
Their religious or devotional realisations are incontestably
more vivid; and it is probable that, while a father is most
moved by the death of a child in his presence, a mother

generally feels most the death of a child in some distant land. But, though more intense, the sympathies of women are commonly less wide than those of men. Their imaginations individualise more; their affections are, in consequence, concentrated rather on leaders than on causes; and if they care for a great cause, it is generally because it is represented by a great man, or connected with some one whom they love In politics, their enthusiasm is more naturally loyalty than patriotism In history, they are even more inclined than men to dwell exclusively upon biographical incidents or characteristics as distinguished from the march of general causes. In benevolence, they excel in charity, which alleviates individual suffering, rather than in philanthropy, which deals with large masses and is more frequently employed in preventing than in allaying calamity.

It was a remark of Winckelmann that 'the supreme beauty of Greek art is rather male than female;' and the justice of this remark has been amply corroborated by the greater knowledge we have of late years attained of the works of the Phidian period, in which art achieved its highest perfection, and in which, at the same time, force and freedom, and masculine grandeur, were its pre-eminent characteristics. A similar observation may be made of the moral ideal of which ancient art was simply the expression. In antiquity the virtues that were most admired were almost exclusively those which are distinctively masculine. Courage, self-assertion, magnanimity, and, above all, patriotism, were the leading features of the ideal type; and chastity, modesty, and charity, the gentler and the domestic virtues, which are especially feminine, were greatly undervalued. With the single exception of conjugal fidelity, none of the virtues that were very highly prized were virtues distinctively or pre-eminently feminine. With this exception, nearly all the most illustrious women of antiquity were illustrious chiefly because they overcame the natural conditions of their sex.

It is a characteristic fact that the favourite female ideal of the artists appears to have been the Amazon.[1] We may admire the Spartan mother, and the mother of the Gracchi, repressing every sign of grief when their children were sacrificed upon the altar of their country, we may wonder at the majestic courage of a Porcia and an Arria; but we extol them chiefly because, being women, they emancipated themselves from the frailty of their sex, and displayed an heroic fortitude worthy of the strongest and the bravest of men. We may bestow an equal admiration upon the noble devotion and charity of a St. Elizabeth of Hungary, or of a Mrs. Fry, but we do not admire them because they displayed these virtues, although they were women, for we feel that their virtues were of the kind which the female nature is most fitted to produce. The change from the heroic to the saintly ideal, from the ideal of Paganism to the ideal of Christianity, was a change from a type which was essentially male to one which was essentially feminine. Of all the great schools of philosophy no other reflected so faithfully the Roman conception of moral excellence as Stoicism, and the greatest Roman exponent of Stoicism summed up its character in a single sentence when he pronounced it to be beyond all other sects the most emphatically masculine.[2] On the other hand, an ideal type in which meekness, gentleness, patience, humility, faith, and love are the most prominent features, is not naturally male but female. A reason probably deeper than the historical ones which are commonly alleged, why sculpture has always been peculiarly Pagan and painting peculiarly Christian, may be found in the fact, that sculpture is especially suited to represent male beauty, or the beauty of strength, and painting female beauty, or the beauty of soft-

---

[1] See Pliny, *Hist. Nat.* xxxiv. 19.

[2] 'Tantum inter Stoicos, Serene, et ceteros sapientiam professos interesse, quantum inter fœminas et mares non immerito dixerim.'—*De Const. Sapientis*, cap. i.

ness; and that Pagan sentiment was chiefly a glorification of the masculine qualities of strength, and courage, and conscious virtue, while Christian sentiment is chiefly a glorification of the feminine qualities of gentleness, humility, and love. The painters whom the religious feeling of Christendom has recognised as the most faithful exponents of Christian sentiment have always been those who infused a large measure of feminine beauty even into their male characters; and we never, or scarcely ever, find that the same artist has been conspicuously successful in delineating both Christian and Pagan types. Michael Angelo, whose genius loved to expatiate on the sublimity of strength and defiance, failed signally in his representations of the Christian ideal; and Perugino was equally unsuccessful when he sought to pourtray the features of the heroes of antiquity.[1] The position that was gradually assigned to the Virgin as the female ideal in the belief and the devotion of Christendom, was a consecration or an expression of the new value that was attached to the feminine virtues.

The general superiority of women to men in the strength of their religious emotions, and their natural attraction to a religion which made personal attachment to its Founder its central duty, and which imparted an unprecedented dignity and afforded an unprecedented scope to their characteristic virtues, account for the very conspicuous position that female influence assumed in the great work of the conversion of the Roman Empire. In no other important movement of thought was it so powerful or so acknowledged. In the ages of

---

[1] This is well illustrated, on the one side, by the most repulsive representations of Christ, by Michael Angelo, in the great fresco in the Sistine Chapel (so inferior to the Christ of Orgagna, at Pisa, from which it was partly imitated), and in marble in the Minerva Church at Rome; and, on the other side, by the frescoes of Perugino, at Perugia, representing the great sages of Paganism. The figure of Cato, in the latter, almost approaches, as well as I remember, the type of St. John.

persecution female figures occupy many of the foremost places in the ranks of martyrdom, and Pagan and Christian writers alike attest the alacrity with which women flocked to the Church, and the influence they exercised in its favour over the male members of their families. The mothers of St. Augustine, St. Chrysostom, St. Basil, St. Gregory Nazianzen, and Theodoret, had all a leading part in the conversion of their sons. St. Helena, the mother of Constantine, Flacilla, the wife of Theodosius the Great, St. Pulcheria, the sister of Theodosius the Younger, and Placidia, the mother of Valentinian III., were among the most conspicuous defenders of the faith. In the heretical sects the same zeal was manifested, and Arius, Priscillian, and Montanus were all supported by troops of zealous female devotees. In the career of asceticism women took a part little if at all inferior to men, while in the organisation of the great work of charity they were pre-eminent. For no other field of active labour are women so admirably suited as for this; and although we may trace from the earliest period, in many creeds and ages, individual instances of their influence in allaying the sufferings of the distressed,[1] it may

---

[1] In that fine description of a virtuous woman which is ascribed to the mother of King Lemuel, we read: ' She stretcheth out her hand to the poor; yea, she reacheth forth her hands to the needy.' (Proverbs xxxi. 20.) I have already quoted from Xenophon the beautiful description of the Greek wife tending her sick slaves. So, too, Euripides represents the slaves of Alcestis gathering with tears around the bed of their dying mistress, who, even then, found some kind word for each, and, when she died, lamenting her as their second mother. (Eurip. *Alcest.*) In the servile war which desolated Sicily at the time of the Punic wars, we find a touching trait of the same kind. The revolt was provoked by the cruelties of a rich man, named Damophilus, and his wife, who were massacred with circumstances of great atrocity; but the slaves preserved their daughter entirely unharmed, for she had always made it her business to console them in their sorrow, and she had won the love of all. (Diodor. Sic. *Frag.* xxxiv.) So, too, Marcia, the wife of Cato, used to suckle her young slaves from her breast. (Plut. *Marc. Cato.*) I may add the well-known sentiment which

be truly said that their instinct and genius of charity had never before the dawn of Christianity obtained full scope for action. Fabiola, Paula, Melania, and a host of other noble ladies devoted their time and fortunes mainly to founding and extending vast institutions of charity, some of them of a kind before unknown in the world. The Empress Flacilla was accustomed to tend with her own hands the sick in the hospitals,[1] and a readiness to discharge such offices was deemed the first duty of a Christian wife.[2] From age to age the impulse thus communicated has been felt. There has been no period, however corrupt, there has been no Church, however superstitious, that has not been adorned by many Christian women devoting their entire lives to assuaging the sufferings of men; and the mission of charity thus instituted has not been more efficacious in diminishing the sum of human wretchedness, than in promoting the moral dignity of those by whom it was conducted.

Among the Collyridian heretics, women were admitted to the priesthood. Among the orthodox, although this honour was not bestowed upon them, they received a religious consecration, and discharged some minor ecclesiastical functions under the name of deaconesses.[3] This order may be traced to the Apostolic period.[4] It consisted of elderly virgins, who were set apart by a formal ordination, and were employed in assisting as catechists and attendants at the baptism of women, in visiting the sick, ministering to martyrs

---

Virgil puts in the mouth of Dido: 'Haud ignara mali miseris succurrere disco.' There are, doubtless, many other touches of the same kind in ancient literature, some of which may occur to my readers.

[1] Theodoret, v. 19.

[2] See the beautiful description of the functions of a Christian woman in the second book of Ter-

tullian, *Ad Uxorem.*

[3] See, upon the deaconesses, Bingham's *Christian Antiquities*, book ii. ch. 22, and Ludlow's *Woman's Work in the Church.* The latter author argues elaborately that the 'widows' were not the same as the deaconesses.

[4] Phœbe (Rom. xvi. 1) described as a διάκονος.

in prison, preserving order in the congregations, and accompanying and presenting women who desired an interview
with the bishop. It would appear, from the evidence of
some councils, that abuses gradually crept into this institution,
and the deaconesses at last faded into simple nuns, but they
were still in existence in the East in the twelfth century.
Besides these, widows, when they had been but once married,
were treated with peculiar honour, and were made the
special recipients of the charity of the Church. Women
advanced in years, who, either from their single life or from
bereavement, have been left without any male protector in
the world, have always been peculiarly deserving of commiseration. With less strength, and commonly with less
means, and less knowledge of the world than men, they are
liable to contract certain peculiarities of mind and manner to
which an excessive amount of ridicule has been attached, and
age in most cases furnishes them with very little to
compensate for the charms of which it has deprived them.
The weight and dignity of matured wisdom, which make
the old age of one sex so venerable, are more rarely found
in that of the other, and even physical beauty is more
frequently the characteristic of an old man than of an old
woman. The Church laboured steadily to cast a halo of
reverence around this period of woman's life, and its religious
exercises have done very much to console and to occupy it.

In accordance with these ideas, the Christian legislators
contributed largely to improve the legal position of widows in
respect to property,[1] and Justinian gave mothers the guardian-

---

[1] A very able writer, who takes
on the whole an unfavourable
view of the influence of Christianity on legislation, says: 'The
provision for the widow was
attributable to the exertions of the
Church, which never relaxed its
solicitude for the interests of wives
surviving their husbands, winning,
perhaps, one of the most arduous
of its triumphs when, after exacting for two or three centuries an
express promise from the husband
at marriage to endow his wife,
it at last succeeded in engrafting
the principle of dower on the

ship of their children, destroying the Pagan rule that guardianship could only be legally exercised by men.[1] The usual subservience of the sex to ecclesiastical influence, the numerous instances of rich widows devoting their fortunes, and mothers their sons, to the Church, had no doubt some influence in securing the advocacy of the clergy; but these measures had a manifest importance in elevating the position of women who have had, in Christian lands, a great, though not, I think, altogether a beneficial influence, in the early education of their sons.

Independently of all legal enactments, the simple change of the ideal type by bringing specially feminine virtues into the forefront was sufficient to elevate and ennoble the sex. The commanding position of the mediæval abbesses, the great number of female saints, and especially the reverence bestowed upon the Virgin, had a similar effect. It is remarkable that the Jews, who, of the three great nations of antiquity, certainly produced in history and poetry the smallest number of illustrious women, should have furnished the world with its supreme female ideal, and it is also a striking illustration of the qualities which prove most attractive in woman that one of whom we know nothing except her gentleness and her sorrow should have exercised a magnetic power upon the world incomparably greater than was exercised by the most majestic female patriots of Paganism. Whatever may be thought of its theological propriety, there can be little doubt that the Catholic reverence for the Virgin has done much to elevate and purify the ideal of woman, and to soften the manners of men. It has had an influence which the worship of the Pagan goddesses could never possess, for these had been almost destitute of moral beauty, and especially of that kind of moral beauty which is peculiarly feminine.

---

customary law of all Western Europe.'—Maine's *Ancient Law*, p. 224.

[1] See Troplong, *Influence du Christianisme sur le Droit*, pp. 308–310.

It supplied in a great measure the redeeming and ennobling element in that strange amalgam of religious, licentious, and military feeling which was formed around women in the age of chivalry, and which no succeeding change of habit or belief has wholly destroyed.

It can hardly, I think, be questioned that in the great religious convulsions of the sixteenth century the feminine type followed Catholicism, while Protestantism inclined more to the masculine type. Catholicism alone retained the Virgin worship, which at once reflected and sustained the first. The skill with which it acts upon the emotions by music, and painting, and solemn architecture, and imposing pageantry, its tendency to appeal to the imagination rather than to the reason, and to foster modes of feeling rather than modes of thought, its assertion of absolute and infallible certainty, above all, the manner in which it teaches its votary to throw himself perpetually on authority, all tended in the same direction. It is the part of a woman to lean, it is the part of a man to stand. A religion which prescribes to the distracted mind unreasoning faith in an infallible Church, and to the troubled conscience an implicit trust in an absolving priesthood, has ever had an especial attraction to a feminine mind. A religion which recognises no authority between man and his Creator, which asserts at once the dignity and the duty of private judgment, and which, while deepening immeasurably the sense of individual responsibility, denudes religion of meretricious ornaments, and of most æsthetic aids, is pre-eminently a religion of men. Puritanism is the most masculine form that Christianity has yet assumed. Its most illustrious teachers differed from the Catholic saints as much in the moral type they displayed as in the system of doctrines they held. Catholicism commonly softens, while Protestantism strengthens, the character; but the softness of the first often degenerates into weakness, and the strength of the second into hardness. Sincerely Catholic nations are distinguished for their reverence, for their habitual and vivid perceptions of religious things, for the warmth of their emotions, for a certain amiability of disposition, and a certain natural courtesy and refinement of manner that are inexpressibly winning. Sincerely Protestant nations are distinguished for their love of truth, for their firm sense of duty, for the strength and the dignity of their character. Loyalty and humility, which are especially feminine, flourish chiefly in the first; liberty and self-assertion in the second. The first are most prone to superstition, and the second to fanaticism. Protestantism, by purifying and dignifying marriage, conferred a great benefit upon women; but it must be owned that neither in its ideal type, nor in the general tenor of its doctrines or devotions, is it as congenial to their nature as the religion it superseded.

Its complete suppression of the conventual system was also, I think, very far from a benefit to women or to the world. It would be impossible to conceive any institution more needed than one which would furnish a shelter for the many women who, from poverty, or domestic unhappiness, or other causes, find themselves cast alone and unprotected into the battle of life, which would secure them from the temptations to gross vice, and from the extremities of suffering, and would convert them into agents of active, organised, and intelligent charity. Such an institution would be almost free from the objections that may justly be urged against monasteries, which withdraw strong men from manual labour, and it would largely mitigate the difficulty of providing labour and means of livelihood for single women, which is one of the most pressing, in our own day one of the most appalling, of social problems. Most unhappily for mankind, this noble conception was from the first perverted. Institutions that might have had an incalculable philanthropic value were based upon the principle of asceticism, which makes the sacrifice, not the promotion, of earthly happiness its aim, and binding vows produced much misery and not a little vice. The convent became the perpetual prison of the daughter whom a father was disinclined to endow, or of young girls who, under the impulse of a transient enthusiasm, or of a transient sorrow, took a step which they never could retrace, and useless penances and contemptible superstitions wasted the energies that might have been most beneficially employed. Still it is very doubtful whether, even in the most degraded period, the convents did not prevent more misery than they inflicted, and in the Sisters of Charity the religious orders of Catholicism have produced one of the most perfect of all the types of womanhood. There is, as I conceive, no fact in modern history more deeply to be deplored than that the Reformers, who in matters of doctrinal innovations were often so timid, should have levelled to the dust, instead of attempting to regenerate, the whole conventual system of Catholicism.

The course of these observations has led me to transgress the limits assigned to this history. It has been, however, my object through this entire work to exhibit not only the nature but also the significance of the moral facts I have recorded, by showing how they have affected the subsequent changes of society. I will conclude this chapter, and this work, by observing that of all the departments of ethics the questions concerning the relations of the sexes and the proper position of women are those upon the future of which there rests the greatest uncertainty. History tells us that, as civilisation advances, the charity of men becomes at once warmer and more expansive, their habitual conduct both more gentle and more temperate, and their love of truth more sincere ; but it also warns us that in periods of great intellectual enlightenment, and of great social refinement, the relations of the sexes have often been most anarchical. It is impossible to deny that the form which these relations at present assume has been very largely affected by special

religious teaching, which, for good or for ill, is rapidly
waning in the sphere of government, and also, that certain
recent revolutions in economical opinion and industrial
enterprise have a most profound bearing upon the subject.
The belief that a rapid increase of population is always
eminently beneficial, which was long accepted as an axiom
by both statesmen and moralists, and was made the basis of
a large part of the legislation of the first and of the decisions
of the second, has now been replaced by the directly opposite
doctrine, that the very highest interest of society is not to
stimulate but to restrain multiplication, diminishing the
number of marriages and of children. In consequence of
this belief, and of the many factitious wants that accompany
a luxurious civilisation, a very large and increasing proportion of women are left to make their way in life without any
male protector, and the difficulties they have to encounter
through physical weakness have been most unnaturally and
most fearfully aggravated by laws and customs which, resting on the old assumption that every woman should be a
wife, habitually deprive them of the pecuniary and educational
advantages of men, exclude them absolutely from very many
of the employments in which they might earn a subsistence,
encumber their course in others by a heartless ridicule or by
a steady disapprobation, and consign, in consequence, many
thousands to the most extreme and agonising poverty, and
perhaps a still larger number to the paths of vice. At the
same time a momentous revolution, the effects of which can
as yet be but imperfectly descried, has taken place in the
chief spheres of female industry that remain. The progress
of machinery has destroyed its domestic character. The
distaff has fallen from the hand. The needle is being rapidly
superseded, and the work which, from the days of Homer to
the present century, was accomplished in the centre of the
family, has been transferred to the crowded manufactory.[1]

[1] The results of this change have been treated by Miss Parkes

The probable consequences of these things are among the most important questions that can occupy the moralist or the philanthropist, but they do not fall within the province of the historian. That the pursuits and education of women will be considerably altered, that these alterations will bring with them some modifications of the type of character, and that the prevailing moral notions concerning the relations of the sexes will be subjected in many quarters to a severe and hostile criticism, may safely be predicted. Many wild theories will doubtless be propounded. Some real ethical changes may perhaps be effected, but these, if I mistake not, can only be within definite and narrow limits. He who will seriously reflect upon our clear perceptions of the difference between purity and impurity, upon the laws that govern our affections, and upon the interests of the children who are born, may easily convince himself that in this, as in all other spheres, there are certain eternal moral landmarks which never can be removed.

---

in her truly admirable little book better than by any other writer called *Essays on Woman's Work*, with whom I am acquainted.

INDEX.

Spinoza, his remark on death, i. 203 Anecdote of him, 289

Staël, Madame de, on suicide, ii. 59

Statius, on the first night of marriage, i. 107, *note*

Stewart, Dugald, on the pleasures of virtue, i. 32, *note*

Stilpo, his scepticism and banishment, i. 162. His remark on his ruin, 191.

Stoics, their definition of conscience, i. 83. Their view of the animation of the human fœtus, 92. Their system of ethics favourable to the heroic qualities, 128. Historical fact in favour of the system, 128. Their belief in an all-pervading soul of nature, 162. Their pantheistic conception of the Deity, 163. Their conception and explanation of the prevailing legends of the gods, 163. Their opinion as to the final destruction of the universe by fire, and the resuscitation of souls, 164. Their refusal to consult the oracles, 165. Stoicism the expression of a type of character different from Epicureanism, 172. Rome pre-eminently the home of Stoicism, 172. Account of the philosophy of the Stoics, 177. Its two essentials — the unselfish ideal and the subjugation of the affections to the reason, 177. The best example of the perfect severance of virtue and interest, 181. Their views concerning the immortality of the soul, 182–184. Taught men to sacrifice reputation, and do good in secret, 186. And distinguished the obligation from the attraction of virtue, 186. Taught also that the affections must be subordinate to the reason, 187–191. Their false estimate of human nature, 192. Their love of paradox, 192. Imperfect lives of many eminent

Stoics, 193. Their retrospective tendencies, 193. Their system unfitted for the majority of mankind, 194. Compared with the religious principle, 195. The central composition of this philosophy, the dignity of man, 195. High sense of the Stoics of the natural virtue of man, and of the power of his will, 195, 196. Their recognition of Providence, 196. The two aspects under which they worshipped God, 198. The Stoics secured from quietism by their habits of public life, 199–201. Their view of humanity, 202. Their preparations for, and view of, death, 202. Their teaching as to suicide, 212, 13, *et seq.* Contrast between Stoicism and Roman luxury, 225, 226. The Stoical philosophy quite capable of representing the cosmopolitan spirit, 239, 240. Stoicism not capable of representing the softening movement of civilisation, 241. Influence of the eclectic spirit on it, 244. Stoicism becomes more essentially religious, 245. Increasingly introspective character of later Stoicism, 247. Marcus Aurelius the best example of later Stoicism, 249–255. Effects of Stoicism on the corruption of Roman Society, 291, 292. It raised up many good Emperors, 292. It produced a noble opposition under the worst Emperors, 293. It greatly extended Roman law, 294. The Stoics considered as the consolers of the suffering, advisers of the young, and as popular preachers, 308. Rapid decadence of Stoicism, 317, 318. Difference between the Stoical and Egyptian pantheism, 324. Stoical naturalism superseded by the theory of dæmons, 331. Theory that the writings of the Stoics

ary virtues differing in different ages, nations, and classes, 154, 155. Four distinct motives leading men to virtue, 178-180. Plato's fundamental proposition that vice is to virtue what disease is to health, 179. Stoicism the best example of the perfect severance of virtue and self-interest, 181. Teachings of the Stoics that virtue should conceal itself from the world, 186. And that the obligation should be distinguished from the attraction of virtue, 186. The eminent characteristics of pagan goodness, 190. All virtues are the same, according to the Stoics, 192. Horace's description of a just man, 197. Interested and disinterested motives of Christianity to virtue, ii. 3. Decline of the civic virtues caused by asceticism, 139. Influence of this change on moral philosophy, 146. The importance of the civic virtues exaggerated by historians, 147. Intellectual virtues, 188. Relation of monachism to these virtues, 189, et seq.

Vitalius, St., legend of, and the courtesan, ii. 320

Vivisection, ii. 176. Approved by Bacon, 176, note

Volcanoes, how regarded by the early monks, ii. 221

Vultures, why made an emblem of nature by the Egyptians, i. 108, note

W AR, its moral grandeur, i. 95. The school of the heroic virtues, 173. Difference between foreign and civil wars, 232. Antipathy of the early Christians to a military life, ii. 248. Belief in battle being the special sphere of

Providential interposition, 249. Effects of the military triumphs of the Mohammedans, 251. Influences of Christianity upon war considered, 254. Improved condition of captives taken in war, 256

Warburton, on morals, i. 15, note, 17, note

Waterland, on the motives to virtue and cause of our love of God, quoted, i. 9, note, 15, note

Wealth, origin of the desire to possess, i. 23. Associations leading to the desire for, for its own sake, 25

Western Empire, general sketch of the moral condition of the, ii. 14

Widows, care of the early Church for, ii. 366

Will, freedom of the human, sustained and deepened by the ascetic life, ii. 123

Wine, forbidden to women, i. 93, 94, note

Witchcraft, belief in the reality of, i. 363. Suicide common among witches, ii. 54

Wollaston, his analysis of moral judgments, i, 76

Women, law of the Romans forbidding women to taste wine, i. 93, 94, note. Standards of female morality of the Jews, Greeks, and Romans, 103, 104. Virtues and vices growing out of the relations of the sexes, 143. Female virtue, 143. Effects of climate on this virtue, 144. Of large towns, 146. And of early marriages, 145. Reason for Plato's advocacy of community of wives, 200. Plutarch's high sense of female excellence, 244. Female gladiators at Rome, 281, and note. Relations of female devotees with the anchorites, ii. 120, 128, 150. Their condition in savage life, 276. Cessa-

THE END.

AMERICAN
SPHINX

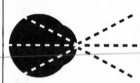

This Large Print Book carries the
Seal of Approval of N.A.V.H.

AMERICAN SPHINX

The Character
of Thomas Jefferson

JOSEPH J. ELLIS

G.K. Hall & Co. • Thorndike, Maine

Copyright © 1996 by Joseph J. Ellis

All rights reserved.

Published in 2000 by arrangement with Vintage Books, a division of Random House, Inc.

G.K. Hall Large Print American History Series.

The text of this Large Print edition is unabridged.
Other aspects of the book may vary from the original edition.

Set in 16 pt. Plantin by Warren S. Doersam.

Printed in the United States on permanent paper.

Library of Congress Cataloging-in-Publication Data

Ellis, Joseph J.
   American sphinx : the character of Thomas Jefferson / Joseph J.
Ellis
     p. cm.
   Originally published: New York : A.A. Knopf, 1997.
   Includes bibliographical references.
   ISBN 0-7838-9076-1 (lg. print : hc : alk. paper)
   1. Jefferson, Thomas, 1743–1826 — Psychology. I. Title.
E332.2 .E45   2000
973.4'6'092—dc21   00-036969

MILLER MEMORIAL LIBRARY
2901 DIXWELL AVENUE
HAMDEN, CONNECTICUT 06518

LP
92
JEFFERSON

For Edmund S. Morgan

MILLER MEMORIAL LIBRARY
2901 DIXWELL AVENUE
HAMDEN, CONNECTICUT 06518

CONTENTS

PREFACE AND ACKNOWLEDGMENTS

ANY ASPIRING BIOGRAPHER of Jefferson, recognizing the ink already spilled and the libraries already filled, might do well to recall the young Virginian's famous words of 1776. Which is to say that no one should undertake yet another book on Thomas Jefferson for "light and transient causes." In fact "prudence dictates" and "a decent respect of the opinions of mankind requires" that the publication of all new books about that man from Monticello be accompanied by a formal declaration of the causes that have impelled the author to undertake the effort.

My own defense would begin over thirty years ago, when I entered graduate school at Yale to study early American history. It is impossible to avoid Jefferson while attempting to master the story of the American Revolution, since his career crisscrosses the major events of the era. And his ideas, or at least the ideas for which he became the most eloquent spokesman, define

7

the central themes of the story of the emerging American republic. Moreover, I was a native Virginian who, like Jefferson, had graduated from the College of William and Mary. I even had reddish blond hair like Jefferson and had learned how to disguise my insecurities behind a mask of enigmatic silence. It was therefore natural for me, once ensconced in the former cradle of New England Puritanism and Federalism, to identify with Jefferson's edgy doubts about the arrogant austerities and quasi-Arctic climate of New England.

My eventual mentor in graduate school, Edmund S. Morgan, even had a huge Jefferson portrait on his office wall, the luminous Rembrandt Peale likeness of 1800, which looked down on our seminar sessions with otherworldly authority that I found oddly reassuring. Jefferson and I were kindred spirits, I told myself, allies in this alien world where a southern accent seemed inversely correlated with one's seriousness of purpose. This youthful infatuation for Jefferson eventually went the way of my southern accent, never completely gone altogether but relegated to the blurry margins, where it lost its distinctive character. Like any young love, however, it became a permanent part of my emotional inventory.

Not that I actually knew very much about Jefferson's life or thought. My affinity for Jefferson was more personal than scholarly. Only once, when I was scouting about for a dissertation topic, did I consider working on Jefferson. My recollection is that C. Vann Woodward, a fellow southerner also recently arrived in New Haven — though as a mature and not just budding historian — alerted me to the dangers. One should not attempt biography until a bit further down the trail of life, he suggested. As for Jefferson, he was such a sprawling and famously elusive subject that any young historian who sallied forth after him was like the agile youth sent forward against impossible odds in a story about the tragic casualties of war. This excellent advice had the immediate sound of truth. I did not give Jefferson any serious scholarly consideration for another twenty-five years.

As a college teacher I assigned books about Jefferson in my courses, and I developed formal lectures on the Declaration of Independence and Jefferson's paradoxical stance on slavery. But it was not until I began research for a book on John Adams that I probed beneath the surface of the Jefferson correspondence. It was an odd way for a Virginian to come home again, arriving at Monticello by way of Quincy, but that is how it happened.

Adams had a truly special relationship with Jefferson that developed out of their common cause against English imperial rule and their different roots in the regional cultures of New England and Virginia. As a result, Adams admired, even loved Jefferson; they sustained a fifty-year friendship that culminated in an exchange of letters in their twilight years that most historians regard as the intellectual capstone to the achievements of the revolutionary generation. But Adams also disagreed profoundly with Jefferson's version of the American Revolution. Indeed he thought that Jefferson's entire political vision rested on a seductive set of attractive illusions. The more I read, the more I concluded that Adams was right. For the first time I began to see Jefferson critically and ironically.

My clinching commitment to a book-length study of Jefferson came in the process of writing an essay for the inaugural issue of *Civilization* about Jefferson's somewhat problematic place in contemporary American culture. If my work on Adams had given me a new perspective, my essay for *Civilization* gave me a fresh appreciation of Jefferson's resonance as an American icon. One could work for several years on Adams and enjoy splendid isolation. But working on Jefferson was like entering a crowded room in which there were always several ongoing conversations, and the constant buzz suggested that more was at stake than the resolution of merely historical questions. Jefferson was electromagnetic. He symbolized the most cherished and most contested values in modern American culture. He was one of those dead white males who still mattered.

These evolving thoughts became not just the reasons for writing a book about Jefferson but also the decisive influences on the shape of the